BRANCH, JUMP, CALL, and CASE INSTRUCTIONS

(Unless noted otherwise, operand is one byte displacement)

SIGNED and UNSIGNED BRANCH INSTRUCTIONS

Signed Branch Instructions	Unsigned Branch Instructions	
BEQL	BEQLU	Branch if EQUal
BNEQ	BNEQU	Branch if Not EQual
BLSS	BLSSU	Branch if LeSS
BGTR	BGTRU	Branch if Greater
BLEQ	BLEQU	Br if Less or EQual
BGEQ	BGEQU	Branch if Greater or EQual

CONDITION CODE BRANCH INSTRUCTIONS

BNEQ	Branch if Z clear (result Not Equal to zero)
BEQL	Branch if Z Set (result EQuaL to zero)
BCC	Branch if C Clear (no unsigned overflow)
BCS	Branch if C Set (signed overflow)
BVC	Branch if V Clear (no signed overflow)
BVS	Branch if V Set (signed overflow)
BGEQ	Branch if N clear (result is not negative)
BLSS	Branch if N set (result is negative)

UNCONDITIONAL BRANCHES and JUMPS

BRB	disp	BRanch with Byte displacement
BRW	disp	BRanch with Word displacement
JMP	adr	JuMP (general operand specifier)

SUBROUTINE CALLS and RETURN

BSBB	disp	Branch to SuBroutine with Byte displacement
BSBW	disp	Branch to SuBroutine with Word displacement
JSB	adr	Jump to SuBroutine (general operand specifier)
RSB		Return from SuBroutine (no operand)

PROCEDURE CALLS and RETURN (See Chapter 8)

CALLG	arglist,dst	CALL procedure with General arg list
CALLS	numarg,dst	CALL procedure with arguments on Stack
RET		RETurn from procedure

ADD, COMPARE, and BRANCH INSTRUCTIONS

(N=Z=V=*, C=-)
(disp is a word displacement)

ACBx	limit,add,index,disp	index ← index + add, branch if add GEQ 0 and index LEQ limit or add LSS 0 and index GEQ limit

Byte	Word	Long	F_flt	D_flt	G_flt	H_flt
ACBB	ACBW	ACBL	ACBF	ACBD	ACDG	ACDH

ADD or SUBTRACT ONE and BRANCH INSTRUCTIONS

(disp is a byte displacement, lim and index are longwords)

AOBLSS	lim,index,disp	index = index + 1, BR if index LSS lim
AOBLEQ	lim,index,disp	index = index + 1, BR if index LEQ lim
SOBGTR	index,disp	index = index - 1, BR if index GTR 0
SOBGEQ	index,disp	index = index - 1, BR if index GEQ 0

BRANCH ON LOW BIT (scr is a longword)

BLBC	scr,disp	branch if low bit (bit 0) clear
BLBS	scr,disp	branch if low bit (bit 0) set

CASE INSTRUCTIONS (for multiway branching)

CASEB	str,index,lim,disp[0],	tmp ← index - str
CASEW	disp[1],	if tmp LEQU lim, BR disp[tmp]
CASEL	disp[lim]	else no branch

BIT STRING BRANCH INSTRUCTIONS - see Bit String Instructions

LONGWOR...

ADWC	ad...		
SBWC	su...		
ASHL	cnt,src,dst	dst...	
ROTL	cnt,scr,dst	dst ← ROTATE(src)	ROTate Long cnt bits
PUSHL	src	-(SP) ← src	PUSH Long
INDEX	sub,low,high,size,indexin,indexout		see COMPUTE INDEX

QUADWORD AND OCTAWORD INSTRUCTIONS

ASHQ	cnt,src,dst	dst ← src * 2**cnt	Arithmetic SHift
CLRQ	dst	dst ← 0	CLeaR
CLRO	dst	dst ← 0	CLeaR
MOVQ	src,dst	dst ← src	MOVe
MOVO	src,dst	dst ← src	MOVe
MOVAQ	src,dst	dst ← ADR(src)	MOVe Address
MOVAO	src,dst	dst ← ADR(src)	MOVe Address
PUSHAQ	src	-(SP) ← ADR(src)	PUSH Address
PUSHAO	src	-(SP) ← ADR(src)	PUSH Address
EMUL	mulr,muld,add,prod		Extended MULtiply (see Ch 6.3)
EDIV	divr,divd,quo,rem		Extended DIVide (see Ch 6.3)

COMPUTE INDEX

INDEX	sub,low,high,size,indexin,indexout	(see Chapter 7.5)

indexout ← (indexin + sub*size)
if indexout LSS low or indexout GTR high, trap

SIGNED CONVERT INSTRUCTIONS excluding Packed (N=Z=V=*, C=0)

Description

CVTxy	src,dst	dst ← src	ConVerT scr (type x)

Instructions

to from	Byte	Word	Long	F_flt	D_flt	G_flt	H_flt
Byte		CVTBW	CVTBL	CVTBF	CVTBD	CVTBG	CVTBH
Word	CVTWB		CVTWL	CVTWF	CVTWD	CVTWG	CVTWH
Long	CVTLB	CVTLW		CVTLF	CVTLD	CVTLG	CVTLH
F-flt	CVTFB	CVTFW	CVTFL		CVTFD	CVTFG	CVTFH
D_flt	CVTDB	CVTDW	CVTDL	CVTDF			CVTDH
G_flt	CVTGB	CVTGW	CVTGL	CVTGF			CVTGH
H_flt	CVTHB	CVTHW	CVTHL	CVTHF	CVTHD	CVTHG	

PACKED CONVERT INSTRUCTIONS (N=Z=V=*, C=0)

to from	Packed	Long	Leading	Trailing
Packed		CVTPL	CVTPS	CVTPT
Long	CVTLP			
Leading	CVTSP			
Trailing	CVTTP			

OTHER CONVERSIONS

UNSIGNED CONVERSIONS
(MOVe Zero extended)

to from	Word	Long
Byte	MOVZBW	MOVZBL
Word		MOVZWL

FLOATING to LONGWORD
ROUNDED CONVERSIONS

to from	Long
F_flt	CVTRFL
D_flt	CVTRDL
G_flt	CVTRGL
H_flt	CVTRHL

VAX

assembly language and architecture

Charles Kapps
Temple University

Robert L. Stafford
Temple University

PWS-KENT
Publishing Company
Boston, Massachusetts

PWS–KENT
Publishing Company

20 Park Plaza
Boston, Massachusetts 02116

PWS-KENT Publishing Company is a division of Wadsworth, Inc.

The "VAX-11 Programming Card," shown in Appendix F and (in a condensed version) on the endpapers, is used courtesy of Digital Equipment Corporation. Copyright, Digital Equipment Corporation, 1983. All rights reserved. Reprinted by permission.

VAX, VAX/VMS, PDP, VT52, VT/100, VT/200, and DEC are trademarks of Digital Equipment Corporation. UNIX is a trademark of Bell Laboratories, Inc. Ada is a trademark of the U.S. Department of Defense. IBM is a registered trademark of International Business Machines Corporation. CDC is a registered trademark and Cyber is a trademark of Control Data Corporation.

Library of Congress Cataloging in Publication Data

Kapps, Charles A.
  VAX assembly language and architecture.

  Includes index.
  1. VAX (Computer) 2. VAX (Computer)—
Programming. 3. Assembler language (Computer program
language) 4. Computer architecture. I. Stafford,
Robert L. II. Title.
QA76.8.V37K36 1985   001.64   85-3494
ISBN 0-87150-837-0

ISBN 0-87150-837-0

Sponsoring Editor: Karin Ellison
Production Editor: Helane Manditch-Prottas
Interior Design: Trisha Hanlon
Cover Design: Helane Manditch-Prottas
Text Composition: Graphic Typesetting Service
Text Printing and Binding: Halliday Lithograph
Cover Photo: Courtesy of Unitrode/Steve Grohe/The Picture Cube
Cover Printing: John P. Pow Co.

Printed in the United States of America.
  93 94 — 10 9 8 7

Preface

This book is designed for a one-semester course in assembly language programming for the VAX family of computers. We assume that people who use this book will have some familiarity with computer programming in a higher-level language such as Pascal or FORTRAN. However, minimal assumptions have been made in this regard, and the basics of machine organization are covered very thoroughly. Our motivational philosophy is to knit theory and practice firmly together. We have made every effort to develop a conceptual understanding of the VAX architecture while leading the student to early hands-on experience with the machine. This approach should also be ideal for individuals who wish to use the text as a self-study guide for learning the assembly and machine language of the VAX family.

The VAX family was chosen not only because of its popularity, but because we believe that the architecture is ideal for learning. The organizational consistency makes the VAX an easy computer to program in assembly language. The richness of the architecture makes it easy to use the assembly language for complicated problems. This feature also makes the VAX ideal as a basis for learning the architecture of other machines. By focusing on a single computer family, we were able to include advanced topics such as floating-point and decimal operations, system level input and output, interfacing to higher-level languages, and operating system functions. These topics extend the scope of the book into the larger field of computer science.

Our major goal is to make the book both accessible and relevant for the reader and the instructor. For example, an abridged version of the VAX instruction set is printed on the inside covers for easy reference. In the early chapters, methods are shown that enable students to run simple programs on the computer. Routines are provided for input and output in assembly language as well as in higher-level languages. Later, input and output using VAX/VMS system services are described. In addition to discussing input and output, the appendices cover methods for running and debugging programs, creating programs using the EDT editor, and using VAX/VMS commands.

The organization of the chapters follows:

- Chapters 1 and 2 contain background information for persons who may have limited experience with computers.
- Chapters 3, 4, and 5 introduce the basic concepts of VAX architecture and assembly language. By the end of Chapter 5, the use of processor registers and simple subroutines has been covered so that the reader can start running fairly complex programs.
- Chapters 6, 7, and 8 present intermediate material that focuses on the manipulation of data. This includes more sophisticated operations with numbers, the processing of alphabetic information, and arrays.
- Chapters 9–13 present the more advanced topics of subroutines and global symbols, macros and conditional assembly, system level input and output, and floating-point, character, and packed decimal operations. These chapters can be covered in any order or omitted.
- Chapters 14 and 15 tie together the advanced topics to form an introduction to systems architecture, operating systems, and systems programming.

Chapters 1–7 are intended for use in the order presented. The order of the remaining chapters can be varied according to the following graph of chapter dependencies.

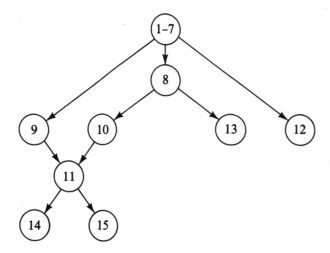

We extend sincere appreciation to the people who helped us during the preparation of this material. Steven Lipshutz provided us with systems support during preparation of the manuscript. Joe Yeager of Philadelphia College of Textiles and Science class-tested early versions of the manuscript.

We benefited from the comments of the following people who reviewed all or parts of the manuscript: Gabriel Barta, Geneva, Switzerland; Daniel A. Cañas, University of Texas at Austin; George W. Gorsline, Virginia Polytechnic Institute and State University; Paul S. LaFollette, Jr., Temple University; Mike G. Murphy, University of Houston Downtown College; David D. Riley, University of Wisconsin, LaCrosse; John Roach, Virginia Polytechnic Institute and State University; Paul W. Ross, Millersville College; and Richard Spillman, Pacific Lutheran University.

We would like to acknowledge Pat DeSpirito for her dedication and patience as well as her ability to decipher our handwriting.

We would like to thank David Goldstein for his work on the exercises.

We would also like to thank Integrated Circuit Systems and Temple University for access to computer resources and documentation.

At PWS Publishers, we are particularly grateful to our editor, Karin Ellison, and to our production editors, Betty O'Bryant and Helane Manditch-Prottas.

Finally, special thanks are due to Lawrence J. Kenah of Digital Equipment Corporation who, in addition to reviewing our manuscript, provided valuable advice and detailed insights into the VAX architecture and the VMS operating system.

We dedicate this book to Christianne, Judy, Marcia, and Sarah.

Charles Kapps
Robert L. Stafford

Contents

Introduction

1.1 Overview

The purpose of this chapter is to provide background material and establish a context for the remainder of the text. In order to place the VAX computer system in perspective, the history which led to its development is summarized. Finally, a simplified method for running assembly language programs is presented. This material assumes some familiarity with a higher-level language such as FORTRAN or Pascal.

1.2 History
The Early Days

The history of automatic computers goes back much farther than many people realize. In the 1830s and 1840s, an English mathematician by the name of Charles Babbage attempted to build an automatic computer based on gears and punched cards. Unfortunately, Babbage was never able to complete his analytic engine. Later in the century, however, an American named Herman Hollerith developed a punched card tabulating system that was used with the 1890 U.S. census.

Punched card tabulating equipment based on Hollerith's designs came into extensive use in the early part of the twentieth century. This equipment, which uses the initials EAM for Electronic Accounting Machinery, was made of electrical and mechanical parts (motors, switches, solenoids, relays, gears, clutches, ratchets, and so forth).

Although modern equipment is considerably different from the early EAM equipment, the original Hollerith standards are still used for punched cards. (See page 228 for more detail on Hollerith codes.)

One major drawback to the EAM equipment was that it consisted of a conglomeration of special purpose machines—card duplicators, tabulators, sorters, and collators. These were all specially wired to perform a specific task. Any variability in the system was accomplished by wiring configurations through plug boards. These plug boards allowed the user to route data and control information in much the same way that a switchboard operator routes telephone calls.

The next big step in computing came around 1940, when a more general and convenient method for controlling computations was developed by Howard Aiken at Harvard University. The Mark I computer was essentially a cross between a giant adding machine and a player piano. The entire control of the machine was "programmed" by punching appropriate patterns of holes in several player-pianolike scrolls.

Electronic Computers

Like its predecessors, the Mark I computer was electromechanical. In other words, electricity was only used to move mechanical parts. These moving parts, in turn, activated switches that controlled the electric currents. At best such mechanical operations require about one one-thousandth of a second, and often may require much more. The solution to such relative slowness was to replace the mechanical switches with electronic switches. An **electronic switch** is one that has no moving parts. The switching is accomplished by applying electrostatic or magnetic fields to the materials or empty space where the electrical conduction is taking place. In 1940, the available active element for an electronic switch was the vacuum tube.

Shortly after the Mark I was in operation, Presper Eckert and John Mauchly built the first large scale electronic computer, called the ENIAC, at the University of Pennsylvania. Because a vacuum-tube switch is capable of operating in one one-millionth of a second, the ENIAC had the potential of being 1000 times faster than the Mark I. As computers became faster, they began to tax people's ability to make use of the speed. In fact, one of the early computer scientists was reputed to have said that six ENIACs would keep all the mathematicians in the country busy forever, just in finding problems for them to solve.

In order to perform a given computational process on the ENIAC, it was necessary to plug in a large number of wires in a certain configuration, a time-consuming process. The next innovation was the idea that a computational process should be specified by a **computer program** that resides in memory along with the data. In addition to making computers easier to use, an **internally stored program** makes it possible for the computer program to modify itself as it executes. (Although this was important with early computers, modern computers have been designed with instruction sets so that modification is no longer necessary. In fact, program modification is usually considered undesirable for several reasons, one of which is difficulty in debugging such programs.)

In the past, many people have credited John von Neumann of Princeton University with developing the idea of the internally stored program. However, recent evidence indicates that Eckert and Mauchly deserve at least as much credit as von Neumann. In any case, the computer field owes a great debt to all three individuals.

The Solid State Era

In the late 1950s and early 1960s, transistors began to replace the vacuum-tube switches in computers. Transistors had five distinct advantages over vacuum tubes: they were smaller, they consumed much less energy, they were faster, they were less expensive, and they were more reliable.

Although there is no fundamental difference between transistor computers and vacuum-tube computers, the five advantages of transistors had a tremendous economic impact, which led to two opposing trends in computer design:

1. First, it became feasible to build very large and powerful "supercomputers." Early examples of these were the IBM 7094, CDC 6600, and DEC PDP-6.*

2. It also became feasible, for the first time, to build small, inexpensive "minicomputers." These computers were low enough in cost that small laboratories could afford to have them for dedicated use, so that one user could have the computer all to him/herself. (The large computers were so expensive that use had to be scheduled and shared.) Early examples of minicomputers were the IBM 1620, Royal McBee RPG 4000, and DEC PDP-5.

The proliferation of both kinds of computers started the extensive use of computers, and computers began to become better understood.

---

* Some people may argue the appropriateness of the term "supercomputer" for these examples. However, in the early mid-1960s, they were pretty "super."

Consequently, the architecture and organization of later computers reflect an improved understanding; however, the organization principles have remained basically unchanged since the days of the first general purpose machines.

Integrated Circuits

Transistors are made by implanting small amounts of impurities in a semiconductor crystal such as silicon. Early transistors were all individually packaged in a small metal or plastic container with contact leads protruding. Because the actual transistor was much smaller than its package, much space was wasted. Integrated circuits, on the other hand, are made by forming many transistors on the surface of a silicon wafer. Wiring is then photographically applied right on the surface of the wafer. This allows extremely complex circuits to be constructed in a very small space. (At present, it is possible to have hundreds of thousands of transistors on a "chip" less than 1 cm^2 in area.)

The advent of integrated circuits completely revolutionized the economics of computers. Large computers have become less expensive and minicomputers have become more sophisticated, so that now it is sometimes difficult to distinguish one from the other. We also have the so-called "microcomputers," in which an entire computer can be placed on a single silicon chip that can be sold for only a few dollars. Originally, microcomputers were rather crude, but recent advances have blurred the distinction between microcomputers and minicomputers.

At present, integrated-circuit technology is still developing, and one can only guess where the future will lead.

Other Hardware Advances

The physical components that make up a computer system are collectively referred to as **computer hardware**. The previous subsections primarily dealt with advances in processor design and implementation. Paralleling this, although perhaps not so dramatic, have been advances in other hardware devices such as memories and peripheral equipment.

Memory design has followed a similar history from electromechanical designs to integrated circuits. On the other hand, many peripheral devices such as printers, terminals, and magnetic tape units have not improved as much. As a result, peripheral devices are by far the most expensive parts of most computer systems.

1.3 Developments in Computer Software

Machine and Assembly Language

To build a computer, designers first select a particular set of orders or instructions and then construct a machine that will carry out or execute programs comprised of these instructions. The instructions are called **machine language instructions** and the resulting programs are called **machine language programs**. Notice that the machine language instructions of one machine are usually totally different from the machine language instructions of another machine.

Machine languages are usually numerical languages that are awkward for human beings to use. For example, the VAX machine language instruction to add the contents of one memory cell (in this case the memory cell called 00000400) to the contents of another memory cell (called 00000500) can be encoded as

00000500 9F   00000400 9F   C0

where C0 is the operation code for a particular kind of addition and 9F specifies that the preceding symbols are names of memory cells.

In the early 1950s, assembly languages were developed to ease the burden on programmers. In an **assembly language,** names are substituted for numbers. For example, the preceding VAX machine language instruction might be rewritten in assembly language as follows:

ADDL2   BONUS,SALARY

The advantage of using names instead of numbers should be obvious.

Before an assembly language program can be executed, it must be translated into machine language. This translation is basically a clerical process that involves substituting the correct number for each of the names (that is, substituting C0 for ADDL2 in the previous example). However, this is exactly the kind of problem that is easily solved with a computer. Therefore, the designer of an assembly language creates a program, called the **assembler,** that will read a user's assembly language program and translate it into machine language.

Higher-Level Languages

In the mid 1950s, the first higher-level languages were developed. Unlike an assembly language, a higher-level language is not associated with any particular machine language or computer model. Instead, the designer of a higher-level language concentrates on developing a language that is convenient for solving a certain class of computing problems. Then the designer builds a translator, called a **compiler,** to translate a user's program into a given machine language.* If it is desired to use the higher-level language on a computer with a different machine language, a second translator is constructed that translates the same higher-level language program into machine language suitable for the second computer. Thus the user of a higher-level language does not have to know the machine language of the computer being used. In addition, it is possible to transfer a program written in a higher-level language from one computer to another without rewriting the program (assuming that the necessary translators are available).

The difference between assembly language and higher-level languages can also be described in terms of the translation process. Each assembly language instruction is generally translated into one machine language instruction. In contrast, each statement in a higher-level language may be translated into many machine language statements.

In the late 1950s and throughout the 1960s, a variety of higher-level languages became popular. The first of these was FORTRAN (FORmula TRANslation), which was developed by a group headed by John Backus at IBM. FORTRAN was designed to help people solve *scientific problems* where a large number of calculations are required, as opposed to *data processing problems* where a large number of input and output operations (such as reading and printing) are necessary. In order to solve data processing problems, COBOL (COmmon Business Oriented Language) was designed by a committee sponsored by the Department of Defense. In 1960, an international group of computer experts met to develop a new language for scientific problems. (The original specifications for FORTRAN were written in 1954, and a great deal had been learned about language design in the intervening years.) The result was the programming language ALGOL 60 (ALGOrithmetic Language). In the mid-1960s, IBM developed the language PL-I (Programming Language I), which was designed for both scientific programming problems and data processing applications. At about the same time, John Kemeny and Thomas Kurtz at Dartmouth College developed BASIC (Beginners' All purpose Symbolic Instruction Code). Although BASIC resembles a simplified version of FORTRAN, it was specifically designed to be used from an interactive time-sharing terminal. Other languages that are now in common use include APL (A Programming Language), which is also designed to be used from a time-sharing terminal, LISP, which is used in many

---

* Some higher-level languages are interpreted, which is a step-by-step translation during program execution.

artificial intelligence applications, and Pascal and Modula II, which resemble simplified versions of ALGOL. One of the newer higher-level languages is called Ada, and it incorporates features from many other languages. It should be noted that this list of programming languages is far from exhaustive. There are literally hundreds of programming languages. Many are specialized languages designed for a particular class of problems such as simulation.

Why Study Assembly Language?

Higher-level languages are easier to use than assembly language. In addition, higher-level languages can generally be transported from one computer system to another without rewriting the program. Why then should people still write programs in assembly language?

In some cases, a user may wish to use features of a computer that are not accessible from available higher-level languages. This situation often occurs in developing operating system software, especially in the portions involving input, output, and other machine-dependent resources. In such cases it becomes necessary to use assembly language for at least some sections of the program.

For some applications, using a carefully written assembly language program to solve a given problem will be more efficient (in terms of running time and/or memory space used) than a carefully written program in a higher-level language. This often overrides the fact that assembly language programs may require more programmer time to write, debug, test, and modify than an equivalent program written in a higher-level language. The selection of a language is an economic question, and the various costs for the particular application must be examined in order to make a rational decision. With current costs, it appears that higher-level languages will be the correct choice in the majority of applications, but that assembly language is still appropriate for a significant number of applications where speed or memory usage is very important.

In addition, there are important reasons for knowing (as opposed to programming in) assembly language. To a large extent, the purpose of a higher-level language is to "hide" the complexity of the machine from the average programmer or user. However, the higher-level language is generally not completely successful in burying the complexity. As a result, the higher-level language may produce unexpected results such as arithmetic overflow, and apparently simple changes in a higher-level language program may result in large changes in running time or memory usage. A knowledge of assembly language is useful for understanding and predicting these results. Such knowledge is particularly useful when a higher-level language program is transported from one machine to another. Finally, computer scientists should know assembly languages in order to really understand how a computer functions.

Exercise Set 1

Exercise questions marked by an asterisk (*) will require outside reading.

1. Identify the following persons, and name their major accomplishment.
   a. Herman Hollerith
   b. Howard Aiken
   c. Presper Eckert
   d. John Mauchly
   e. John von Neumann
   f. John Backus
   *g. John Atanasoff
   *h. Augusta Ada Byron (Countess of Lovelace)
   *i. Nicolas Wirth

*2. Using reference material other than this text, write a short (one page or so) biography of any of the persons named in Exercise 1.

3. Vacuum-tube computers have been completely replaced by solid-state computers. This is true to the extent that there are very few if any vacuum-tube computers in practical operation anywhere in the world today. To account for this, name as many disadvantages of vacuum-tube computers as you can.

*4. One of the important names in the founding of computer science is Grace Hopper. What is she best known for? And how do her accomplishments differ from those referred to in Exercise 1?

1.4 The VAX Family of Computers
Digital Equipment Corporation

Digital Equipment Corporation, or DEC (pronounced deck) as it is commonly known, was formed in 1957. During the 1960s, the company produced a variety of computers. The first computer that Digital designed was called the PDP-1. Subsequent computers were numbered sequentially up to the PDP-15. However, for various reasons the PDP-2, PDP-3, and PDP-13 were never marketed. (The letters PDP stand for Programmed Data Processor.)

In the 1960s, DEC pioneered the development of computers that cost less than $100,000. Because even small computers at that time cost more than $100,000, these "smaller than small" computers became known as minicomputers. Digital became and still remains the dominant company in the minicomputer field.

In addition to minicomputers, Digital also developed much larger, time-sharing computers that were designed to provide computer access for 100 or more simultaneous users. Computers in this category include the PDP-10 (now called the DECsystem-10) and the DECSYSTEM-20. Digital is currently the second largest computer manufacturer, with IBM being the largest.

The PDP-11 Computer

In 1970, DEC introduced a minicomputer called the PDP-11. These computers were intended to replace the PDP-5/PDP-8 family of mini-computers that were then becoming obsolete. (However, an integrated-circuit implementation of the PDP-8 is the basis of DEC's DEC-mate series of small business computers.)

The PDP-11 is called a **16-bit** minicomputer. The 16-bit designation means that most operations deal with a unit of information that consists of 16 binary digits. (See Chapters 2 and 3.) This is also called the **word size** of the processor. To a certain extent, the word size determines the speed at which the processor can operate. It also tends to determine the price. While a 32-bit machine is likely to be faster than a 16-bit machine, it is also likely to be more expensive.

During the 1970s, the PDP-11 evolved into a family of computers. All of the computers in this family used the same machine language, but they spanned several orders of magnitude in price and performance. For example, some members of this family are too small to be called minicomputers, so they are classified as microcomputers. (The DEC Professional 300 series of personal computers is a part of the PDP-11 family.) Other members, such as the PDP-11/70, are much larger computers that are capable of serving up to 50 or more simultaneous time-sharing users. Computers such as the PDP-11/70 are really too large to be called minicomputers and are sometimes called **super-minis.**

The VAX Family

The VAX family of computers is the successor to the larger PDP-11 computers. The name VAX is an acronym for **Virtual Address eXtension,** which indicates that this computer family uses a complicated technique for managing computer memory. Although VAX computers can execute PDP-11 machine language code, they are really 32-bit machines instead of 16-bit machines and they normally use a different machine language, which is referred to as **native code.**

The VAX family includes computer systems such as the VAX-11/730, the VAX-11/750, the VAX-11/780, and the VAX-11/782 computer systems. All of these computer systems execute the same VAX machine language. However, the models designated by the larger numbers (such as the VAX-11/785) are much more powerful and expensive than the lower model numbers (such as the VAX-11/730). Some of these models are shown in Figure 1.1. While it is possible to acquire a VAX system for under $100,000, it is also possible to configure a $1,000,000 VAX system. At the smaller end of the VAX family are the MicroVAXs, which can be configured for $20,000 or less (see Figure 1.2).

VAX computer systems are used in a variety of environments. For example, they may be used to provide general time-sharing services for up to 100 or more simultaneous users. They are also used in science and engineering for more specialized activities such as

Figure 1.1 A VAX-11/730 computer system with other VAX-11 family members, the 750, 780, and 782. (Courtesy of Digital Equipment Corporation.)

Figure 1.2 A MicroVAX I computer system. (Courtesy of Digital Equipment Corporation.)

Computer Aided Design and Computer Aided Manufacture (CAD/CAM).
These highly computer-bound applications involve solving problems
which use much computer time even on very fast computers. As a
result, one single VAX may only support a few CAD/CAM users at a
time.

In general, the VAX computers are designed to perform a variety
of general data processing functions where high speed at moderate

cost is important. The VAX operating system, called **VMS** for **Virtual Memory System,** supports both interactive and batch users and allows many VAX and other computers to be connected together in a network for operation sharing. Programming on the VAX can be done using a variety of higher-level programming languages such as FORTRAN, COBOL, BASIC, Pascal, PL-I, APL, and so forth, as well as in assembly language, which is the topic of this book.

Systems Software

Although it would be possible to enter one's own programs into a machine without an operating system, various areas such as input, output, file management, and language translation would require much programming effort. As a result, virtually all computer users purchase a packaged set of programs for their computer for running the system. This is **systems software**. Systems software falls into several categories:

1. Monitors. These programs coordinate and direct the execution of all other programs.
2. Utility programs. These programs are invoked by user commands for such purposes as creating or modifying files, assigning input and output devices, obtaining status information, and so forth.
3. System subroutines. These subroutines are called by user programs to perform system functions such as those described in category 2.
4. Language processors. These enable the user to write programs in various languages: assembly language, FORTRAN, Pascal, and so forth.
5. Special library packages. These allow one to use special mathematical functions, statistical functions, graphics control, and so forth.

An **operating system** normally contains programs in categories 1 through 3, and user-selected features of 4 and 5. Since systems software requires a considerable development effort, one must pay a license fee to use an operating system. The cost of these licenses may be thousands of dollars.

The operating system that is provided by Digital Equipment Corporation is called VAX/VMS. A significantly different operating system that may be used with the VAX computer is called UNIX. This book will assume the use of the VAX/VMS operating system.

1.5 Getting Started
An Assembly Language Program

With a knowledge of a higher-level language, it is possible to create and run simple assembly language programs. For example, Figure 1.3 shows a simple program in three languages: Pascal, FORTRAN, and MACRO, the assembly language for the VAX computer. Line numbers, such as 1. and 2., have been added to these programs. Note that these line numbers are not part of any of the three programs.

A given type of statement in one programming language may have no analogous statement in another language. When this occurs in the programs shown in Figure 1.3, the comment NOT NEEDED is used so that the remaining lines in the programs will still correspond. As the figure shows, comments in Pascal are bracketed by the characters (* and *), while comments in FORTRAN begin with the character C in the first position of a line. In assembly language, any line that begins with a semicolon (;) is treated as a comment.

Symbols such as J, K, and DIF are called **variable names** in higher-level languages such as Pascal and FORTRAN. In assembly languages, they are called **symbolic addresses.** In the previous three programs, lines 3, 4, and 5 have the same effect. They indicate that the variables (symbolic addresses) J, K, and DIF are the names of memory cells that will contain 32-bit integers. (The statement J:.BLKL 1 declares J to be name of a BLocK of Longwords of length 1. In the VAX assembly language, a **longword** is simply a 32-bit integer.)

Similarly, lines 7 through 10 in the three programs have the same effect. In all three programs, DIF will contain the value 8 after line 10 is executed. Notice that assignment statements such as J: = 20;

Figure 1.3 A sample program in three languages

	Pascal		FORTRAN		Assembly Language	
1.	PROGRAM SAMPLE;	1.	C NOT NEEDED IN FORTRAN	1.	;NOT NEEDED IN MACRO	
2.	VAR	2.	C NOT NEEDED IN FORTRAN	2.	;NOT NEEDED IN MACRO	
3.	J : INTEGER;	3.	INTEGER J	3. J:	.BLKL	1
4.	K : INTEGER;	4.	INTEGER K	4. K:	.BLKL	1
5.	DIF : INTEGER;	5.	INTEGER DIF	5. DIF:	.BLKL	1
6.	BEGIN	6.	C NOT NEEDED IN FORTRAN	6.	.ENTRY	START,0
7.	J := 20;	7.	J=20	7.	MOVL	#20,J
8.	K := 12;	8.	K=12)	8.	MOVL	#12,K
9.	DIF := J;	9.	DIF=J	9.	MOVL	J,DIF
10.	DIF := DIF-K;	10.	DIF=DIF-K	10.	SUBL2	K,DIF
11.	(*NOT NEEDED IN Pascal*)	11.	STOP	11.	$EXIT_S	
12.	END.	12.	END	12.	.END	START

or J = 20 move information from right to left while the VAX assembler moves information from left to right. The statement MOVL #20, J should be read as "Move the number 20 to the longword J." Similarly, the statement SUBL K,DIF should be read as "Subtract the longword in K from the longword in DIF (leaving the result in the longword DIF)."

Figure 1.4 shows the program "skeleton" for a simple assembly language program. The lowercase letters mark the symbols and lines that the user must fill in to create an executable program. Notice that the various fields are lined up to form vertical columns. This convention is quite easy to follow by using the tab positions on most DEC terminals. This alignment is not required by the assembler but is necessary as a practical matter so that programs are readable. In the next to last statement in the program, notice that the sixth character in the name $EXIT_S is the underscore (_), not a minus sign (−).

Communicating with the VAX

The normal method of communicating with a VAX computer system is by using an interactive terminal. There are two basic types of terminals—**hard-copy** terminals and **VDT** terminals. Hard-copy terminals produce printed output (the hard copy) and resemble typewriters. VDTs (Video Display Terminals) resemble a keyboard attached to a television set. Appendix A describes how to run assembly language programs.

Assembly Language Instructions

Assembly language instructions such as

```
MOVL    J,DIF
```

consist of two parts or fields. The first field is called the **operation code** or **opcode field.** It contains operation codes such as MOVL or SUBL2. The second field is called the **operands field**. This field may contain symbolic addresses (variable names) such as J and DIF as well as constants such as #20 and #12. The operands are separated by commas. The number of operands depends on the operation code.

The assembly language of a VAX computer has several hundred operation codes. For example, the instruction

```
ADDL2   BONUS,WAGE
```

```
name1:      .BLKL       1           ;RESERVE SPACE FOR name1
name2:      .BLKL       1           ;RESERVE SPACE FOR name2
 . . .
namen:      .BLKL       1           ;RESERVE SPACE FOR namen
            .ENTRY      START,1     ;ENTRY POINT FROM VAX/VMS
            instruction 1           ;program documentation
            instruction 2

            . . .
            instruction k
            $EXIT_S                 ;RETURN TO VAX/VMS
            .END        START       ;START IS THE ENTRY ADDRESS
```

Figure 1.4 An assembly language skeleton

will cause the longword contained in BONUS to be added to the longword in WAGE with the result being placed in longword WAGE. It is analogous to the statement WAGE:=WAGE+BONUS; in Pascal or WAGE=WAGE+BONUS in FORTRAN. (BONUS and WAGE are assumed to be declared as integers.) Similarly, the instruction

```
ADDL3 BILL,TAX,TOTAL
```

will cause the longwords in BILL and TAX to be added together and the result will be stored in the longword TOTAL. This statement is analogous to the statement TOTAL:=BILL+TAX; in Pascal or TOTAL=BILL+TAX in FORTRAN. The contents of BILL and TAX are unchanged and the previous contents of TOTAL are lost.

Several assembly language instructions are listed next, along with analogous statements in Pascal and FORTRAN. The variables A, B, C, and D are assumed to be declared as integers in Pascal and FORTRAN. The symbolic addresses A, B, C, and D are assumed to be declared with .BLKL 1 in assembly language.

Assembly Language	Pascal	FORTRAN
MOVL #100,A	A:=100;	A=100
MOVL A,B	B:=A;	B=A
ADDL2 #10,B	B:=B+10;	B=B+10
ADDL3 #40,A,C	C:=40+A;	C=40+A
SUBL2 B,C	C:=C-B;	C=C-B
SUBL3 #30,A,D	D:=A-30;	D=A-30
SUBL3 B,#200,D	D:=200-B;	D=200-B

Notice that the last assembly language statement on the last line, SUBL3 B,#200,D should be read as "Subtract the longword in B from the number 200 and place the result in D."

The following assembly language statements contain a variety of errors. The effects of these errors are described in more detail in Chapter 4 and Appendix A.

Assembly Statement	Error
MOVL 100,A	Number sign (#) omitted
MOVL A,#100	Last operand cannot be a constant
ADDL2 A B	Comma required between operands
ADDL3 A,B	ADDL3 requires three operands
MOVE A,B	MOVL, not MOVE
SUB2L A,B	SUBL2, not SUB2L
ADDL4 A,B,C,D	No ADDL4 operation code

The sophistication of higher-level languages usually requires that a single statement be translated into several machine language instructions. On the other hand, most assembly language statements are translated into machine language on a one-to-one basis. This is the fundamental difference between assembly languages and higher-level languages. In the previous examples, the higher-level languages were chosen for their simplicity to make their implementation in assembly language obvious. In most cases, the translation is not so simple. For example, the statement $A := B + C - D - 10$; in Pascal can be implemented with the following assembly language statements

```
ADDL3  B,C,A
SUBL2  D,A
SUBL2  #10,A
```

Exercise Set 2

1. After reading Appendix A, assemble and execute the assembly language program in Figure 1.3.

2. Reenter the program in Exercise 1 as making the following modifications and attempt to assemble and execute the modified program. (Note that the changes are not cumulative.) Each modification introduces an error into the program. Describe the effect of each error. That is, does the error produce an error message from the assembler, the linker, or during execution, or does it simply produce incorrect results?

   a. Remove line 3 (J:.BLKL 1) so that J is not declared.

   b. Remove the colon from line 4 so that it becomes K .BLKL 1.

c. Remove the number sign from line 7 so that it becomes MOVL 20, J.

d. Change line 7 to MOVL 700, J.

e. Change line 9 to MOVL #J,DIF.

3. Write and run an assembly language program that is equivalent to the following FORTRAN and Pascal programs.

FORTRAN

```
INTEGER J, K, L
J=15
K=22
L=J-K+9
STOP
END
```

Pascal

```
PROGRAM THREE;
VAR
   J, K, L:INTEGER;
BEGIN
   J := 15;
   K := 22;
   L := J-K+9;
END.
```

4. Write and run an assembly language program that is equivalent to the following FORTRAN and Pascal programs. Notice that multiplication can be achieved with successive addition. Your program should use a temporary longword to store the sum of J and K during execution. When your program exits, J and K should still contain 15 and 9 respectively.

FORTRAN

```
INTEGER J, K, L
J=15
K=9
L=3*(J+K)
STOP
END
```

Pascal

```
PROGRAM FOUR;
VAR
   J, K, L:INTEGER;
BEGIN
   J := 15;
   K := 9;
   L := 3*(J+K);
END.
```

5. Write and run an assembly language program that is equivalent to the following FORTRAN and Pascal programs. (Hint: K can be computed from J with fewer than 10 additions.)

FORTRAN

```
INTEGER J,K
J=50
K=32*J
STOP
END
```

Pascal

```
PROGRAM FIVE;
VAR
   J,K:INTEGER;
BEGIN
   J := 50;
   K := 32*J;
END.
```

6. Solve Exercise 5 assuming that K: = 23*J. (Hint: 23 = 16 + 4 + 2 + 1, so compute 1*J, 2*J, 4*J, and 16*J and add the results.)

7. There are two instructions called MULL2 and MULL3 which multiply two numbers. The format of these instructions is

Assembly Language	Pascal	FORTRAN
MULL2 #10,B	B:=10*B;	B=10*B
MULL3 #40,A,C	C:=40*A;	C=40*A
MULL2 A,B	B:=A*B;	B=A*B
MULL3 A,B,C	C:=A*B;	C=A*B

Solve Exercise 5 by making use of the MULL2 or MULL3 instruction.

Numbers, Counting, and Logic in a Computer

2.1 Introduction

Digital computers manipulate information under the control of a computer program. The way in which the information is represented inside the computer is an important issue. In this chapter, we will see how binary integers and boolean values are represented in the memory of a VAX computer. Later chapters will show how other information—alphabetic information, floating point numbers, and simple data structures such as arrays—is represented.

2.2 Number Systems

Historical Aspects

Throughout history, people have devised many and varied methods for reckoning or counting. Even today we can still find people using such primitive methods of counting as placing stones in a bag or carving notches in a stick. In contrast with the primitive schemes, we can find the elaborate Roman numeral system which is now used mostly for show. However, the number system with which all of us are most familiar is the decimal or Arabic system.* Figure 2.1 shows some examples of numbers represented in various systems.

Decimal Notation

Another feature of our traditional number representation systems is that the schemes of representation tend to use groupings of fives and tens. This causes us to regard 5, 10, and their multiples and powers as extremely important numbers with almost magical properties. After all, it is very easy to multiply or divide a number by 10. It is not so easy to do those same operations with 8, 9, 11, or 12.

The fact is that the only reason that the numbers 5 and 10 have any special properties is because the representations of the numbers are based on tens. Number representations can be based upon numbers other than 10. For example, the fact that there are 60 seconds in a minute and 60 minutes in an hour is a vestige of a base 60 (sexagesimal) number system that was used by the Babylonians more than 4000 years ago. The use of the words "dozen" for 12 and "gross" for 144 illustrates the use of a base 12 counting system. There is really no particular advantage to a base 10 system. The only reason that fives and tens received such importance in number representation is that humans are endowed with ten fingers (five per hand), and the base 10 system most likely evolved from people counting on their fingers. Since computers do not have five-fingered hands, there is no special advantage to fives or tens in a computer. In fact, the contrary is true. Computers can be built to operate more efficiently if they operate using number-representation systems based on numbers other than 10.

Counting in Other than Decimal Notation

As we introduce other number systems, we will review the basic concepts of the decimal system. This includes counting, addition, and subtraction, as well as the interpretation of number representations. In the **decimal system,** numbers are expressed in the form of a string of symbols chosen from a collection of ten **digits:** 0, 1, 2, 3, 4, 5, 6, 7, 8, and 9. Counting is performed by starting with 0, and writing down

---

* Arabic numerals were introduced to the European culture in the twelfth century by means of a Latin translation of a book by the Arabic mathematician Muhammad ibu-Musa al-Khwarizmi (ca. A.D. 780-850). A corruption of al-Khwarizmi's name gives us the word **algorithm,** meaning a well-defined, step-by-step process for solving a problem.

Figure 2.1 Several systems of number representations

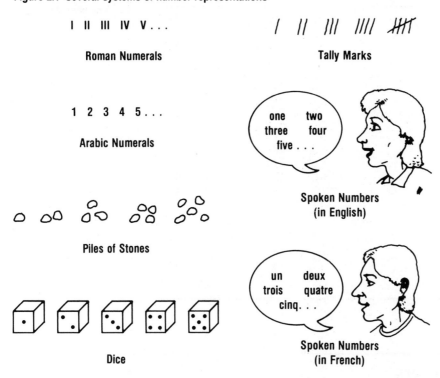

I II III IV V . . .

Roman Numerals

/ // /// //// ⊬⊬

Tally Marks

1 2 3 4 5 . . .

Arabic Numerals

one   two
three four
five . . .

**Spoken Numbers
(in English)**

Piles of Stones

Dice

un   deux
trois quatre
cinq. . .

**Spoken Numbers
(in French)**

successive digits, such as, 0, 1, 2. When we get up to 9, we have used every digit, and we continue by going back to 0 and placing a 1 to the left to get 10, 11, 12, and so forth. When we get to 19, we set the 9 to 0 and count once with the digit on the left to get 20, and so on. When a sequence of 9s occurs on the right, they all go back to 0 and a count, or carry, is propagated to the left. Thus, after 3999, we get 4000.

As stated in the preceding section, there is nothing sacred about the number 10, nor is there any magic about using a set of ten digits. Suppose there were only six digits. This might be the number system we would be using if people had three fingers on each hand rather than five. This system would be called the **base 6** number system.

In the base 6 number system we have six digits: 0, 1, 2, 3, 4, and 5. Counting is basically the same in base 6 as in decimal, except that since there are no 6s, 7s, 8s, or 9s, we must revert to 0 and produce a carry when 5 is reached. Thus, the next number after 5 is 10; after 15 we get 20; and after 255 we get 300. Table 2.1 shows how one could count from 0 to 36 in the base 6 number system.

Decimal	Base 6		Decimal	Base 6	Table 2.1 Counting in the base 6 number system
0	0		19	31	
1	1		20	32	
2	2		21	33	
3	3		22	34	
4	4		23	35	
5	5		24	40	
6	10		25	41	
7	11		26	42	
8	12		27	43	
9	13		28	44	
10	14		29	45	
11	15		30	50	
12	20		31	51	
13	21		32	52	
14	22		33	53	
15	23		34	54	
16	24		35	55	
17	25		36	100	
18	30				

2.3 Binary Numbers
The Need for Binary Numbers

In the previous section, the base 6 number system was introduced as a means of showing how counting can be done in bases other than 10. However, a much more important, though stranger looking, system is the **base 2** or **binary** number system.

Recall that our use of the decimal number system is based upon the primitive practice of counting on our fingers. In other words, the original human hardware available for counting was fingers. Since fingers are used in a ten-state fashion, we perceive the base 10 number system as natural for human use. The use of base 5 and base 20 (the score) by some societies has a similar origin.

The question now is, "What is natural for the computer?" Clearly, computers do not have fingers and thus would have no propensity toward using the decimal system. What is natural for computers is dependent upon the kinds of operations that occur within the various parts of a computer. As we look at the workings of a digital computer, virtually every operation consists of one or more events that either happen or fail to happen. If you look at a certain region of a punched card, that area can either have a hole punched through it or it can fail to have a hole punched through it. There are just two alternatives and no others. A hole cannot be halfway punched. A physical event that can only occur in one of two ways (such as a hole either existing or not existing) is called a **binary** event.* Table 2.2 lists several different binary events.

Event	States
A key on a keyboard	Can be **pressed** or **not pressed**
Hole in punched card	Can be **punched** or **not punched**
A toggle switch	Can be **on** or **off**
A light bulb	Can be **lighted** or **dark**
A digital signal on a wire	Can have **high voltage** or **low voltage**

Table 2.2 Examples of binary events

Binary Counting

The binary number system operates in much the same way as the decimal or base 6 systems, except that there are only two digits, 0 and 1. When you count, you start at 0 as usual. The next number is 1, but you cannot go further since there are no more digits. Therefore, you must go back to 0 and carry a 1 to the next place, giving us 10 in binary for 2 in decimal. Table 2.3 illustrates binary counting up to 32.

Binary Arithmetic

Binary addition and subtraction follow the same scheme that is normally used for decimal arithmetic. First, a rule is needed for adding together two binary digits. Although techniques analogous to those used with decimal digits could be used, it is easier simply to memorize the following table.

0 + 0 = 00 (zero with no carry)
0 + 1 = 01 (one with no carry)
1 + 0 = 01 (one with no carry)
1 + 1 = 10 (zero with a carry)

---

* Readers may note that it is possible for events such as hole punches to be multistate rather than just two-state. For example, three or four or more differently shaped holes could be punched. However, for computer design, this is not usually practical because the construction of a device that is capable of reliably recognizing several different hole shapes would be considerably more expensive than a device that merely has to recognize the presence or absence of a hole.

Decimal	Binary		Decimal	Binary	
0	0		17	10001	**Table 2.3 Counting in binary**
1	1		18	10010	
2	10		19	10011	
3	11		20	10100	
4	100		21	10101	
5	101		22	10110	
6	110		23	10111	
7	111		24	11000	
8	1000		25	11001	
9	1001		26	11010	
10	1010		27	11011	
11	1011		28	11100	
12	1100		29	11101	
13	1101		30	11110	
14	1110		31	11111	
15	1111		32	100000	
16	10000				

A similar set of rules can be developed for subtraction. Figure 2.2 shows some sample binary calculations.

Binary numbers can be interpreted in much the same way that decimal numbers are interpreted. Since there are just two digits, the value of each digit is weighted by a power of 2. Thus, the binary number 11010 is equal to

$$(1 \times 16) + (1 \times 8) + (0 \times 4) + (1 \times 2) + (0 \times 1) = 16 + 8 + 2 = 26$$

Similarly,

$$1011 = (1 \times 8) + (0 \times 4) + (1 \times 2) + (1 \times 1) = 8 + 2 + 1 = 11$$

a.
```
    101
 +   10
    111
```

b.
```
    110
 -   10
    100
```

c.
```
  11010
 +  1011
 100101
```

d.
```
  11001
 -  1101
   1100
```

e.
```
  11111
 +   101
 100100
```

f.
```
 100000
 -   1011
  10101
```

Figure 2.2 Binary calculations

And finally,

$$100101 = (1 \times 32) + (0 \times 16) + (0 \times 8) + (1 \times 4) + (0 \times 2) + (1 \times 1)$$

This is $32 + 4 + 1 = 37$. Note also that $37 = 11 + 26$, as might be expected from example c in Figure 2.2. A list of the powers of 2 is shown on the endsheets at the back of the book.

2.4 Base Conversions

Basic Algorithms

There are two methods that are frequently used for converting numbers from one base to another. One of these methods uses multiplication and the other uses division. The multiplication method is used to convert a number from one base into the base in which arithmetic is being performed. While people normally use base 10 for performing arithmetic, most computers use base 2. The division method is used to convert a number from the base in which arithmetic is being performed into some other base.

Multiplication Method

The first method is based upon the use of powers to define numbers. For example, in decimal, the digits of a number are weighted by 1, 10, 100, 1000, and so forth. In binary they are weighted by powers of two; 1, 2, 4, 8, 16, 32, and so forth. In general, in the base b system the digits are weighted by powers of b. Therefore, given the base b number

$$d_4\, d_3\, d_2\, d_1\, d_0$$

The interpreted value would be

$$d_4 * b^4 + d_3 * b^3 + d_2 * b^2 + d_1 * b + d_0$$

Now computationally, it usually pays to rewrite this formula in a way that does not require the individual computation of each power of the base. The rewritten formula is

$$(\,(\,(\,(0 * b + d_4) * b + d_3) * b + d_2) * b + d_1) * b + d_0$$

The reader may verify that this formula is numerically equivalent to the first. Note that the term $0 * b$ is simply 0, and could be left off, but is included here to make the algorithm simpler to describe. The algorithm for computing this can be stated in English as follows:

1. Set ANSWER to 0
2. Start at the left-most digit of the number to be converted
3. Multiply ANSWER by b
4. Get the next digit of the number and add it to the ANSWER
5. If there are any more digits, go back to Step 3. Otherwise ANSWER contains the converted number.

As an example, let us see how the binary number 10110 could be converted to decimal. The following shows the digits left and the values of answers at each step of the algorithm.

Step	Answer	Digits Left
1	0	—
2	0	10110
3	0	10110
4	1	0110
5	1	0110
3	2	0110
4	2	110
5	2	110
3	4	110
4	5	10
5	5	10
3	10	10
4	11	0
5	11	0
3	22	0
4	22	—
5	22	done 10110 binary is 22 decimal

Division Method

The division method for number conversion works in almost the reverse manner. As we all know, if you take a decimal number and divide it by 10, the remainder will equal the right-most digit of the number. The quotient will be the remaining digits on the left. Thus, if 3754 is divided by 10, the remainder is 4 and the quotient is 375. This same principle applies if a base b number is divided by b. The remainder will be the right-most base b digit, and the quotient will be the remaining base b digits on the left.

Because the quotient contains the remaining digits, this method can be repeated to convert the entire number. The following steps give the algorithm for converting the number N to base b.

1. n gets the number N
2. q (uotient), r (emainder) is computed from n/b
3. r is output as the next digit going from right to left
4. n gets q. If n is not equal to zero, go to Step 2. Otherwise we are done.

Using this algorithm to convert the decimal number 25 to binary, we would have the following step sequence:

Step	n	q	r	Output	Converted Number
1	25				
2	25	12	1		
3	25	12	1	1	1
4	12	12	1		1
2	12	6	0		1
3	12	6	0	0	01
4	6	6	0		01
2	6	3	0		01
3	6	3	0	0	001
4	3	3	0		001
2	3	1	1		001
3	3	1	1	1	1001
4	1	1	1		1001
2	1	0	1		1001
3	1	0	1	1	11001
4	0	0	1		11001 the answer is 11001

Note that we used the multiplication algorithm to convert from binary to decimal, and the division algorithm to convert from decimal to binary. The reason for this is that our native form of arithmetic is decimal. To state this as a general rule, we would say that the multiplication algorithm should be used to convert numbers from any base into the base used for normal arithmetic. The division algorithm should be used to convert from the base used for normal arithmetic to some other base. For human use, this means converting in and out of decimal. However, inside computers such as the VAX, the native form of arithmetic is usually binary. Therefore, in a computer program, we could expect to see the multiplication algorithm used for converting from decimal to binary and the division algorithm used to convert from binary to decimal. This is the exact opposite of what was done in the previous examples.

2.5 Hexadecimal Encoding

Purpose for Encoding

It may be noted that the lower the base of the number system, the fewer possible values for a single digit: 10 for decimal, 6 for base 6, and 2 for binary. Because there are fewer possibilities for each digit, the digits carry less information. As a consequence, numbers represented in the base 6 system tend to require more digits than the same numbers represented in decimal. For example, 10000 in base 6 represents the number 1296 in decimal. The problem is even more severe with binary numbers. For example, the number 71230, as expressed in decimal, comes out as 10001011000111110 in the binary system. There are more than three times as many digits in the binary representation of this number as there are in the decimal representation. It is usually the case that a binary number will have about 3⅓ times as many digits as the same number expressed in decimal.

A single binary digit contains the smallest possible amount of digital information and is usually referred to as a **bit** for **b**inary dig**it**. Because binary numbers tend to be very long, they are very difficult for humans to deal with. Consider your seven-digit telephone number. If it were translated into binary, it would have approximately twenty-three digits or bits. How many people would be able to remember their own telephone number, much less dial a string of twenty-three 1s and 0s without making a mistake? Even professional computer programmers, who have been practicing for many years, are not usually capable of dealing very well with large binary numbers. How then can people and machines communicate?

Method for Encoding

One solution comes in the form of **hexadecimal encoding.** With hexadecimal encoding, a large binary number is split into groups of four bits starting from the right. For the binary number 10001011000111110, this would be done in the following manner:

0001   0001   0110   0011   1110

Note that since the original number contains 17 bits and 17 is not a multiple of 4, it was necessary to pad the left end of the number with three 0s to fill out the left-most group of four. This does not change the number because appending 0s to the left of the number does not change its value.

The next step is to consider each group of four bits as a 4-bit binary number. Four bits can be arranged in 2^4 or 16 ways. Therefore, we need a set of 16 simple symbols for representing the 16 possible bit patterns. The standard way of doing this is to use the 10 decimal digits and the letters A through F. These are the **hexadecimal** symbols.

The next step is to replace each group of four binary digits with the equivalent hexadecimal symbol (see Figure 2.3). Applying this rule to the previous binary string produces the following:

0001	0001	0110	0011	1110	Binary number
1	1	6	3	E	Hexadecimal encoding

Thus, the hexadecimal representation of the binary string is 1163E.

Although one could think of hexadecimal encoding as simply a code for making binary numbers easier to remember, it also serves as a number system in its own right, specifically the base 16 number system. The problem with hexadecimal numbers or numbers in any base higher than 10 is that more than 10 number symbols are needed to represent the different digits. As a result, we can get numbers that do not really look like numbers, like 1163E. However, remembering

Binary Grouping	Hexadecimal Encoding
0000	0
0001	1
0010	2
0011	3
0100	4
0101	5
0110	6
0111	7
1000	8
1001	9
1010	A
1011	B
1100	C
1101	D
1110	E
1111	F

Figure 2.3 Hexadecimal encoding

the basic rule for counting, step through all the digits in order until the highest digit value is reached and then carry a count to the next digit position. In the case of the hexadecimal system, the highest digit value is 15, for which the symbol is F. Therefore, in hexadecimal, the next number after F is 10, the next number after FF is 100, and the next number after B7CFFF is B7D000. Table 2.4 shows how to count in binary and hexadecimal up to 100 (decimal). Note the correspondences between the binary and the hexadecimal.

In order to simplify the representation of numbers in the VAX computer, hexadecimal is used extensively in such places as assembly language, memory dumps, and file dumps. It is obvious that a number such as 6EA7 cannot be decimal, and therefore on the VAX it would be safe to assume that this number is hexadecimal. However, things would not be so obvious with a number such as 1734, which could be interpreted as either decimal or hexadecimal. In order to avoid confusion, hexadecimal numbers in VAX assembly language programs are prefixed by the symbol ^X. Numbers without the ^X prefix are normally assumed to be decimal. In keeping with this notation, the remainder of this book will use ^X to prefix hexadecimal numbers when appropriate to avoid confusion. Thus, if the previous two numbers needed marking to show that they were hexadecimal, we would write them as ^X6AE7 and ^X1734.

Hexadecimal Addition and Subtraction

In many cases it is useful to add or subtract hexadecimal numbers by hand. One approach to addition is to convert the digits in each column to decimal, add the decimal digits, and then convert the decimal sum to hexadecimal. Consider, for example, the following addition problem.

```
   C  8  A
+  A  B  3
```

The right-most or units column contains ^XA and ^X3. Converting to decimal, ^XA + ^X3 equals 10 + 3 or 13 decimal. Converting back to hexadecimal, 13 equals ^XD, which means that the sum of ^XA and ^X3 is ^XD with no carry to the next digit position. At this point, the addition appears as follows:

```
      0          carry
   C  8  A
+  A  B  3
         D
```
(This example is continued on the next page.)

Table 2.4 Decimal, binary, and hexadecimal

Decimal	Binary	Hex.	Decimal	Binary	Hex.	Decimal	Binary	Hex.	Decimal	Binary	Hex.
1	1	1	26	11010	1A	51	110011	33	76	1001100	4C
2	10	2	27	11011	1B	52	110100	34	77	1001101	4D
3	11	3	28	11100	1C	53	110101	35	78	1001110	4E
4	100	4	29	11101	1D	54	110110	36	79	1001111	4F
5	101	5	30	11110	1E	55	110111	37	80	1010000	50
6	110	6	31	11111	1F	56	111000	38	81	1010001	51
7	111	7	32	100000	20	57	111001	39	82	1010010	52
8	1000	8	33	100001	21	58	111010	3A	83	1010011	53
9	1001	9	34	100010	22	59	111011	3B	84	1010100	54
10	1010	A	35	100011	23	60	111100	3C	85	1010101	55
11	1011	B	36	100100	24	61	111101	3D	86	1010110	56
12	1100	C	37	100101	25	62	111110	3E	87	1010111	57
13	1101	D	38	100110	26	63	111111	3F	88	1011000	58
14	1110	E	39	100111	27	64	1000000	40	89	1011001	59
15	1111	F	40	101000	28	65	1000001	41	90	1011010	5A
16	10000	10	41	101001	29	66	1000010	42	91	1011011	5B
17	10001	11	42	101010	2A	67	1000011	43	92	1011100	5C
18	10010	12	43	101011	2B	68	1000100	44	93	1011101	5D
19	10011	13	44	101100	2C	69	1000101	45	94	1011110	5E
20	10100	14	45	101101	2D	70	1000110	46	95	1011111	5F
21	10101	15	46	101110	2E	71	1000111	47	96	1100000	60
22	10110	16	47	101111	2F	72	1001000	48	97	1100001	61
23	10111	17	48	110000	30	73	1001001	49	98	1100010	62
24	11000	18	49	110001	31	74	1001010	4A	99	1100011	63
25	11001	19	50	110010	32	75	1001011	4B	100	1100100	64

In the middle or 16s column, ^X8 + ^XB equals 8 + 11 or 19. Converting back to hexadecimal, 19 equals 16 + 3 or ^X13. Thus, the sum of ^X8 and ^XB is equal to ^X3 with a carry to the next higher digit position. (There will be a carry whenever the decimal sum of the digits is 16 or greater.) The addition now appears as follows:

```
    1  0      carry
    C  8  A
+   A  B  3
       3  D
```

Finally, in the left-most or 256s column, ^X1 + ^XC + ^XA equals 1 + 12 + 10 or 23. Since 23 equals 16 + 7, 23 decimal equals ^X17 or ^X7 with a carry to the next higher digit position. The completed addition is

```
 1  1  0      carry
    C  8  A
+   A  B  3
 1  7  3  D
```

Subtraction is performed in a similar manner. To subtract the numbers

    C 8 A
 — A B 3

begin with the right-most or units column. ^XA – ^X3 equals 10 – 3 or 7 decimal, which equals ^X7. (Because 10 is larger than 3, no borrow is required from the next higher column.) The subtraction appears as follows:

       0   borrow
    C 8 A
 — A B 3
            7

In the middle or 16s column, ^X8 – ^XB equals 8 – 11. Because 8 is less than 11, it is necessary to borrow 16 from the next higher column. Thus, ^X8 – ^XB equals 16 + 8 – 11 or 13 with a borrow. In hexadecimal, this is ^XD with a borrow. The subtraction has now reached the following point.

   –1 0   borrow
    C 8 A
 — A B 3
       D 7

Finally, in the left-most or 256s column, ^C minus ^A minus the borrow is equal to ^X1 and the completed subtraction appears as follows:

   –1 0   borrow
    C 8 A
 — A B 3
     1 D 7

The subtraction can be checked by verifying that ^XAB3 plus ^X1D7 equals ^XC8A.

Exercise Set 1

1. Making use of information available in dictionaries and encyclopedias, describe three historical number systems other than the Roman and Arabic. How do these number systems compare in

a. Ease of learning.

b. Use for computational purposes.

c. Use for representing large numbers.

2. Continue the hexadecimal and binary counting sequences shown in Table 2.3 until you reach the equivalent of 200 decimal.

3. Perform the following binary additions.

a.		**b.**		**c.**	
	101		110		101
+	11	+	101	+	101

d.		**e.**		**f.**	
	10111		11011		11101
+	1010	+	1001	+	101

g.		**h.**		**i.**	
	1011011		110101101		110101100011
+	101101	+	10110010	+	101100011010

4. Using the same pairs of numbers as in Exercise 3, perform binary subtraction rather than addition.

5. Give the decimal equivalent of the following binary numbers.

a. 101	**b.** 11010
c. 111010	**d.** 101110
e. 110011	**f.** 1011101
g. 1100011	**h.** 1101111
i. 11100101	**j.** 1110101011
k. 101110100001	**l.** 11001010101110

6. Give the hexadecimal equivalents of the binary numbers shown in Exercise 5.

7. Perform the following hexadecimal additions.

a.		**b.**		**c.**	
	7F		E3		E3
+	32	+	1A	+	AA

d.		**e.**		**f.**	
	A7B		5E4		E8B
+	82	+	39D	+	C8D

g.		**h.**		**i.**	
	A5B9		48FD		2B89
+	276	+	3CFF	+	FFF

8. Using the same pairs of numbers as in Exercise 7, perform hexadecimal subtraction rather than addition.

9. Convert the following hexadecimal numbers to decimal.

   a. ˆXA   b. ˆX10   c. ˆX100

   d. ˆX1F   e. ˆX2A   f. ˆX45

   g. ˆXA4   h. ˆXC8   i. ˆXDA

   j. ˆX1374   k. ˆX1A3D   l. ˆXF3DE

10. Convert the following decimal numbers to binary.

   a. 10   b. 15   c. 24

   d. 37   e. 42   f. 51

   g. 85   h. 97   i. 128

   j. 1000   k. 3555   l. 5999

11. Convert the decimal numbers in Exercise 10 to hexadecimal. Use the ˆX notation with your answers.

*12. Show how to count to the equivalent of 200 decimal in the base 7 number system. In the base 7 system, how can you tell even numbers from odd numbers? Is there a simple rule, as in decimal?

2.6 Two's Complement Arithmetic
Fixed Register Arithmetic

Our discussion so far has assumed that there are no size limitations on the numbers. However, in a computer, arithmetic is generally performed in devices called **registers.** A **register** is a device which contains the representation of a number. A familiar example of a register is the automobile odometer, which registers the accumulated mileage traveled. The odometer is made of wheels with digits around them which can be rotated to display any number from 0 through 99,999 miles. It is important to note the fixed upper boundary. Most registers in computers have a fixed number of parts and, therefore, there is a fixed upper boundary to the size of the number that can be represented. For example, most operations in the VAX are limited to 8, 16, or 32 binary digits or bits. As a result, you can get some strange results, as happens when an old automobile has gone more than 100,000 miles and registers a very "low" mileage.

Consider, for example, a small machine with 5-bit binary registers. Five bits can be arranged in 2^5 or 32 ways. Therefore, one could

00000	0	01000	8	10000	16	11000	24
00001	1	01001	9	10001	17	11001	25
00010	2	01010	10	10010	18	11010	26
00011	3	01011	11	10011	19	11011	27
00100	4	01100	12	10100	20	11100	28
00101	5	01101	13	10101	21	11101	29
00110	6	01110	14	10110	22	11110	30
00111	7	01111	15	10111	23	11111	31

Figure 2.4 Five-bit unsigned numbers

use such a register to count from 0 to 31 decimal or 00000 to 11111 in binary. Since counting only involves positive numbers, such an interpretation of the contents of a register is called an **unsigned** interpretation and such numbers are called **unsigned numbers.** Any attempt to count beyond 31 will cause the register to wrap around to 0, producing an incorrect result as happens when the odometer of an automobile passes 99,999 miles. This error is called **unsigned overflow.** Figure 2.4 shows all thirty-two 5-bit numbers along with their unsigned decimal interpretation.

However, it actually turns out that the overflow property can be used to represent negative numbers. Consider again the machine with 5-bit binary registers. We will look at what happens when we add 11101 or decimal 29 to various numbers such as 7, 8, and 9. Figure 2.5 shows this arithmetic in binary. It should be noted in each case that a carry is lost off the answer because we are restricted to five bits.

Two's Complement Negative Numbers

Examining the results in Figure 2.5, we can see that when we add 11101 to the binary representation of either 7, 8, or 9, the result is 3 less than the original number. It is as if we had subtracted 3. This works for other examples as well. As a result, in a 5-bit system, 11101 can be thought of as a negative 3. Similarly, 11111 behaves like -1, 11110 behaves like -2, and so on.

11101	=	29		11101	=	29		11101	=	29
+ 00111	=	7		+ 01000	=	8		+ 01001	=	9
00100	=	4		00101	=	5		00110	=	6

Figure 2.5 Addition in a 5-bit register

Representing **signed numbers** in this way is called the **two's complement** system. The name derives from the fact that the negative of a number is obtained by subtracting the number from the power of 2 which is just too large to fit in the register. For example,

$$
\begin{array}{rcl}
100000 & & \\
-\quad\ 00011 & = & 3 \\
\hline
11101 & = & -3
\end{array}
$$

Another way of computing the two's complement of a number is to change all of the 0s in the number to 1s and vice versa, and then add 1. For example,

```
00011  =  3
11100  Interchange 0s and 1s
11101  Add 1 to get -3
```

Figure 2.6 shows all 32 possibilities of 5-bit numbers with their signed decimal interpretations. As the figure illustrates, the leading bit is used to designate the sign: 1 means negative, and 0 means positive. Note that this means that numbers like 11101, which might be interpreted as large unsigned numbers, are in fact negative numbers in the two's complement system. From Figure 2.6 it can be seen that the 5-bit, two's complement system is capable of representing negative numbers from -1 to -16. Positive numbers have the range from 0 to 15. Note that there is a representation for -16 but not for $+16$. This lack of symmetry is due to the fact that the representation for 0 is included with the positive numbers. Any attempt to generate a signed number less than -16 or greater than $+15$ in this representation results in an error called **signed overflow.**

It is important to realize that the same rules of addition are used for both signed and unsigned arithmetic. The difference is the

10000	-16	11000	-8	00000	0	01000	8
10001	-15	11001	-7	00001	1	01001	9
10010	-14	11010	-6	00010	2	01010	10
10011	-13	11011	-5	00011	3	01011	11
10100	-12	11100	-4	00100	4	01100	12
10101	-11	11101	-3	00101	5	01101	13
10110	-10	11110	-2	00110	6	01110	14
10111	$-\ 9$	11111	-1	00111	7	01111	15

Figure 2.6 Five-bit two's complement numbers

way in which the numbers are interpreted. Consider, for example, the following addition:

```
  11000
+ 00101
  11101
```

With the unsigned interpretation, this addition is equivalent to the decimal addition $24 + 5 = 29$. With the signed addition, it is equivalent to $-8 + 5 = -3$.

2.7 Number Representations on the VAX
Bytes, Words, and Longwords

As previously noted, most operations on the VAX operate on groups of 8, 16, or 32 binary digits or bits. A group of 8 bits is called a **byte**, a group of 16 bits is called a **word**, and a group of 32 bits is called a **longword.**

The information contained in a **byte** may be directly represented as 8 binary digits, such as

00111010

Usually, however, the information in a byte is represented as two hexadecimal digits. The byte shown previously would be represented in hexadecimal as

3A

Notice that binary and hexadecimal are just different ways of representing the information contained in a byte. Within the computer, a byte is actually represented in binary. The hexadecimal representation is used for human convenience.

The word "byte" is actually a pun developed in the late 1950s to refer to a mouthful of bits. The second letter was changed to "y" because the printed words "bit" and "bite" are easy to confuse. Continuing the pun, a group of four bits is sometimes called a **nibble** or sometimes a **nybble.**

Although 8 bits is a convenient amount of information for some purposes, it is inconveniently small for others. For example, 8 bits can only be arranged in 2^8 or 256 different ways. If an 8-bit byte is used to represent an unsigned number, it is only possible to represent integers from 0 through 255 (decimal). The range for signed numbers is from -128 to $+127$.

To avoid this problem, the VAX uses 2, 4, 8, or even 16 bytes to store larger quantities of information. In the VAX computer, the information contained in two bytes is called a **word.** Since each byte consists of 8 bits (or 2 hexadecimal digits), a word consists of 16 bits (or 4 hexadecimal digits) of information. The following shows how the word ^X1A2B would be represented in binary.

```
0001 1010 0010 1011
   1    A    2    B
```

The next larger unit of information is a **longword** that consists of 2 words or 4 bytes. Since each byte consists of 2 hexadecimal digits or 8 bits, a longword consists of 8 hexadecimal digits or 32 bits. The following shows how the longword ^X1A2B3C4D would be represented in binary.

```
0001 1010 0010 1011 0011 1100 0100 1101
   1    A    2    B    3    C    4    D
```

Even larger units of information are the **quadword** and the **octaword.** As its name implies, a quadword consists of 4 words or 8 bytes. A quadword is represented with 16 hexadecimal digits or 64 bits. An octaword consists of 8 words, which is 16 bytes or 32 hexadecimal digits or 128 bits. In this book, the most frequently used units of information will be the byte and the longword. The various quantities of information that are used on the VAX computer are summarized in Table 2.5.

On almost all modern computers, a byte refers to 8 bits of information. However, the number of bits in a word depends on the manufacturer and the model of the computer. For example, on the DEC-SYSTEM 10 and the DECsystem 20, a word refers to 36 bits of information, while a word on a large IBM computer almost always refers to 32 bits of information. The word size on the VAX computer was defined as 16 bits to be consistent with the definition of a word on the earlier PDP-11 family of computers described in Chapter 1.

As the previous examples illustrate, the hexadecimal representation for bytes, words, and longwords is much more compact than the binary representation. As a result, the VAX operations will usually be described in terms of the hexadecimal representation. This is possible because, in many instances, the hexadecimal representation and

		Length in		
	Bits	**Hexadecimal Digits**	**Bytes**	**Words**
Byte	8	2	1	
Word	16	4	2	1
Longword	32	8	4	2
Quadword	64	16	8	4
Octaword	128	32	16	8

Table 2.5 Units of information on the VAX

the binary representation give equivalent results. The following is an example of adding two bytes.

Binary Encoding	**Hexadecimal Encoding**
0010 1110	2E
+ 0100 1111	+ 4F
0111 1101	7D

The sum of the hexadecimal encodings, ^X2E and ^X4F is ^X7D, which is the hexadecimal encoding of the binary answer.

As we proceed, hexadecimal encodings will be used for just about everything. This is true to the extent that there is a tendency to start thinking that the VAX is a hexadecimal computer rather than a binary computer. This is not the case, however, and, as we shall see, there are certain operations such as the boolean operations described in Section 2.8 that can most easily be understood in terms of the actual binary representation. For a vast majority of the VAX operations, however, it is quite acceptable to think in terms of the much more compact hexadecimal representation.

Signed and Unsigned Bytes

The 8 bits in a byte can be used to represent signed or unsigned numbers. Table 2.6 shows how hexadecimal bytes between ^X00 and ^XFF can be interpreted as unsigned or signed numbers. As shown in the table, unsigned numbers range from 0 to 255 with ^X00 representing 0 and ^XFF representing 255. For signed numbers, the two's complement representation is used. Signed numbers range from −128 to +127. Note that ^X80 represents −128, ^XFF represents −1, ^X00 represents 0, and ^X7F represents +127.

Hexadecimal Contents	Unsigned Interpretation	Signed Interpretation
00	0	0
01	1	1
02	2	2
03	3	3
04	4	4
05	5	5
.	.	.
.	.	.
.	.	.
7C	124	124
7D	125	125
7E	126	126
7F	127	127
80	128	−128
81	129	−127
82	130	−126
83	131	−125
.	.	.
.	.	.
.	.	.
FC	252	−4
FD	253	−3
FE	254	−2
FF	255	−1

Table 2.6 The range of signed and unsigned byte operands with decimal equivalents

With 5-bit numbers, we noted that the same addition rules are used for signed and unsigned numbers. The same result holds for signed and unsigned bytes. The difference is in the way that the numbers are interpreted. For example, if ˆXFC and ˆX02 are added, the result is ˆXFE. With the unsigned interpretation, this corresponds to adding 252 to 2 to get 254. With the signed interpretation, this corresponds to adding −4 to 2 to get −2.

Overflow errors are possible with either interpretation. For example, the sum of ˆXFF and ˆX03 is ˆX02. (What would normally be the correct unsigned sum, ˆX102, will not fit in a byte.) For signed numbers, this is correct because the sum of −1 and 3 is 2. However, for unsigned numbers, the result is incorrect because 255 plus 3 is certainly not equal to 2, and we say that **unsigned overflow** has occurred. Similarly, the sum of ˆX7E and ˆX04 is ˆX82. In this case, the unsigned result is correct (126 plus 4 is equal to 130) but the signed result is incorrect (126 plus 4 is not equal to −126) and we say that **signed**

overflow has occurred. Obviously, either kind of overflow condition indicates that an arithmetic operation may have produced an incorrect result. Chapter 6 explains how to test for overflow.

Signed and Unsigned Words and Longwords

In addition to bytes, the VAX can also manipulate 16-bit words, 32-bit longwords, and, to some extent, 64-bit quadwords. This allows arithmetic with a greater range of numbers. For example, when bytes, words, and longwords are used to represent unsigned integers, their ranges are as follows:

	Byte	Word	Longword
Zero	^X00	^X0000	^X00000000
Maximum value	^XFF or 255	^XFFFF or 65,535	^XFFFFFFFF or 4,294,967,295

The minimum (most negative) and maximum numbers that are used when bytes, words, and longwords are used to represent signed integers are shown in the following chart. Some intermediate values, including −2, −1, 0, +1, and +2 are also shown.

	Byte	Word	Longword
Minimum value	^X80 or −128	^X8000 or −32,768	^X80000000 or −2,147,483,648
Minimum plus one	^X81 or −127	^X8001 or −32,767	^X80000001 or −2,147,483,647
Minus two	^XFE	^XFFFE	^XFFFFFFFE
Minus one	^XFF	^XFFFF	^XFFFFFFFF
Zero	^X00	^X0000	^X00000000
Plus one	^X01	^X0001	^X00000001
Plus two	^X02	^X0002	^X00000002
Maximum minus one	^X7E or +126	^X7FFE or +32,766	^X7FFFFFFE or +2,147,483,646
Maximum value	^X7F or +127	^X7FFF or +32,767	^X7FFFFFFF or +2,147,483,647

As the tables show, words and longwords are just like bytes except that the added bits allow larger numbers to be represented. Arithmetic operations on word or longword operands can produce signed or unsigned overflow in the same way that byte operations can produce overflow.

2.8 Boolean Logic

Values and Operations

In the nineteenth century, an English mathematician named George Boole developed algebraic methods for dealing with the logical values of true and false. When working with computers, it is quite useful at times to interpret the binary 1 and 0 as the **Boolean values** of true and false.

In order to manipulate the Boolean value, it is necessary to have **Boolean operations.** The basic Boolean operations are **AND, OR,** and **NOT.** The **AND** and **OR** combine the truth values of two sentences together in much the same way that is done in English. For example, **a AND b** is true if and only if both **a** and **b** are true. Similarly **a OR b** is true when **a** or **b** is true or if both **a** and **b** are true. The **NOT** operation reverses the truth value; thus, **NOT a** is true if **a** is false, and **NOT a** is false if **a** is true. Figure 2.7 shows all of the possible combinations of operations for the three Boolean operators. As is done in most computer usage, true is represented as 1 and false as 0.

Tables of a Boolean operation such as the one shown in Figure 2.7 are called **truth tables** and can be used to define any Boolean operation other than the basic three previously shown. For example, another commonly used Boolean operation is the **exclusive OR.** This is defined as the same as **OR** but is false when both operands are true. The truth table for **exclusive OR** is

```
0 exclusive OR 0 = 0
0 exclusive OR 1 = 1
1 exclusive OR 0 = 1
1 exclusive OR 1 = 0
```

It turns out that any Boolean operation can be formed from the basic three: **AND, OR,** and **NOT.** For example

a exclusive OR b = (a OR b) AND NOT (a AND b)

Multibit Operations

The VAX computer includes instructions for performing Boolean operations on bytes, words, and longwords. When used in this way, Boolean operations are extended to operate in a bit-by-bit manner across

0 AND 0 = 0	0 OR 0 = 0	NOT 0 = 1	
0 AND 1 = 0	0 OR 1 = 1	NOT 1 = 0	
1 AND 0 = 0	1 OR 0 = 1		
1 AND 1 = 1	1 OR 1 = 1		

Figure 2.7 Boolean Operations

corresponding bits in a byte, word, or longword. For example, with two longwords we could have the following operation.

```
        1011 0111 1100 1010 0000 0000 1111 1111
OR      0010 0101 0101 0011 0000 1111 0000 1111
        1011 0111 1101 1011 0000 1111 1111 1111
```

Note that each bit of the result is the **OR** of the two corresponding bits above it. There are operations other than purely logical ones that can make use of Boolean operations this way. For example, the following operation illustrates the use of **AND** to mask out (set to zero) the left-most 16 bits in a longword.

```
        1011 0111 0000 1111 1111 0000 1010 1111   longword
AND     0000 0000 0000 0000 1111 1111 1111 1111   mask
        0000 0000 0000 0000 1111 0000 1010 1111   result
```

Finally, note that if the **NOT** operation is applied to the bits of a longword, it will invert each bit, or change each 1 to a 0 and each 0 to a 1.

2.9 Other Encodings
Octal Encoding

The trend in most computers has been for information to be stored in binary registers having multiples of 8, including 8, 16, 32, and 64 bits. Since these numbers are all divisible evenly only by 1, 2, 4, and 8, the only possible encodings which split up the registers evenly would be binary, base 4, hexadecimal, and base 256. As we discussed before, binary results in very long numbers. Base 4 is not much better, and base 256 would be impossibly difficult to learn. As a result, hexadecimal is the popular number system for most present generation computers.

However, in the past generation of computers, it was more popular to have a multiple of six bits in the register size. As a result, the base 8, or **octal** number system was usually preferred, because binary numbers are then split up into groups of three bits. Among machines which used octal for representing binary numbers were all of Digital Equipment Corporation's major products prior to the VAX, the CDC computers, and most of the IBM 7000 series machines.

To convert a binary number to octal, it is merely necessary to separate the bits into groups of three starting at the right. Zeros may be added to the left to insure that there is an exact multiple of three bits. Then each group of three digits is replaced with its numerical equivalent. This can be found from the first half of Figure 2.5 which was used for hexadecimal conversion. For example, the binary number 1101110011100010 can be converted to octal as follows

001	101	110	011	100	010
1	5	6	3	4	2

Octal has one advantage over hexadecimal in that it is easier to learn and it is easier to do arithmetic by hand in octal than in hexadecimal. However, because of its grouping by threes, octal does not fit conveniently into the byte, word, longword structure of the VAX. Octal does have some importance for VAX users because of the compatibility that the VAX has with the earlier PDP-11 family of computers described in Chapter 1. Documentation for the PDP-11 is mostly in octal in order to maintain compatibility with other Digital Equipment Corporation products that were being manufactured at the time that the PDP-11 was introduced.

One's Complement

As previously described, two's complement numbers can be negated by inverting all of the bits and then adding 1. For example, the following shows how to generate the 8-bit representation of -3.

```
  00000011  =   3
  11111100  =   NOT 00000011
+        1
  11111101  =   -3 in two's complement
```

In contrast, some computers form negative numbers by simply inverting the 0 and 1. On such computers, negating a number can be accomplished with the **NOT** operation. For example, the 8-bit representation of − 3 is **NOT** 00000011 or 11111100. This system is called the **one's complement** system because a number may also be negated by subtracting the number from all 1s. For example,

```
  11111111
− 00000011  =    3
  11111100  =  − 3 in one's complement
```

Of particular note in the one's complement system is that there are two representations of 0. For bytes, they are 00000000 and its complement 11111111. The two representations of 0 may require programmers to be cautious if they are checking to see if a result is 0. The arithmetic operations of addition and subtraction, as well as multiplication and division, must be modified somewhat if one's complement notation is used. However, since very few computers use one's complement arithmetic, these topics will not be discussed here.*

Other Representations

Numbers can be represented in other ways as well. For example, four bits can be used to represent a decimal digit in the following manner; four bits can, of course, be arranged in 16 different ways. If six of these possibilities are considered to be "illegal," the remaining ten "legal" arrangements result in a ten-position switch that can represent a single decimal digit. With this system, the string of binary digits

0001   1000   1001   0010   0000   0100

represents the decimal number 189204 (where 0000 represents the decimal digit 0, 0001 represents the decimal digit 1, and so on). This representation is called the **binary coded decimal** or **packed decimal** representation. Another representation is based on scientific notation and is called **real** or **floating point** representation. It is similar to the exponent notation used to represent large numbers in higher-level languages such as FORTRAN or Pascal as well as in scientific calculators (for example, 3.84536E + 08).

Finally, the emphasis on representing numbers may give a reader the impression that computers are mainly used to perform arithmetic computations. This is simply not true. Strings of binary digits can

* The CDC Cyber computers are notable examples of one's complement machines.

be used to represent any physical event that can be detected. For example, many computer terminals are capable of printing 95 separate characters (including the blank space). Seven bits of information can be arranged in 2^7 or 128 ways. Thus seven bits are sufficient to represent any one of the 95 printable characters with $128 - 95$ or 33 combinations that can be used to represent the special function keys such as RETURN or TAB. Indeed, Chapter 8 will use such a 7-bit code in order to process strings of characters. These coding techniques are very important. For example, they are used when higher-level language programs and assembly language programs are translated into machine language.

Similarly, there are 88 keys on a standard piano. Seven bits of information could therefore be used to designate the pressing of a particular key. (Additional bits may, of course, be required to indicate such things as the time at which the key was pressed, the velocity at which the key was struck, and the length of time that the key was held down.) With such coding techniques, it is possible to write programs for analyzing music or even composing music.

As a final example, it is possible to represent pictures in terms of strings of bits. To do this, a grid pattern with perhaps 1000 rows and 1000 columns is drawn on top of a photograph. From each of the 1 million square areas on the photograph, the amount of light that is reflected is measured and the result converted to a binary number. [If 64 different shades can be detected, the light reflected from each square might be converted to a 6-bit number where 000000 (base 2) represents white, 111111 (base 2) represents black, and the other combinations represent various shades of gray.] The picture has now been converted into a form that can be processed by computer. Photographs from satellites and certain kinds of X ray and other medical images are regularly processed by computers using similar encodings.

Exercise Set 2

1. Show the signed decimal equivalents for the 64 binary combinations in a 6-bit two's complement number system.

2. Add the following pairs of 8-bit two's complement numbers showing carries, including carries that are lost because of the fixed register size of 8 bits. Show the signed number equivalents of both numbers and the result in decimal with each problem.

a. 00000011
00000101

b. 00001011
11111100

c. 11111101
11111010

d. 11101100
11111111

e. 00100111
11011011

f. 10011101
00100101

3. Repeat Exercise 2 but subtract the second number from the first instead of adding. Show borrows, including those that are lost.

4. Convert the numbers in Exercise 2 to hexadecimal and perform the byte additions in hexadecimal showing carries, including carries that are lost off the left end of the number.

5. Repeat Exercise 4 but use hexadecimal subtraction instead of addition. Show borrows, including those that are lost.

6. Each of the following longwords represents a signed number. Give the decimal equivalent. (For some of these numbers, the multiplication algorithm for base conversions described in Chapter 2 will have to be used.)

   a. 0000 000 F
   b. FFFF FFF 0
   c. 0000 0100
   d. FFFF FF00
   e. 0000 1000
   f. FFFF F000
   g. 00ABCDEF
   h. FFABCDEF

7. Convert each of the following bytes, words, and longwords to hexadecimal.

   a. 0011 0111
   b. 1010 0001
   c. 0111 1100
   d. 1110 1111
   e. 0011 1001 1110 0101
   f. 1010 1011 1111 0010
   g. 0011 1011 1110 1111 0101 1000 1101 0001
   h. 1101 1110 0110 1001 1000 1110 0101 1110

8. Each of the following bytes represents a signed number between −128 and 127. Give the decimal equivalent. (Hint: Compute the two's complement of the negative numbers.)

   a. 01
   b. FF
   c. 0F
   d. 1A
   e. FA
   f. A0
   g. 7A
   h. 83

9. Assume that each of the bytes in Exercise 8 represents an unsigned number between 0 and 255. Give the decimal equivalent.

10. For the pairs of binary numbers shown in Exercise 2, show the results of the multibit Boolean operations, AND, OR, and exclusive OR.

11. Show how to count to the equivalent of 200 decimal in octal.

12. Give the octal equivalents of the binary numbers shown in Exercise 7.

Processor and Memory Structure

3.1 Introduction

The operation of most computers involves the transmission of data and control information back and forth between the **processor** and **memory**. The programmable control information is normally referred to as **machine language.** In order to execute a program, that program must be in the machine language for the particular computer being used. As computers have evolved, machine languages have become more and more complex and difficult for humans to work with. As a result, assembly languages and higher-level languages have been developed, which are then translated into machine language for execution. Of the various languages supported by a computer system, assembly language is the closest to machine language. Therefore, in order to understand assembly language properly, it is necessary to have an understanding of the machine language into which the assembly language programs are translated. This chapter describes the basic organization of the VAX computer, its processor, its memory, and the way that the machine language controls some basic operations.

3.2 The Organization of a Computer

Figure 3.1 illustrates the important parts of a simple digital computer: an **input device,** an **output device,** a **memory,** and a **central control unit** or **processor.** The **input device** permits us to put information into the computer. Simple input devices include the buttons

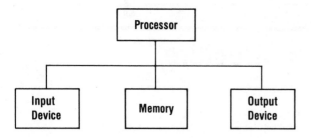

Figure 3.1 A simple
computer

or keys on an electronic calculator or typewriter-style keyboard. The **output device** allows us to get results back from the computer. Simple output devices include the lighted numerals on an electronic calculator, typewriter-like printers, and the screen of a video display terminal. The **memory** is used for storing information. Generally, memory may be thought of as a set of **cells**, each of which contains a number. (In addition to main memory, most computers have auxiliary storage devices such as magnetic disks for storing additional information.) The input device, the output device, and the memory are all connected by electrical wires to a central control unit called the **processor.** By sending electrical signals on these wires, the processor can

1. Ask the input device to get or **read** information and make that information available to the processor or memory.
2. Ask the output device to **print** a particular item of information.
3. Ask memory to save or **store** a particular item of information in a particular memory cell.
4. Ask memory to retrieve or **fetch** the item of information that was previously stored in a particular memory cell.

In this simple computer, the input device, the output device, and the memory are passive devices. They do not do anything unless they are told to do something by the processor. The processor is the active device that controls the transfer of numbers between itself and the other devices. The sequence of operations that the processor performs is determined by a set of **instructions** that form a **computer program.** The job of a programmer is to set up an appropriate set of instructions that direct the processor to perform the operations necessary to solve a particular problem.

3.3 Memory Representation on the VAX Computer

Binary Representation of Memory

Memory on the VAX computer can be viewed as a large number of **memory cells,** each of which contains an 8-bit byte. Since each memory cell can contain an 8-bit byte, we will refer to the contents of each memory cell as a **memory byte** or simply a **byte.** A byte in a memory cell is usually represented as two hexadecimal digits (^X00 to ^XFF).

Each memory cell is identified by a number called the **address** of the memory cell. The address of a memory cell allows the cell to be uniquely identified and can be thought of as being analogous to the street address of a building. A street address allows you to find or identify a particular building; a memory address allows you to find or identify a particular memory cell.

On the VAX computer, an address is a 32-bit binary number. The 32-bit addresses are normally represented as eight hexadecimal digits. For example, assume that address ^X00ABCDEF contained the byte ^X35. In hexadecimal this would appear as

Hexadecimal Contents	Hexadecimal Address
35	00ABCDEF

We are displaying the address on the right and the contents on the left because that is the way the VAX assembler does it. The reason for this will become apparent later. Notice that two numbers are associated with each memory byte—the address, which is 32 bits long, and the contents, which is 8 bits long.

Since 32 binary digits can be arranged in 2^{32} or 4,292,967,296 different ways, a VAX computer program could conceivably address up to 4,294,967,296 different memory bytes (approximately 4 billion bytes or 4 gigabytes). The first byte in memory has the address ^X00000000 and the last byte has the address ^XFFFFFFFF. Figure 3.2 illustrates the possible contents of the first 11 bytes of memory.

Memory as a Collection of Bytes, Words, and Longwords

As noted in Chapter 2, a VAX computer manipulates **words, longwords,** and **quadwords** in addition to bytes. A 16-bit word is stored in memory in two consecutive bytes. The following example shows

Hexadecimal Contents	Hexadecimal Address
90	00000000
9F	00000001
34	00000002
12	00000003
00	00000004
00	00000005
9F	00000006
EF	00000007
CD	00000008
0B	00000009
00	0000000A

Figure 3.2 An example of hexadecimal representation of memory

how the word ^X1234 would be stored in memory bytes ^X00000002 and ^X00000003.

Hexadecimal Contents	Hexadecimal Address
34	00000002
12	00000003

Note that the word that is being represented is ^X1234, not ^X3412. The VAX computer stores the low-order hexadecimal digits of the word, such as ^X34, in the byte with the lower address (^X00000002) and the high-order digits of the word (^X12) in the higher address (^X00000003). When words are represented in this manner, it is necessary to read the bytes "from the bottom up." It is to avoid this problem that listings of data on the VAX are usually read from right to left. Therefore, words in memory are frequently represented as follows:

Hexadecimal Contents	Hexadecimal Address
1234	00000002

When this representation is used, only one address is listed. However, it is understood that memory byte ^X00000002 contains ^X34 and that byte ^X00000003 contains ^X12. It is to remind programmers of this that programs such as the assembler list the address to the *right* of the contents.

A 32-bit longword is stored in memory as four consecutive bytes. The following example shows how the longword ^X000BCDEF would be stored in memory beginning at address ^X00000007.

Hexadecimal Contents	Hexadecimal Address
EF	00000007
CD	00000008
0B	00000009
00	0000000A

Notice that it is again necessary to read the bytes "from the bottom up." The longword beginning in address ^X00000007 is ^X000BCDEF, not ^XEFCD0B00. To eliminate this awkwardness, longwords in memory are frequently represented as follows:

Hexadecimal Contents	Hexadecimal Address
000BCDEF	00000007

The programmer must remember that, in this case, the longword actually occupies bytes ^X00000007 through ^X0000000A and that the low order digits, ^XEF, are contained in byte ^X00000007.

A 64-bit quadword is stored in memory in eight consecutive bytes. An even longer unit of information, the 128-bit octaword, is stored in memory in sixteen consecutive bytes.

Assume that the eleven bytes in Figure 3.2 represent three bytes, two words, and one longword as follows:

1. Addresses ^X00000000, ^X00000001, and ^X00000006 contain bytes,
2. Addresses ^X00000002 and ^X00000004 mark the beginning of words, and
3. Address ^X00000007 is the beginning of a longword.

The information in Figure 3.2 can be represented more compactly as shown in Figure 3.3. This is the format that will generally be used in the remainder of this book. However, it is important to

Hexadecimal Contents	Hexadecimal Address
90	00000000
9F	00000001
1234	00000002
0000	00000004
9F	00000006
000BCDEF	00000007

Figure 3.3 Compact representation for memory

realize that Figures 3.2 and 3.3 contain exactly the same information. They are simply different representations of the same memory contents. Figure 3.3 may seem to imply that the contents of memory byte ^X00000006, ^X9F will be treated as a byte. However, it is quite possible for a program to treat a given memory byte as a byte at one time, as part of a word at another time, and as part of a longword at still another time. There is simply no way to look at a byte in memory and determine how it will be used.

Address Versus Contents of Memory

It is important to avoid confusion between the address of a byte, word, or longword and the contents of the byte, word, or longword in memory. Longwords can be particularly confusing because both memory addresses and longwords are 32 bits long. For example, the following shows several longwords that are stored in memory beginning at address ^X00001000.

Hexadecimal Contents	Hexadecimal Address
0 0 0 0 1 2 3 4	00001000
A 3 B4 F 3 0 3	00001004
0 0 0 0 1 0 0 0	00001008
0 0 0 0 0 0 0 0	0000100C
F F F F F F F F	00001010

In the second line, ^X00001004 is the starting address of the longword and ^XA3B4F303 is the contents. It is possible to change the contents of a memory cell, but never its address. In other words, the contents of a memory cell are variable but the address of a memory cell is fixed.

The distinction between addresses and contents is complicated by the fact that the contents of one memory cell is frequently the address of another memory cell. For example, the longword ^X00001000 in address ^X00001008 could represent the address ^X00001000. In this case, we say that the contents of the longword in ^X00001008 **points to** the longword ^X00001234 in address ^X00001000.

The use of such pointers is very common and extremely important. If a program is to manipulate objects in memory, the addresses of these objects must be available and these addresses, along with the rest of the computer program, are stored in memory. Furthermore, pointers and addresses are the bases for the construction of many data structures. Confusion between the address of a memory cell and the contents of the memory cell is one of the most common errors in writing assembly language programs.

3.4 Processor Use of Memory
Fetch and Store Operations with Memory

Memory is controlled by the processor. The processor can either ask memory to **fetch** the byte in a particular memory cell, or **store** a particular byte in a particular memory cell. A fetch does not change the contents of the designated memory location, but a store does. In order to perform a fetch, the processor sends memory the address of the desired memory location, and memory responds by sending the processor the contents of the addressed cell. For example, using the data from Figure 3.3, if the processor asked memory to fetch the byte in memory cell ^X00000006, memory would respond by sending the number ^X9F back to the processor. Memory cell ^X00000006 would still contain ^X9F.

In order to perform a store, the processor sends memory the address of the desired memory cell along with a number that is to be placed in the designated cell. Again using data from Figure 3.3, assume that the processor asked memory to store the byte ^X1B in memory cell ^X00000006. The old contents of memory cell ^X00000006 would be lost or destroyed, and ^X1B would become the new contents. There would be no record of the fact that memory cell ^X00000006 ever contained ^X9F. If the processor subsequently asked memory to fetch the byte in memory cell ^X00000006, memory would respond by sending back the new contents, ^X1B.

Fetch and store operations with larger quantities of information such as words and longwords proceed in a similar fashion. Again using the data from Figure 3.3, assume that the processor asks memory to fetch the contents of the **word** beginning at address ^X00000002. Memory responds by sending the processor the contents, ^X34, of address ^X00000002 as well as the contents, ^X12, of address ^X00000003. The processor combines the two bytes to form the word ^X1234. Similarly, if the processor asks memory to fetch the longword beginning at address ^X00000007, memory responds by sending the processor the contents of bytes at addresses ^X00000007, ^X00000008, ^X00000009, and ^X0000000A. The processor assembles these four bytes to form the longword ^X000BCDEF. If the processor asked memory to fetch the longword beginning in ^X00000004, memory would respond by sending the processor the four bytes in ^X00000004 through ^X00000007, which the processor would assemble into the longword ^XEF9F0000.*

---

* To achieve higher speed, VAX computer systems actually transfer two or four bytes at a time (depending on the model) between the processor and memory. However, the 16- or 32-bit data paths are transparent to the programmer.

The fetch and store operations are the only operations that memory can perform. For example, memory cannot perform an addition. If it is desired to add two numbers in memory, both must be fetched into the processor and the result must then be stored back in memory.

The ADD Byte Instruction

As previously noted, the processor is the active device that controls the transfer of numbers back and forth between itself and the other devices that form the computer, such as memory. The programmer, in turn, controls the processor by writing a set of instructions, called a program, that the processor executes. For example, the following instruction will cause the processor to add the 8-bit byte contained in memory cell ^X00001001 to the 8-bit byte contained in memory cell ^X00001003, and place the 8-bit result in memory cell ^X00001003.

```
ADDB2    ^X00001001,^X00001003
```

Note that this instruction does **not** cause the processor to add ^X00001001 to ^X00001003 to get ^X00002004. Rather, this instruction causes the *contents* of memory bytes ^X00001001 and ^X00001003 to be added, and the sum to be placed in memory byte ^X00001003. The processor executes this instruction in four steps.

Step 1 Fetch the byte in memory cell ^X00001001.
Step 2 Fetch the byte in memory cell ^X00001003.
Step 3 Add the bytes fetched during Steps 1 and 2.
Step 4 Store the resulting sum in memory cell ^X00001003.

The bytes in addresses ^X00001001 and ^X00001003 are called **operands** because they are "operated on" by the ADDB2 instruction.

The SUBTRACT Byte, MOVE Byte, and RETURN Instructions

The SUBB2 (SUBtract Byte, 2 operands) and the MOVB (MOVe Byte) instructions are similar to the ADDB2 (ADD Byte, 2 operands) instruction. To execute the instruction

```
SUBB2    ^X00001FFF,^X00000500
```

the processor performs the following steps:

Step 1 Fetch the byte in memory cell ^X00001FFF.

Step 2 Fetch the byte in memory cell ^X00000500.

Step 3 Subtract the byte fetched in Step 1 from the byte fetched in Step 2.

Step 4 Store the resulting difference in memory cell ^X00000500.

To execute the instruction

```
MOVB    ^X00001000,^X00001003
```

the processor performs the following two steps:

Step 1 Fetch the byte in memory cell ^X00001000.

Step 2 Store the byte fetched during Step 1 in memory cell ^X00001003.

A program is simply a sequence of instructions. For example, the program in Figure 3.4 will set the contents of memory byte ^X00001003 equal to the sum of the bytes in addresses ^X00001000, ^X00001001, and ^X00001002.

The processor executes the instructions in Figure 3.4 one after the other. The RET (for RETurn) returns control of the processor from the current program to the program that initiated execution of the current program. If the program is a main program running under the VAX/VMS operating system, the RET instruction returns control of the processor to VAX/VMS.

Assume, for example, that memory initially contains the following information:

Contents	Address
1A	00001000
26	00001001
05	00001002
??	00001003

[The two question marks indicate that we don't care about (or don't know) the initial contents of byte ^X00001003.] The first instruction

Instruction 1	MOVB	^X00001000,^X00001003
Instruction 2	ADDB2	^X00001001,^X00001003
Instruction 3	ADDB2	^X00001002,^X00001003
Instruction 4	RET	

Figure 3.4 A simple program

in Figure 3.4 will move ˆX1A to byte ˆX00001003; the second instruction adds ˆX26 to ˆX00001003, changing its contents to ˆX1A + ˆX26
or ˆX40; and the third instruction adds ˆX05, changing the contents
of byte ˆX00001003 to ˆX40 + ˆX05 or ˆX45. When the program returns,
memory will have the following contents:

Contents	Address
1A	00001000
26	00001001
05	00001002
45	00001003

3.5 Machine Language Programs
Machine Language Codes

One question that should arise at this point is where the computer
program physically exists. In our previous description of the computer, there was one place for holding information, the memory. The
memory therefore can be used for storing computer programs. However, since the memory cells are only capable of storing binary strings,
the specific processor instructions must be encoded using a binary
code. The following table shows the operation codes for the instructions MOVB, ADDB2, SUBB2, and RET. Each two-digit hexadecimal
number in the table represents an 8-bit binary operation code.

Operation Name	Operation Code
MOVB	90
ADDB2	80
SUBB2	82
RET	04

In addition to operation codes, the VAX uses **operand specifiers**
to indicate how the operands (the bytes to be moved, added, or subtracted) can be found. The simplest way to designate an operand is
to provide the 32-bit address of the operand. (This is the method that
we have been using throughout the chapter.) This method of finding
an operand is called **absolute addressing.** The code or operand specifier 9F is used to specify absolute addressing.

The following example shows how a MOVB instruction is coded
as a string of hexadecimal digits.

90   9F   00001000   9F   00001003

The operation code, 90, specifies a MOVB instruction. The first operand specifier, 9F, indicates that a 32-bit address will be provided, and ^X00001000 is that 32-bit address. The second operand specifier, 9F, indicates that another 32-bit address will be provided and ^X00001003 is the 32-bit address. If this instruction were placed in memory beginning at address ^X00001004, it would appear as follows:

Comment	Contents	Address
Operation code—MOVB	90	00001004
Operand specifier—a 32-bit address follows	9F	00001005
Address from which byte is to be fetched	00001000	00001006
Operand specifier—a 32-bit address follows	9F	0000100A
Address to which byte is to be stored	00001003	0000100B

Instructions in this all numerical format are called **machine language instructions.** Note that when this MOVB instruction is coded in machine language, it is eleven (decimal) bytes long. The operation code occupies one byte, and it requires five bytes to locate each of the two operands—one byte for the operand specifier and four bytes for the 32-bit address.

In order to save space, the previous MOVB instruction can be listed as follows:

Contents	Address
00001003 9F 00001000 9F 90	00001004

Instructions in this format should be read from right to left. The address at which the instruction starts, ^X00001004, is at the end of the line. The information to the left of the address specifies the contents of addresses ^X00001004 through ^X0000100E. Proceeding from right to left, the operation code is ^X90, the operand designator byte for the first operand is ^X9F, the address from which a byte is to be fetched is ^X00001000, the operand designator byte for the second operand is ^X9F, and the address into which a byte is to be stored is ^X00001003. This is the representation that will normally be used for machine language instructions in the remainder of this book. Note that the two representations of the MOVB instruction contain exactly the same information about the contents of memory. The only thing that differs is the format.

The ADDB2 and SUBB2 instructions have a format that is identical to MOVB. (The only difference is that a different operation code is used.) In contrast, the RET instruction is only one byte long because

Comment	Contents		Address	
A byte of data		1A	00001000	Figure 3.5 Standard format for a machine language program
A byte of data		26	00001001	
A byte of data		05	00001002	
Sum will go here		??	00001003	
MOVB inst	00001003 9F 00001000 9F	90	00001004	
ADDB2 inst	00001003 9F 00001001 9F	80	0000100F	
ADDB2 inst	00001003 9F 00001002 9F	80	0000101A	
RET inst		04	00001025	

RET does not have any operands. Figure 3.5 shows how the program in Figure 3.4 would look in machine language.

If the processor were directed to begin executing instructions at address ^X00001004, the processor would

1. Execute the MOVB instruction that begins in address ^X00001004.
2. Execute the ADDB2 instruction that begins in address ^X0000100F.
3. Execute the ADDB2 instruction that begins in address ^X0000101A.
4. Execute the RET instruction that begins (and ends) in address ^X00001025.

As the result of executing these four instructions, memory byte ^X00001003 would be set to ^X45.

3.6 The Program Counter

Up to this point we have described the way that numbers, including data and machine language instructions, are stored in memory. In addition to this primary or main storage, the VAX processor itself contains a small number of very high speed storage areas. To distinguish the very limited storage areas inside the processor from the much larger storage area in memory, the storage areas in the processor are called **processor registers**, or simply **registers.**

Although there are varieties of storage areas inside the VAX processor, most programmers are primarily concerned with 16 registers called the **general registers.** Since each of the 16 general registers is 32 bits long, each of the general registers contains a longword (four bytes). To distinguish one general register from another, they are numbered from 0 to 15 in decimal (or from ^X0 to ^XF). Note that these processor registers are quite different from memory cells. Each cell in memory can only contain an 8-bit byte. If a 32-bit longword is to be stored in memory, four memory cells are required. In contrast, each general register contains a longword so that the 16 registers contain a total of 16 longwords or 64 bytes.

Despite its name, general register 15 is used for a very special purpose. (As we shall see later, general registers 12, 13, and 14 are used for special purposes as well.) As the processor executes each machine language instruction, it uses register 15 to address the next instruction. As a result, processor register 15 is called the program counter, or simply the PC. To see how the program counter works, the first 15 bytes of the machine language program presented in Figure 3.5 are shown next.

	Memory	
Contents	**Address**	**Processor**
1A	00001000	00001004 PC
26	00001001	
05	00001002	
??	00001003	
90	00001004	
9F	00001005	
00	00001006	
10	00001007	
00	00001008	
00	00001009	
9F	0000100A	
03	0000100B	
10	0000100C	
00	0000100D	
00	0000100E	
. . .	0000100F	

In order to execute the program that begins in address ^X00001004, it is necessary to load the address ^X00001004 into the PC as shown. The VAX/VMS operating system does this when control is passed to the machine language program. The processor then executes the MOVB instruction beginning at address ^X00001004 by performing the following seven steps.

Step 1 Fetch the 8-bit operation code. Because the program counter contains ^X00001004, the processor fetches the byte, ^X90, that is contained in address ^X00001004 and assumes that the byte is an operation code. In addition, the processor adds one to the program counter so that the program counter now contains ^X00001005. (We say that the program counter now points to address ^X00001005.)

Step 2 Fetch the operand specifier byte. Because the operation code fetched in Step 1 is the operation code for a MOVB instruction, the processor next fetches the byte, ^X9F, that is currently pointed to by the PC and assumes that it is an operand specifier byte. The program counter is incremented by one so that it now points to address ^X00001006.

Step 3 Fetch the address of the first operand. The operand specifier byte fetched in Step 2, ^X9F, indicates that the program counter points to the address of the operand. In other words, the four bytes following the operand specifier byte represent the address of the operand. The processor fetches the four bytes in addresses ^X00001006 through ^X00001009 and assembles the four bytes to form the address ^X00001000. During this process, the program counter is incremented by four so that it now points to address ^X0000100A.

Step 4 Fetch the first operand. Because of the address that was fetched in Step 3, the processor fetches the byte, ^X1A, contained in address ^X00001000.

Step 5 Fetch the operand specifier byte for the second operand. Because the MOVB instruction requires two operands, the processor fetches the byte, ^X9F, that is pointed to by the PC (which contains ^X0000100A) and interprets the byte as an operand specifier byte. The processor also increments the PC to ^X0000100B.

Step 6 Fetch the address of the second operand. Because of the 9F fetched in Step 5, the processor fetches the contents of bytes ^X0000100B through ^X0000100E and assembles the four bytes to form the address ^X00001003. In addition, four is added to the PC so that it now contains ^X0000100F.

Step 7 Execute the move. The processor stores the byte fetched in Step 4, ^X1A, into the address fetched in Step 6, ^X00001003. This completes the execution of the MOVB instruction. Because this step does not modify the PC, the PC still contains ^X0000100F.

When the processor finishes executing an instruction, it simply fetches the byte pointed to by the PC (and increments the PC) and assumes that the byte is a new operation code. (After the processor finished Step 7 cited previously, it will fetch the contents of ^X0000100F and assume that it is a new operation code.) The sequence of steps that the processor performs next depends on the new operation code. If the operation code specifies a MOVB instruction, the processor will perform the previous seven steps. If the new operation code specifies an ADDB2 or a SUBB2 instruction, the processor will perform a sequence of nine steps. The first six steps are identical to the first six steps for the MOVB instruction shown previously. The remaining three steps are

Step 7 Fetch the second operand. The processor fetches a byte from memory using the address that was fetched in Step 6.

Step 8 Perform the addition or subtraction. The processor adds (or subtracts) the byte fetched in Step 4 to (from) the byte fetched in Step 7.

Step 9 Store the result. The processor stores the byte computed in Step 8 into the memory byte whose address was fetched in Step 6.

In executing a program, the processor blindly fetches and executes machine language instructions until (1) a RETurn instruction is reached, (2) the computer operator manually halts the machine, or (3) some error condition forces the processor to terminate execution of the program.

3.7 Execution Errors

As we have just seen, the contents of a memory byte can be interpreted or used in a variety of different ways. In Figure 3.5 for example, some bytes were treated as operation codes, others were treated as operand specifier bytes, others were treated as one byte of a four-byte address, and still others were treated as operands. It is not possible to examine the contents of a memory byte and determine how the contents should be interpreted. If a given memory byte contains ^X9F, the contents could represent

1. A PUSH Address of Byte (PUSHAB) operation code. (The PUSHAB instruction will be explained in Chapter 9.)
2. The operand specifier byte 9F.
3. One of the four bytes in the longword address ^X9F9F9F9F.

4. An unsigned byte operand that represents the decimal number 159.

5. A signed byte operand that represents the decimal number −97.

It is important to distinguish between operation codes, operand specifier bytes, addresses, and operands because different rules apply to each. The operation code directs the processor to perform some operation such as MOVB, ADDB2, SUBB2, or RET. Since each operation code is eight bits long, there are potentially 2^8 or 256 different operation codes.* User programs may use the vast majority of operation codes. However, certain operation codes (including the HALT instruction with the operation code ˆX00) are classified as **privileged instructions** and may only be executed by the parts of the operating system that have special privileges. If a user attempts to execute a privileged instruction, an error called a **reserved instruction trap** occurs and control is returned to VAX/VMS.

An operand specifier byte specifies the way in which an operand is to be located. Since the operand specifier byte is eight bits long, there are potentially 2^8 or 256 different ways of locating an operand. The only operand specifier byte described to this point is ˆX9F. With this operand specifier, the longword address of the operand immediately follows the operand specifier byte. As noted previously, this method of finding an operand is called **absolute addressing.** Some of the other 255 possible values for the operand specifier byte are illegal. Attempts to use an illegal value will produce a **reserved addressing mode fault** which will return control to VAX/VMS.

Addresses are 32-bit longwords that can range from ˆX00000000 to ˆXFFFFFFFF in hexadecimal. However, the VAX/VMS operating system generally restricts the addresses that user programs may access. Any attempt to violate these restrictions results in an error called an **access control violation fault.**

Any hexadecimal byte from ˆX00 to ˆXFF is a legal byte operand. As noted in Chapter 2, these bytes can represent signed and unsigned numbers. It is important to realize that there is only one ADDB2 instruction. For example, if ˆXFC and ˆX02 are added, the result is ˆXFE. With the unsigned interpretation, this corresponds to adding 252 to 2 to get 254. With the signed interpretation, this corresponds to adding −4 to 2 to get −2.

---

* Actually, several operation codes function as "escape codes" which indicate that a special operation code can be found in the following byte. This allows many additional operation codes to be defined. Current VAX computers implement a total of approximately 300 operation codes.

Overflow errors are possible with either interpretation. For example, the sum of ^XFF and ^X03 is ^X02. (What would normally be the correct sum, ^X102, will not fit in a byte.) For signed numbers, this is correct because the sum of −1 and 3 is 2. However, for unsigned numbers, the result is incorrect because 255 plus 3 is certainly not equal to 2, and we say that **unsigned overflow** has occurred. The VAX does not consider unsigned overflow to be an error. Chapter 6 explains how to test for unsigned overflow.

Similarly, the sum of ^X7E and ^X04 is ^X82. In this case, the unsigned result is correct (126 plus 4 is equal to 130) but the signed result is incorrect (126 plus 4 is not equal to −126) and we say that **signed overflow** has occurred. If a special bit (called the IV bit) in the processor is set, signed overflow will generate an error called an **arithmetic trap.** Otherwise no error will occur. Chapter 6 also shows how the programmer can test for the signed overflow error.

As noted previously, the VAX can manipulate 16-bit word operands, 32-bit longword operands, and, to some extent, 64-bit quadword operands in addition to byte operands. Arithmetic operations on word or longword operands can produce signed or unsigned overflow in the same way that byte operations can produce overflow.

Exercise Set 1

1. In Figure 3.3, specify the hexadecimal value of each of the following:
   a. The word that begins in address ^X00000000.
   b. The word that begins in address ^X00000001.
   c. The word that begins in address ^X00000008.
   d. The longword that begins in address ^X00000000.
   e. The longword that begins in address ^X00000001.
   f. The longword that begins in address ^X00000005.

2. Define each of the following terms:
   a. operation code
   b. operand specifier byte
   c. operand
   d. program counter
   e. processor register
   f. general register
   g. execution error
   h. machine language instruction
   i. machine language program

3. Assume that memory bytes ^X0200 through ^X0203 contain the following:

Contents	Address
1F	00000200
05	00000201
FF	00000202
3F	00000203

Describe the effect of executing each of the following machine language instructions. For each instruction, list the address and the new contents of any bytes that are changed. (The effects are not cumulative. Addresses ^X0200 through ^X0203 are set to the values shown before each instruction is executed.)

a. 00000203 9F 00000200 9F 90

b. 00000201 9F 00000200 9F 80

c. 00000202 9F 00000200 9F 80

d. 00000200 9F 00000201 9F 82

e. 00000203 9F 00000203 9F 82

3.8 Some Additional Machine Language Instructions

Description of Machine Language Instructions

In order to describe machine language instructions, we will use a notation that is similar to the notation that Digital Equipment Corporation uses in its documentation for the VAX computer system. For example, the four instructions that have been described to this point are

Symbolic Opcode	Opcode	Operands	Operation (description)
ADDB2	80	add, sum	sum←sum + add
SUBB2	82	sub, dif	dif←dif − sub
MOVB	90	src, dst	dst←src
RET	04		return to the calling program

The first line describes the ADDB2 instruction. The symbolic operation code, ADDB2, represents an ADD Byte instruction with two operands. The opcode column indicates that the operation code for ADDB2 is ^X80. The "add" and "sum" in the operands field can be thought of as variable names in a higher-level language such as FORTRAN or Pascal. The names are used in the operation or description column to describe what the operation code does. In this case, the description, sum←sum + add, indicates that the first operand, called "add," is added to the second operand, called "sum," and that the resulting sum is placed in "sum," the second operand.

The other instructions are described in a similar manner. The description for SUBB2 (SUBtract Byte, 2 operands) is "dif←dif – sub." This means that the second operand, "dif," receives the difference between the original value in the second operand, "dif," and the value in the first operand, "sub" (for SUBtrahend or the number to be subtracted). In the description of the MOVB instruction, "src" means SouRCe and refers to an operation that will be fetched or read and "dst" means DeSTination and refers to an operand that will be stored or written.

Two things should be noted about these descriptions of the machine language instructions. First, they should be read in the normal order (from left to right) as opposed to machine language (which should be read from right to left). Second, the descriptions of the VAX instructions, which are listed on the inside cover of this book and appendix F, are in this format.

Additional Instructions

The ADD instruction will be used to illustrate the way in which individual instructions belong to families. In Chapter 1, the instruction ADDL2 (ADD Longword, 2 operands) was introduced. As one might expect, the ADD family includes instructions for adding words. The description of these instructions is

Symbolic Opcode	Opcode	Operands	Operation
ADDB2	80		
ADDW2	A0	add, sum	sum←sum + add
ADDL2	C0		

These instructions will be referred to as the ADD2 family of instructions.

Also in Chapter 1, the ADDL3 instruction (ADD Longword, 3 operands) was introduced. The ADD family also includes three operand instructions for adding bytes and words as well. The description of the ADD3 family is

Symbolic Opcode	Opcode	Operands	Operation
ADDB3	81		
ADDW3	A1	add1, add2, sum	sum←add1 + add2
ADDL3	C1		

For example, the machine language instruction

00000800 9F   00001000 9F   00001200 9F   C1

would cause the longword beginning at ^X00001200 to be added to
the longword beginning at ^X00001000 with the sum stored in the
longword beginning at ^X00000800. If A, B, and C were symbolic
names for the addresses ^X00000800, ^X00001000, and ^X00001200,
then this statement could be written in assembly language as follows:

```
ADDL3   C,B,A
```

The SUB family is similar to the ADD family. Six members of this
family are described as follows:

Symbolic Opcode	Opcode	Operands	Operation
SUBB2	82		
SUBW2	A2	sub, dif	dif←dif − sub
SUBL2	C2		
SUBB3	83		
SUBW3	A3	sub, min, dif	dif←min − sub
SUBL3	C3		

The MOV family contains the following members:

Symbolic Opcode	Opcode	Operands	Operation
MOVB	90		
MOVW	B0	src, dst	dst←src
MOVL	D0		
MOVQ	7D		

The MOVQ (MOVe Quadword) instruction moves a 64-bit quadword.

3.9 Additional Operand Specifiers

Immediate Addressing

An operand specifier byte specifies the way in which an operand is
to be located. The operand specifier byte that we have been using,
^X9F, indicates that the **absolute addressing** mode is to be used. As
we have seen, this mode specifies that the address of the operand is

contained in the longword that immediately follows the operand specifier byte.

The **immediate addressing** mode is similar to absolute addressing except that the operand itself, rather than the address of the operand, immediately follows the operand specifier byte. The operand specifier byte ^X8F is used to specify immediate addressing. Consider, for example, the following machine language instruction.

Second Operand	First Operand	Opcode
00000800 9F	50 8F	80

The operation code, ^X80, specifies an ADDB2 (ADD Byte, 2 operands) instruction. The first operand specifier byte, ^X8F, indicates that immediate addressing is to be used. The following byte contains ^X50, which **is** the first operand. (In the remaining five bytes of the instruction, absolute addressing is used to specify that the second operand is the contents of address ^X00000800.) As a result, this instruction will add ^X50 to the contents of memory byte ^X00000800. If memory byte 00000800 contained ^X60 before the execution of this instruction, it would contain ^XB0 after the instruction were executed.

In a similar manner, the following instruction will cause the number ^X01234567 to be added to the longword beginning at address 00000A00.

Second Operand	First Operand	Opcode
00000A00 9F	01234567 8F	C0

Because the operation code ^XC0 or ADDL2 requires a longword operand, the immediate operand (in this case 01234567) is contained in the four bytes that follow the operand specifier byte. Note that memory cell ^X01234567 is not involved in the execution of this instruction in any way.

Operands that are contained inside a machine language instruction, such as 50 and 01234567 in the previous examples, are called **immediate operands.** (Since the operands are "inside" the machine language instruction, they are immediately available as soon as the instruction is fetched.)

In assembly language, the number sign, #, can be used to specify immediate addressing. For example, in the assembly language statements

```
ADDB2    #80,ALPHA
ADDL2    #1000,BETA
```

the number sign on the first operand will cause the assembler to use immediate addressing when these statements are translated into machine language.

Relative Addressing

The absolute addressing mode (^X9F) that has been used throughout this chapter allows every addressable location to be accessed. However, it is wasteful. For example, the machine language program in Figure 3.5 is reproduced next as Figure 3.6. Note that most of the bytes of the program in Figure 3.6 are used for the addresses. (The program is 38 bytes long and 24 bytes are used for addresses.)

Another method of addressing, called **relative addressing,** can be much more efficient. In relative addressing, an operand is addressed by giving the difference between the actual address and the current value of the program counter. This difference is called a **displacement.** In effect, the displacement tells how much earlier or later the operand occurs from the current location. (Recall that the PC contains the location of the current instruction or instruction segment.)

To see how relative addressing works, examine Figure 3.7. The program in Figure 3.7 is identical to the program in Figure 3.6 except that relative addressing is used instead of absolute addressing. In Figure 3.7, the operand specifier byte ^XAF is used instead of ^X9F. The ^XAF means that a single byte is used to specify the address. If the byte is negative (as a two's complement number), it means that the operand occurs that many bytes earlier in memory. If the byte is positive, it means that the operand occurs that many bytes later in memory.

Consider, for example, the MOVB instruction in Figure 3.7. The operation code, ^X90, is in address ^X00001004. Address ^X00001005 contains ^XAF, which specifies that the first operand will be found using relative addressing. The following address, ^X00001006, contains ^XF9, the displacement. The signed number ^XF9 is equal to

Comment	Contents		Address	Figure 3.6 Standard format for a machine language program
A byte of data		1A	00001000	
A byte of data		26	00001001	
A byte of data		05	00001002	
Sum will go here		??	00001003	
MOVB inst	00001003 9F 00001000 9F	90	00001004	
ADDB2 inst	00001003 9F 00001001 9F	80	0000101F	
ADDB2 inst	00001003 9F 00001002 9F	80	0000101A	
RET inst		04	00001025	

−7. By the time the displacement has been fetched from memory, the program counter will have been incremented so that it contains ˆX00001007. Therefore, the address of the first operand of the MOVB instruction is

$$
\begin{array}{r}
00001007 \\
-7 \\
\hline
00001000
\end{array}
$$

Note that the operand address, ˆX00001000, is identical to the first operand address of the MOVB instruction in Figure 3.6. Figuring out the addresses for the remaining operands is left as an exercise for the reader. (See Exercise 3 on page 73.)

Using relative addressing instead of absolute addressing reduces the size of the program from 38 to 20 bytes. This makes the program not only smaller, but also faster, since fewer fetches are required for its execution. However, the use of bytes for relative addresses can only work for small programs since a byte can only be used to reference forward 127 or backward 128 locations from the current location counter value. To avoid this problem, the VAX allows the use of words or longwords for relative addresses. These addressing modes are distinguished by the operand specifier bytes ˆXCF and ˆXEF respectively. The use of word displacements or longword displacements will make the program longer, but it will also allow the addressing of any location in a program, no matter how large.

The byte, word, and longword relative addressing modes will be seen in programs written in assembly language in the next chapter and are explained in more detail in Chapter 7. As we shall see, relative addressing has other advantages, in addition to the speed and space advantages. As a result, when the assembler translates statements such as

```
MOVB     A,B
ADDL3    C,D,E
```

Comment	Contents					Address
A byte of data					1A	00001000
A byte of data					26	00001001
A byte of data					05	00001002
Sum will go here					??	00001003
MOVB inst	FA	AF	F9	AF	90	00001004
ADDB2 inst	F5	AF	F5	AF	80	00001009
ADDB2 inst	F0	AF	F1	AF	80	0000100E
RET inst					04	00001013

Figure 3.7 A machine language program using relative addressing

into machine language, it uses relative addressing rather than absolute addressing. Notice that the use of relative addressing does not require any additional work by the programmer because the assembler computes the displacements.

Exercise Set 2

1. Assume that memory addresses ^X0200 through ^X020F contain the following longwords.

Contents	Address
0000000F	00000200
FFFFFFFF	00000204
00000100	00000208
00000001	0000020C

Describe the effect of executing each of the following machine language instructions. For each instruction, list the address and the new content of any longword that is changed. (The effects are not cumulative. Addresses ^X0200 through ^X020F are set to the values shown before each instruction is executed.)

a. 00000208 9F 00000200 9F D0

b. 00000208 9F 00000200 8F D0

c. 00000204 9F 0000020C 9F C0

d. 00000204 9F 0000020C 8F C0

e. 0000020C 9F 00000204 9F C2

f. 00000204 9F 00000010 8F 00000208 9F C1

g. 00000204 9F 00000208 9F 00000020 8F C3

h. 00000208 9F 00000200 9F 7D

2. What hexadecimal values will be contained in the longwords beginning at ^X0200, ^X0204, ^X0208, and ^X020C when the following program returns to the operating system? (Execution begins at address ^X0210.)

Instruction	Address
00000200 9F 00000020 8F D0	00000210
00000204 9F 00000040 8F D0	0000021B
00000208 9F 00000200 9F 00000204 9F C1	00000226
0000020C 9F 00000208 9F 0000000F 8F C3	00000236
04	00000246

3. In Figure 3.7, compute the operand addresses for the remaining five operands. Compare the operand addresses with the operand addresses in Figure 3.6.

4. Beginning at address ^X0200, write a machine language program that is equivalent to the following Pascal or FORTRAN program.

FORTRAN	Pascal
INTEGER J, K, L	PROGRAM FOUR;
J=15	VAR
K=22	J,K,L:INTEGER;
L=J-K+9	BEGIN
STOP	J := 15;
END	K := 22;
	L := J-K+9;
	END.

5. Assemble the following program and examine the machine language program in the assembly listing. Identify the operation codes, operand specifiers, addresses, and numbers in the resulting printout. (The .ENABLE statement on the first line directs the assembler to use the absolute addressing mode described in this chapter.)

```
          .ENABLE   ABSOLUTE
J:        .BLKL     1
K:        .BLKL     1
DIF:      .BLKL     1
          .ENTRY    ADDRESS,0
FIRST:    MOVL      #512,J
          MOVL      #64,K
          SUBL3     K,J,DIF
LAST:     $EXIT_S
          .END      ADDRESS
```

6. Repeat Exercise 5, omitting the line which says .ENABLE ABSO-LUTE. This will allow the assembler to use relative addressing. Explain each relative address and show that it will produce the proper effective address during execution.

4

Operation of the Assembler

4.1 Introduction

Programming in machine language is difficult for a programmer. For example, in order to add a longword called **TAX** to a longword called **TOTAL**, a programmer would have to write a machine language instruction such as

Operand	Operand	Opcode
E4 AF	F2 AF	C0

In creating this instruction, the programmer must remember that ^XC0 is the operation code for the ADDL2 instruction and ^XAF is the operand specifier byte for byte relative addressing. In addition, the programmer must compute the byte displacement to access the longword TAX (assumed to be ^XF2 in this example) and the longword TOTAL (assumed to be ^XE4). In order to appreciate the problems that face a programmer, it is worth noting that the VAX has several hundred different operation codes. Furthermore, it is not unusual for a computer program to use several thousand memory cells.

Assembly languages relieve some of the demands on a programmer's memory by using **symbolic names** instead of numbers. For example, the preceding machine language instruction could be written in assembly language as

```
ADDL2    TAX,TOTAL
```

A computer program, called the **assembler**, translates the assembly language program into machine language by substituting appropriate numbers for the symbolic names and special symbols. For the

74

preceding assembly language statement, the assembler would substitute ^XC0 for ADDL2, ^XAF and ^XF2 for TAX, and ^XAF and ^XE4 for TOTAL. Note that assembly language statements are read from left to right in the normal fashion. The previous assembly language statement should be read as "Add the longword beginning at TAX to the longword beginning at TOTAL, storing the result in the longword beginning at TOTAL."

In addition to allowing the programmer to use symbolic names, the assembler also performs computational services such as computing displacements and converting numbers from one base into another.

Typically, each type or model of computer has its own assembly language. Indeed, there are sometimes different assembly languages for a given type or model of computer. In fact, there are at least two different assemblers for the VAX. One is the assembler program that is associated with the UNIX operating system. The second is an assembler called **VAX-11 MACRO** or simply **MACRO** that is supplied by the manufacturer of the VAX, Digital Equipment Corporation, as part of the VMS operating system. The VAX-11 MACRO assembler is the one that will be described in this book.

4.2 An Assembly Language Example
An Assembly Language Program

Figure 4.1 shows an assembly language program that adds the bytes 26, 38, and 5 and places the resulting sum, 69, in SUM. As the figure shows, assembly language statements are composed of four fields. The first field is called the **label** field and it is used to define symbolic addresses such as A, B, C, SUM, and START. The second field is the **operation code** or **opcode** field, which may contain symbolic operation

Label	Opcode	Operands	Comments
A:	.BYTE	26	;A BYTE OF DATA
B:	.BYTE	38	;A BYTE OF DATA
C:	.BYTE	5	;A BYTE OF DATA
SUM:	.BLKB	1	;SPACE FOR ONE BYTE
START:	.WORD	0	;A WORD CONTAINING 0
	MOVB	A,SUM	;SUM:=A
	ADDB2	B,SUM	;SUM:=SUM+B
	ADDB2	C,SUM	;SUM:=SUM+C
	RET		;RETURN
	.END	START	

Figure 4.1 An assembly language program

codes such as MOVB, ADDB2, and RET. In addition, this field may contain **assembly directives** such as .BYTE, .BLKB, .WORD, and .END that direct the assembler to take some special action. The third field is the **operands** field that may be used to specify the operands of an instruction. For example, in the instruction

```
ADDB2    B,SUM    ;SUM:=SUM+B
```

the operands B and SUM specify that the byte beginning at address B is to be added to the byte beginning at address SUM. Finally, the **comments** field is used to document the program.

If this program is assembled, the assembler will translate the assembly language program into machine language. Figure 4.2 shows a segment of the assembly language listing.

In Figure 4.2, the assembly language source code is listed on the right side. The machine language translation is listed on the left side. To assist in interpreting error messages, the assembler assigns a line number to each line as shown in the center of the figure.

Line number six of the program listing is

Machine Language				Assembly Language			
Contents	Addr	Line	Label	Opcode	Operands	Comments
F8 AF F7 AF	90	0006	6		MOVB	A,SUM	;SUM:=A

The assembler has translated the symbolic operation code MOVB to the machine language operation code ^X90 and placed it in address ^X00000006 which the assembler shortens to 0006 in the listing.

Figure 4.2 An assembly language listing

Machine Language				Assembly Language			
Contents	Addr	Line	Label	Opcode	Operands	Comments
	1A	0000	1	A:	.BYTE	26	;A BYTE OF DATA
	26	0001	2	B:	.BYTE	38	;A BYTE OF DATA
	05	0002	3	C:	.BYTE	5	;A BYTE OF DATA
	00000004	0003	4	SUM:	.BLKB	1	;SPACE FOR ONE BYTE
	0000	0004	5	START:	.WORD	0	; A WORD CONTAINING 0
F8 AF F7 AF	90	0006	6		MOVB	A,SUM	;SUM:=A
F3 AF F3 AF	80	000B	7		ADDB2	B,SUM	;SUM:=SUM+B
EE AF EF AF	80	0010	8		ADDB2	C,SUM	;SUM:=SUM+C
	04	0015	9		RET		;RETURN
		0016	10		.END	START	

Addresses in the text may be similarly shortened, when it is clear
what is intended. In order to access operand A, the assembler selected
the byte relative addressing mode (operand specifier ^XAF) and computed the correct byte displacement (^XF7). For the operand SUM,
the assembler used byte relative addressing with the displacement
^XF8. Lines seven through nine are processed in a similar manner,
starting with the next available address, 000B.

Line one of the assembly listing is

Machine Language			Assembly Language			
Contents	Addr	Line	Label	Opcode	Operands	Comments
1A	0000	1	A:	.BYTE	26	;A BYTE OF DATA

The assembly directive, .BYTE is used to reserve space and to specify
a value for a byte. Unless directed otherwise, the assembler begins
assigning addresses at ^X0000. As a result of the label A in this statement, A is a symbolic way of referring to address ^X0000. As a result,
A is called a **symbolic address.** By default, the assembler assumes
that the value following .BYTE is a decimal number. The assembler
thus converts 26 to ^X1A so that it can be placed in address ^X0000.
Lines two and three are processed in a similar manner.

In the fourth line of the listing, the .BLKB (BLocK Byte) directive
is used to reserve space for a byte without specifying an initial value.
The value following .BLKB specifies the number of bytes to reserve.
(The assembly language statement .BLKB 20 would reserve space for
an array of 20 bytes.) In this case, the value is one so that SUM is
simply the symbolic name of a byte whose contents is not specified
when execution of the machine language program starts. The number
00000004 that appears in the contents field of the machine language
portion of the listing indicates that the next available address for the
assembler is ^X00000004. This information is not actually part of the
machine language program, but is used by other systems software in
the process of preparing the machine language program for execution.
The programmer should assume that the contents of memory location
SUM are undefined when execution of the machine language program
begins.

The .WORD directive in the fifth line of the program is similar
to the .BYTE directive except that .WORD reserves space and provides a value for a 16-bit word. Symbolic address START is the **entry
address** of the program. The VAX/VMS operating system treats user
programs as if they were subroutines or procedures and transfers
control to them using the CALLS or CALLG instruction described in
Chapter 9. These instructions require a 16-bit mask which is normally
equal to zero for main programs. The full function of this mask is

explained in Chapter 9. The first instruction to be executed immediately follows the mask.

The .END directive in line ten marks the physical end of the
program. The symbol START following .END identifies START as
the entry address of the program.

4.3 The Assembly Process

Symbol Tables

The translation or assembly process is basically one of substituting
numbers for names. The substitution process makes extensive use of
two tables: the **permanent symbol table** and the **user symbol table.**
The permanent symbol table contains the values for symbols that do
not change, such as the operation codes and assembly directives. A
small section of the permanent symbol table is shown next.

Permanent Symbol	Hexadecimal Value
ADDB2	80
ADDB3	81
ADDL2	C0
ADDL3	C1
ADDW2	A0
ADDW3	A1

The user symbol table contains values for the symbols, such as
labels, that the user creates. For example, the user symbol table for
the program in Figure 4.2 is shown next. The user symbol table shows
the numerical value that is associated with each symbol. That is, A
is a symbolic name for address ^X0000, B is the symbolic name for
address ^X0001, and so forth.

User Symbol	Hexadecimal Value
A	00000000
B	00000001
C	00000002
START	00000004
SUM	00000003

In the assembly listing, the symbol table is shown in alphabetical
order as shown here.

Simple Translation

When the permanent symbol table and the user symbol table are available, the assembly process proceeds as follows. The assembler scans the program line by line. When a symbol is found in the operation code field, the permanent symbol table is searched to see if it is an operation code or an assembly directive. Assembly directives cause an appropriate section of code in the assembler to be executed.

Operation codes are processed in the following manner. For each operation code, the permanent symbol table contains the numerical operation code as well as information about the number and type of operands. The assembler places the numerical operation code in the machine language program and then processes any operands. Using fairly simple rules, the assembler places the appropriate information in the machine language program. This may include operand specifier bytes and displacements. The user symbol table is searched as necessary to determine the value of any symbols used in the operand field.*

Creating the Symbol Table

The previous section assumed that the permanent symbol table and the user symbol table were available. The permanent symbol table does not vary from one program to another. Because of this, the permanent symbol table is "built in" to the assembler.

In contrast, the user symbol table varies from program to program. As a result, the assembler must create the user symbol table. MACRO does this by assuming that **numbers are to be placed in consecutive bytes in memory.** Again, by using fairly simple rules, the assembler can calculate the number of bytes generated by each line of assembly language code. By assuming that the first byte that is generated is to be placed in address ^X00000000, the assembler can determine the exact address of each instruction or data location in the program. Since some of these lines in the program contain a label, the labels can be identified with addresses to form the user symbol table.

More specifically, the assembler creates the user symbol table by keeping track of a single quantity—the address of the next available memory byte. The assembler maintains the current value of this

---

* For symbols in either the operation field or the operands field, the VAX-11 MACRO assembler actually searches the user symbol table first. If the symbol is not found, the assembler searches the permanent symbol table. This order of search allows users to redefine symbols appearing in the permanent symbol table.

quantity in a longword called the **location counter.** (Advanced programmers often write programs in sections. In order to facilitate this, the VAX assembler allows the use of multiple location counters, with one for each program section.)

The location counter is normally initialized to ^X00000000. The assembler scans the assembly language program from beginning to end using the following rules:

Rule 1   When the assembler encounters a symbol followed by a colon (such as START:, A:, or SUM:), a symbolic address is being defined. The assembler inserts the symbolic address into the user symbol table along with the current value of the location counter. The value of the location counter is not changed.

Rule 2   When the assembler encounters a symbol in the operation code field, it adds an appropriate quantity to the location counter. The appropriate quantity is simply the number of bytes of machine language code that the symbol in the operation code field and its operands will generate. For example,

Opcode	Operand	Appropriate Quantity
.BYTE	57	1
.WORD	0	2
.BLKB	1	1
.END	START	0
MOVB	A,SUM	Length of instruction varies
ADDB2	B,SUM	Length of instruction varies
RET		1

The length of instructions such as MOVB and ADDB2 depends on the addressing modes used and the rules used by the assembler for selecting an operand specifier byte. In Figure 4.2, the MOVB and ADDB2 instructions require five bytes each. Applying these rules to the program in Figure 4.2 will generate the symbol table shown.

It should be noted that the location counter is to the assembler what the program counter is to the processor during execution. However, it is also important to note the differences. The location counter is a memory cell (a longword) inside a program called the assembler. It determines where the next byte generated by an assembly language program will be placed in memory. The program counter is a very special register (i.e., a very special piece of hardware) inside the processor of the VAX computer. It determines the starting address of the next machine language instruction to be executed.

Two-Pass Assembly

Figure 4.3 contains a revised version of the program in Figure 4.1. The only difference between this version and the previous one is that the directives reserving space for the longwords A, B, C, and SUM have been moved to the end of the program.

Consider what happens when this program is assembled. The second line of the program contains the statement MOVB A,SUM. In attempting to generate machine language code for this line, the assembler can substitute the numeric operation code ^X90 for the symbolic operation code MOVB. However, it cannot compute operand specifier bytes and displacements for the symbols A and SUM because A and SUM are symbolic addresses that will not be entered into the symbol table until the sixth and ninth lines of the assembly program are reached.

To solve this problem, the assembler uses two passes. This means that the assembler reads through the assembly language program **twice.** The first time, no machine language code is generated because address definitions are missing. However, addresses can be determined as the program is read and the user symbol table is generated. Then in a second pass through the program, the machine language code is produced.

The process of constructing the user symbol table by scanning the assembly language program is called **pass 1** of the assembly process. The machine language program is produced during **pass 2**. During pass 2, the assembler scans the assembly language program a second time and, using the permanent and user symbol tables, substitutes numbers for symbolic names to create the machine language program.

Even with two passes, there is a problem in computing displacements. For example, the instruction in the second line of the program, MOVB A,SUM, can be anywhere from five to eleven bytes long depending on whether byte, word, or longword relative address-

Label	Opcode	Operands	Comments
START:	.WORD	0	;A WORD CONTAINING 0
	MOVB	A,SUM	;SUM:=A
	ADDB2	B,SUM	;SUM:=SUM+B
	ADDB2	C,SUM	;SUM:=SUM+C
	RET		;RETURN
A:	.BYTE	26	;A BYTE OF DATA
B:	.BYTE	38	;A BYTE OF DATA
C:	.BYTE	5	;A BYTE OF DATA
SUM:	.BLKB	1	;SPACE FOR ONE BYTE
	.END	START	

Figure 4.3 A revised assembly language program

ing is used to reference symbols A and SUM. During pass 1, the assembler must decide on an instruction length in order to assign values to symbolic addresses. If the symbols A and SUM had been assigned values earlier in the program, the assembler could easily determine whether byte, word, or longword relative addressing should be used to reference addresses A and SUM. In this program, however, A and SUM are defined later in the program and, on the first pass through the program, the assembler has no way of knowing how far away from the MOVB instruction A and SUM will turn out to be.

To solve this problem, the assembler selects longword relative addressing instead of byte or word relative addressing whenever an undefined symbol is encountered during pass 1.* As shown in Figure 4.4, this significantly increases the length of a program. (The program in Figure 4.2 is ^X16 or 22 bytes long while the functionally identical program in Figure 4.4 is ^X28 or 40 bytes long.)

To avoid this inefficiency, VAX assembly language programmers normally place the data areas in front of the program areas when relative addressing is being used as shown in Figure 4.1. Programs with a structure similar to the program in Figure 4.3 should not be used.

Figure 4.4 A revised assembly language listing

Machine Language				Assembly Language			
	Contents	Addr	Line	Label	Opcode	Operands	Comments
	0000	0000	1	START:	.WORD	0	;A WORD CONTAINING 0
00000027'EF	00000024'EF	90 0002	2		MOVB	A,SUM	;SUM:=A
00000027'EF	00000025'EF	80 000D	3		ADDB2	B,SUM	;SUM:=SUM+B
00000027'EF	00000026'EF	80 0018	4		ADDB2	C,SUM	;SUM:=SUM+C
		04 0023	5		RET		;RETURN
		1A 0024	6	A:	.BYTE	26	;A BYTE OF DATA
		26 0025	7	B:	.BYTE	38	;A BYTE OF DATA
		05 0026	8	C:	.BYTE	5	;A BYTE OF DATA
	00000028	0027	9	SUM:	.BLKB	1	;SPACE FOR ONE BYTE
		0028	10		.END	START	

* The assembler generally allows the programmer to override assembler defaults. In this case, the programmer can specify byte, word, or longword relative addressing by B^, W^, and L^ respectively in front of an operand. For example, the instruction ADDB3 B^X,W^Y,L^Z directs the assembler to use byte, word, and longword relative addressing for X, Y, and Z respectively.

4.4 A Complete Assembly Language Program

If the assembly language program in Figure 4.1 is assembled, linked, and executed, it will properly compute that the sum of 26, 38, and 5 equals 69. However, the program contains elements that are considered to be poor programming practice and poor programming style. A much improved version of this program is shown in Figure 4.5. The first change from Figure 4.1 is the use of the .TITLE directive in the first line of the program. As noted in Chapter 1, the .TITLE directive is not required for program execution, but its use is strongly recommended for proper program documentation. The symbol following the .TITLE directive, in this case IMPROVED, becomes the name of the program. Any symbols following the name (in this case ASSEMBLY LANGUAGE PROGRAM) are treated as comments.

As lines 2 through 6 illustrate, a line beginning with a semicolon is treated as a comment line. Blank comment lines such as line 5 are useful in visually dividing a program into sections.

The .ENTRY directive in the thirteenth line is the preferred method of identifying the entry point of a program. The statement .ENTRY START,0 in Figure 4.5 replaces the statement START: .WORD 0 in Figure 4.1. The first symbol following the .ENTRY directive (in this case START) is the entry address of the program. In addition to causing START to be entered into the symbol table, .ENTRY also marks START as a special address (in this case the entry address that

```
Label     Opcode    Operands       Comments
          .TITLE    IMPROVED ASSEMBLY LANGUAGE PROGRAM
;DESCRIPTION         COMPUTE 26+38+5 AS AN EXAMPLE
;PROGRAMMER          KAPPS AND STAFFORD
;VERSION DATE        JULY 1, 1985
;
;DATA AREA
A:        .BYTE     26             ;A BYTE OF DATA
B:        .BYTE     38             ;A BYTE OF DATA
C:        .BYTE     5              ;A BYTE OF DATA
SUM:      .BLKB     1              ;SPACE FOR ONE BYTE
;
;PROGRAM AREA
          .ENTRY    START,0        ;ENTRY ADDRESS IS
          MOVB      A,SUM          ;SUM:=A
          ADDB2     B,SUM          ;SUM:=SUM+B
          ADDB2     C,SUM          ;SUM:=SUM+C
          $EXIT_S                  ;RETURN
          .END      START
```

Figure 4.5 An improved assembly language program

the VAX/VMS operating system uses to transfer control to the program). In addition, .ENTRY generates a 16-bit mask that is used by the CALLS and CALLG instructions as previously described. The zero following START specifies that the value of this mask is zero, just as it was when the .WORD directive was used.

The final difference between Figures 4.1 and 4.5 is that the RET instruction has been replaced by the symbolic name $EXIT_S. This is the preferred way to return control to the VAX/VMS operating system. $EXIT_S is neither an operation code (such as MOVB) nor an assembly directive (such as .ENTRY). Rather, it is the name of a **macro.** A macro is simply some lines of code that have been given a name and stored in a place that is known to the assembler. When you use the name of the macro (in this case $EXIT_S) in a program, the assembler automatically replaces the macro name with the lines of code. In the case of the $EXIT_S macro, the lines of code return control to VAX/VMS. In order to emphasize that the assembly language for the VAX computer includes this macro feature, Digital Equipment Corporation chose to call the assembler VAX-11 MACRO. Macros will be covered in detail in Chapter 10.

4.5 The Syntax of VAX-11 MACRO Assembly Language

Symbolic Names

Assembly language statements must satisfy certain **rules of syntax** that are required by the assembler. One set of rules concerns the symbolic names created by the programmer, such as A, B, C, SUM, and START in Figure 4.5. Symbolic names can be from 1 to 31 characters long. Symbolic names may be formed from the letters of the alphabet (A–Z), the digits (0–9), and three special symbols: the dollar sign ($), the period (.), and the underscore (_). However, symbolic names must not begin with a digit (0–9). The following are legal symbolic names.

```
X
TAX
R2D2
THISISALONGSYMBOLICNAME
A_MORE_READABLE_LONG_NAME
JULY_4_1776
$14.96
```

The following symbolic names are not legal for the reasons indicated.

Illegal Name	Reason
4_JULY_1776	Name begins with a digit
WAGE RATE	Name contains the illegal character "space"
GROSS-PAY	Name contains the illegal character "minus sign"
$1,234.56	Name contains the illegal character "comma"
THIS_NAME_IS LONGER_THAN_31_CHARACTERS	

It is strongly recommended that symbolic names be chosen with care. Meaningful names such as WAGE, HOURS_WORKED, and MONTH can make an assembly language program easier to debug and maintain. In addition, the dollar sign should **not** be used in symbolic names. The VAX/VMS operating system uses the dollar sign in symbolic names that are used for special system functions, and names that contain dollar signs are reserved for system software. If the user accidentally uses one of these names, errors or unexpected results may be produced. For example, the macro $EXIT_S generates a call to a system program named SYS$EXIT. If the user defined a symbolic address called SYS$EXIT, $EXIT_S would not operate normally.

The Label Field

The label field contains labels or the names of symbolic addresses. Each label is the symbolic name (address) of a location in memory. (Generally, the remaining fields on each line specify the contents of one or more bytes beginning at the designated location.) The label should be a valid symbolic name that is followed by a colon (:).* By convention, labels are normally typed at the beginning of a line, but may appear anywhere on a line provided they are not preceded by any nonblank character. Generally, it is only necessary to place a label on a line if the line is referred to by some other line in the program.

The Operation Code Field

The operation code field may begin anywhere after the label if the statement begins with a label. Otherwise, it is the first nonblank field on the line. However, by convention, the operation code field begins at the first tab stop which is normally the ninth character position.

---

* Spaces or tabs may appear between the name and the colon. This allows programmers to line up the colons on separate lines if they wish.

As a result, the operation code fields in a program line up, making the program easier to read. (Normally the tab stops occur every eight spaces, i.e., in character positions 9, 17, 25, 33, . . . , .)

When a statement begins with a label that is longer than seven characters, the label may be placed on a separate line so that the operation code field can still begin at the first tab stop. For example, to reserve space for an instruction called A_LONG_NAME, use the following two lines.

Label	Opcode	Operands

```
A_LONG_NAME:
         ADDL2      READ_VALUE,X_TOTAL
```

Some programmers use this format for all instruction labels, regardless of the length of the name.

The operation code field may contain three types of symbols:

1. Symbolic operation codes such as MOVL and SUBL2
2. Assembly directives such as .TITLE, .BLKB, .ENABLE, and .END
3. Macro names such as $EXIT_S

Notice that all three types of names conform to the rules listed for user-created symbolic names.

The Operands Field

The operands field may begin at any position after the operation code field provided there is at least one space or tab between the operation code field and the operands field. However, by convention, the operands field usually begins at position 17, the second tab position. The operands field consists of a number of operands separated by commas. The number of operands depends on the contents of the operation code field. The directive .BLKB requires one operand, the operation code ADDB3 requires three operands, and the operation code RET requires that there be no operands. If the user specifies an inappropriate number of operands, the assembler will generate an error message.

The assembler will also generate error messages for absurd operation code and operand combinations. For example, the statement

Label	Opcode	Operands

```
J:       .BLKL      #1
```

will generate an error message because the number sign (#) is an operand specifier byte that is only relevant when the operation code field contains an operation code. Similarly, the statement

Label	Opcode	Operands
FIRST:	MOVL	#5,#3

will generate an error because it doesn't make sense to replace the immediate operand 3 with the immediate operand 5. (A constant cannot have its value changed.)

Comments

A comment must start with a semicolon(;). Anything after the semicolon is ignored in the sense that it is not considered to be part of the assembly language program. Comments can begin anywhere on a line after the operand (or after the operation code field if there are no operands). It is often desirable to make an entire line a comment by placing a semicolon at the beginning of the line.

4.6 Additional Features of the Assembler
Number Conversions

The assembler can perform a wide variety of services to the programmer. One of these services is the processing of numbers in various bases. Normally, numbers in an assembly program are interpreted as decimal numbers. However, if a number is preceded by the characters ^X, the number is interpreted as a hexadecimal number. For example, the effects of the following instructions are identical.

```
MOVL    #64,K
MOVL    #^X40,K
```

Either instruction will move 64 decimal (which is 40 hex) to the longword K. It is for this reason that we have been using the ^X to distinguish hexadecimal numbers in the text.

Similarly, a number that is preceded by the characters ^B is interpreted as a binary number. For example, all of the following are equivalent.

```
MOVL      #24,K
MOVL      #^X18,K
MOVL      #^B11000,K
```

Any one of the three can be used to move the constant 24 decimal to the longword K. The programmer is free to select the one that is most meaningful and convenient for the application at hand.

Incorrectly typed numbers may generate assembly errors. The following numbers are incorrect for the reason indicated.

Number	Reason
^B1012	Binary numbers must be composed of 0s and 1s
1O	The letter "O" has been used instead of the digit "0"
X1234ABCD	The caret "^" has been omitted
123,456	The comma is not legal within numbers

The .BYTE, .WORD, and .LONG Directives

As explained in Section 4.2, the .BYTE directive is used to reserve space and provide an initial value to a byte location. For example,

```
BOND:    .BYTE    007
MAX_BYTE:
         .BYTE    ^XFF
UPDOWN:
         .BYTE    ^B10101010
```

will initialize BOND, MAX _ BYTE, and UPDOWN to 7, ^XFF or 255, and ^B10101010 or 170 respectively. During the assembly process, each line would cause one to be added to the location counter and one byte of information would be added to the machine language program. The largest legal operand for the .BYTE directive is 255.

Similarly, the .WORD directive is just like the .BYTE directive except that it is used to provide an initial value for a 16-bit word. For example, the statements

```
YEAR:    .WORD    1984
MAX_WORD:
         .WORD    ^XFFFF
GROSS:   .WORD    144
```

will initialize YEAR, MAX_WORD, and GROSS to 1984, ^XFFFF or 65535, and 144 respectively. During pass 1 of the assembly process, each of these lines causes 2 to be added to the location counter. During pass 2, the operands are converted to hexadecimal if necessary and placed in the next two bytes of the machine language program. Notice that ^XFFFF or 65535 is the largest legal operand for the .WORD directive.

Similarly, the .LONG directive is used to initialize 32-bit long-words. Unlike some computers, the .BYTE, .WORD, and .LONG directives may follow one another in any order. For example, the statements

```
HOMERS:
        .BYTE    61
MAX_LONG:
        .LONG    ^XFFFFFFFF
PERMUTES:
        .WORD    5040
```

will initialize the byte HOMERS to 61, the longword MAX_LONG to ^XFFFFFFFF, which is approximately 4 billion, and the word PER-MUTES to 5040. Collectively, these statements will add 7 to the location counter and generate 7 bytes of machine language code.

There are now two very different ways of setting a byte, word, or longword to a particular value. For example, assume that a long-word called COUNT is to contain 10. This could, of course, be accomplished with a .LONG directive:

```
COUNT:    .LONG    10
```

However, it could also be accomplished by the pair of statements:

```
COUNT:    .BLKL    1
          ...
          MOVL    #10,COUNT
```

If the first method is used, COUNT is initialized once by the assembler at assembly time. If the second method is used, the MOVL instruction can be placed in a loop and used repeatedly to COUNT to 10. The second method is equivalent to the statements COUNT = 10 or COUNT: = 10; in FORTRAN or Pascal. The first method is analogous to the statement DATA COUNT/10/ in FORTRAN. There is no equivalent to the first method in standard Pascal.

In selecting between these methods, the following guidelines are recommended.

1. If COUNT contains a constant that is not modified by the program, then using the .LONG directive is probably a better choice

than using the MOVL instruction because it saves memory space and time.

2. If COUNT contains a variable that is modified by the program, then the MOVL instruction should be used. The reason is that this program may, at some later time, be executed several times as part of a larger program. If .LONG were used to initialize COUNT, COUNT would only be initialized properly for the first execution.

The .BLKB, .BLKW, and .BLKL Directives

As shown in earlier programs, the .BLKB and .BLKL directives are used to reserve space for bytes and longwords. Similarly, the .BLKW directive is used to reserve space for words. Consider, for example, the following statements:

```
ALPHA:   .BLKB   1
BETA:    .BLKL   1
GAMMA:   .BLKW   1
THETA:   .BLKB   1
```

These four directives will reserve space for two bytes (ALPHA and THETA), one word (GAMMA), and one longword (BETA). Collectively, they will cause $1 + 1 + 2 + 4 = 8$ to be added to the location counter.

As described in Chapter 7, the various $.BLK_x$ directives can be used to reserve space for arrays. For example, the statement

```
VECTOR:  .BLKL   20
```

will cause VECTOR to be the starting address of an array of 20 long-words. This statement will cause $4 * 20 = 80$ to be added to the location counter.

Simple Expressions

A variety of types of symbolic names have been described. The types include labels (symbolic addresses), symbolic operation codes, assembly directives, and macros. All of these types of symbols are fairly complicated objects with their own sets of rules. It would be convenient to have a way of allowing a symbol to simply represent a number.

Assembly expressions allow symbols to represent numbers. If the statement

Label   Opcode   Operand
```
FACTORIAL_7=5040
```

is placed in an assembly language program, then the number 5040 will be substituted for any subsequent occurrence of the symbol FACTORIAL_7. For example, the following MOVL instruction

Label   Opcode   Operand
```
FACTORIAL_7=5040
       · · ·
       MOVL    #FACTORIAL_7,ANS
```

will generate the same machine language code as the instruction

```
MOVL    #5040,ANS
```

Within the assembly process, the equal sign (=) is very similar to the colon (:). During pass 1, the colon causes the symbol preceding it to be entered into the user symbol table with the current value of the location counter. The equal sign also causes the symbol preceding it to be entered into the user symbol table. However, the value that is entered is simply the value on the right hand side of the equal sign. Symbolic names that represent numbers (FACTORIAL_7) should be defined (FACTORIAL_7=5040) before they are used (MOVL #FACTORIAL_7,ANS). By convention, they are generally defined at the beginning of the program just after the .TITLE directive. Symbol definitions such as FACTORIAL_7=5040 can be placed anywhere on the line. However, by convention they appear at the beginning of a line.

The use of symbols that represent numbers has two important advantages, readability and maintainability. To see how the use of symbols improves readability, consider the following statement.

```
MOVL    #12,COUNT
```

This statement indicates that something is being counted but it does not indicate what is being counted. After all, the #12 could refer to (1) the number of units in a dozen, (2) the number of inches in a foot, (3) the number of months in a year, (4) the number of disciples at the Last Supper, (5) the number of years before one becomes a teenager, or (6) the number of notes in a piano octave. Defining symbols such as:

```
DOZEN=12
INCHES_IN_FOOT=12
MONTHS_IN_YEAR=12
DISCIPLES_AT_SUPPER=12
PRE_TEEN_YEARS=12
NOTES_IN_OCTAVE=12
```

allows the programmer to write statements such as:

```
MOVL     #NOTES_IN_OCTAVE,COUNT
```

which are much more meaningful.

Finally, the use of symbols to represent numbers allows the program to be maintained more easily. For example, programs for accounting and inventory control at a doughnut shop would probably use the number 12 many times to convert between units and dozens of units. If this software were transferred to a shop where a dozen referred to a baker's dozen, it would be necessary to examine the program to determine which of the 12s should be changed to 13s. If the program had been written properly, it would only be necessary to change the statement DOZEN = 12 to DOZEN = 13. If this example seems far-fetched, remember that many programs will eventually need to be converted from the English measuring system (pound, foot, quart) to the metric system (gram, meter, liter). The use of symbols to represent numbers can make such conversions much easier.

The statement DOZEN = 12 in assembly language is equivalent to the following statements in FORTRAN and Pascal:

FORTRAN   **Pascal**

```
PARAMETER (DOZEN=12)      CONST DOZEN=12;
```

Symbol definitions in assembly language such as A = 7 appear to be similar to assignment statements in higher-level languages such as A = 7 (or A: = 7 in Pascal). However, they are very different. In assembly language, **all expressions are evaluated at assembly time.** The statement A = 7 causes the symbol A to be entered into the symbol table with a value of 7. When the assembler finds subsequent occurrences of the symbol A, the value 7 is immediately substituted.

In most higher-level languages, **expressions are evaluated at execution time.** During compilation, an assignment statement such as

A = 7 or A: = 7; is actually translated into a machine language such as MOVL #7 ,A. During execution, this instruction causes the number 7 to be moved to memory cell A.

Numbers and Addresses

From our discussion so far, we know that the user symbol table can contain two very different types of objects—symbols that represent addresses and symbols that represent numbers. Addresses are very special numbers that are subject to a variety of restrictions. For example, machine language addresses are 32-bit unsigned numbers. In addition, VAX system managers, using features of the VAX hardware and software, usually restrict the addresses that a programmer can use. Violating these restrictions during program execution will produce an addressing error. Numbers, of course, are not subject to these restrictions.

Although numbers and addresses are quite different, the symbols that represent them are quite similar. The major difference between them is that address symbols are usually entered into the symbol table with a colon (:) while numbers are usually entered with an equal sign (=). As a result, it is easy to use a number as an address and vice versa. For example, in the following statements

```
MILE=5280
         , , ,
         MOVL     MILE,COUNT
```

the programmer has inadvertently omitted the symbol # from the operand MILE. As a result, the symbol MILE, while defined as a number (MILE = 5280), is used as an address in the MOVL instruction. During execution, the MOVL instruction will attempt to fetch the longword beginning at address 5280 or ^X14A0. The effect of such errors is difficult to predict. Depending on the particular situation, they may generate assembly error messages, execution error messages, or simply incorrect answers.

An error also occurs if the symbol # is inadvertently included. For example, in the following statements

```
ALT:     .BLKL    1
         , , ,
         MOVL     #ALT,COUNT
```

the symbol # does not belong in front of the operand ALT. When the MOVL instruction is executed, COUNT will receive the address of

ALT rather than its contents. While there are occasions where addresses are treated as data, the VAX has special instructions for dealing with this. (See Chapter 7.) Therefore it is usually considered poor programming to use the symbol # with an address symbol.

Exercise Set 1

1. Assemble the programs in Figures 4.1 and 4.3 and examine the assembly language listings to see if they correspond to the machine language listings in Figures 4.2 and 4.4 respectively. Assemble the program in Figure 4.5 and compare the listing with the one generated from the program in Figure 4.1.

2. Execute the three programs assembled in Exercise 1 and confirm that the byte SUM contains ^X63 when each of the three programs returns.

3. In the following assembly language program, specify in hexadecimal the values that symbolic addresses A through H will contain before execution begins.

```
A:        .BYTE     20
B:        .BYTE     128
C:        .BYTE     -128
D:        .WORD     128
E:        .WORD     -128
F:        .LONG     ^X128
G:        .BYTE     ^B10000000
H:        .LONG     4096
          .ENTRY    INST,0
          $EXIT_S
          .END      INST
```

4. Using the DEBUG facility, use the MACRO, LINK, and RUN commands to load the program in Exercise 3 into memory. Instead of using the DEBUG command GO to execute the program, use commands such as E/BYTE A and E/LONG F to verify your answers to Exercise 3. (See Section 1.5 and Appendix A.)

5. Assemble, link, and execute the following program using the DEBUG facility. In order to see the machine language program, use the DEBUG command E/BYTE FIRST:LAST which prints the bytes between addresses FIRST and LAST. (Notice that the program has been loaded into memory beginning at address ^X0200.) Identify the operation codes, operand specifiers, addresses, and numbers in the resulting printout. Verify that the byte rel-

ative addresses still point to the appropriate locations even though the program begins at address ^X0200.

```
J:          .BLKL      1
K:          .BLKL      1
DIF:        .BLKL      1
            .ENTRY     ADDRESS,0
FIRST:      MOVL       #512,J
            MOVL       #64,K
            SUBL3      K,J,DIF
LAST:       $EXIT_S
            .END       ADDRESS
```

*6. In the program shown in Figure 4.3, the assembler used longword relative addressing to access A, B, C, and SUM because these addresses were defined at the end of the program. Is it possible to design a three-pass assembler so that byte or word relative addressing is used whenever possible, even when addresses are used before they are defined?

4.7 The Linker

Debugging one large program is usually much more difficult than debugging several small programs. As a result, good programmers usually break up a large program into a number of smaller **modules.** When a problem is split up in this fashion, one of the modules is designated as the **main program** that will initially receive control during execution. The other modules are, in turn, called by the main program, and are called **subprograms** or **subroutines.** There are several instructions in the VAX machine language for calling subroutines and returning from them. Some of these instructions will be described in the next chapter.

It is even possible for the programs to be written in different languages. For example, a main program called A could be the machine translation of a FORTRAN program, while a subroutine called B could be the machine language translation of an assembly language program. By breaking a large problem into smaller subproblems, the programmer can select the best language for solving each subproblem.

Since two modules in the same machine language program cannot occupy the same memory locations, it is necessary to make sure that each module occupies its own set of addresses. This cannot be accomplished by the assembler or higher-level language translators because they do not normally have information about the other modules that will make up the combined program. A program called the **linker** is used to solve this problem.

The linker does two things. First, it moves or **relocates** the various modules that make up a program so that they occupy nonconflicting areas of memory. Second, it makes addresses defined in one module available to other modules as required. (Such addresses are required to transfer control from one module to another.) The linker derives its name from the fact that it links together interdependent machine language modules to create a single machine language program that is ready for execution.

Assembly language programs are normally expected to be processed by the linker even if there is only to be one module. Because of this, the output of the assembler is not in a form that is ready for execution. This output is called an **object** module and is stored in what is called an **OBJ file.** The output of the higher-level language translators such as the FORTRAN or Pascal compilers is also in the form of an OBJ file.

The linker reads OBJ files as input, relocates, and links the object modules to produce a single program that is ready to be executed. A program in this form is called an **executable image** and is stored in an **EXE file.**

At the end of Chapter 3, we noted that relative addressing has significant advantages over absolute addressing in addition to its speed and space advantages. Another advantage is that using relative addressing within a module means that those addresses do not have to be modified when the module is relocated. Within a module, the distance (displacement) between an instruction and the data it references does not change just because the module is relocated. In contrast, if an instruction contains the absolute address of another location within the module, that address will change if the module is relocated. As a result, absolute addresses must be marked by the assembler in the OBJ file so that the linker can modify the address in creating the EXE file. (Modules which require no address modification by the linker are called **position independent.** This important topic is discussed in detail in Chapters 7 and 15.)

4.8 Running a Sample Program
A Sample Program

As an illustration, an assembly language program will be assembled, linked, and executed. It will be assumed that the programmer is using an interactive timesharing terminal of some type.

In the example that follows, the programmer has the name

JOHNDOE. It is assumed that the programmer has used one of the
editors available on the **VAX** computer to create a file called
SAMPLE.MAR. If the user entered a DIRECTORY or DIR command,
the results would be as follows:

```
$ DIR
Directory DISK$USER:[JOHNDOE]

SAMPLE.MAR;1

Total of 1 file.
$
```

Notice that the characters that are typed by the user are underlined.
On the last line, the dollar sign ($) indicates that **VAX/VMS** is ready
to accept another command.

The user can examine the file SAMPLE.MAR by listing it on his
terminal with the **TYPE** command.

```
$ TYPE SAMPLE.MAR
        .TITLE   SQUARES -TABLE OF SQUARES-
        .DISABLE GLOBAL                        ;FLAG UNDEFINED SYMBOLS
;COMPUTE A TABLE OF SQUARES USING FINITE DIFFERENCES
;AUTHOR - JOHN DOE
;VERSION DATE - JULY 31, 1985
SECOND_DIF=2                                   ;CONSTANT SECOND DIFFERENCE
FIRST_DIF_INIT=1                               ;INITIAL FIRST DIFFERENCE
SQUARE_INIT=1                                  ;SQUARE OF ONE
FIRST_DIF:                                     ;VARIABLE FIRST DIFFERENCE
        .BLKL    1
SQUARE_1:                                      ;WILL GET ONE SQUARED
        .BLKL    1
SQUARE_2:                                      ;WILL GET TWO SQUARED
        .BLKL    1
SQUARE_3:                                      ;WILL GET THREE SQUARED
        .BLKL    1
        .ENTRY   BEGIN,0                        ;ENTRY POINT
        MOVL     #FIRST_DIF_INIT,FIRST_DIF      ;INITIALIZE FIRST DIFFERENCE
        MOVL     #SQUARE_INIT,SQUARE_1          ;COMPUTE FIRST SQUARE
        ADDL2    #SECOND_DIF,FIRST_DIF          ;UPDATE FIRST DIFFERENCE
        ADDL3    FIRST_DIF,SQUARE_1,SQUARE_2    ;COMPUTE SECOND SQUARE
        ADDL2    #SECOND_DIF,FIRST_DIF          ;UPDATE FIRST DIFFERENCE
        ADDL3    FIRST_DIF,SQUARE_2,SQUARE_3    ;COMPUTE THIRD SQUARE
        $EXIT_S                                 ;RETURN
        .END     BEGIN
$
```

This program computes the squares of the numbers one through three by using the method of differences. This method relies on the fact that if we compute the differences between successive squares, they form the series 1, 3, 5, 7, ... Note that the difference between successive differences in this series is the constant number two. The following table shows how this operates:

Squares	0		1		4		9		16		. . .
First difference		1		3		5		7		. . .		
Second difference			2		2		2		. . .			

To compute the next square in the sequence, add the constant 2 to the last difference, 7, to get 9. Then add 9 to the last square, 16, to get 25.

Assembling the Program

The assembly language program can be assembled with the command $ MACRO/DEBUG/LIST SAMPLE. The symbols /DEBUG and /LIST after the MACRO command provide additional input to the assembler. /DEBUG informs the assembler that the user wishes to use the DEBUG feature when the program is executed. /LIST requests the assembler to produce a listing of the assembly and machine language programs.

The effect of the MACRO command can be seen by examining the directory.

```
$ MACRO/DEBUG/LIST SAMPLE
$ DIR

Directory DISK$USER:[JOHNDOE]

SAMPLE.LIS;1          SAMPLE.MAR;1          SAMPLE.OBJ;1

Total of 3 files.
$
```

The new file SAMPLE.OBJ contains the machine language version of the program. No attempt should be made to type or list this file because it is formatted as a binary rather than a character file. The new file SAMPLE.LIS contains the assembly language listing. By default, the assembler uses the file type .OBJ for object files and .LIS for listing files. Since the file SAMPLE.LIS is formatted as a character file, it can be typed on the user's terminal as follows:

```
$ TYPE SAMPLE.LIS
SQUARES                        -TABLE OF SQUARES-           24-JUN-1985 20:00:43  VAX-11 Macro V03-00    Page   1
                                                            24-JUN-1985 19:54:02  DISK$USER:[JOHNDOE]SAMPL(1)
                                 0000      1          .TITLE   SQUARES  -TABLE OF SQUARES-
                                 0000      2          .DISABLE GLOBAL                         ;FLAG UNDEFINED SYMBOLS
                                 0000      3 ;COMPUTE A TABLE OF SQUARES USING FINITE DIFFERENCES
                                 0000      4 ;AUTHOR - JOHN DOE
                                 0000      5 ;VERSION DATE - JULY 31, 1985
                       00000002  0000      6 SECOND_DIF=2                                     ;CONSTANT SECOND DIFFERENCE
                       00000001  0000      7 FIRST_DIF_INIT=1                                 ;INITIAL FIRST DIFFERENCE
                       00000001  0000      8 SQUARE_INIT=1                                    ;SQUARE OF ONE
                                 0000      9 FIRST_DIF:                                       ;VARIABLE FIRST DIFFERENCE
                       00000004  0000     10          .BLKL    1
                                 0004     11 SQUARE_1:                                        ;WILL GET ONE SQUARED
                       00000008  0004     12          .BLKL    1
                                 0008     13 SQUARE_2:                                        ;WILL GET TWO SQUARED
                       0000000C  0008     14          .BLKL    1
                                 000C     15 SQUARE_3:                                        ;WILL GET THREE SQUARED
                       00000010  000C     16          .BLKL    1
                                 0000     17          .ENTRY   BEGIN,0                        ;ENTRY POINT
           EA AF    01 D0        0012     18          MOVL     #FIRST_DIF_INIT,FIRST_DIF      ;INITIALIZE FIRST DIFFERENCE
           EA AF    01 D0        0016     19          MOVL     #SQUARE_INIT,SQUARE_1          ;COMPUTE FIRST SQUARE
           E2 AF    02 C0        001A     20          ADDL2    #SECOND_DIF,FIRST_DIF          ;UPDATE FIRST DIFFERENCE
  E3 AF  E1 AF  DF AF  C1        001E     21          ADDL3    FIRST_DIF,SQUARE_1,SQUARE_2    ;COMPUTE SECOND SQUARE
           D7 AF    02 C0        0025     22          ADDL2    #SECOND_DIF,FIRST_DIF          ;UPDATE FIRST DIFFERENCE
  DC AF  DA AF  D4 AF  C1        0029     23          ADDL3    FIRST_DIF,SQUARE_2,SQUARE_3    ;COMPUTE THIRD SQUARE
                                 0030     24          $EXIT_S                                 ;RETURN
                                 0039     25          .END     BEGIN


SQUARES                        -TABLE OF SQUARES-           24-JUN-1985 20:00:43  VAX-11 Macro V03-00 Page   2
Symbol table                                               24-JUN-1984 19:54:02  DISK$USER:[JOHNDOE]SAMPL(1)


BEGIN             00000010 RG D  01
FIRST_DIF         00000000 R  D  01
FIRST_DIF_INIT =  00000001    D
SECOND_DIF     =  00000002    D
SQUARE_1          00000004 R  D  01
SQUARE_2          00000008 R  D  01
SQUARE_3          0000000C R  D  01
SQUARE_INIT    =  00000001    D
SYS$EXIT          ******** G     01
```

```
                          +----------------+
                          ! Psect synopsis !
                          +----------------+
                          (this section of listing omitted)
                             +-----------------------+
                             ! Performance indicators !
                             +-----------------------+
                          (this section of listing omitted)
                             +-------------------------+
                             ! Macro library statistics !
                             +-------------------------+
                          (this section of listing omitted)

There were no errors, warnings or information messages.
/DEBUG/LIST SAMPLE
$
```

The assembly and machine language listings are straightforward with the exception of lines 18, 19, 20, and 22. From what has preceded, one would expect the assembly language statement

```
MOVL  #FIRST_DIF_INIT,FIRST_DIF
```

to generate the machine language instruction

Operand	Operand	Opcode	Address
EE AF	00000001 8F D0		0012

where ^X0012 is the starting address, ^X8F is the operand specifier byte for immediate addressing, and ^X00000001 is the number FIRST_DIF_INIT which equals 1. However, the code that is actually generated at line 18 is

Operand	Operand	Opcode	Address
EA AF	01	D0	0012

In brief, there are two ways of specifying immediate operands—the long way and the short way. The short way is only usable for small numbers. The range is 0 to 63. Any other numbers must use the long method with an operand specifier byte of ^X8F. The short method is called **literal mode** and allows the number to be stored in the operand specifier byte itself. Operand specifier bytes ^X00 through ^X3F are used for this purpose. Literal mode is explained in more detail in Chapter 7, page 190.

Following the assembly language listing, the assembler prints the user symbol table. The entry

```
FIRST_DIF          00000000   R   D   01
```

indicates that the symbol FIRST_DIF has a value of ^X00000000. The R following the address indicates that FIRST_DIF is a **relocatable address** that will be relocated when the program is relocated. The D means that this symbolic name will be available to the debugger. The 01 refers to something called a **program section.** Program sections are described in Chapter 9.

The relocatable address BEGIN is different from the other addresses in the program because it is defined with the .ENTRY directive. As such, the address BEGIN is defined in this program but the symbol BEGIN can be referenced by other programs (such as VAX/VMS). Symbols that are defined in this program but are avail-

able to other programs are called **global symbols** and the characters
RG identify BEGIN as a relocatable global symbol.

The last line of the symbol table contains the entry

```
SYS$EXIT          ********    G        01
```

This symbol is generated by the macro $EXIT_S that was used to
return control to VAX/VMS. $EXIT_S actually generates instructions
that cause control to be transferred to the address SYS$EXIT, which
is an address that is defined by the VAX/VMS operating system. Because
it is used in this program but defined in another program, it is called
a global (G) symbol. The characters ******** indicate that the symbol SYS$EXIT is currently undefined. Global symbols are described
in Chapter 9.

As the symbol SYS$EXIT shows, the assembler does not neces-
sarily consider undefined symbols to be errors. By default, the assembler classifies undefined symbols as global symbols and assumes that
the linker will somehow find values for the undefined symbols. Although
this is a nice feature, it means that some user errors such as misspelled
symbols will not be detected by the assembler. This feature can be
turned off by inserting the following statement at the beginning of
an assembly language program.

```
.DISABLE   GLOBAL   ;FLAG UNDEFIND SYMBOLS
```

When this statement is included, the assembler generates an error
message when it finds an undefined user symbol. (The symbol
SYS$EXIT will not generate an error message because the macro
$EXIT_S has defined SYS$EXIT as external.)

The actual effect of the /DEBUG parameter on the MACRO command can now be described. In creating the object file, the assembler
includes information about global symbols. The rest of the symbol
table is discarded at the end of assembly. The /DEBUG parameter
directs the assembler to include the entire symbol table as part of
the object file. This allows the programmer to use symbolic names
when the program is executed with the DEBUG feature.

Linking the Program

The program can be linked by entering the VAX/VMS command
LINK/DEBUG SAMPLE. The effect of the LINK command can be
seen by examining the user's directory.

```
$ LINK/DEBUG SAMPLE
$ DIR

Directory DISK$USER:[JOHNDOE]

SAMPLE.EXE;1         SAMPLE.LIS;1         SAMPLE.MAR;1         SAMPLE.OBJ;1

Total of 4 files.
$
```

The new file, SAMPLE.EXE is the executable version of the user's machine language program. In translating the object program SAMPLE.OBJ into the executable program SAMPLE.EXE, the linker relocates the program so that it begins at address ^X0200 instead of ^X0000. The relocation process is simple because relative addressing has been used throughout the program. The reason for performing this relocation is described in the section on programming errors and debugging. The /DEBUG parameter on the LINK command specifies that the programmer wishes to use the DEBUG facility when the program SAMPLE.EXE is to be executed.

Executing the Program

The user's program can now be executed by entering the command RUN SAMPLE. Because the /DEBUG parameter was specified on the LINK command, control is passed to the DEBUG program instead of to the user program. (It is also possible to activate the debugger by using the RUN command RUN/DEBUG SAMPLE.) The debugger program lists two lines of information and then responds with the prompt message DBG>.

```
$ RUN SAMPLE

                    VAX-11 DEBUG Version 3.4-2

%DEBUG-I-INITIAL, language is MACRO, module set to 'SQUARES'
DBG>
```

In the same way that the VAX/VMS operating system uses the character $ to indicate that the user should enter a VAX/VMS command, the debugger uses DBG> to indicate that a debugger command should be entered. Usually, the GO command is entered at this point, which causes the user's program to be executed.

```
DBG>GO
routine start at SQUARES\BEGIN
%DEBUG-I-EXITSTATUS, is '%SYSTEM-S-NORMAL, normal successful completion'
DBG>
```

The normal procedure at this point is to examine the contents of memory using the E (for Examine) command. For example,

```
DBG>E SQUARE_1
SQUARES\SQUARE_1:   00000001
DBG>E SQUARE_2
SQUARES\SQUARE_2:   00000004
DBG>E/DEC SQUARE_3
SQUARES\SQUARE_3:   9
DBG>
```

The command, E SQUARE_1 shows that the longword SQUARE_1 in the program SQUARES (SQUARES\SQUARE_1) contains ^X00000001 while the second command, E SQUARE_2 shows that SQUARE_2 contains ^X00000004. Finally the third command, E/DEC SQUARE_3 shows the contents of SQUARE_3 is 9 decimal, the expected result. Notice that, while the assembler uses decimal as the default number system, the debugger defaults to hexadecimal.

The debugger can be used to examine the contents of memory locations that contain instructions. For example, the command

```
DBG>E BEGIN+2
SQUARES\BEGIN+02:   EAAF01D0
DBG>
```

shows the first instruction in the program. (Since BEGIN is the entry point of the program, it is the starting address of the 16-bit (two byte) mask. Since the first instruction to be executed immediately follows the mask, it must begin in address BEGIN + 2.) Examining the longword from the right, ^XD0 is the operation code, ^X01 is the literal operand ^X01, ^XAF is the second operand specifier byte, and ^XEA is the byte displacement.

The debugger has no way of determining whether a given address contains a byte, a word, a longword, or an instruction. Unless otherwise specified, the examine commands display the contents of a longword. Bytes and words may be examined with the commands E/BYTE and E/WORD respectively. The command E/INST (for instruction) can be used to examine instructions. Recall that the symbol table is available to the debugger because the /DEBUG parameter was included in the MACRO command. As a result, the debugger can partially reconstruct the assembly language statement from the machine language program. For example,

```
DBG>E/INST BEGIN+2
SQUARES\BEGIN+02:   MOVL    #01,B^SQUARES\FIRST_DIF
DBG>
```

Notice that the second operand in the instruction begins with the symbols B^. These symbols indicate that byte relative addressing is being used to reference address FIRST_DIF in program SQUARES.

The examine command can be used to examine the contents of absolute (numerical) addresses. The following six examine commands examine the contents of various memory locations between ^X0000 and ^X020A.

```
DBG>E 0
%DEBUG-W-NOACCESSR, no read access to virtual address 00000000
DBG>E 1FF
%DEBUG-W-NOACCESSR, no read access to virtual address 000001FF
DBG>E 200
SQUARES\FIRST_DIF:   00000005
DBG>E 204
SQUARES\SQUARE_1:   00000001
DBG>E/WORD 210
SQUARES\BEGIN:   0000
DBG>E/INST 212
SQUARES\BEGIN+02:   MOVL    #01,B^SQUARES\FIRST_DIF
DBG>EXIT
$
```

As the first two commands illustrate, it is not possible to examine the contents of addresses from ^X0000 to ^X01FF. The programmer has no need to access these locations because the linker has relocated the program so that it begins in address ^X0200. The third command, E 200, causes the debugger to print the longword beginning at address FIRST_DIF. Because of the relocation, symbolic address FIRST_DIF is now equivalent to numerical address ^X0200. By selecting appropriate addresses the contents of SQUARE_1, BEGIN, and BEGIN + 2 are also shown. Finally, the EXIT command is used to return control to VAX/VMS.

Programming Errors and Debugging

Programming errors in assembly language programs can yield a variety of types of error messages. To demonstrate the effects of errors, several errors will be introduced into line 19 of the previous assembly language program. The correct version of this line is

```
MOVL    #SQUARE_INIT,SQUARE_1   ;COMPUTE FIRST SQUARE
```

In the line shown next, the operation code MOVL has been misspelled as MOV.

```
MOV     #SQUARE_INIT,SQUARE_1   ;COMPUTE FIRST SQUARE
```

As a result, the assembler is unable to find a value for the symbol MOV. The result is the following error message:

```
$ MACRO SAMPLE
                                0016    19      MOV     #SQUARE_INIT,SQUARE_1   ;COMPUTE FIRST SQUARE
%MACRO-E-UNRECSTMT, Unrecognized statement

There were 1 error, 0 warnings and 0 information messages, on lines:
   19 (1)
```

A similar message would be generated if the colon following a label were omitted.

Very different types of errors can occur if a number is used as an address. For example, in the next line, the programmer has forgotten to place the symbol # in front of the symbolic name SQUARE_INIT.

```
MOVL    SQUARE_INIT,SQUARE_1   ;COMPUTE FIRST SQUARE
```

This does not generate an assembler or linker error. Rather, during execution, the program will attempt to fetch the longword beginning at absolute address ^X00000001. Because the user is not permitted to access the first ^X200 bytes of memory, the following error message will be generated.

```
$ MACRO SAMPL
$ LINK SAMPL
$ RUN SAMPL
%SYSTEM-F-ACCVIO, access violation, reason mask=00, virtual address=00000001, PC=0000021A, PSL=03C00000
%TRACE-F-TRACEBACK, symbolic stack dump follows
module name     routine name                    line      rel PC     abs PC

SQUARES         , BLANK ,                                  0000001A   0000021A
```

The fact that the virtual address equals ^X00000001 is an indication that the programmer should look for a statement that could possibly generate that address. The address listed under "abs PC", ^X0000021A, is the address that was contained in the program counter at the time the error was detected. Examining locations around ^X021A with the debugger may help to locate the error. The address listed under "rel PC", ^X0000001A, is the PC address relative to the beginning of the module. Examining addresses around ^X001A in the assembly language listing may also help to locate the error (see the assembly listing on page 99.) The address "abs PC" is ^X200 greater than "rel PC" because the linker has relocated the module to address ^X0200.

A variety of programming errors, such as a missing # sign, are likely to generate small illegal addresses. As long as the addresses are less than ^X0200, VAX/VMS will terminate execution of the user program as soon as the program attempts to reference the illegal address. In fact, this is the primary reason that VAX/VMS relocates main programs to address ^X0200 and makes smaller addresses inaccessable to the program.

The use of addresses as numbers can produce programs that execute without error but produce incorrect results. For example, consider the effect of changing line 6 in the program from SQUARE_INIT = 1 to SQUARE_INIT = ^X210. If the program with the incorrect operand, SQUARE_INIT, is rerun, it will assemble, link, and execute without producing an error message. However, the values of SQUARE_1, SQUARE_2, and SQUARE_3 will be wildly incorrect. What has happened is that the programmer, in using a number as an address, has accidentally generated a valid address. The program attempts to fetch the longword beginning at absolute address ^X0210. Because the program has been relocated to address ^X0200, address ^X0210 is the longword that begins ^X10 bytes from the beginning of the program. The longword is, in fact, ^X01D00000. The first four digits, ^X01D0, are the first four digits of the machine language instruction on line 18 of the assembly listing and the last four digits, ^X0000, are the 16-bit mask generated in line 17 (see the assembly listing on page 99).

Debugging assembly language programs is more difficult than debugging programs that are written in higher-level languages. When programmers have difficulty finding errors, it is sometimes necessary to examine the assembly program character by character to find an error. Particular care should be given to symbols that generate operand specifier bytes such as #.

Exercise Set 2

1. Using DEBUG commands such as E 1000, E 2000, E 4000, E 8000, E 10000, etc., determine the highest address that you are allowed to access on your VAX/VMS computer. Can you use the DEBUG program to convert the resulting hexadecimal answer to decimal?

2. Assemble, link, and execute the program that computes the squares of one, two, and three and use the debugger to verify that the answers are correct. Then repeat the process with each of the following errors. Describe the effect of each error. Does the error produce an assembly error, a link error, an execution error, or does it simply generate incorrect results?

   a. Remove the colon after the label FIRST_DIF in the ninth line.

   b. Misspell the label in the ninth line, FIRST_DIF, as FIRST_DIFF.

   c. Remove the .DISABLE GLOBAL directive in the second line and repeat part (b).

   d. Eliminate the statement .BLKL 1 in the fourteenth line (the line after the label SQUARE_2).

   e. Eliminate the statement $EXIT_S in line 24.

3. Modify the program that computes the squares of one, two, and three so that it computes the squares of the integers one through six.

4. Write a program similar to the SQUARES program that computes the cubes of the integers from one to six. (Hint: To discover the algorithm, write down the series 1, 8, 27, 64, 125, . . . and then, with pencil and paper, compute the first, second, and third order differences.)

Program Control Features

5.1 Introduction

Higher-level languages provide control structures that allow the programmer to conditionally execute one or more statements depending on the values of data within the program. In Pascal or FORTRAN, this is accomplished with the IF-THEN-ELSE statement. These statements are translated into conditional branch instructions that are part of the machine language instruction of the VAX.*

Similarly, higher-level languages provide structures for repeatedly executing sections of programs. Repeated sections of programs are called **loops.** In Pascal loops are created with FOR or WHILE statements. In FORTRAN, DO statements are used to create loops. Such statements could be translated into the same conditional branch instructions that are used to implement IF-THEN-ELSE statements. However, the VAX architecture provides additional instructions that are specifically designed to implement loops. This chapter shows how conditional statements and loops are written in assembly language.

Another topic discussed in this chapter is the use of the 16 general registers inside the processor. This chapter will look also at how to write subroutines for the VAX. Although this topic is covered in considerable detail in Chapter 9, we will take a brief look at simple cases of subroutine use. Here, the reader is shown how to use subroutines to read and print numbers.

---

* Some Pascal compilers translate Pascal programs into an intermediate language called p-code that is then interpreted. However, the VAX/VMS Pascal compiler translates Pascal programs into VAX machine language programs.

5.2 Branching
An IF-THEN Example

Figure 5.1 contains segments of Pascal and FORTRAN programs that are designed to set the variable MINAB equal to the minimum of the variables A and B. Notice the INTEGER declarations at the beginning of both programs. The integer declaration causes the Pascal and FORTRAN compilers to reserve 32-bit longwords for the variables (symbolic addresses) MINAB, A, and B. In addition, the contents of MINAB, A, and B will be treated as signed 32-bit integers. Because VAX/VMS Pascal and FORTRAN use longwords as the default length for integers, we will use longwords for most integers in the remainder of this book. In addition, when variables are used in Pascal and FORTRAN program segments, they should be assumed to be 32-bit signed integers unless noted otherwise.

The preceding Pascal and FORTRAN segments could be translated into the assembly language segment shown in Figure 5.2. Notice that this is a program segment rather than a complete program. A variety of assembly directives and instructions, as well as the $EXIT_S macro, are left off for the sake of brevity.

The two instructions after the ;BEGINNING OF CONDITIONAL comment are CMPL A, B and BLEQ NEXT. CMPL stands for CoMPare Longword and BLEQ stands for Branch if Less than or EQual to. The machine language translation of these instructions tells the processor to compare the longwords A and B and then branch or go to the instruction that begins in symbolic address NEXT if the signed longword in A is less than or equal to the signed longword in B. If the longword in A is greater than the longword in B, the processor will execute the instruction that immediately follows the BLEQ instruction (in this case, the instruction MOVL B,MINAB).

Pascal

```
. . .
VAR
   MINAB, A, B : INTEGER;
. . .
MINAB := A;
IF A > B THEN
   MINAB := B;
. . .
```

FORTRAN

```
. . .
INTEGER MINAB, A, B
. . .
MINAB = A
IF (A.GT.B) THEN
   MINAB = B
ENDIF
. . .
```

Figure 5.1 An example of branching

```
          ' ' '
MINAB:    .BLKL    1              ;32-BIT SIGNED INTEGER
A:        .BLKL    1              ;32-BIT SIGNED INTEGER
B:        .BLKL    1              ;32-BIT SIGNED INTEGER
          ' ' '
          MOVL     A,MINAB        ;MINAB:=A
;BEGINNING OF CONDITIONAL
          CMPL     A,B            ;COMPARE A AND B AND
          BLEQ     NEXT           ; BRANCH IF B>=A
          MOVL     B,MINAB        ;MINAB:=B
;END OF CONDITIONAL
NEXT:     ' ' '
```

Figure 5.2 Branching in
VAX/VMS MACRO

The process of performing a conditional branch using the technique shown in Figure 5.2 involves two separate processes that require two separate instructions. First, values must be compared and then a conditional branch can occur based upon the result of the comparison. In this case, the CMPL (CoMPare Longword) compares the longwords A and B. Then, the BLEQ (Branch if Less than or EQual to) instruction branches to location NEXT if the comparison (in this case A less than or equal to B) is true. Note that the BLEQ instruction itself does not state what is being compared with what. The assumption is that this instruction will be preceded by an instruction such as CMPL.

Notice that the condition being tested in the assembly language program is the reverse of the condition in Pascal and FORTRAN. In all three programs, the programmer wishes to set MINAB equal to B if and only if A is greater than B. In the Pascal and FORTRAN programs, the programmer tests for the condition (A greater than B) where something is to be done (set MINAB equal to B). In assembly language, however, the programmer must test for the opposite condition (A less than or equal to B) and then branch when the opposite condition is true.

Finally, notice that the last line of the program segment begins with the symbolic address NEXT. Higher-level languages such as Pascal and FORTRAN usually distinguish between **variable names** that refer to memory locations containing data and **statement labels** that refer to memory locations containing instructions. Assembly languages do not make this distinction. During assembly, the colon following NEXT on the last line of Figure 5.2 causes NEXT to be entered into the symbol table as a symbolic address. As a result, NEXT is the starting address of the instruction that follows the MOVL B,MINAB instruction.

Signed Conditional Branches

The BLEQ instruction belongs to a family of six **signed branch** instructions. The six family members are:

Symbolic Opcode	Numerical Opcode	Description
BNEQ	12	Branch if the first operand is Not EQual to the second operand
BEQL	13	Branch if the first operand is EQuaL to the second operand
BGTR	14	Branch if the first operand is GReaTer than the second operand
BLEQ	15	Branch if the first operand is Less than or EQual to the second operand
BGEQ	18	Branch if the first operand is Greater than or EQual to the second operand
BLSS	19	Branch if the first operand is LeSS than the second operand

When used following a compare instruction, these six branch instructions can be used to implement the six relational operators in Pascal and FORTRAN. These six relational operators are

Pascal Relational Operator	=	<>	<	>=	<=	>
FORTRAN relational operator	.EQ.	.NE.	.LT.	.GE.	.LE.	.GT.
VAX signed branch instruction	BEQL	BNEQ	BLSS	BGEQ	BLEQ	BGTR

Each operator and branch instruction is paired with its opposite. Note that BLSS is the opposite of BGEQ and that BLEQ is the opposite of BGTR.

The order of the operands in a compare instruction is important. That is, the effect of the instructions

```
CMPL    A,B
BGTR    ALPHA
```

is very different from the effect of

```
CMPL    B,A
BGTR    ALPHA
```

The first pair of instructions branches when the longword beginning in address A is greater than the longword in B, while the second pair of instructions branches when the longword in B is greater than the longword in A.

In fact, the assembly language program segment in Figure 5.2 can be rewritten as follows:

```
        MOVL     A,MINAB         ;MINAB:=A
;BEGINNING OF CONDITIONAL
        CMPL     B,A             ;COMPARE B AND A AND
        BGTR     NEXT            ; BRANCH IF B > A
        MOVL     B,MINAB         ;MINAB:=B
;END OF CONDITIONAL
NEXT:    , , ,
```

In this example, notice that the order of operands in the CMPL instruction has been reversed (B,A instead of A,B) and that the branch condition has been reversed (BGTR rather than BLEQ). Either assembly segment may be used to implement the Pascal or FORTRAN statements in Figure 5.1.

An IF-THEN-ELSE Example

The Pascal and FORTRAN program segments in Figure 5.1 can be rewritten using an IF-THEN-ELSE structure as shown in Figure 5.3. An assembly language program that mimics the IF-THEN-ELSE structure is shown in Figure 5.4.

In the assembly language program in Figure 5.4, the CMPL and BGTR statements cause a transfer of control to address AGTRB (the else part) if the longword beginning at A is greater than the longword beginning at B. If A is not greater than B, the VAX processor will execute the instruction that immediately follows the BGTR instruction which, in this example, is MOVL A,MINAB. After executing the MOVL instruction, the processor executes the BRB (BRanch with Byte displacement) instruction on the following line. This statement causes an unconditional transfer of control to symbolic address NEXT. If the BRB instruction were not present, the program would not oper-

Pascal	FORTRAN
| ```
, , ,
IF A <= B THEN
   MINAB := A
ELSE
   MINAB := B;
, , ,
``` | ```
, , ,
IF (A.LE.B) THEN
   MINAB = A
ELSE
   MINAB = B
ENDIF
, , ,
``` |

Figure 5.3 Revised branching example

```
;BEGINNING OF CONDITIONAL IF A <= B
        CMPL    A,B             ;COMPARE A AND B
        BGTR    AGTRB           ; BRANCH IF A > B
;THEN
        MOVL    A,MINAB         ;MINAB:=A
        BRB     NEXT
;ELSE
AGTRB:  MOVL    B,MINAB         ;MINAB:=B
;END OF CONDITIONAL
NEXT:     , , ,
```

Figure 5.4 Revised program in VAX/VMS MACRO

ate properly because, after setting MINAB equal to A, the processor would next execute the statement MOVL B,MINAB, thereby setting MINAB equal to B. The unconditional branch instruction BRB is analogous to the unconditional GO TO statement in Pascal or FOR-TRAN. The reason for the byte displacement in the instruction name "branch with byte displacement" will be explained when the machine language format of the branch instructions is described.

Notice that the assembly language segment in Figure 5.2 is simpler than the segment in Figure 5.4 because it only uses one branch instruction instead of two. In addition, the segment in Figure 5.2 uses less memory and will execute more rapidly. As a result, an optimizing compiler will translate the IF-THEN-ELSE structure shown in Figure 5.3 into a machine language structure similar to that shown in Figure 5.2.

Local Symbols

It is important for programmers to select meaningful names for symbolic addresses. For example, if a given longword contains the gross wage of an individual, a symbolic name such as GWAGE, GROSS_WAGE, or GWAGEL* is a much better choice than a name like K. Similarly, the first instruction in a block of instructions that computes the deductions from an employee's paycheck should be given a name such as DEDUCT.

However, in very long programs, it can be difficult for the programmer to generate unique, meaningful symbolic names. A long assembly language program may contain hundreds of symbolic names,

---

* Some programmers like to incorporate the letters L, W, or B in their symbols to indicate that the symbol is a longword, word, or byte.

and the programmer may accidentally use the same symbolic name for two different addresses, thereby producing an assembler error message. There are a variety of solutions to this problem. One is to break the large program into smaller programs which can be assembled separately and then linked together into a single machine language program. This is discussed in Chapter 9. A second possibility is to use larger symbolic names such as WAGE_LOOP or TAX_LOOP. A third possibility is to use a special symbol called a **local symbol.**

A local symbol is a symbolic address that consists of a series of digits followed by a dollar sign, such as 1$, 57$, or 999$. The following program segment uses local symbols called 10$, 20$, and 30$ in setting MINONE equal to the minimum of longwords A, B, and C.*

```
MINABC:  CMPL     A,B
         BLSS     10$
         MOVL     B,MINONE
         BRB      20$
10$:     MOVL     A,MINONE
20$:     CMPL     C,MINONE
         BGTR     30$
         MOVL     C,MINONE
30$:
MINXYZ:  , , ,
```

The symbols 10$, 20$, and 30$ are called local symbols because they can only be referred to between addresses MINABC and MINXYZ. In other words, the definition of normal symbols such as MINABC and MINXYZ limits the scope of local symbols such as 10$, 20$, and 30$. An attempt to branch to address 10$ from an instruction before MINABC or after MINXYZ would generate an assembly error for an undefined symbol.

Note that the label 30$ is on an otherwise blank line, followed by the label MINXYZ on the next line. As a result, both labels refer to the same location, namely the starting address of the next instruction in the program. The BGTR 30$ instruction could have been written BGTR MINXYZ without any difference in the assembled program. However, use of the symbol 30$ is preferred since MINXYZ is a label

---

* It is customary to choose numbers that are multiples of 10. This way, insertions can be made while still keeping the numbers in order. The actual numerical values have no significance, but it is easier to debug a program which is organized in an orderly fashion.

which has nothing to do with the program segment MINABC, but is the beginning of some unrelated section of the program.

Because local symbols are only defined between two ordinary symbols such as MINABC and MINXYZ, local symbol names can be reused many times in a program. For example, the following program segment sets MINONE equal to the minimum of A, B, and C and then sets MINTWO equal to the minimum of X, Y, and Z.

```
MINABC: CMPL    A,B             ;MINONE=MIN(A,B,C)
        BLSS    10$
        MOVL    B,MINONE
        BRB     20$
10$:    MOVL    A,MINONE
20$:    CMPL    C,MINONE
        BGTR    30$
        MOVL    C,MINONE
30$:
MINXYZ: CMPL    X,Y             ;MINTWO=MIN(X,Y,Z)
        BLSS    10$
        MOVL    Y,MINTWO
        BRB     20$
10$:    MOVL    X,MINTWO
20$:    CMPL    Z,MINTWO
        BGTR    30$
        MOVL    Z,MINTWO
30$:
NEXTMIN: . . .
```

Because the local symbols 10$, 20$, and 30$ in the first half of the program segment become undefined as soon as the label MINXYZ is encountered, their reuse in the second half of the program segment does not generate multiple definition errors.

In the remainder of this book, local symbols will be used in many program segments. However, whenever a block of code performs a function that might be referenced from elsewhere in the program, the block will be given a normal symbolic name (e.g. MINABC and MINXYZ in the previous example). Programming style precludes the excessive use of local symbols, since the use of large numbers of them over several pages of listings would make a program unreadable. They are intended to be used more or less exclusively for **trivial** symbols which are used for branches forward or backward over a few lines of code. Local symbols also have an important use within macros, as will be discussed in Chapter 10.

5.3 Condition Codes

The CMP Family of Instructions

The CMP family of instructions is described as follows:

Symbolic Opcode	Numerical Opcode	Operands	Operation
CMPB	91 ⎫		
CMPW	B1 ⎬	src1, src2	src1 − src2
ĊMPL	D1 ⎭		

The family includes instructions for comparing bytes and words as well as longwords. For example, the instructions

```
CMPB     BYTE_1 ,BYTE_2
BLSS     10$
```

will branch to 10$ if the signed value in BYTE_1 is less than the signed value in BYTE_2.

  The machine language format of these instructions is similar to the format of the MOV and SUB families. (Note that the operation codes for MOVB, MOVW, and MOVL are ^X90, ^XB0, and ^XD0 respectively.) The operation code is followed by two operand specifiers. Each operand specifier begins with an operand specifier byte that determines how each operand can be found. As a result, any of the addressing modes, including literal, immediate, relative, or absolute addressing, can be used with the CMP family of instructions.

  Literal or immediate operands may be used for either the first or second operand. For example,

```
CMPW     #21 ,ALPHA
BLSS     20$
```

will branch to 20$ if the number 21 is less than the contents of the word at address ALPHA. The instruction

```
CMPL     WAGE ,#1000
BLSS     NOTAX
```

will branch to NOTAX if the longword at address WAGE is less than 1000.

  As the description of the CMP family indicates, a compare instruction actually performs a subtraction. Unlike the SUB family, which subtracts the first operand from the second, the CMP family subtracts the second operand from the first. (Note that the description is src1 − src2.) Also, unlike the SUB family, the result of the subtraction produced by executing a CMP instruction is discarded. However, the processor saves four items of information about the subtraction. These items indicate

1. Whether or not the result of the subtraction was zero. The processor stores this information in a bit called the **Z bit.**
2. Whether or not the result of the subtraction was negative. The processor stores this information in a bit called the **N bit.**
3. Whether or not the subtraction produced a signed overflow. The processor stores this information in a bit called the **V bit.** (V stands for oVerflow.)
4. Whether or not the subtraction produced an unsigned overflow. The processor stores this information in a bit called the **C bit.** (C stands for Carry.)

Collectively, these four bits are called the **condition codes** and they are stored in a special register inside the processor called the **processor status longword.** Collectively, the condition code bits contain **all** of the information necessary to determine whether or not a conditional branch instruction should transfer control (branch).

The following shows a CMPL instruction that is followed by a conditional branch instruction.

```
CMPL    SCORE,#90
BGEQ    A_GRADE
```

During execution, the CMPL instruction directs the processor to subtract 90 from the longword in address SCORE. The processor sets the four condition code bits based on the subtraction (erasing their previous value) and discards the results of the subtraction. Then the BGEQ instruction examines the condition code bits in order to determine whether or not to transfer control to A_GRADE. The condition code values that cause each conditional branch instruction to transfer control are described in Chapter 6.

Setting the Condition Codes

Each conditional branch requires that the condition codes be set before the branch can have meaning. In the previous examples, this was accomplished by a member of the CMP family of instructions.

However, there are a number of other ways to set the condition code bits.

One of these ways is to perform an arithmetic operation. Every arithmetic instruction automatically causes the processor to set the condition codes based on the results of the arithmetic operation. For example, the instruction ADDL2 A,B automatically tests the value being stored in B. The result is almost as if the pair of instructions

```
ADDL2    A,B
CMPL     B,#0
```

were executed. Since this is true of all arithmetic instructions, the same applies to the other five members of the add family of instructions, the six members of the subtract family, and (although no computation is performed) the four move instructions.

As a result, conditional branch instructions can be used following members of the add, subtract, or move families. The move instructions set the condition codes by comparing the value moved with zero. Therefore the following instructions will cause a branch to statement 30$ if the value stored in B is greater than or equal to zero.

```
MOVL     A,B
BGEQ     30$
```

The preceding pair of statements copy the longword from A to B and branch to 30$ **if B is greater than or equal to zero.** If B is to be compared to a number other than zero, a CMPL instruction should be inserted.

Although the conditional branch instructions examine the values of the condition code bits, they do not alter the value of these bits. As a result, it is possible to have several conditional branch instructions following a move, add, subtract, or compare instruction. Consider, for example, the following SUBL3 instruction.

```
         SUBL3    A,B,C
         BGTR     30$
         BEQL     20$
10$:      , , ,

20$:      , , ,

30$:      , , ,
```

The SUBL3 instruction will subtract the longword in A from a copy of the longword in B and place the resulting difference in longword C. In addition, the SUBL3 instruction will set the condition codes based on the longword stored in C. As a result, the BGTR will cause a transfer of control to 30$ if C is greater than zero. If C is equal to zero, the processor will drop through the BGTR instruction and the BEQL instruction will transfer control to 20$. If C is less than zero, the processor will drop through both branch instructions to the instructions that begin in 10$.

In a similar manner, the following lines will cause a transfer to statements 40$, 50$, or 60$ depending on whether the longword at D is less than, equal to, or greater than 50 respectively.

```
          CMPL      D,#50
          BGTR      60$
          BEQL      50$
40$:        , , ,

50$:        , , ,

60$:        , , ,
```

5.4 Machine Language Format of the Branch Instructions
Relative Addressing

The branch family has a different machine language format than the rest of the VAX machine language instructions. To begin with, there is no operand specifier byte. The conditional branch instructions are, with a few exceptions, 16 bits or 2 bytes long. The first byte contains an 8-bit operation code and the second byte contains an 8-bit **displacement** that indicates where the processor is to branch. Since the displacement is only 8 bits long, there are only 2^8 or 256 different displacements. As noted in Chapter 3, an 8-bit relative displacement can only reference addresses that are between -128 and 127 bytes away from the address in the program counter. However, this is not a serious restriction because there are instructions that allow longer branches.

As noted in Chapter 3, the concept of relative addressing is quite simple. Assume, for example, that you are on a superhighway that has 100 exits numbered from 00 to 99. Further assume that you have stopped your car at exit 32 to give directions to a lost motorist. In giving directions to the motorist, you might say, "Get off at exit 35" or "Get off at exit 25." In doing so, you are using absolute addressing. However, you could also say, "Go ahead 3 exits" (since 32 + 3 = 35) or "Go back 7 exits" (since 32 − 7 = 25). In doing so, you are using relative addressing. That is, you are telling the motorist to go backward or forward a certain number of exits from where the motorist is currently standing.

The branch instructions operate in a similar manner. The branch instructions direct the processor to go backward or forward a certain number of bytes from the address contained in the program counter. The 8-bit displacement is interpreted as an 8-bit signed number. The displacement can therefore represent decimal numbers between − 128 and + 127 (see Table 2.6 on page 40). The branch instructions can therefore direct the processor to branch backward up to 128 bytes or forward up to 127 bytes.

The operation of the branch instruction is straightforward. Assume that the following BRB (unconditional BRanch with Byte relative addressing) begins in address 00000400

Instruction	Address
50 11	00000400

The processor fetches the BRB operation code of ^X11 from address ^X0400 and then fetches the displacement of ^X50 from address ^X0401. By this time, the program counter has been incremented to ^X0402. The processor adds ^X50 to ^X0402 to get ^X0452 and places the sum in the program counter. As a result, the processor will fetch its next instruction from address ^X0452.

Since the displacements are interpreted as signed numbers, displacements between ^XFF and ^X80 direct the processor to branch backward. For example, the instruction

Instruction	Address
B0 11	0000400

causes the processor to branch backward to address ^X000003B2.

The assembler computes the displacements, and so the programmer need only remember the following items. The branch instruction directs the processor to branch backward or forward a certain number of bytes. Because the displacement is a signed 8-bit number, displacements range from − 128 to + 127 (decimal). Since the program counter has been incremented by two before the displacement is added to it, it is only possible to branch backward − 126 or forward +129 from the starting address of the branch instruction. Within an assembly language program, the programmer simply types a branch instruction such as BRB. If the address is between 126 bytes behind the branch instruction and 129 bytes ahead of the branch instruction, the assembler computes the correct displacement. Otherwise, the assembler issues an error message to indicate that the address is too far away to be reached with the branch instruction.

The BRW and JMP Instructions

The VAX provides the BRW (unconditional BRanch with Word displacement) instruction to handle cases where the branch address is too far away from the branch instruction. BRW is just like BRB except that the operation code is followed by a 16-bit displacement instead of an 8-bit displacement. As a result, the BRW instruction can branch backward up to 32765 or forward up to 32770 bytes from the address of the BRW instruction. For example, the instruction

Instruction	Address
5000 31	00000400

will cause the processor to branch to ^X00005403. The operation code for BRW is ^X31. By the time the processor has fetched the 16-bit signed displacement ^X5000, the program counter has been incremented to ^X00000403. The processor adds the positive displacement ^X5000 to ^X00000403 and places the sum, ^X00005403, in the PC. As a result, the processor will fetch its next operation code from address ^X00005403.

To see how the BRW instruction is used, consider the following example:

```
CMPL    A,B
BLSS    ALPHA
 .  .  .
```

If the branch address (ALPHA) is too far away from the BLSS instruction to be reached with a byte displacement, the assembler will print an error message. The programmer could rewrite the preceding statements as

```
        CMPL    A,B
        BGEQ    10$
        BRW     ALPHA
10$:     .  .  .
```

In rewriting the statements, notice that it was necessary to change the BLSS instruction into its opposite, BGEQ.

The JMP (for JuMP) instruction is even more global. Unlike the branch family of instructions, the JMP instruction has a format that is consistent with the rest of the VAX machine language instructions. JMP is a single-operand instruction in which the operation code is followed by an operand specifier byte. For example, consider the following instruction:

Instruction	Address
00010000 EF 17	00004000

The operation code for the JMP instruction is ^X17. The operand specifier byte, ^XEF, specified longword relative addressing. By the time the longword displacement, ^X00010000, has been fetched from memory, the program counter will have been incremented to ^X00000406. Therefore, this instruction will branch to address ^X00000406 plus ^X00010000 or ^X00010406.

When assembling a JMP instruction with relative addressing, the assembler will default to longword relative addressing for forward jumps. For backward jumps, the assembler will use byte, word, or longword relative addressing as needed.* The use of byte relative or word relative addressing with the JMP instruction doesn't make a great deal of sense because the instructions BRB (BRanch with Byte displacement) or BRW (BRanch with Word displacement) will achieve the same result and is one byte shorter. The JMP with longword relative addressing can be used to transfer control to an address that cannot be reached with a BRW instruction (i.e. an address that is more than approximately 32000 bytes away). For example, the preceding program segment that branched to ALPHA could be rewritten as follows:

```
          CMPL    A,B
          BGEQ    10$
          JMP     ALPHA
10$:      . . .
```

---

* As noted in Chapter 4, the programmer can override the default by preceding the address symbol with B^, W^, or L^ to generate byte, word, or longword relative addresses respectively.

However, if programs are modularized properly, there should seldom, if ever, be a need to branch to an address that far away.

The real advantage of the JMP instruction is that it allows the use of a wide variety of addressing modes. These modes allow the JMP instruction to easily implement complicated control structures. Addressing modes are described in more detail in Chapter 7. The descriptions of the BRB, BRW, and JMP instructions are

Symbolic Opcode	Numerical Opcode	Description
BRB	11	Unconditional transfer of control using byte displacement
BRW	31	Unconditional transfer of control using word displacement
JMP	17	Unconditional transfer of control using an operand specifier byte to determine the addressing mode

5.5 Additional Instructions
The CLR Family of Instructions

In writing programs, it is frequently necessary to set the contents of a memory cell to zero. This can be accomplished with a member of the MOV family. For example, the MOVL instruction

```
MOVL    #0,ALPHA
```

will set the longword beginning in ALPHA to zero. The same result can be achieved with a SUBL2 instruction.

```
SUBL2   ALPHA,ALPHA
```

To save time and space and to make assembly language programs more readable, the VAX instruction set includes a CLR (for CLeaR) family of instructions. For example, the instruction

```
CLRL    ALPHA
```

will set the longword beginning in address ALPHA to zero. This instruction is not only simpler to use than MOVL #0,ALPHA but it is more efficient since only one operand needs to be specified. The CLR family includes the following instructions:

Symbolic Opcode	Numerical Opcode	Operands	Operation
CLRB	94		
CLRW	B4	dst	dst←0
CLRL	D4		
CLRQ	7C		

These instructions can be used to clear bytes, words, longwords, and 64-bit quadwords.

The CLR family of instructions provides examples of one-operand instructions just as MOVL is an example of a two-operand instruction and ADDL3 is an example of a three-operand instruction. The machine language translation of these instructions has the expected format. The operation code is followed by a single-operand specifier. The operand specifier begins with an operand specifier byte that indicates how the operand can be found. The remaining instructions in this section are also single-operand instructions with a similar machine language format.

The INC and DEC Family of Instructions

Another common function is adding one to the contents of a memory location. The instruction

```
ADDL2    #1,ALPHA
```

can be replaced by the INCL (for INCrement Longword) instruction

```
INCL    ALPHA
```

Similarly, the DECL (for DECrement Longword) instruction is used to subtract one from the contents of a memory longword. For example, the instruction

```
DECL    ALPHA
```

is equivalent to the instruction SUBL2 #1,ALPHA. However, the DECL instruction is shorter, faster, and it produces more readable assembly language programs.

The descriptions of the INC and DEC families are

Symbolic Opcode	Numerical Opcode	Operands	Operation
INCB	96 ⎫		
INCW	B6 ⎬	sum	sum←sum + 1
INCL	D6 ⎭		
DECB	97 ⎫		
DECW	B7 ⎬	dif	dif←dif − 1
DECL	D7 ⎭		

As these descriptions imply, instructions are available for incrementing or decrementing bytes, words, and longwords.

The TST Family of Instructions

Assume that a programmer wishes to set a longword B equal to A plus one and then branch to statement 10$ if A is equal to zero. The statements

```
ADDL3   A,#1,B
BEQL    10$
```

will not achieve the desired result because the condition code bits reflect the value of B rather than A and the BEQL instruction will branch if B is equal to zero. The statements

```
ADDL3   A,#1,B
CMPL    A,#0
BEQL    10$
```

will achieve the desired result.

Notice that the only purpose of the CMPL instruction is to set the condition code bits according to the longword at A. The VAX architecture includes a TST family of instructions for just this purpose. The program segment can be rewritten as follows:

```
ADDL3   A,#1,B
TSTL    A
BEQL    10$
```

The TSTL (for TeST Longword) instruction simply fetches the longword beginning at A, uses the fetched value to set the condition code bits, and then discards the fetched value. The contents of the longword A is not affected.

The descriptions for the TST family of instructions are

Symbolic Opcode	Numerical Opcode	Operands	Operation
TSTB	95 ⎫		
TSTW	B5 ⎬	src	src − 0
TSTL	D5 ⎭		

The operands field indicates that the operand called src (for SouRCe) is fetched and that the operand may be either a byte, a word, or a longword. In the operation field, the src − 0 indicates that the processor subtracts zero from the source and sets the condition codes based on the result. Although subtracting zero from the source does not change the value of the source, it does set the condition codes and it shows how the TST instructions could be implemented in the hardware inside the processor.

5.6 Looping

It is easy to create looping structures by using the conditional branch instructions. For example, the following program segment will compute the sum of the integers from one to ten.

```
SUM_TEN_TO_ONE:
        CLRL    SUM
        MOVL    #10,J
10$:    ADDL2   J,SUM
        DECL    J
        BNEQ    10$
20$:     . . .
```

In this program segment, the longword SUM will contain the sum of the integers and the longword J is used as the loop counter. The loop shown is a down-counting loop. The longword J is initialized to ten outside the loop by the MOVL #10,J instruction. Within the loop, the instruction DEC J subtracts one from J on each pass through the loop. For the first nine passes, J is greater than zero and the BNEQ #10$ instruction transfers control to 10$. On the tenth pass through the loop, J contains zero and the processor drops through the BNEQ instruction to the instruction that begins at 20$. When this statement is reached, longword SUM will contain 10 + 9 + 8 + 7 + 6 + 5 + 4 + 3 + 2 + 1 or 55.

This program segment can be further simplified by using the SOBGTR (Subtract One and Branch if the result is GreaTeR than zero) instruction. This implementation is shown next. The SOBGTR instruction requires two operands. The first operand must reference a longword and the second operand is the branch address. When the instruction is executed, the longword is automatically decremented. If the longword is still greater than zero, a branch occurs to the address specified by the second operand. As with other branch instructions, the branch address is represented as an 8-bit displacement.

```
SUM_TEN_TO_ONE:
        CLRL     SUM
        MOVL     #10,J
10$:    ADDL2    J,SUM
        SOBGTR   J,10$
        , , ,
```

The SOBGEQ instruction (Subtract One and Branch if Greater than or EQual to zero) is identical to SOBGTR except that it will branch when the first operand contains zero.

Assembly language programmers frequently use down-counting loops that exit when the loop counter reaches zero. In higher-level languages, however, up-counting loops are generally used. For example, the following loop skeletons in FORTRAN and Pascal vary the loop counter from 5 to 25. In both programs, J is assumed to be declared as an integer.

FORTRAN

```
      DO 100 J=5,25

         body of loop
100   CONTINUE
```

Pascal

```
FOR J := 5 TO 25 DO
   BEGIN
      body of loop
END;
```

Similar loops can be constructed in assembly language using the AOBLEQ (Add One and Branch if Less than or EQual to) instruction. This instruction requires three operands. The first operand is a longword that specifies the limit for the index (e.g., 25). The second operand is a longword that serves as the index of the loop (e.g., J). Finally, the third operand is a byte displacement. The assembly language implementation of the FORTRAN and Pascal programs is

```
        MOVL     #5,J
10$:
            body of loop
        AOBLEQ    #25,J,10$
```

The preceding AOBLEQ instruction increments the longword J and
then compares J with the longword #25. If J is less than or equal to
25, the branch to 10$ is taken. The AOBLSS instruction is just like
the AOBLEQ instruction except that the branch is taken only if the
index is LeSS than the limit.

5.7 Processor Registers
Assembly Language Notation

As we noted in Chapter 3, the VAX processor contains 16 **general
registers,** each of which is 32 bits in length. These registers are designated registers 0 through 15 in decimal or ^X0 through ^XF in hexadecimal. Despite their name, general registers 12 through 15 (^XC
through ^XF) serve special purposes. For example, register 15 is the
program counter which enables the processor to keep track of where
it is as it executes each instruction. However, registers 0 through 11
are for general use and can be used to hold data of various lengths.

In Chapter 7, we will see how processor registers are used with
a variety of addressing modes. In this section, we will introduce an
addressing mode called **register addressing.** In register addressing,
the operand is in the register instead of in the memory. Using registers
in this way makes your programs both shorter and more efficient.

In order to make the processor registers easy to use, the permanent symbol table in the assembler defines the following symbols:

Symbol	Meaning
R0	Register addressing with register 0
R1	Register addressing with register 1
. . .	
R9	Register addressing with register 9
R10	Register addressing with register 10 (^XA)
R11	Register addressing with register 11 (^XB)
AP or R12	Register addressing with register 12 (^XC)
FP	Register addressing with register 13 (^XD)
SP	Register addressing with register 14 (^XE)
PC	Register addressing with register 15 (^XF)

To help the programmer remember that processor registers 12 through 15 are reserved for special purposes, they are referred to by the names AP (Argument Pointer), FP (Frame Pointer), SP (Stack Pointer), and PC (Program Counter). The assembler allows register 12 to be referenced as either AP or R12.

With these symbols defined, the use of the processor registers is straightforward. For example, the following instruction will copy the longword in register 3 and place the copy in register 8.

```
MOVL    R3,R8
```

The symbol R3 specifies that the source operand is in general register 3 and R8 specifies that the destination of the longword is register 8. Similarly, the following instruction will add the longword beginning in memory address A to the longword in register 2 and place the sum in register 0.

```
ADDL3   A,R2,R0
```

Although each of the general registers contains a 32-bit longword, it is possible to use the general registers with byte and word operands as well. To illustrate this, assume that processor registers 3 and 8 contain the following longwords

Longword	Register
11223344	Register 3
55667788	Register 8

The instruction, MOVL R3,R8, will move the longword in register 3 into register 8, thereby changing the contents of register 8 to ^X11223344. However, if a MOVB instruction were used instead of the MOVL instruction, then the processor would copy the low-order byte in register 3 into the low-order byte position in register 8. The upper 24 bits in register 8 would not be altered. Thus, the instruction MOVB R3,R8 would change the contents of register 8 to ^X55667744. Similarly, word instructions only reference or modify the lower two bytes (16 bits) in a register. The upper two bytes are not involved in the execution of the instruction in any way. Thus, the instruction MOVW R3,R8 would change the contents of register 8 to ^X55663344.

Some Examples

It is legal to use a mixture of different operand specifier bytes in a single instruction. For example, each of the following is a valid instruction.

```
MOVB      A,R1
ADDW3     R1,#50,R10
SUBL2     R7,C
CMPL      R4,#20
SUBB3     #50,A,R11
INCW      R4
```

However, instructions such as BLEQ R5 are illegal. Since the branch instructions do not have an operand specifier byte, register addressing cannot be used. In addition, the instruction JMP R5 would also be illegal even though it does have an operand specifier byte. The reason is that it is only possible to execute code out of memory, and therefore, it is illegal to jump to a register.

To see how the use of processor registers can improve execution speed, consider the following program segment which sets the long-word A equal to B + C − D − 5.

```
ADDL3     B,C,A
SUBL2     D,A
SUBL2     #5,A
```

Consider the number of times that the longword in memory cell A is fetched or stored. The ADDL3 stores a result into A. Both SUBL2 instructions fetch from and then store into A. The following sequence of instructions uses register R0 to eliminate all three fetches from and all but one store into A.

```
ADDL3     B,C,R0
SUBL2     D,R0
SUBL3     #5,R0,A
```

The revised assembly language segment appears to be longer because of the added operand in the third instruction. As we shall see, however, register addressing actually uses less memory than byte relative addressing. As a result, the revised segment actually requires less memory than the original segment.

Registers have important uses within loops. Frequently referenced values should be kept in registers. For example, one of the

assembly segments that added the integers from ten to one is reproduced next.

```
SUM_TEN_TO_ONE:
        CLRL    SUM
        MOVL    #10,J
10$:    ADDL2   J,SUM
        SOBGTR  J,10$
        . . .
```

Using R0 in place of J and R1 in place of SUM, this segment becomes

```
SUM_TEN_TO_ONE:
        CLRL    R1
        MOVL    #10,R0
10$:    ADDL2   R0,R1
        SOBGTR  R0,10$
        MOVL    R1,SUM
        . . .
```

Even though it was necessary to add the instruction MOVL R1,SUM
after the end of the loop, the revised program is shorter and uses less
memory than the original.

Register Addressing

The preceding examples show how register addressing is used in
assembly language. When register operands are translated to machine
language, the number of the register (^X0 to ^XF) becomes part of the operand specifier byte. For example, the instruction MOVL R8,R3 would
generate the following machine language code if it were assembled
into memory beginning at address ^X0400.

Operand	Operand	Opcode	Address
58	53	D0	04000

Notice that the machine language translation is only three bytes long.
^XD0 is the operation code for the MOVL instruction. The first oper-
and specifier byte, ^X53, specifies that the source operand is the 32-
bit longword in general register 3. The second operand specifier byte,
^X58, indicates that the longword will be placed in general register
8, destroying the previous longword in register 8.

Register addressing illustrates the way that operand specifier bytes are coded for other addressing modes. An operand specifier byte specifies the way in which an operand is to be located. An operand specifier byte consists of two hexadecimal digits. The hexadecimal digit on the right (0 to F) specifies one of the 16 general registers inside the processor. The hexadecimal digit on the left is called the **mode** and indicates the way in which the general register is used in locating the operand.

Mode	Register	
m m m m	r r r r	8 bits in an operand and specifier byte

The only exception to this format is literal addressing mode which stores a 6-bit constant in the operand specifier byte.

Register addressing is specified by setting the mode bits to ^B0101 or ^X5. Any operand specifier byte from ^X50 to ^X5E specifies register addressing. The register digit specifies the number of the register that contains the operand. For example, the assembly operands R0 and R11 will assemble into the operand specifier bytes ^X50 and ^X5B respectively.

Since the mode digit consists of four bits, the VAX architecture could include a total of 16 modes (^X0 through ^XF). As described in Chapter 7, however, the VAX uses modes ^X0 through ^X3 for literal addressing. The remaining 12 modes (^X4 through ^XF) along with the literal-addressing mode are called the **general-register addressing modes.** The two general-addressing modes that have been introduced are

Operand Specifier Byte	Name	Meaning
00-3F	Literal	The operand specifier byte contains a 6-bit constant. The assembler selects this mode when an operand consists of a number sign followed by a small constant or a symbol that represents a small constant (#1, #20, etc.).
50-5E	Register	The operand is in the processor general register specified by the second hexadecimal digit (^X0 to ^XE) in the operand specifier byte. The assembler selects this mode whenever an operand consists of a register symbol (R3, R10, SP, etc.).

Notice that the range of operand specifier bytes for register addressing is ^X50–^X5E, not ^X50–^X5F. Because of the way that the program counter is incremented during execution of an instruction, register addressing (^X5F) should never be used with the program counter. In fact, only modes ^X8 through ^XF should be used with the program counter. Because the program counter is such a special register, modes ^X8 through ^XF are called **program-counter addressing modes** when they are used with the program counter. The five program-counter addressing modes that we have used are

Operand Specifier Byte	Name	Meaning
8F	Immediate	The operand is contained in bytes following the operand specifier byte. The assembler selects this mode when a number sign is followed by a number or a symbol representing a number that is too large for literal mode (#100, #123456, etc.).
9F	Absolute	The address of the operand is contained in the four bytes following the operand specifier byte. (The assembler selects absolute addressing when the operand begins with the symbols @#; e.g., @#EXTNAME.)
AF	Byte relative	A one-byte displacement follows the operand specifier byte.
CF	Word relative	A one-word displacement follows the operand specifier byte.
EF	Longword relative	A longword displacement follows the operand specifier byte.

The assembler selects one of the relative-addressing modes when a symbol or number is used as the operand (WAGE, 20$, etc.). With each of the program counter addressing modes, information needed to locate the operand immediately follows the operand specifier byte. The program counter is used in these modes because, after the operand specifier byte is fetched, the program counter points to the byte that immediately follows the operand specifier byte. The operation of these modes is described in Chapter 7.

5.8 Subroutines
Calling and Returning

The topic of subroutines is covered in considerable detail in Chapter 9. However, subroutines are being introduced at this point for two purposes. First, subroutines are important for the proper structure of programs, and what follows will enable the reader to write some simple subroutines. Second, Appendix B shows some input/output subroutines that can be incorporated into programs. Using these subroutines will allow the reader to start writing some more sophisticated programs.

There are three concerns with subroutines. First, there must be some means of jumping to the subroutine. Second, there must be a means of jumping back to the calling program. To call a subroutine whose name is SUB, the VAX instruction JSB SUB can be used. (JSB means Jump to SuBroutine.) To return, the instruction RSB (Return from SuBroutine) can be used. Third, there is the problem of passing information between the main program and the subroutine. This problem is covered extensively in Chapter 9. However, for now we will use the simple method of passing information back and forth using the general registers in the processor. For example, the main program can move data to R0, R1, . . . , before calling the subroutine and the subroutine can return with results left in the general registers. This method works well for simple problems, but it is too simplistic for more sophisticated problems, as will be seen in Chapter 9.

Input and Output

Appendix B contains some input/output subroutines called IOINIT, RNUM, and PNUM. Subroutine IOINIT performs certain initialization functions that must be performed before input or output can take place. IOINIT performs functions similar to the OPEN statement in some higher-level languages. In order to perform the initialization functions, execute the instruction

```
JSB      IOINIT
```

Note that this instruction should only be executed once during the execution of a program.

Subroutine RNUM reads a hexadecimal longword from the user's computer terminal and places the 32-bit value in R0. PNUM prints out on the user's terminal the hexadecimal and decimal value of the contents of R0. (If batch processing is being used, RNUM reads a longword from a batch input stream and PNUM places the contents of R0 in the batch log file.) Therefore, to read a number and store its value in X, execute the instructions

```
JSB     RNUM
MOVL    RO,X
```

To print the value of X, execute the instructions

```
MOVL    X,RO
JSB     PNUM
```

Of course, the subroutines IOINIT, RNUM, and PNUM must be copied from Appendix B and be included as part of your program.

Calling a subroutine is analogous to taking a temporary detour. For example, the main program in Figure 5.5 is designed to read two numbers and place the sum in memory longword SUM. (Do not worry about the instructions such as PUSHR #^M<R0,R1> in the subroutines. Many of these instructions have not yet been described, but are covered in later chapters.) When the processor executes the first JSB RNUM instruction, the processor temporarily stops executing the main program and transfers control to subroutine RNUM (see the arrow labeled A). When the processor reaches the RSB instruction at the end of RNUM, control is automatically transferred to the instruction following the JSB instruction, which in this case is a MOVL R0,A instruction (see arrow B). When the processor executes the second JSB RNUM instruction, control is again transferred to subroutine RNUM (see arrow C). Finally, the RSB instruction at the end of RNUM transfers control back to the MOVL R0,B instruction in the main program (see arrow D).

The JSB instruction, like the JMP instruction, causes a transfer of control. (The machine language format of the JSB is just like the format for JMP except that the operation code is ^X16 instead of ^X17.) However, the JSB instruction also provides a mechanism for returning, at some later time, to the statement immediately following the JSB instruction. The RSB instruction uses the information saved by the JSB in order to return. (RSB is a one-byte instruction with an operation code of ^X05.)

Subroutines represent a powerful technique for breaking a large program into more manageable parts. If misused, however, they can lead to errors that are difficult to detect. Assume, for example, that the programmer used the statement JMP RNUM instead of JSB RNUM to transfer control to subroutine RNUM. The subroutine would exe-

Figure 5.5　A main program with subroutines

```
          .TITLE   SHOW_SUBS
;PROGRAM TO READ A AND B AND PRINT SUM := A + B
;DATA BLOCK
A:        .BLKL    1
B:        .BLKL    1
SUM:      .BLKL    1
;MAIN PROGRAM
          .ENTRY   START,0          ;START IS ENTRY POINT
          JSB      IOINIT           ;CALL IOINIT TO PREPARE FOR I/O
          JSB      RNUM             ;READ NUMBER INTO R0
          MOVL     R0,A             ; AND STORE IN A
          JSB      RNUM             ;READ A SECOND NUMBER INTO R0
          MOVL     R0,B             ; AND STORE IN B
          ADDL3    A,B,SUM          ;SUM := A + B
          MOVL     SUM,R0           ;MOVE SUM TO R0
          JSB      PNUM             ; AND PRINT
          $EXIT_S                   ;AND EXIT
;
; RNUM AND PNUM AND IOINIT CONSTANTS
          . . .
;
; RNUM, PNUM, AND IOINIT VARIABLE SPACE
;
; INITIALIZATION ROUTINE
IOINIT: PUSHR  #^M<R0,R1>
          . . .
        RSB
;
; PRINT NUMBER ROUTINE
PNUM:     PUSHR  #^M<R0,R1>
          . . .
        RSB
;
; READ NUMBER ROUTINE
RNUM:     PUSHR  #^M<R1>
          . . .
        RSB
;END OF COMBINED PROGRAM - ENTRY ADDRESS IS START
          .END     START
```

A

B

C

D

cute properly until the RSB instruction at the end of the subroutine was reached. The RSB instruction assumes that a previous JSB instruction has saved the return address. Because no such address was saved, the RSB instruction will return control to a garbage location, producing unpredictable results. A similar result may occur if the programmer forgets to put a $EXIT_S instruction at the end of the main program and drops through the main program into the subroutine.

Additional Subroutine Call Instructions

Subroutines are so important that the VAX instruction set includes five machine language instructions for transferring control to a subroutine. The instructions are JSB, BSBB, BSBW, CALLG, and CALLS. The instructions BSBB (Branch to SuBroutine with Byte displacement) and BSBW (Branch to SuBroutine with Word displacement) are similar to the JSB instruction except that the format of the branch family of instructions is used. The BSBB instruction consists of a one-byte operation code followed by a byte containing an 8-bit relative address. BSBW consists of a one-byte operation code followed by two bytes containing a 16-bit relative address. When control is transferred to a subroutine with either a JSB, BSBB, or a BSBW instruction, the subroutine should end with an RSB instruction. When a subroutine is called with CALLG or CALLS, the subroutine should end with an RET instruction.

It is possible for subroutines to be **nested.** For example, a main program could call a subroutine named SUBA, which in turn could call a subroutine named SUBB. The subroutine SUBB will return control to SUBA, which will in turn return control to the main program.

General register 14 is used by the five instructions that transfer control to subroutines to facilitate nesting. Register 14 is called the **stack pointer** or **SP** because it points to an area in memory called the stack. It is called the stack because its use is similiar to a stack of dishes or a stack of books. If one were to add a dish to a stack of dishes, one would normally place the new dish on the top of the stack. If one were asked to remove a dish from a stack of dishes, one would normally remove the dish that was on top of the stack. As a result, the dish that one would naturally remove is the dish that was most recently added to the stack. The call instructions use the SP as a pointer to place the return address on the top of the stack. The return instruction obtains the return address from the top of the stack. As a result, a stack is the correct storage technique for nested subroutines. If program MAIN calls subroutine SUBA, and SUBA calls subroutine SUBB, the return address on the top of the stack will be the return address to SUBA. As a result, the return instruction at the end of SUBB will correctly return control to SUBA and the return instruction at the end of SUBA will return control to MAIN. In Chapter 9 we will see that there are many other important uses for the stack.

In order to maintain standardized calling procedures for subroutines written in various languages, the CALLS, CALLG, and RET instructions are provided. These provide a more complex system for saving information in addition to the return address. In addition to the SP, these instructions use registers 12 and 13. The overall operation of these instructions is explained in Chapter 9. The names of the special registers are

Register	Symbol	Name	Function
12	AP	Argument Pointer	For passing arguments
13	FP	Frame Pointer	For saving the stack pointer
14	SP	Stack Pointer	For saving return address and other data
15	PC	Program Counter	Points to the next instruction to be executed

Subroutine Example

As an example of how to use IOINIT, RNUM, and PNUM and how you might write your own subroutine, let us look at the following problem. The problem is to read three numbers and print out the largest. Although our method for solving this problem may seem far-fetched and overcomplicated, it is a generalizable technique that will actually simplify larger problems.

From what we have seen previously, we already have subroutines for initializing the input/output process, reading a number, and printing a number. In addition, we will write a subroutine that finds the larger of two numbers, which will be named MAX. When MAX is called, it will compare the value of R0 with R1 and put the larger longword in R0. Figure 5.6 shows this subroutine.

```
;
; SUBROUTINE MAX SETS R0 TO THE MAXIMUM OF R0 AND R1
;
MAX:     CMPL     R0,R1          ;IS R0 GREATER THAN R1
         BGEQ     10$            ;YES, RETURN R0 AS MAX
         MOVL     R1,R0          ;NO, THEN R1 IS MAX
10$:     RSB                     ;RETURN TO MAIN PROGRAM
```

Figure 5.6 Subroutine to find the maximum of two numbers

Now, the main program can call IOINIT, RNUM, MAX, and PNUM to read the three numbers and print the largest. Figure 5.7 shows what the main program would look like.

Finally, Figure 5.8 shows how the main program and the subroutines can be combined to form a single program. Notice that the constant and variable areas for IOINIT, RNUM, and PNUM are placed in front of subroutines IOINIT, RNUM, and PNUM. This allows the assembler to use byte relative and/or word relative addressing instead of longword relative addressing. Also notice that there is only one .END assembly directive and that it is placed after the last subroutine. For the time being, we will combine the main program and its subroutines into a single assembly language program. Later, in Chapter 9, we will see how assembly language programs that are independently assembled can be combined and even included with independently compiled programs that are written in higher-level languages such as FORTRAN or Pascal.

Figure 5.7 Main program for finding the largest of three numbers

```
;
;THIS MAIN PROGRAM READS THREE HEX LONGWORDS
;AND PRINTS THE LARGEST
;
        .ENTRY  START,0
        JSB     IOINIT          ;INITIALIZE RNUM AND PNUM
        JSB     RNUM            ;READ A
        MOVL    R0,R2           ;PUT A IN R2
        JSB     RNUM            ;READ B
        MOVL    R0,R1           ;PUT B IN R1
        JSB     RNUM            ;READ C INTO R0
        JSB     MAX             ;R0=MAX(B,C)
        MOVL    R2,R1           ;PUT A IN R1
        JSB     MAX             ;R0=MAX(A,R0)
        JSB     PNUM            ;PRINT R0
        $EXIT_S                 ;RETURN TO VAX/VMS
```

```
          .TITLE     LARGEST OF THREE
;
;THIS MAIN PROGRAM READS THREE HEX LONGWORDS
;AND PRINTS THE LARGEST
;
          .ENTRY     START,0          ;ENTRY POINT IS START
          JSB        IOINIT           ;INITIALIZE RNUM AND PNUM
          JSB        RNUM             ;READ A
          MOVL       R0,R2            ;PUT A IN R2
          JSB        RNUM             ;READ B
          MOVL       R0,R1            ;PUT B IN R1
          JSB        RNUM             ;READ C INTO R0
          JSB        MAX              ;R0=MAX(B,C)
          MOVL       R2,R1            ;PUT A IN R1
          JSB        MAX              ;R0=MAX(A,R0)
          JSB        PNUM             ;PRINT R0
          $EXIT_S                     ;RETURN TO VAX/VMS
;
;SUBROUTINE MAX SETS R0 TO THE MAXIMUM OF R0 AND R1
;
MAX:      CMPL       R0,R1            ;IS R0 GREATER THAN R1
          BGEQ       10$              ;YES, RETURN R0 AS MAX
          MOVL       R1,R0            ;NO, THEN R1 IS MAX
10$:      RSB                         ;RETURN TO MAIN PROGRAM
;
;RNUM AND PNUM AND IOINIT CONSTANTS
          . . .
;
;RNUM, PNUM, AND IOINIT VARIABLE SPACE
;
;INITIALIZATION ROUTINE
IOINIT:   PUSHR      #^M<R0,R1>
          . . .
          RSB
;
;PRINT NUMBER ROUTINE
PNUM:     PUSHR      #^M<R0,R1>
          RSB
;
;READ NUMBER ROUTINE
RNUM:     PUSHR      #^M<R1>
          . . .
          RSB
;END OF COMBINED PROGRAM, ENTRY ADDRESS IS START
          .END       START
```

Figure 5.8 Complete program for finding the largest of three numbers

Exercise Set 1

1. Write an assembly language program that reads 20 numbers and prints out the sum of the 20 numbers. Use the read and print routines shown in Appendix B for doing the exercise.

2. **a.** Write an assembly language program that reads three numbers. The program then prints out

   - 0 if all three numbers are different
   - 1 if any two of the three are the same
   - 2 if all three numbers are the same

   b. Rewrite the program so that it loops 20 times, printing out the results for 20 sets of 3 numbers.

   c. Rewrite the program so that it reads N, the number of sets of three numbers, and then loops N times.

3. Write an assembly language program that reads three numbers and prints them out in ascending order.

4. Write a program for Exercise 3 using a subroutine that takes the numbers in R0 and R1 and swaps them if necessary so that the contents of R0 will be less than or equal to the contents of R1 upon exit.

5. Write an assembly language program that reads 20 numbers and prints out the largest. Use the subroutine MAX shown in Figure 5.6. Rewrite the program so that it reads N, the number of numbers, and then finds the largest of the N numbers.

6. Using a loop and the method of differences described in Chapter 4, write a program that prints the squares of the integers from one to fifty.

7. Write a program similar to the program in Exercise 6 that prints the cubes of the integers from one to fifty.

8. An inventor constructs a robot whose sole purpose is to construct more robots just like itself. The way that the robot functions is that it spends two days collecting enough raw materials to build three robots. It spends the next three days producing robots, one per day. It then becomes inactive and does nothing more. Each new robot is immediately activated and goes through the five-day building cycle, as did the original. Write an assembly language program that prints out the number of robots in existence at the end of each day for 20 days from the activation of the first robot. (Hint: Robots behave differently depending on their age. Keep a tally of how many robots there are in each age group.)

VAX Arithmetic

6.1 Introduction

In previous chapters, we have seen how to add and subtract signed and unsigned numbers, and how to test and compare signed numbers. In this chapter, we will look at more of the properties of signed and unsigned numbers, as well as deal with overflow, multiplication, division, and multiple precision. We will see more instructions, and see how they can simplify programming. We will also further examine the test, compare, and branch instructions and see how they operate.

6.2 Signed and Unsigned Numbers
Operation and Interpretation

One of the advantages of the two's complement number system is that the same addition and subtraction algorithms can be used for both signed and unsigned numbers. (This is not true of some other signed number systems used in various computers.) Although this result may seem remarkable, it can be illustrated quite easily. For this purpose, it is convenient to use 4-bit numbers rather than 8-, 16-, or 32-bit numbers because the number of combinations is so much smaller.

Four bits can be arranged in 2^4 or 16 ways. As shown in Figure 6.1, the 16 combinations can be arranged in a circular pattern to produce something that resembles the face of a 16-hour clock with the binary number 0000 at the 12 o'clock position. A pointer is used to designate one of the 16 binary numbers. Adding one to a number is defined as moving the pointer ahead one position. Subtracting one is defined as moving the pointer backward one position.

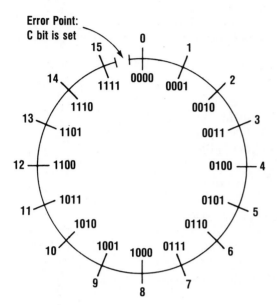

Figure 6.1 Unsigned arithmetic

If a one is added 16 times in succession, the pointer will make a complete circle and return to its starting position. Mathematicians call this a **modulo 16** counting system.* However, we might call this an error because X plus 16 is obviously not equal to X. In order to make this counting system consistent, it is necessary to agree on an error point somewhere around the clock dial.

For example, it is possible to locate the error point between 1111 and 0000. Whenever one is added to 1111 or one is subtracted from 0000, an error called **unsigned overflow** has occurred. With the error point specified, the various binary patterns can be given decimal interpretations. If the binary pattern 0000 represents the decimal number zero, it will be found that the pattern 1111 must represent decimal 15. The result is, of course, the unsigned number system.

However, it is possible to place the error point at some other position on the clock face. In particular, the error point can be placed between 0111 and 1000 as shown in Figure 6.2. If one is added to 0111 or one is subtracted from 1000, an error called **signed overflow** has occurred. If the binary patterns are now given a decimal interpretation, it is found that the patterns now represent decimal numbers between −8 and +7. (Note that if the binary pattern 0000 rep-

---

* As defined here, this clock analogy only applies to adding or subtracting positive numbers.

resents zero, we are compelled by the definition of subtraction to interpret the pattern 1111 as -1.) The result is, of course, the familiar two's complement number system.

Binary numbers on the VAX-11 computer are interpreted in exactly the same way except that 8, 16, or 32 bits are used instead of 4. The actual number of bits is determined by whether a byte, word, or longword instruction is used. The error point for unsigned longword overflow is between ^XFFFFFFFF and ^X00000000 and the error point for signed longword overflow is between ^X7FFFFFFF and ^X80000000.

The reasons a programmer would choose one system over the other depend on the needs of that particular part of the problem. As will be shown in Chapter 7, addresses are sometimes used as data to compute locations in an array. Since the address ^X80000000 is considered to be a higher address than ^X7FFFFFFF, these values should be treated as unsigned numbers. On the other hand, if negative numbers could possibly be generated, then signed numbers should be used.

Detecting Overflow

In order for the programmer to detect the two kinds of overflow, there are two condition switches located in the processor. These are called the C bit and the V bit. The C bit is set (to 1) whenever a Carry is produced out of the high-order bit of the result during an arithmetic operation. This is the same as unsigned overflow as shown in Figure 6.1. The C bit is cleared (to 0) if no carry (or unsigned overflow) occurred. The V bit is set if signed oVerflow occurs as shown in Figure 6.2, and is cleared if no signed overflow occurs.

In order for the C and V bits to be useful, there must be a means of testing their state. There are four instructions for doing this:

Symbol	Meaning
BCS	Branch if C is Set (if C = 1)
BCC	Branch if C is Clear (if C = 0)
BVS	Branch if V is Set (if V = 1)
BVC	Branch if V is Clear (if V = 0)

As an example of how these bits are used, the following program segment adds two signed longwords, and then branches to ERROR if the result overflowed, as would be the case if it were less than $-2,147,483,648$ or greater than $+2,147,483,647$.

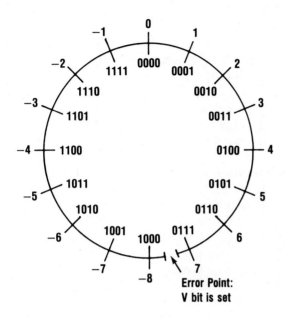

Figure 6.2 Signed arithmetic

```
ADDL2    A,B      ;ADD A AND B
BVS      ERROR    ;EXIT ON OVERFLOW
         .
         .
         .
ERROR:   .                 ;PRINT ERROR MESSAGE
```

Note that these four branch instructions are like the other branch instructions and have a limited range of locations to which they can branch; that is, 128 bytes before the program counter or 127 bytes after. If ERROR were more than 128 bytes from the BVS instruction, a JMP or BRW instruction would be needed. For example,

```
ADDL2    A,B      ;ADD A AND B
BVC      10$      ;IF NO OVERFLOW, CONTINUE
JMP      ERROR    ;EXIT ON OVERFLOW
10$:     .
         .
         .
ERROR:   .                 ;PRINT ERROR MESSAGE
```

Other Condition Switches

We have already seen the use of two condition switches, the C bit and the V bit. There are two other condition switches in the VAX, the N bit and the Z bit. The four condition switches are collectively known as the **condition codes.** The purpose for the N and Z bits is to simplify testing the conditions that result whenever an arithmetic operation is performed. In Chapter 5, we discussed testing and comparing. The following material shows what was really happening with the conditional branches.

The N bit is set whenever the result of an operation is negative. This is true even for such simple operations as MOVL. After a MOVL instruction, the N bit will be set if the number being moved is negative. The N bit will be cleared if the number is positive. In effect, the N bit will be the same as the sign bit or most significant bit of the result. However, overflow may cause the actual stored sign bit of the result, as well as the N bit, to be wrong.

The Z bit is somewhat similar. The Z bit will be set if the result of an operation is zero. It will be cleared if the result is *not* zero. In a way that is similar to the N bit, the Z bit also reflects the actual result even if overflow occurs. As for the other condition code bits, the N and Z bits can be tested by branch instructions. One slight difference is that the mnemonic operation codes reflect the use of the conditional branch instruction rather than the name of the condition code. The following four instructions complete the list of single-condition code branches.

Symbol	Meaning
BNEQ	Branch if previous result is *not equal* to zero; that is, if Z is clear
BEQL	Branch if previous result is *equal* to zero; that is, if Z is set
BGEQ	Branch if previous result is *greater than or equal* to zero; that is, if N is clear
BLSS	Branch if previous result is *less than zero;* that is, if N is set

Note that these are the same instructions that were discussed in Chapter 5. In order to complete the set, the following two instructions operate on a combination of condition codes.

Symbol	Meaning
BGTR	Branch if the previous result is *greater than zero;* that is, both N and Z are clear
BLEQ	Branch if the previous result is *less than or equal* to zero; that is, either N is set or Z is set.

Data-Handling Instructions

The data-handling instructions cause the condition code bits to be set and cleared according to what is appropriate for the result of the data operation. Instructions such as MOVL, CLRL, and the Boolean operations cannot cause overflow. Therefore, these instructions clear the V bit but leave the C bit unchanged. This operation is what was referred to as **testing** in Chapter 5. Data-handling instructions are those which deal with data, such as MOVL, ADDL, SUBL, and so on. These are opposed to control instructions such as JMP, BRB, BNEQ, and so on, which may examine the condition code bits, but do not deal with data, and therefore do not set or clear condition code bits.

Among the data-handling instructions, there are two odd sets, TSTL, TSTW, TSTB and CMPL, CMPW, CMPB. While these were described partially in Chapter 5, the details of how they work center around the condition codes. TSTL picks up a piece of data, looks at it, sets condition codes appropriately, and then does nothing else. The data looked at is not modified or used in any other way. The TSTL instruction will always clear both V and C bits because looking at a number cannot cause either kind of overflow. The N and Z bits will be set appropriately, depending on whether the data looked at are negative or zero.

The CMPL instruction is similar. This instruction looks at two pieces of data. That is, the instruction CMPL A,B causes B to be subtracted from A. The result is looked at for the purpose of setting condition code bits, and then the result is thrown away. The result is not stored anywhere, and neither A nor B is modified. Of course, this allows the CMPL instruction to be used in exactly the way it was used in earlier chapters. For example,

```
CMPL      A,B
BEQL      10$
```

Note that the instructions BGEQ, BGTR, BLSS, and BLEQ should not be used with unsigned numbers. For example, as an unsigned number, the longword ^XFFFFFFFF is larger than the longword ^X00000000. However, a comparison followed by BGTR will tell you the opposite because ^XFFFFFFFF will be considered a negative number, namely −1. To solve this, four unsigned conditional branch instructions are provided.

Symbol	Meaning
BGTRU	Branch if *greater than;* Unsigned
BGEQU	Branch if *greater than or equal;* Unsigned
BLEQU	Branch if *less than or equal;* Unsigned
BLSSU	Branch if *less than;* Unsigned

These instructions only make sense if used in conjunction with a compare instruction; therefore, the following instructions could be used in order to branch to 10$ if A is greater than B in an unsigned sense.

```
CMPL    A,B
BGTRU   10$
```

A curious thing to note is that the BLSSU instruction is identical to the BCS instruction. The assembler uses the same operation code for both, namely ^X1F. See Exercise 6 on page 152.

Comparing or testing for equality is the same for signed and unsigned numbers. However, in order to avoid having to remember when to use signed or unsigned branches, the assembler provides the mnemonics BEQLU and BNEQU which in fact assemble to the same operation codes as BEQL and BNEQ, respectively. That way the assembly language programmer can be consistent and always use the U if he is using unsigned numbers.

Data and Sign Conversion Instructions

It is often useful to be able to use a mixture of byte information, word information, and longword information in the same problem. Difficulty occurs, however, if you try to add or subtract values of different kinds. For example, you cannot directly add a byte to a word. In order to add a value, which is stored in a byte, to a word, it is necessary to extend the byte out to be a 16-bit word. That word can then be added to the other word. For example, the following instruction could be used to add a byte B to a word W.

```
CLRW    R0            ;CLEAR LOW BITS OF R0
MOVB    B,R0          ;THEN SET LOW ORDER 8 BITS TO B
ADDW2   R0,W          ;AND ADD EIGHT BIT NUMBER TO W
```

In addition to requiring three instructions, this sequence requires an extra place to hold a word. R0 is used here, but a word location in memory would work just as well. The CLRW instruction clears 16 bits to zero. Then the byte B is moved into the lower eight bits of the word which is then added as a word to W.

One problem with this method is that it assumes that the byte is an unsigned number. This will not work if you consider the byte to be signed, since the upper eight bits of the word are always zero because of the CLRW instruction. That means that R0 is always treated as a positive number which will be in the range from 0 to 255. In order to make this work for signed numbers, it would be necessary to check the sign of the byte, and if it is negative, set the high-order bits of the word in R0 to ones instead of zeros. This could be done with the following instruction.

```
        CLRW    R0              ;CLEAR LOW BITS OF R0
        TSTB    B               ;UNLESS B IS NEGATIVE
        BGEQ    10$
        MOVW    #-1,R0          ;THEN BITS SHOULD BE ONES
10$:    MOVB    B,R0            ;PUT B IN LOW 8 BITS
        ADDW2   R0,W            ;AND ADD SIGNED VALUE TO W
```

As we can see, this is already quite involved. Because of this, the VAX includes a set of convert instructions which copy signed bytes, words, or longwords to areas of different sizes. The following list of instructions includes the conversions which apply to integer operands. In addition, there are conversions which apply to floating point operands, and these are discussed in Chapter 12.

Symbol	Meaning
CVTBW	ConVerT Byte to Word
CVTBL	ConVerT Byte to Longword
CVTWB	ConVerT Word to Byte
CVTWL	ConVerT Word to Longword
CVTLB	ConVerT Longword to Byte
CVTLW	ConVerT Longword to Word

Effectively, these instructions operate in the same way as the MOV family of instructions, except that the size of the source and destination operands are different. These instructions affect the N and Z bits as described before. The C bit is always cleared to zero. The V bit is set if the result is too large to fit in the destination space as a signed number. Clearly, this can only happen on those instructions which move a larger object to a smaller space, such as CVTWB. The source word can be greater than 127 or less than −128, but this would not fit into the destination byte.

As an example of how these instructions operate, we can rewrite the preceding program which adds a signed byte to a word.

```
CVTBW   B,R0
ADDW2   R0,W
```

This works because the convert instructions, such as CVTBW, which move a smaller object to a larger space, will extend the sign bit over the extra space. For example, ^X03 will expand to ^X0003 but ^X83 will expand to ^XFF83.

Another similar set of instructions is used to reverse the algebraic sign of a number. Effectively, these instructions are similar to the FORTRAN or Pascal statement.

FORTRAN	Pascal
X = -Y	X := -Y;

The instructions are

Symbol	Meaning
MNEGB	Move NEGative Byte
MNEGW	Move NEGative Word
MNEGL	Move NEGative Longword

The instructions are two-operand instructions which move the two's complement negative of the source to the destination. For example,

```
MNEGL    X,R0
```

would move the negative of X in the 32-bit two's complement form to R0.

These instructions treat the N and Z bits normally to show the sign of the result and whether or not it is equal to zero. The V bit is set if the result cannot be expressed. Remember that two's complement negative numbers always go one further than positive numbers. For example, the most negative word is −32768 or ^X8000, whereas the largest positive number is +32767 or ^X7FFF. Therefore, there is no negative of the word ^X8000. The V bit will be set to indicate this.

The C bit is a little odd. It is set if the result is not zero. This may not seem to make sense, but it is useful for negating multiple precision numbers. (See the section on multiple precision later in this chapter.) In effect, the logic is that negating the number is the same as subtracting it from zero. For example, the instruction

```
MNEGL    X,R0
```

will set the C bit to the same value as the following pair of instructions.

```
CLRL     R0
SUBL2    X,R0
```

(In fact all four condition codes N, Z, V, and C will be the same in either case.) If the longword in X is not zero, the SUBL2 instruction will set the C bit because subtracting a nonzero number from zero always produces unsigned overflow.

The convert, and obviously, the move negative instructions apply to signed numbers. In addition, it may be useful to move unsigned numbers to larger fields in order to add an unsigned byte to a long-word. The convert instructions such as CVTBL cannot reliably be used for this purpose, because the byte will be treated as being signed rather than unsigned.

One solution to the problem is to use a pair of instructions to convert the unsigned byte to a longword. For example,

```
CLRL    RO
MOVB    B,RO
```

However, there is a set of instructions which achieve the same thing faster and with less code. They operate like the convert instructions except that they treat the operands as unsigned integers. Also, they only provide for moving a smaller operand to a larger one. The set is

Symbol	Meaning
MOVZBW	MOVe Zero-extended Byte to Word
MOVZBL	MOVe Zero-extended Byte to Longword
MOVZWL	MOVe Zero-extended Word to Longword

These instructions clear the more significant bits of the destination operand to zero, and move the source operand into the less significant bits. The N and V bits are all cleared to zero. Clearly there cannot be overflow and since zero is moved into the sign bit of the destination, N must be zero. The C bit is unchanged.

It may seem odd that there are no instructions for converting unsigned numbers to a smaller field such as is done with the CVTLB instruction for signed conversion. However, the same effect can be had by using the ordinary move instructions. For example,

```
MOVB    L,B
```

will move the last eight bits of the longword source L to the byte destination B. In fact, this will work for signed as well as unsigned operands. However, the CVTLB instruction does have an advantage with regard to error detection, since the V bit is set if the result will not fit in the space provided. Unfortunately, there is no similar test for unsigned numbers, since the V bit is reserved for signed numbers, and the C bit is normally used for a single carry bit, and not for general overflow.

Exercise Set 1

1. Show the decimal equivalents of the following hexadecimal words interpreted both as unsigned numbers and as 16-bit two's complement, signed numbers.

   a. ^X00FD   **b.** ^XFFFD   **c.** ^X7FFF

   d. ^XF716   **e.** ^X8000   **f.** ^X8001

   g. ^X80FD   **h.** ^X7655   **i.** ^X6EEF

2. Show the 16-bit two's complement negative of each of the numbers in Exercise 1 as would be computed by the MNEGW instruction. Also state the resulting values of the N, Z, V, and C bits in each case.

3. Show the results of adding the following pairs of hexadecimal words as they would be added using the ADDW3 instruction. Also state the resulting values of the N, Z, V, and C bits in each case.

   a. ^X011A   **b.** ^X6A5A   **c.** ^X6E5D
       ^X00FD   ^X7FEC   ^XFFEB

   d. ^XFFFF   **e.** ^X7FFF   **f.** ^XD7B7
       ^XFFFF   ^X8001   ^X6DF8

4. Do the same as for Exercise 3, except subtract the **first** number from the **second** as would be computed using the SUBW3 instruction.

5. Show that when signed two's complement overflow occurs, the sign bit of the result is the opposite of what it should be.

6. Explain why the BLSSU instruction is the same as BCS. Which unsigned branch instruction is the same as BCC? Explain.

7. Given the following list of possible contents for R0, state the new contents of R0 and the values for the N, C, V, and Z bits after executing the instructions INCL R0, DECL R0, INCW R0 , DECW R0.

   a. ^X7FFFFFFF   **b.** ^X80000000   **c.** ^XFFFFFFFF
   d. ^X00000000   **e.** ^X00000001   **f.** ^X80000001

*8. Write a subroutine that prints out four numbers which are either ^X00000000 or ^X00000001, indicating the values of the N, Z, V, and C bits. (Note: The JSB instruction does not affect the condition codes, nor does any branch or jump. However, instructions such as MOVL do change them. There are special instructions not yet discussed in the text which might simplify this exercise, but do not use them here. Rather, write the program in the form of a branch tree.) Also write a main program which tests the subroutine by doing various calculations and then calls the subroutine to print the results after each calculation.

6.3 Multiplication and Division
Basic Instructions

There are two sets of instructions for performing integer multiplication on the VAX: the basic instructions and the extended instructions. The basic instructions are intended for simple multiplication and division of bytes, words, or longwords as they stand. The extended instructions that will be discussed later allow extension to unlimited precision and for obtaining additional operations such as the remainder from division. The basic multiplication and division instruction set consists of the following instructions:

```
MULB2    DIVB2
MULB3    DIVB3
MULW2    DIVW2
MULW3    DIVW3
MULL2    DIVL2
MULL3    DIVL3
```

These instructions operate in much the same way that the two- and three-operand add and subtract instructions operate. For example, the instruction

```
MULL3    A,B,C
```

would multiply longwords A and B together and place the result in the longword C. Similarly,

```
MULB2    X,Y
```

would multiply the bytes X and Y and store the result as a byte in Y. One thing to note about these instructions is that the result of multiplication tends to produce large results. Therefore, care must be taken to avoid overflow. This is especially true with the multiply byte instructions which have a very limited range of possible magnitudes for the product.

The divide instructions operate in a similar way except that, as with subtraction, the order of the operands is important. These instructions always divide the first operand *into* the second. Consequently, the instruction

```
DIVL3     A,B,C
```

divides the longword A into the longword B and places the quotient into the longword C. Similarly, the instruction

```
DIVB2     X,Y
```

divides the byte X into the byte Y and leaves the quotient in the byte Y.

There is a notable difference, however, between addition and subtraction versus multiplication and division. There is no difference between the basic operations of adding or subtracting signed numbers and adding or subtracting unsigned numbers. As we have seen, the only real difference is in how we detect and treat overflow. On the other hand, multiplication and division of signed numbers is significantly different from multiplication and division of unsigned numbers.

All the instructions for multiplication and division described in this section are designed to operate on **signed** numbers. The treatment of signs follows the normal rules of algebra. Multiplication or division of numbers with like signs produce a positive product or quotient. Multiplication or division of numbers with unlike signs produces a negative product or quotient.

Integer division, however, presents a special problem in that the results of the division may not come out to be even whole numbers. The VAX integer division instructions described in this section use the same conventions for dealing with this problem as do most higher-level languages such as FORTRAN or Pascal. Fractional parts of the quotient are truncated so that the result is always "rounded" toward zero. This is true for both positive and negative results. Therefore, 7 divided by 2 is truncated to 3. Similarly, -7 divided by 2 is truncated to -3.

Finally, there is the question of how these instructions affect the condition codes. As might be expected, the N and Z bits are set or cleared to show whether the product or quotient is negative or zero. In either case, this means the stored product or quotient, and disregards any bits lost because of overflow or truncation.

The V bit is set to show overflow. It is easy to see where overflow can occur with multiplication, since the results of multiplication tend to be large. The V bit will be set if the product is too large in magnitude to fit in the data space provided for the result. In other words, byte products must be greater than or equal to ^X80 and less than or equal to ^X7F. Word products must be in the range from ^X8000 through ^X7FFF, and longword products must be in the range from ^X80000000 through ^X7FFFFFFF.

It may be less clear how overflow occurs in division, since quotients are usually smaller in magnitude than the divisor, which already fits in the data space. One obvious exception is division by zero. Clearly, an attempt to divide by zero will cause the V bit to be set. There is, however, one other exception. This is a result of the inherent asymmetry of the two's complement number system. Recall that the largest magnitude negative number has no positive counterpart. Bytes range from -128 to $+127$; words range from $-32,768$ to $+32,767$; and longwords range from $-2,147,483,648$ to $+2,147,483,647$. Therefore, in word arithmetic, there is no negative of $-32,768$. As a result, the DIVW2 or DIVW3 instruction will cause overflow if an attempt is made to divide $-32,768$ by -1. There is an analogous effect in the byte and longword versions of the divide instruction, and all will cause the V bit to be set.

Finally, there is the matter of the C bit. However, recall that the C bit is used primarily for unsigned operations, and these multiplication and division instructions are used only for signed arithmetic. Therefore, these instructions *always* clear the C bit to zero, no matter what results are produced.

Extended Multiply and Divide Instructions

In general, when two n-bit numbers are multiplied together, the result may be as large as $2 * n$ bits long. In order to account for this possibility along with its counterpart in division, the VAX includes two extended instructions for multiplication and division. The extended multiply instruction multiplies two 32-bit signed numbers together to produce a 64-bit signed result. The extended division instruction divides a 64-bit dividend by a 32-bit divisor, producing a 32-bit quotient and a 32-bit remainder.

More specifically, the extended multiply instruction operates as follows:

```
EMUL    A,B,C,D
```

A, B, C, and D are general operands. A and B are the 32-bit multiplier and multiplicand. D is the 64-bit product which is stored in a **quad-word.** C is a 32-bit signed quantity which is added to the 64-bit product. This instruction is often used for such things as base conversions, where a multiply and accumulate function is taking place. For that reason, the EMUL instruction includes this operand. If you have nothing to add to the product, the instruction can always be written in the form

```
EMUL     A,B,#0,D
```

Note that this instruction makes our first practical use of quad-words. In Chapter 3 we stated that information can be moved about in units of 8, 16, 32, and 64 bits with the instructions MOVB, MOVW, MOVL, and MOVQ, respectively. The MOVQ instruction moves a quadword or 64 bits or 8 bytes. This is not all that significant with memory locations since it is just an extension of the other multibyte moves, MOVW and MOVL. However, with registers there is a potential problem, since the registers are designed to contain 32 bits. Therefore, when a quadword operand is a register reference, the register and the next higher register are used. Consequently, the instruction

```
MOVQ   .  X,R0
```

would move the low-order 32 bits of X to R0, and the higher-order 32 bits of X to R1. Similarly, the instruction

```
EMUL     A,B,#0,R3
```

would place the 64-bit product of A and B in registers R3 and R4.

The extended divide instruction operates in somewhat the reverse of the extended multiplication. A quadword dividend is divided by a longword divisor. This produces a longword quotient and a longword remainder. The format of the instruction is

```
EDIV     D,E,F,G
```

D is the longword divisor and E is the quadword dividend. F is the longword quotient and G is the longword remainder. Unless it is zero, the sign of the remainder is chosen so that it is the same as the sign of the dividend. Since all operands are signed with this instruction, the expected sign of the quotient follows the rules of algebra. If the dividend and the divisor have the same sign, the expected sign of the quotient is positive. If the dividend and the divisor have differing signs, the expected sign of the quotient will be negative. The actual sign of the quotient may not be the same as the expected sign if it happens to be zero or if there is overflow.

Overflow can occur for two reasons. As one would expect, division by zero will cause the V bit to be set. However, note that division of a 64-bit number by a 32-bit number is **not** guaranteed to produce a 32-bit result. For example, ^X000123456789ABCD divided by ^X0000100 is ^X00000123456789AB with a remainder of ^X000000CD. Note that the remainder is always less in magnitude than the dividend, and thus must fit in 32 bits. The quotient in this case is still too large to fit in 32 bits, and thus, overflow will result.

A final thing to note about the extended multiply and divide instructions is that there is a kind of symmetry between them. Specifically, the accumulation operand of the EMUL instruction is somewhat the complement of the remainder in the EDIV instruction. For example, consider the extended divide

```
EDIV    D,E,F,G
```

As long as there is no overflow, the extended multiply

```
EMUL    D,F,G,X
```

will produce a quadword result, X, which is identical to the quadword dividend, E, input to the EDIV instruction.

With these instructions, the N and Z bits indicate the properties of the product of EMUL and the quotient of EDIV. The V bit shows if overflow occurs with EDIV, but overflow is impossible with EMUL, since two 32-bit operands can always be multiplied and have a result with no more than 64 bits. As with the basic multiply and divide instructions, the C bit is always cleared.

6.4 Multiple Precision Arithmetic
Double Precision Representation

As we have seen earlier, there are addition and subtraction instructions for 8-bit bytes, 16-bit words, and 32-bit longwords. Bytes and words are quite restrictive in the range of numbers that can be dealt with, but even longwords have a finite limit to their size. Unsigned longwords have values from 0 through 4,294,967,295. Signed longwords have values from $-2{,}147{,}483{,}648$ through $+2{,}147{,}483{,}647$. Although the ranges of these numbers may seem to be large enough for most purposes, there are some problems which require larger numbers. In order for a computer system to be general it must be capable of handling problems with any size number.

There is only one way to represent a number that will not fit in a single location, and that is to use several locations to store the number. The next obvious step in this direction is use two locations for a number. This is called **double precision.**

A double-precision number can simply be thought of as a 64-bit number or quadword. The 64-bit number can be stored in two longwords with the upper 32 bits in one longword and the lower 32 bits in the second longword. It is often easiest to think of this pair of 32-bit longwords as a single 64-bit quadword. In doing so, it becomes apparent that both signed and unsigned 64-bit numbers can be represented. All that is necessary is to generalize the concept of two's complement arithmetic to apply to 64 rather than 32 bits. As before, the left-most bit of the entire number is the sign. This would be the sign bit of the most significant 32-bit longword of the pair of longwords used for representing the number. (Note that the sign bit of the less significant 32-bit longword is simply a bit in the middle of the number, and is not related to the sign of the overall number.)

Double-Precision Addition and Subtraction

The ability to store double-precision numbers is of little use unless it is also possible to perform arithmetic with these larger numbers. Actually, the basic arithmetic processes can be implemented quite simply as can be seen from the following examples. In order to keep these examples simple, we will assume that we are dealing with 6-digit **decimal** numbers in a machine that has 3-digit decimal words.

Consider the following addition

```
    | 1  2  3|   | 4  5  6|
  + | 1  1  2|   | 2  3  3|
    ---------    ---------
    | 2  3  5|   | 6  8  9|
```

Here we see that the right half of the sum is equal to the sum of the right halves of the numbers being added. Similarly, the left half of the sum is the sum of the left halves of the numbers being added.

It should be noted, however, that this is not a general solution, because unsigned overflow can occur when the right halves of the numbers are added together. For example,

```
                1       Overflow carry
      ┌─────────┐      ┌─────────┐
      │ 1  2  3 │      │ 7  8  9 │
  +   ┌─────────┐      ┌─────────┐
      │ 1  1  2 │      │ 5  6  6 │
      └─────────┘      └─────────┘
      ┌─────────┐      ┌─────────┐
      │ 2  3  6 │      │ 3  5  5 │
      └─────────┘      └─────────┘
```

What has to be done here is to add the overflow carry to the sum of the left halves.

A similar process is used for subtraction.

```
                1       Borrow
      ┌─────────┐      ┌─────────┐
      │ 2  3  6 │      │ 3  5  5 │
  −   ┌─────────┐      ┌─────────┐
      │ 1  1  2 │      │ 5  6  6 │
      └─────────┘      └─────────┘
      ┌─────────┐      ┌─────────┐
      │ 1  2  3 │      │ 7  8  9 │
      └─────────┘      └─────────┘
```

Here an unsigned overflow occurs when you try to subtract 566 from 355 because an unsigned number cannot be negative. Because of that overflow, a one has to be borrowed from the difference of the most significant halves.

Add and Subtract With Carry Instructions

The methods just described also work when using binary arithmetic with 32-bit longword registers. In the VAX, the C bit indicates the presence of a carry when you add (or subtract) the least significant halves. Therefore, all that has to be done is to add (or subtract) the C bit to (or from) the most significant half of the result. You could of course do this by testing the C bit and then either incrementing or decrementing the result register. However, the VAX designers thought that multiple-precision arithmetic was important enough that they provided instructions for that purpose. For addition,

Symbol	Meaning
ADWC	ADd With Carry

This instruction adds the longword source operand and the C bit to the longword destination. For subtraction,

Symbol	Meaning
SBWC	SuBtract With Carry

This subtracts the longword source operand and the C bit from the longword destination.

These two instructions could be used along with the other arithmetic instructions to add the 64-bit number A to the 64-bit number B. The numbers A and B will be contained in VAX longwords AL, AR, BL, and BR where L and R refer to the left and right halves, respectively. The code for double precision is

```
ADDL2    AR,BR
ADWC     AL,BL
```

Similarly, A can be subtracted from B by the following code:

```
SUBL2    AR,BR
SBWC     AL,BL
```

Either of these programs can be extended to work with triple precision for 96-bit numbers, or even higher precision. All that is necessary is to use successive ADWC or SBWC instructions for the more significant parts.

6.5 The Multiplication and Division Algorithms

The Shift Instructions

In the decimal number system it is easy to multiply or divide by 10 or any power of 10 such as 100, 1000, 10000, and so forth. All you have to do is add zeros on the right to multiply, or drop off digits from the right to do integer division. In a register, this appears in the form of a shift of the number to the left for multiplication or to the right for division. For example, in a machine with 10-digit **decimal** registers

     0000057342   times 1000 is   0057342000

and

     0000057342   divided by 100 is   0000000573

This principle applies to number systems of any base when multiplied or divided by powers of the base. Therefore, numbers in a binary computer can be multiplied or divided by 2^n by shifting the number left or right n binary places. For example, in a 16-bit word

0000010011011110   times 8_{10} or 1000_2 is   0010011011110000

and

0000010011011110 divided by 4_{10} or 100_2 is   0000000100110111

These examples show what happens with positive numbers. The question remains, however, as to what shifting does with negative numbers. With left shifts, there is no problem, since

1111111111111000 is -8

and

1111111111110000 is -16

The only problem that would occur would be if so many left shifts were done that the left-most or sign bit were zeroed out. However, this is simply the overflow case and is in effect the same as would result if a positive number were shifted left and bits were lost off the left end, or if a one were shifted into the sign position. This kind of overflow is the kind that always results when an attempt is made to store a result whose magnitude is too large to fit in the space provided.

To sum things up, signed numbers can be multiplied or divided by a power of two by shifting the number to the left or right. When shifting to the left, zeros are brought in to fill the vacated bit positions. When shifting to the right, however, the sign bit is replicated in the vacated spaces. The reason for this can be seen by looking at two cases.

	0000000000010000 = 16		1111111111110000 = -16
divide by 4	0000000000000100 = 4	divide by 4	1111111111111100 = -4
	zeros are brought in		ones are brought in

There are two instructions in the VAX which can be used to perform this kind of operation. They are

```
ASHL    N,A,B
```

and

```
ASHQ    N,X,Y
```

In either case, N is a signed byte which gives a count of bit positions to be shifted. If N is positive, a left shift occurs; if N is negative, a right shift occurs. This is in effect the same as multiplying by 2^n or 2^{-n}. The instruction ASHL takes the longword operand A and shifts it by N and stores the result in the longword B. The instruction ASHQ is the same, except that the operands X and Y are quadwords or 64 bits.

These instructions set the N and Z bits according to the value of the result. The V bit will be set if a left shift produces a result with too large a magnitude to be stored in the destination operand. The C bit is cleared, because these instructions are assumed to be dealing only with signed data.

One point should be made about lost bits that occur during a right shift. Clearly, if a positive number is shifted right, the lost bits correspond to a fractional remainder. Dropping these bits causes the same kind of truncation that occurs with FORTRAN integer division using the "/" operator or Pascal integer division using the DIV operator. Unfortunately, this is not the case when a negative number is shifted right. This can be seen from the following example:

$$111 \ldots 1111011101 = -35$$
shifted right 3 times
$$111 \ldots 1111111011 = -5$$

From FORTRAN or Pascal integer arithmetic, -35 divided by 8 is -4, not -5. The reason for this is that right shifting causes two's complement numbers to be rounded downward, in the algebraic sense. Therefore -4.375 is rounded downward to the next *more negative* integer, -5. In order to make this kind of division correspond to FORTRAN or Pascal integer division, additional instructions would be required. See Exercise 6 on page 167.

While on the subject of shift instructions, there is another shift instruction which is used primarily for packing and unpacking data from a longword. We have seen how a longword can be subdivided into bytes. However, it is sometimes useful to subdivide longwords into pieces with odd numbers of bits. It then becomes necessary to shift the longword to align the pieces. Chapter 8 covers the need for this kind of operation. This instruction operates in much the same way as the arithmetic shifts, except that instead of extending the sign or shifting in zeros, lost bits from one end are shifted back to the other end. The instruction effectively treats the longword operand as if the ends were wrapped around each other. The form of the instruction is

```
ROTL    N,A,B
```

Here, as with the ASHL instruction, N is a byte which counts the shifts. The longword is rotated N places and stored in the longword B. The direction of rotation is left if N is positive and right if N is negative. For example, ^X12345678 rotated 12 times left would give ^X45678123. Recall that each hexadecimal digit is four bits; therefore, a shift of 12 bits gives a shift of 3 hexadecimal places. Shifts which are not multiples of four bits cannot be illustrated as easily by using the hexadecimal form for the numbers. While the N and Z bits operate normally for the ROTL instruction, V and C have no meaning. The actual rule is that V will be zero and C will be left unchanged.

General Multiplication and Division Algorithms (Optional Section)

VAX users do not have to be concerned with the algorithms for multiplication and division because they are implemented by hardware in the VAX processor. However, some smaller computers do not have multiplication and division instructions. These computers include certain models of the PDP-11 family of computers as well as most computer systems based on 8-bit microprocessors. On these computers, multiplication and division must be implemented in software. The following section illustrates how such software can be written.

The shifting operations described previously are the basis for almost all efficient multiplication and division algorithms. The reason for this can be seen by looking at how multiplication and division operate in the binary number system.

Essentially, binary multiplication operates in much the same way as decimal multiplication except that it is easier, because the only numbers to multiply by are zero and one, and it is quite simple to multiply by either. For an example, let us use a 4-bit "word" size for simplicity's sake. Then, to multiply 0110 by 0101 we get

```
      0110
×     0101
      0110
     0000
    0110
   0000
  00011110    8-bit product
```

The eighth bit, the zero on the left, is there because of a possible carry.

Notice that this operation consists of a sequence of shifts followed by possible adds of the multiplicand. The shifted multiplicand is added to the product if the corresponding bit of the multiplier is one. If the bit is zero, no addition takes place. The classical way of implementing this algorithm involves the use of three registers. Two hold the multiplicand and the multiplier; the other is used for accumulating the product and is called the accumulator. The accumulator and multiplier registers are actually combined for shifting purposes as one long register. The double length product will eventually reside in these two registers.

Since the accumulator is the high end of the register, everything is shifted right so that the first accumulation ends up shifted to the low end of the register pair. Shifting right to do multiplication may seem odd, but the example should make it clear that this is the correct direction. In words, the algorithm for multiplication can be stated as follows:

Step 1. Load the multiplier in the multiplier register, the multiplicand in the multiplicand register, and clear the accumulator to zero.

Step 2. If the least-significant bit of the multiplier register is one, add the multiplicand to the accumulator.

Step 3. Shift the accumulator-multiplier register pair one place to the right.

Step 4. Repeat Steps 2 and 3 the number of times that there are bits in the multiplier register.

Step 5. The double length product is now in the accumulator-multiplier register pair.

As an example, we can see how the multiplication of 0110 and 0101 would appear at each step of this algorithm. The symbols AC, MP, and MC refer to the accumulator, multiplier, and multiplicand registers, respectively.

	AC	MP	MC
1.	0000	0101	0110
2.	0110	0101	
3.	0011	0010	
2.	0011	0010	
3.	0001	1001	
2.	0111	1001	
3.	0011	1100	
2.	0011	1100	
3.	0001	1110	
5.	product = 00011110		

There are two things to note about this algorithm. First, as stated, overflow can occur when the multiplicand is added to the accumulator. This can be avoided by adding one more bit to the accumulator. The reader may verify that one bit is enough to guarantee that no overflow problems occur.

Second, this algorithm was stated for unsigned numbers. However, slight modifications can correct this. The problem of a negative multiplicand can be handled easily by having the right shift do sign extensions as is done with the ASH family of instructions. A negative multiplier creates a slightly different problem. Recall that an n-bit negative two's complement number x must be interpreted as $x - 2^n$. One way to account for this is that at Step 5 in the algorithm, if the original multiplier was negative, then subtract the multiplicand from the accumulator. Since we have just shifted the product right after adding the 2^{n-1} coefficient, the subtraction will correspond to -2^n times the multiplicand.

Figure 6.3 shows a program which uses the preceding algorithm to perform signed multiplication in much the same way that the EMUL instruction operates. The program multiplies the 32-bit signed numbers in R0 and R1, leaving the quad length product in R0 and R1. Note that the two MOVL instructions at 30$ could be replaced by a single MOVQ MP,R0. This is actually preferable, and the two instructions were only used to make the process clearer. The reader should note also the use of a new instruction, BLBC. This is actually one of a pair of instructions.

Figure 6.3 Multiplication program

```
MP:      .BLKL     1              ;MULTIPLIER
AC:      .BLKL     1              ;ACCUMULATOR (MUST FOLLOW MP)
MC:      .BLKL     1              ;MULTIPLICAND
MULT:    CLRL      AC             ;CLEAR AC
         MOVL      R1,MP          ;AND SET UP MULTIPLIER
         MOVL      R0,MC          ;AND MULTIPLICAND
         MOVB      #32,R0         ;AND BIT COUNT
10$:     BLBC      MP,20$         ;CHECK LOW BIT OF MP
         ADDL2     MC,AC          ;IF 1 ADD MULTIPLICAND
20$:     ASHQ      #-1,AC,AC      ;SHIFT EVERYTHING RIGHT
         DECB      R0             ;AND LOOP 32 TIMES
         BNEQ      10$
         TSTL      R1             ;TEST ORIGINAL MP
         BGEQ      30$            ;UNLESS POSITIVE
         SUBL2     MC,AC          ;SUBTRACT MC FOR -2**N
30$:     MOVL      MP,R0          ;RETURN QUAD PRODUCT
         MOVL      AC,R1          ;TO R0 AND R1
         RSB
```

Symbol		Meaning
BLBC	A,LOC	Branch on Low Bit Clear
BLBS	A,LOC	Branch on Low Bit Set

The BLBC instruction will branch to LOC if the low-order or least-significant bit of A is zero. Since this is the lowest bit, it does not matter if A is a byte, word, longword, or quadword. The BLBS instruction branches if the low-order bit is one. These instructions are usually used to test for error flags set in programs. However, it turns out that they are especially useful for this algorithm in Step 2.

Another thing to note is that no provision has been made for the extra bit in the AC needed to prevent overflow problems. Consequently this program will not work if the magnitude of the multiplicand is too great. It is possible to fix this problem by adding a few instructions. See Exercise 9 on page 168.

Division can be performed by an algorithm which is essentially a reversal of the multiplication algorithm. However, some added checks must be made to take care of overflow and division by zero. Again a double length shift register is used which will be divided into two parts, the accumulator and the quotient register. To prevent overflow, the accumulator should have one extra bit, as in the multiplication algorithm. Initially, the double length dividend is loaded into the double length shift register. The following algorithm develops.

Step 1. Load the double length dividend into the accumulator (high half) and the quotient register (low half). Load the divisor in the divisor register.

Step 2. If the divisor is less than or equal to the accumulator part of the dividend, exit with an overflow or divide-by-zero flag.

Step 3. Shift the accumulator-quotient register *left* one place.

Step 4. If the dividend is less than or equal to the accumulator, subtract it from the accumulator and set the low-order bit of the quotient register to one.

Step 5. Repeat Steps 3 and 4 the number of times that there are bits in the quotient register.

Step 6. The quotient register now holds the quotient, and the accumulator holds the remainder.

As stated, this algorithm operates on unsigned numbers. The algorithm can be modified to operate on signed numbers. See Exercise 11 on page 168.

Exercise Set 2

1. Multiply the following pairs of signed hexadecimal words and indicate which operations would cause overflow with the MULW2 instructions.

   a. ^X0014
   ^X002F

   b. ^X00FC
   ^X0088

   c. ^XFFFF
   ^X0001

   d. ^XFFFF
   ^X0002

   e. ^XFFFF
   ^XFFFF

   f. ^XFF01
   ^XFEFF

2. Divide the following pairs of signed hexadecimal words and show which are not valid operations.

   a. ^X0DCB/^X002C

   b. ^X0163/^X7716

   c. ^X0B8C/^X0000

   d. ^X0000/^X0B8C

   e. ^XFFF8/^XFFFB

   f. ^X8000/^XFFFF

3. The area of a triangle is $A = bh/2$ where b is the length of the base and h is the height. Write a VAX assembly language program which reads values for b and h and computes and prints the value for A. The program should loop unless a value of zero is entered for b. Use longword arithmetic.

4. Write a VAX assembly language program which reads a list of numbers and prints the average. The length of the list can vary, but will be terminated when the value zero is read. (This zero is not included as one of the averaged values.)

5. A **prime** number is an integer greater than or equal to two which has no divisors other than one and itself. Write a VAX assembly language program which prints out the first 50 prime numbers.

6. Show how the ASHL instruction could be augmented with additional instructions so that right shifts will truncate fractions for either positive or negative numbers.

7. Write a VAX assembly language program which reads ten pairs of longword numbers which are treated as double precision (64-bit) signed numbers. Your program prints the largest and smallest number pair.

8. Observe the program shown in Figure 6.3. How could the program be modified to include an additive operand such as the third operand of the EMUL instruction? Make this modification and write a main program which reads a number of triples of numbers and multiplies/accumulates them using first the mod-

ified subroutine and then the EMUL instruction. The program should print both sets of results for comparison.

*9. In addition to the modifications made in Exercise 7, make whatever modifications are necessary to account for the fact that the accumulator is one bit too short to avoid overflow. Run your program with some worst case examples and verify that the results are always the same as those computed by the EMUL instruction.

10. Write and test a VAX assembly language program for dividing unsigned numbers using the algorithm on page 166.

*11. How can the unsigned division algorithm on page 166 be modified to divide signed numbers? Implement the algorithm as a VAX assembly language subroutine and verify that it produces the same results as the EDIV instruction. What about the problem when the accumulator is really one bit too short, so that bad results may occur if the magnitude of the divisor is too large? Can these problems be accounted for? Test your program with some worst case data.

Arrays

7.1 Introduction and Review

Most readers are already familiar with the concept of an array as used in higher-level languages such as Pascal or FORTRAN. The programmer has a collection of data that is to be processed in some related way. Furthermore, the programmer wishes to have the entire collection of data in memory at the same time. In this chapter, we will see how arrays are created and processed in assembly language on a VAX computer system. In addition, the complete set of addressing modes available on a VAX will be described.

Sorting a set of numbers into ascending order is an example of a problem that may be solved by using an array. Since we (supposedly) do not know the actual order of the numbers being read, we cannot print a single number until all of the numbers have been read in. After all, the last number read in could be the smallest, and therefore, the first to be printed out. Figures 7.1(a) and 7.1(b) show an example of just such a program written in Pascal and FORTRAN, respectively. The program reads a list of 20 numbers, sorts them so that they are now rearranged in increasing order, and finally prints the rearranged list. Notice that this program performs three processes: reading, sorting, and printing. These three areas are identified by the remark and comment lines in the programs. The sorting method used in this program is one version of the popular selection sorting technique. If the reader is not already familiar with this method of sorting, it is suggested that the program be examined step by step as an exercise.

The first statement is of special note in both versions of this program. These statements are nonexecutable and simply inform the

(a) Pascal.   Figure 7.1 Sorting program

```
PROGRAM SORT(INPUT,OUTPUT);
VAR J,K,L,M : INTEGER;
    LIST : ARRAY[1..20] OF INTEGER;
BEGIN
(*READ UNSORTED NUMBERS*)
    FOR J := 1 TO 20 DO READLN (LIST[J]);
(*SORT NUMBERS*)
    FOR L := 1 TO 19 DO BEGIN
        FOR K := L+1 TO 20 DO BEGIN
            IF (LIST[L] > LIST[K]) THEN BEGIN
                M := LIST[L];
                LIST[L] := LIST[K];
                LIST[K] := M;
            END;
        END;
    END;
(*PRINT SORTED NUMBERS*)
    FOR J := 1 TO 20 DO WRITELN (LIST[J]);
END.
```

(b) FORTRAN

```
      PROGRAM SORT
      INTEGER LIST(1:20), J, K, L, M
C READ UNSORTED NUMBERS
      READ *, (LIST(J), J=1,20)
C SORT NUMBERS
      DO 20 L=1,19
        DO 10 K=L+1,20
          IF(LIST(L).GT.LIST(K)) THEN
            M=LIST(L)
            LIST(L)=LIST(K)
            LIST(K)=M
          END IF
10      CONTINUE
20      CONTINUE
C PRINT SORTED NUMBERS
      PRINT *, (LIST(J), J=1,20)
      STOP
      END
```

compiler about the number of memory locations that must be set aside for the array LIST.

As we have already seen, in assembly language programs we must make an allocation of every location that is being used for data. This is usually done with the .BLKL 1 assembly directive. In the next section, we will see how locations are allocated for arrays.

Another point to note about these FORTRAN and Pascal programs is that, in the various operations in the executable part of the program, the variable identifier LIST is used with a **subscript** or **index** which points to the specific location in the array. This is required because we are always referring to a single location and not a whole array. This is usually the case in assembly language. Although some machines, including the VAX, have instructions which are capable of moving a whole array, most machine-level operations deal with a single location at a time. Therefore, a means is needed for identifying a single location out of an array. This will be shown in the next section.

7.2 Arrays in Assembly Language
Storage Allocation

As we just saw, some means is needed to allocate or set aside a number of locations when dealing with an array. Although it might be possible to do this in many quite arbitrary ways, the simplest method is to use a contiguous block of memory locations. Successive locations in the block correspond to successive locations in the array.

The way of allocating a block of memory in the VAX assembly language is to use the directives .BLKL, .BLKW, or .BLKB. However, as used previously, these directives always had the value one in the operand field, indicating the assignment of one longword, word, or byte. For an array, a larger number can be used to indicate a larger block of memory. The assembler then reserves space for that number of data items at that point in the program. For example, .BLKL 10 would have the effect of allocating ten longwords that are placed one after the other (see Figure 7.2).

Now, in order to be able to refer to the array, there must be a symbolic name. This can be accomplished by placing a label XYZ on the .BLKL directive. As explained in Chapter 4, this causes the symbolic address XYZ to be entered into the user symbol table with the current value of the location counter. As a result, the symbolic address XYZ refers to the first longword of the array. The assembly directive .BLKL 20 causes 20 times 4 or 80 to be added to the location counter.

```
XYZ:      .BLKL    10        XYZ:      .BLKL    1        ;XYZ(1)        Figure 7.2 .BLKL directive
This directive produces              .BLKL    1        ;XYZ(2)
the allocation on the right.         .BLKL    1        ;XYZ(3)
                                     .BLKL    1        ;XYZ(4)
                                     .BLKL    1        ;XYZ(5)
                                     .BLKL    1        ;XYZ(6)
                                     .BLKL    1        ;XYZ(7)
                                     .BLKL    1        ;XYZ(8)
                                     .BLKL    1        ;XYZ(9)
                                     .BLKL    1        ;XYZ(10)
```

Address Expressions

Now that we have allocated space for an array, we are confronted with the problem of accessing a specific location in an array. The first location of the array is really no problem because the name of the array refers to the first location. Therefore, we could clear the first location of the longword array XYZ by executing the instruction CLRL XYZ. However, this does not solve the problem of how to access other locations in the array, such as the second, third, or fourth locations.

One solution is through the use of **address expressions.** Since longwords require four-byte locations, the address of the second location of the array XYZ is four higher than the address of XYZ. Similarly, the third and fourth locations of XYZ have addresses eight and twelve higher than the address of XYZ. Therefore, we can refer to these addresses symbolically as XYZ + 4, XYZ + 8, and XYZ + 12. We could thus clear the first four locations of the array XYZ with the following instructions:

```
CLRL      XYZ
CLRL      XYZ+4
CLRL      XYZ+8
CLRL      XYZ+12
```

Note that in assembly language expressions, the symbol XYZ always refers to the address of XYZ and never to its contents. This is very important when we consider an instruction like MOVL XYZ+4,A. At first glance, this might seem analogous to the Pascal or FORTRAN statement A:=XYZ+4; or A=XYZ+4. However, this is clearly wrong, because we do not mean the contents of XYZ with four added; we mean the contents of the longword four-byte locations higher than

XYZ. Thus, the analogous Pascal or FORTRAN statement would be A: = XYZ[2]; or A = XYZ(2).

Note that address expressions can be used in assembly language just about anywhere an ordinary symbol or number can be used. The expression can be quite complex, but it must result in a meaningful quantity such as an address or a constant number. This will be covered in more detail in Chapter 10. For the time being, we will just limit ourselves to the most common case of an address plus or minus one or more numbers or symbols that are defined to be constant numbers.

Although the use of address expressions is very important when dealing with arrays, there is a serious limitation. These expressions are evaluated at assembly time, and therefore cannot involve any numbers that would change during execution. This means that although we can refer to specific locations in an array such as XYZ[1], XYZ[2], and so on, we cannot refer to a variable or arbitrary location in an array such as XYZ[J]. Consequently, although we could clear out an array with a succession of CLRL instructions, we do not yet have a means of writing a loop that would do that.

Register-Deferred Mode

What is needed is a means of producing the *effect* of an address expression which is computed at the time that the program is being executed. In order to facilitate this, most modern computers have special addressing modes. The address that is actually used for a fetch or store operation is called the **effective address.** With the relative-addressing mode, for example, a displacement is added to the value in the program counter to generate an effective address. The VAX architecture allows an effective address to be generated with a variety of addressing modes. One of the simplest is the **register-deferred** mode. To use this mode, the program computes the numerical value of an address and places it in a register. Then, when register-deferred addressing is used, the numerical value contained in the register is used as the address of the operand (the effective address).

In the VAX, 15 of the 16 general registers, namely R0, R1, . . . , R11, AP, FP, and SP, can be used for register-deferred addressing. (Register 15, the program counter, may not be used for register-deferred addressing.) In order to use an instruction such as CLRL in the register-deferred mode, the assembly language operand consists of a register symbol enclosed in parentheses. For example, the instruction CLRL (R3) specifies register-deferred addressing with register 3. The

effective address is the value contained in the general register. If
register 3 contained ^X00001000, the instruction would clear the longword beginning in address ^X1000.

As an example, let us see how the instruction CLRL (R3) functions at the machine language level. The translation of the instruction
will require just two bytes, one for the operation code and one for
the operand specifier byte. The instruction will be assembled into the
following machine language instruction.

63 D4

The operation code for CLRL is ^XD4. The byte ^X63 means register-
deferred mode with register R3. (The ^X6 specifies register-deferred
mode and ^X3 specifies R3.)

Now, before we can say what this instruction does, we must
know the contents of R3. Let us suppose that at the time that the
VAX is about to execute this instruction, R3 contains ^X00001E84.
Since the effective address is ^X1E84, the CLRL instruction operates
on this location, and the longword in location ^X00001E84 is cleared
to zero. Note that the contents of R3 are not modified by the CLRL
instruction, so that R3 still contains ^X00001E84 after the CLRL
instruction is executed.

Figure 7.3 shows a program segment that clears an entire array
of 50 longwords. Several things to note are:

1. Register R0 is loaded with the starting address of the array XYZ
   using the new instruction MOVAL (MOVe Address of Longword).
2. Each time through the loop, four is added to R0 so that it points
   to the next longword in the array.
3. To avoid confusion, a second register, R1, is used to count the
   number of times through the loop. Using a second register may
   seem wasteful, and, as we shall see, the second register will not
   be needed when additional addressing modes are introduced.

Figure 7.3 Register deferred mode

```
XYZ:    .BLKL 50                    ;ARRAY LOCATION
          . . .
CLEAR:  MOVAL   XYZ,R0              ;R0 IS THE POINTER REGISTER
        CLRL    R1                  ;R1 IS THE LOOP COUNTER
10$:    CLRL    (R0)                ;CLEAR ARRAY LOCATION
        ADDL2   #4,R0               ;INCREMENT POINTER
        AOBLSS  #50,R1,10$          ;LOOP UNTIL 50 LOCATIONS ARE CLEARED
```

The MOVA Family of Instructions

The MOVAL instruction used in the program in Figure 7.3 is one of a family of instructions designed specifically for loading addresses for uses such as register-deferred addressing. The MOVAL instruction differs from the MOVL instruction in that the MOVL moves the **contents** of a longword to a destination, whereas MOVAL moves the **address** of a longword to the destination. MOVAL is one member of the **move address** family which includes the following instructions:

Symbol	Meaning
MOVAB	MOVe the Address of a Byte
MOVAW	MOVe the Address of a Word
MOVAL	MOVe the Address of a Longword
MOVAQ	MOVe the Address of a 64-bit Quadword
MOVAO	MOVe the Address of a 128-bit Octaword

Since an address on the VAX is 32 bits long, all five of these instructions move a 32-bit value to a longword destination. It may seem odd that there are five such instructions, since an address is an address regardless of whether the address points to a byte, word, longword, or whatever. In fact, in the example in Figure 7.3, the program would operate no differently had the MOVAL instruction been replaced by a MOVAB instruction. However, as more complex addressing modes are introduced later in this chapter, it will become apparent why more than one such instruction is needed.

To see the value of the move address family, it is useful to examine the effect of the following three instructions:

```
1. MOVL    A,R0
2. MOVL    #A,R0
3. MOVAL   A,R0
```

Assume that the symbol A is defined in assembly language as follows and that the assembler assigns the numerical address ^X00000444 to symbolic address A.

```
A:      .LONG    ^X00112233
```

If the linker relocates the module containing A so that it begins in address ^X0200, then, during execution, A is a symbolic name for address ^X00000444 plus ^X0200 or ^X00000644 (see the discussion of relocation in Chapter 4). In machine language, A would appear as follows:

Contents	Address
00112233	00000644

The first instruction, MOVL A,R0, will move the contents of the longword at A to R0 so that R0 will contain ˆX00112233 after the instruction is executed. Because the instruction uses one of the forms of relative addressing to reference address A, the relocation of the program to ˆX0200 does not require any modification of the program. (If A and the MOVL A,R0 instruction are in the same module, the distance between them does not change when the module is relocated.)

For the second instruction, MOVL #A,R0, the assembler uses immediate addressing for the "constant" A, whose value in the symbol table is ˆX00000444. As a result, the longword ˆX00000444 becomes part of the instruction. When the linker relocates the program so that it begins in address ˆX0200, the linker adds ˆX0200 to the longword in the instruction so that it becomes ˆX00000644. As a result, the instruction will move ˆX00000644 (the address that A represents at execution time) to R0.

The third instruction, MOVAL A,R0, also moves ˆX00000644 to R0. However, this instruction uses one of the forms of relative addressing to generate the address A, and thus, this instruction does not have to be modified when the program is relocated.

On many computers, such as the PDP-11 family, instructions similar to MOVL #A,R0 are used to obtain addresses within a module. All such addresses must be modified if the program is relocated. In contrast, the VAX architecture was specifically designed to make it easy to write **position-independent** programs that can be relocated without modification. This is why the MOVAL family of instructions was included in the VAX instruction set. As a result, it is considered poor programming practice to use instructions such as MOVL #A,R0 that use immediate addressing with a symbolic address.

A Sorting Program

As a final example in this section, the program in Figure 7.1 might be rewritten in assembly language as shown in Figure 7.4. The example does not include input or output, but just the sorting portion. In the assembly language program, R3 and R4 are used to hold the loop counters L and K respectively. However, L in the higher-level language program varies from 1 to 19 while R3 in the assembly language program varies from 0 to 18. Similar comments apply to K and R4. R2 in the assembly language program, like variable M in the higher-level language programs, is used as a temporary storage area when

Figure 7.4 Assembly language, sorting problem

```
SIZE=20
LIST:     .BLKL    SIZE                  ;SPACE FOR ARRAY
          .
          .
          .
SORT:     MOVAL    LIST,R0               ;LEFT POINTER IN R0
          CLRL     R3                    ;R3 IS OUTER LOOP COUNTER, L
10$:      MOVL     R0,R1                 ;RIGHT POINTER IN R1 EQUALS
          ADDL2    #4,R1                 ; LEFT POINTER PLUS 4
          MOVL     R3,R4                 ;R4 IS INNER LOOP COUNTER, K
          INCL     R4                    ; WHICH IS INITIALIZED TO L+1
20$:      CMPL     (R0),(R1)             ;COMPARE LIST(LEFT) AND LIST(RIGHT)
          BLEQ     30$                   ;IF LESS OR EQUAL, OK
          MOVL     (R0),R2               ;OTHERWISE SWAP
          MOVL     (R1),(R0)             ; TWO LIST ELEMENTS
          MOVL     R2,(R1)               ; USING R2 AS TEMPORARY, M
30$:      ADDL2    #4,R1                 ;INCREMENT RIGHT POINTER
          AOBLSS   #SIZE,R4,20$          ;LOOP UNTIL DONE
          ADDL     #4,R0                 ;INCREMENT LEFT POINTER
          AOBLSS   #SIZE-1,R3,10$        ;LOOP UNTIL DONE
```

two elements are swapped. Register-deferred addressing is used with registers R0 and R1 to access the elements in the array. Notice the use of the MOVAL instruction to load the address LIST into R0.

Exercise Set 1

1. Given that general registers R0, R1, and R2 contain the following hexadecimal values

R0	^X00001111
R1	^X00000E24
R2	^X0000FFC4

   and that the symbols ABC, PQW, and XYZ correspond to the following addresses

ABC	^X00001000
PQW	^X0000C4E0
XYZ	^XFFFFFFF8

what are the effective addresses of the following clear instructions; that is, what locations would be cleared when they are executed?

a. CLRL   PQW   b. CLRL   PQW+24

c. CLRL   ABC+^XE4   d. CLRL   ABC+300

e. CLRL   (R0)   f. CLRL   XYZ+1046

g. CLRL   (R1)   h. CLRL   XYZ+^X300

i. CLRL   (R2)   j. CLRL   XYZ+100

2. Assemble each of the instructions in Exercise 1 to machine language assuming that the instruction begins at address ^X00000346.
3. Convert the program segment shown in Figure 7.4 to a complete sorting program. Use the RNUM and PNUM subroutines shown in Appendix B to complete the missing input and output sections. Run the program with sample data.
4. The flowchart on page 179 describes a sorting algorithm known as the **bubble sort:**
   a. How does this sorting program work? Show an example with four or five elements.
   b. How does this sorting program differ from the selection sort shown in Figure 7.4?
   c. Which method is more efficient, or is there any difference?
   d. What advantages or disadvantages are there, one over the other, if any?
5. Write an assembly language program segment (such as was done in Figure 7.4) for the bubble sort program shown in Exercise 4.
6. Write and run a complete bubble sort program adding input and output sections using the subroutines given in Appendix B.

7.3 Other Addressing Modes
Auto-Increment Addressing

As can be seen from the previous examples, when scanning through an array using register-deferred addressing, it is necessary to update the pointer in the register by adding some number every time through the loop. Also, with longword arrays, the number added each time is four since the programs are stepping through successive longwords in an array. In order to facilitate this and to make many programs

Bubble sort flowchart

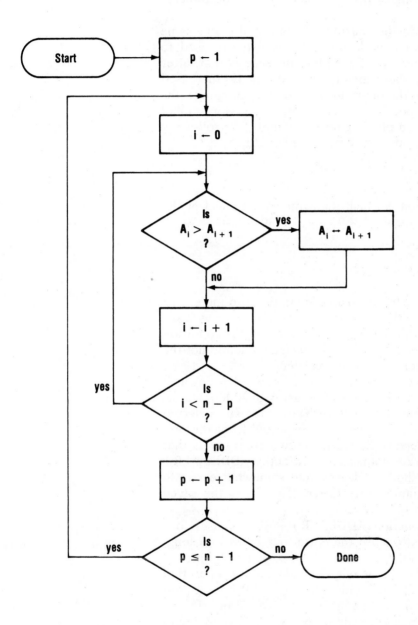

* n is the number of items to be sorted.
* A is the array of data to be sorted.

much more efficient, the VAX has an addressing mode where this increment takes place automatically. This is called the **auto-increment mode.**

The auto-increment mode operates in essentially the same way as the register-deferred mode in that a register is used to hold the address of the operand. The only difference is that, after executing the instruction, the register involved will be increased by the number of bytes in the operand. In assembly language, the auto-increment mode is specified by enclosing a register symbol in parentheses followed by a plus sign. For example, the following CLRL instruction uses the auto-increment mode with register 0.

```
CLRL     (R0)+
```

The effect of this instruction is much the same as the effect of the following pair of instructions.

```
CLRL     (R0)
ADDL2    #4,R0
```

There are, however, two things to note about the auto-increment mode. The first is simply that the auto-increment mode requires fewer instructions. The second is that, with auto-increment, the condition codes are determined by the operand of the instruction, and not the increment process or the contents of the register.

For an example of how auto-increment can be used, let us look at a program which sums the elements of an array of 20 longwords. Figure 7.5 shows how this could be done with either register-deferred or auto-increment addressing. As would be expected from the preceding discussion, the difference between the two programs is that the auto-increment version does not need the instruction ADDL2 #4,R0. This makes the program shorter, clearer, and somewhat easier to write, and it also runs significantly faster. (Note that the saved instruction is inside a loop.)

Notice that the instruction ADDL2 (R0)+,SUM causes four to be added to R0. This is because there are four bytes in a longword. In order for the auto-increment mode to work on all kinds of arrays, the amount of the increment depends on the operation code. Thus, ADDB2 (R0)+,SUM would increment R0 by one and ADDW2 (R0)+,SUM would increment R0 by two. Similarly, instructions that operate on quadwords or octawords would increment the register by eight or sixteen respectively.

This explains in part why there is more than one MOVA instruction. The instructions in the MOVA family can be used with any

Figure 7.5 Two programs to add 20 numbers

(a) Register-Deferred Version			(b) Auto-Increment Version		
SIZE=20			SIZE=20		
SUM:	.BLKL	1	SUM:	.BLKL	1
DATA:	.BLKL	SIZE	DATA:	.BLKL	SIZE
	...			...	
SUMV1:	MOVAL	DATA,R0	SUMV2:	MOVAL	DATA,R0
	CLRL	R1		CLRL	R1
	CLRL	SUM		CLRL	SUM
10$:	ADDL2	(R0),SUM	10$:	ADDL2	(R0)+,SUM
	ADDL2	#4,R0			
	AOBLSS	#SIZE,R1,10$		AOBLSS	#SIZE,R1,10$

addressing mode. Thus, it would be possible to have the instruction
MOVAL (R0)+,R3. This instruction would cause **the address in** R0
(rather than the longword pointed to by R0) to be moved to R3. R0
would then be incremented by four. Assume, for example, that R0
pointed to a longword at memory address A before the instruction
was executed. After executing the instruction MOVAL (R0)+,R3, R3
would point to the longword in address A and R0 would point to the
longword following in address A+4. To allow such address computations to operate properly with data of different lengths, the members of the MOVA family will auto-increment by different amounts
as follows:

Instruction		Increment of R0
MOVAB	(R0)+,R3	1
MOVAW	(R0)+,R3	2
MOVAL	(R0)+,R3	4
MOVAQ	(R0)+,R3	8
MOVAO	(R0)+,R3	16

It may seem that there is very little need to use the auto-increment
mode with a member of the MOVA family. However, one use for such
a mode is the generation of address lists for subroutines. This use is
discussed in Chapter 9.

Auto-Decrement Addressing

In order to deal with the fact that it is often necessary to access the
elements of an array in reverse order, the VAX has another addressing
mode called the **auto-decrement mode.** The auto-decrement mode is

essentially the same as the auto-increment mode, with the general register being decremented or reduced by four, two, or one for long-word, word, or byte instructions respectively. Another difference is due to the need for symmetry between the two modes. In the auto-increment mode, the general register is incremented **after** it is used. In the auto-decrement mode, the general register is decremented **before** it is used. This means that the auto-decrement instruction exactly undoes what the auto-increment does. This is important when an array is used as a **stack.** As noted in Chapter 5, a stack is analogous to a stack of dishes in that the first item removed is the most recently added item. (If dishes are added and removed from the top of a stack of dishes, the dish at the top of the stack is always the most recently added dish.) As we shall see in Chapter 9, the symmetry between auto-increment mode and auto-decrement mode allows programmers to easily implement stacks.

In assembly language, the auto-decrement mode is indicated as

```
CLRL    -(R3)
```

This instruction would cause R3 to be decremented by four, and then the location that R3 is pointing to would be cleared. Note that the designers of the assembly language require the minus sign at the beginning of the operand, whereas in the auto-increment mode, the plus sign is at the end of the operand. This is to remind programmers that decrementing takes place before use, whereas incrementing takes place after use. The single instruction given earlier has the same effect as the following pair of instructions.

```
SUBL    #4,R3
CLRL    (R3)
```

As an example of the use of auto-decrement mode, Figure 7.6 shows a program that copies a 20-longword array A to another array B, and reverses the order of the longwords. Notice that the instruction MOVAL B+BYTES,R1 loads register R1 with the address of the longword that immediately follows the last longword in the array B. (If the 20 longwords in the array occupy locations ^X0400, ^X0404, ^X0408, . . ., ^X044C, the address loaded into R1 is ^X0400 plus the constant BYTES. Since BYTES equals 20 times 4 which is 80 decimal or ^X50, the address loaded into R1 is ^X0400 plus ^X50 or ^X00000450.) However, because auto-decrement addressing is used in the MOVL instruction, R1 is auto-decremented to ^X00000450 minus ^X4 or ^X0000044C before the first item is stored into array B.

```
SIZE=20                          ;ARRAY CONTAINS 20 LONGWORDS
BYTES=SIZE*4                     ;WHICH OCCUPY 80 BYTES
A:      .BLKL   SIZE
B:      .BLKL   SIZE

           . . .
REVERSE:
        MOVAL   A,R0             ;POINTS TO START OF ARRAY A
        MOVAL   B+BYTES,R1       ;POINTS TO END OF ARRAY B
        CLRL    R2               ;LOOP COUNTER (0 TO SIZE-1)
10$:    MOVL    (R0)+,-(R1)
        AOBLSS  #SIZE,R2,10$
```

Figure 7.6 A program for reversing an array

Displacement Mode

Figure 7.7 shows an example of a program segment in which each element of an array (except the last) is set equal to the element that follows it. This is an operation that might be performed if the first item were being deleted.

Figure 7.8 (a) shows how this program could be implemented in assembly language using auto-increment addressing. Note that three registers are used. R0 is used to point to A[I], R1 is used to point to A[I+1], and R2 is used as a loop counter that varies from zero to VSIZE−1. Notice that VSIZE is assumed to be the address of a longword (a variable) rather than a constant, so that the instruction AOBLSS VSIZE,R2,10$ rather than AOBLSS #VSIZE,R2,10$ must be used to end the loop. Since both R0 and R1 are incremented together, they start out with a difference of four and continue to have a difference of four at every step in the program.

In order to avoid the need for using two or more registers on such occasions, the VAX has a set of modes called **displacement modes.** Displacement modes allow for a fixed offset from an address in a register. In assembly language, this is specified with an operand that consists of a number (or a symbol that represents a number) followed by a register symbol enclosed in parentheses. Thus, the instruction CLRL 16(R0) will clear the contents of the longword that is 16 locations higher than the address contained in R0. If R0 con-

Pascal
```
FOR I:= 1 TO VSIZE-1 DO
 BEGIN
  A[I] := A[I+1];
 END;
```

FORTRAN
```
DO 10 I=1,VSIZE-1
   A(I)=A(I+1)
10 CONTINUE
```

Figure 7.7 Programs to move data in an array

Figure 7.8 Using displacement mode

(a) Auto-Increment Mode Version	(b) Displacement Mode Version

```
              MOVAL   A,R0                           MOVAL   A,R0
              MOVAL   A+4,R1
              CLRL    R2                             CLRL    R2
              SUBL3   #1,VSIZE,R3                    SUBL3   #1,VSIZE,R3
      10$:    MOVL    (R1)+,(R0)+            10$:    MOVL    4(R0),(R0)+
              AOBLSS  R3,R2,10$                      AOBLSS  R3,R2,10$
```

tained ^X000003A4, the longword at address ^X000003B4 would be cleared.

Figure 7.8(b) shows how the assembly language program in Figure 7.8(a) could be rewritten using displacement mode, thereby saving a register. One possible source of confusion with this program is that the instruction MOVL 4(R0),(R0)+ uses R0 in both operands (once with auto-incrementation). Confusion can occur as to exactly when R0 is incremented. The rule is that the operands of an instruction are processed one at a time in the order that they appear in the instruction. Therefore, since the auto-incrementation occurs on the second operand, it will not affect the computation of the effective address for the first operand.

The following example is a rather weird way of rewriting the program in Figure 7.8(b) so that the auto-increment mode is used on the first operand.

```
              MOVAL   A+4,R0
              CLRL    R2
              SUBL3   #1,VSIZE,R3
      10$:    MOVL    (R0)+,-8(R0)
              AOBLSS  R3,R2,10$
```

Note that the second operand should be pointing to an address that is four less than the first. Because R0 will have already been incremented by four, the displacement on the second operand must be −8. This also shows that displacements are two's complement numbers and can therefore be negative.

In order to save memory space, there are three displacement modes. The first uses a byte displacement in the range −128 to +127. The second uses word displacement with a range from −32768 to +32767. The third uses longword displacement and can address any location in memory.

If the magnitude of the displacement is small enough to fit in a byte, i.e. between −128 and +127, the assembler will chose byte displacement. If the displacement is out of this range, a word or longword will be used. The assembler will use a longword displacement if it does not know how big the number is. (This can happen when the symbol is defined later in the program.) The choice of the assembler can be overridden by placing a control symbol in front of the address field. The control symbols are

B^   Byte displacement
W^   Word displacement
L^   Longword displacement

For example, the instruction

```
CLRL    W^X(R3)
```

will be assembled with word displacement regardless of whether or not X fits in a word. Usually, this will lead to errors in cases when an insufficient size is chosen. The use of the control symbols shown previously is therefore not recommended for most programs.

In the last example on page 184, R0 was initialized by the MOVAL A+4,R0 instruction to point to the address A+4. This was to avoid the temptation to combine the displacement mode with the auto-increment mode to produce an operand specifier such as 4(R0)+. There is no such mode on the VAX and an operand such as 4(R0)+ will generate an assembly error. Expressions such as A+4 and modes such as −8(R0) may look complicated but the preceding program performs the same series of operations during execution as the program in Figure 7.8(b). Note that expressions such as A+4 are computed by the assembler and require no computation during program execution.

Index-Register Mode

Although the displacement, register-deferred, auto-increment, and auto-decrement modes provide a rich variety of ways to deal with arrays, each has its own disadvantages. The register-deferred, auto-increment, and auto-decrement modes are fine for scanning through a single array. However, these modes are not quite so useful for selecting random locations in an array, and are even more awkward when more than one array is involved. For example, with the register-deferred mode, the Pascal or FORTRAN sequence

Pascal

```
I := arbitrary value;
 . . .
A[I] := B[I] + C[I];
```

FORTRAN

```
I = arbitrary value
 . . .
A(I) = B(I) + C(I)
```

would require separate computation of the addresses of A(I), B(I), and C(I), and placement of these values in three separate registers so that the instruction

```
ADDL3  (R2),(R3),(R1)
```

could be executed. As a side note, the value of I would have to be multiplied by four, assuming that A, B, and C have been declared as INTEGER arrays. The resulting code in assembly language would appear as follows:

```
MULL3    I,#4,R4            ;BYTE OFFSET INTO R4
MOVAL    A-4,R1             ;ADDRESS OF A[I] TO R1
ADDL2    R4,R1
MOVAL    B-4,R2             ;ADDRESS OF B[I] TO R2
ADDL2    R4,R2
MOVAL    C-4,R3             ;ADDRESS OF C[I] TO R3
ADDL2    R4,R3
ADDL3    (R2),(R3),(R1)     ;A[I] := B[I] + C[I]
```

In the MOVAL instructions, notice that four is subtracted from symbolic addresses A, B, and C. This is because Pascal and FORTRAN arrays normally use one for the lower subscript. Therefore, the assembly language symbol A is used for the address of A[1] or A(1). If the index I contains one, the MULL3 instruction places the offset I*4 or ^X00000004 into R4 and the three ADDL2 instructions will leave registers R1, R2, and R3 pointing to addresses A, B, and C respectively. The address A − 4 is called the **base address** of array A because it is the address to which an offset is added in order to compute the address of a particular element in the array. Similarly, addresses B − 4 and C − 4 are the base addresses for arrays B and C.

The need to initialize three separate registers takes a significant amount of time and space. Clearly, the auto-increment and auto-decrement modes do not help in this problem, unless later steps in the program do sequential scanning of the arrays A, B, and C. The solution to this problem involves the use of a new mode called the **index-register mode.** To write this same code using the index-register mode we would have

```
MOVL     I,R0
ADDL3    B-4[R0],C-4[R0],A-4[R0]
```

Note that the syntax looks almost like the syntax of a statement in a higher-level language. In the ADDL3 instruction, each operand is specified by a base address such as B − 4 or C − 4, followed by a register symbol enclosed in square brackets, such as [R0].

The effective address is computed by adding an offset which is four times the value of the index register (in this case R0) to the base address. Therefore, the program does not need to multiply I by four. Note that the value of R0 is multiplied by four because ADDL3 is a longword instruction. If the index-register mode is used for a word or byte operand, the multiplication is automatically by two or one, and if the operand is a quadword, the multiplication is automatically by eight.

Unlike all of the other addressing modes, the index mode is always used in conjunction with one of the other modes. The other mode is used to generate the base address to which the offset computed from the index is added. In this case, one of the forms of relative addressing will be used to generate the base addresses A − 4, B − 4, and C − 4. As a result, the ADDL3 instruction is position-independent. Furthermore, if A, B, and C are close enough to the ADDL3 instruction, the assembler will use byte- or word-relative addressing for A − 4, B − 4, and C − 4. As a result, the instruction length may be as little as 10 to 13 bytes.

As was stated earlier, the index-register mode is used in conjunction with other modes so that an instruction such as

```
CLRL    (R2)+[R0]
```

could be written. This would compute an effective address by adding the address in R2 to four times the value of R0, and clearing that location. Then, R2 would also be incremented by four.

Figure 7.9 shows how the program from Figure 7.5 could be rewritten using the index-register mode. As can be seen from Figure

(a) Register-Deferred Mode Version

```
SIZE=20
SUM:    .BLKL   1
DATA:   .BLKL   SIZE

        . . .
ADDUP:  MOVAL   DATA,R0
        CLRL    R1
        CLRL    SUM
10$:    ADDL2   (R0),SUM
        ADDL2   #4,R0
        AOBLSS  #SIZE,R1,10$
```

(b) Index-Register Mode Version

```
SIZE=20
SUM:    .BLKL   1
DATA:   .BLKL   SIZE

        . . .
ADDUP:  CLRL    R0
        CLRL    R1
        CLRL    SUM
10$:    ADDL2   DATA[R0],SUM
        INCL    R0
        AOBLSS  #SIZE,R1,10$
```

Figure 7.9 Adding 20 numbers using the index-register mode

7.9, there is not much difference between the two versions, except that the index register version increments R0 by one instead of four. However, the index-register version is conceptually simpler because R0 contains an index rather than an address.

Another advantage of the index-register mode can be seen by looking at what happens with R0 and R1. In the program in Figure 7.9(a), R0 contains an address and R1 contains a loop counter. In the index-register example in Figure 7.9(b), R0 contains the index and R1 contains the loop counter. Close examination of the index-register version shows that R0 and R1 contain the same value. Both are initialized to zero outside the loop and both are incremented by one each time through the loop. Since they contain the same value, one of the registers is unnecessary and the program segment can be rewritten as

```
ADDUP:  CLRL     R0
        CLRL     SUM
10$:    ADDL2    DATA[R0],SUM
        AOBLSS   #SIZE,R0,10$
```

7.4 General-Register Addressing Modes
Review

Table 7.1 shows the addressing modes that have been described in this chapter. (Note that register addressing has also been included.) All of these modes are **general-register addressing modes** that are designed to be used with all of the general registers (with the possible exception of the program counter, register 15). In the table, the name of the mode is listed on the left side. On the right side, the use of the mode in assembly language is illustrated with a CLRL instruction using R3 as the general register.

In order to interpret the middle columns in Table 7.1, recall that each machine language instruction consists of a numerical operation code followed by an appropriate number of operand specifiers. Each operand specifier consists of an operand specifier byte that may be followed by additional information, such as a displacement, depending on the operand specifier byte. The operand specifier byte, in turn, consists of two hexadecimal digits. The second hexadecimal digit specifies the general register that is to be used in locating the operand. The first hexadecimal digit in the operand specifier byte is the **mode** digit that specifies how the register will be used in locating the operand.

Table 7.1 General-register address modes

Name	Spec Byte	Opcode	Assembly Language
Register	53	D4	CLRL R3
Register-deferred	63	D4	CLRL (R3)
Auto-decrement	73	D4	CLRL -(R3)
Auto-increment	83	D4	CLRL (R3)+
Byte-displaced	xx A3	D4	CLRL D(R3)
Word-displaced	xxxx C3	D4	CLRL D(R3)
Longword-displaced	xxxxxxxx E3	D4	CLRL D(R3)
Byte-relative indexed	xx AF 43	D4	CLRL A[R3]
Word-relative indexed	xxxx CF 43	D4	CLRL A[R3]
Longword-relative indexed	xxxxxxxx EF 43	D4	CLRL A[R3]

Notes: The symbol A refers to an address and D refers to a displacement. The assembler will choose byte, word, or longword modes for A and D depending upon the size of the value.

In the middle columns of Table 7.1, the operation code for the CLRL instruction, ^XD4, appears in the opcode field. The byte to the left, under the heading "Spec Byte," is the operand specifier byte. In each case, the second digit of the operand specifier byte is ^X3 because R3 is used as the general register. The first digit is the mode digit. As the table shows, mode ^X5 specifies register addressing, mode ^X6 specifies register-deferred addressing and so on.

Notice that the register-deferred, auto-decrement, and auto-increment modes (modes ^X6, ^X7, and ^X8 respectively) are very similar in that the register contains, at some point, the address of the operand. With the register-deferred mode, the contents of the register are not altered. With auto-decrement mode, the register is decremented before it is used, and with the auto-increment mode, the register is incremented after it is used.

Modes ^XA, ^XC, and ^XE are the mode digits for byte-, word-, and longword-displacement addressing respectively. The assembler generates a byte, word, or longword displacement and places it in memory immediately after the operand specifier byte. In Table 7.1, the displacements are represented by the symbols xx, xxxx, and xxxxxxxx.

Recall that the program counter points to the various bytes in an instruction as the instruction is executed. When execution of an instruction has been completed, the program counter must point to the beginning of the next instruction. To achieve this, the byte-, word-, and longword-displacement modes automatically add one, two, or four respectively to the program counter in order to "skip over" the displacement in the instruction. The addition to the program counter is automatic regardless of the general register that is being used for displacement addressing. For example, in the instruction

```
CLRL    L^X(R3)
```

the longword-displacement mode will add four to the program counter to "skip over" the four-byte displacement. As a result, the program counter will properly point to the starting address of the next instruction. (Note that the content of R3 is unchanged.) The programmer does not have be concerned with this addition because the various displacement modes take care of it automatically.

The last three entries in Table 7.1 show three examples of indexed addressing (mode 4). Unlike all of the other modes, the index-addressing mode must be used in conjunction with some other addressing mode. Instructions that use indexed addressing by itself, such as CLRL [R3], are illegal. With indexed addressing, the register contains an index that is used to compute an offset. The second addressing mode supplies an address that the offset can be added to. Register-, literal-, and immediate-addressing modes cannot be used with the index-addressing mode because they do not generate an operand address that the offset can be added to.

In Table 7.1, indexed addressing is used in conjunction with relative addressing. The operand specifier byte for the index mode with register 3, ^X43, is immediately followed by the operand specifier byte for byte-, word-, or longword-relative addressing (^XAF, ^XCF, and ^XEF respectively). The relative-addressing modes specify the base address of the array and the index-addressing mode specifies the index of the desired element within the array.

Literal Mode

Eight modes are shown in Table 7.1. These are 4, 5, 6, 7, 8, A, C, and E. Clearly, there should be other modes to account for the unused possibilities. As noted in Chapter 5, operand specifier bytes from ^X00 to ^X3F are used for the **literal mode.** This mode is characterized by the high-order two bits of the operand specifier byte being zero. When in this mode, the remaining six bits are interpreted as an unsigned 6-bit immediate value. This allows small immediate operands in the range 0 to 63 to be specified within a single byte. The value of a literal must be positive. The assembler automatically chooses literal mode for small, positive immediate operands. Therefore, an instruction such as

```
MOVL    #5,R0
```

can be assembled in three bytes

50   05   D0

An instruction with a larger immediate operand, such as

```
MOVL    #64,R0
```

is assembled using immediate mode and would require seven bytes

50   00000040   8F   D0

Since literals are unsigned, small, negative immediate operands should be avoided. This can usually be done by choosing the right instruction. For example, MNEGL #5,R0 is preferred to MOVL #−5,R0 because it will result in a three-byte instruction instead of a seven-byte instruction.

Deferred Modes

As we saw in Section 7.2, there is a mode called the register-deferred mode. In this mode, the contents of the register are not used as the operand, but as the address of the operand. There are four more deferred modes which apply to the auto-increment mode and the three displacement modes, which are shown in Table 7.2.

In each case, an address is computed in the same way as is done for the non-deferred modes. A longword is fetched from this address, and the contents of the longword are used as the **address** of the operand for the instruction. In the case of auto-increment deferred, the register is incremented by four. This is true regardless of the instruc-

Name	Spec Byte	Opcode	Assembly Language
Auto-increment deferred	93	D4	CLRL @(R3)+
Byte-displacement deferred	B3	D4	CLRL @D(R3)
Word-displacement deferred	D3	D4	CLRL @D(R3)
Longword-displacement deferred	F3	D4	CLRL @D(R3)

Table 7.2 Register-deferred modes

Note: The symbol D refers to a displacement. The assembler will choose byte, word, or longword displacement for D depending upon the size of the value.

Table 7.3 VAX general register-addressing modes

Mode	Spec Byte	Opcode	Assembly Language	
Literal	50 05	D0	MOVL	#5,R0*
Indexed	.... xx 43	D4**	CLRL	A[R3]
Register	53	D4	CLRL	R3
Register-deferred	63	D4	CLRL	(R3)
Auto-decrement	73	D4	CLRL	-(R3)
Auto-increment	83	D4	CLRL	(R3)+
Auto-increment deferred	93	D4	CLRL	@(R3)+
Byte-displacement	xx A3	D4	CLRL	D(R3)
Byte-displacement deferred	xx B3	D4	CLRL	@D(R3)
Word-displacement	xxxx C3	D4	CLRL	D(R3)
Word-displacement deferred	xxxx D3	D4	CLRL	@D(R3)
Longword-displacement	xxxxxxxx E3	D4	CLRL	D(R3)
Longword-displacement deferred	xxxxxxxx F3	D4	CLRL	@D(R3)

* Literal mode can only be used on source operands.

** The symbol .... xx indicates the appropriate addressing mode for A.

Note: The symbol D refers to a displacement. The assembler will choose byte, word, or longword displacement for D depending upon the size of the value.

tion type, because the register is always pointing to an address, and addresses are always longwords. These deferred-addressing modes are used primarily for table look-up schemes that use a table of addresses. The addresses in the table point to the operands or to more complex data structures.

Table 7.3 shows a full list of the VAX general register-addressing modes.

7.5 Program-Counter Addressing Modes

In previous chapters, we described a variety of addressing modes that used the program counter. These modes are called **program-counter addressing modes** and they are summarized in Table 7.4. A MOVL instruction is used to illustrate immediate addressing while a CLRL instruction is used for the other addressing modes. In the second line, notice that the symbols @# are used in the instruction CLRL @#A to specify the absolute addressing mode that was used in Chapter 3. In the table, the operand specifier bytes are ^X8F, ^X9F, ^XAF, ^XCF, and ^XEF. In each case, the ^XF indicates that the program counter is being used to locate the operand. The x's following the operand specifier byte represent the hexadecimal digits that must follow the operand specifier byte.

It is not desirable to use the program counter as though it were a general register because unpredictable results can occur. However, there is a set of useful ways that the program counter can be used, as shown in Table 7.4. As an instruction is decoded by the VAX processor, the program counter is incremented as each byte is fetched. That means that at any stage of instruction decode, the program counter points to the next byte to be examined. How this works can be seen by examining the execution of the instruction

```
MOVL    #100,R0
```

In machine language, this becomes

```
50    00000064    8F    D0
```

The operand specifier byte, ^X8F, specifies that auto-increment addressing is to be used with register ^XF, the program counter.

Let us suppose that this instruction is located beginning at location ^X00000300. Then we can show a byte-by-byte list of the addresses as follows:

Contents	Address
D0	0300
8F	0301
64	0302
00	0303
00	0304
00	0305
50	0306

Table 7.4 Program-counter addressing modes

Mode	Spec Byte		Opcode	Assembly Language	
Immediate	50 xxxxxxxx	8F	D0	MOVL	#K,R0*
Absolute	xxxxxxxx	9F	D4	CLRL	@#A
Byte-relative	xx	AF	D4	CLRL	A
Word-relative	xxxx	CF	D4	CLRL	A
Longword-relative	xxxxxxxx	EF	D4	CLRL	A

* Immediate mode can only be used on source operands.

Note: The symbol A refers to an address and K refers to a constant. The assembler will choose byte, word, or longword modes for A depending upon the size of the value.

As the instruction begins to be executed, the program counter will contain ^X0300. The operation code, ^XD0, will be fetched and the program counter is incremented to ^X0301. ^XD0 is recognized as being the operation code for MOVL. This instruction requires two operands, so that the VAX processor will continue by fetching the first operand. The next byte, the ^X8F at address ^X0301, is fetched and the program counter is incremented to ^X0302. This byte is the operand specifier byte. In the operand specifier byte, ^X8 means that the mode is auto-increment, and ^XF means that register 15 or the PC is involved. Since the content of the PC is ^X0302, the longword contents beginning at ^X0302 are fetched. Thus ^X00000064 is the source operand for the MOVL instruction. However, since the mode is auto-increment, the PC is now incremented by four, becoming ^X0306. Instruction decode now continues at location ^X0306, and ^X50 is fetched. This is the operand specifier byte for the destination and it indicates that register addressing is to be used with R0. Therefore, ^X00000064 is moved to R0.

As this example shows, immediate addressing is simply the auto-increment mode using the program counter as a general register. A similar analysis will show that some modes are not useful with the program counter. For example, the machine language instruction

50   00000064   6F   D0

is identical to the preceding machine language instruction except that register-deferred addressing (mode 6) is used in place of auto-increment addressing. The operand, ^X00000064, would be fetched but the program counter would not be properly incremented to point to the next operand specifier byte, ^X50. Auto-decrement addressing (mode 7) would not even fetch the operand ^X00000064 properly because the program counter would be decremented before it was used. For these and other reasons, modes 4 through 7 are not used with the program counter.

However, modes 8 through 15 (^X8 through ^XF) are used with the program counter. The following shows how the five program-counter modes in Table 7.4 are implemented with general-register modes.

Program Counter Mode	Implementation
Immediate	Auto-increment mode using the PC
Absolute	Auto-increment deferred mode using the PC
Byte-relative	Byte-displacement mode using the PC
Word-relative	Word-displacement mode using the PC
Longword-relative	Longword-displacement using the PC

To see how the byte-relative mode is implemented using the byte-displacement mode with the program counter, assume that the following three-byte instruction begins in memory address ^X0300.

Contents	Address
D4	0300
AF	0301
F1	0302

When the contents of ^X0300 is fetched and interpreted as an instruction, it is the CLRL instruction, which requires one operand. The operand specifier byte is ^XAF which is the byte-displacement mode with register R15, the program counter. The one-byte displacement, ^XF1 is fetched. In two's complement notation, this is −15 which is added to the program counter to produce an effective address. Since the program counter has been incremented with the fetching of each byte, it now contains ^X0303, or one beyond the displacement byte which was the last byte fetched. *Therefore, the effective address is computed by adding the sign extension of ^XF1 to ^X0303 to get

^X00000303
^XFFFFFFF1
^X000002F4

Thus, the longword at location ^X02F4 is cleared. This is the normal addressing scheme used for the instruction

```
CLRL    A
```

Word-relative and longword-relative addressing operate in a similar manner. The assembler will normally choose the best relative addressing scheme if the value of the address is known. If the value of the address is not known, the assembler will use longword displacement to be on the safe side. There are essentially two reasons that the assembler would not know an address. The first is that it involves global relocation, which is described in Chapter 9. The other reason is that the symbol used for the address or used in the address expression has not yet been defined in the program. For this reason, it is usually recommended to define all of the data regions before the program on the VAX. This will help minimize forward references which will result in excessive use of longword displacements.

---

* As previously noted, a displacement mode always increments the PC over the displacement, regardless of the register (^X0 to ^XF) used in the operand specifier byte.

Mode	Spec Byte		Opcode	Assembly Language	
Immediate	50 xxxxxxxx	8F	D0	MOVL	#K,R0*
Absolute	xxxxxxxx	9F	D4	CLRL	@#A
Byte-relative	xx	AF	D4	CLRL	A
Byte-relative deferred	xx	BF	D4	CLRL	@A
Word-relative	xxxx	CF	D4	CLRL	A
Word-relative deferred	xxxx	DF	D4	CLRL	@A
Longword-relative	xxxxxxxx	EF	D4	CLRL	A
Longword-relative deferred	xxxxxxxx	FF	D4	CLRL	@A

Table 7.5 VAX program-counter addressing modes

* Immediate mode can only be used on source operands.

Note: The symbol A refers to an address and K refers to a number. The assembler will choose byte, word, or longword modes for A depending upon the size of the value.

Deferred displacement modes can also be used with the program counter. This means that the located longword is used as an address rather than the operand. This is sometimes referred to as **indirect addressing.** Deferred displacement would be used for the following instruction:

```
CLRL    @A
```

In this case, A would not be cleared, but rather A would be assumed to be a longword in memory containing the address of the location to be cleared.

Table 7.5 shows a full list of the VAX program-counter addressing modes.

7.6 Multiple-Dimensioned Arrays
Storing Arrays in Memory

As experience with Pascal or FORTRAN may have shown, arrays are often needed with multiple dimensions. Most frequently, this is seen in the form of the matrix (see Figure 7.10).

Since the computer memory is organized in the form of a linear string, more complex data structures such as matrices must be mapped or translated into the linear format. For a structure as simple as a matrix, the usual thing to do is to subdivide the matrix into a number of one-dimensional arrays or strings. This can be done either by stringing out the rows of the matrix one after the other, or by stringing

$$
\begin{array}{llll}
A_{11} & A_{12} & A_{13} & \ldots & A_{1n} \\
A_{21} & A_{22} & A_{23} & \ldots & A_{2n} \\
A_{31} & A_{32} & A_{33} & \ldots & A_{3n} \\
\;\cdot & \;\cdot & \;\cdot & & \;\cdot \\
\;\cdot & \;\cdot & \;\cdot & \cdots & \;\cdot \\
\;\cdot & \;\cdot & \;\cdot & & \;\cdot \\
A_{m1} & A_{m2} & A_{m3} & \ldots & A_{mn}
\end{array}
$$

Figure 7.10 A classical $m \times n$ matrix

out the columns. Basically, it makes little difference which way is chosen. Most FORTRAN systems store matrices columnwise but VAX Pascal stores arrays by row. Table 7.6 shows how a 5 × 7 matrix of longword integers might be stored in the VAX in the FORTRAN manner starting at location ^X00003C00. For Pascal, consider that the matrix is 7 × 5 instead, and reverse the order of all the subscripts so that A(I,J) in FORTRAN becomes A[J,I] in Pascal. Also, the words "row" and "column" should be interchanged in the discussion that follows.

From Table 7.6, it can be seen that any array element $A_{i,j}$ can be accessed by adding the proper offset to the base address ^X00003C00. The offset can easily be derived from the formula $4[i - 1 + 5(j - 1)]$. For example, if the matrix element A_{36} is desired, $i = 3$ and $j = 6$. Therefore, the offset is

$$4[3 - 1 + 5(6 - 1)] = 108_{10} = \text{^X6C}$$

The resulting address is ^X00003C6C.

Table 7.6 Memory map of a 5 × 7 matrix

Address	Matrix Element	Address	Matrix Element	Address	Matrix Element
^X00003C00	A_{11}	^X00003C30	A_{33}	^X00003C60	A_{55}
^X00003C04	A_{21}	^X00003C34	A_{43}	^X00003C64	A_{16}
^X00003C08	A_{31}	^X00003C38	A_{53}	^X00003C68	A_{26}
^X00003C0C	A_{41}	^X00003C3C	A_{14}	^X00003C6C	A_{36}
^X00003C10	A_{51}	^X00003C40	A_{24}	^X00003C70	A_{46}
^X00003C14	A_{12}	^X00003C44	A_{34}	^X00003C74	A_{56}
^X00003C18	A_{22}	^X00003C48	A_{44}	^X00003C78	A_{17}
^X00003C1C	A_{32}	^X00003C4C	A_{54}	^X00003C7C	A_{27}
^X00003C20	A_{42}	^X00003C50	A_{15}	^X00003C80	A_{37}
^X00003C24	A_{52}	^X00003C54	A_{25}	^X00003C84	A_{47}
^X00003C28	A_{13}	^X00003C58	A_{35}	^X00003C88	A_{57}
^X00003C2C	A_{23}	^X00003C5C	A_{45}		

The derivation of this formula is straightforward. The matrix is stored in memory with the first column occupying the first five memory longwords, the second column occupying the next five memory longwords, and so on. Thus, the jth column begins $5(j - 1)$ longwords from the start of the array. The ith longword in the column will be located $i - 1$ longwords from the beginning of the column or $i - 1 + 5(j - 1)$ longwords from the beginning of the array. (The first element in a column is obviously zero longwords past the beginning of the column.) Multiplication by four is necessary because longword addresses increase by fours.

Scanning Arrays on the VAX

Arrays are often scanned by row, by column, or diagonally. In these cases, it is often possible to index through these arrays without having to perform so much arithmetic. Clearly, if we were going to scan down the matrix columns one after the other, we would be doing the same thing as simple indexing through an array of 35 elements. Therefore, any of the techniques described in previous sections could be used.

Quite often (and this distinguishes a matrix from a one-dimensional array) a special operation must be performed at the end of scanning each column. For example, we might be trying to find the sums of the numbers in each column. This can easily be accomplished by including a second counter that tests for the ends of the columns. Figure 7.11 shows how a program could scan down the columns of the 5×7 matrix.

As the mode following the statement label 20$ indicates, the index-addressing mode is used to access elements in the matrix. Because the index mode takes care of multiplying the index by the length of the operand, this skeleton can be used with byte, word, and quadword arrays as well as longword arrays. This will be true of all of the examples in this section.

At first glance, scanning across the rows of a matrix may seem more complex than scanning down a column. However, it is in fact not any harder, and with some tricks, it may even be easier. To scan across a row merely means incrementing by an appropriate number. Referring back to Table 7.5, we can see that elements A_{11}, A_{12}, A_{13}, A_{14}, and so on are at location ^X00003C00, ^X00003C14, ^X00003C28, ^X00003C3C, and so on. Each is 20_{10} or ^X14 locations from the previous one. (^X14 is decimal 20 or four times the number of rows in the matrix. This is the number of bytes per column, and there are four bytes per longword.)

Because the index register addressing mode will multiply the index by four, it is merely necessary to increment the index register by five each time. The problem is knowing how to initialize the pointer

```
ROWS=5
COLS=7
SIZE=ROWS*COLS

          ⠆ ⠆ ⠆
          CLRL     R1              ;INDEX REGISTER
10$:      any processing for the beginning of a column

          ⠆ ⠆ ⠆
          CLRL     R2              ;COUNTER REGISTER
20$:      any processing on the array element A[R1]

          ⠆ ⠆ ⠆
          INCL     R1              ;INCREMENT INDEX
          AOBLSS   #ROWS,R2,20$    ;END OF THE COLUMN?
          End of column processing

          ⠆ ⠆ ⠆
          CMPL     R1,#SIZE
          BLSS     10$
```

Figure 7.11 A program for scanning down the columns of a 5 × 7 matrix

register at the beginning of each row. One method for doing this would be to have a dummy index register that scans down the first column. See Figure 7.12 for an example of this kind of approach.

There is, however, a rather simple trick of arithmetic that can make the dummy counter unnecessary. Figure 7.13 shows how this operates. The first row of the matrix is processed by successively adding five to the index in R1. Since the matrix has 5 times 7 or 35 elements, the final total will be 35. When the contents of R1 reach 35, the first row has been processed. Subtracting 34 sets the contents of R1 to 1, the correct index for the first element in the second row.

```
ROWS=5
COLS=7
SIZE=ROWS*COLS

          ⠆ ⠆ ⠆
          CLRL     R2              ;SET UP DUMMY INDEX
10$:      beginning of row processing

          ⠆ ⠆ ⠆
          MOVL     R2,R1           ;SET UP REAL INDEX
20$:      operate on matrix element A[R1]

          ⠆ ⠆ ⠆
          ADDL2    #ROWS,R1        ;ADD 5 TO GET TO NEXT ROW
          CMPL     R1,#SIZE        ; ELEMENT AND TEST FOR
          BLSS     20$             ; END OF ROW
          end of row processing

          ⠆ ⠆ ⠆
          AOBLSS   #ROWS,R2,10$    ;INCREMENT DUMMY
```

Figure 7.12 Program for scannning rows of a 5 × 7 matrix

```
ROWS=5
COLS=7
SIZE=ROWS*COLS
        + + +
        CLRL      R1              ;INDEX REGISTER
10$:    beginning of row processing
        + + +
20$:    operate on matrix element A[R1]
        + + +
        ADDL      #ROWS,R1        ;ADD 5 TO GET TO NEXT ROW
        CMPL      R1,#SIZE        ; ELEMENT AND TEST JUST
        BLSS      20$             ; AS BEFORE
        end of row processing
        + + +
        SUBL      #SIZE-1,R1      ;END OF ROW, SO SUB 34
        CMPL      R1,#ROWS        ; FROM INDEX AND TEST
        BLSS      10$
```

Figure 7.13 Improved program for scanning the rows of a 5 × 7 matrix

The INDEX Instruction

In order to simplify the access of elements of two dimensional arrays, the VAX has a complex instruction called **INDEX**. The **INDEX** instruction not only aids in the computation of the indexing formula $[i - 1 + 5(j - 1)]$ but also provides for subscripts to start at differing values and checks to determine that the index is in the range defined for the array. The instruction has extendability so that it is usable for arrays with any number of dimensions. The **INDEX** instruction has six longword operands

```
INDEX   SUB,LOW,HIGH,SIZE,IXIN,IXOUT
```

The instruction computes

```
IXOUT := (IXIN+SUB)*SIZE
```

and produces an error trap if

```
SUB < LOW  or  SUB > HIGH
```

Figure 7.14 shows how the program of Figure 7.13 could be rewritten using the INDEX instruction. To scan columns instead of

Figure 7.14 Use of the INDEX instruction for scanning the rows of a 5 × 7 matrix

```
ROWS=5
COLS=7
        • • •
        CLRL    R1                          ;ROW NUMBER (0 TO ROWS-1)
10$:    CLRL    R2                          ;COLUMN NUMBER (0 TO COLS-1)
20$:    INDEX   R2,#0,#COLS-1,#ROWS,#0,R0   ;R0:=R2*ROWS
        INDEX   R1,#0,#ROWS-1,#1,R0,R0      ;R0:=(R0+R1)*1
        operate on matrix element A[R1]

        • • •
        AOBLSS  #COLS,R2,20$
        AOBLSS  #ROWS,R1,10$
```

rows, it is merely necessary to interchange the initialization and increment of R1 and R2.

The advantage of the INDEX instruction is that it can be used to access the elements of a matrix in an arbitrary order. As long as R1 contains a row index I with a value from zero to ROWS − 1 and R2 contains a column index J with a value from zero to COLS − 1, the statements

```
20$:    INDEX   R2,#0,#COLS-1,#ROWS,0,R0    ;R0:=R2*ROWS
        INDEX   R1,#0,#ROWS-1,#1,R0,R0      ;R0:=(R0+R1)*1
```

operate on matrix element A[R1]

can be used to access the matrix element A[I,J] or A(I,J).

Exercise Set 2

1. Given that R0 contains ˆX00001200 and that memory has the following contents:

Contents	Address
ˆX0000120C	ˆX000011F4
ˆX000011F8	ˆX000011F8
ˆX000011F4	ˆX000011FC
ˆX0000120C	ˆX00001200
ˆX00001208	ˆX00001204
ˆX00001200	ˆX00001208
ˆX000011F4	ˆX0000120C

what are the new contents of memory and R0 after each of the following instructions? (Assume the previously given contents for **each** instruction.)

a. CLRL R0

b. CLRL (R0)

c. CLRL (R0)+

d. CLRL -(R0)

e. MOVL R0,(R0)

f. MOVL (R0),R0

g. MOVL (R0)+,(R0)+

h. MOVL (R0)+,(R0)

i. MOVL (R0)+,-(R0)

j. MOVL -(R0),-(R0)

k. MOVL @(R0)+,R0

l. MOVL @(R0)+,@(R0)+

2. Assemble each of the instructions in Exercise 1 into machine language.

3. Rewrite the program(s) from Exercises 3, 5, or 6 in the previous section of exercises (pages 177-179) so that maximum use is made of the auto-increment or auto-decrement modes.

4. Rewrite the program(s) from Exercises 3, 5, or 6 in the previous section of exercises (pages 177-179) so that maximum use is made of the index-register mode.

5. Write a program that reads 35 numbers in the order that they would be if scanning a 5×7 matrix across the rows. Print out the numbers in the order they would have if scanning the matrix down the columns.

*6. A two-dimensional array can be scanned by row or by column. What are the corresponding ways that a three-dimensional array can be scanned? Write a program that reads 60 numbers forming a $3 \times 4 \times 5$ array, and then print out the 60 numbers in all the different ways that the array can be scanned. (Do not consider all possible reversals of direction.)

Alphabetic Information

8.1 Representing Alphabetic Information
Introduction

So far in our discussion, we have dealt with how to perform the numeric calculations. Nothing has been said about alphabetic information, even though it should be clear that there must be some way of dealing with alphabetic data. After all, the assembler, the operating system, and the Pascal and FORTRAN compilers all deal with statements that are strings of alphabetic characters. Furthermore, since these processors are really just ordinary computer programs, any program should be able to manipulate alphabetic data. The immediate question is how alphabetic information is represented in the computer. The answer is that characters are encoded as binary numbers that have a unique representation for each character of the alphabet. As this must also include numerals and punctuation, the term **alphanumeric** characters is sometimes used. The actual encoding used is completely arbitrary. In other words, the interpretation of the character code is completely determined by the design of the input/output device used for reading or printing the characters. With the VAX, the most frequently used code is the one that was originally standard for teletypewriters but now is used for all kinds of input and output devices. This code is called **ASCII** which means *American Standard Code for Information Interchange*. Another character code is called EBCDIC, which is derived from Hollerith punched card code, and will be discussed later.

This chapter concentrates on the basic techniques for manipulating characters as well as the individual bits that make them up.

Character strings are discussed as arrays of bytes and are processed using techniques introduced in the previous chapters. In Chapter 13, we will see that the VAX architecture includes instructions which can manipulate entire strings of characters in one operation.

The ASCII Code System

As just stated, the ASCII code system originated from use with teletypewriters. As such, each code represents the pressing of some combination of keys on a typewriterlike keyboard. (Note that, as on most typewriters, pressing more than one key at a time is usually illegal or ineffective.* The exceptions are the SHIFT and CONTROL keys which do not produce a code themselves, but are used in combination with other keys.) With a typewriter, every key you press causes the printing mechanism to do something; that is, type a character, space, carriage return, and so on. Similarly, every implemented ASCII code causes the printing mechanism on the teletypewriter to do such an operation. In order to type a message on a typewriter, you must press the keys in a sequence. For the computer program to type a message on a teletypewriter, the program must provide the teletypewriter with a sequence of ASCII codes.

The most commonly used standard at present is the 7-bit ASCII system. It uses 2^7 or 128 codes, of which 95 are used for printing characters, and 33 are used for control operations such as carriage return and line feed. The 95 printing characters consist of the following:

- 26 Uppercase letters
- 26 Lowercase letters
- 10 Numerals
- 1 Blank space
- 32 Punctuation marks

The 32 punctuation marks are:

! " # $ % & ´ ( ) * + , − . / < > : ; = ? @ [\ ] _ ^ ` { | } ~

Note here that some of the older or less expensive teletypewriters and printers are only capable of printing 64 characters, which are

---

* Some terminals have a roll-over feature so that if more than one key is struck it is treated as a sequence of single keystrokes.

- 26 Uppercase letters
- 10 Numerals
- 1 Blank space
- 27 Punctuation marks
  (the marks ` { | } ~ are excluded)

Although these terminals are obsolete, many of them still exist. As a result, the VAX/VMS command language does not distinguish between uppercase and lowercase letters and does not use the five punctuation marks that are missing on these terminals.

A newer ASCII standard uses eight bits instead of seven. The 8-bit ASCII code is capable of representing 256 different codes, thus allowing a greatly expanded alphabet to be represented. The additional 128 codes permit the representation of foreign language alphabets and graphic symbols.

In 7-bit ASCII, only a few of the 33 control characters are commonly used. The most common of these are:

- BEL   Rings the bell on the typewriter
- BS   Backspaces the typewriter*
- HT   Horizontal tab*
- LF   Line feed, advances the paper one line
- VT   Vertical tab**
- FF   Form feed, advances the paper to a new page*
- CR   Carriage return, moves the print mechanism back to the beginning of the line

At this point, the reader may wonder what the other 26 control characters do. For the most part, with computer equipment, they do nothing. (Many of them are used as control codes for message switching and sending telegrams. In fact, this is what teletypewriters were originally used for.) In most equipment, the unused control characters are ignored. For example, a teletypewriter with no horizontal tab feature will do nothing when sent a horizontal tab character. As a consequence, these characters can be used for software functions. For example, the VAX operating system can replace a horizontal tab with space characters so that the program, in effect, simulates a tab operation. This is an optional function which can be selected by users whose output device has no built-in tab function.

---

* Some equipment is not capable of this function.

** Most equipment is not capable of this function.

Table 8.1 The ASCII character set

^X00	NUL	^X10	DLE	^X20	SP	^X30	0	^X40	@	^X50	P	^X60	`	^X70	p
^X01	SOH	^X11	DC1	^X21	!	^X31	1	^X41	A	^X51	Q	^X61	a	^X71	q
^X02	STX	^X12	DC2	^X22	"	^X32	2	^X42	B	^X52	R	^X62	b	^X72	r
^X03	ETX	^X13	DC3	^X23	#	^X33	3	^X43	C	^X53	S	^X63	c	^X73	s
^X04	EOT	^X14	DC4	^X24	$	^X34	4	^X44	D	^X54	T	^X64	d	^X74	t
^X05	ENQ	^X15	NAK	^X25	%	^X35	5	^X45	E	^X55	U	^X65	e	^X75	u
^X06	ACK	^X16	SYN	^X26	&	^X36	6	^X46	F	^X56	V	^X66	f	^X76	v
^X07	BEL	^X17	ETB	^X27	´	^X37	7	^X47	G	^X57	W	^X67	g	^X77	w
^X08	BS	^X18	CAN	^X28	(	^X38	8	^X48	H	^X58	X	^X68	h	^X78	x
^X09	HT	^X19	EM	^X29	)	^X39	9	^X49	I	^X59	Y	^X69	i	^X79	y
^X0A	LF	^X1A	SUB	^X2A	*	^X3A	:	^X4A	J	^X5A	Z	^X6A	j	^X7A	z
^X0B	VT	^X1B	ESC	^X2B	+	^X3B	;	^X4B	K	^X5B	[	^X6B	k	^X7B	{
^X0C	FF	^X1C	PS	^X2C	,	^X3C	<	^X4C	L	^X5C	\	^X6C	l	^X7C	|
^X0D	CR	^X1D	GS	^X2D	–	^X3D	=	^X4D	M	^X5D	]	^X6D	m	^X7D	}
^X0E	SO	^X1E	RS	^X2E	.	^X3E	>	^X4E	N	^X5E	^	^X6E	n	^X7E	~
^X0F	SI	^X1F	US	^X2F	/	^X3F	?	^X4F	O	^X5F	_	^X6F	o	^X7F	DEL

Since 7-bit ASCII is a 7-bit code, each character is represented as a 7-bit binary number. The first 32 numbers are used for 32 of the 33 control characters, ^X00 through ^X1F. Blank space is ^X20; the decimal digits 0–9 are ^X30 through ^X39; uppercase letters occupy ^X41 through ^X5A; lowercase letters, ^X61 through ^X7A; punctuation is assigned in an ad hoc manner to the otherwise unused codes from ^X21 through ^X7E. All this leaves one control character to be assigned to ^X7F. This character is called Rub Out or DEL (for DELete) and had a special importance in the days of hand-prepared paper tape. If you make a mistake typing, you can backspace a paper tape punch, but you cannot erase the holes. You can, however, punch more holes. Therefore, a special character was created called Rub Out or DEL with a code of all ones (^X7F). This character would cause all holes to be punched across the tape, and was generally ignored by the input processors. Because of this traditional usage, the VAX operating system uses DEL or Rub Out as a software backspace to erase mistakes. Table 8.1 shows the entire 128-character ASCII code in hexadecimal.

The ASCII Keyboard

Because of the size of the ASCII alphabet (128 characters), it is not usually practical to assign one key for each character. As a consequence, it is normal to use a combination of keys to obtain some of the symbols. For example, a shift key is used to distinguish between uppercase and lowercase letters. The shift key also serves to distinguish between certain punctuation marks and numerals, as is done on most ordinary typewriters. Therefore, even though a terminal has only uppercase letters, it will still have a shift key.

Figure 8.1 shows the layout of the keyboard of a typical terminal. Note that this keyboard has very few keys for control characters, and typically, carriage return, line feed, tab, backspace, escape, and delete are the only ones. The first four are needed because they are typewriter functions that are used just to do ordinary typing. The latter two serve no particular hardware function, but are used extensively for software purposes, as mentioned before for delete.

The reader may well wonder how one might produce other control characters. Note that near the lower left-hand corner of Figure 8.1, there is a key marked **CTRL** (for control). This key is much like the shift key in that it has no particular function of its own, but is held down while another key is pressed. The basic function of the control key is to force the two most significant bits of the character code to zero. Thus, for example,

- Control @ is ^X00 or NUL
- Control A is ^X01 or SOH
- Control B is ^X02 or STX
- Control C is ^X03 or ETX

Note that all of the control characters except DEL can be produced this way. This includes carriage return (control M) and line feed (control J). DEL is somewhat odd, being all ones, and therefore usually

Figure 8.1 Typical ASCII keyboard

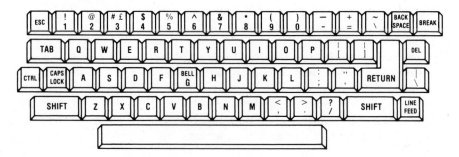

is given a separate key. In any case, since the control key forces bits to zero, it could not be used to create DEL.

Many keyboards also have a special locking key that may be marked ALL CAPS. This key causes the keyboard to behave like an uppercase-only keyboard. Much of the existing software is designed to be compatable with older terminals that can only handle 64 printing characters. Locking the ALL CAPS key allows use of a 95-character terminal as though it were a 64-character terminal. (Without such a switch, you would have to hold the shift key down most of the time while using such software.) In Table 8.1, notice that the code for each lowercase letter is ^X20 higher than the code for the corresponding uppercase letter. For example, the code for "a" is ^X61 and the code for "A" is ^X41. The ALL CAPS key, in effect, subtracts ^X20 from the codes for lowercase letters. The subtraction is usually implemented by clearing bit 5 of the binary code for lowercase letters. The VAX operating system is capable of simulating the ALL CAPS key in software, making its use unnecessary for many cases.

Devices Other Than Teletypewriters

The ASCII code is a **serial** (character-by-character) code that was originally designed for use with teletypewriters which are character-by-character typing machines. Even so, the ASCII code is quite useful for such devices as line printers and video display terminals or VDTs. VDT terminals are sometimes called **CRT**s because the major component is a **cathode ray tube.**

Even though these devices are designed for high-speed multi-character operations, information is usually fed to them one character at a time in order to simplify interconnections. Line printers and VDTs usually handle information in units of a line or a page at a time; as such, they do not have a typing carriage to return as does a teletypewriter. However, in order to be compatible with normal ASCII, carriage return and line feed are used to terminate a line and to advance to the next line. Therefore, for the most part, these devices may be treated as if they were ordinary teletypewriters.

Some devices have special capabilities. Printers may allow the programmer to advance the paper to the top of a new page. CRTs may have functions such as screen erase, cursor control, and scroll versus page mode. A **cursor** is a flashing marker that indicates where text is to be entered on the screen. The cursor usually moves to the right as you type, but some CRTs allow the cursor to be repositioned anywhere on the screen. **Scrolling** allows the user to add lines to the bottom of the screen by rolling the remaining text up, losing the top line. These special capabilities usually operate through some protocol of control characters. For example, the string of seven characters.

(escape)[5;39f

causes a VT-100 or any terminal that implements what is called the **ANSI standard escape sequence** to move the cursor to the 39th character position of the fifth line on the screen. The particular manual for the device should be consulted for such information.

Storing Characters in the VAX

Individual characters are stored as bytes in the VAX. When using the 7-bit ASCII code, the VAX/VMS operating system normally sets the high-order bit in each byte to zero. A string of characters is normally stored as an array of bytes. Consequently, if it were desired to type the message, **HELLO!!!** on a single line, we would need the characters H, E, L, L, O, !, !, and !. These eight characters would require an array of eight bytes. If this array were called STRING and began at location ^X00000400, it would appear as shown in Figure 8.2. This data could be entered into an assembly language program using the .BYTE directive, as follows:

```
STRING: .BYTE    ^X48,^X45,^X4C,^X4C,^X4F,^X21,^X21,^X21
```

One thing of special note with byte arrays is that when bytes or smaller data items are packed into longer data items such as longwords, the **least** significant bits are filled in first. Consequently, the bytes appear to be ordered backward. For example, if this array of

Content	Address	Character	Symbolic Address
^X48	^X0400	H	STRING
^X45	^X0401	E	STRING+1
^X4C	^X0402	L	STRING+2
^X4C	^X0403	L	STRING+3
^X4F	^X0404	O	STRING+4
^X21	^X0405	!	STRING+5
^X21	^X0406	!	STRING+6
^X21	^X0407	!	STRING+7

Figure 8.2 ASCII character string

eight bytes were considered to be packed into an array of two longwords, they would appear as

Contents	Address	Symbolic Address
^X4C4C4548	^X0400	STRING
^X2121214F	^X0404	STRING+4

It is for this reason that assembly listings show their object code
representations reading from right to left. Thus, the assembly listing
of the preceding byte directive would list the bytes as

```
21 21 21 4F 4C 4C 45 48    0400
```

Admittedly, this is somewhat awkward and it takes some getting used
to. However, this problem exists in one form or another on all byte-
oriented computers, and the VAX notation is, perhaps, less confusing
than many other representations.

8.2 Manipulating Characters
Bytes and Byte Instructions

Inside the VAX, the codes for characters are simply numerical quantities in the range from 0 to 255 (if they are thought of as unsigned)
just like any other kind of byte. Referring back to Figure 8.2, we can
see that the application of various byte instructions such as MOVB,
INCB, DECB, ADDB2, and so forth can be used to manipulate the
characters of the string. For example, the instruction

```
MOVB    STRING+5,STRING+2
```

will move the code ^X21 stored at location STRING + 5 or ^X405 to
location STRING + 2 or ^X402. The bytes in the array string would
have the contents shown in Figure 8.3. When printed, this would form
the line of print, **HE!LO!!!.** Similarly, the instruction

```
ADDB2    #5,STRING+3
```

would cause the number ^X4C in location STRING + 3 to become
^X51. This is the ASCII code for the character **Q**. Consequently, if the
string were now printed, it would appear as, **HE!QO!!!.**

Contents	Address	Symbolic Address
^X48	^X400	STRING
^X45	^X401	STRING+1
^X21	^X402	STRING+2
^X4C	^X403	STRING+3
^X4F	^X404	STRING+4
^X21	^X405	STRING+5
^X21	^X406	STRING+6
^X21	^X407	STRING+7

Figure 8.3 Storage of a character string

The important thing to remember is that, as far as the VAX processer is concerned, a character string is nothing more than an array of 8-bit numerical quantities. The interpretation of these quantities to be codes for characters is strictly a function of the input and output devices and of the software. Consequently, it is the responsibility of the programmer to restrict operations on character strings to those which make sense. It is difficult to differentiate the operations which make sense from those which do not. It all depends on the context of the problem. Going back to the previous example, the number five was added to the letter "L" to get the letter "Q." Out of context, this might not seem to be a very useful operation, and in fact, it was not intended to be so. However, operations of this sort might be useful in encryption, or even changing character codes from ASCII to some other code for a non-ASCII input/output device. See the section at the end of this chapter on "Other Character Representations."

Assembly Language Conventions for Character Strings

In the previous section, we introduced the idea of inserting a character string into a program using the .BYTE directive. In order to enter character strings in this fashion, it is necessary to look up each character of the text in a table such as Table 8.1 on page 206. Clearly this would be a burdensome task if the program contained very many character strings. In order to simplify putting character strings in the program, the VAX-MACRO assembler has a directive called .ASCII. This directive allows character strings to be inserted into the program. Character strings are enclosed in quotes in a manner similar to that used in many higher-level languages. For example, the character string which was introduced with

```
STRING: .BYTE    ^X48,^X45,^X4C,^X4C,^X4F,^X21,^X21,^X21
```

could be entered with the following instead:

```
STRING: .ASCII   "HELLO!!!"
```

The memory contents produced in either case would be identical.

There is a problem if the string being defined contains nonprinting characters such as the tab character (^X09), carriage return (^X0D), the bell character (^X07), and so on. Although some nonprinting characters can be included in the string being defined, it is poor programming practice. This is because it is difficult to determine which characters are actually in the string. To solve this problem, the .ASCII directive allows byte expressions to be enclosed in angle brackets, < and >. For example, suppose the string HELLO!!! were to be preceded by two tab characters and followed by a bell character. Transmitting this string to a terminal will cause the word HELLO!!! to appear beginning at the second tab stop and the bell in the terminal would be made to ring. The following .ASCII directive could be used to create this string.

```
ALARM_STRING:
     .ASCII   <^X09><^X09>"HELLO!!!"<^X07>
```

Notice that the array ALARM_STRING contains 11 ASCII characters.

Of course, a better style would be to define symbols for the tab character and the bell character and use the symbols instead of the actual hexadecimal numbers. This might then appear as follows:

```
     TAB = ^X09
     BEL = ^X07
     . . .
ALARM_STRING:
     .ASCII   <TAB><TAB>"HELLO!!!"<BEL>
```

One obvious problem here is that, as stated, it would be impossible to have a character string which included quote marks between the quotes. The solution to this is that VAX-MACRO allows the use of alternative quote marks. In particular, the first printable character other than < is interpreted to be a start of a quote. The second occurrence of the same character forms an end of quote. Therefore, the preceding string could be entered in either of the following ways:

```
ALARM_STRING:
     .ASCII   <TAB><TAB>/HELLO!!!/<BEL>
```

or

```
ALARM_STRING:
        .ASCII    <TAB><TAB>XHELLO!!!X<BEL>
```

Clearly each choice allows every possibility other than itself. However, to be standard, most programmers limit their choices to just a few, such as ", ', or /.

When transmitting successive lines to a terminal, it is necessary to separate successive lines with the control characters carriage return, ^X0D, and line feed, ^X0A. In most circumstances, the VAX/VMS operating system inserts these characters for the user. Therefore, it is unnecessary to include them in the character string in most cases. With many other computer systems, users must explicitly include these control characters. Chapter 11 discusses line formatting in detail.

To see how character strings could be used, let us look at a program segment that sends each character of the character string, STRING, to a subroutine called PROCESS. The characters are passed one at a time in R0. It is not necessary to know what PROCESS does, except that it takes one character at a time and does something. Perhaps it prints the character, perhaps it puts the character into a buffer. Using what we have seen so far, we could write the program as follows:

```
STRING:    .ASCII    "HELLO!!!"
           . . .
PASS:      CLRL      R1
10$:       MOVB      STRING[R1],R0
           JSB       PROCESS
           AOBLSS    #8,R1,10$
```

One problem with this program is that the AOBLSS instruction contains the immediate operand #8 which tells how many characters there are in the array, STRING. This raises a difficulty if the programmer ever changes the character string, STRING. In this case, he must always remember to change the #8 to the length of the new string.

One solution to this problem is to use a symbolic expression to compute the length of the string. Note that if the address of the array is subtracted from the address of the next available location, the difference will be the number of byte locations in the array. For example, referring back to Figure 8.3 on page 211, it can be seen that the byte array occupies addresses ^X400 through ^X407. Therefore, the next available location is ^X408, which differs from ^X400 by eight, which is the length of the array. This could be incorporated into the preceding program as follows:

```
STRING:    .ASCII    "HELLO!!!"
STRINGEND:
           . . .
PASS:      CLRL      R1
10$:       MOVB      STRING[R1],R0
           JSB       PROCESS
           AOBLSS    #STRINGEND-STRING,R1,10$
```

This program will assemble to the same binary code as the previous version. However, since the expression STRINGEND-STRING is substituted for 8, the assembler will automatically place the string length into the AOBLSS instruction. Consequently, STRING can be modified without any further changes to the program. For example, if the string to be processed were changed to GOOD BYE!!! the first two lines would become:

```
STRING:    .ASCII    "GOOD BYE!!!"
STRINGEND:
```

The string would now be 11 bytes long. If STRING were assigned the address ^X400 as before, STRINGEND would be assigned address ^X40B. Then the expression STRINGEND-STRING would have the value ^XB or 11 in decimal.

Another method for solving this problem is to use a sentinel value for flagging the end of a string. Zero is a good value to use for character strings, since zero is the code for NULL which is ignored by most systems. The VAX/11 assembler provides for this with the directive .ASCIZ. This is the same as .ASCII except that an extra byte of zero is added to the end of the string. Therefore

```
STRING: .ASCIZ   "HELLO!!!"
```

is the same as

```
STRING: .ASCII    "HELLO!!!"<0>
```

The following program shows how the zero sentinel byte could be used to write a program with the same effect as the previous example, namely to call PROCESS, passing every character from a string as a byte in R0.

```
STRING: .ASCIZ    "HELLO!!!"
           . . .
PASS:   MOVAL     STRING,R1
10$:    MOVB      (R1)+,R0
        BEQL      20$
        JSB       PROCESS
        BRB       10$
20$:
```

This method clearly has advantages when variable length strings or internally generated strings are used. It also makes it easy to use the auto-increment mode on the MOVB instruction.

   There is still another method for dealing with character strings. While somewhat complex, the method has advantages when passing character strings to subroutines, and is used as a standard technique by higher-level languages manipulating character strings on the VAX. This is explained in more detail in Chapter 9. The method involves attaching a descriptor to the ASCII string. A descriptor consists of two longwords. The first is broken into two words. The first word gives the size of the string in bytes. The second word gives some codes that would identify the information to systems software as a character string. The second longword gives the address of the first byte of the character string. The descriptor format is generated using the .ASCID directive. For example, the following .ASCID directive

```
STRING: .ASCID    "HELLO!!!"
```

is equivalent to the following code using previously discussed directives

```
STRING: .WORD     20$-10$        ;LENGTH = 8
        .WORD     ^X010E         ;SPECIAL CODES
        .ADDRESS  10$            ;ADDRESS OF STRING
10$:    .ASCII    "HELLO!!!"     ;CHARACTER STRING
20$:
```

The directive .ADDRESS is used to store an address into a longword in memory. In operation, this directive is very similar to the .LONG directive except that .LONG should only be used with constant data and .ADDRESS should be used for relocatable addresses. Either directive would place the address 10$ in a longword. However, .ADDRESS should be used for relocatable addresses because it provides additional information to the assembler and the linker.

The following program shows how the previous example could be rewritten using a descriptor instead of direct access.

```
STRING:  .ASCID    "HELLO!!!"
              . . .
PASS:    CLRL      R1
         MOVZWL    STRING,R2
10$:     MOVB      @STRING+4[R1],R0
         JSB       PROCESS
         AOBLSS    R2,R1,10$
```

Note that access to STRING in the MOVB instruction is one level more indirect than it was in the previous example. STRING+4 is the address of the longword that contains the starting address of the ASCII string and @STRING+4 is the address of the first byte of the string. Thus, the source operand of the MOVB instruction is @STRING+4[R1]. Also note that the MOVZWL instruction was used to convert the unsigned 16-bit word in string into an unsigned longword that is placed in R2. This conversion is required by the AOBLSS instruction, which requires longwords for its first two operands.

Exercise Set 1

1. With a teletypewriter or CRT connected in LOCAL mode (that is, not connected to a computer, but talking to itself), explore the effects of all of the keys. Also, use the shift and/or control key with all of the other keys, and describe the effects. In particular:

   a. Does your machine have uppercase and lowercase? If not, what is the effect of shifting a letter? Is it possible to type all letters with shift held down? If there is lowercase, is there a shift lock key? An all caps key? What is the difference?

   b. What is the effect of the control key? Which control characters do anything? What do they do? Do you always notice the effect?

   c. Some terminals respond to "escape" followed by other characters. See if you can notice their responses.

2. Perform the steps outlined in Exercise 1 with the terminal connected to the VAX operating system. How do you explain the different results obtained between Exercises 1 and 2?

8.3 Simplified Input and Output

The whole subject of input and output is extremely complex and much of it is beyond the scope of this text. Some of the details of input and output are covered in Chapter 11. However, it is necessary to be able to communicate with running programs. This section is intended to convey in a minimal way a scheme to enable users to read from and output to their terminal. This is done through the use of three subroutines called IOINIT, RLINE, and PLINE.

These routines are part of the same package of routines described in Appendix B and introduced in Chapter 5. In fact, IOINIT is the same routine that was used to initialize RNUM and PNUM. This routine also initializes RLINE and PLINE, and must be called before either of them are used. IOINIT must not be called more than once, even if all four input/output routines are being used.

Just as RNUM and PNUM are used to read and print numbers, RLINE and PLINE are used to read and print strings of characters in a line. Both routines assume that the main program has a buffer or an array for storing the characters. For RLINE, this array will receive the characters from the line being read. For PLINE, this array contains the characters being printed. In addition, PLINE needs to know how many characters are to be printed, and RLINE needs to know how much space is available in your array for input. Finally, when RLINE returns, the main program must be able to determine just how many characters were actually read. This information is passed back and forth using R0 and R1. R0 is used to hold the address of the character buffer, and R1 is used for size information.

For example, in order to print the character string HELLO! the following code could be used

```
STRING: .ASCII  "HELLO!"
STRINGEND:
        . . .
        MOVAL   STRING,R0
        MOVZWL  #STRINGEND-STRING,R1
        JSB     PLINE
```

Note that the length loaded into R1 is a word. That is because it is used as a word in PLINE. The instruction MOVZWL is used for two reasons. First, it is poor programming practice to leave garbage in the upper half of a register and the MOVZWL instruction will set the high-order 16-bits to zero. Second, the assembler will generate a warning message if the value of the expression STRINGEND-STRING is greater than 65535 or 2^{16} minus 1. Note also that no carriage return or line feed is provided. Since PLINE prints lines, the line control is taken care of automatically by the normal input processes of the VAX/VMS operating system. Any carriage returns or line feeds which were included would cause extra lines to be printed.

The calling sequence of PLINE lends itself well to the use of string descriptors as can be seen from this alternative method for printing the same string

```
DSTRING:       .ASCID   "HELLO!"
       . . .
       MOVL    DSTRING+4,R0   ;CONTENTS OF DSTRING+4 IS ADDRESS
       MOVZWL  DSTRING,R1     ;WORD AT DSTRING IS LENGTH
       JSB     PLINE
```

The subroutine RLINE operates in a similar way. The main difference is that RLINE expects to be given a maximum buffer size. This is so that the program will be protected from someone typing a long line which could extend beyond the end of the buffer and over-write the program area. As an example of how RLINE operates, the following code could be used to read an input line into an 80-character buffer.

```
BSIZE=80
BUFFER: .BLKB    BSIZE
       . . .
       MOVAL    BUFFER,R0 ;ADDRESS OF BUFFER TO R0
       MOVZWL   #BSIZE,R1 ;SIZE OF BUFFER TO R1
       JSB      RLINE
```

When RLINE returns, three things will have happened.

1. The characters read will have been placed in the byte array BUFFER. Since RLINE operates by line, there will be no control characters such as carriage return or line feed in the input string stored in BUFFER.
2. The actual number of characters read will be stored as a word in R1. This could be zero if only a carriage return were typed, or it could be as large as 80 if that many characters were typed. However, it will never be greater than the original value of R1, no matter how many characters were typed.
3. An error code is returned as a byte in R0.

There are a number of reasons that an error could occur during input. The three most common would be that more characters were typed than will fit in the buffer; that a read was attempted beyond the end of the input data (most likely on a batch system); or that there is some sort of program error such as forgetting to call IOINIT. The error code is provided so that your program can check for this happening. For example, some programs are designed to read until they run out of data. This error code could be used to terminate such a program. The way that the error code operates is that if R0 contains the number 1 (as a word) then the program operated normally, and there is no error. Any other value indicates some sort of error. This is the standard error handling procedure for routines in the VAX/VMS operating system. The number of different error values is extremely large, and the best thing to do is to let the operating system describe the error to you. This can be done by passing the error code to the system on the $EXIT_S line. In this case, this would appear as $EXIT_S R0. The error code should be checked by your program with instructions such as:

```
        ' ' '
        JSB     RLINE
        CMPW    R0,#1
        BEQL    10$
        $EXIT_S R0
10$:    next instruction
```

Note that the pair of instructions CMPW R0,#1 and BEQL 10$ can be replaced by a single instruction which is introduced in the next section. Note also that RLINE is the only one of the five input/output routines in this package which returns an error code. The other routines all ignore errors. Chapter 11 gives a more detailed description of error codes and how to make use of them.

8.4 Bit Manipulation Instructions
The Need to Manipulate Bits

It is often quite useful to pack information into words or bytes in various size parcels. Here are some examples of pieces of words or bytes that have already been discussed as having some special significance.

1. Bit 31 of a longword, bit 15 of a word, or bit 7 of a byte gives the algebraic sign.
2. Bit 0 of a word or byte tells if the number being represented is odd or even.
3. Bits 5 and 6 of an ASCII character code tell whether the character is uppercase, or lowercase, or a control character, or in the main block of numeric and punctuation characters.

The BIS, BIC, and BIT Family of Instructions

In order to create or examine little packets of information of the kind described previously, the VAX has been supplied with three families of instructions. They are designed to set or clear specific bits in a word or to test specific bits. The three instruction families are as follows:

Symbol	Meaning
BIS	BIt Set
BIC	BIt Clear
BIT	BIt Test

Each instruction family includes instructions for the various operand sizes, and the BIS and BIC families can operate with two or three operands. The full set is

Symbolic Opcode	Numerical Opcode	Operands	Operation
BISB2	88		
BISW2	A8	mask, dst	dst ← dst OR mask
BISL2	C8		
BISB3	89		
BISW3	A9	mask,src,dst	dst ← src OR mask
BISL3	C9		
BICB2	8A		
BICW2	AA	mask,dst	dst ← dst AND (NOT mask)
BICL2	CA		
BICB3	8B		
BICW3	AB	mask,src,dst	dst ← src AND (NOT mask)
BICL3	CB		
BITB	93		
BITW	B3	mask,src	src AND mask
BITL	D3		

The first operand of each instruction is a **mask** that is used to select certain bits in the second operand. In the two-operand versions of the BIS and BIC families, the result is stored in the second operand. The three-operand version stores the result in the third operand. This is like ADDL2 versus ADDL3. For example, the BISW2 instruction causes each bit of the second-operand word to be set to a one if the corresponding bit in the mask word is a one. The bits in the second operand that correspond to zeros in the mask are not changed. As the description shows, this is a bit-by-bit OR operation of the mask with the second operand. For example, consider the following 16-bit binary numbers before and after the execution of a BISW2 instruction.

```
X = 1101   1110   0001   0001
Y = 1100   0101   0110   1000    Before BISW2 X,Y


X = 1101   1110   0001   0001
Y = 1101   1111   0111   1001    After BISW2 X,Y
```

Note that the mask is unchanged. In the three-operand version BISW3 X,Y,Z the value of Y would remain unchanged, and the result would be stored in Z.

The BICW2 instruction is similar, except that bits of the second operand are cleared to zero if the corresponding bit of the mask is a one. This operation is like the Boolean AND operation of the one's complement (NOT) of the mask with the second operand (see Chapter 2). The preceding example will now be reshown, using the BICW2 instruction.

```
X = 1101   1110   0001   0001
Y = 1100   0101   0110   1000    Before BICW2 X,Y

X = 1101   1110   0001   0001
Y = 0000   0001   0110   1000    After BICW2  X,Y
```

The BIT family of instructions is quite different. It is like the CMP family of instructions in that no computed result is stored. Instead, both families are used to set condition codes. For the BIT family, a computed result is determined that has a one in a given bit position only if **both** operands have ones in the corresponding position. This is the Boolean AND operation. If there are no ones in the entire computed result, the condition code Z will be set, and this can be tested with the BEQL and BNEQ instructions. If the most significant bit of the computed result is one, then N will be set, and this can be tested with the BLSS and BGEQ instructions. Since an overflow or carry cannot occur, these condition codes would not normally be used. However, in order to be consistent with how most programmers would want to use the branch instructions, V is always cleared and C is left unchanged. The BIC and BIS families set the condition codes in the same manner except that the N and Z bits depend on the value stored in the destination rather than on the value of the temporary result.

Again using the same values of X and Y, here is an example of how the BITW instruction operates.

```
X = 1101   1110   0001   0001
Y = 1100   0101   0110   1000   Before and after BITW X,Y

temp = 1100   0100   0000   0000   after BITW X,Y (temp not stored)
```

The BITW X,Y instruction leaves X and Y unchanged. The temporary result, which is not stored, is used to set the condition codes as follows:

N = 1
Z = 0
V = 0
C = Previous value before BITW instruction

Note that use of the Z bit can be confusing. The Z bit is set to one (or true) if the temporary result is equal to zero. This means that every bit selected by the mask was equal to zero in the source.

The XOR Instruction

A similar bit manipulation family is XOR family. This family instruction computes the bit-by-bit **exclusive-OR** of two operands and stores the result either into the second or the third operand depending upon whether the two- or three-operand version of the instruction is used. The exclusive-OR of two bits is defined as 1 if either of the two input bits is 1 **but not** both. This can be seen in the following table.

0 exOR 0 = 0
0 exOR 1 = 1
1 exOR 0 = 1
1 exOR 1 = 0

Using the same example of X and Y from the previous section, we can see how the XORW2 instruction works.

```
X = 1101   1110   0001   0001
Y = 1100   0101   0110   1000      Before XORW2 X,Y


X = 1101   1110   0001   0001
Y = 0001   1011   0111   1001      After XORW2 X,Y
```

The reader should note the similarities and differences between the BIS and XOR families. BIS is the **inclusive**-OR, while XOR is the **exclusive**-OR.

The complete family of XOR instructions is

Symbolic Opcode	Numerical Opcode	Operands	Operation
XORB2	8C $\Big\}$		
XORW2	AC	mask,dst	dst←dst XOR mask
XORL2	CC		
XORB3	8D $\Big\}$		
XORW3	AD	mask,src,dst	dst←src XOR mask
XORL2	CD		

The MCOM Instructions

The last set of bit manipulation instructions is the MCOM (for Move COMplement) family which simply reverses all of the bits in the source operand and stores it in the destination. That is, 1 bits are changed to 0, and 0 bits are changed to 1. For example, the instruction MCOMW X,Y will have the following effect:

```
X = 1101   1110   0001   0001      Before MCOMW X,Y

Y = 0010   0001   1110   1110      After MCOMW X,Y
```

The MCOM and MNEG families of instructions are actually quite similar. MNEG is used to obtain the negative of a signed two's complement number. The MCOM instructions could be used to obtain the negative of a one's complement number as described in Chapter 2. However, the VAX uses the two's complement system for signed numbers rather than the one's complement system. As a result, the MCOM instructions are usually only used for bit manipulation purposes. In actuality, the two's complement negative can be computed by adding one to the one's complement negative. The three instructions in this set are:

Symbolic Opcode	Numerical Opcode	Operands	Operation
MCOMB	92		
MCOMW	B2	src,dst	dst ← NOT src
MCOML	D2		

Examples Using Bit Manipulation

Figures 8.4 and 8.5 show two examples of program segments that use the bit manipulation instructions. The first, in Figure 8.4, extracts the third hexadecimal digit of the longword N and returns it as a single byte character code in R0.

The program segment in Figure 8.5 computes what is called a **parity bit.** As previously noted, the ASCII code that we are using is a 7-bit code. However, when ASCII characters are transmitted between computers and input/output devices, an eighth bit is sometimes added in order to obtain error detection. This bit is called a **parity bit** and is set to a one or a zero in order to make the total number of ones in the 8-bit code an even number. This is called **even parity.** Now, if noise or a malfunction causes one of the ones to change to a zero, or one of the zeros to change to a one, the total number of ones becomes an odd number (**odd parity**), and this error is detectable. (Note: Some systems generate odd parity, and then even parity means there is an error. The VAX hardware and software can communicate with terminals that use odd parity, even parity, or no parity at all.) Since the VAX hardware and software process parity bits for the user, the user is not normally aware of their existence.

The program segment in Figure 8.5 takes a 7-bit ASCII code in R0 and determines whether there is an odd or an even number of ones in the code. A parity bit is the added bit in position 7 to produce a byte with odd parity.

```
N:        .BLKL  1
G_DIG_3:  MOVL   N,R0                   ;PUT NUMBER IN R0
          BICL2  #^XFFFFF0FF,R0         ;CLEAR ALL BUT 3RD DIGIT
          ASHL   #-8,R0,R0              ;SHIFT RIGHT 8 PLACES
          BISB2  #^X30,R0               ;MAKE AN ASCII CODE
          CMPB   R0,#^X39               ;IS DIGIT DECIMAL
          BLEQ   10$                    ;YES, LEAVE AS IS
          ADDB2  #^X41-^X30-10,R0       ;NO, COVERT TO A-F
10$:      RSB                           ;AND RETURN
```

Figure 8.4 Program to print the third hexadecimal digit of a word

Figure 8.5 Subroutine to generate a byte with odd parity

```
;
;SUBROUTINE ODDGN GENERATES A BYTE WITH ODD PARITY
;
MASK:   .BLKB   1
TEST:   .BLKB   1
ODDGN:  BICB2   #^X80,R0        ;CLEAR PARITY BIT
        MOVB    #1,MASK         ;START WITH MASK OF 1
        MOVL    #7,R1           ;7 BITS IN CODE
        CLRB    TEST            ;TEST WILL INDICATE PARITY
10$:    BITB    MASK,R0         ;TEST FOR BIT
        BEQL    20$             ;SKIP IF ZERO
        INCB    TEST            ;TEST COUNTS ONES
20$:    ASHB    #1,MASK,MASK    ;MOVE MASK BIT
        SOBGTR  R1,10$          ;COUNT SEVEN BITS
        BITB    #1,TEST         ;TEST PARITY
        BNEQ    30$             ;IF PARITY ALREADY ODD WE ARE DONE
        BISB2   #^X80,R0        ;OTHERWISE SET PARITY BIT
30$:    RSB                     ;RETURN WITH RESULT IN R0
```

A final example uses various features of the bit manipulation and shift instructions with character strings. This program (shown in Figure 8.6) reads in an unsigned decimal number that has been read in using the line read routine, RLINE. The value of the decimal number is placed in location DATA. Because no check is made of the number of characters typed in, the result could overflow a longword. Similarly, no error checks are made. If the user types characters other than decimal digits, the result will be meaningless.

Note the general way that this program works. It starts out with the contents of DATA equal to zero. Then each time a digit is picked up, the number in DATA is multiplied by ten and the value of the digit is added. For example, suppose we type in 573: the number in DATA is 0 and the first digit is 5; the number in DATA times 10 is still 0, plus 5 is 5. Now the next digit is 7. DATA times 10 is 50, plus 7 is 57. The last digit is 3. DATA times 10 is 570; add three and we get 573. The character count ends the process. See Chapter 2 page 25 for a description of this algorithm. The examples in Figures 8.4, 8.5, and 8.6 can be rewritten to be more efficient. For example, in Figure 8.6, the instructions

```
MULL2   #10,DATA        ;DATA=DATA*10
ADDL2   R0,DATA         ;ADD IN DIGIT
```

Figure 8.6 Decimal read subroutine

```
;
;READS A DECIMAL NUMBER AND LEAVES IT IN R0
;
BSIZE=80
BUFFER:  .BLKB    BSIZE
DATA:    .BLKL    1
READ:    MOVAL    BUFFER,R0          ;READ A LINE OF TEXT
         MOVZWL   #BSIZE,R1          ;USING RLINE
         JSB      RLINE              ;R1 WILL HAVE STRING LENGTH
         MOVAL    BUFFER,R2          ;GET LOCATION OF INPUT LINE
         CLRL     DATA               ;INITIALLY ANSWER IS ZERO
10$:     DECL     R1                 ;CHECK CHARACTER COUNT
         BLSS     20$                ;AND EXIT IF DONE
         MOVB     (R2)+,R0           ;GET CHARACTER
         BICL     #^XFFFFFFF0,R0     ;STRIP EXTRA BITS
         MULL2    #10,DATA           ;DATA=DATA*10
         ADDL2    R0,DATA            ;ADD IN DIGIT
         BRB      10$                ;GET NEXT DIGITS (IF ANY)
20$:     MOVL     DATA,R0            ;GET RESULT
         RSB                         ;AND RETURN
```

can be replaced with a single EMUL instruction which was introduced in Chapter 6. This and other improvements are left as exercises
for the reader.

The BLBS and BLBC Instruction

As we saw in the multiplication example at the end of Chapter 6 and
in the example in Figure 8.5, it is fairly common to want to test the
least significant bit of a number. For this reason, there are two instructions just for that purpose.

Symbol	Meaning
BLBS	Branch if Low Bit is Set
BLBC	Branch if Low Bit is Clear

These instructions examine the low-order bit of a byte, word, longword, or quadword and branch to an address if the bit is one (for
BLBS) or zero (for BLBC). It does not normally matter whether the

addressed item is a word or byte, or whatever, because the low-order bit is in the low-order byte, and bytes, words, longwords, or quad-words are all accessed by giving the address of the low-order byte. (However, if the index register or auto-increment modes are used, the operand is treated as a longword in the sense that the register is multiplied or incremented by four.) As an example of how to use the BLBS instruction, the instruction

```
BLBS      X,50$
```

will branch to 50$ if the least significant bit of X is one. The BLBS instruction could be used with the program in Figure 8.5 to save an instruction. Note that the last four instructions of this program are

```
        BITB      #1,TEST
        BNEQ      30$
        BISB      #^X80,R0
30$:    RSB
```

These could be changed to

```
        BLBS      TEST,30$
        BISB      #^X80,R0
30$:    RSB
```

thus saving an instruction. Note that this instruction has an 8-bit displacement, thus limiting the range of the branches as with other conditional branch instructions.

Another application for these instructions is in connection with the system error codes described in the section on the RLINE sub-routine. It was noted that the normal return value was one. However, all other error codes are set up to be even numbers. This allows the BLBS or BLBC instruction to be used to check for errors. Thus, the error check code shown on page 219 could be simplified as follows:

Original Form

```
        ...
        JSB       RLINE
        CMPW      R0,#1
        BEQL      10$
        $EXIT_S   R0
10$:    ...
```

Form with BLBS

```
        ...
        JSB       RLINE
        BLBS      R0,10$
        $EXIT_S   R0
10$:    ...
```

8.5 Other Character Representations
Hollerith Code

Although ASCII is the most popular character encoding for use with the VAX, other encodings are worthy of note. Of special importance is the encoding used on punched-card equipment. This is also known as **Hollerith** code because of its developer, Herman Hollerith, who introduced the use of punched cards for tabulating the 1890 U.S. Census.

The basis of Hollerith code is a paper card that is the same height and width as the dollar bill in use at the time. Rectangular holes can be punched in the card in any of 80 column positions horizontally, and any of 12 row positions vertically (see Figure 8.7).

Each column is used for a single character; therefore, a card can contain 80 encoded characters. Since there are 12 rows, and since, conceivably, any possible combination of 12 punches is possible, the punched-card code could accommodate an alphabet with as many as $2^{12} = 4096$ different characters. In practice, however, if you punch too many holes in a card, it starts looking like, and having the physical strength of, a piece of cheesecloth. Consequently, the codes are restricted so that normally no column has more than three punches in it.*

The rows on the card are numbered (from top to bottom) 12, 11, 0, 1, 2, 3, 4, 5, 6, 7, 8, and 9, respectively. The codes for the numerals 0 through 9 are punched with a single punch in the corresponding row (that is, the code for 5 is a punch in the 5 row, or a **five punch**). Letters are formed by combining one punch in rows 1–9 (a **numeric punch**) with a second punch in rows 12, 11, or 0 (a **zone punch**). This gives $9 \times 3 = 27$ possibilities, of which 26 are used. Figure 8.8 gives a table of codes for the alphabet. Note that the one code left out is 0–1, a code in the middle of the table. Hollerith left this code out because he feared that his machinery might tear a card with two adjacent rows being punched. In addition, the single punches 12, 11, and no punch at all are used for &, -, and blank space.

Modern Card Codes

Later, as data processing became more sophisticated, a need for more punctuation arose. This need was met by extending the range of the numeric punches from 9 to 15 by using an 8 punch in combination

---

* There are some exceptions to this rule, notably special-purpose cards such as end-of-file cards, binary cards, and some extended alphabet codes that may include lowercase letters and control characters.

Figure 8.7 Hollerith card

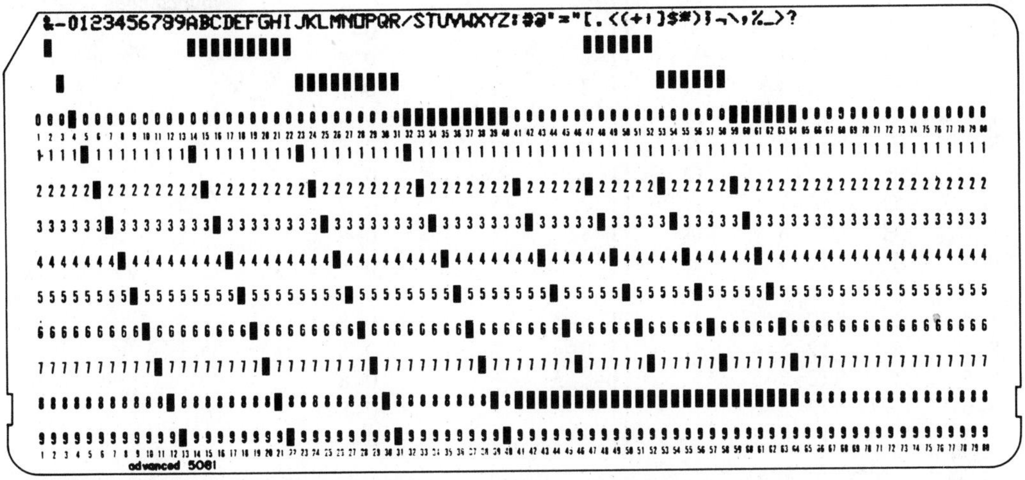

with a punch from 2 through 7. For example, an 8–5 punch has a decimal value of 13. In addition, the gentler modern equipment allows the 0–1 punch to be used. This gives a total possibility of 64 characters.

Assignment of punctuation to punch configurations is pretty much arbitrary, and there are, in fact, several different assignments. Figure 8.9 shows the most popular card code. This code is often called **029 code** because it was first introduced on the IBM model 29 keypunch. In some ways, however, the name 029 code is a misnomer, because IBM makes model 29 keypunches with a variety of different code assignments. In particular, this code assignment is found in the IBM model 029–EH keyboard. However, note that the assignment of numerals and alphabetic characters is standard; only punctuation changes.

The 64-character 029 code is a subset of an 8-bit code called EBCDIC (pronounced ebb-sa-dick, which is an acronym for Extended Binary Coded Decimal Interchange Code). The eight bits provide for

A	1–12	J	1–11	Unused	1–0
B	2–12	K	2–11	S	2–0
C	3–12	L	3–11	T	3–0
D	4–12	M	4–11	U	4–0
E	5–12	N	5–11	V	5–0
F	6–12	O	6–11	W	6–0
G	7–12	P	7–11	X	7–0
H	8–12	Q	8–11	Y	8–0
I	9–12	R	9–11	Z	9–0

Figure 8.8 Hollerith code for the alphabet

	No punch						
Space		&	12	-	11–0	0	
1	1	A	12–1	J	11–1	/	0–1
2	2	B	12–2	K	11–2	S	0–2
3	3	C	12–3	L	11–3	T	0–3
4	4	D	12–4	M	11–4	U	0–4
5	5	E	12–5	N	11–5	V	0–5
6	6	F	12–6	O	11–6	W	0–6
7	7	G	12–7	P	11–7	X	0–7
8	8	H	12–8	Q	11–8	Y	0–8
9	9	I	12–9	R	11–9	Z	0–9
:	8–2	¢	12–8–2	!	11–8–2	unused	0–8–2
#	8–3	.	12–8–3	$	11–8–3	,	0–8–3
@	8–4	<	12–8–4	*	11–8–4	%	0–8–4
|	8–5	(	12–8–5	)	11–8–5	–	0–8–5
=	8–6	+	12–8–6	;	11–8–6	>	0–8–6
"	8–7	|	12–8–7	¬	11–8–7	?	0–8–7

Figure 8.9 IBM 029-EH keypunch code

a possible 2^8 or 256 combinations. In addition to the 64 characters of the 029 code, EBCDIC includes lowercase letters as well as a variety of control characters. The EBCDIC code is shown in Figure 8.10 as a table with 32 rows and 8 columns. The row specifies the right-most five bits while the column specifies the left-most three bits. For example, the capital letter A occupies the second position in the seventh column. Thus, the binary code for an A consists of the bits 110 (from the column) followed by 00001 (from the row) or 11000001. Notice that many combinations are not assigned to any symbol or control character. EBCDIC is the standard code on large IBM computers as well as computers made by other manufacturers. The gaps between the codes for I and J and the codes for R and S are designed to maintain compatability with earlier codes derived from the Hollerith punch card code.

Exercise Set 2

1. Given that the contents of A, B, C, and D, are

```
A   ^X0F0F0F0F
B   ^XF0F0F0F0
C   ^X12345678
D   ^X87654321
```

Right-most	Left-most Three Bits								Figure 8.10 EBCDIC code
Five Bits	000	001	010	011	100	101	110	111	
00000	NUL	DS	Sp	-					
00001	SOH	SOS		/	a		A		
00010	STX	FS			b	s	B	S	
00011	ETX				c	t	C	T	
00100	PF	BYP			d	u	D	U	
00101	HT	LF			e	v	E	V	
00110	LC	ETB			f	w	F	W	
00111	DEL	ESC			g	x	G	X	
01000					h	y	H	Y	
01001					i	z	I	Z	
01010	SMM	SM	¢						
01011	VT	CU2	.	,					
01100	FF		<	%					
01101	CR	ENQ	(	_					
01110	SO	ACK	+	>					
01111	SI	BEL	|	?					
10000	DLE		&					0	
10001	DC1				j		J	1	
10010	DC2	SYN			k		K	2	
10011	TM				l		L	3	
10100	RES	PN			m		M	4	
10101	NL	RS			n		N	5	
10110	BS	UC			o		O	6	
10111	IL	EOT			p		P	7	
11000	CAN				q		Q	8	
11001	EM				r		R	9	
11010	CC		!	:					
11011	CU1	CU3	$	#					
11100	IFS	DC4	*	@					
11101	IGS	NAK	)	'					
11110	IRS		;	=					
11111	IUS	SUB	¬	"					

what would be the effect on A, B, C, and D and the condition codes N, Z, C, and V after executing each of the following instructions on the original contents?

a. BISL2 A,B

b. BICL2 A,C

c. BICL2 C,A

d. BISL2 B,C

e. BITL2 C,D

f. BITL2 C,C

2. Write and run a program that reads characters typed in and prints each character out seven times on a line. The program terminates when it reads a blank (zero length) line.

3. Write a program which reads a line. The program then prints out the line alternately forward and backward seven times. The line length may vary, but would not be longer than 80 characters.

4. Write a program to run in the batch stream which reads characters from data cards. It types the characters back out replacing **all** control characters (including carriage return and line feed) with an asterisk and the letter that would be typed with "control" to get the control character. Follow each control-J or *J with a carriage return and line feed. What control characters does the batch stream insert into your data? Can control characters be punched onto cards? If so, how?

5. Write a subroutine that reads 32-bit binary numbers as a sequence of 32 ASCII 1s and 0s followed by carriage return/line feed. The subroutine returns with the binary value in R0.

6. Write a subroutine that takes the value of R0 and prints it out as a 32-bit binary number. Print one number per line as the subroutine is called successively.

7. Combine the subroutines of Exercises 5 and 6 with a main program that tests the subroutines by calling them several times.

8. Write a subroutine that prints out signed decimal numbers. Modify the subroutine in Figure 8.6 to read signed decimal numbers. Write a main program that tests these subroutines by calling them a number of times. The printout routine should not print leading zeros.

9. Rewrite the programs in Figures 8.4, 8.5, and 8.6 to be more efficient, using the following suggestions in addition to any that you may think of:

    a. In Figure 8.4, solve the problem by indexing into an array of sixteen characters from the string "0123456789ABCDEF".

    b. In Figure 8.5, use the BLBS or BLBC instructions for testing bits in a byte. If speed is more important than space, could a table of 256 bytes be employed to effect?

    c. In Figure 8.6, use the EMUL instruction to replace the MULL2 and ADDL2 instructions.

10. Each of the following program segments performs a simple operation. However, logical instructions are used and the operation being performed is not necessarily obvious. For each segment, identify the operation or function.

a.
```
XORL2    A,B
XORL2    B,A
XORL2    A,B
```
(relation of new A and
B to original values)

b.
```
MOVL     A,B
XORL2    B,B
```
(value of B)

c.
```
MOVL     A,B
DECL     B
MCOML    B,B
```
(relation of B to A)

d.
```
MOVL     A,B
XORL2    #-1,B
INCL     B
```
(relation of B to A)

e.
```
10$:     XORL3   A,B,C
         MCOML   A,A
         BICL2   A,B
         MOVL    C,A
         ASHL    #1,B,B
         BNEQ    10$
```
(relation of C to original
values of A and B)

*11. Write a program that reads a body of text. The program then prints out the number of times each printable character occurred in the text. Your answers should be printed in decimal using a routine such as written for Exercise 8. Your printout should resemble

```
A   APPEARED     129     TIMES
B   APPEARED     17      TIMES
C   APPEARED     18      TIMES
```

Subroutines

9.1 Introduction

In previous chapters, we have seen the use of simple subroutines for performing frequently repeated operations, such as reading or printing lines or numbers. Subroutines are very important in the structure of computer programs. In this chapter, we will examine the details of how the calling and returning processes function. We will also see how subroutines access data from the main program, and how complex subroutine structures can be tied together and joined with programs written in higher-level languages. The latter item is, perhaps, the most important. One of the most significant uses of assembly language is to augment such languages as Pascal or FORTRAN to allow operations that would be difficult or impossible in the higher-level language alone. In addition, with VAX/VMS, main programs written in assembly language can call subroutines written in higher-level languages. This allows assembly language programs easy access to such higher-level language functions as formatted input and output. This chapter will discuss the standardized calling method that allows programs written in different languages, including assembly language, to communicate with one another.

9.2 Calling a Subroutine
Review of the JSB Instruction

In Chapter 5, it was stated that a subroutine could be called by using the instruction

```
JSB ADDR
```

Furthermore, the subroutine returned to the main program with the instruction

RSB

The explanation given in Chapter 5 was that the JSB instruction used the stack pointer (register 14 or SP) to save the program counter (register 15 or PC) in an area of memory called the stack. The value of the PC that is saved on the stack is the address of the instruction that follows the JSB instruction. This is the instruction to execute after the subroutine returns.

This explanation is true, but incomplete. For example, we have already seen programs in which subroutines called other subroutines. When subroutines are nested in this manner, a whole array of return addresses must be saved. This raises the question of how each RSB instruction gets the correct return address from the stack.

Using the Stack

In order to use an array to store return addresses, there must be a pointer that indicates where the data are being stored. General register number 14, or the SP (for Stack Pointer), is always used for this purpose. The reader can now see why there were cautions against using register 14. Random use of register 14 could cause very strange things to happen at the next subroutine call or return.

An array that is accessed by sequentially adding and removing data in the following manner is called a **stack.** The operation of a stack is analogous to a stack of plates in a cafeteria. In order to save an item of information, a new plate is obtained from somewhere, a 32-bit binary number is printed on the plate, and the plate is placed on top of the stack of plates. To retrieve an item from the stack, the plate on the top of the stack is removed and the number on the plate is examined. Notice that plates are always added and removed from the **top** of the stack. As a result, the plate that is removed is always the plate that was most recently added. For example, in the following figure, three quantities labeled A, B, and C are first saved on the stack and then removed from the stack.

			C			
		B	B	B		
	A	A	A	A	A	
———	———	———	———	———	———	———
Empty	Add item	Add item	Add item	Remove top	Remove top	Remove top

Although C was the last item to be placed on the stack, it is the first item to be removed. This Last In, First Out sequence is often abbreviated as **LIFO.**

Register 14 is called the **stack pointer** because it points to the top of the stack. For example, assume that the first longword on the stack is stored in memory location ˆX7FFC8FFC. Since the first longword will be stored at address ˆX7FFC8FFC, register 14 contains ˆX7FFC9000 when the stack is empty.

	Address	Contents
	ˆX7FFC8FF4	??????
	ˆX7FFC8FF8	??????
	ˆX7FFC8FFC	??????
register 14 ˆX7FFC9000	→ˆX7FFC9000	??????

In order to save a longword on the stack, subtract four from register 14 and store the item in the resulting address. If longword A is saved on the stack, the result will be:

	Address	Contents
	ˆX7FFC8FF4	??????
	ˆX7FFC8FF8	??????
register 14 ˆX7FFC8FFC	→ˆX7FFC8FFC	A
	ˆX7FFC9000	??????

To save longword B on the stack, subtract four from register 14 and place longword B at the resulting address.

	Address	Contents
	ˆX7FFC8FF4	??????
register 14 ˆX7FFC8FF8	→ˆX7FFC8FF8	B
	ˆX7FFC8FFC	A
	ˆX7FFC9000	??????

Retrieving an item from the stack is just the reverse of saving an item. Fetch the contents of the memory cell whose address is contained in register 14 and then add four to register 14. After longword B is fetched, the stack will appear as follows:

	Address	Contents
	ˆX7FFC8FF4	??????
	ˆX7FFC8FF8	??????
register 14 ˆX7FFC8FFC	→ˆX7FFC8FFC	A
	ˆX7FFC9000	??????

Notice that memory longword ^X7FFC8FF8, which used to contain B, now contains ??????. Memory cells that used to contain an item on the stack may contain meaningless information after the item is removed from the stack. The programmer should assume that this is true on most if not all computer systems. The particular implementation of a stack may allow hardware or software to overwrite memory locations in the stack after the item has been removed.

Removing another item from the stack retrieves item A and leaves the stack empty.

	Address	Contents
	^X7FFC8FF4	??????
	^X7FFC8FF8	??????
	^X7FFC8FFC	??????
register 14 ^X7FFC9000	→^X7FFC9000	??????

Because return addresses are saved on the stack, subroutines can be nested without difficulty. For example, a main program called ALPHA might call a subroutine called BETA. BETA in turn might call a subroutine GAMMA, and GAMMA might then call subroutine DELTA. By the time subroutine DELTA is executing, three return addresses have been saved on the stack—the return addresses to ALPHA, BETA, and GAMMA. Because of the last in, first out property of the stack, the return address that is removed from the stack when DELTA is completed will be the return address to GAMMA. Similarly, GAMMA will return to BETA, and BETA will return to ALPHA. As we shall see later in the chapter, the use of the stack for storing return addresses even allows a subroutine to call itself. Such subroutines are called **recursive.**

A longword can be placed on the stack with the instruction

```
MOVL    X,-(SP)
```

Similarly, a longword can be removed from the stack with the instruction

```
MOVL    (SP)+,X
```

Actually, users can employ these two instructions for placing data on the stack and thereby use the stack for storing temporary data. As an example of this, imagine a subroutine that uses R2, R3, and R4 for internal computation. However, also assume that the main program is using these registers and does not want the subroutine to change them. The subroutine must then save the values of R2, R3, and R4, and restore them when returning. This is a very common use for the stack. Although almost any available location could be used to save a register, there are important advantages to using the stack. When the stack is used for temporary storage, those memory cells are only used until the item is removed from the stack, at which time the memory space is available for other purposes. Memory and time are also conserved because MOVL R2,−(SP) is a short instruction, but MOVL R2,SAVE is a longer instruction because it includes an address. For these and other reasons that will become apparent later on, good programming practice on the VAX requires that the stack be used for such purposes.

Figure 9.1 shows a subroutine that saves registers R2, R3, and R4 on the stack. Note the label RETN. In order to return, you must either branch to RETN or execute instructions that have the same effect. It would be catastrophic to execute RSB **without** restoring the contents of the registers. The RSB instruction takes the top of the stack to be the return address. If the registers had not been restored, the top of the stack would have contained the saved value of R4, and **not** the return address. The general rule is that any subroutine may use the stack for storing data, **but** whatever a process adds to the stack, it must remove before executing RSB, nothing more, nothing less.

In point of fact, pushing data on the stack and especially saving registers on the stack are so important that there are several instructions especially designed to help in doing this. The first is the PUSH LONG instruction.

```
PUSHL    X
```

Figure 9.1 Using the stack to save registers

```
START:      MOVL       R2,-(SP)            ;SAVE REGISTERS
            MOVL       R3,-(SP)            ;R2, R3, AND R4
            MOVL       R4,-(SP)            ;ON STACK

               .
               .
               .

RETN:       MOVL       (SP)+,R4            ;RESTORE REGISTERS
            MOVL       (SP)+,R3            ;NOTE REVERSE ORDER
            MOVL       (SP)+,R2            ;LAST ON STACK IS FIRST OFF
            RSB                            ;SUBROUTINE RETURN
```

This instruction pushes a longword onto the stack. In actuality, this instruction has the same effect as the instruction

```
MOVL    X,-(SP)
```

However, the PUSHL instruction is clearer, operates somewhat more efficiently, and requires one byte less memory. For these reasons, the PUSHL instruction is preferred.

Two other stack instructions are designed for the wholesale saving of general registers on the stack. These instructions refer to registers by using a 16-bit mask for selecting a subset of the 16 general registers. The instructions are

```
PUSHR    MASK
```

and

```
POPR    MASK
```

The operand identified as MASK is a 16-bit word. Each bit in the word refers to a general register. Bit 0 refers to R0, bit 1 refers to R1, and so forth through bit 14 referring to register 14 (the SP). Since register 15 (PC) is the program counter it would not normally be saved on the stack except with a subroutine call instruction. For this reason, bit 15 of the mask is ignored and is always treated as zero by these instructions. In addition, great care should be exercised with registers AP, FP, and SP (registers 12, 13, and 14 respectively). Attempting to save these registers on the stack and restoring their values directly is likely to upset irrevocably the flow of control of your program. These registers have special functions, and when they are saved, it must be in specially prescribed ways. This will be explained more fully later in this chapter in the section on the CALLS and CALLG instructions.

The way the PUSHR instruction works is that each register whose corresponding bit in the mask is a one will be pushed onto the stack. For example,

```
PUSHR    #^X0047
```

will cause R0, R1, R2, and R6 to be saved on the stack because the number ^X0047 has ones in bit positions 0, 1, 2, and 6 because its binary representation is

```
0000 0000 0100 0111
```

Consequently, the instruction, PUSHR #^X0047 is equivalent to the set of instructions

```
PUSHL    R6
PUSHL    R2
PUSHL    R1
PUSHL    R0
```

Note that the registers are pushed on the stack in inverse order of register number. The POPR instruction undoes what the PUSHR instruction does. Therefore the instruction

```
POPR     #^X0047
```

is equivalent to

```
MOVL     (SP)+,R0
MOVL     (SP)+,R1
MOVL     (SP)+,R2
MOVL     (SP)+,R6
```

An apparent difficulty of using this instruction is the awkwardness of setting up the mask word. In order to simplify this procedure, the VAX MACRO assembler has a special operator for generating masks. It is the ^M operator. It has the appearance

```
^M<register list>
```

The register list is simply a list of register names separated by commas. Using this operator, the PUSHR #^X0047 instruction could be rewritten as

```
PUSHR    #^M<R0,R1,R2,R6>
```

This is clearly preferable, because it identifies, explicitly, which registers are being saved or restored.

It should be noted that, so far, all of our demonstrations of use of the stack have involved pushing or popping longwords. Although it is possible to use the stack with any size data, such as bytes or words, the VAX operates much more efficiently if the stack pointer is aligned to a longword boundary. In other words, the stack pointer value should be a multiple of four. Since the system always starts your program with the stack pointer aligned to a longword boundary, it will stay that way if you only push or pop longwords. It is still possible, however, to use the stack to save bytes or words and still keep longword alignment. To do this use the convert or zero-fill instructions. For example, a byte can be saved on the stack with the instruction

```
MOVZBL    BYTE,-(SP)
```

The byte can be restored with the instruction

```
CVTLB     (SP)+,BYTE
```

These instructions are described in Chapter 6, pages 149 ff. Notice that the auto-increment and auto-decrement modes are used with a longword operand so that the stack will be incremented or decremented by four.

Since the stack is just an array in memory, the question arises as to where the array is. This depends on the operating system. In the VAX/VMS system, programs are normally loaded starting at address ^X00000200. The stack starts at a high address such as ^X7FFC9000 and proceeds backward in memory. (The actual starting address is determined by your VAX/VMS operating system.)

Passing Information Between a Main Program and Subroutines

In most cases, the function of a subroutine is to perform some computation based on one or more pieces of information. The results of this computation may also be in the form of one or more pieces of information. These pieces of information must be communicated from the main program to the subroutine and vice versa.

In Chapter 5, a very simple method of communication was used for the RNUM and PNUM subroutines. The number being passed to or from the subroutine was placed in R0. This method is usable whenever there are only a few (no more than 12) longwords of information being passed back and forth. The first longword is placed in R0, the second in R1, and so on up through R11 (if necessary). The subroutine would be programmed to look for the information in the appropriate register. As many as 12 results could be transmitted back in the same way.

Obviously, this method of passing information has serious limitations when dealing with large amounts of data or arrays. The limitation of 12 registers for storage can be overcome by using specially set aside areas of memory that serve as communications areas. However, this does not really work well for large amounts of data because it requires loading and storing all of the locations at each subroutine call. This could entail an excessive amount of computing.

One solution to this problem is especially useful when dealing with arrays. Here, instead of passing the values in the array, the main program passes the address of the array. The subroutine then uses this address in order to access the data in the array. This method was used in Chapter 8 with the RLINE and PLINE subroutines. As another example of how this works, Figure 9.2 shows a subroutine that adds up an array of 100 numbers. The main program passes the **address** of the array to the subroutine via R1. The **value** of the result is passed back using R0. Thus, we are using a combination of both methods. The calling sequence for this program would be

```
MOVAL    ARRAY,R1
JSB      SUMUP
MOVL     R0,ANS
```

where ARRAY is the label of the array of the numbers to be added together, and ANS is the location that ultimately receives the result.

Of special note here is the fact that, in addition to the advantages just discussed, passing addresses rather than data is a much more general method of communication. For one thing, addresses can be used bidirectionally. In other words, if the subroutine has the address of a main program location, it can use that address both for accessing data and for sending results back to the main program. This was done with RLINE and PLINE. RLINE returns data, while PLINE accesses data.

In summary, we can say that transmitting values is a quick and simple technique that is very useful for subroutines that deal with only a few pieces of data. Transmitting addresses is needed for subroutines using many pieces of data. These techniques are referred to

```
SIZE=100
SUMUP:   PUSHR    #^M<R1,R2>    ;SAVE R1 AND R2
         MOVL     #SIZE,R2      ;R2 GETS ITEM COUNT
         CLRL     R0            ;CLEAR SUM
1$:      ADDL2    (R1)+,R0      ;ADD ITEM TO SUM
         DECL     R2            ;DECREMENT COUNT
         BNEQ     1$            ;LOOP UNTIL DONE
         POPR     #^M<R1,R2>    ;FROM STACK
         RSB                    ;RETURN
```

Figure 9.2 Subroutine for summing an array

as **call by value** and **call by reference** respectively. Later in this chapter, we will see an even more general method for transmitting data referred to as **call by descriptors.**

Exercise Set 1

For Exercises 1, 2, and 3, assume that R0 contains ^X00000256, R1 contains ^XFFFFF624, R2 contains ^XFFFFFFFC, and the following memory locations contain:

Address	Contents
^X7FFC8FF0	^X123 45678
^X7FFC8FF4	^X000 002FC
^X7FFC8FF8	^X000 00005
^X7FFC8FFC	^X000 04212
^X7FFC9000	^XFFFFFFFE

Also assume that the SP contains ^X7FFC8FF8 and that the original value of the SP was ^X7FFC9000. The value of the PC is ^X4E3. The address of SUB is ^X67F.

1. What values are contained on the stack?
2. What locations would change, and what would be the new contents after execution of each of the following instructions (use the values specified earlier for each instruction):

a.	PUSHL	R0	**b.**	MOVL	(SP)+,R1
c.	CMPL	(SP)+,(SP)+	**d.**	JSB	SUB
e.	JSB	@R0	**f.**	RSB	
g.	ADDL2	R2,SP	**h.**	MOVL	(SP),-(SP)
i.	PUSHR	#^M<R0,R1>	**j.**	POPR	#^M<R1,R2>

3. Which of the following instructions represent normal use of the stack? Which are abnormal and may produce unpredictable results owing to the fact that the operating system may periodically interrupt your program and modify locations below the stack pointer? Which instructions are catastrophic and will most likely result in program failure? Which instructions will generate assembly errors? Explain your answers. Use the values described in Exercise 1 for each instruction and show the resulting changes in contents.

a. MOVL   R0,(SP)+   **b.** CMPL   -(SP),-(SP)

c. JSB   (SP)+   **d.** JSB   @(SP)+

e. JSB   SP   **f.** INCL   SP

g. DECL   SP   **h.** MOVL   4(SP),R0

i. MOVL   (SP)+,PC

4. Write a subroutine similar to SUMUP, shown in Figure 9.2. However, your program will have a second input in R2 giving the size of the array to be summed. Then write a main program that reads 10 numbers, prints them, and calls your subroutine to sum them up, and then does the same with 20 numbers.

5. Write a program that reads in a variable number of numbers (up to 100), sorts them, and prints out the sorted array. This program should be split into various subroutines, one for each of the major functions. Array addresses, sizes, and all other data should be passed in the general registers at each subroutine call.

9.3 Independent Assembly and Global Symbols

The Need for Independent Assembly

When writing a program of any appreciable size, it is most important to break the program down into a number of pieces of manageable size which are called **modules.** The more independent these modules are, the easier it is to write, test, and debug each one. When every module is debugged, it is reasonable to deal with debugging the total program.

In order to deal with programming in this fashion, it is important to be able to treat each module as a separate program. This means that each of the smaller programs must be able to be assembled by itself. Consequently, it must have all its own locations completely defined within the module, like any program. In other words, there must not be any undefined symbols.

On the other hand, these program modules are intended to be combined to form a single program. This means that although the modules may be **highly** independent, they cannot be completely independent. There must be some form of communication between the programs. This is accomplished by means of **global symbols.**

Global Symbols

A global symbol is a symbolic address that is defined in one program but accessible to other independently assembled programs. Although global symbols can be used for almost anything that ordinary symbols are used for, they are most frequently used for subroutine names.

For example, a program module may contain a subroutine named READ. If this subroutine is to be called from one of the other program modules, the symbol READ must be global. The definition of global symbols is accomplished by means of the .ENTRY directive, the .GLOBAL directive, or by using two colons after the symbolic label. The .GLOBAL directive is followed by a symbol, or by several symbols separated by commas. The effect is to mark the symbols as global symbols in the assembler's user symbol table. For example,

```
.GLOBAL START,PRINT,SORT_TABLE
```

would cause the symbols START, PRINT, and SORT_TABLE to be marked as global so that these addresses would be available to other program modules.

The .ENTRY directive that we have been using since Chapter 1 automatically declares the symbol being defined as global. Furthermore, a symbolic address can be defined to be global by following it with two colons instead of one when it appears in the label field. Thus, the following lines of code are all equivalent ways of beginning a program and defining START to be a global symbol that can be accessed from other independently assembled program modules.

```
1.              .ENTRY    START,0

2.              .GLOBAL   START
     START:     .WORD     0

3. START::      .WORD     0
```

If a symbol such as START is used in a module but is defined elsewhere, the symbol should be identified as an external global symbol in the module. This is done by using the .EXTERNAL directive. For example, the directive

```
.EXTERNAL PRINT,GET_SYMBOL,REMOVE
```

marks symbols PRINT, GET_SYMBOL, and REMOVE as external global symbols that are used in the current module but are defined elsewhere. This prevents the assembler from generating an error mes-

sage for an undefined symbol. Instead, a special code is generated in
the object file which indicates that values for these externally defined
addresses must be obtained when all of the modules are combined
by the linker to form a single program.

Linking with Global Symbols

The process of combining all of the program modules together and
resolving global symbols is performed by a system program called
the **linker.*** The linker does two things. First, it relocates each program module to a successive block of memory. Note that the relocation address will be different for each module, and will depend on
how much memory was required by the preceding modules.

Second, the linker resolves the global references. Here the linker
is finishing a process that the assembler could not do because of
external global symbols. As in assembling, linking requires two passes
through the object files. In the first pass, a symbol table is constructed
for all defined global symbols. In the second pass, the missing addresses
corresponding to external global symbols are supplied by looking
them up in the symbol table generated during the first pass. If global
symbols remain undefined, it means that one of several errors has
occurred. The programmer may have forgotten to declare a symbol
as a global symbol; a symbol may have been misspelled; a module
may have been forgotten, and so on. The linker will produce an error
message for each undefined symbol.

In addition, most systems have a provision for subroutine libraries. This is a file of object modules that the linker will search to try
to resolve undefined global symbols. A module will not be loaded
from the library unless it is needed to satisfy an otherwise undefined
global symbol.

Figures 9.3 and 9.4 illustrate the use of global symbols. In the
subroutine (Figure 9.4), two colons are used to declare READ to be
a global symbol that is referenced by some other module (in this case
the main program). If READ were not declared to be a global symbol
in the subroutine, no assembly error would occur. However, in trying
to resolve the reference to READ in the main program, the linker
may search a subroutine library, looking for an object module called
READ. If the library contains a READ routine, the results during
execution would be unpredictable. After all, who knows what some-

---

* This linker is the same linker discussed in the section on relocation in Chapter 4
  (pages 95 ff). The reader is referred to this section to review the relocation concept.

```
.TITLE     MAIN          A MAIN PROGRAM MODULE
.EXTERNAL  READ          ;READ IS USED BUT NOT DEFINED
.ENTRY     START,0
...
JSB        READ          ;THIS LINE USES READ
...
.END       START         ;NOTE TRANSFER ADDRESS
```

Figure 9.3 A main program module

body else's program named READ might do? The programmer, therefore, may have great difficulty locating the error. In order to avoid this problem, the subroutine libraries in VAX/VMS use global names containing a dollar sign. For example, the square root routine is called MTH$SQRT and the routine called by $EXIT_S is called SYS$EXIT. This is why we cautioned against the use of dollar signs in user-created symbolic names.

In the main program (Figure 9.3), READ is declared by the .EXTERNAL directive to be an external global symbol. This indicates that the linker will substitute a numerical address for READ in the instruction JSB READ. If the .EXTERNAL directive were omitted, the assembler would flag READ as an undefined symbol. It is for this reason that we included the .DISABLE GLOBAL line in our earlier program. Without this line, the assembler automatically declares all undefined symbols to be external global symbols. It is a good idea to keep the .DISABLE GLOBAL line in your program, since the automatic declaration of global symbols delays the finding of misspelled symbol names.

The difference between the .END statements in Figures 9.3 and 9.4 is significant. The main program module must have a transfer or starting address on the .END statement, but none of the other modules should have anything following .END. This is because there cannot be more than one starting place for an entire program.

Figure 9.4 A subroutine module

```
        .TITLE     SUB1          A SUBROUTINE MODULE
;NOTE THAT READ:: DECLARES READ TO BE GLOBAL
READ::  PUSHR      #^M<R0>           ;BEGINNING OF READ SUBROUTINE
        ...
        POPR       #^M<R0>
        RSB
        .END                     ;NOTE NO TRANSFER ADDRESS
```

9.4 Procedure Calling
The CALLG and CALLS Instructions

Up until now, subroutine calling was done using the JSB, BSBW, and
BSBB instructions and returning with the RSB instruction. This is
the simple method for calling subroutines. A much more sophisticated
subroutine calling procedure is supported by the VAX. This allows a
single call and return instruction to automatically take care of all of
the following functions:

1. Normal handling of the program counter to allow calling and
   returning as is done with JSB and RSB.
2. Passing of argument lists for subroutine calls.
3. Selective saving and restoring of registers and condition codes.
4. Stacking of information needed for nested subroutine calls.
5. Marking of critical points in the stack which allows a subroutine
   traceback and other error procedures to be accomplished.
6. Completely restoring the stack during the return operation. This
   eliminates much of the danger caused by extraneous data being
   left on the stack.
7. Cleaning up of the stack in a way that allows an argument list
   to be placed on the stack and automatically removed at return.

In order to accomplish all this, there are two special registers
in addition to the program counter, (PC or register 15) and the stack
pointer (SP or register 14). These are the **argument pointer** (AP or
register 12) and the **frame pointer** (FP or register 13).

The argument pointer is used to point to an array which contains
a number of longwords which are being passed from the calling program to the called program. These longwords can be any kind of data,
but usually are addresses which in turn point to the data items or
arrays which are being passed to the subroutine. As mentioned before,
passing addresses has the advantage of allowing data transmission
both to and from the subroutine. Also, for reasons which will be
clearer later, the first longword on the argument list is usually a
number which tells how many more longwords there are on the list.
Among other things, this allows subroutines to have a varying number
of arguments as with the FORTRAN function MAX0 or the UCSD
Pascal function CONCAT.

The frame pointer is used to save the value of the stack pointer,
so that a return may be effected even though the subroutine may have

left data on the stack. Recall that subroutines called with JSB must remove anything that they pushed on the stack before they execute the RSB instruction. Because of the frame pointer, subroutines called with CALLS or CALLG are not subject to this restriction. The frame pointer is also used by the operating system for unwinding a list of subroutine calls in order to trace back to the main program in case of an error.

As was mentioned earlier, user programs should not modify the argument pointer or frame pointer except in ways described in this section. The instructions described in this section automatically save and restore these registers in standard ways. Any other use can cause unpredictable results.

In order to use this method of subroutine calling, a subroutine is called with the instruction **CALLG** or **CALLS.** The subroutine returns to the main or calling program with the instruction **RET.** The CALLG and CALLS instructions save all the necessary registers on the stack, and set up the AP and FP. The subroutine being called must tell the CALLG or CALLS instruction which registers it wants saved in the group R0, R1, . . . , R11. The CALLG and CALLS instructions always save the AP, FP, SP, and PC (registers 12, 13, 14, and 15). The way that the subroutine indicates which registers it wants saved is through bits in a 16-bit word called the **procedure-entry mask.** The procedure-entry mask word is actually the entry address of the subroutine. The first instruction to be executed will be two bytes higher than the location addressed by the CALLG or CALLS instruction. By convention, R0 and R1 are not saved under VMS.

The procedure-entry mask works in much the same way that the register mask works with the PUSHR or POPR instruction (see page 239). The main difference is that only registers R0 through R11 can be saved. Each bit corresponds to a register. As with PUSHR and POPR, the ^M operator can be used to generate a procedure-entry mask. For example, ^M<R2,R3> will cause R2 and R3 to be saved. Since register 12 through register 15 are automatically saved, bits 12 through 15 serve other purposes. Bits 12 and 13 are not used and *must* be zero. Bits 14 and 15 cause the integer overflow and decimal overflow traps to be set, respectively. These traps are used to detect errors. If the particular error occurs and the bit controlling the trap is set, control will be transferred to the VAX/VMS operating system. This is described more fully in Chapter 15. For now, we will set all four of these bits at zero.

For example, to call a subroutine using the CALLG instruction, your program would have a longword array as its argument list. The calling sequence could then appear as follows:

```
        .EXTERNAL  SUBR
        . . .
ARGLST: .LONG      3              ;THERE ARE 3 ARGUMENTS
        .ADDRESS   A              ;A IS ADDR OF FIRST ARGUMENT
        .ADDRESS   B              ;B IS ADDR OF SECOND ARGUMENT
        .ADDRESS   C              ;C IS ADDR OF THIRD ARGUMENT
        . . .
        CALLG      ARGLST,SUBR
        . . .
```

Note that the directive .LONG is used to place the constant three into
a longword while the directive .ADDRESS is used for placing the
addresses A, B, and C into longwords.
    The subroutine could be written as follows:

```
SUBR:: .WORD     ^M<R2,R3,R4>  ;SAVE AND RESTORE R2-R4
       MOVL      4(AP),R2      ;R2 GETS ADDR OF FIRST ARGUMENT
       MOVL      8(AP),R3      ;R3 GETS ADDR OF SECOND ARGUMENT
       MOVL      12(AP),R4     ;R4 GETS ADDR OF THIRD ARGUMENT
       . . .
       RET
```

Note that the first word of the subroutine is not an instruction but
is the entry mask word. The notation ^M<...> operates in the same
manner as it does with the PUSHR and POPR instructions.
    When this program is entered, the AP is pointing to the argument
list, and 4(AP) will point to the first argument (not counting the longword which has the argument count). Similarly, 8(AP) points to the
second argument and 12(AP) to the third argument. Therefore, the
instruction MOVL 4(AP),R2 will move the first entry on the argument list to R2. However, note that the first entry on the argument
list is the **address** of A. If you wanted the actual value of A (perhaps
it is a 16-bit word), we could use deferred addressing on R2 such as
MOVW (R2), ..., or if we do not really care about the address, we
could access the data directly with the instruction MOVW @ 4(AP),
... and then get the data without involving R2 at all.
    The .ENTRY directive that we have used to identify the entry
point of a main program can be used for any program or subroutine
that is called with the CALLS or CALLG instructions. For example,
the directive

```
.ENTRY    START,0
```

causes the assembler to do three things.

1. It enters symbolic address START into the user symbol table as the address of the next available location.
2. It makes START a global symbol.
3. It inserts a word of code using the second argument to form an entry mask.

Since the operating system does not rely on a program saving registers, we have always used zero for the entry mask. However, note that the reason we used this directive in the first place is that the VAX operating system treats our main program as a subroutine which it calls using the CALLS or CALLG instruction.

We can use the .ENTRY directive in the preceding subroutine to produce the following equivalent code:

```
.ENTRY     SUBR,^M<R2,R3,R4>
MOVL       4(AP),R2      ;R2 GETS ADDR OF FIRST ARGUMENT
MOVL       8(AP),R3      ;R3 GETS ADDR OF SECOND ARGUMENT
MOVL       12(AP),R4     ;R4 GETS ADDR OF THIRD ARGUMENT
  .  .  .
RET
```

The CALLS instruction is similar to the CALLG instruction. However, in order to facilitate the use of variable argument lists, CALLS assumes that the argument list will be located on the stack. The CALLS instruction will place the number of arguments at the top of the argument list, and the entire argument list will be removed from the stack when RET is executed. Therefore, the calling program does not have to worry about removing the words from the stack. The same subroutine call from the preceding example could be effected by the following sequence using CALLS:

```
  .  .  .
PUSHAL     C
PUSHAL     B
PUSHAL     A
CALLS      #3,SUBR
  .  .  .
```

The instruction PUSHAL is used to place the addresses of A, B, and C on the stack. Just as the instruction

```
PUSHL      X
```

is equivalent in effect to

```
MOVL       X,-(SP)
```

the instruction

```
PUSHAL     A
```

is equivalent in effect to

```
MOVAL      A,-(SP)
```

and is used as the more efficient means for placing addresses on the stack. Note that the normal inversion of the stack means that the third argument is pushed on the stack first.

In Chapter 7, we saw that MOVAL was part of a family of instructions including MOVAB, MOVAW, MOVAL, MOVAQ, and MOVAO. In a similar way, PUSHAL is a member from the following family of instructions:

Symbol	Meaning
PUSHAB	PUSH Address of Byte
PUSHAW	PUSH Address of Word
PUSHAL	PUSH Address of Longword
PUSHAQ	PUSH Address of Quadword
PUSHAO	PUSH Address of Octaword

9.5 Interfacing Assembly Language and Higher-Level Languages

The Need for Combining Assembly Language and Higher-Level Language Programs

Higher-level languages usually provide for three types of program modules. These are main programs, subroutines or procedures, and functions. As implemented under VAX/VMS, these program modules may be independently compiled or translated into object modules. Communication between object modules is accomplished by means of global names for subroutines and functions. Since the object modules produced by VAX/VMS compilers have exactly the same format as those produced by the assembler, it is possible to interchange main programs, subroutines, and functions written in higher-level languages with modules written in assembly language as long as the VAX/VMS programming conventions are followed.

There are various reasons why one would want to write an assembly language subroutine to be called by a higher-level language program. First, there are certain operations that are not particularly easy in some higher-level languages. These include bit operations on words (masking, packing, and so on), and multiple-precision arithmetic other than that which is provided for in these languages. Second, some operations are excluded from most higher-level languages. These include nonstandard input/output, interfacing to nonstandard devices, and access to absolute memory locations.

Similarly, there are various reasons for calling higher-level language routines from assembly language. For example, most higher-level languages provide simplified means for performing input and output. Appendix C shows input/output routines written in higher-level languages that may be called from assembly language main programs. In addition, higher-level languages provide an easy way to evaluate complex mathematical expressions.

VAX/VMS Calling Convention

The VAX/VMS calling convention is a standard method for transferring control and information between a calling program and a called program. This standard is used by the higher-level languages implemented as part of the VAX/VMS operating system. These languages include BASIC, BLISS, C, COBOL, FORTRAN, Pascal, and PL/I. The convention is also used to obtain services from the VAX/VMS operating system.

The standards for some languages, such as BASIC and Pascal, do not provide for the independent compilation of subroutines and functions. However, since independent compilation is such an important programming concept, many implementations of these languages provide language extensions to allow for calling externally compiled or assembled program modules. In particular, the VAX/VMS implementations of the previously listed languages include such extensions where necessary. As standard FORTRAN does not require any extensions, we will use FORTRAN modules to introduce the VAX/VMS calling convention. The extensions required to use Pascal modules will also be described. For other languages, the appropriate VAX/VMS language reference manual should be consulted.

FORTRAN Calling Conventions

When writing an assembly language subroutine that is to interface with FORTRAN programs, it is necessary to use the calling and returning conventions that are part of the VAX/VMS procedure calling standard. It is also necessary to know the way that data are passed back and forth. This is done primarily by using the argument lists described for the CALLS and CALLG instructions.

The simplest case is a subroutine that has no arguments in the call. Such a subroutine would be called in FORTRAN using a statement such as

```
CALL      XSUB
```

The object code generated by the FORTRAN compiler is exactly what the assembler would generate for

```
.EXTERNAL XSUB
. . .
CALLS     #0,XSUB
```

The CALLS instruction has an operand of #0 because the subroutine has no arguments. This means that the subroutine should have the simple structure shown in Figure 9.5.

The next topic to deal with is the communication of data between FORTRAN programs. There are two ways that a FORTRAN main program can communicate with a subroutine. The first is by means of an argument list; the second is through common blocks. Common blocks will be discussed in a later section.

In FORTRAN, argument lists are transferred by passing addresses, as described earlier in this chapter for the CALLG and CALLS instruction. As an example, a FORTRAN program having the statement CALL YSUB(A,B,C) will set aside an array of four longwords. There is one longword for each of three addresses, and one longword at the beginning of the array that gives the number of arguments. Figure 9.6(a) gives the equivalent assembly language for the FORTRAN statement CALL YSUB(A,B,C). This implementation assumes that the var-

```
.TITLE  XSUB           SAMPLE SUBROUTINE
.ENTRY  XSUB,^M<. . .>
. . .
RET
.END
```

Figure 9.5 A FORTRAN callable subroutine

```
        .EXTERNAL YSUB        ;ALL SUBROUTINES ARE GLOBAL
        . . .
ARGS:   .LONG     3           ;NUMBER OF ARGUMENTS
        .ADDRESS  A           ;ADDRESS OF A
        .ADDRESS  B           ;ADDRESS OF B
        .ADDRESS  C           ;ADDRESS OF C
        . . .
A:      .BLKL     1           ;LOCATION OF A
B:      .BLKL     1           ;LOCATION OF B
C:      .BLKL     1           ;LOCATION OF C
        . . .
        CALLG     ARGS,YSUB   ;CALL SUBROUTINE
```

Figure 9.6(a) Assembly language equivalent for CALL YSUB(A,B,C) using CALLG

iables A, B, and C are declared in the FORTRAN program as a data type that occupies a longword. For example, the declaration INTE-GER A,B,C would cause the variables A, B, and C to be signed long-word integers. (See the VAX/VMS FORTRAN reference manual.) Figure 9.6(b) shows how the same calling sequence could be written using the CALLS instruction. The difference is that the argument list is built on the stack each time the subroutine is called. The number of arguments is given in the argument list so that a subroutine could deal with a variable number of arguments. This also makes calling with the CALLG instruction compatible with calling with the CALLS instruction. (Other computer systems use different conventions for detecting the number of arguments, such as using a special value to mark the end of the argument list.)

Figure 9.7 illustrates a subroutine that adds the elements of an array A and places the sum in S. Note that the program changes both R0 and R1. However, this is all right because the VAX/VMS calling convention allows it. Standard calling procedures allow subroutines to modify the contents of R0 and R1. The reason for this will be

```
        .GLOBAL   YSUB        ;ALL SUBROUTINES ARE GLOBAL
        . . .
A:      .BLKL     1           ;LOCATION OF A
B:      .BLKL     1           ;LOCATION OF B
C:      .BLKL     1           ;LOCATION OF C
        . . .
        PUSHAL    C           ;BUILD THE ARGUMENT LIST
        PUSHAL    B           ;NOTE THAT THE LAST ARGUMENT
        PUSHAL    A           ;IS FIRST ON THE STACK
        CALLS     #3,YSUB     ;CALL SUBROUTINE
```

Figure 9.6(b) Assembly language equivalent for CALL YSUB(A,B,C) using CALLS

FORTRAN Subroutine

```
SUBROUTINE SUM(S,A)
INTEGER S,I,A(10)
S=0
DO 10 I=1,10
   S=S+A(I)
10 CONTINUE
RETURN
END
```

Figure 9.7 Relation of FORTRAN to assembly language

Equivalent Assembly Language Subroutine

```
        .TITLE    SAMPLE
        .ENTRY    SUM,^M<R2>
        MOVL      8(AP),R0      ;R0 GETS ADDRESS OF A
        CLRL      R2            ;WILL ACCUMULATE SUM
        CLRL      R1            ;SET INDEX TO ZERO
10$:    ADDL2     (R0)+,R2      ;R2:=R2+A(I)
        AOBLSS    #10,R1,10$    ;LOOP UNTIL DONE
        MOVL      R2,@4(AP)     ;STORE RESULT IN S
        RET                     ;RETURN
        .END
```

explained in the section on FORTRAN and Pascal functions. All the other registers must be saved. Therefore, if the subroutine uses R2, R3, and R5, bits 2, 3, and 5 must be set in the entry mask word, with .ENTRY SUB,^M<R2,R3,R5>. In Figure 9.7, only R2 must be saved.

The CALLG instruction uses the AP to point to the argument list. Therefore, 4(AP) and 8(AP) refer to the second and third locations of the list. These locations contain the **addresses** of the arguments (S and A in the FORTRAN or Pascal program). Since 4(AP) refers to the address of S, @4(AP) refers to the contents of S. Therefore, when the instruction MOVL R2,@4(AP) is executed, the contents of R2 is copied to S.

Pascal Calling Conventions

The normal way of declaring a procedure in Pascal is to use a procedure declaration such as:

```
PROCEDURE NAME (argument declarations);
BEGIN
   procedure body
END;
```

These statements must be within the body of the program which calls the procedure, of course. In order to tell Pascal that you are not providing the procedure body but rather expect the procedure to be an external subroutine, the following is all that need be done: Replace the procedure body section along with its BEGIN and END with the keyword EXTERNAL which is an extension to standard Pascal. Therefore, the preceding procedure could be written as

```
PROCEDURE NAME (argument declarations);
EXTERNAL;
```

Note that the argument declarations still must be included, even though this information does not appear to be used inside the Pascal program itself. However, the Pascal compiler performs error checking and type compatability verification, and therefore the compiler wants to see this information.

As an example of how this can be used, consider a Pascal program which calls an external procedure called YSUB which has three integer arguments. The program could be written as shown in Figure 9.8. This program will generate a calling sequence to a global symbol YSUB in exactly the same manner that FORTRAN did in the illustrations given in Figures 9.6(a) and 9.6(b).* Therefore, an assembly language program written for this calling sequence would work equally well with FORTRAN or Pascal.

One major point of difference to note is that VAX Pascal stores two-dimensional arrays by row, whereas FORTRAN stores them by column. (See Chapter 7.) In higher-dimensioned arrays, the same principles apply. Pascal varies the last subscript first; FORTRAN varies the first subscript first.

```
PROGRAM MAIN(INPUT,OUTPUT)
VAR
 A,B,C : INTEGER;
 . . .
PROCEDURE YSUB(VAR X,Y,Z : INTEGER);
EXTERNAL;
 . . .
 YSUB(A,B,C)
 . . .
```

Figure 9.8 Pascal call of an external procedure

---

* Here, we are speaking about the effects of the instructions. The actual sequence of instructions may vary, but will be equivalent just as the instructions in Figures 9.6a and 9.6b are equivalent.

FORTRAN and Pascal Functions

From the descriptions found in most FORTRAN and Pascal hand-books, one could imagine that function subprograms are entirely dif-ferent from subroutine subprograms. In fact, there is only one real difference. Functions return a single value that is available for use in an expression. This value may occupy one byte or it may occupy as many as two longwords for double-precision or complex data types. These words are always returned in the general registers R0 and R1. R1 is only used if more than one longword is needed. Argument lists for functions are implemented in exactly the same way as for sub-routines or procedures. Thus, we can see that the subroutine SUM of Figure 9.7 or its Pascal equivalent could be rewritten as a function as shown in Figure 9.9. Note that since the function is of INTEGER type and thus returns a 32-bit binary number, only R0 is needed for the result to be available to the calling program. The difference in the main program would be that, instead of the statement CALL SUM(S,A) or SUM(S,A), there would be a statement such as S = ISUM(A) or S: = ISUM(A);. In the Pascal function, the MODULE statement is an extension to standard Pascal that allows for the independent com-pilation of functions and procedures. In addition, all procedures and functions which are called globally must be preceded by [GLOBAL] as shown in Figure 9.9. See the VAX/VMS Pascal reference manual.

FORTRAN Common Blocks

FORTRAN has two methods for passing data back and forth between main programs and subroutines. The first we have seen is through argument lists. The other method that FORTRAN programs can use to communicate is by means of common blocks. If a main program and subroutine both contain the statement

```
COMMON   /DBLK/X,Y,Z
```

the X, Y, and Z refer to the same locations in the two programs,*
and thus communication can take place without argument lists or arrays of addresses being passed. The method operates by declaring the common block name as a global name, and a special array is set aside that is large enough for the variables in the common block. This space is set aside in each program, but the linker is designed to **overlay** blocks with the same global name. (That is, the common

---

* It is assumed that X, Y, and Z are declared consistently in both programs.

Figure 9.9 Equivalent of a FORTRAN or Pascal function

FORTRAN Function   **Pascal Function**

```
                                    MODULE SAMPLE(INPUT,OUTPUT)
                                    TYPE
                                        NMBS = ARRAY[1..10] OF INTEGER;
        INTEGER FUNCTION ISUM(A)    [GLOBAL]FUNCTION ISUM(VAR A : NMBS):INTEGER;
        INTEGER A(1:10),J           VAR
        ISUM=0                          J : INTEGER;
        DO 10 J=1,10                BEGIN
          ISUM=ISUM+A(J)              ISUM := 0;
10      CONTINUE                    FOR J:=1 TO 10 DO ISUM := ISUM + A[J];
        RETURN                      END;
        END                         END.
```

                   Equivalent Assembly Language Subroutine
```
        .TITLE      SAMPLE          SAMPLE FUNCTION
        .ENTRY      ISUM,^M<R2,R3>
        MOVL        4(AP),R3        ;R3 GETS ADDRESS OF A
        CLRL        R2              ;R2 IS COUNTER
        CLRL        R0              ;CLEAR SUM
10$:    ADDL2       (R3)+,R0        ;ADD A(J) TO SUM
        AOBLSS      #10,R2,10$      ;LOOP TEN TIMES
        RET                         ;RETURN
        .END
```

blocks in the various programs are assigned to the same area of memory.) This insures that the programs all refer to the same locations.

Figure 9.10 shows the assembly language equivalent of the FORTRAN COMMON statement. The **.PSECT** directive establishes that what follows is to go in a particular **program section.** The name DBLK identifies the particular section. The remaining nine parameters indicate that the section (or block) is:

1. Position independent. Since this is assumed to be numeric data, the actual addresses it occupies are irrelevant.
2. Overlaid as opposed to concatenated. The X, Y, and Z in this block are to occupy the same locations as the X, Y, and Z in blocks with the same name in other programs. Concatenated sections would be placed one after another and would use separate space.

Figure 9.10 The assembly language equivalent of a common block

FORTRAN
```
INTEGER X,Y(25),Z
COMMON /DBLK/X,Y,Z
```

Equivalent Assembly Language
```
        .PSECT      DBLK,PIC,OVR,REL,GBL,SHR,NOEXE,RD,WRT,LONG
X:      .BLKL       1
Y:      .BLKL       25
Z:      .BLKL       1
        .PSECT
```

3. Relocatable as opposed to absolute. In assembly language, it is possible to have absolute program sections, but in FORTRAN everything user defined is relocatable.

4. Global as opposed to local. If this section is to be accessible to other program modules, the name DBLK must be global.

5. Sharable. This data is sharable by other processes.

6. Nonexecutable. This is data, not executable code.

7. Readable. It is allowed to be read.

8. Writable. It is allowed to be written into or modified.

9. Longword aligned. This may improve efficiency of execution.

Although some of these options may not be implemented to do anything at present (such as 6 and 7), they must be specified or default values will be used. Error messages will result if the linker finds conflicting attributes for program sections with the same name.

After the .PSECT line, a sequence of labeled .BLKL's is given for the variables in the block. It is possible to use data-generating lines (such as .LONG). This would have the same effect as a FORTRAN BLOCK DATA module. Locations in the block would have data loaded in them, but care would have to be taken to avoid overwriting data specified in a different module. In order to avoid this problem, the FORTRAN standard prohibits the use of DATA statements for variables in common blocks, except in the BLOCK DATA module.

A block ends either when another .PSECT is encountered, or at the .END at the end of the program. If a .PSECT has no argument, it indicates that assembly is to go back to the regular program section. On the other hand, a subsequent .PSECT could have arguments, indicating the definition of another common block.

FORTRAN-77 Character Data Type

Since objects in FORTRAN character data type are of arbitrary length, they must be handled somewhat differently from fixed length objects such as reals or integers. In order to solve the problem of obtaining length information, the calling procedure for character arguments is somewhat more complicated than that described for ordinary variables in the preceding sections. Instead of the argument list containing the address of the data, it contains the address of a **descriptor.** As noted in Chapter 8, a descriptor is a two-longword block of data which contains the length information and the address of the actual data. There is also a code which identifies the object as character data. This allows descriptors to be used for other kinds of data, although standard use of FORTRAN only uses descriptors for character data.

A full discussion of descriptors is very complex and is well beyond the intended level of this book. However, the example in Figure 9.11 shows how descriptors are used to pass a simple character variable to a subroutine.

The descriptor contains a 16-bit word of 20 giving the length of the character string, an 8-bit byte of 14 which is a code saying this is a character string descriptor, an 8-bit byte of 1 saying that this is an unsubscripted variable (array descriptors are much more complex and give all the data about the structure of the array), and finally, there is a longword giving the address of the character string.

Obviously, R0 and R1 cannot be used for receiving the results of a character function which could be a very long string. As a result,

Figure 9.11 Passing character data

```
      FORTRAN                        Assembly Language
CHARACTER*20 A        A:     .BYTE     20        ;CHARACTER STRING
. . .                        . . .
CALL XYZ(A)           ARGS:  .LONG     1         ;ARGUMENT LIST
                             .ADDRESS  ADESC

                             . . .
                      ADESC: .WORD     20        ;STRING LENGTH
                             .BYTE     14        ;CHARACTER TYPE
                             .BYTE     1         ;UNSUBSCRIPTED
                             .ADDRESS  A         ;STRING LOCATION

                             . . .
                             CALLG     ARGS,XYZ
```

character functions are treated like subroutines. In other words, the string result is added as an extra argument at the beginning of the string. Thus, a call to the character function CFUN which might appear as

```
A=CFUN(B,C,D)
```

would be treated as if it were written

```
CALL CFUN(A,B,C,D)
```

9.6 Recursive Functions

For certain types of problems, such as language processing and artificial intelligence, **recursive functions** are important. In brief, a recursive function is a function that calls itself. Recursive functions developed from recursive definitions used in mathematics.

As an example of a recursive definition, consider the factorial function. An engineer might be content to define n factorial (or $n!$) as the product of the integers from 1 through n. ($0! = 1$ would be considered a special case.) However, while this definition is sufficient for computation, it is not in a very usable form for mathematical proofs. A mathematician would prefer the following definition:

$$0! = 1$$
$$n! = n * (n - 1)! \text{ if } n > 0$$

The first line indicates that zero factorial ($0!$) is equal to one, while the second line indicates that n factorial ($n!$) is equal to n times $(n-1)$ factorial. Definitions of this sort are amenable to use in a form of proof called **mathematical induction.** Inductive proofs have importance in computer science for proving program correctness.

While standard FORTRAN has no provision for recursive functions, most of the newer higher-level languages allow them. For example, ALGOL, APL, and Pascal are among the languages that allow function subprograms or subroutine subprograms to call themselves. Figure 9.12 shows a recursive Pascal function that computes factorials. Since this external function follows the VAX/VMS calling procedure, this function could be called by a Pascal, FORTRAN, or assembly language main program.

```
MODULE EXTFUN(INPUT,OUTPUT);
  [GLOBAL] FUNCTION FAC(N : INTEGER) : INTEGER;
    BEGIN
      IF N=0 THEN
        FAC := 1
      ELSE
        FAC := N*FAC(N-1);
    END;
  END.
```

Figure 9.12 Pascal factorial program

In order for a recursive program to work, it must save all the necessary data when the program calls itself. Note that fixed locations could not be used to save such information because the information would be overwritten during the next recursive call. Since a recursive program calls itself, it must be able to return to itself. Note also that there must be an eventual path through the function to the original calling program. Otherwise, an endless loop will result.

The VAX stack provides assembly language users with the most important tool for recursive programming. In order for recursive functions to work, required data must be saved on a stack every time the routine calls itself. The data items are then removed from the stack when the routine returns to itself. Figure 9.13 shows how the recursive factorial function in Figure 9.12 could be written in assembly language. Note that this program has two pieces of necessary information that must be saved on the stack. One item is the argument

```
         .TITLE   FACTORIAL ROUTINE
TEMP:    .BLKL    1                     ;TEMP LOCATION FOR N-1
         .ENTRY   FAC,0
         MOVL     @4(AP),R0             ;N IN R0
         BNEQ     10$                   ;SKIP ON UNLESS ZERO
         MOVL     #1,R0                 ;ZERO FACTORIAL IS 1
         RET
10$:     PUSHL    R0                    ;SAVE N ON STACK
         SUBL3    #1,R0,TEMP            ;N-1 IN TEMP
         PUSHAL   TEMP                  ;SET UP CALL ARGUMENT LIST
         CALLS    #1,FAC
         MULL2    (SP)+,R0              ;COMPUTE N*(N-1)FACTORIAL
         RET                           ;RETURN WITH RESULT IN R0
         .END
```

Figure 9.13 Recursive assembly language factorial routine

value N, and the other is the return address and calling frame, which are, of course, automatically saved on the stack.

As this function is entered, N is placed in R0 and N − 1 is placed in the temporary location TEMP. The program then tests to see if N is zero, in which case the result 0! = 1 is left in R0. If n is not equal to zero, the address of TEMP is pushed on the stack so that FAC can compute (N − 1)!. Care must be taken here, as the recursive call to FAC will destroy the value of TEMP. Normally, recursive programs should save such locations on the stack and restore them upon return. However, since TEMP is not used any further, it need not be saved. When control is returned, the value of (N − 1)! is in R0. This is multiplied by N which was saved in the stack and the result, N*(N − 1)! which equals N!, is left in R0.

Exercise Set 2

1. Write a subroutine similar to SUMUP, shown in Figure 9.2. However, your program will have a second input argument giving the size of the array to be summed. Then write a main program that reads 10 numbers, prints them, calls your subroutine to sum them up, and then does the same with 20 numbers. Each subroutine, including RNUM and PNUM (if used), must be independently assembled as separate modules that are linked together with global symbols. See Exercise 4, page 244.

2. Write a program that reads in a variable number of numbers (up to 100), sorts them, and prints out the sorted array. This program should be split into various independently assembled subroutines for each of the major functions. The separate subroutine modules should be linked using global symbols. Array addresses, sizes, and so on, should be passed in the general registers at each subroutine call. See Exercise 5, page 244.

3. The following is a proposed method for generating positive random numbers in the range 1–32767

   a. Start with any positive integer in the range.

   b. For each generated number: (i) Shift the original number left once. (ii) If the two high-order bits are both 1 or both 0, set the low-order bit to 0. If one of the bits is 1 and the other is 0, set the low-order bit to 1. In other words, the low-order bit becomes the exclusive OR of the sign bit and bit 14 of the shifted word. (iii) Then clear the sign bit to 0.

Write a FORTRAN or Pascal callable subroutine or function for generating such pseudo-numbers. Test your subroutine by calling it several hundred times and printing the results. Can you think of any other means of testing the randomness of these numbers? If so, incorporate them into your program.

4. Write a FORTRAN or Pascal callable subroutine that is called by the FORTRAN or Pascal statement

FORTRAN   **Pascal**

CALL   LOCS(A)   LOCS(A)

where A is a three-location INTEGER array. Your subroutine fills in A with the following:

– A(1) The memory address of the instruction that will be returned to when RET is executed.
– A(2) The location of the parameter list.
– A(3) The location of A itself.

Write a FORTRAN or Pascal main program that tests this subroutine. Verify its results from loading maps, symbol tables, and so on, as best as you can.

5. A recursive function known as Ackermann's function is defined over the nonnegative integers as follows:

$A(0,n) = n + 1$ for $n > 0$
$A(m,0) = A(m - 1,1)$ for $m > 0$
$A(m,n) = A[m - 1, A(m,n - 1)]$ for m and $n > 0$

Write a recursive subroutine in assembly language for computing Ackermann's function.

6. Write a FORTRAN or Pascal callable function that calls the recursive Ackermann's function of Exercise 5, above, and test it with a main program that calls the function for various values. (Warning: Do not use numbers larger than three for the arguments.)

7. Write a sorting program such as described in Exercise 2, on page 264 except that:
   a. The input and output subroutines and main program should be written in FORTRAN.
   b. The sorting program should be in assembly language.
   c. All arguments should be passed by placing them in common blocks.

Macros and Conditional Assembly

10.1 Introduction

This chapter introduces some features of the assembler which are of a higher-level nature and which go far beyond the basic assembly process of generating machine language code. Macros are means of generating large amounts of complex code with only a few simple statements. Conditional assembly allows variability in the code generated based upon control parameters which can govern the overall structure of a program or the expansion of macros. The macro feature is used in assemblers for virtually all modern machine languages. Essentially, macros are named blocks of program text that are parameterized and can be inserted at various places in a program. As such, macros are not specifically an assembly language feature because any language could be extended to make use of named blocks of program text. However, only a few higher-level languages have macro features, and so macros are often associated with assembly language.

This chapter will show the reader the fundamentals of writing macros and using conditional assembly. It should be noted, however, that these topics can become very complex, and the material in this chapter is only the beginning. In Chapter 11 we will see that there are a large number of macros that have been written to help the programmers make use of the **system services** of the VAX/VMS operating system. System services are programs and subroutines which allow the user to perform system-oriented tasks such as input and output. The system services macros or just **system macros** are stored in a library which is available to the assembly language programmer.

For the most part these macros are used to generate the calling sequences and argument lists for the system services routines. One such macro, which we have already been using, is $EXIT_S that generates a call to a subroutine called SYS$EXIT.

10.2 Repetitive Blocks of Code
The Need for Assembly Time Repetition

Quite often while solving a problem employing assembly language, one finds that large areas of a program are highly repetitive. Now the first reaction that should come to mind is that loops and subroutines are used for avoiding repetition. Although this is true, there are occasions when neither loops nor subroutines are the best method. A list of some possible reasons why loops or subroutines may be undesirable on occasion follows:

1. Programs with loops and subroutines will run slower than programs with equivalent repeated code. This is because loops need extra instructions for counting, indexing, testing exit conditions, and branching back. Similarly, subroutines have to be called and returned from; arguments have to be passed; and registers must be saved. On those occasions when speed is critical, subroutines and loops may need to be avoided (especially at the innermost nested levels of the program).

2. Although repetition in form may be called for, exact repetition may not. This situation could be handled by a subroutine with a complex argument structure, but often this is not a desirable solution. If the underlying process is very simple, the overhead of passing arguments and calling a subroutine may involve more overall code than if the desired code were simply repeated.

3. Finally, the code that is repeated may be data rather than instructions. Assume, for example, that an array is to be filled entirely with 5s. One way to handle this would be with an initialization routine that stores 5s over the array. Sometimes, however, initialization routines are inconvenient, and it is preferable just to assemble the array with the elements initialized to 5 by repeating the directive **.LONG 5** several times.

The preceding reasons are not intended to be exhaustive, but to give several ideas why one might have repetitive parts of a program instead of looping. It was this motivation that led to the development of **macro assemblers.** As we shall see in this chapter, the implementation of macros is so sophisticated that other uses will also become apparent.

Repeat Blocks

The simplest form of repetition that assembly language deals with is the **repeat block.** A repeat block is a block of code that is repeated verbatim some number of times. An example of the need for this is the case given before—an array filled with 5s. This could be assembled by placing a number of **.LONG 5** lines one after the other.

As a convenience to the user, the VAX assembly language has a special assembly directive for indicating repeats. The .REPT directive is used in the following context:

```
.REPT       expression
.
.           block of code
.
.ENDR
```

The block of code is repeated over and over, the number of times being given by the value of the expression following the .REPT directive. Figure 10.1(a) shows how a block of seven longwords containing the number 5 could be assembled using the .REPT directive. Figure 10.1(b) shows the equivalent code. Note that although this example has only one line between .REPT and .ENDR, there is no definite limit* and any needed amount of code is acceptable.

Also note the fact that the lines in the repeat block are repeated without change. There is no variability in the lines of text. This does **not** mean, however, that there is no room for variability in the generated machine language. Expressions and definitions can be used to produce variable results as is shown in the next section.

Repeat Blocks Using the Location Counter

Suppose that a programmer wished to create an array of 100 pairs of longwords. The first longword in each pair contains the starting address of the next pair of longwords. The second longword initially

---

* The only limit would be that the assembler's storage capability would eventually fill up.

(a) Repeat Block

```
.REPT    7
.LONG    5
.ENDR
```

(b) Equivalent Code

```
.LONG    5
.LONG    5
.LONG    5
.LONG    5
.LONG    5
.LONG    5
.LONG    5
```

Figure 10.1 Use of repeat block

contains zero. This arrangement of data is known as a singly linked list and is often used for data that must be rearranged. To rearrange data, one need only move several pointers or addresses. The data words themselves are not moved.*

This structure could be created with the following statements:

```
10$:      .ADDRESS           20$
          .LONG    0
20$:      .ADDRESS           30$
          .LONG    0
30$:      .ADDRESS           40$
          .LONG    0
40$:      .ADDRESS           50$
          .LONG    0
50$:      . . .
```

Clearly, this example is a repetitive structure, but it is not exact repetition because each of the addresses is different. In order to accomplish the preceding with repeat blocks, we use the special symbol period or **dot (.).** The dot symbol is called the **location counter.** As we saw in Chapter 4, the location counter in the assembler keeps track of the next available location. Since this location keeps changing, the value of dot keeps changing. For example, when assembling longwords, the value of dot is the address of the longword currently being assembled. The address of the next longword in memory can be designated by the expression dot plus four ($.+4$). The longword after that will have address ($.+8$). Using this, the linked list structure can be generated as shown in Figure 10.2.

---

* The VAX has a number of instructions specifically designed for manipulating data in linked lists. However, they are somewhat complex and extraneous to the topics at hand. Therefore, the reader is referred to Chapter 13 and the *VAX Architecture Handbook* for details on their use.

```
,REPT       100
,ADDRESS    ,+8
,LONG       0
,ENDR
```

Figure 10.2 Linked list
structure

Repeat Blocks with Other Symbols

Although it is often possible to represent variable data in terms of
complex expressions involving the symbol dot, sometimes it is quite
difficult if not nearly impossible to do so. In such cases, another
method of defining variable data may prove useful. This method
involves definition of symbols using the equal symbol (=). We have
already used the equal symbol to define assembly parameters in the
form of SIZE = 10. For the most part defining symbols with = and :
are similar. There is, however, one important difference. If a symbol
is defined more than once using :, it is a multiple-definition error;
and the program will be flagged with error messages. On the other
hand, symbols defined with = may be redefined with a subsequent
= . These definitions are repeated on both passes of assembly, and
the symbol will take on the new value for the remaining lines of
program after its redefinition.

Figure 10.3 shows how the list structure of Figure 10.2 could be
implemented by redefining symbols with = rather than using the dot
symbol. While this example may seem somewhat more complex, it
has the advantage of more generality. Consider, for example, the
problem of filling an array of eight longwords with the values of the

Figure 10.3 Linked list with redefined symbols

Repeat Block	Equivalent of Repeat Block	Equivalent with K Evaluated
`K=0`	`K=0`	
`A:` `,REPT` `100`	`A:`	`A:` `,ADDRESS` `A+8`
`K=K+8`	`K=K+8`	`,LONG` `0`
`,ADDRESS` `A+K`	`,ADDRESS` `A+K`	`,ADDRESS` `A+16`
`,LONG` `0`	`,LONG` `0`	`,LONG` `0`
`,ENDR`	`K=K+8`	`,ADDRESS` `A+24`
	`,ADDRESS` `A+K`	`,LONG` `0`
	`,LONG` `0`	`, , ,`
	`K=K+8`	
	`,ADDRESS` `A+K`	
	`,LONG` `0`	
	`, , ,`	

```
K = 1
F = 1
            .REPT      8
            .LONG      F
K = K + 1
F = F * K
            .ENDR
```

Figure 10.4 An array of
factorials

factorials of 1 through 8. Redefinition in a repeat block gives a simple, straightforward method for generating such an array (see Figure 10.4).

Note the fact that neither K nor F in Figure 10.4 is a location or even the name of a location. They are simply symbols that are assigned numeric values in the symbol table. They are not used as the address of an instruction or piece of data. Also note that computations such as K = K + 8 or K = K + 1 or F = F*K are computed at assembly time, not at execution time. These lines in the program do not produce any executable code.

This feature of assembly language can be a source of confusion, because higher-level languages, such as FORTRAN or Pascal, consider K = K + 8 or K: = K + 8; to be executable statements which are translated into machine language instructions such as ADDL2 #8,K. In assembly language, on the other hand, the statement K = K + 8 is a symbol table operation that occurs at assembly time and causes no computation to occur at execution time.

This distinction is easier to understand when the symbols represent addresses. In a higher-level language, a statement such as K = L + 4 (or K: = L + 4) will cause the **contents** of address K to be set equal to the contents of address L plus four. In assembly language, the statement K = L + 4 will cause K to be the address of the longword that follows the longword L.

10.3 Symbolic Expressions
Review of Expressions

In previous chapters, symbolic expressions have been used in a simple form. Usually these expressions have been limited to something of the form A − 6 or A + 6, meaning the address six locations before or after A. When dealing with repeat blocks, macros, and conditional assembly, much more complexity is needed to give more power from expressions. For one thing, we should recall that symbols need not be used exclusively for addresses. Symbolic names can be used for numbers that can be used for any purpose.

The assembly language programmer must be extremely careful to understand the relationships between the assembly process itself and program execution. For example, as stated above, the line of assembly code $K = K + 1$ does not cause K to be incremented at execution time. As stated above, it does not even cause the generation of any executable machine language code. What it does do is to cause the entry for K in the assembler's symbol table to be incremented. Do not confuse $K = K + 1$ with INCL K. They are entirely different statements.

It is also important to note that there is a distinction between symbols for values that change when the program is relocated, symbols for values that do not change, and global symbols that are defined in other modules. For example, symbols used for addresses in the current module have values that must be changed when the program is relocated to an execution area. Such symbols are called **relocatable.** The values of symbols used for numbers do not change during relocation. In addition, there are addresses that have fixed values. These addresses are called **absolute addresses** and are used by the operating system for accessing special purpose locations as described in Chapter 15. Symbols for values that do not change when the program is relocated are called **absolute.** Symbols in the symbol table are distinguished as being relocatable or absolute. A third kind of symbol is the global symbol, but since global symbols are much more complex, they will not be considered further in this section.

Rules for Forming Expressions

Expressions can be used in assembly language almost anywhere that a number or value is required. Expressions are formed by combining symbols and numbers with the operators $+$, $-$, $*$, and $/$, almost as in Pascal or FORTRAN. Parentheses can be used, except that angle brackets ($<$ and $>$) are used for left and right parentheses. It is extremely important to note that there is no operator precedence. Expressions are evaluated from left to right, with parentheses having their usual effect. For example, $X + Y * <A + <5 * B / K>>$ would be an acceptable expression. Because of the left-to-right evaluation, the expression $1 + 2 * 3$ is equal to 9, not 7. (The assemblers for some computers do not follow these rules.)

Just as symbols have types, expressions will have those same types. Rather than enumerate an exhaustive set of rules for determining the type of expressions, the following is a set of commonsense guidelines that will handle all but the most unusual cases.*

1. An expression must evaluate to something that can be entered in the symbol table. Thus, it should be one of the following:
   a. A number, or an absolute address.
   b. An address of a location within the program, or a location that is displaced a fixed amount from a location in the program; for example, the location 100 bytes beyond the end of your program.
   c. A global address plus or minus a fixed number.
2. An expression composed entirely of numbers and absolute symbols will be absolute.
3. A relocatable symbol plus or minus an absolute value will be a relocatable expression. The reason is that a location that is a fixed amount from some location in a program will move (and therefore have to be relocated) as the program is moved.
4. The difference between two relocatable symbols defined in the same program section is **absolute.** The reason is that the difference between two addresses is the number of locations between those two addresses. If both are relocatable and in the same program section, then both will change by the same amount when the program section is moved. Therefore, the number of locations between them will remain **fixed.**

The preceding rules can, of course, apply to the subexpressions of a complex expression. In addition, there are two rules that apply to the use of multiplication and division.

5. With multiplication, at least one operand should be absolute. Then the multiplication can be thought of as a repeated addition. For example, if A, B, and C are relocatable, consider the following expression: $<3*A> - <2*B> - C$. This could be rewritten as: $A + A + A - B - B - C$, which is equivalent to $A - B + A - B + A - C$. Note that each subexpression is the difference between two relocatables and is therefore absolute. Therefore, the entire expression is absolute.
6. With division, both operands should be absolute. It is hard to imagine anything else making sense. However, this does not

---

* Expressions which do not fall within these simple rules or which involve global symbols will be flagged by the VAX assembler as *complex*. Complex expressions are evaluated by the linker.

preclude the use of division in complex expressions that involve relocatable parts. For example, if the difference between two addresses was desired in longwords rather than in bytes, the following expression would work: <A − B>/4. Note that this is really the quotient of two absolute subexpressions (assuming that A and B are relocatable). Also note that the preceding expression is preferable to the seemingly equivalent <A/4> − <B/4>. Although this expression may work on the VAX in some contexts, where the evaluation is performed by the linker, it may give problems or produce errors in contexts where the assembler must determine the value.

An Example Using Expressions

The use of expressions and symbols that are numbers is important for ordinary assembly language programming because it gives the programmer the ability to modify the program easily and because it makes the program easier to read and document. For example, consider a program that prints out a message and surrounds the message with three layers of asterisks, such as

```
*************************
*************************
*************************
*** THIS IS A MESSAGE ***
*************************
*************************
*************************
```

Because of the conspicuous presentation of this message, it must be very important. Figure 10.5 illustrates a subroutine for printing this message.

By using symbols and expressions, modifications can be made to the program quite easily. For example, if the message were to be surrounded by five layers of asterisks instead of three, all that would need to change is the sixth line of the program, which would now state BOXES = 5. If the asterisks were to be changed to at signs (@), the fifth line of the program could be changed to read MARK = ˆA"@". The operator ˆA is used to define a value to be equal to the ASCII code for the string of characters which follows. Thus, ˆA"@" has the value of the ASCII code for the at sign which is ˆX40. The program is assumed to use a global subroutine PLINE for printing a character stored as a byte in R0.

Figure 10.5 Message-printing subroutine

```
;SUBROUTINE MPRINT TO PRINT A MESSAGE SURROUNDED BY BOXES
;
        .TITLE  MPRINT          MESSAGE PRINT
        .EXTERNAL               PLINE
MARK=^A"*"
BOXES=3
MSG:    .ASCII  "THIS IS A MESSAGE"
EMSG:
MSG_LENGTH=EMSG-MSG+<2*BOXES>
MSG_BUF:
        .BLKB   MSG_LENGTH
;
        .ENTRY  MPRINT,^M<R2>
        BSBW    HORIZ           ;PRINT HORIZONTAL STRIPES
        MOVAB   MSG_BUF,R1
        BSBW    VERT            ;PUT VERTICAL MARKS IN BUFFER
        MOVAB   MSG,R0
        MOVAB   EMSG,R2         ;R2 MARKS END OF STRING
10$:    MOVB    (R0)+,(R1)+     ;MOVE CHARACTER FROM MSG TO BUFFER
        CMPL    R0,R2           ;TEST FOR END OF STRING
        BNEQ    10$
        BSBW    VERT            ;FINAL VERTICAL MARKS IN BUFFER
        BSBW    PBUF            ;PRINT MESSAGE LINE
        BSBW    HORIZ           ;PRINT HORIZONTAL STRIPES
        RET
;
HORIZ:  MOVL    #BOXES,R2       ;R2 IS COUNT OF LINES
10$:    CLRL    R0              ;R0 IS INDEX IN BUFFER
20$:    MOVB    #MARK,MSG_BUF[R0];PUT MARK IN BUFFER
        AOBLSS  #MSG_LENGTH,R0,20$;LOOP UNTIL BUFFER FULL
        BSBW    PBUF            ;PRINT LINE OF MARKS
        SOBGTR  R2,10$          ;PRINT #BOXES LINES
        RSB
;
VERT:   MOVL    #BOXES,R0       ;INSERT #BOXES MARKS
10$:    MOVB    #MARK,(R1)+     ;R1 POINTS INTO BUFFER
        SOBGTR  R0,10$          ;LOOP UNTIL #BOXES INSERTED
        RSB
;
PBUF:   PUSHR   #^M<R0,R1>      ;SAVE R0 AND R1 ON STACK
        MOVAL   MSG_BUF,R0      ;R0 POINTS TO BUFFER
        MOVZWL  #MSG_LENGTH,R1  ;R1 CONTAINS LENGTH
        JSB     PLINE           ;PRINT THE LINE
        POPR    #^M<R0,R1>      ;RESTORE R0 AND R1
        RSB
;
        .END
```

275

The Effect of Two Assembly Passes

A final consideration involved with expressions and the use of expressions concerns the order in which symbols are defined and used. Recall that two passes are needed in the assembly process because an instruction may refer to a symbolic address that is defined later on in the program. There are, however, cases where a value must be known on the first pass. In such cases, the symbols used in expressions for such a value must have been defined previously.

Essentially, since the symbol table is generated in the first pass, any symbols used in ways that affect the values in the symbol table must be defined before being used. A simple example of such a case is the direct definition case, which will usually result in an error. For example,

```
A=B
B=5
```

will leave A undefined at the end of the first pass, and during much of the second pass. Clearly, this problem could be fixed easily by exchanging the two lines.

A more complex problem arises when an expression is used in a way that affects the size of the program. If such an expression contains undefined symbols, it will adversely affect all subsequent addresses for the remainder of the program. For example,

```
X:          .BLKL    A
Y:          .BLKL    1
A=5
```

Since A is undefined on the first pass, the assembler will not know how many longwords to set aside for the array X. For lack of anything better to do, the assembler uses 0 for undefined symbols. Therefore, the address Y will be the same as the address X. However, on the second pass, A is defined as 5 so the address Y will come out to be 20 greater than the address X. This discrepancy will be flagged with a message such as, "Expression is not absolute." The reason for this message is that undefined expressions are assumed by the assembler to be global or relocatable symbols which will be defined later.

Furthermore, whenever an expression is used in such a manner that its value must be known at assembly time, the expression not only must consist of entirely predefined symbols, but also must be simple enough to be evaluated by the assembler. For obvious reasons, therefore, complex expressions that must be evaluated by the linker cannot be used.

Exercise Set 1

1. Show how the following repeat blocks would assemble in machine language. Assume that they are loaded starting at location ^X1200.

   a.   `.REPT     5`
        `.ADDRESS .+5`
        `.ENDR`

   b. `.REPT     7`
        `.LONG     5`
        `.ADDRESS .-4`
        `.ENDR`

   c. `K=0`
        `.REPT     4`
     `K=K+4`
        `.ADDRESS.+K`
        `.ENDR`

   d. `K=0`
        `.REPT     5`
     `K=K+1`
        `.REPT     K`
        `.LONG     K*3`
        `.ENDR`
        `.ENDR`

2. Write a repeat block that generates an array of 100 longwords labeled NUMBS. This array should be set to contain the numbers 1 through 100.

   a. Do the problem using dot expressions.

   b. Do the problem using symbol redefinition with =.

3. Assume that $I=2$, $J=3$, and $K=5$ are defined values for the assembly language symbols, I, J, and K. What are the values of the following expressions in hexadecimal?

   a. `I*J+K`

   b. `I+J*K`

   c. `J/I+2`

   d. `I+J/K`

   e. `I+<J*K>/K`

   f. `I+<<J*K>+K>`

   g. `I+J*<I+J>`

   h. `<I+J>*I+J`

4. Assume that A, B, and C are relocatable symbols (that is, labels that refer to locations in the program). Also, I, J, and K are absolute symbols (that is, symbols that refer to fixed numbers). Which of the following expressions are absolute, relocatable, or neither (i.e., complex)?

   a. `A+I`

   b. `B-K`

   c. `A-B`

   d. `A+B`

   e. `A+K-B`

   f. `<A-B>+<A-C>`

   g. `<A-K>+<A-J>`

   h. `<A+K>+<<B-C>*4>`

5. The following program produces a number of errors due to improper order definitions. Indicate which statements are mis-

placed and which statements would be flagged with errors. (Note: Even though this is not a program, because there are no executable lines, reordering the statements could cause it to assemble without error.)

```
I=3
A:          .BLKL    K
B:          .BLKL    D-C
C:          .BLKL    I
D:          .BLKL    K+I
K=J
J=I+5
            .END
```

6. Reorder the statements in the program in Exercise 5, so that it could be assembled without assembly errors.

10.4 Macros
A Simple Macro

Macros are complex blocks of program text that can be repeated a number of times in a program. Unlike repeat blocks, the repeated code generated by a macro need not all be in one place but may be placed at various points in the program. Also unlike repeat blocks, macros allow considerable variability to the repeated code.

Essentially, macros are named blocks of code. Anywhere the name is used in the operation field, the block of code will be inserted into (copied into) the program. In addition, there may be **parameters,** or symbols, that are modified or substituted for each time the macro is invoked, or **called.**

As an example, note that there is no instruction on the VAX for adding 64-bit integers. Suppose that the problem that you are working on requires double precision arithmetic. (See Chapter 6, pages 158ff.) Therefore, it would be necessary to have the equivalent of the following lines of code whenever you added quadwords.

```
ADDL3      A,B,C
MOVL       A+4,C+4
ADWC       B+4,C+4
```

Now, it would be convenient to have this block of code generated by using a symbol, such as ADDQ3. In order to do this, we must first

```
.MACRO    ADDQ3    A,B,C
ADDL3     A,B,C
MOVL      A+4,C+4
ADWC      B+4,C+4
.ENDM     ADDQ3
```

Figure 10.6 Simple macro
definition

define the block to be a macro with the name ADDQ3. We will use
the symbols A, B, and C for the parameter names. Any symbol names
are usable as long as they are not confused with any other symbols
in the program.

After the names are chosen, we must then define the macro. This
starts out with the directive .MACRO ADDQ3 A,B,C and is followed
by the lines of code to be generated each time the macro is called.
Finally, the directive .ENDM ADDQ3 is used to signal the end of the
macro definition. The name of the macro, ADDQ3, is placed on the
.ENDM line to aid the assembler and programmer in dealing with
nested macros, which are discussed later in this chapter. Figure 10.6
shows the full macro definition.

Macro Definition versus Macro Expansion

The macro definition itself does not cause any code to be placed into
the program. Code is generated only when the macro is **called.** The
macro call consists of the name of the macro, which is used as if it
were an opcode, followed by the arguments to be substituted for the
parameters. Figure 10.7 shows a number of examples of macro calls
along with the effective generated code. Figure 10.7(a) shows a simple
straightforward macro call, where the symbols X, Y, and Z are to be
substituted for parameters A, B, and C. In Figure 10.7(b), A, B, and
C are substituted for themselves, which causes no confusion.

In Figure 10.7(c), COST, PROFIT, and PRICE are substituted for
A, B, and C, showing that the number of characters substituted need
not be the same as in the parameter name. A key point here is that
character strings are substituted, not addresses. It would be improper
to say that the address of PRICE is substituted for the address A. In
fact, the symbol A may never even be used as an address. What happens is that the macro processor replaces all of the substitutable
parameters with the argument **character strings.** The resulting code
is then processed by the assembler as normal assembly language.

Figure 10.7(d) shows how character string substitution operates.
Here, the character strings $X+4$, $Y+8$, and $Z+12$ are substituted for
A, B, and C. Note here that the substitution is purely a character

Macro Call		Generated Code	
a. ADDQ3	X,Y,Z	ADDL3	X,Y,Z
		MOVL	X+4,Z+4
		ADWC	Y+4,Z+4
b. ADDQ3	A,B,C	ADDL3	A,B,C
		MOVL	A+4,C+4
		ADWC	B+4,C+4
c. ADDQ3	COST,PROFIT,PRICE	ADDL3	COST,PROFIT,PRICE
		MOVL	COST+4,PRICE+4
		ADWC	PROFIT+4,PRICE+4
d. ADDQ3	X+4,Y+8,Z+12	ADDL3	X+4,Y+8,Z+12
		MOVL	X+4+4,Z+12+4
		ADWC	Y+8+4,Z+12+4

Figure 10.7 Simple macro calls and expansion

string substitution. The string $X+4$ is substituted for A, even in the expression $A+4$. Therefore, we get $X+4+4$ for the substitution, not $X+8$.

Because of the way that this particular macro was written in Figure 10.6, the arguments must be addresses or expressions for addresses. Other addressing modes such as R0, @8(AP), and X[R1] cannot be used because they would produce the following kinds of expressions which are illegal in the contexts used:

```
R0+4
@8(AP)+4
X[R1]+4
```

The macro in Figure 10.8 is a suggested rewrite of the macro in Figure 10.6 which will work for most of the addressing modes.

By putting the operands of the instructions on the stack to do the arithmetic, the symbols substituted from the macro arguments do not have to appear in expressions. Furthermore, they are used only

```
.MACRO   ADDQ3      A,B,C
MOVQ     B,-(SP)
MOVQ     A,-(SP)
ADDL2    (SP)+,4(SP)
ADWC     (SP)+,4(SP)
MOVQ     (SP)+,C
.ENDM    ADDQ3
```

Figure 10.8 Rewrite of macro in Figure 10.6

once and with quadword instructions. This would be important if the substitutable argument was something like (R5)+, or even X[R1]. Using the macro with the arguments, R0, @8(AP), and X[R1], we would have

```
ADDQ3     R0,@8(AP),X[R1]
```

which would expand to

```
MOVQ      @8(AP),-(SP)
MOVQ      R0,-(SP)
ADDL2     (SP)+,4(SP)
ADWC      (SP)+,4(SP)
MOVQ      (SP)+,X[R1]
```

The use of the stack in this example is a little bit tricky and involves careful examination of the effects of the operands −(SP), (SP)+, and 4(SP). It is suggested that you work out some examples of your own, noting the contents of the stack at each instruction. (See Exercise 5 on page 288.) It should be noted that this macro will not work properly with addressing modes involving the SP. However, it should work for all other addressing modes.

Macro Parameters in Other Fields

It is important to understand that when macros are called, they are **expanded** by replacing the parameter occurrences with the argument character strings. It should be noted that parameters can occur anywhere within the macro definition and are identified by the use of the name surrounded by punctuation of some sort. Figure 10.9 shows

(a) Definition

```
        .MACRO   TEST   ABC,DEF,HIJ
ABC:    DEF      HIJ
        INCL     HIJ
        .ENDM    TEST
```

(b) Macro Call

```
        TEST     LOOP1,CLRL,COUNT
```

(c) Macro Expansion

```
LOOP1:  CLRL     COUNT
        INCL     COUNT
```

Figure 10.9 A macro with various substitutable parts

a macro definition and expansion that illustrates how various fields can be substituted.

First, note that the lines of code in the macro definition do not constitute correct assembly code by themselves. The first line contains DEF in the opcode field, which is not a legal VAX instruction. However, DEF is a substitutable parameter, and in the macro expansion, DEF does not occur but is replaced with CLRL, which is a legal VAX opcode.

Another point this example shows is that labels can be substitutable. In fact, it is almost always necessary for a label that appears in a macro definition to be a substitutable parameter. Suppose that ABC were not substitutable; then if the macro was called two or more times, ABC would appear as a label more than once and would result in a multiple-definition error.

10.5 Conditional Assembly

Definition of Conditional Assembly

Often, especially in large programs, portions of code are sometimes needed and sometimes not needed. Examples include

1. Portions of a program that are needed for debugging and not needed when the program is running.
2. Macros and subroutines that are needed for one model of computer but not needed, or differ for another model.
3. Code that is needed to support optional computer features.
4. Portions of a macro that need to be expanded for some arguments, but not for others.

Code that is not needed can be removed from the program to save memory. However, it is not necessarily an easy task to remove code from a program. Editing out areas of a large program is a risky proposition at best. There is always the chance of removing too much or of removing the wrong things. It is also difficult to go back to the original code if you change your mind. **Conditional assembly** is a method for dealing with these problems.

Conditional assembly allows a certain identified block of code in a program to be included or to be ignored by the assembler. The block of code is called a **conditional block** and is delimited by two assembly directives. The beginning of the block is marked by .IF and the end by .ENDC. The .IF directive includes a description of a logical condition. If the condition is true, the code in the conditional block is assembled into the program. Otherwise, the entire block is skipped over as if it did not exist.

Example of Conditional Assembly

Figure 10.10 shows a simple example of a conditional block. The value of the symbol TEST determines whether or not the block of code is assembled. If TEST is **not equal** to 0, then the code is assembled. Otherwise it is skipped over.

Of special note is the fact that the block of code contains the definition of the label XCODE. Consequently, if this block of code is skipped over, references to the symbol XCODE would result in an error flag for an undefined symbol. To prevent this, it would be necessary either to

1. Include all references to XCODE in conditional blocks that are also **skipped** when TEST equals 0, or
2. Include an alternative definition for XCODE that is **included** when TEST equals 0.

Also note that this conditional block generates machine instructions and therefore affects the location counter. Therefore, the symbol TEST must be defined earlier in the program. Usually symbols that control conditional blocks are defined with the equal sign (=) early in the program where they can be easily accessed for modification.

Figure 10.10 uses the relational operator NOT_EQUAL for **not equal**. As would be expected, the six arithmetic relations EQUAL, NOT_EQUAL, LESS_THAN, LESS_EQUAL, GREATER_EQUAL, and GREATER (for equal, not equal, less than, less than or equal, greater than or equal, and greater than) are all usable. They all compare their argument expression with zero. The syntax is

```
.IF        relation, expression
```

```
         .IF      NOT_EQUAL,TEST
         MOVL     X,Y
XCODE:   INCL     R0
         ADDL2    W,R1
         .ENDC
```

Figure 10.10 Conditional block

For example,

```
.IF      GREATER_EQUAL,X-5
```

will skip over code unless the value of the expression $X - 5$ is greater than or equal to zero. In other words, X must be greater than or equal to 5 in order for the conditional code to be assembled.

Other Conditional Assembly Codes

In addition to the preceding arithmetic conditions, there are six symbolic conditions. These are

1. DEFINED The condition is true if the argument is a defined symbol. For example, .IF DEFINED,XYZW will generate code if XYZW is a defined symbol in the symbol table.
2. NOT_DEFINED This is the opposite of DEFINED.
3. BLANK The condition is true if the following macro parameter is substituted with blanks. For example, consider the following macro.

```
.MACRO  NULL    X,Y,Z
.IF     BLANK,Y
.LONG   X,Z
.ENDC
.ENDM   NULL
```

The macro call NULL 5, ABC,6 will generate no code, whereas NULL 5,,6 will generate two longwords of code. Note that if .LONG has more than one argument, multiple longwords will be generated.

4. NOT_BLANK This is the opposite of BLANK.
5. IDENTICAL This condition code is true if the following two macro type arguments are identical character strings after macro parameter substitution.
6. DIFFERENT This is the opposite of IDENTICAL.

Clearly, the last four conditional assembly codes are only usable within a macro definition. In fact, one of the main uses of conditional assembly is within macros. Conditional assembly can be used to control the lines of code that are assembled depending upon argument values, or even upon the number of times the macro is called. For example, consider a macro which generates the calling sequence for a subroutine called SUBR. This subroutine has three arguments which are passed in an argument list using the standard VAX/VMS calling sequence described in the previous chapter. Because of the nature of SUBR, the second and third arguments are optional; however, SUBR still requires an argument list of three longwords. If an argument is being explicitly passed, its address must be in the list; if the argument is being left out, the illegal address zero is put in the list. Figure 10.11 shows how such a macro might be written.

Note that the macro in Figure 10.11 tests to see if B and C are blank. If so, the number zero is pushed on the argument list. Otherwise, the appropriate address is pushed on the stack. Note that one thing must be done for BLANK and another for NOT_BLANK. This is much like the IF-THEN-ELSE structure used in higher-level languages. In fact, the VAX assembler has an else for conditional assemblies. It is .IF_FALSE. This directive causes code to be assembled if it was being skipped, or skipped if it was being assembled. There are also two more similar conditional directives: .IF_TRUE which puts the conditional assembly back to its original condition and .IF_TRUE_FALSE which causes code to be assembled regardless of the condition. Figure 10.12 shows how the macro in Figure 10.11 could be rewritten somewhat more concisely using .IF_FALSE so that the full reverse condition need not be spelled out.

```
.MACRO   DO_SUBR   A,B,C
.EXTERNAL   SUBR
.IF      NOT_BLANK,C
PUSHAL   C                 ;PUSH ADDRESS OF C
.ENDC
.IF      BLANK,C
PUSHL    #0                ;OR ZERO
.ENDC
.IF      NOT_BLANK,B
PUSHAL   B                 ;PUSH ADDRESS OF B
.ENDC
.IF      BLANK,B
PUSHL    #0                ;OR ZERO
.ENDC
PUSHAL   A                 ;PUSH REQUIRED ADDRESS OF A
CALLS    #3,SUBR           ;THEN CALL SUBR
.ENDM    DO_SUBR
```

Figure 10.11 A macro for calling a subroutine

```
,MACRO   DO_SUBR   A,B,C
,EXTERNAL   SUBR
,IF      NOT_BLANK,C
PUSHAL   C                   ;PUSH ADDRESS OF C
,IF_FALSE
PUSHL    #0                  ;OR ZERO
,ENDC
,IF      NOT_BLANK,B
PUSHAL   B                   ;PUSH ADDRESS OF B
,IF_FALSE
PUSHL    #0                  ;OR ZERO
,ENDC
PUSHAL   A                   ;PUSH REQUIRED ADDRESS OF A
CALLS    #3,SUBR             ;THEN CALL SUBR
,ENDM    DO_SUBR
```

Figure 10.12 Rewrite of macro for calling a subroutine

10.6 Nesting and Recursion

Without exploring the subject in depth, we can note that conditional blocks can be nested within other conditional blocks, and macro definitions can appear within macros. The .IF–.ENDC and .MACRO–.ENDM directives must occur in pairs like parentheses. This pairing allows complex structures for multiple decisions and for macros that define other macros when called to be constructed. In addition, the use of the macro name on the .ENDM directive helps make nesting clear.

Also note that macro expansions can call other macros. This causes no problem because, after expansion, control is returned to the assembler proper which may encounter additional macro calls. This produces additional generated code that is simply added to whatever is already there.

An interesting point here is that a macro may call itself. This forms a kind of loop where the macro is expanded repeatedly. However, as in normal programming loops, there must be a way to end the loop. Thus, if a macro does call itself, that call must be within a conditional block which eventually is skipped over. Macros of this sort are called **recursive macros**, since they behave in much the same way as recursive subroutines, which were described in Chapter 9. Figure 10.13 shows a recursive macro for generating a table of numbers from 1 through N by calling the macro TABLE N. Note that TABLE calls the macro TAB, which is the recursive macro. In the .IF line, N is enclosed by parentheses because it might be replaced by an expression.

Figure 10.13 A recursive macro

```
;
;MACRO FOR GENERATING A TABLE OF CONSECUTIVE NUMBERS
;
        .MACRO  TABLE  N
TABK=1                                  ;INITIALIZE TABK
        TAB     N                       ;START PROCESS
        .ENDM   TABLE
;
;RECURSIVE MACRO TO BE USED BY TABLE
;
        .MACRO  TAB    N
        .IF     LESS_EQUAL,TABK-<N>  ;HAVE WE GENERATED ENOUGH
        .LONG   TABK                 ;NO, PRODUCE LONGWORD
TABK=TABK+1
        TAB     N                    ;GENERATE MORE RECURSIVELY
        .ENDC
        .ENDM   TAB
```

Exercise Set 2

1. Given the following macro definitions:

```
.MACRO  ORD    A,B
MOVL    A,B
CLRL    A
SUBL2   B,A
.ENDM   ORD
.MACRO  SPEC   A,B,C
MOVL    #A,AA
B       A,C
CLRB    C+6
.ENDM   SPEC
```

show the assembly language expansions resulting from the following macro calls:

a. ORD   SUM,TOTAL   b. ORD   R0,(R1)+

c. ORD   A[R0],B   d. ORD   B,A

e. SPEC   XMAX,MOVL,W   f. SPEC   1000,ADDL2,C+6

g. SPEC   X,ORD,1000   h. SPEC   B,ORD,A

2. Assuming that the symbols A and B are defined as A = 5 and B = 7, what code, if any, is assembled by the following conditional assemblies?

```
a.  ,IF      EQUAL ,A-3         b.  ,IF      NOT_EQUAL ,A-3
    MOVL     X,Y                    MOVL     #3,W
    ,ENDC                          ,ENDC

c.  ,IF      GREATER ,B         d.  C=0
    MOVL     R,R0                   ,IF                  LESS_THAN ,B-4
    ,ENDC                          C=1

                                   ,ENDC
                                   ,IF      EQUAL ,C
                                   MOVL     H,Q
                                   ,ENDC

e.  C=0                         f.  C=0
             ,IF      EQUAL ,B               ,IF      NOT_EQUAL ,B
    C=1                            C=1

             ,IF      EQUAL ,C               ,IF      EQUAL ,C-1
             MOVL     U,V                    MOVL     I,J
             ,ENDC                          ,ENDC
             MOVL     L,M                    MOVL     G,F
             ,ENDC                          ,ENDC
```

3. Write a two-argument version of the macro ADDQ3 shown in Figure 10.6 on page 279. This macro should be called ADDQ2 and cause the first quadword argument to be added to the second, just as ADDL2 adds one longword to another. What addressing modes work with your macro? Which do not? Is there any way to make the macro work with all addressing modes?

4. Rewrite the macro of Exercise 3, so that it includes conditional assembly directives that check to see if the first argument is #1. If so, the code can be simplified considerably. For example, the INCL instruction could be used instead of ADDL2 and there would be no source operand to deal with.

5. Referring to Figure 10.8, you are given the following macro definition:

```
,MACRO   ADDQ3      A,B,C
MOVQ     B,-(SP)
MOVQ     A,-(SP)
ADDL2    (SP)+,4(SP)
ADWC     (SP)+,4(SP)
MOVQ     (SP)+,C
,ENDM    ADDQ3
```

Show the expansion of the macro call

```
ADDQ3    X,Y,Z
```

Go through the instructions generated by the expansion as they would occur during execution. Show how the contents of the quadwords X, Y, and Z and the stack change as each instruction is executed.

6. Imagine that there is a simple computer with an architecture similar to the VAX in that it has a memory of 32-bit two's complement longwords. However, it only has one general register called "the accumulator." All operations must operate through the accumulator and there are ten instructions, as follows:

LDA   M   Load memory location M into the accumulator.

STA   M   Store the accumulator into location M.

ADDA   M   Add the contents of M to the accumulator.

SUBA   M   Subtract the contents of M from the accumulator.

JUMP   M   Jump to location M.

JMI   M   Jump to location M if the accumulator is negative.

JZ   M   Jump to location M if the accumulator is 0.

READ   Read a number into the accumulator.

PRINT   Print out the value of the accumulator.

STOP   Stop execution.

The following program prints out the first 10 powers of two by computing 2X as X + X:

```
         .TITLE  HYPOTHETICAL COMPUTER PROGRAM
START:   LDA     MTEN      ;INITIALIZE COUNT TO
         STA     COUNT     ;NEGATIVE 10
         LDA     ONE       ;INITIALIZE POWER
         STA     POWER
LOOP:    LDA     POWER     ;MULTIPLY POWER BY TWO
         ADDA    POWER
         STA     POWER
         PRINT             ;PRINT POWER
         LDA     COUNT     ;INDEX COUNT
         ADDA    ONE
         STA     COUNT
         JMI     LOOP      ;LOOP WHILE NEGATIVE
         STOP              ;AND THEN STOP
MTEN:    .LONG   -10       ;INITIAL VALUE OF COUNT
ONE:     .LONG   1         ;THE CONSTANT ONE
COUNT:   .BLKL   1         ;VARIABLE DATA AREA
POWER:   .BLKL   1
         .END    START
```

Write a set of macros that simulates this hypothetical machine by replacing each instruction with VAX instructions that have an equivalent effect. Test your macros with the sample program.

*7. Write a program for the hypothetical machine described in Exercise 6 that reads two signed numbers and multiplies them together producing a signed result. Is it possible to make your program efficient even though there is no shift instruction in the hypothetical machine? Test your program with the macros you wrote for Exercise 6.

10.7 Advanced Macro Techniques

Keyword Arguments

There are two methods used by the VAX assembler for identifying the arguments in a macro call. The simpler one is the one which we have been using. This identifies the arguments by their relative positions. Arguments passed in this method are called **positional arguments.** For example, in the following macro definition and call:

```
.MACRO   MAC      A,B,C
.  .  .
.ENDM    MAC
.  .  .
MAC      XXX,YYY,ZZZ
```

the argument XXX would be substituted for A,YYY for B, and ZZZ for C. The matching is order dependent.

The other method is called **keyword argument passing.** Here the names used in the original macro are matched to the argument using an equal sign. For example, using the preceding example, the following call:

```
MAC      B=YYY,C=ZZZ,A=XXX
```

would again substitute XXX for A, YYY for B, and ZZZ for C. However, because the substitutions are identified by name or keyword, the order is not important; and in fact, this illustration intentionally has the arguments out of order. The price that is paid for the ability to scramble the order is that more typing is required. However, there are often advantages which outweigh the extra typing.

The main purpose for this kind of macro call is that complex macros, such as the system macros described in Chapter 11, often have many arguments, and it is difficult to keep track of the order in which they were specified in the original definition. This problem is compounded by the fact that software is often revised so that such macros need modification. Another factor is that quite often, many of the parameters in a complex macro are optional and need only be specified under special circumstances. As a result, the positional notations would require many commas as place markers for the unused or blank arguments. For example, consider a macro called **GENERATE** which has 15 substitutable parameters. If only two arguments, the sixth and the thirteenth, were given for a specific call, the positional method of calling the macro might appear as

```
GENERATE    ,,,,,FTAB,,,,,,,XLOC
```

Note that there are fewer than fourteen commas because XLOC is being substituted for the thirteenth parameter, and since nothing need be specified for the fourteenth and fifteenth parameters, the trailing commas are not needed. However, if the sixth parameter had been named FUNC, and the thirteenth VALUE, the macro could be called using the explicit names in the following way:

```
GENERATE    FUNC=FTAB,VALUE=XLOC
```

Using this method, it is not necessary to know how many parameters there were in the original macro definition, nor what their relative positions were. In addition, the use of mnemonic symbols for keywords such as FUNC and VALUE helps make a program understandable.

As a result, the system programming manuals for the VAX/VMS system usually prefer to define the system macros in terms of keyword arguments rather than positional arguments. More examples of how this is done are shown in the next chapter, which describes system macros that are used for input and output.

Default Parameter Substitution

As was seen in the previous section, it is not uncommon, especially with system macros, to have blank arguments in a macro call. As might be expected, what normally happens is that blank arguments cause **nothing** to be substituted for the corresponding parameters. The parameter name is deleted, and nothing is put in its place. For example, consider the following macro definition:

```
.MACRO   ADDX   A,B,C
ADDL3    A,B,C
.ENDM    ADDX
```

If this macro were called

```
ADDX     SUM,,TOTAL
```

the expansion would be

```
ADDL3    SUM,,TOTAL
```

which would be an erroneous code (unless, of course, ADDL3 had been redefined as a macro). It might be intended in some cases that a macro such as this would have a special meaning in the case of a blank argument. For example, this macro could be defined so that if the middle argument is left blank, the instruction would be assembled to add the number one to the first argument. This could be accomplished by conditional assembly using the .IF BLANK, . . . directive. However, this usually requires the addition of quite a few lines to the macro. For example, the previous macro would become

```
.MACRO   ADDX   A,B,C
.IF      BLANK,B
ADDL3    A,#1,C
.IF_FALSE
ADDL3    A,B,C
.ENDC
.ENDM    ADDX
```

Clearly, using this technique with a complex macro which had several arguments that had special meaning when blank, could require an extraordinary amount of code. For example, consider the GENERATE macro in the previous section. If each blank argument doubles the amount of code, there could be 2^{15} lines of code.

There is a simpler way. This is **default parameter substitution.** With default parameter substitution, a string is provided for each parameter so that if a blank argument is placed in the macro call, the default string is used instead. The default strings are placed in the parameter list of the macro definition, using an equal sign. To see how this works, consider again the **ADDX** macro, which could be redefined as

```
.MACRO  ADDX  A,B=#1,C
ADDL3   A,B,C
.ENDM   ADDX
```

Here, B is given the default substitution string #1. Therefore, the macro call

```
ADDX    SUM,,TOTAL
```

would expand as

```
ADDL3   SUM,#1,TOTAL
```

However, if a nonblank argument is used for B, it is used normally, so that

```
ADDX    SUM,FIVE,TOTAL
```

would expand as

```
ADDL3   SUM,FIVE,TOTAL
```

Generated Local Symbols

In this section we describe another kind of default substitution for missing or blank arguments. Recall that earlier in this chapter, it was advised that care be taken in using labels inside a macro definition. The reason is that if the macro is called many times in the program, the label would end up being multiply defined. One solution for this problem is to make sure that the label is a substitutable parameter. Then the programmer can provide his own unique symbol for the label each time the macro is called. For example, consider the following macro for clearing an array of N longwords:

```
        .MACRO  CLEAR  A,N,L
        CLRL    R0
L:      CLRL    A[R0]
        AOBLSS  N,R0,L
        .ENDM   CLEAR
```

Given the following call

```
        CLEAR   ARRAY,#20,30$
```

the expansion would be

```
        CLRL    R0
30$:    CLRL    ARRAY[R0]
        AOBLSS  #20,R0,30$
```

This works perfectly well. However, it requires that the programmer be constantly aware of parts of the macro which are not
directly important to the overall purpose of the macro, namely that
of finding a unique symbol for L. Care must be taken in choosing an
argument which will work. Here, for example, it is important that .
the symbol 30$ is not used as a label elsewhere in the current local
symbol block.

The solution to this problem is to have the assembler generate
its own local symbols. This can be done by placing a question mark
in front of the name of the parameter in the macro definition line. In
particular, the above macro could be redefined as

```
        .MACRO  CLEAR   A,N,?L
        CLRL    R0
L:      CLRL    A[R0]
        AOBLSS  R0,N,L
        .ENDM   CLEAR
```

If a parameter is flagged with a question mark and a blank
argument is used in the macro call, the assembler will generate its
own local symbol. Generated local symbols all have the form of a
large number (at least 30000) followed by a dollar sign. The assembler
starts with 30000 and uses successive numbers 30001, 30002, . . . ,
each time a symbol needs to be generated. Thus, for example, the
following macro call:

```
CLEAR   ARRAY,#20
```

would be expanded as follows

```
          CLRL    R0
30015$:   CLRL    ARRAY[R0]
          AOBLSS  R0,#20,30015$
```

This assumes that there have been 15 previous local symbols generated, thus bumping the count to 30015.

Of course, there may be occasions when the programmer wants
to access a label externally from the macro. In this case, an explicit

use of the symbol will override the generation of any symbol. Thus, the following macro call:

```
CLEAR   ARRAY,#20,30$
```

would be expanded as it was above, with 30$ being substituted for L, and no symbol would be generated.

Character Manipulations in Macros

Normally, the symbols used for substitutable parameters in macros are identified by being surrounded by space or punctuation of some sort. Thus, in the following macro:

```
.MACRO  EVER    A,B
MOVB    A,B
.ENDM   EVER
```

the B in MOVB would not be substituted for, but the B in A,B would.

Most of the time, this gives the desired result, but sometimes it is useful to be able to create symbols by **concatenating** or joining symbols together. This can be accomplished in macros by using the apostrophe which has a special function in macro expansion. The apostrophe is a punctuation mark, and therefore would delimit a parameter name. However, in the expansion of a macro, apostrophes which are next to the name of a substitutable parameter are deleted. The following macro illustrates the use of the apostrophe.

```
.MACRO  SLIDE   A,B,X
MOV'X   A,B
.ENDM   SLIDE
```

The apostrophe in MOV'X delimits X as being substitutable, and since the apostrophe is next to a substitutable parameter, it will be deleted. This means that the expansion of the macro call

```
SLIDE   #5,DATA,L
```

would be

```
MOVL    #5,DATA
```

Sometimes, it is desirable to keep the apostrophe in the macro expansion. This is possible, since an apostrophe which is not next to a substitutable parameter is left in the expansion. This may sometimes require the use of two or three apostrophes in the macro in order to leave one remaining. For example, the following macro definition and call:

```
.MACRO   STRING   X,Y
.ASCII   /X'''Y/
.ENDM
STRING   DON,T
```

would be expanded as

```
.ASCII   /DON'T/
```

The reason for using the apostrophe is to avoid unnecessary punctuation. Sometimes, the reverse problem occurs. It is desired to pass argument strings to macros which contain punctuation, such as commas. This is a little difficult, because the string A,B looks like two arguments, rather than one. The solution to this problem is to use angle brackets (<and>) around the argument in the macro call. If an argument in a macro call is enclosed in angle brackets, the angle brackets are removed, and whatever string is inside is used as the substitution string for the macro. The string can contain spaces, commas, and even pairs of angle brackets. As an example of how this might be used, consider the following macro:

```
.MACRO   WHAT    A,B
A        B
.ENDM    WHAT
```

if called with the following

```
WHAT     MOVL,<SRC,DEST>
```

the expansion would be

```
MOVL     SRC,DEST
```

Notice that one level of brackets is removed, but if there were others inside they would be retained. This can be seen from the expansion of the following call:

```
WHAT     WHAT,<ADDL3,<R0,#2,R5>>
```

This will expand to

```
WHAT     ADDL3,<R0,#2,R5>
```

which in turn will be expanded to

```
ADDL3    R0,#2,R5
```

It is possible to define alternative delimiters, so that odd numbers of angle brackets can be used inside an argument. However, the reader is referred to the *VAX/VMS Macro Language Reference Manual* for further details.

Line Extensions

As we have seen in the previous sections, there is a considerable amount of information that can be put into macro definitions and macro calls. One problem that can immediately be seen is that there may not be enough room on a line to accomodate all the parameters, default values, or arguments in a macro definition or call. The solution to this problem is the use of line extensions which serve the same function as do continuation lines in a FORTRAN program. The way that extensions operate in the VAX assembly language is that if the last argument on a line consists solely of a minus sign, then the next line is considered to be an extension or continuation line. Successive extension lines are allowed, each using a minus sign at the end. The minus signs themselves are deleted from the final interpretation of the line of code. As an example, the following macro call:

```
DOMAC    A=ARG1,B=ARG2,C=ARG3,D=ARG4
```

could be written

```
DOMAC    A=ARG1,-
         B=ARG2,-
         C=ARG3,-
         D=ARG4
```

The semicolon that is used before a comment has the effect of an end-of-line marker. Therefore, comments can be used within each line of an extended line. For example, the previous macro call could be rewritten:

```
DOMAC    A=ARG1,-          ;FIRST ARGUMENT
         B=ARG2,-          ;NEXT ARGUMENT
         C=ARG3,-          ;AND SO ON
         D=ARG4            ;ETC.
```

Exercise Set 3

1. Given that the definition of a macro begins with the line

```
.MACRO PROB EXP,TOTAL,SUM,MAX
```

   show how each of the following macro calls could be rewritten
   using keyword argument passing instead of positional argument
   passing.

   a. PROB   A,B,C,D
   b. PROB   A+5,B(R5)[R3],-(SP),#27
   c. PROB   A,,,D
   d. PROB   ,R5,<A,B>,LONGSYMBOL
   e. PROB   ,,(SP)+
   f. PROB   <A,B,C,D>

2. Given that the definition of a macro begins with the line

```
.MACRO SECOND CHAN,ADS,ORK,W
```

   convert the following keyword macro calls to the equivalent positioned argument macro calls.

   a. SECOND   CHAN=A,ADS=B,ORK=C,W=D
   b. SECOND   ADS=A,ORK=B,CHAN=C,W=D
   c. SECOND   ADS=ORK,ORK=W,CHAN=ADS,W=CHAN
   d. SECOND   ADS=(R5+,W=-(SP)
   e. SECOND   CHAN=<A,B>
   f. SECOND   W=<A,B>

3. Given the following macro definition:

```
        .MACRO  TEST    ARRAY=BLOCK,SIZE=#100,ANS=R0,?LABEL
        CLRB    ANS
        PUSHR   #^M<R1,R2>
        MOVAB   ARRAY,R1
        CLR     R2
LABEL:  XORB2   (R1)+,ANS
        AOBLSS  R2,SIZE,LABEL
        POPR    #^M<R1,R2>
        .ENDM   TEST
```

   show the expansions for the following macro calls using 30000$
   for generated local symbols.

   a. TEST   ARRAY=LIST

   b. TEST   SIZE=#25

   c. TEST   ARRAY=BLOCK,SIZE=SIZE

   d. TEST

   e. TEST   A,B,C,D

   f. TEST   LABEL=X,ANS=CSUM

4. Given the following macro definitions:

```
.MACRO  WHATEVER  A
A
.ENDM   WHATEVER
```

show the full expansion for the following macro calls listing all intermediate steps.

   a. WHATEVER   HALT

   b. WHATEVER   <ADDL3 A,B,C>

   c. WHATEVER   <3$: ADDL2 1,R0>

   d. WHATEVER

   e. WHATEVER   WHATEVER

   f. WHATEVER   <WHATEVER <CLRL R0>>

5. Write a macro which expands to produce instructions to add four longwords, A,B,C, and D, together to produce a sum, ANS. The macro will have five substitutable parameters, A, B, C, D, and ANS. Each of these parameters will have a default value as follows:

```
A       X
B       #100
C       (R1)+
D       #0
ANS     R0
```

System Input and Output

11.1 Introduction

In Chapter 8, a simplified form of input and output was described which allowed programmers to read strings of characters from the programmer's terminal and to write strings of characters to the terminal. In this chapter, we will examine more the use of the VAX/VMS input and output system services which allow full control of the data formats, the use of devices other than the terminal, and the use of logical devices. In addition, we will look at file structures, file-structured operations, methods for dealing with errors that may occur with input/output, and other system operations.

There are numerous ways that a sophisticated computer system like VAX/VMS allows users to perform input and output. These ways tend to operate at varying levels depending upon the needs of the user. At the higher-level end of the scale are the input and output schemes used in higher-level languages such as FORTRAN with its READ, WRITE, FORMAT, and other statements. It is assumed that the reader is already somewhat familiar with this form of input and output. At the low end of the scale is machine language input and output. This involves setting bits and fields in special registers which are a part of each peripheral device. In fact, all input and output must ultimately result in operations at this lowest level. However, a multiuser system such as the VAX/VMS system has protection mechanisms which prevent users from using this low-level input/output directly, since doing so would interfere with other users' input/output. As a result, only the operating system itself can access the device registers. Chapter 15 describes how some of these functions operate.

VAX assembly language programmers who do not have operating system privileges can perform input and output operations at two intermediate levels which are between the machine language and the higher-level language operations. The first of these methods uses the **queued input/output** system, called **QIO.** The second uses the **record manager services,** called **RMS.** The QIO system operates at the lower of these two levels and allows reading and writing raw information from or to a device. The RMS system operates at a somewhat higher level and provides for file-structured operations. This chapter will cover some of the basic operations of both systems. However, the reader should keep in mind that these topics are quite complex, and our treatment is in no way exhaustive. For a full treatment the appropriate manuals should be consulted.*

11.2 Using System Services

The normal method for using most system functions such as input/output operations is by calling a system service routine. System service routines on the VAX/VMS system can be called by routines written in higher-level languages as well as in assembly language. Since the calling sequences are often quite complicated, system macros are provided to simplify the use of these routines. These macros are defined on a library file which is searched whenever the program calls a macro that has not been defined within the program itself. In order to distinguish system macros from user-defined macros, the system macros have names that begin with a dollar sign. An example of such a system macro which we have already used is $EXIT_S. In the case of $EXIT_S, the "_S" indicates that the macro is expanded using the CALLS instruction. There is a similar macro, $EXIT_G which uses the CALLG instruction. In fact, most of the macros described in this chapter have an "_S" and a "_G" version. The "_S" versions usually have extensive argument lists which describe what is to be put on the stack prior to execution of the CALLS instruction. The "_G" versions usually only have one argument which points to the argument list, but this means that the argument list must be set up separately. In order to simplify things, this chapter will make use of the easier to use, though sometimes less efficient, "_S" versions.

Recall the use of the underline character. Both dollar sign and underline are characters which can be used in VAX-MACRO labels, symbols, and macro names. As far as the assembler is concerned, they

---

* *VAX-11 Record Manager Services Reference Manual, VAX/VMS System Services Reference Manual, VAX/VMS I/O User's Guide.*

are just characters in the alphabet. Programmers can use these characters as pseudo-punctuation and thereby split a long symbolic name into several symbolically meaningful pieces. The use of the underline character is not restricted to system programs, but its use is encouraged to split long symbols for easier reading. For example, the symbol INPUT_OUTPUT_ROUTINE is preferred to INPUTOUTPUTROU-TINE. On the other hand, the dollar sign symbol is reserved for system use and should not be used in user-defined symbols, because confusion can result.

Most of the system macros expand into calling sequences for system subroutines. The calling sequences could, of course, be generated without the macros, but the process of setting up the calls is greatly simplified by use of the macros. The calling sequences use the standard form of argument lists described in Chapter 9, and consequently, these subroutines can be called by programs written in higher-level languages such as FORTRAN or Pascal. The argument lists can either be placed on the stack or in an array in a fixed memory location.

Although most of the macros are used to generate calling sequences to system subroutines, there are some system macros which are used to generate tables of data. Two of these macros are $FAB and $RAB which are used to define files and records when the record manager system, which is described later in this chapter, is used. Others are used to set up the argument lists when the "_G" versions of the macros are used.

In addition to setting up subroutine calling sequences and data tables, many of the system macros define long lists of symbols. These symbols are used so that programmers can use symbolic names rather than numeric codes to indicate operations or relative locations of pieces of data in a table. For example, the symbol IO$_READVBLK is a symbol which can be used in the $QIOW_S macro to indicate that the desired queued input/output function is to read a virtual block.

11.3 Queued Input/Output Requests

The queued input/output requests are used for simple, unstructured input and output functions from an input device or to an output device. The term **device** is used to mean a source of input or destination for output connected to the computer such as a teletypewriter terminal, a printer, a disk drive, or a tape drive. For the purposes of this chapter we will restrict our use of "devices" to the user's terminal device.

Assigning a Channel

Specific devices are identified by names defined in the system. The names SYS$INPUT and SYS$OUTPUT usually are used to mean the user's teletypewriter terminal. SYS$INPUT is used for input, and SYS$OUTPUT is used for output. When a device name is passed to the system, the system must look up the information describing the parameters needed to access that particular device. Clearly, it would be very inefficient to look up this information every time an operation was to be performed on the device. In order to avoid having to do this, the system is designed to look the information up once and make the information accessible through an internal array. Each entry in the array contains information necessary to use the device or a pointer to a place where the information can be found. The entries in the array are referred to as **channels,** and these relative locations in the array are **channel numbers.** In order to get the system to look up the device information and assign a channel number, the system macro $ASSIGN _S is used. The $ASSIGN_S macro has two required keyword arguments, DEVNAM and CHAN. DEVNAM is the address of the descriptor for a character string which spells out the device name. (See Chapters 8 and 9 for an explanation of .ASCID type string descriptor.) CHAN is the address of a longword which will receive the channel number assigned by the system. Figure 11.1 shows how a program could load the longword CH1 with a channel number for the SYS$INPUT device. In addition to the two required arguments shown in the $ASSIGN_S call in Figure 11.1, there are two optional arguments. These are an access mode and mailbox name.

The four access modes on the VAX are user, supervisor, executive, and kernel. The access mode parameter allows the program to lower the privileges of operations on a channel to those of a lower-access mode. This would provide a means of protection from system programs which are performing operations being called in by a lower-level user. However, since it is most likely that readers of this book would be restricted to user mode, the lowest-level mode, there is no need to use the access mode argument.

```
CH1:        .BLKL       1
CHNAME:     .ASCID      "SYS$INPUT"
            .
            .
            .
            $ASSIGN_S   DEVNAM=CHNAME,CHAN=CH1
```

Figure 11.1 Assigning a channel number

The mailbox name argument is used to assign a mailbox to receive error or other messages about a channel. Mailboxes are pseudo-input/output devices which are used to allow one program or process to send messages asynchronously to another. In this case, a mailbox could be set up to receive changes in status of a channel which occur even though no input or output is happening at a particular time. For example, suppose that the device assigned to a channel is a dial-up line. A mailbox could be used to inform a program that the dial-up line user has hung up the connection. Conceivably, the hang-up could occur at anytime, and the program could get immediate notice via the mailbox handler. Again, the use of mailboxes goes beyond the intended level of this book and will not be covered further.

Queued Channel Operation

Input and output operations are accomplished through the $QIO_S and the $QIOW_S macros. These macros stack up requests to perform the desired input/output operations on a queue which is used by the system to determine which operations are to be performed. For the most part, input and output operations take much longer to perform than internal machine operations. For example, the VAX can execute millions of instructions in the time it takes for a user at a terminal to type in one command. As a result, the VAX operating system usually only initiates input/output operations, and then proceeds to do other operations until the input/output is completed.

The $QIO_S and $QIOW_S macros operate on these principles. The subroutine called by $QIO_S returns to the calling program immediately after having initiated the request. The program is then free to do computation unrelated to the input/output requested. There are a number of ways for determining if the requested input/output has been completed, and the program must use one of these before it can be sure that operations related to the input or output can be performed.

The $QIOW_S macro is used when the program has nothing that can be done until the data is available. In this case, it must *wait* for the input or output to be completed. However, note that this waiting is not really waiting as far as the machine is concerned. In any multiuser system such as the VAX, computation can usually be performed on other users' programs while your program is waiting for the completion of an input/output request.

Both $QIO_S and $QIOW_S have the same set of parameters. Two of these are always required. They are

1. CHAN   The channel number
2. FUNC   A code for the desired function

The channel number is normally obtained from the location which was loaded by the $ASSIGN_S macro. The input/output function is specified by a numeric code which identifies the function. Whenever $QIO_S or $QIOW_S is called, a set of symbols is defined for identifying all of these functions. Referring to the functions by their symbolic names rather than their actual numeric values has two advantages. First, the character strings used for the symbols tend to describe the operation and help to make your program self-explanatory. Second, a revised VAX/VMS system could conceivably use different values. With symbolic names reassembly of the program would automatically correct all the function codes. Some examples of function codes are

1. IO$_READVBLK   READ Virtual BlocK
2. IO$_READLBLK   READ Logical BlocK
3. IO$_READPBLK   READ Physical BlocK
4. IO$_WRITEVBLK   WRITE Virtual BlocK
5. IO$_WRITELBLK   WRITE Logical BlocK
6. IO$_WRITEPBLK   WRITE Physical BlocK
7. IO$_SETMODE   SET MODE
8. IO$_SETCHAR   SET CHARacteristics

These function codes and modification to the codes will be discussed in more detail later in this section. Depending upon which function code is used, there may be up to six function-dependent parameters identified, P1, P2 . . . P6. For example, with reading and writing, P1 is the address of an array or buffer where the data will be placed or where the data will come from. P2 is the size of the buffer in bytes. Figure 11.2 shows how a message could be written to SYS$OUTPUT. The $ASSIGN_S is the same as used in Figure 11.1.

Note that the function code and the message size are preceded by number signs. This is because the macro expands to include the instructions PUSHL FUNC and PUSHL P2. This allows the parameters to be substituted by either a number preceded by a number sign, the address of a location which contains the value, or even some register name or addressing mode that locates the value.

Note also that the message string contains a line feed and carriage return. This is necessary because this calling sequence just outputs the characters given without any formatting. Normally, the

```
CR=^X0D                                                    Figure 11.2 Typing out a
LF=^X0A                                                    message
CH1:            .BLKL         1
CHNAME:         .ASCID        "SYS$OUTPUT"
MESSAGE:        .ASCII        <LF>"Here is a message."<CR>
MESSAGE_END:
MESSAGE_SIZE=MESSAGE_END-MESSAGE
                    .
                    .
                    .
                $ASSIGN_S     DEVNAM=CHNAME,CHAN=CH1
                    .
                    .
                    .
                $QIOW_S       CHAN=CH1,FUNC=#IO$_WRITEVBLK,-
                              P1=MESSAGE,P2=#MESSAGE_SIZE
                    .
                    .
                    .
```

VAX/VMS operating system operates input and output in units of records which correspond to lines of print and which do not require control characters. In most cases, record formatting is preferred because it is more efficient. However, for the time being, our discussion is limited to character formatting so that we can keep our attention closer to terminal behavior. The $QIO macros have a parameter called P4 which can be used to produce automatic formatting of various kinds, and this will be discussed in more detail later.

This program also uses the function IO$_WRITEVBLK to perform the output operation. This operation writes a **virtual block** of information. If output is to a disk, **virtual blocks** are defined relative to a file origin, whereas **logical blocks** are defined relative to the device itself. **Physical blocks** are defined as the physical blocks on a tape or disk and may be of a different size from the logical blocks. For compatibility, logical blocks on file-structured devices are uniformly set to be 512 bytes, even though the medium may actually have the physical arrangement of information blocked differently. In general, the writing of physical and logical blocks is only needed for implementation of system functions, and system security could be breached if casual users were able to access physical or logical blocks on the system disk. As a consequence, IO$_READLBLK, IO$_WRITELBLK, IO$_READPBLK and IO$_WRITEPBLK can only be used by priveleged users.

11.4 Terminal Input/Output
Queued Input Operation

Terminal input has one complication not usually encountered with output. At the time that output is to be printed, the program has determined exactly how many characters there are in the output buffer. This is true for single line output, multiline output, or even if only a part of a line is to be written. However, with input, the number of characters on a line are not usually determined by the program, but rather the person at the terminal. Therefore, the program must be able to determine exactly how many characters were typed by the terminal operator. There are a number of ways of determining this; however, we will summarize these into three methods.

Reading an Entire Line The first two methods are based upon the assumption that an entire line is to be read at a time. The third method operates with the program reading one character at a time. This latter method of input is used when each character typed may function as a control character causing some sort of operation by itself. An example of this kind of program is a screen editor, such as EDT (see Appendix E).

If input is to be read one line at a time, a buffer that is at least as long as the longest acceptable input line must be provided for storing the line. If the user's terminal has an 80-character screen, then it is reasonable to restrict input lines to be no longer than a screen line. Therefore an 81-byte buffer would be adequate. Note that one extra character is necessary in order to hold the carriage return at the end of the 80-character line. The first two methods of input use such a buffer. In fact, usually memory is not so scarce, and a slightly oversized buffer is preferred, just to be on the safe side. In the first method, the input line is read, and then the buffer is scanned character by character searching for the termination character. The termination character is normally the carriage return (the ASCII code ^X0D). However, any control character which is enterable (except tab, line feed, form feed, vertical tab, and backspace) will normally cause termination of a line.* Parameter P4 can be used to alter the list of characters that are interpreted as meaning the termination of a line. Any set of characters in the alphabet can be chosen; however, use of other than the standard set of termination characters is rarely

---

* Because of their special functions, control-Q, control-S, control-Y, and several other control characters are not normally enterable characters in that they cannot be entered into a character string being read in normal mode.

needed, and the reader is referred to the *VAX/VMX Input/Output User's Guide* for details on these functions.

Since there are a number of possible termination characters, checking each character against all possibilities could be quite time consuming. This leads to the second method of determining the length of the input string. As the operating system must check each character against termination characters as they are read in and count their array locations, a count of nontermination characters exists and is in fact available to the programmer via a quadword called the **input/output status block** or IOSB. The second word of the IOSB quadword is a count of the number of bytes transferred, not counting the termination character. Figure 11.3 shows the lines necessary to read a line from the terminal and to have the byte count of the line available at the location BCOUNT. The remaining three words of the IOSB contain status information that may be necessary for more complex data operations. Again the reader is referred to DEC's manuals for more information.

Whether the code shown in Figure 11.3 is for the first or second method depends upon what the program does with the information obtained by the $QIOW_S operation. If BUFFER is searched for a termination character, it is the first method; if BCOUNT is used to obtain a character count, it is the second method. Since BCOUNT, and therefore SBLOK, are not needed for the first method, the two lines that define them as well as the IOSB argument can be omitted from the program in Figure 11.3.

```
CH1:            .BLKL           1
CHNAME:         .ASCID          "SYS$INPUT"
BUFFER:         .BLKB           100
SBLOK:          .BLKQ           1
BCOUNT=SBLOK+2                  ;SECOND WORD OF IOSB
                 .
                 .
                 .
                $ASSIGN_S       DEVNAM=CHNAME,CHAN=CH1
                 .
                 .
                 .
                $QIOW_S         CHAN=CH1,FUNC=#IO$_READVBLK,-
                                P1=BUFFER,P2=#100,IOSB=SBLOK
                 .
                 .
                 .
```

Figure 11.3 An example of terminal input

Reading One Character at a Time The third method of input is to read one character at a time. The simplest way to do this is to make the buffer size one byte. Then, as soon as the person at the terminal types a single character, the buffer will be full, and the input will be terminated even though no termination character was typed. The $QIOW _S will return to the program with that one character, and the program can process it as appropriate. This will allow the program to process one character at a time and respond immediately on a character-by-character basis, as does EDT in the screen mode. However, one problem that arises in this mode is that delete and control-U no longer operate as we have been accustomed.

Normally, as input is typed, it is held in an area of the operating system called the **type-ahead buffer.** At some point, the characters delete and control-U tell the operating system to delete characters or lines from the type-ahead buffer. When an input is active, information will be transferred from the type-ahead buffer to the user's buffer whenever there is enough to fill the buffer, or when a termination character is encountered. If the character buffer is one single byte, as soon as the type-ahead buffer receives one single character, it is transmitted immediately to the user's program. Therefore, there will not be any data in the type-ahead buffer for delete or control-U to operate on, and thus, these characters have no effect.

As a result, in single character mode it is usually necessary for a program to do all its input editing, and therefore to process delete and control-U, itself. One problem is that under normal operations delete and control-U are not transmitted to the user's program. Consequently, the program is unaware that the user is typing DEL to delete characters or control-U to delete the whole line. This can be deceiving because the display on the terminal screen may appear as if the delete or control-U were really working. One solution to this problem is to enter a modified mode where delete and control-U are not processed by the system, but passed to the program as ordinary characters. This can be done by using the modification code IO$M_NOFILTR. The bits in this code are combined with the IO$_READVBLK using the Boolean OR operator (!) so that the function is written

```
FUNC=IO$_READVBLK!IO$M_NOFILTR
```

Figure 11.4 shows a program segment which reads characters one at a time and places them into a buffer. Carriage return is the terminal character. If delete is typed, one character (if any are there) is removed from the buffer, and the sequence backspace-space-backspace is typed in order to remove the character from the terminal screen. If control-U is typed, the delete function is repeated until the buffer is empty (and the corresponding characters are removed from the screen). The program assumes that CH1 and CH2 have been assigned to the SYS$INPUT and SYS$OUTPUT devices as in the earlier examples.

Interactive Terminal Use

Whenever a program is communicating with an interactive terminal, it is important for the program and the terminal to maintain some sort of a dialog so that the user and the program stay in synchronization with each other. Failure to do this often occurs when someone first writes a program to be run interactively. The programmer issues the command to run the program and nothing happens. The computer appears to be dead. The programmer soon discovers that the program was in fact running, but waiting for input. The solution, of course, is to precede each read in the program with a command to type out some sort of prompt message to tell the user that input is expected.

These prompting messages can be simple or complex depending upon how much information the user needs to know in order to make the correct input response. For example, the VAX/VMS operating system prompts with the messages "User:" and "Password:" when the user is logging in, and very specific responses are required. Once logging in is completed, a simpler prompt of "$" is normally used and which is understood to be a request for any VAX/VMS terminal command. User programs use their own distinctive prompts. Many of the editors such as TECO and EDT use "*" to prompt for a command. The debugger prompts with "DBG>".

In order to facilitate the use of input prompt messages such as these, $QIO supports an additional read command, IO$_READPROMPT. This command uses two additional parameters, P5 and P6. P5 specifies the address of a prompt string and P6 gives the length of the prompt string. The prompt string can be any string of characters, but should probably begin with carriage return and line feed so that the prompt message is sure to be on a new line. Figure 11.5 shows a program segment which reads into a 100-character buffer after having prompted with the message "Enter data -". Except for the prompt message, IO$_READPROMPT functions exactly like IO$_READVBLK. The program in Figure 11.5 assumes that CH1 was assigned a channel number as in the previous examples. Also note the use of the IOSB argument as described above.

It should be noted that IO$_READPROMPT is not necessary to generate prompts since a read could always be preceded in the program by a normal write using IO$_WRITEVBLK. However, there are

Figure 11.4 Single character input

```
        .
        .
        .
CR = ^X0D
BS = ^X08
CTLU = ^X15
DEL = ^X7F
BSB:    .ASCII  <BS>" "<BS>
BUFFER: .BLKB   100
CHBUF:  .BLKB   1
        .
        .
        .
READ:   MOVL    R5,-(SP)
        CLRL    R5              ;INITIALIZE BUFFER POINTER
10$:    $QIOW_S CHAN=CH1,FUNC=#IO$_READVBLK!IO$M_NOFILTR,-
                P1=CHBUF,P2=#1
        MOVB    CHBUF,BUFFER[R5] ;PICKUP CHARACTER
        INCL    R5              ;AND BUMP THE POINTER
        CMPB    CHBUF,#CR       ;CARRIAGE RETURN?
        BEQL    20$
        CMPB    CHBUF,#DEL      ;DELETE?
        BEQL    30$
        CMPB    CHBUF,#CTLU     ;CONTROL-U?
        BEQL    40$
        CMPL    R5,#100         ;ROOM LEFT IN BUFFER?
        BLSSU   10$             ;YES
        JMP     ERROR           ;NO
20$:    MOVL    R5,R0           ;RETURN LENGTH OF STRING IN R0
        MOVL    (SP)+,R5        ;RESTORE R5
        RSB                     ;RETURN

30$:    DECL    R5              ;BACK UP OVER DELETE
        BEQL    10$             ;EXIT IF BUFFER EMPTY
        BSBB    60$             ;DELETE CHARACTER
        BRB     10$             ;AND EXIT
40$:    DECL    R5
50$:    TSTL    R5              ;IS BUFFER EMPTY?
        BEQL    10$             ;YES, ALL DONE
        BSBB    60$             ;NO, DELETE CHARACTER
        BRB     50$             ;TRY FOR ANOTHER
60$:    DECL    R5              ;DELETE CHARACTER
        $QIOW_S CHAN=CH2,FUNC=#IO$_WRITEVBLK,-
                P1=BSB,P2=#3    ;ERASE CHARACTERS FROM SCREEN
        RSB                     ;RETURN
```

Figure 11.5 Input with a prompt message

```
CR = ^X0D
LF = ^X0A
PROMPT:         ,ASCII     <CR><LF>"Enter data - "
PROMPT_END:
PROMPT_LOC:
                ,ADDRESS   PROMPT
BUFFER:         ,BLKB      100
SBLOK:          ,BLKQ      1
BCOUNT=SBLOK+2

                ,
                ,
                ,
                $QIOW_S    CHAN=CH1,FUNC=#IO$_READPROMPT,-
                           P1=BUFFER,P2=#100,IOSB=SBLOK,-
                           P5=PROMPT_LOC,P6=#PROMPT_END-PROMPT
                ,
                ,
                ,
```

several advantages to using the read with prompt function. First, it is somewhat more efficient, since it requires only one call to $QIO. Second, since the prompt message is linked to the read, the operating system knows to override the effect of control-O and even to reissue the prompt if the user types control-U.

11.5 Additional Queued Input/Output Considerations

Errors

So far in all our examples, there was an assumption that everything was perfectly all right and that there was no need to worry about errors. As anyone experienced in computers knows, this is a bad assumption. Errors can occur for all kinds of reasons. In fact, the program that works the first time it is run is an extreme rarity, even for simple programs. As a result, users of the input/output system services should be prepared to deal with errors.

Some types of errors that can occur are: A device name could be misspelled, an unassigned channel number might be used, a function might be attempted for which the user does not have the privilege of use, or there could be an input/output error on the device being used. In many cases, when an error occurs in a system routine, the routine will print an error message and cause execution of the program to stop. This should be a familiar occurrence to most users of higher-level languages. However, the routines called by the system macros do not operate this way. The philosophy is that sophisticated programmers who would be using these routines would have their own means for dealing with errors. For example, a program might search for an available device by attempting to assign different devices until a successful assignment is made. As a result, if the routine is unable to execute the requested function successfully, it stops without taking further action and returns to the calling program with an error indication.

All these system routines use the register R0 for returning error information. If the low-order bit (bit number 0) of R0 is one, then there was a normal return. If the low-order bit in R0 is zero, then an error was found. The low-order bit of R0 can easily be tested using the BLBC or BLBS instructions. Therefore, in order to test if an assignment was successful, the following code could be used.

```
        $ASSIGN_S  DEVNAM=NAME,CHAN=CH1
        BLBS       R0,10$    ;ERROR?
        JMP        ERROR     ;YES, SO EXIT
10$:                         ;NO, SO CONTINUE
```

If the low-order bit of R0 is not equal to one, the low-order three bits indicate the severity of the error, and the remaining bits contain a code identifying the error. Each error has a defined symbolic name. For example, SS$_NOPRIV is the code signalling that the user had insufficient privilege for the attempted operation. However, for most cases, the only reason for needing to know the actual error code would be to be able to print an error message which informs the user as to the reason for the error. Since there are hundreds of different error codes, writing a program to print all the possible error messages would be a considerable effort. However, error messages can be requested from the operating system by placing an argument on the $EXIT_S macro. If this is done, the operating system will check the value of the argument and if the low-order bit is zero, it will print an error message explaining the reason for the error. Thus, the following error routine could be used with the previous three lines of code.

```
ERROR:  $EXIT_S  R0
```

Then if R0 is set to SS$_NOPRIV, a message such as

```
SYSTEM-F-NOPRIV, No privilege for attempted operation, reason . . .
```

will be printed at the user's terminal or in the batch log.

Logical Device Names

When writing a program, it is usually not a good idea to include the specific name of a physical device in the code of the program. The reason is that from one user to the next, the actual device you are using may change. For example, a user may enter the SHOW TERMINAL command to determine that the particular port logged into is TTC3. That means that TTC3 is the device name to use when assigning a channel for input or output to the terminal.

However, it would be unwise to write your program to specify the device name with the line

```
.ASCID          "TTC3"
```

The problem is that when you log off today and log in again tomorrow (or even later today), the port assigned to your terminal might be TTD4 instead of TTC3. Since TTC3 is probably assigned to some other user, your program will no longer work and will cause a privilege violation error.

One possible solution is, rather than including the device name as constant data in the program, have the user type the name as input data. There are two problems with this idea. The first is that it is inconvenient for the users to have to enter this data since users would not necessarily know what device they are logged into unless they take the pains to use the SHOW command to find out. However, the second problem is actually a logical dilemma. How can the program communicate with the terminal to find out the device name for the terminal if it does not know the name for the terminal? The solution to the problem is to use logical device names rather than physical device names.

A logical device name is a character string which is assigned instead of the physical device name. These names may be chosen by the user and assigned to a device using the ASSIGN command. For example, if the user wanted to use SCOPE to refer to the terminal, the following command could be used

```
ASSIGN TTC3: SCOPE
```

This is a system command which is entered at the terminal in response to the $ prompt.

If such an assignment were made, the program could use the name SCOPE to assign a channel to TTC3. The program could be written

```
NAME:     ,ASCID    "SCOPE"
CH:       ,BLKL     1
          ,
          ,
          ,
          $ASSIGN_S    DEVNAM=NAME,CHAN=CH
```

This solves the second problem of not being able to get the program to assign a channel without having the terminal's physical name, but still requires that the user know the physical name in order to type the assign command. One solution to this is that several logical device names are automatically assigned whenever a user logs onto the system. In one example so far, we have been using the logical names SYS$INPUT and SYS$OUTPUT. These names are automatically assigned to the appropriate input and output devices for normal input and output. For an interactive user, these are both assigned to the user's terminal. For the batch system, they are assigned to the batch stream input and output.

Therefore, the better way to encode the above programming example may be

```
NAME:     ,ASCID    "SYS$INPUT"
CH:       ,BLKL     1
          ,
          ,
          ,
          $ASSIGN_S    DEVNAM=NAME,CHAN=CH
```

This will automatically assign channel CH to the user's terminal.

Output Formatting

One of the more difficult tasks of programming is preparing output to be in a suitable format for easy reading. This involves the insertion of messages, and the conversion of numbers from internal form to a suitable base, usually decimal or sometimes hexadecimal. Most higher-level languages have some provision for controlling output format. FORTRAN, of course, uses the FORMAT statement, COBOL uses the

PICTURE statement, and Pascal uses the colon designations in the output lists.

In assembly language, the formatting of input and output normally requires that the programmer write some extensive character manipulation programs. In order to simplify this task, the VAX/VMS system includes some routines for output formatting which can be called by the use of the system routine, $FAO_S. This program operates in much the same manner as FORTRAN does with FORMAT statements, in that there is a control string which describes the output format. However, an entirely different set of codes is used. The remainder of this section describes some of the more useful of the control codes for $FAO_S. For a complete description, the reader is referred to the *VAX/VMS System Services Reference Manual*.

The $FAO_S routine can be called in several ways, but the simplest involves three necessary parameters and a set of optional parameters. The necessary parameters are CTRSTR, OUTBUF, and OUTLEN. CTRSTR is the address of the descriptor of a character string containing the control string. This is probably an .ASCID string. OUTBUF is the address of the descriptor of a byte array for holding the converted output. This descriptor can be assembled as two longwords: one contains the length of the byte array and the other the address of the byte array where the output will be stored. OUTLEN is the address of a word which will receive the length of the converted character string. Note that the length field of the OUTBUF descriptor determines the maximum size of the output string. The actual string generated by $FAO_S may be smaller. The value of the OUTLEN word will give the actual length. Note that if $FAO_S completes successfully, this value will always be less than or equal to the length given in the buffer descriptor. If an attempt is made to generate a larger string, a truncated string will be returned, along with an error value in R0.

The control string contains a sequence of character strings and format specifiers which determine the output format. Any character string which is not recognized as a format control directive is treated as a character string to be inserted in the output. Such strings are not enclosed in separate quotes as with a FORTRAN FORMAT statement. All format control directives are preceded with an exclamation point. Therefore, any character string not preceded by an exclamation point is just passed to the output buffer.

After an exclamation point, an optional length value and a one- or two-character code are used for the format specifier. For example, SL is the code for converting a longword to decimal with a sign. Therefore, the following control string could be used to print an answer.

```
.ASCID   "THE ANSWER IS !10SL(DECIMAL)."
```

This would be equivalent to the following FORTRAN FORMAT statement.

```
100    FORMAT('THE ANSWER IS',I10,'(DECIMAL)')
```

Figure 11.6 gives a partial list, including some of the more important format control codes, used by $FAO_S. For a complete description of the use of $FAO_S, the reader is referred to the *VAX/VMS System Services Reference Manual*.

Each of the control codes may have a length inserted between the exclamation point and the two-letter control descriptor. This is a decimal number which gives the width of the field in characters. If a length such as !6SL is provided, the converted value will be expanded or truncated to fit into exactly six spaces. If no length is provided, the length of the field will be adjusted to the minimum size needed for the number. Note, however, that if the buffer length is not large enough, truncation will occur anyway.

A final thing to note with these codes is that they require values to convert. This is true in FORTRAN, where every I6 must have a matching variable to convert. This is done in the $FAO_S by providing parameters, P1, P2, P3, ... Up to twenty parameters can be specified. Each parameter is set equal to an address of a location containing the value to be converted. Consequently, if A, B, and C contain a byte, a word, and a longword which are to be converted to decimal, the code in Figure 11.7 could be used.

It is obvious that the data conversion control strings, such as !SW, would require a parameter, but it should be noted that the date and time conversion codes also require a parameter. This is because they can be used not only for converting the current time and date, but also converting prestored times and dates, as might be used for identifying versions of files or systems. The simplest use of these conversions is to print out the current time and date. For these cases,

Code	Function
!XB	Convert byte to hexadecimal
!XW	Convert word to hexadecimal
!XL	Convert longword to hexadecimal
!SB	Convert byte to signed decimal
!SW	Convert word to signed decimal
!SL	Convert longword to signed decimal
!%T	Insert time of day into buffer
!%D	Insert date and time of day into buffer

Figure 11.6 $FAO_S format control codes

Figure 11.7 $FAO_S example

```
CR=^X0D
LF=^X0A
CSTR:      .ASCID    <LF>"BYTE !SB WORD !SW LONGWORD !SL "<CR>
BDES:      .LONG     80,BUF
BUF:       .BLKB     80
BSIZ:      .BLKL     1
A:         .BLKB     1
B:         .BLKW     1
C:         .BLKL     1
           .
           .
           .
           $FAO_S    CTRSTR=CSTR,OUTBUF=BDES,OUTLEN=BSIZ,-
                     P1=A,P2=B,P3=C
```

a parameter equal to #0 must be used. Therefore, the following code could be used to print the present time of day.

```
TSTR:      .ASCID    <LF>"TIME=!%T,"<CR>
           .
           .
           .
           $FAO_S    CTRSTR=TSTR,OUTBUF=BDES,OUTLEN=BSIZ,-
                     P1=#0
           $QIO_S    CHAN=CH1,FUNC=IO$WRITEVBLK,-
                     P1=BUF,P2=BSIZ
```

It is assumed that symbols defined in Figures 11.3 and 11.7 still apply.

Exercise Set 1

1. Write a program using $QIOW_S to read a line that has been typed in and to print it back out five times.

2. Write a program which reads in a character string of up to 30 characters and then attempts to open a channel using that character string as a device name. Then use PNUM to print out the channel number assigned, if any, and the error code left in R0.

3. Use the VAX/VMS ASSIGN command to assign the logical name XXX to your current terminal designation. For example, if your current terminal is TTA3:, enter the command,

```
ASSIGN   TTA3   XXX
```

Then assign YYY to be XXX and ZZZ to be YYY with the commands

```
ASSIGN   XXX   YYY
ASSIGN   YYY   ZZZ
```

Use the program you wrote for Exercise 2, above, to attempt to assign channel numbers to your terminal and to XXX, YYY, and ZZZ. Are all assignable? If not, how many levels of logical names are usable?

4. Rewrite the IOINIT, RNUM, and PNUM subroutines described in Appendix B so that they use $QIOW_S and the related routines instead of $PUT and $GET as used in the appendix version.

5. Repeat Exercise 4; however, redo the algorithms so that there is no array for the input string, but rather input characters are read one character at a time. This would also require that the program include code for processing delete and control-U.

11.6 Files and Records
Mass Storage Devices

In order for a computer to have general practicality, it must be capable of storing large amounts of information on some sort of **mass storage device.** Various kinds of mass storage devices have been used in large computer systems. The most common mass storage devices used for the VAX are magnetic disk and magnetic tape. Information is written onto these devices as a sequentially organized arrangement of blocks. Privileged users can access disks and tapes block by block using the $QIO operations on channels assigned to a disk or a tape. However, nonprivileged users will use other methods for accessing this kind of information. The remainder of this chapter will be directed to this latter kind of input and output.

While both disks and tapes have a sequential, block-organized data structure, the physical attributes of the two kinds of devices are quite different, giving a radically different nature to the way the devices are used. Tapes are long narrow strips of magnetic recording material rolled up on reels. A length of 2400 feet by a width of one-half inch is standard for an industry-compatible, full-sized reel. Blocks of information are placed one after another down the length of the tape. Figure 11.8 shows this organization.

The tape is read or written onto by moving the tape past a fixed magnetic recording **head** in a manner which is similar to that used in a home audio tape recorder. In order to read information at the end of the tape, it is necessary to spool the tape forward 2400 feet. If information were then required at the beginning of the tape, the tape would then have to be rewound back the same 2400 feet. Needless to say, this would take a considerable amount of time (perhaps as much as several minutes). For this reason, data on magnetic tapes are not usually accessed randomly, but in a predetermined sequence.

Disks are made up of one or more circular platters which are coated with a magnetic recording material in a band around the surfaces of the disk. These bands make up the recording surfaces of the disk. Information is recorded in circular tracks around each recording surface. There may be more than 1000 tracks on each surface, and each track is written in a number of fixed-length blocks called **sectors.** In industry-standard magnetic tape, the blocks have no fixed places, but occupy varying amounts of space as they are written. Disk sectors on the other hand, occupy fixed locations on the tracks. This can be achieved by physical marks, such as slots or holes on the disk or by recorded marks on the tracks themselves. The first method is called hard sectoring, and the second soft sectoring. Before

Figure 11.8 Magnetic tape organization

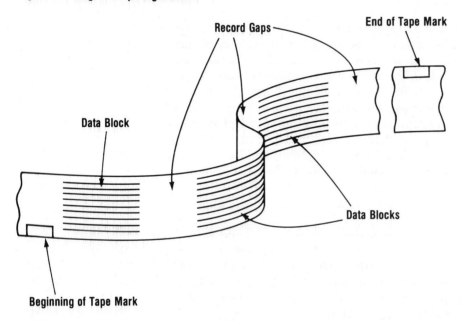

a soft-sectored disk can be used it must be **formatted** by writing the sector location marks on every track. Figure 11.9 shows the typical arrangement of a multiplatter disk.

Because of this arrangement, each block of information on a disk can be located by a specific address which has the following parts:

1. Platter number
2. Surface on the platter (upper or lower)
3. Track number on a surface
4. Sector number on a track

Disks are normally read by a system of read/write heads. Usually there is one head per surface, although there may be more on some disk systems. These heads move in and out and are positioned over the track being read. The disk itself is continuously rotating, and access to a sector requires waiting until the desired sector passes under the read/write head.

The disk heads move in and out very quickly, requiring only a fraction of a second to move from the inner most tracks to the outer most tracks. In addition, the disks spin quite rapidly, making from 5 to 100 revolutions each second. The result is that the disk system can access any block of information on the disk in a fraction of a second. Compare this with the magnetic tape which may require several minutes to go from one end to the other. As a consequence,

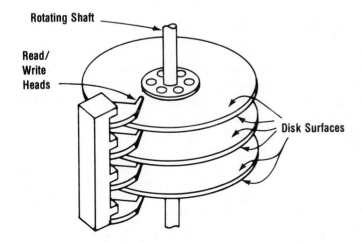

Figure 11.9 Multiplatter disk

it is only practical to use tapes in a **sequential** fashion, going from one end to the other. On the other hand, disks can be used in a **random access** fashion; that is, blocks can be accessed at random wherever they are located on the disk.

An even more important consideration in the sequential nature of tapes and the random nature of disks concerns the writing of information. As mentioned before, disks have hard- or soft-sector marks which exactly locate the blocks of information on the disk. Normal magnetic tapes have no such marks. As a consequence, information can only be written on a tape sequentially. Further, it is not normally possible to go back and rewrite a block of information in the middle of a tape without corrupting all of the information that follows. On the other hand, any sector on the disk can be written into without affecting the information in any other sector.

Files

Usually, the amount of information capable of being stored on a mass storage device is much larger than is needed for a single application. As a result, it is customary to partition mass storage devices into a number of collections of information called **files.***

Because of the sequential nature of magnetic tape, the files on a magnetic tape consist of contiguous collections of blocks which are identified at each end by special labelling blocks, called **labels.** Among other kinds of information, the labels contain the file names used by the programmer for identifying the file. For reasons described in the previous section, the sequential nature of tape operations allows the adding of labels and files to the tape, but once a file is written on a tape, it cannot be modified or deleted.

Disks on the other hand are capable of random input and output operations. As a result, a disk file can be composed of random blocks of information scattered around on various sectors of the disk. When files are written, the input/output system must locate unused sectors for the blocks of the file. Disk files can be modified or deleted. If a file is deleted, its blocks become available as unused sectors on the disk. To keep track of all of these operations requires a system of **directories. A directory** is an area of the disk that contains information regarding the locations of files, the locations of blocks, and so forth. Furthermore, most large disks are used to service more than one user.

---

* There are some applications which require so much information that it will not fit on a single disk or tape. Thus, the information must be extended over several such devices. These are referred to as *multivolume files*.

Since each user may have his own directory of files, there may even be a directory of directories.

If this sounds somewhat complex, that is the intent. Writing programs to maintain files on a disk is not only extremely complex, it is dangerous. A disk containing 100,000 blocks of information can be rendered totally useless by the loss of one block of information in a directory. With information scattered around on the disk, the directory must be well maintained and securely protected in order to find anything. As a consequence, it is rare for users of a system to do any of this sort of programming. In fact, there are protection schemes which prevent any but the most privileged program levels from performing any operations that could corrupt directory information on a disk. For this reason, users' access to disk files is normally accomplished through the use of system programs that operate at a somewhat higher level than the QIO operations described in the earlier part of this chapter. In particular, in the VAX/VMS system, file input/output is accomplished through use of the **Record Manager Services,** or **RMS,** which is described in Section 11.7.

Records

Just as disks and tapes are subdivided into files, it is usually necessary to subdivide files into smaller amounts of information, called **records.** Historically, records were synonymous with blocks, because a block is the smallest unit of information that can be read in a single, physical device operation. However, it was rapidly learned that the units of information which are convenient for a programming application to deal with are not the same as physical block sizes. The result was that either programs operated very inefficiently because small amounts of information were stored in blocks capable of holding much more, or the programmer had to restructure programs to make efficient use of the mass storage devices. In most cases, the programmer would just as soon leave such a task for someone else. As a consequence, most sophisticated input/output systems break files down into records which can be specified to correspond to the needs of the application. These records are then packed to fit efficiently into the physical block structure of the particular input/output device.

A **record** therefore, is the amount of information from a file that is convenient to handle at one time. The most common form of a record would be a line that is typed in or printed out. Most often, records are read in or written out one after another. This is called **sequential access.** However, some applications require the ability to read records from any point in a file. This is called **random access.**

Most operating systems provide for random access of records in a file stored on a random access device.

In order to use standard system software for reading and writing operations, the programmer must identify the structure of the file. Some of the features that must be identified are

1. Fixed-length records versus variable-length records
2. Record length (for fixed-length records)
3. Sequential access versus random access
4. Kind of random access (for random access files)
5. Other properties such as file size, whether the file contains ASCII or binary data, and so forth

In the VAX/VMS system, these operations are performed by a system called RMS which is described in the next section.

11.7 The VAX/VMS Record Manager Services (RMS)

The VAX/VMS Record Manager Services (**RMS**) is designed to perform file-structured operations. They are a collection of those system routines needed by most programs for file input and output. As with queued input/output, RMS operations are accomplished through the use of a number of system subroutines which are invoked by macros. Essentially, there are two kinds of macros used by RMS. One kind generates data blocks which contain all of the necessary information about the files or about particular records in a file. The other kind of macro generates executable code that calls the subroutine necessary to perform the RMS operation.

File Access Blocks

File access blocks are blocks of data which contain all the information about a file that a user must provide in order to perform input or output to the file. This block contains, among other things, the name of the file and information about organization, access methods, and record types. The file access block is generated by use of a data-generating macro called $FAB. If the file is of the most common type, sequential access with variable-length records, then most of the block will be specified by default, and all that needs to be specified is the file name.

File names are strings of characters which specifically identify a file. A full file name has the following parts:

1. Node name—identifies the particular VAX in a network of VAX's
2. Device name—identifies which disk, tape, etc. is being used
3. Directory name—identifies the directory or subdirectory used, because a disk may have many directories or subdirectories
4. File name—identifies a particular file, along with 5 and 6
5. File type—identifies the use of the file; i.e., MACRO program, FORTRAN program, object file, etc.
6. Version number—identifies the file version when a file may have been modified or rewritten

These parts of a file name are identified by separating punctuation such as :, [ ] , and ;. Thus, a full file name might appear as

```
TEMPVAX::DPA2:[KANDS.PROGS]EXAMPLE.MAR;4
```

The parts of this description are

1. Node name—TEMPVAX
2. Device name—DPA2
3. Subdirectory—PROGS in directory KANDS
4. File name—EXAMPLE
5. File type—MAR
6. Version number—4

Since a full file name can be quite lengthy, most of the parts are implied by default if they are not specified. The normal default specifications are

1. Node name—node on which the program is running
2. Device name—default disk for the user's login
3. Directory/Subdirectory—default directory for the user's login
4. File name—none
5. File type—none
6. Version number—highest for the file

Most of these defaults are controlled through logical names automatically assigned at log on. These defaults can be changed through use of the DEFINE command. In addition, special default values can

be specified in the file access block. As a consequence, if the above
file met all the default conditions, it could be referred to simply as

```
EXAMPLE.MAR
```

Similarly, we can generate a file access block which would allow
the above file to be read from or written to, using sequential access,
with the following macro call

```
F1:    $FAB    FNM=<EXAMPLE.MAR>
```

Note that the angle brackets are a required part of the syntax.

This macro call generates two things. The first is the actual file
access block. However, the file access block does not actually contain
the file name because the block is fixed length and can only contain
fixed-length data. As a consequence, the file access block contains the
address and length of the file name string as a longword and a word.
The actual file name is stored as an .ASCII string in a separate program section called $RMSNAM. Note that the RMS system requires
that file access blocks and record access blocks (to be discussed in
the next section) be longword aligned. That is, the starting address
must be a multiple of four. In order to ensure that the file access
blocks and record access blocks are longword aligned, it is best to
put them in program sections of their own. For example, the following
sequence could be used.

```
       .PSECT    IOBLOCKS,LONG
F2:    $FAB      FNM=<FILE1.TYP>
F3:    $FAB      FNM=<FILE2.TYP>
       .
       .
       .
       .PSECT
```

Note that a program can have any number of file access blocks. However, it must have one block for each file that is in use at any particular
time.

Note also that the file names used by a file access block can
contain logical as well as actual names for portions or all of a file
specification. For example, the following kinds of calls could be made
to the $FAB macro.

```
F4:    $FAB      FNM=<SYS$INPUT>
F5:    $FAB      FNM=<USER:FILE.TYP>
```

Use of the logical names SYS$INPUT and SYS$OUTPUT will allow input and output to come from and go to the user's terminal. If the program is run in batch, SYS$INPUT and SYS$OUTPUT refer to the batch stream input and output.

Record Access Blocks

Record access blocks are used to provide all of the information necessary to read or write a particular record on a file. The information associated with a record access block includes the following:

1. Reference to the file access block for the file being read or written
2. Location in memory for a buffer for the record
3. Size of the record
4. Size of the buffer
5. Information needed to locate the record, if the file has random access.
6. Prompt messages for terminal input
7. Timing information which allows simultaneous operations of several files

Some of this information must be supplied by the user's program to the RMS system. Other information is provided by RMS to the user's program. Which is which depends upon whether the operation involved is input or output. For example, when writing variable-length records, the actual record length is determined by the user's program. However, when reading variable-length records, the length is determined by what is actually on the file.

As with file access blocks, most of the information in a record access block can be specified by default when sequential files are being read or written. For a sequential file with variable-length records, the following three items are necessary, and usually suffice:

1. File
2. Buffer location
3. Buffer size in bytes

Using this information, the $RAB macro can be used to generate a record access block. In order to write a record, the following macro call could be used:

```
R1A:    $RAB    FAB=OUTFILE,RBF=OUTBUF,RSZ=OBS
```

Here the symbols have the following meanings:

Symbol	Meaning
OUTFILE	Label on the $FAB macro for the file being written
OUTBUF	Label on the .BLKB or .ASCII where the data being written is stored
OBS	Symbol or number or expression for the size of the string (record) being written

In order to read a record, the following kind of macro call is needed:

```
R1A:    $RAB      FAB=INFILE,UBF=INBUF,USZ=IBS
```

In this case the symbols have the following meanings:

Symbol	Meaning
INFILE	Label on the $FAB macro for the file being read
INBUF	Label on the .BLKB where the input record is to be stored
IBS	Size of the input buffer

Note that IBS is not the size of the record, which could be larger or smaller. It is the maximum amount of space available for storing the record. Therefore, if an attempt is made to read a larger record, information will be lost. To show that this has occurred, the warning value having the symbol RMS$_RTB will be returned in R0. (See the earlier section on error returns and the later section on RMS operations.)

Note that RBF and RSZ are used for output and UBF and USZ are used for input. Why this is so will be made clear later.

As with file access blocks, record access blocks should be longword aligned. This is most easily accomplished by placing them all in the same, longword-aligned, program section. Figure 11.10 shows code that could provide the file and record access blocks for terminal output.

Note that the record access blocks labeled R2C has no RSZ specification. This is because, as would be the case in most programs, the length of the string being written is not known until that point in the execution of the program when the writing is about to take place. There are means for providing missing pieces of information during the execution of a program. This applies to file access blocks as well as record access blocks and this allows for variability in all items, including file names, buffer addresses, record sizes, and so forth.

```
        .PSECT   IOBLOK,LONG
F1:     $FAB     FNM=<SYS$INPUT>
F2:     $FAB     FNM=<SYS$OUTPUT>
R1A:    $RAB     FAB=F1,UBF=IBUF,USZ=80
R2A:    $RAB     FAB=F2,RBSF=MSGA,RSZ=MSGAE-MSGA
R2B:    $RAB     FAB=F2,RBF=MSGB,RSZ=MSGBE-MSGB
R2C:    $RAB     FAB=F2,RBF=OBUF
        .PSECT
MSGA:   .ASCII   "MESSAGE A"
MSGAE:
MSGB:   .ASCII   "MESSAGE B"
MSGBE:
IBUF:   .BLKB    80
OBUF:   .BLKB    132
```

Figure 11.10 Typical definition of file and record access blocks

11.8 Using RMS
RMS Operations

The purpose of the file and record access blocks is to provide information needed to read and write records on a file. Therefore, the basic operations associated with files is reading and writing. However, in order to use these operations, it is necessary to perform some associated operations for initialization and termination of the operations. Using the simplest cases, RMS input/output can be performed using six macros which generate appropriate subroutine calls. These macros are

1. $OPEN   Performs the directory searches and other operations necessary to enable the RMS system to read records from an already existing file.*

2. $CREATE   Prepares space on a disk and in the directory for a new file that can be written on.* This is used instead of $OPEN for creating new output files.

3. $CONNECT   Connects a file to a record stream. This completes the opening process for record operations on a file and connects the record access block to the file access block and the record stream. This operation must be done for every file after it has been opened or created but before any of the other operations can be per-

---

* Analogous operations occur if the file is on magnetic tape, a terminal, or some other device.

formed using the record access block. If more than one record access block is being used for the file, the most recently connected one will be the only one that is active. Therefore, before a new record access block can be used, it must be connected. The previous one must be disconnected using the $DISCONNECT macro. $CONNECT causes the system to establish internal buffers appropriate to the physical block and logical record structures of the file.

4. $GET   Reads a record into an input buffer.

5. $PUT   Writes a record from an output buffer.

6. $CLOSE   Terminates operation on a file and allows the file access block to be used for input or output on another file. When a $EXIT_S macro is executed, all open files are automatically closed. However, it is better programming practice to close open files explicitly. Although VAX/VMS is very good about closing files for the user, information written on an output file sometimes can be lost if a program bombs before the output file is closed. It is the closing of the file that completes the directory entries for the file.

In the simplest cases, these macros need only refer to a file access block or record access block because all the pertinent information is contained in the access blocks. Since $OPEN, $CREATE, and $CLOSE are file operations, they refer to the file access block. Similarly, $CONNECT, $GET, and $PUT refer to the record access block.

Assuming that file access blocks and record access blocks were set up as shown in Figure 11.10, read operations could be performed on SYS$INPUT using the following steps in the executable part of your program.

```
$OPEN       FAB=F1     ;OPENS THE FILE
$CONNECT    RAB=R1A    ;CONNECTS R1A TO ITS FAB
 .
 .
 .
$GET        RAB=R1A    ;THIS STATEMENT CAN BE
 .                     ;REPEATED, OR BE IN A LOOP
 .
 .
$CLOSE      FAB=F1     ;DONE AT THE END OF
$EXIT_S                ;THE PROGRAM
```

Similarly, output to SYS$OUTPUT could be performed with the following code.

```
$CREATE    FAB=F2     ;OPENS THE FILE FOR OUTPUT
$CONNECT   RAB=R2A    ;CONNECTS R2A
    ,                 ;NOTE THAT R2B OR R2C CANNOT BE
    ,                 ;USED UNLESS CONNECTED
    ,
$PUT       RAB=R2A    ;THESE STATEMENTS CAN
    ,                 ;BE EXECUTED REPEATEDLY
    ,
    ,
$PUT       RAB=R2B    ;IN ANY ORDER, OR
    ,                 ;IN LOOPS
    ,
    ,
$PUT       RAB=R2C
    ,
    ,
    ,
$CLOSE     FAB=F2     ;DONE AT THE END OF
$EXIT_S               ;THE PROGRAM
```

Program Use of Access Blocks

As was mentioned earlier, the $FAB and $RAB macros are used to set up the constant part of file and record access blocks. However, there may be variable portions of these blocks, such as buffer addresses, record sizes, and file name strings, that cannot be defined at assembly time, and thus must be dealt with at execution time. In order to do this, it is simply necessary to locate the appropriate longwords, words, bytes, or bits in the access blocks and change or examine them. Keeping in mind the philosophy of how things are done in the VAX/VMS operating system, these locations in the access blocks are all identified symbolically, rather than by their actual locations.

When the $FAB and $RAB macros are called, a number of symbols are defined which give the locations of the various parts of the access block relative to the start of the block. The symbols used for the parameters discussed so far in this section are

Symbol	Meaning
FAB$L_FNA	Longword for the address of ASCII file name string
FAB$B_FNS	Byte for the size of file name string
RAB$L_FAB	Longword for the address of file access block in the record access block
RAB$L_RBF	Longword for the address of record buffer
RAB$W_RSZ	Word for the size of record buffer in bytes
RAB$L_UBF	Longword for the address of user buffer
RAB$W_USZ	Word for the size of user buffer in bytes

As an example of how this could be used, let us imagine a subroutine for writing a character string to a file. The subroutine will be called using the standard calling sequences described in Chapter 9. The subroutine will have two arguments. The first will be the address of a descriptor for a character string to be written. The second argument will be the address for the file access block of the (already open) file where the output is to be written. Figure 11.11 shows this subroutine. Recall that a character string descriptor contains two longwords. The first word of the first longword contains the length. The second longword contains the address of the character string.

Note that the symbols defined above give the addresses relative to the start of the access block. Therefore, to address a parameter such as RSZ, it was necessary to produce the effective address, RBLOCK + RAB$W_RSZ.

In general, it is preferable to use a scheme such as this to print out messages. If a separate record access block for each message is used, valuable memory is wasted.

Control of Terminals and Printers

On a terminal or printer, a record normally takes on the form of a line of characters. From our experience so far, control characters such as carriage return or line feed are used to delimit the ends of lines. While some operating systems also use these control characters to delimit ends of records, RMS normally does not. The reason is that RMS is intended for more general kinds of information. If information in general is considered to be an arbitrary string of bytes, then numerical values such as ^X0D could be ordinary pieces of data within a string. However, since ^X0D also happens to be the code for carriage return, confusion would result if this were also interpreted as the end-of-record control character. To get around this, the internal representation of records written by RMS contain an extra, one-word byte

Figure 11.11 Subroutine for writing out a string

```
          .TITLE    STRING WRITE ROUTINE
          .PSECT    SWIOBLOCK,LONG
RBLOCK:   $RAB                                   ;BLANK RAB TO BE FILLED
          .PSECT
          .ENTRY    STRINGWRITE,0
          MOVL      8(AP),RBLOCK+RAB$L_FAB  ;LOAD ADDRESS OF FAB
          MOVL      4(AP),R0                ;GET POINTER TO DESCRIPTOR
          MOVL      4(R0),RBLOCK+RAB$L_RBF  ;LOAD ADDRESS OF STRING
          MOVW      (R0),RBLOCK+RAB$W_RSZ   ;LOAD STRING SIZE
          $CONNECT  RAB=RBLOCK              ;MAKE SURE RBLOCK IS CONNECTED
          $PUT      RAB=RBLOCK              ;WRITE THE STRING
          RET
          .END
```

count which gives the number of bytes of information in the record. Normally, the user does not see this byte count as part of the record. Instead, when a $GET is executed, the byte count is stored at relative address RAB$W_RSZ in the record access block.

One exception to this is with input from a terminal. Since input from a terminal is being generated by a human typist, the use of byte counts would be very awkward. Instead carriage return is normally used to terminate lines. However, in order to make terminal input compatible with other input, RMS removes the carriage return, and instead returns a byte count through relative location RAB$W_RSZ as with other reads. Since most control characters can be used to terminate input records from a terminal, the user may wish to find out which one was really typed.* Did the typist actually type carriage return, or was it control-W or control-G or something else? This can be determined, because, RMS saves the actual termination character in the relative low-order byte location of the word RAB$W_STV0.

When writing a file which is to be printed, it is permissable to include control characters in the character strings. These control characters, such as carriage return, line feed, and form feed, will have their normal functions. However, the inclusion of termination characters in output records has the tendency to make output not be

---

* It is possible for a programmer to select his own set of termination characters. However, the normal set of termination characters includes all control characters except those used in text such as tab, line feed, backspace, and vertical tab, and those with special control functions, ^C, ^O, ^Q, ^R, ^S, ^U, ^Y, and delete.

compatible with input, where the termination characters are removed. There is a way around this. In fact, the method has three variations.

In order to avoid having line termination control characters explicitly in the output record, a parameter is placed in the file access block which identifies the file as being intended for eventual printing. Then, when the file is finally printed or sent to a terminal, the appropriate control characters are sent to the printer. The three ways of doing this have differing degrees of complexity depending upon the complexity of output required. The first method simply places a carriage return and line feed between every line. The second uses FORTRAN carriage control characters, and the third uses more complex control words which are beyond the scope of this chapter. In order to choose one of these, one of the following RAT (Record ATribute) parameters is placed in the $FAB macro for the file.

1. `$FAB  FNM=<SYS$OUTPUT>,RAT=<CR>` For carriage return/line feed between lines. When this file is printed, each line will be preceded by line feed and ended with a carriage return.

2. `$FAB  FNM=<SYS$OUTPUT>,RAT=<FTN>` For **FORTRAN** carriage control characters. The first character in each line is deleted from the print out and is used to control vertical spacing on the printer. The normally accepted carriage control characters on the VAX are
   space—single space before printing
   0—double space before printing
   1—eject page before printing
   +—no space before printing (over print lines)
   $—no carriage return at end of line (This is for prompts at a terminal.)

3. `$FAB  FNM=<SYS$OUTPUT>,RAT=<PRN>` For complex printer control. See the *VAX-11 Record Management Services Reference Manual* for further information on this kind of printer control.

Terminal Prompts

As was discussed in the first half of this chapter, input from a terminal usually requires some kind of prompt messages. Without prompt messages, the terminal user is in effect flying blind and may become confused as to what input the program is expecting. Of course, prompts can be issued by outputting records to SYS$OUTPUT in the normal fashion. However, there are several disadvantages to prompting in this way.

1. If SYS$OUTPUT is reassigned, in order to save what normally could be terminal output, then the prompt will appear in the wrong place.
2. If the program is to be run in batch, the prompts are unnecessary and will tend to clutter up the output.
3. Because every read becomes two operations, this adds to the complexity of the program.

In order to avoid these problems, prompts can be issued automatically by the $GET command. To do this requires three additions to the record access block. The first is the setting of a flag to indicate that a prompt is desired. The second and third are the specification of a prompt message string and giving its length. These three items can be put into the record access block with the following arguments:

1. `ROP=<PMT>`   Flag a prompt request
2. `PBF=string label`   Identifies prompt string
3. `PSZ=size`   Indicates prompt string length

As an example, the following code could be used in a program to issue the prompt "Enter data - " whenever input data is to be read from the terminal.

```
RSIZE=8
        .PSECT   IOBLOCK,LONG
INFILE: $FAB     FNM=<SYS$INPUT>
INREC:  $RAB     FAB=INFILE,UBF=IBLK,USZ=RSIZE,-
                 ROP=<PMT>,PBF=PRMSG,PSZ=PRNSGE-PRMSG
        .PSECT
PRMSG:  .ASCII   "Enter Data - "
PRMSGE:
IBLK:   .BLKB    RSIZE
```

Then, whenever the macro, $GET RAB=INREC is executed, the prompt message will be issued, and the program will wait for input to be typed.

As with the other parameters we have seen, PBF and PSZ can be loaded into the record access block at execution time. As before, these parameters are located by symbols which give the addresses relative to the start of the record access block. The symbols which locate PBF and PSZ are

Symbol	Meaning
RAB$L_PBF	Longword for the address of the prompt message
RAB$B_PSZ	Byte for the size of the prompt message

Note that the size of the prompt message is specified in a field of only one byte. This is because it is assumed that prompt messages will not be very long, and therefore, one byte is enough.

Error Conditions

As with many other system subroutines, those called by the RMS routine return an error status value through R0. An error can be detected by the fact that the low-order bit of R0 is not one. As before, the simplest way to test for this is with the BLBC instruction. For the most part, if an error is detected, the program should just exit. The macro $EXIT_S R0 will give you a useful error message as long as the error code is still in R0.

However, one of these error codes can be useful for certain kinds of file operations. Its symbolic value is RMS$_EOF. This value is left in R0 if an attempt is made to read past the end of a file. This can be used for reading a file when it is not known how long the file is. The program keeps reading until RMS$_EOF appears in R0, and then proceeds to other processing. As an example of how this might work, the following code could be used.

```
$GET    RAB=INFILE
CMPL    R0,#RMS$_EOF
BEQL    DONE
BLBC    R0,ERROR
```

The program will proceed to DONE if the end of file is read and to ERROR for any other error. If no error occurs, the program will continue to the next instruction.

Programming Example

As an example of how the RMS operates, Figure 11.12 shows a program which copies one file to another in much the same way that the system command COPY FILEA FILEB operates. The program is written to prompt the user for the names of input and output files.

Figure 11.12 Input-Output programming example

```
           .TITLE    FILE COPY PROGRAM
           NSIZE=40                              ;MAX SIZE OF NAME
           RSIZE=80                              ;MAX SIZE OF RECORD
           .PSECT    IOBLOCK,LONG
TRMFAB:    $FAB      FNM=<SYS$INPUT>             ;FOR GETTING FILE NAME
INFAB:     $FAB                                  ;FILE NAMES WILL BE
OUTFAB:    $FAB      RAT=<CR>                     ;SUPPLIED LATER
TRMRAB:    $RAB      FAB=TRMFAB,ROP=PMT,USZ=NSIZE   ;OTHER PARAMETERS TO COME
INRAB:     $RAB      FAB=INFAB,UBF=RBUFFER,USZ=RSIZE
OUTRAB:    $RAB      FAB=OUTFAB,RBF=RBUFFER      ;SIZE TO COME
           .PSECT
PMT1:      .ASCII    "Enter input file name - "
PMT1S=,-PMT1                                     ;COMPUTE MESSAGE SIZE
PMT2:      .ASCII    "Enter output file name - "
PMT2S=,-PMT2                                     ;COMPUTE MESSAGE SIZE
NAME1:     .BLKB     NSIZE
NAME2:     .BLKB     NSIZE
RBUFFER:   .BLKB     RSIZE
;
           .ENTRY    START,0
           $OPEN     FAB=TRMFAB                  ;OPEN AND CONNECT
           $CONNECT  RAB=TRMRAB                  ;THE TERMINAL
           MOVAB     NAME1,TRMRAB+RAB$L_UBF      ;SET NAME BUFFER
           MOVAB     PMT1,TRMRAB+RAB$L_PBF       ;PROMPT STRING
           MOVB      @PMT1S,TRMRAB+RAB$B_PSZ     ;AND PROMPT LENGTH
           $GET      RAB=TRMRAB                  ;GET INPUT FILE NAME
           MOVAB     NAME1,INFAB+FAB$L_FNA       ;PUT IN INPUT FAB
           MOVB      TRMRAB+RAB$W_RSZ,INFAB+FAB$B_FNS ;SET SIZE
           $OPEN     FAB=INFAB                   ;OPEN INPUT FILE
           BLBS      R0,10$                       ;CHECK FOR ERROR
           JMP       ERROR
10$:       $CONNECT  RAB=INRAB                   ;AND CONNECT INPUT FILE
           BLBS      R0,20$                       ;CHECK FOR ERROR
           JMP       ERROR
20$:       MOVAB     NAME2,TRMRAB+RAB$L_UBF      ;NOW SET UP
           MOVAB     PMT2,TRMRAB+RAB$L_PBF       ;TO GET OUTPUT
           MOVB      @PMT2S,TRMRAB+RAB$B_PSZ     ;FILE NAME
           $GET      RAB=TRMRAB
           MOVAB     NAME2,OUTFAB+FAB$L_FNA      ;AND OPEN
           MOVB      TRMRAB+RAB$W_RSZ,OUTFAB+FAB$B_FNS     ;OUTPUT
           $CREATE   FAB=OUTFAB                  ;FILE
           BLBS      R0,30$                       ;CHECK FOR ERROR
           JMP       ERROR
```

(continued on next page)

Figure 11.12 (continued)

```
30$:          $CONNECT   RAB=OUTRAB
              BLBS       R0,40$                          ;CHECK FOR ERROR
              JMP        ERROR
;
;HERE IS WHERE THE COPY LOOP RESIDES
;
40$:          $GET       RAB=INRAB                       ;READ A RECORD
              CMPL       R0,#RMS$_EOF                    ;END OF FILE?
              BEQL       50$                             ;YES
              BLBC       R0,ERROR                        ;NO, OTHER ERROR?
              MOVW       INRAB+RAB$W_RSZ,OUTRAB+RAB$W_RSZ
                                                         ;GET RECORD SIZE
              $PUT       RAB=OUTRAB                      ;AND WRITE THE RECORD
              BLBS       R0,40$                          ;LOOP IF NO ERROR
50$:          $CLOSE     FAB=INFAB                       ;AT END OF FILE
              $CLOSE     FAB=OUTFAB                      ;CLOSE FILES
              $EXIT_S                                    ;AND EXIT
;
ERROR:        $EXIT_S    R0                              ;ERROR EXIT
;
              .END       START
```

Exercise Set 2

1. Given the following relative locations in a FAB or RAB, answer these questions for each one.

   –What is it used for?
   –Does it appear in a FAB or RAB?
   –Is it a byte, word, or longword?
   –Is its value required or optional?
   –Is it a value provided by the program? If so, when is it used?
   –Is it a value the system returns to the program? If so when?

   a. FAB$L_FNA   **b.** FAB$B_FNS
   c. RAB$L_PBF   **d.** RAB$B_PSZ
   e. RAB$L_RBF   **f.** RAB$W_RSZ
   g. RAB$L_UBF   **h.** RAB$W_USZ

2. Write a program which reads a number of records from a terminal using RMS macros and prints them back out in the reverse order from that read in. For example, if you type in "HELLO, HOW ARE YOU?," the program will print "?UOY ERA WOH ,OLLEH." The program will loop reading and printing until a record of zero length is read, at which time it will exit. Format

the printout by adding carriage returns and line feeds to the output records.

3. Write a program which reads a file from a disk which has FORTRAN carriage control characters at the beginning of each line. The file will be copied to the system through the logical device name SYS$PRINT. The printed output will have the normal page spacing that would be expected on printed output. (If SYS$PRINT is not available for student use, your instructor may direct you to use SYS$OUTPUT or some other output file.) Hint: Make use of the RAT (Record ATribute) parameter.

4. Repeat Exercise 3, above, but do not use the RAT parameter. Instead, your program will strip and interpret the carriage control characters, and insert the ASCII control characters, CR, LF, and FF, as appropriate, to get the expected printout.

5. Consider an employee data base, where there are up to 20 employees in the file. Each employee has a record which has five parts:

   a. Employee number—2 digits
   b. Employee's name—25 characters
   c. Employee's address—100 characters (can include carriage return and line feed)
   d. Employee's social security number—9 digits 2 dashes
   e. Employee's salary—8 digits and a decimal point

   Draw a flowchart for a system which accepts and executes the following one-letter commands:

   A   Create a new file with 20 blank records.
   B   Locate and print out a record, given its record number.
   C   Allow the user to enter or change the name field.
   D   Allow the user to enter or change the address field.
   E   Allow the user to enter or change the social security number field.
   F   Allow the user to enter or change the salary field.
   G   Rewrite the old record with the new information.
   H   Terminate the run and close the file(s).

*6. Use additional information, which is not available in this chapter but is available in the *VAX-11 Record Manager Services Reference Manual,* to write an assembly language program which implements the system described in Exercise 4, above. The program should use a random access file which has 20 records which can be read or written in any order.

Floating-Point Numbers

12.1 Introduction

In Chapter 6, numbers were discussed in terms of the basic integer representation. The integer representation is an example of a **fixed-point** representation because the decimal point is assumed to be in a fixed place. (If a 32-bit longword contains an integer, the decimal point is assumed to be to the right of the rightmost bit in the longword.) Although the fixed-point representation of numbers is useful for many purposes, it is awkward for many problems which involve very small fractional quantities, as well as very large quantities. Such problems are common in science and engineering, as well as other fields.

Floating-point representation was developed to efficiently represent fractional quantities and very large quantities. Floating-point representation is similar to scientific notation in that, in both systems, numbers are represented as a series of significant digits times a number raised to a power.

In this chapter, we will see how fractional quantities are handled in general and how this is done with the VAX in particular. We will examine the floating-point representations available on the VAX and the instructions that manipulate these representations.

12.2 Fixed- and Floating-Point Numbers

In order to use fixed- and floating-point numbers effectively, it is important to understand the principles of their operation. In order to keep the discussion simple at first, we will discuss fixed- and floating-point in terms of a decimal representation. We will then go into VAX representation and see how some rather clever tricks are employed to make the representation efficient.

There are various ways to express fractional quantities. The most basic method is in terms of pairs of integers such as 1/2, 5/12, and 537/8946. This method of representing fractions could be implemented quite easily in a computer. However, it is not normally used in computation because of an inherent awkwardness. Instead, a preferred method is to restrict fractions to a set of standard denominators, such as tenths, hundredths, thousandths, and so on. Because these denominators are powers of 10, fractions using them are called **decimal fractions.** They are usually represented with a decimal point or **radix point,** such as 5.4, 7.92, and 0.093. There are other fraction schemes using denominators such as 12, 14, 16, 32, and 60. Although some of these are going out of use with the introduction of the metric system, others linger. Most computers use either decimal fractions or binary fractions (which will be discussed later).

Fixed-Point Numbers

In computers, two methods are commonly used for dealing with fractional quantities. These are the **fixed-** and **floating-point** methods. The simpler of these methods is the fixed point. The fixed-point method operates on the basis that often there is a smallest fraction, so there would never be a need to consider anything smaller. A good example of this is money calculation. Most normal U.S. money calculation deals with units of dollars, and the smallest unit considered is one cent, or 1/100 of a dollar.*

Because there is no need to deal with fractions of a cent, the whole problem could be reformulated in terms of integer numbers of cents. For example, $537.23 is the same as 53723 cents. However, since most people get confused when dealing with a large numbers of cents rather than dollars, a preferred method for talking about the same thing is to say that the number 53723 has an assumed decimal point two places from the right. This number therefore represents 537.23 dollars. This is called the fixed-point system because the decimal point is assumed to be at some fixed place in the number.

The fixed-point system is very useful for dealing with money and therefore is used extensively in business languages such as COBOL.

---

* Certain tax computations and interest computations do deal with fractions of cents, such as the mil. The fixed-point scheme described here would have to be modified to handle these cases.

Fixed-point numbers can also be used for scientific calculations by **scaling** the problem into appropriate units. Consequently, scientific problems are often stated in terms of integral numbers of

- Milliamperes
- Microseconds
- Centimeters
- Kilograms
- Tonnes (a metric ton = 1000 kilograms)

The last two items on the list are a variation of the dollars and cents problem described previously, because the decimal point is effectively moved to the right, off the end of the number. Therefore, instead of counting fractions of a unit, we are counting multiples of a unit. At times this is necessary in order to prevent the numbers from becoming so large that multiple precision is required in the machine unnecessarily. For example, if the weight of a supertanker were expressed in milligrams, many digits would be required. Consequently, tonnes or even kilotonnes would be used.

The problem of scaling things to the correct units can be quite complex and was, in fact, one of the hardest parts of programming some of the early computers. The difficulty lies in the fact that many scientific problems involve both very large and very small numbers. For example, a problem involving a nuclear-powered ship might use kilotonnes for the ship, but would use milligrams for the fuel pellets, and thus the units of mass would be inconsistent from one part of the problem to another.

Floating-Point Numbers

A solution to this problem is the use of **floating-point numbers.** A floating-point number actually consists of two parts. One part contains the sign and digits of the number. The other part states where the decimal point is assumed to be. A method similar to this is often used by scientists in normal writing so that their calculations can all be made in standard units. This **scientific notation** represents numbers as certain significant digits times a power of 10. For example,

$$-5.347 \times 10^{15} = -5347000000000000.$$

or

$$4.92 \times 10^{-9} = 0.000000004912$$

In effect, what we have is $\pm a \times 10^{\pm b}$, where a represents the significant digits of the number and b represents a power of ten. Note that there is a sign associated with both a and b.

The representation of floating-point numbers in a computer requires that the two signed numbers $\pm a$ and $\pm b$ be stored somewhere. There must also be an understanding of what the numbers mean. Although it is possible to store the two numbers in two separate memory locations, this is inefficient because b tends to be relatively small and it would be wasteful to make a and b the same size. Instead, some means of packing a and b together is usually used. Let us imagine that we have a machine that has eight-digit, signed, decimal words, such as $+73214692$. (Remember that we will use decimal for a while.)

A nice compromise for packaging a and b into this word would be to use two digits for b and the remaining six for a. This gives us six **significant** digits in the number and a range of values spanning a factor of 10^{99}. Thus, in the computer word $+51314159$, $+314159$ represents a and 51 represent b. There are two questions that arise. The first is "Where is the decimal point assumed to be in a?" Although the decision is arbitrary, most computer manufacturers place it at the far left. Therefore, $a = +0.314159$. The second question is "What happened to the sign of b?" The computer word only has one sign and we used it for a. However, if we are to represent small as well as large numbers, we must have a sign for b as well.

The usual technique is to store in the two digits representing b a number that is a fixed-amount larger than the actual value of b. Using 50 as the fixed amount, the number 50 indicates that b is 0, the number 51 indicates that b is 1, the number 52 indicates that b is 2, and so on. Numbers smaller than 50 represent negative exponents. For example, the number 49 indicates that b is -1, and the number 41 indicates that b is -9. Since the number 51 gives a value for b of 1, the word $+51314159$ represents $+0.314159 \times 10^1$ or simply 3.14159. To distinguish between the two representations of the exponent, the value of b will be called the **true exponent** and the value $b + 50$ will be called the **excess 50** exponent or simply the **excess** exponent. Figure 12.1 shows examples of floating point numbers along with their equivalents.

As we can see from Figure 12.1, there are three explicit portions of a floating-point word—the sign of a, the digits that represent b, and the digits that represent the magnitude of a. The latter is usually referred to as the **fraction part** because of the assumed placement of the decimal point in a. (As noted above, the digits representing b are called the excess exponent.) Figure 12.2 shows the named parts in the floating point format.

Floating Point	Scientific Notation	Normal Decimal
-46134926	-0.134926×10^{-4}	-0.0000134926
$+50934821$	$+0.934821 \times 10^{0}$	0.934821
$+50999999$	$+0.999999 \times 10^{0}$	0.999999
$+51100000$	$+0.100000 \times 10^{1}$	1.00000
-53426910	-0.426910×10^{3}	-426.910

Figure 12.1 Decimal floating-point representation

Sign	Exponent	Fraction

Figure 12.2 Floating-point format

Normalized Floating-Point Numbers

A final note about floating-point representations has to do with **normalization.** From the previous discussion, it can be seen that $+51100000$ represents $0.1 \times 10^{1} = 1$. Similarly, $+54000100$ represents $0.0001 \times 10^{4} = 1$. Consequently, $+51100000$ and $+54000100$ both represent the same number. To prevent possible confusion, most floating-point systems insist that numbers be adjusted so that the leftmost digit of the fraction is **not** 0 (as in $+51100000$). This is called the **normalized** floating-point representation. The primary importance of this requirement, beyond preventing confusion, is that normalized floating-point numbers preserve the maximum number of significant digits. Accuracy or precision could be lost with unnormalized numbers such as $+54000100$. The one exception to the normalization rule is 0, which has a normalized representation of $+00000000$.

We can now look at the range of numbers possible with this floating-point representation. Figure 12.3 shows the range of numbers. Note that there is a gap between $\pm 10^{-51}$ and 0. This means that very small numbers should be avoided since the information content of the word may be insufficient to allow their representation.

Figure 12.3 Range of normalized decimal floating-point numbers

Smallest number	$-99999999 =$	$-0.999999 \times 10^{49} \approx -10^{49}$
Largest negative number	$-00100000 =$	$-0.100000 \times 10^{-50} = -10^{-51}$
Zero	$+00000000 =$	$0.000000 \times 10^{0} = 0$
Smallest positive number	$+00100000 =$	$0.100000 \times 10^{-50} = +10^{-51}$
Largest number	$+99999999 =$	$0.999999 \times 10^{49} \approx +10^{49}$

12.3 Floating-Point Operations
Addition and Subtraction

Being able to represent numbers in the floating-point form is really of no use unless there is some way of performing operations on the numbers. The usual operations available in computers are addition, subtraction, multiplication, and division. (Other mathematical operations and functions are derived from these four.) In this section, we will see how these operations can be performed on the decimal floating-point representations of the previous section.

First, let us consider addition and subtraction. (These operations go together, the only difference being how the signs are treated.) A rule learned early in our schooling, says the first step in adding numbers with decimal points is to line up the points. Thus

$$\begin{array}{r} 573.426 \\ +\quad 8.93425 \end{array} \quad \text{must be rewritten as} \quad \begin{array}{r} 573.426 \\ +8.93425 \\ \hline 582.36025 \end{array}$$

Then simple digit-by-digit addition is performed. A similar kind of rule applies to either scientific notation or floating-point encodings of numbers. Two numbers in this notation cannot be added unless their exponents are first made the same. Therefore, for a similar example,

$$\begin{array}{r} .573426 \times 10^3 \\ +\ .893425 \times 10^1 \end{array} \quad \text{must be rewritten as} \quad \begin{array}{r} .573426\ \ \times 10^3 \\ +\ .00893425 \times 10^3 \\ \hline .58236025 \times 10^3 \end{array}$$

Let us now go through a step-by-step process with these same two numbers in the floating-point format and see how the process could operate in a computer.

Step 1. Align the two numbers one above the other.

$$+53573426$$
$$+51893425$$

Step 2. Unpack the numbers to separate the fraction and exponent parts.

$$53\ \ +573426$$
$$51\ \ +893425$$

Step 3. To line up the smaller number with the larger, exchange the numbers, if necessary, so that the number with the larger exponent is first.

53 +573426
51 +893425

Step 4. Compute the difference in the exponents.

      53 +573426
    − 51 +893425
       2

Step 5. Shift the second number right by the amount of the difference, and make the exponents the same.

53 +573426
53 +008934|25*

Step 6. Add the fraction parts. The exponent of the result remains the same.

53 +573426
53 +008934
53 +582360

Step 7. Repack the result into the floating-point format.

+ 53582360

The result of the addition is 582.36.

Complications with Addition and Subtraction

The process, outlined above, clearly works for the example given. However, two complications can arise that require two additional steps. The first problem is that the sum of two numbers may require

---

* These digits are lost except in double-precision operations. Alternatively, we could round the number up when the left-most digit is 5 or greater. This truncation or rounding results in unavoidable computational error.

more digits than either of the original numbers. For example, suppose we add $+53573426$ and 53698421. When we apply Steps 1 through 5, we find that no shifting was necessary and we get

53 $+573426$
53 $+698421$

Now apply step 6.

53 $+$ 573426
53 $+$ 698421
      $+1271847$

Note that the resulting fraction part has more than six digits. This would prevent us from repacking the word into an eight-digit register. The solution is to shift the fraction part one place to the right and add one to the exponent as follows:

> **Step 6a** 54 $+127184|7^*$
> **Step 7** Repack the result into the floating-point format.

> $+54127184$

The second problem is in a sense the opposite of the above problem. It occurs when subtracting numbers with like signs or adding numbers with unlike signs. Again Steps 1 through 5 are the same; but when we perform the subtraction at Step 6, we may end up with fewer than six digits. For example, if we add $+53573426$ and -53573213, we would have the following at Step 6:

53 $+573426$
53 -573213
53 $+000213$

Note that if we repacked this number, the result would not be normalized. We must therefore normalize the result to get

> **Step 6b** 50 $+213000$

---

* This digit is lost. It could be saved with double-precision arithmetic or used to round up the result to $+127185$. This is similar to what happens in Step 6 and also contributes to unavoidable error.

Note that the trailing zeros indicate a loss of accuracy. This usually happens when two nearly equal numbers are subtracted. Step 6b must take into account that the result could be zero. In that case, the normalized form is

00 +000000

Multiplication and Division

The rules for floating-point multiplication and division come straight from the rules of scientific notation. When you multiply, you add exponents; when you divide, you subtract exponents. The fraction parts are either multiplied or divided. For example

$$(0.5 \times 10^{15}) \times (0.8 \times 10^4) = (0.5 \times 0.8) \times 10^{15+4} = 0.4 \times 10^{19}$$

Similarly,

$$(0.4 \times 10^{19}) / (0.5 \times 10^{15}) = (0.4 / 0.5) \times 10^{19-15} = 0.8 \times 10^4$$

The rules for multiplying floating-point numbers are as follows:

Step 1 Align the two numbers one above the other.

> +65500000
> +54800000

Step 2 Unpack the numbers as for addition.

> 65 +500000
> 54 +800000

Step 3 The fractions are then multiplied. No adjustments are necessary for the exponents or fraction parts. (Note where the decimal point occurs in the result; that is, 0.50×0.80 equals 0.4000.)

> 65   +0.500000
> 54 × +0.800000
>   +0.400000

Step 4 The exponents are added, but each exponent has an excess of 50, so the result would have an excess of 100. Therefore, we must subtract 50.

```
    65
  + 54
   119
  − 50
    69  + 400000
```

Step 5 The result is then repacked.

+ 69400000

Since the fraction parts are always less than 1, the product of two fraction parts must be less than 1. Consequently, the problem that arose in the example of Step 6a in addition does not arise. However, the product could be smaller than 0.1. Therefore, normalization is sometimes necessary. This operates the same way as Step 6b of addition. For example, if + 51150000 is multiplied by + 52200000, we have

Steps 3 and 4:

```
    51       + 0.150000
  + 52   ×   + 0.200000  (Note that 0.15 × 0.20 is equal to 0.0300)
   103         0.030000
  − 50
    53       + 030000
```

Normalization is needed to get

Step 4a: 52 + 300000

which produces a result of + 52300000. Note that the example is, in fact, 1.5 × 20 equals 30.

Division operates in much the same form as multiplication. The details of division are left as an exercise for the reader.

Discussion

This floating-point representation may seem awkward. From left to right, a floating-point number consists of the sign of the fraction, a two-digit exponent in excess 50 representation, and a six-digit fraction. This format was chosen to simplify the process of comparing two floating-point numbers.

Assume that we wish to determine if a floating-point number X is larger than a floating-point number Y. This can be done by computing $Y - X$ with floating-point subtraction and testing to see if the result is negative. However, there is a faster and easier way. Treat the representations of X and Y as if they were signed eight-digit integers and compute $Y - X$ using **integer** subtraction. If the resulting integer is negative, then X (as a floating-point number) is larger than Y. For example, assume that X equals 10.0 and Y equals 1.0. The floating-point representations of X and Y are $+52100000$ and $+51100000$, respectively. Subtracting $+52,100,000$ from $+51,100,000$ as signed integers yields $-01,000,000$ indicating that X (10.0) is larger than Y (1.0). (In this case, X and Y are both positive and the exponent of X exceeds the exponent of Y by 1, so X is larger.)

The reader should verify that this shortcut works for any pair of floating-point numbers provided that both numbers are normalized. In order for this shortcut to work, the exponent must be placed between the sign of the fraction and the fraction itself. This is also the reason that an excess representation (in this case excess 50) is used for the exponent. On computers that do not have a machine language instruction for comparing floating-point numbers, variations of this shortcut are used to generate efficient software for comparing floating-point numbers. On computers that have such instructions, variations of this shortcut may be used to simplify hardware design.

Floating-Point Error Conditions

Various error conditions can occur during floating-point computations. For example, an attempt to divide a floating-point number by zero will produce a **floating divide by zero** error. It is also possible for floating-point operations to produce **floating-point overflow.** As shown in Figure 12.3, the floating-point representation described here can only represent numbers between -10^{49} and 10^{49}. An attempt to generate a number outside this range results in a floating-overflow condition. Consider, for example, the following multiplication:

      +98800000
× +54400000

The fraction part of the answer is .800000 times .400000 or .320000. The excess 50 exponent is 98 plus 54 minus 50 or 102. The correct answer to the multiplication is $.32 \times 10^{52}$. (The excess 50 exponent 102 represents a true exponent of 52.) Since the excess 50 exponent is larger than 99, the exponent will not fit into the two-digit exponent field and floating overflow has occurred.

Consider the following multiplication:

    +02800000
× +40400000

The fraction part of the answer is again .800000 times .400000 or .320000. However, the excess 50 exponent is 02 plus 40 minus 50 or −08. The correct answer to the multiplication is $.32 \times 10^{-58}$. (The excess 50 exponent −08 represents a true exponent of −58.) Since the excess 50 exponent is less than zero, the exponent will not fit into the two-digit field. This condition is called **floating underflow.**

Notice that floating overflow is quite different from floating underflow. Floating overflow means that the absolute value of the result of a floating-point operation is too large to be represented. Floating underflow means that the result is too close to zero to be represented. Floating underflow can occur when two small, nearly equal numbers are subtracted, when two small numbers are multiplied, or when a small number is divided by a large number. (Small and large refer here to magnitude.)

In the floating-point representation that has been described, an excess 50 exponent of 00 indicates that the true exponent is −50. For example, the floating-point number

+00123456

represents the number $.123456 \times 10^{-50}$. An exponent of zero does not have any special significance. The floating-point representation used with a variety of computers follows this convention. However, on other computers including the VAX and the PDP-11, an exponent of zero is treated as a special case. In the VAX, a positive fraction with an exponent of zero is interpreted as having the value zero regardless of the value of the fraction. That is, any floating-point number analogous to

+00??????

is interpreted as zero. The reason for doing this will become clear when the VAX floating-point representations are described.

When exponent of zero is treated in this way, there is a question of how to interpret floating-point numbers that are analogous to

−00??????

Such numbers could be interpreted as negative zero. However, having two versions of zero is inconvenient and can lead to programming errors. Instead, the VAX treats such numbers as **reserved operands.** This simply means that numbers analogous to −00?????? are considered to be illegal floating-point numbers and any attempt to use such numbers in a floating-point computation results in an error condition. A reserved operand can be quite useful. For example, a higher-level language translator can initialize all floating-point variables to a reserved or illegal value. During execution, if the program attempts to reference a floating-point variable without first initializing it, the reserved operand will cause an immediate error.

Exercise Set 1

1. Convert the following numbers into the normalized, decimal, floating-point representation as described in this chapter.

   a. 5
   b. 374
   c. 3.14159
   d. 0.0005
   e. 0.8035×10^{23}
   f. 0.4923×10^{-15}
   g. 8.496×10^{18}
   h. 954.2×10^{-12}

2. Convert the following decimal floating-point numbers to scientific notation and to ordinary decimal notation (no exponent).

   a. $+51300000$
   b. -53742000
   c. $+50894026$
   d. $+45805216$
   e. -56293465
   f. -57100000
   g. $+38950125$
   h. -64790881

3. Perform the indicated operations on the following pairs of decimal floating-point numbers. Show your steps along the way. Express your results as a normalized floating-point number.

   a. $(+53215904) + (+53116895)$
   b. $(+52159099) + (+49889621)$
   c. $(+50912065) - (+54891126)$
   d. $(-52998046) + (-50479138)$
   e. $(-53885304) - (-53885034)$
   f. $(+57900000) \times (+48800000)$
   g. $(+51426931) \times (-44357926)$
   h. $(-43250000) \times (-41250000)$
   i. $(-55255000) / (+51500000)$
   j. $(-41800000) / (-44200000)$

4. List all the steps for performing floating-point division. What conditional steps are there? Is normalization a problem (assume that the operands are normalized)? Does fraction part overflow

occur as in Step 6a of addition? Assuming that the operands are normalized, how much overflow can occur?

5. A popular method for computing square roots on the computer is to use the so-called Newton-Raphson formula. To compute the square root of N, you guess a value (call it X). Then you apply the formula

$$X_{new} = 0.5 \times (X_{old} + N/X_{old})$$

The new value of X will be much closer to the correct square root than the old value. The formula can be applied repeatedly to obtain an answer that is as accurate as desired. The speed of the method depends upon the number of times the formula needs to be applied, and this depends upon the accuracy of the original guess and final accuracy desired.

   a. Mathematically, what is the square root of a number expressed in scientific notation? That is, how are the exponent and fraction of the square root related to the exponent and fraction of the original number?

   b. How could the answer to part (a) provide a simple method for obtaining a good guess for the square root of a floating-point number?

   c. In the worst cases, how far is your guess from the correct answer?

   d. Using the worst cases, how many iterations of the Newton-Raphson formula are needed to produce an answer that is accurate to six digits? (Use a calculator or a computer to test the worst cases.)

*6. Write a VAX assembly language program that reads a character string representing a signed decimal number. The string will consist of a sign, decimal digits, and an imbedded decimal point, such as $+89.462$, -0.009461, and so on. The program will then print out the equivalent normalized, decimal, floating-point representation, such as $+52894620$, -48946100, respectively. Your program should loop to work out at least 20 different examples. Some hints for solving this problem are

   a. Ignore leading zeros (except as noted in hint c).

   b. Stack up the six digits in an array of six bytes.

   c. Count digits before the decimal point or leading zeros after the decimal point in order to determine the exponent.

*7. Repeat Exercise 6, except that your program should accept any legal FORTRAN REAL constant, including E notation.

12.4 VAX Floating-Point Numbers

Binary Floating Point

Floating-point numbers in the VAX operate in much the same way as those described in the previous section. However, since the VAX is a binary computer, floating-point numbers are encoded in binary rather than decimal. This means that the fraction is expressed as a binary number, and that the exponent is a power of 2 rather than a power of 10.

Recall from Chapter 2 that the binary number 11011 is interpreted as follows:

$$11011 = (1 \times 2^4) + (1 \times 2^3) + (0 \times 2^2) + (1 \times 2^1) + (1 \times 2^0)$$
$$= 16 + 8 + 0 + 2 + 1 = 27$$

Binary fractions work much the same way, but with negative exponents. Therefore the binary fraction 0.100011 is interpreted as

$$0.100011 = (1 \times 2^{-1}) + (0 \times 2^{-2}) + (0 \times 2^{-3}) + (0 \times 2^{-4}) + (1 \times 2^{-5}) + (1 \times 2^{-6})$$
$$= 1/2 + 0 + 0 + 0 + 1/32 + 1/64 = 35/64$$

Binary fractions may seem strange at first, but in fact they are used quite commonly—normally inches in the English measuring system are divided into binary fractions. It would not be unusual for a machinist to have a drill with a diameter of 35/64 of an inch. Most home carpentry sets have drills measured in sixty-fourths of an inch up to one fourth of an inch.

One point to note is that not all fractions can be expressed as a binary fraction exactly. We should expect this because of our familiarity with decimal fractions. We all know that one-third cannot be expressed in decimal. The best we can do is something like 0.333333. This is not exact. We can make it better by adding 3s, but no finite number of 3s will make the number exact. As we would expect, it is also impossible to express one-third exactly in binary. However, it may come as a surprise that the fraction one-fifth cannot be expressed exactly either. We are used to decimal where 1/5 = 0.2, but we cannot do this in binary. The following table shows how one-fifth can be defined by bracketing it by binary fractions but will never be equal to any of them:

1/4   > 1/5 > 1/8
1/4   > 1/5 > 3/16
7/32   > 1/5 > 3/16
13/64 > 1/5 > 3/16
13/64 > 1/5 > 25/128

Floating-Point Representation

As in decimal, binary floating-point numbers have an exponent and fraction. Let us look at how these are distributed in a floating-point word. The VAX uses four different floating-point formats, called F_floating, D_floating, G_floating, and H_floating. The four floating-point formats vary in length from a 32-bit longword (F_floating) to a 128-bit octaword (H_floating). In addition, D_floating and G_floating, which are both 64 bits long, differ in the number of bits assigned to the exponent versus the fraction. We will use the 32-bit F_floating format to introduce the VAX floating-point formats.

First we need a sign for the fraction. One bit suffices for this. Next we need an exponent. The VAX F_floating format uses a range from 2^{-128} to 2^{+127}. This is roughly equivalent to a decimal range from 10^{-38} to 10^{+38}—a range that is adequate for a variety of problems in science, engineering, and other fields. Since the range from -128 to $+127$ has 256 steps, eight bits are needed for the exponent.

The VAX uses a method for signs for the exponents that is similar to the excess 50 used in the previous sections. It is, however, an excess 128 decimal (10000000 binary) system. Therefore, we have the following table for exponents:

Decimal Exponent	Binary Representation	Hexadecimal Representation
+127	11111111	FF
+1	10000001	81
0	10000000	80
−1	01111111	7F
−128	00000000	00

The F_floating point numbers are stored in a 32-bit longword. Since the sign requires 1 bit and the exponent 8 bits, 23 bits (32 − 9) are used for the fraction part. For example, consider representing the decimal number .75, or $3/4 \times 2^0$. Since 3/4 is 1/2 plus 1/4, the binary fraction part is .110000 . . . 0000 while the excess 128 exponent part is 10000000 which represents a true exponent of zero. Thus .75 could be represented in binary floating point as:

Sign	Exponent	Fraction
0	10000000	11000000000000000000000

However, the 23-bit fraction part gives just barely enough precision for most computations. As a result, the VAX uses a clever way to add an extra bit, giving 24 bits for the fraction part. Recall that in the normalized floating-point representation, the leading digit of the fraction is never zero. Now, in the binary system, the only two possibilities are zero and one. Therefore, if we exclude zero, the leading digit must be one. If the digit is always one, we need not explicitly say so on every number. Therefore, this bit is left out and is called the **hidden bit.** As a result, .75 is represented as follows:

Sign	Exponent	Fraction
0	10000000	10000000000000000000000

(Note: The leading 1 is hidden)

The only problem with assuming that a certain bit is always one is that we cannot represent zero. Another way to view the problem is to look at the representation of $.5 \times 2^{-128}$. Since the number is positive, the sign bit is zero. Because the true exponent is -128, the excess 128 exponent is 00000000. The binary representation of the fraction 1/2 is .10000000 . . . 0000. However, when the hidden bit is removed, the remaining 23 bits are all zero. As a result, the representation of $.5 \times 2^{-128}$ consists of 32 binary zeros which is the same as the representation of zero.

To solve this problem, the VAX interprets any floating-point number with a sign of zero and an excess exponent of zero as a representation of zero. (This means that $.5 \times 2^{-128}$ cannot be represented as a 32-bit F_floating number). In other words, any F_floating number with the form

Sign	Exponent	Fraction
0	00000000	?????????????????????????

is a representation of an F_floating zero.

As noted in the section on decimal floating-point numbers, this leads to the question of interpreting numbers with a negative sign and an exponent of zero, that is, numbers with the form

Sign	Exponent	Fraction
1	00000000	?????????????????????????

The VAX treats such numbers as reserved operands. Any attempt to use such a number in an F_floating operation will produce an error called a **floating-reserved operand** error. As noted previously, this can be used by higher-level language processors to detect undefined floating-point variables during execution. Assembly language programmers may use reserved operands for the same purpose.

As a final example, consider the F_floating representation of the number $+35/64 \times 2^9$

- The sign bit is 0 for + (1 for −).
- The exponent is 10001001 for +9.
- The fraction is 0.10001100000000000000000 because

$$35/64 = 1/2 + 0/4 + 0/8 + 0/16 + 1/32 + 1/64$$

Packed together into 32 bits, this becomes

Sign	Exponent	Fraction
0	10001001	0001100000000000000000000
		(*Note:* The leading 1 is hidden)

Put together as a 32-bit binary string or longword, this would appear as

0100 0100 1000 1100 0000 0000 0000 0000

or in hexadecimal, ^X448C0000.

At this point, we might expect that the issue was done and that we could just place each F_floating number in a longword. However, there is a problem with this. The VAX was designed in part to be compatable with the PDP-11 computer. The PDP-11 is a 16-bit machine, and 32-bit and 64-bit floating-point numbers in the PDP-11 were stored as sequences of 16-bit words with the **most significant** part coming first. This was unfortunate for the VAX, because the VAX almost universally places the **least significant** parts first. Floating-point numbers are the main exception to this rule. As a consequence, when an F_floating number is stored in a longword, we have to reverse the first 16 bits with the last 16 bits. The result looks rather strange.

Binary	Hexadecimal
0000 0000 0000 0000 0100 0100 1000 1100	^X0000448C

Note that the sign bit ends up being right in the middle of the longword.

To avoid this awkwardness, floating-point numbers can be listed as a sequence of 16-bit words. The number above would be represented in hexadecimal as

Contents	Address
448C	starting address
0000	starting address + 2

In this format, the position of the sign, exponent, and fraction is as follows

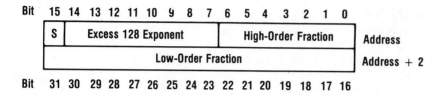

Within each 16-bit word, fraction bits from right to left represent bits of increasing significance.

D, G, and H Floating-Point Numbers

F_floating point numbers are sometimes called **single precision** floating-point numbers. The 8-bit exponent permits numbers in the approximate range of $.29 \times 10^{-38}$ through 1.7×10^{38}. The precision is approximately one part in 2^{23} or approximately seven decimal digits.

D_floating numbers, which are sometimes referred to as **double precision** floating-point numbers, are 64-bits long and therefore occupy a quadword. The D_floating format is identical to F_floating format except that the size of the fraction is increased from 23 bits to 23 plus 32 or 55 bits (not counting the hidden bit). A D_floating number appears as follows:

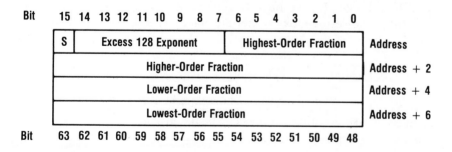

The extra fraction bits permit a precision of approximately one part in 2^{55} or approximately 16 decimal digits. The number $+35/64 \times 2^9$ would appear in D_floating as follows:

Contents	Address
448C	starting address
0000	starting address + 2
0000	starting address + 4
0000	starting address + 6

As a quadword, this would be ^X000000000000448C.

The F_ and D_ floating-point notations used on the VAX are the same as those used on the PDP-11 computers, which have been manufactured by Digital Equipment Corporation for some time. Keeping the floating-point number system the same has helped preserve software compatibility across the product lines. However, there is a new standard for floating-point number systems which was adopted recently by the Institute for Electrical and Electronic Engineers (IEEE).

The IEEE standard floating-point notation is based on the same philosophy as the DEC standard. However, the breakdown of number of bits in the various fields is different. In order to comply with anticipated higher-level language standards using IEEE notation, the VAX has incorporated two new floating-point notations which are based on the IEEE standards. These are called **G_floating point** and **H_ floating point.** G_floating notation uses 64-bits as does the D notation. However, the exponent is somewhat larger and the fraction part correspondingly smaller. This means that G_floating has slightly less precision but much more range than does D notation. (See Table 12.1 for ranges and precisions.) G_floating numbers have the following form:

Bit	15	14 13 12 11 10 9 8 7 6 5 4	3 2 1 0	
	S	Excess 1024 Exponent	Highest	Address
	Higher-Order Fraction			Address + 2
	Lower-Order Fraction			Address + 4
	Lowest-Order Fraction			Address + 6

Bit   63 62 61 60 59 58 57 56 55 54 53 52 51 50 49 48

The excess 1024 exponent is in bit positions 14 through 4 and the highest order fraction bits are in bit positions 3 through 0.

H_floating notation uses 128 bits, which is twice that used by D and G notation. Both the exponent and fraction parts share the extra bits, giving both an extremely wide range of magnitudes as well as a considerable amount of precision. The format of an H_floating number is

Bit	15 14 13 12 11 10 9 8 7 6 5 4 3 2 1 0	
S	Excess 16384 Exponent	Address
	Highest-Order Fraction	Address + 2
	Higher-Order Fraction	Address + 4
	. . .	Address + 6
	. . .	Address + 8
	. . .	Address + 10
	Lower-Order Fraction	Address + 12
	Lowest-Order Fraction	Address + 14

As with F_ and D_ floating, G and H have a one-bit sign, use excess 2^{C-1} notation for the exponent (where C is the number of bits in the exponent), and use a hidden bit in the fraction part. Recall that not representing the hidden bit gives one extra bit of precision over those floating-point notations which represent every bit in the fraction part. Table 12.1 contrasts the properties of the four kinds of floating-point notation.

12.5 Floating-Point Operations on the VAX

In Chapter 6, we saw the full list of integer arithmetic instructions. Basically, these were add, subtract, multiply, and divide. For each arithmetic operation, a family of instructions was described. The instructions in each family included two and three operand versions and versions that operated on 8-bit, 16-bit, and 32-bit integers. As a result, there were six members of each family. For example, the add family of instructions has the following six members:

```
ADDB2      ADDB3
ADDW2      ADDW3
ADDL2      ADDL3
```

When floating-point operations are considered, eight more members are added to each instruction family. The eight members are the two

Table 12.1 VAX floating-point representations

Type	Length Total	Length Sign	Length Exp.	Length Frac*	Magnitude Range	Precision in Decimal Digits
F	32	1	8	23	$.29 \times 10^{-38}$ – 1.7×10^{38}	7
D	64	1	8	55	$.29 \times 10^{-38}$ – 1.7×10^{38}	16
G	64	1	11	52	$.56 \times 10^{-308}$ – $.9 \times 10^{308}$	15
H	128	1	15	112	$.84 \times 10^{-4932}$ – $.59 \times 10^{4932}$	33

* Not counting the hidden bit.

and three operand versions of instructions for performing arithmetic operations on F, D, G, and H floating-point numbers. This results in 32 additional instructions

```
ADDF2   ADDF3   SUBF2   SUBF3   MULF2   MULF3   DIVF2   DIVF3
ADDD2   ADDD3   SUBD2   SUBD3   MULD2   MULD3   DIVD2   DIVD3
ADDG2   ADDG3   SUBG2   SUBG3   MULG2   MULG3   DIVG2   DIVG3
ADDH2   ADDH3   SUBH2   SUBH3   MULH2   MULH3   DIVH2   DIVH3
```

These instructions operate as described earlier, performing the operations indicated on pairs of 32-bit, 64-bit, or 128-bit floating-point numbers. The letters F, D, G, and H in the instruction specify F_floating, D_floating, G_floating, and H_floating operands.

The machine language format of the F and D instructions is the same as the format of the byte, word, and longword arithmetic instructions. The only difference is the use of different machine language operation codes. However, the format of the G and H instructions is slightly different. These instructions were added to the VAX architecture after most of the 8-bit operation codes already had been used for other instructions. As a result, most of the operation codes for the G_ and H_ floating-point operations require two 8-bit bytes. Thus, for example, while the operation code for ADDF2 is ^X40 and the code for ADDD2 is ^X60, the operation code for ADDG2 is ^X40FD and the operation code for ADDH2 is ^X60FD. In fact, all of the operation codes for the G_ and H_ floating-point instructions have ^XFD for the low order 8 bits. This is an escape code. Recall that the low order 8 bits are examined first. By itself, ^XFD is not a valid operation code for any instruction, rather it tells the VAX to fetch another byte to form an extended 16-bit operation code.

In order that floating-point instructions can be followed by conditional branch instructions, the floating-point instructions set the condition codes. The N bit will be set if the result is negative, and the Z bit will be set if the result is zero. The V bit will be set if overflow or underflow occur.

As noted in the section on decimal floating-point numbers, **floating-point overflow** results when an attempt is made to compute a number which is too large in magnitude for the number representation system. For F_floating and D_floating numbers, this magnitude is in the vicinity of 1.7×10^{38}. Many operating systems are set up to terminate execution of a program if floating-point overflow occurs. As a result, the program may not be able to see the V bit set when floating overflow occurs.

Floating-point underflow occurs when an attempt is made to compute a number which is not zero, but is too small in magnitude to be represented in the floating-point notation. (For F_floating and D_floating numbers, the smallest, nonzero floating-point magnitude is approximately $.29 \times 10^{-38}$.) In most cases, underflow will produce a result of zero. However, an excessive number of underflows can be an indication that the numbers in a problem are scaled too small to have significance. For this reason, most operating systems are set up to detect underflows, make the result be zero, but also produce warning messages or an error halt if more than a few (perhaps ten) underflows occur during the execution of a program. The actual value for the maximum count would be a parameter that the user could modify for his run.

So far, we have discussed the N, Z, and V bits. What about the C bit? Since floating-point operations cannot produce a carry in the same sense that integer operations do, the C bit is not used. Thus, the floating-point operations set the C bit to zero.

All of the arithmetic instructions listed above will generate an error called a **floating reserved operand fault** if an attempt is made to use a floating-point number with a sign bit of one and an excess exponent of zero. In fact, almost all of the floating-point instructions behave in this way. (The only exception occurs in a special family of POLY instructions that will be described later.)

In addition to the basic arithmetic operations of add, subtract, multiply, and divide, there are several housekeeping operations. These are move, clear, test, and compare. This gives us the instructions

```
MOVF        CLRF        TSTF        CMPF
MOVD        CLRD        TSTD        CMPD
MOVG        CLRG        TSTG        CMPG
MOVH        CLRH        TSTH        CMPH
```

These instructions have the expected effects of moving a floating-point number from one area of memory to another, clearing the area for a floating-point number, testing to see if a number is negative or zero, and comparing the relative algebraic values of two floating-point numbers.

It might occur to the reader that an F_floating-point number is four bytes, and a longword is also four bytes. Therefore, it might be concluded that MOVF is the same instruction as MOVL, since they both move four bytes from one place to another. However, there are some subtle differences. First, different rules are used to set the condition codes. For MOVL, the Z bit is set if and only if all 32 bits are zero. For a floating-point number, the Z bit is set if the sign bit and the excess exponent are both zero. (The value of the fraction does not matter.) The N bit is set differently because the signs are in different places in the longword. The sign bit for an integer longword is bit 31 (the left-most bit) while the sign bit of a floating-point number is always bit 15 (the high-order bit of the second byte). Finally, the instructions treat reserved operands very differently. A reserved operand has no special significance for the MOVL instruction. However, attempting to move a reserved operand with MOVF instruction will produce a floating reserved operand fault.

Consequently, MOVF and MOVL have different machine language operation codes and are different instructions. On the other hand, clearing an integer location to zero requires the same steps as clearing an F_floating location to zero. Therefore, CLRF is the same instruction as CLRL. That is, the assembly mnemonics CLRF and CLRL are translated into the same machine language operation code. Similar comments apply to the other floating-point formats. For example, MOVQ (MOVe Quadword), MOVD, and MOVG are different instructions but CLRQ, CLRD, and CLRG have the same machine language operation code and are really just different names for the same instruction.

These redundant assembly mnemonics are put into the assembler purely to make life easier for the assembly language programmer. First of all, the programmer is freed from having to remember which instructions are or are not different. (MOVF is different from MOVL, but CLRF is the same as CLRL.) Second, the consistent use of assembly mnemonics helps keep the program well documented.

Other Floating-Point Instructions

In addition to the instructions listed above, there are some additional ones whose integer counterparts have been used in the previous chapters. Again, these come in groups of four for the four types of floating-point numbers. The first set of instructions is

```
MNEGF    MNEGD    MNEGG    MNEGH
```

These instructions move the negative of the source operand to the destination as did the integer "move negated" instructions. Since the process of negating a VAX floating-point number consists merely of flipping the sign bit, these instructions are different from their integer counterparts which operate with two's complement notation.

Another set of instructions is concerned with addressing. These instructions are

```
MOVAF    MOVAD    MOVAG    MOVAH
PUSHAF   PUSHAD   PUSHAG   PUSHAH
```

Since the address of a four-byte block of data does not depend upon the intended use for the data, there is no real difference between the address of a 32-bit floating-point number and a longword. Therefore, MOVAF is identical to MOVAL and PUSHAF is identical to PUSHAL. Similar comments apply to the remaining six instructions.

Constants and Immediate Values

Floating-point instructions can use immediate operands in much the same way that integer instructions can. Thus, for example, the instruction ADDF2 #3.1415927,X will cause the approximate value of pi to be added to the F_floating number X. The syntax for writing floating-point constants, although somewhat more liberal, is essentially the same as that used in FORTRAN. Rather than try to spell out the exact rules here, suffice it to say that any valid representation for a FORTRAN real constant is valid for VAX assembly language. This, of course, includes E notation. For more information, consult the *VAX-11 Macro Language Reference Manual*.

Literal operands can be used with floating-point instructions. As with integer instructions, if the first 2 bits of an operand specifier byte is zero, the remaining 6 bits are used for a restricted, immediate operand. For integers, the restriction is that the number be in the range from 0 to 63. For floating-point operations, the restriction is that the number must be representable in a special 6-bit floating-point notation. Obviously, a highly precise number like 3.1415927 could not be represented in 6 bits. Therefore, the instruction ADDF2 #3.1415927,X will require a full, longword, immediate operand. However, simpler floating-point constants like 1.0 (which are more common) can be represented in the 6-bit notation. Consequently the instruction ADDF2 #1.0,X will assemble in four fewer bytes.

Figure 12.4 shows the 64 floating-point numbers that can be represented as literals. The 6-bit floating-point literal consists of a 3-

Figure 12.4 Floating-point literals

Exponent Bits	Fraction Bits (the leading bit is hidden)							
	000	001	010	011	100	101	110	111
000	$\frac{1}{2}$	$\frac{9}{16}$	$\frac{5}{8}$	$\frac{11}{16}$	$\frac{3}{4}$	$\frac{13}{16}$	$\frac{7}{8}$	$\frac{15}{16}$
001	1	$1\frac{1}{8}$	$1\frac{1}{4}$	$1\frac{3}{8}$	$1\frac{1}{2}$	$1\frac{5}{8}$	$1\frac{3}{4}$	$1\frac{7}{8}$
010	2	$2\frac{1}{4}$	$2\frac{1}{2}$	$2\frac{3}{4}$	3	$3\frac{1}{4}$	$3\frac{1}{2}$	$3\frac{3}{4}$
011	4	$4\frac{1}{2}$	5	$5\frac{1}{2}$	6	$6\frac{1}{2}$	7	$7\frac{1}{2}$
100	8	9	10	11	12	13	14	15
101	16	18	20	22	24	26	28	30
110	32	36	40	44	48	52	56	60
111	64	72	80	88	96	104	112	120

bit characteristic, and a 3-bit fraction part with a hidden bit. No provision is made for negative values or negative exponents. Therefore, the range of fractions is from 1000 (binary) to 1111 binary. (Note that the leading one is hidden so that this only occupies 3 bits of storage.) Since the radix point is assumed on the left, these fractions represent values that range from 1/2 to 15/16 in steps of 1/16. The exponents range from 0 through 7 so that numbers can range with limited steps of precision from $1/2 \times 2^0$, or 1/2, to 15/16 x 2^7, or 120.

In addition to having immediate constants in instructions, it is sometimes useful to have constants located in the data area of a program. This is particularly useful for arrays of constants. With integers, the .BYTE, .WORD, .LONG, and .QUAD assembly directives are used. For real valued constants, the directives .F_FLOATING, .D _FLOATING, .G_FLOATING, and .H_FLOATING are used.* These directives are followed by a variable number of arguments using FORTRAN-style notation. For example, the following directive:

```
.F_FLOATING    1.0,2.0,3.0
```

would generate the following array of longwords

```
^X00004080
^X00004100
^X00004140
```

---

* The directive .FLOAT has the same effect as .F_FLOATING, and the directive DOUBLE has the same effect as .D_FLOATING.

Convert Instructions

In Chapter 6, we saw a set of instructions for moving bytes to words, and words to longwords, and so forth. We will now, extend that set of instructions, not only to allow floating-point operands of one type (such as single precision F_floating) to be converted to a floating operand of another type (such as double precision D_floating), but also to include all the combinations of integer to floating-point and floating-point to integer conversion. Figure 12.5 shows these members of the convert family.

    As would be expected, the fraction part is lost when a real number is moved to an integer field. For the instructions in Figure 12.5, this is done by truncation. There is also the possibility that a real number may be too large to fit into a byte, word, or even a longword integer field. Thus, the possibility of overflow exists. The V bit is used to indicate this as it is for the instructions which move a large integer field to a smaller one, such as CVTWB. Note that precision can be lost with the CVTLF instruction because there are 31 bits of precision in the longword and only 24 bits in the fraction part of an F_floating number.

    Notice that there are no instructions for converting between D_floating and G_floating numbers. To convert from D_floating to G_floating, it is necessary to convert the 64-bit D_floating number to a 128-bit H_floating number and then convert the H_floating number to a 64-bit G_floating number. Similar comments apply to a G_floating to D_floating conversion. The conversions can be performed with the following macros.

```
.MACRO   CVTDG   D_FLT,G_FLT        .MACRO   CVTGD   G_FLT,D_FLT
CVTDH    D_FLT,-(SP)                CVTGH    G_FLT,-(SP)
CVTHG    (SP)+,G_FLT                CVTHD    (SP)+,D_FLT
.ENDM    CVTDG                      .ENDM    CVTGD
```

Figure 12.5 The convert family of instructions

Source Operand Type	Destination Operand Type						
	Byte	Word	Long	F_float	D_float	G_float	H_float
Byte		CVTBW	CVTBL	CVTBF	CVTBD	CVTBG	CVTBH
Word	CVTWB		CVTWL	CVTWF	CVTWD	CVTWG	CVTWH
Long	CVTLB	CVTLW		CVTLF	CVTLD	CVTLG	CVTLH
F_float	CVTFB	CVTFW	CVTFL		CVTFD	CVTFG	CVTFH
D_float	CVTDB	CVTDW	CVTDL	CVTDF			CVTDH
G_float	CVTGB	CVTGW	CVTGL	CVTGF			CVTGH
H_float	CVTHB	CVTHW	CVTHL	CVTHF	CVTHD	CVTHG	

As noted previously, the instructions in Figure 12.5 that convert from a floating format to an integer format truncate any fraction. The VAX provides four additional instructions that round the fraction to the nearest integer. These instructions are

CVTRFL   CVTRDL   CVTRGL   CVTRHL

For example, CVTRFL (ConVerT Rounded F_floating to Longword) will round the floating-point number to the nearest integer and place the result in a longword.

12.6 Complex Floating-Point Instructions

Programs which do a large amount of computation with numerical fractions are often called **number crunchers.** However, even number crunching programs spend much (if not most) of their time doing logical and integer type operations. These include address computations for arrays, counting how many times to go around a loop, and determining where to go next. The lower the level at which these logical operations can be kept, the faster the program will execute. Thus, for example, the looping needed to do multiplication, division, and floating-point operations has long been built into the hardware of high-speed computers. A modern trend is the evaluation of polynomials. A simple polynomial can be defined as

$$A_n X^n + A_{n-1} X^{n-1} + \cdots A_2 X^2 + A_1 X + A_0$$

where A_0 through A_n form an array of constant coefficients, and X is a variable. Since the highest power is n, this is said to be an nth order polynomial. Polynomials are very important in numerical calculations, because many real-valued functions, such as SIN, COS, and EXP, can be approximated with polynomials. For example, the function e^x can be approximated by the polynomial:

$$1 + X + X^2/2! + X^3/3! + X^4/4! + \cdots + X^n/n!$$

By computing this polynomial to a high enough order, any amount of accuracy can be achieved.

The instructions for evaluating polynomials are POLYF, POLYD, POLYG, and POLYH. These instructions have three operands: the floating value X, the integer value of the order of the polynomial, and the address of an array which contains the floating coefficients beginning with the highest order coefficient. There is no specified operand to receive the results. Instead, the results make use of the general registers, R0, R1, R2, ... These instructions also use the general register for temporary storage during computation. Therefore, when these instructions finish, the contents of several of the general registers will be overwritten. POLYF leaves its result in R0, but also overwrites R1, R2, and R3. POLYD and POLYG leave the high order 32 bits of the result in R0 and the low order 32 bits in R1. These instructions also overwrite R2 through R5. POLYH leaves the 128-bit result in R0 through R3 with the highest order bits in R0 and the lowest order bits in R3. POLYH also overwrites R4 and R5.

Note that the use of R0 and R1 for holding a double precision result is the normal method that is used by all D- or G-type instructions when one or more of the operands is a general register. The referenced register will hold the high order 32 bits, and the next higher numbered register will hold the low order 32 bits. Thus, a POLYD instruction could be followed by MOVD R0,ANS or even ADDD2 R0,TOTAL.

As an example of how these instructions operate, let us consider the above polynomial for approximating e^x. Although the accuracy will not be very good unless X is small, let us assume that a fifth order polynomial is good enough. We then will need a table of six coefficients:

```
CTAB:     .F_FLOATING   0.8333333E-2   ;1/5!
          .F_FLOATING   0.04166667     ;1/4!
          .F_FLOATING   0.1666667      ;1/3!
          .F_FLOATING   0.5            ;1/2!
          .F_FLOATING   1.0            ;1/1!
          .F_FLOATING   1.0            ;1/0!
```

Then the instruction POLYF X,#5,CTAB will be able to evaluate the function, leaving the result in R0.

The EMOD (Extended multiply and integerize) family of instructions is used for computing the value of cyclic functions such as trigonometric functions. (As explained below, the letters "MOD" refer to modulus.) Consider the sine of an angle expressed in degrees. Because of the way that the sine function is defined

$$\text{SIN}(X) = \text{SIN}(X+360) = \text{SIN}(X+720) = \text{SIN}(X + N \times 360)$$

where N is any integer. To compute the sine of an angle, the extra multiples of 360 are redundant. To compute the value of cyclic functions, programs generally perform a **range reduction** operation to reduce the input argument to a number between two fixed bounds. For the sine function, for example, the range reduction can be performed by dividing the input argument by 360 (which is the same as multiplying by 1/360), discarding the integer part of the result, and computing the sine based on the fractional part of the result. (In this example, the number 360 is the **MODulus** and the instruction is called EMOD.)

However, the range reduction can result in a loss of significant digits. For example, if reduction is performed on SIN(360001) using F_floating arithmetic, 360001/360 equals 1000 plus 1/360. F_floating numbers only have about 23 bits of precision to begin with. Discarding the integer part, 1000, discards about 10 bits of precision. This means that the fraction only contains about 23 minus 10 or 13 bits of precision.

The EMOD family is designed to solve this problem. Consider, for example, the following EMODF instruction:

```
EMODF    MULT,MULT_EXT,ARG,INT_PART,FRAC_PART
```

The first, third, and fifth operands (MULT, ARG, and FRACT_PART). are F_floating numbers. The second argument, MULT_EXT, is a byte that is used to provide 8 additional fraction bits to augment the 24 fraction bits in MULT. In the example above, the programmer would specify 1/360 to 32 significant digits. The high order 24 digits would become the fraction part of the F_floating number MULT while the 8 low order digits would be placed in the byte MULT_EXT.

When the EMODF instruction is executed, the F_floating argument ARG is multiplied by the extended multiplier (MULT extended by MULT_EXT). The integer part of the result is placed in the integer word INT_PART while the range-reduced result is placed in the F_floating operand FRACT_PART. (POLYF can then use FRACT_PART to compute the sine.) EMODD, EMODG, and EMODH operate in a similar manner. However, the length of the operands (including MULT_EXT and INT_PART) are different.

Exercise Set 2

1. Show how the following numbers would be represented in the 32-bit, F_floating-point number system. Express your answers in hexadecimal.

a. 1.0	**b.** -10.0	**c.** 100.0
d. 0.5	**e.** 0.1	**f.** -0.01

2. Given the following 32-bit floating-point numbers in F_floating notation, show what the values would be in the decimal number system, using FORTRAN notation.

   a. ^X00004080   **b.** ^X00004000
   ç. ^X00003F80   **d.** ^X00006080
   e. ^X0000C080   **f.** ^XCCCC3F4C

3. Show how the numbers in Exercise 1 and 2, above, would be represented in D, G, and H floating-point notation. Express your answer in hexadecimal.

4. As was discussed in Exercise 5 on page 353, the square root of a number N can be approximated by the formula

   $.5 \times (X + N/X)$

   where X is a guess at the square root of N. If X is reasonably close to the square root of N to begin with, the value of this formula will be much closer to the correct value. As a result, if the algorithm produces a good initial guess, several iterations of this formula can yield a result which is good to 15 to 30 decimal places. One simple algorithm for a first guess works as follows:

   a. The representation of a floating point number is

   $f \times 2^C$ where $1/2 \leqslant f < 1$

   b. If one is subtracted from C in order to make it even, the formula becomes

   $f' \times 2^{C'}$ where $1/2 \leqslant f < 2$

   c. Now the square root of this will be

   $\sqrt{f'} \times 2^{C'/2}$

   d. The range of $\sqrt{f'}$ will be approximately

   $0.707 \leqslant \sqrt{f'} \leqslant 1.41$

   e. As a result, a good guess for $\sqrt{f'}$ can be 1, and this will be off by at most 41%.

f. Since the fraction part of a floating-point number cannot be 1, use the largest possible value which is all binary ones.

Write a FORTRAN callable subroutine which has an input value of one D_floating variable, and outputs an array of ten D_floating variables. The program will apply the above algorithm to get an initial guess of the square root of the input value. The program then iterates nine more times using the formula $.5 \times (X + N/X)$ putting each value obtained in the output array. Write a FORTRAN program which calls this subroutine with a variety of input values of differing magnitudes. The FORTRAN program should print out these results along with the results obtained using the DSQRT function from the FORTRAN library for comparison. (Hint: Use masking and shifting operations to divide the exponent by two for the initial guess.) (If you are using a Micro VAX, use G_floating instead of D_floating.)

5. The cosine of X can be computed from the infinite series:

$$COS(x) = 1 - X^2/2! + X^4/4! - X^6/6! + X^8/8! - \cdots$$

This series can be used in a computer to compute the cosine, if a sufficient number of terms is used to guarantee the accuracy needed. Since the series alternates in sign from term to term, the error will be smaller than the first neglected term, once the terms start decreasing in magnitude.

a. How many terms are needed to achieve D_floating accuracy or G if X is in the range $-\pi \leqslant X \leqslant \pi$?

b. Write a FORTRAN callable subroutine or function which computes the cosine using the above polynomial for D_ or G_floating or values. Compare your results with those computed by the FORTRAN library function DCOS.

Do not store the coefficients as an array, but compute them iteratively as you evaluate the polynomial. Do not use the POLYD or POLYG instruction for this exercise.

6. Repeat Exercise 5, above, except your program should contain an array of constant coefficients and use the POLYD or POLYG instruction. Note that since there are no odd powers in the cosine series, it would imply that every other coefficient is zero. This means that half the multiplications and additions are by zero. Can anything be done easily to prevent this inefficiency?

7. Repeat Exercise 5 or 6, above, but restrict the range of X to be $-\pi/2 \leqslant x \leqslant \pi/2$. Now, how many terms are needed to achieve D_ or G_floating accuracy? Is there a simple way to adjust the input argument using trigonometric identities so that the cosine of any angle can be computed even though the range is restricted? If so, incorporate it into your program.

8. Suppose that the CVTFL instruction did not exist. Write a program which uses shifting and masking to convert F_floating numbers to longwords.

9. Repeat Exercise 8 but for the CVTLF instruction.

10. Repeat Exercise 8 but for the CVTDG instruction.

Character, Decimal, and Other Instructions

13.1 Introduction

This chapter describes some of the more complicated instructions that are part of the VAX architecture. For example, the architecture includes instructions for manipulating character strings. With these instructions, it is possible to perform operations such as moving a character string, comparing two character strings, or searching a character string for a particular substring. Many of these techniques were described in Chapter 8. However, the instructions described in this chapter allow these functions to be performed with a single instruction.

Another set of instructions supports decimal numbers and decimal arithmetic. To represent decimal numbers, the VAX architecture includes a number representation called **packed decimal** representation. With this representation, a number is stored as a string of bytes in which each byte represents two decimal digits. Instructions are available for performing arithmetic operations on packed decimal numbers, which are particularly important in business data processing.

Yet another set of instructions supports the formatting of numerical information for input and/or output. A numeric string is a character string that contains numerical information in one of several formats provided by the VAX architecture. Instructions are available for converting packed decimal numbers to numeric strings and vice versa. The EDIT instruction provides a flexible way of converting decimal numbers to character strings. Finally, the VAX architecture includes instructions for manipulating bit fields and double-linked lists.

Many of the instructions described in this chapter were included in the VAX architecture to support higher-level languages. However, many of these instructions perform functions that are generally useful in any programming environment. Their use in assembly language programs can save significant amounts of processor time and memory space.

13.2 The MOVC Family
The MOVC3 Instruction

As we saw in Chapter 8, a character string is a consecutive sequence of bytes in memory which is specified by two attributes—the address of the first byte of the string and the length of the string. Figure 13.1 contains a program segment that will copy a source character string to a destination character string. The source string begins in address SOURCE, the destination string begins in address DEST, and the length of the string is specified by LENGTH. Because a MOVZWL instruction is used to load the length into R0, the length is an unsigned word and the source and destination strings can be from 0 to 65535 bytes long. When the loop exits, register R0 will contain zero, R1 will point to the byte that follows the last byte of the source string, and R3 will point to the byte that follows the last byte of the destination string.

There is an instruction on the VAX called MOVC3 which has much the same effect as the program segment in Figure 13.1. For example, the instruction

```
MOVC3    #LENGTH,SOURCE,DEST
```

will copy #LENGTH bytes from SOURCE to DEST. In addition, the MOVC3 instruction will use processor registers R0, R1, and R3 in the same way as the program segment in Figure 13.1. After the MOVC3 instruction is executed, processor registers R0 through R5 will contain the following:

- R0   Zero
- R1   Address of the first byte following the source string
- R2   Zero
- R3   Address of the first byte following the destination string
- R4   Zero
- R5   Zero

Figure 13.1 Copying a
character string

```
LENGTH=any number from 0 to 65535
SOURCE: .BLKB    LENGTH
DEST:   .BLKB    LENGTH
         . . .
        MOVAB    SOURCE,R1      ;POINTER TO SOURCE STRING
        MOVAB    DEST,R3        ;POINTER TO DESTINATION STRING
        MOVZWL   #LENGTH,R0     ;LENGTH IS UNSIGNED WORD
        BEQL     20$            ;HANDLE ZERO LENGTH STRING
10$:    MOVB     (R1)+,(R3)+
        SOBGTR   R0,10$
20$:     . . .
```

Note that the MOVC3 instruction modifies processor registers R0 through R5 even if the registers do not appear as operands of the instruction. Most of the instructions described in this chapter make implicit use of some or all of the registers R0 through R5. (The POLY instruction described in Chapter 12 also makes implicit use of registers R0 through R5.) Since these instructions destroy the previous contents of registers R0 through R5, the programmer must exercise caution when using these registers.

The following notation will be used to describe instructions and their use of registers

```
MOVC3     len,        srcadr,     dstadr
          R0 = 0      R1 = a      R3 = a        (R2 = R4 = R5 = 0)
```

a = address following last byte of string

The name "len" represents the operand that specifies the length of the strings while "srcadr" and "dstadr" represent the source and destination addresses. The symbols R0 = 0 under len indicate that R0 is used to hold the length and that R0 contains zero when the instruction terminates. The symbols (R2 = R4 = R5 = 0) indicate that the instruction clears these registers even though they are not directly associated with a particular operand.

The MOVC5 Instruction

There is an instruction similar to MOVC3 called MOVC5 which is designed to move a source string to a destination string when the strings may have different lengths. The format of the instruction is

```
MOVC5      srclen,srcadr,fill,dstlen,dstadr
           R0=a R1=b    R2=0 R3=b           (R4=R5=0)
```

a = number of unmoved bytes if the source length is greater than
the destination length, zero otherwise
b = address of byte following last byte of string

The first and fourth operands (srclen and dstlen) are unsigned 16-bit
words that specify the lengths of the source and destination strings.
If srclen is greater than dstlen, only the first dstlen bytes from the
source string are moved to the destination. If srclen is less than dstlen,
srclen bytes are moved from the source to the destination. The
remaining dstlen minus srclen bytes of the destination are loaded
with the fill character specified by the third operand.

For example, assume that the source and destination strings are
defined as follows:

```
SOURCE:    .ASCII    /A SHORT STRING/
SOURCE_END:
SRC_LEN= SOURCE_END-SOURCE
DST_LEN= 25
DEST:      .BLKB      DST_LEN
```

Then executing the instruction

```
MOVC5    #SCR_LEN,SOURCE,#^A"*",#DST_LEN,DEST
```

will set the destination string to

```
A SHORT STRING***********
```

The third operand, #^A"*", illustrates how an ASCII string can be
used as an operand. The operand #^A"*" has the same effect as the
operand #42 or #^X2A because 42 or ^X2A is the ASCII code for the
character "*". Because the source string is 14 bytes long while the
destination string is 25 bytes long, the last 11 characters in the source
string are set to the fill character, in this case "*".

The MOVC5 instruction sets the condition codes based on the
relative lengths of the source and destination strings. In particular,

- N is set if srclen is less than dstlen as a signed number.
- Z is set if srclen is equal to dstlen.
- V is cleared.
- C is set if srclen is less than dstlen as an unsigned number.

Except for the V bit, the condition codes are set as though the instruction

```
CMPW      srclen,dstlen
```

had been executed after the MOVC5 instruction. The unsigned branch instruction can therefore be used after a MOVC5 instruction to branch on the relative lengths of the two strings. To be consistent with the MOVC5 instruction, the MOVC3 instruction sets the condition codes to reflect a comparison of two strings of equal length. Thus MOVC3 clears N, V, and C and sets Z.

Use of the MOVC Family

The MOVC5 instruction is the preferred way to fill a block of memory with the fill character. This can be done by using a zero length source string. For example, assume that the following area of memory is to be initialized to spaces (^X20).

```
BUFLEN=a number from zero to 65535
BUFFER:  .BLKB    BUFLEN
```

Spaces can be moved to BUFFER with the instruction

```
MOVC5     #0,any,#^X20,#BUFFLEN,BUFFER
```

The second operand, "any," is the starting address of the source character string. Since the length of the source string is zero, the address is never referenced and any address, including zero, is valid. One convention is to use the location counter symbol (.) for the second operand. A better convention is to use the stack pointer (SP) for the second operand because this operand only requires a single byte.

The MOVC3 and MOVC5 instructions contain three types of operands—32-bit addresses, 16-bit unsigned string lengths, and, in the case of MOVC5, an 8-bit fill character. Any of the addressing modes described in Chapter 7 can be used for the length or fill operands. However, the address operands require addressing modes that generate a 32-bit address. Thus register, literal, and immediate addressing cannot be used with address operands.

With both the MOVC3 and MOVC5 instructions, the source and destination strings may overlap. Consider, for example, the following:

```
STRING:   ASCII    /ABCDEF/
          . . .
          MOVC3    #5,STRING,STRING+1
```

If the MOVC family operated on a character-by-character basis as shown in Figure 13.1, the byte in STRING would be moved to STRING + 1, the new value in STRING + 1 would be moved to STRING + 2, and so on. As a result, the character in address STRING would be propagated through the remaining five bytes and the string would contain AAAAAA after execution.*

However, the implementation of the MOVC family on the VAX operates as though the source string is first moved to a temporary string which is then moved to the destination string. As a result, STRING will contain AABCDE after the MOVC3 instruction is executed.

13.3 Character String Instructions

The character string instructions such as MOVC3 and MOVC5 can efficiently implement character string operations in higher-level languages. However, the word "character" in the instruction name is misleading because these instructions are not restricted to a particular character code or even to characters of any kind. They are general purpose instructions for manipulating arrays of bytes.

Assume, for example, that a program contains the following two longword arrays:

```
ELEMENTS=any number from 0 to 16383
ARRAY_ONE:    .BLKL    ELEMENTS
ARRAY_TWO:    .BLKL    ELEMENTS
```

The instruction

```
MOVC5    #0,(SP),#0,#4*ELEMENTS,ARRAY_ONE
```

can be used to set all of the longwords in **ARRAY_ONE** to zero. (Since the first operand specifies that the length of the first character string is zero, the address of the first string does not matter. As a result, register deferred addressing with the stack pointer, (SP), was used for the second operand.)

---

* On the IBM 360 and its successors, the instruction analogous to MOVC3 is MVC (for MoVe Characters). MVC implements the move on a character-by-character basis and MVC is used to propagate a byte through a string.

The longwords in ARRAY_ONE can be copied to ARRAY_TWO with the instruction

```
MOVC3     #<4*ELEMENTS>,ARRAY_ONE,ARRAY_TWO
```

(The MOVC3 instruction is the recommended way of moving a block from one area of memory to another.) Similarly, the instruction

```
MOVC3     #<<4*ELEMENTS>-4>,ARRAY_ONE+4,ARRAY_ONE
```

has the effect of setting ARRAY_ONE[I] equal to ARRAY_ONE[I + 1] for I varying from 1 to ELEMENTS-1. (The operand #<<4*ELEMENTS>-4> is equivalent to the operand #4*ELEMENTS-4. The angle brackets, which are normally used to modify operator precedence, are included here for readability.)

All of the character string instructions use some of the registers R0 through R5. As we shall see, character string instructions can have up to three strings as operands. This requires up to three string addresses and three string lengths. When execution of a character string instruction begins, the processor fetches the operands and loads the string lengths and string addresses into registers R0 through R5. (Because the operands are fetched before any of the general registers are loaded, the operands themselves may be in the general registers including registers R0 through R5.) Registers R0 through R5 are loaded with the following information:

- R0   Length of the first string
- R1   Starting address of the first string
- R2   Length of the second string (if needed)
- R3   Starting address of the second string (if needed)
- R4   Length of the third string (if needed)
- R5   Starting address of the third string (if needed)

Depending on the number of strings involved, the character string instructions may use R0 through R1, R0 through R3, or R0 through R5.

At the start of execution of a character string instruction, the instruction loads registers R0 through R1, R0 through R3, or R0 through R5, destroying the previous contents. During execution of a character string instruction, the processor increments addresses in the odd-numbered registers and decrements lengths in the even-numbered registers in a manner appropriate for the particular instruction. When execution of the instruction terminates, the contents of the registers can be used for further processing.

There is another reason that the character string instructions use the general registers. As explained in Chapter 14, an executing program may be interrupted so that the processor can respond to an event that has higher priority than the current program. Most VAX machine language instructions have short execution times, and the processor normally waits until execution of the current instruction has been completed before beginning the interrupt process. However some instructions, including the character string instructions, may have lengthy execution times. (Even on a VAX computer system, it can take a significant fraction of a second to move 65,535 bytes.) To allow the VAX to respond quickly to external events, instructions with lengthy execution times are designed to be interrupted before execution of the instruction has been completed. Because the character string instructions use R0 through R5 for temporary storage, the interrupt process is fast and efficient. When a character string instruction is interrupted in the middle of execution, most of the information required to resume execution of the instruction is in the general registers.

13.4 The CMPC Family

The CMPC (CoMPare Character string) family consists of two instructions, CMPC3 and CMPC5. Like all of the compare instructions, the CMPC instructions simply set the condition codes. The CMPC3 and CMPC5 instructions have the same format as the MOVC3 and MOVC5 instructions. For example, the instruction

```
CMPC3     #10,ALPHA,BETA
```

performs a sequence of up to ten byte comparisons

```
CMPB      ALPHA,BETA
CMPB      ALPHA+1,BETA+1
CMPB      ALPHA+2,BETA+2
  .  .  .
CMPB      ALPHA+9,BETA+9
```

The sequence of comparisons is terminated when two unequal bytes are found or, if the character strings are equal, after all of the bytes have been compared. As a result, the condition codes indicate whether the first string is greater than, equal to, or less than the second character string.

The CMPC3 instruction modifies the contents of general registers R0 through R3. When the strings are equal, R1 points to the byte following the last byte in the first string, R3 points to the byte following the last byte in the second string, and R0 and R2 are zero. When the strings are unequal, however, R1 and R3 point to the bytes that resulted in the unequal comparison and R0 contains the number of bytes remaining in each of the strings **including** the byte that caused the unequal comparison. Consider, for example the following:

```
GAMMA:    .ASCII   /ABCDEF/
DELTA:    .ASCII   /ABCDXY/
          . . .
          CMPC3    #6,GAMMA,DELTA
```

After the comparison, R0 contains 2, which indicates that there were two bytes left in each string when a difference was found. R1 points to the byte containing "E", R3 points to the byte containing "X", and R2 contains zero.

The CMPC5 instruction is designed to compare two strings that may have different lengths. The CMPC5 instruction has the same operand format as the MOVC5 instruction. The CMPC5 instruction operates as though the shorter of the two character strings was extended with fill characters to equal the length of the longer string. Consider, for example, the following strings:

```
ONE:    .ASCII   /ABC/
TWO:    .ASCII   /ABC**!/
```

The strings that are compared by each of the following instructions are illustrated to the right of each instruction.

Instruction		String Comparison	Notes	N	Z	V	C
CMPC5	#3,ONE,#^A"$",#6,TWO	ABC$$$ < ABC**!	$ < *	1	0	0	1
CMPC5	#3,ONE,#^A"*",#6,TWO	ABC*** > ABC**!	* > !	0	0	0	0
CMPC5	#6,TWO,#^A"$",#3,ONE	ABC**! > ABC$$$	* > $	0	0	0	0
CMPC5	#6,TWO,#^A"*",#3,ONE	ABC**! < ABC***	! < *	1	0	0	1

If the character strings are equal, the Z bit is set to one and the N and C bits are zero. If the strings are unequal, the N and C bits are set depending on the bytes that caused the unequal comparison. N is set if the byte from the first string is less than the byte from the second as a signed number string while C is set if the first byte is less than the second byte as an unsigned number.

At the beginning of execution of the CMPC5 instruction, the lengths of the two strings are placed into registers R0 and R2 and the starting addresses are placed into R1 and R3. If the strings are equal, R0 and R2 will contain zero when the instruction terminates and R1 and R3 will point to the bytes that immediately follow the last byte in their respective strings.

If the strings are unequal, R0 and R2 indicate the number of bytes remaining in their respective strings including the byte that caused the unequal comparison. (If the unequal byte is one of the appended fill characters, the corresponding register will contain zero.) R1 and R3 point to the byte that caused the unequal comparison. (If the unequal byte is one of the appended fill characters, the corresponding register will point to the byte following the last byte of the string.)

With a MOVC5 instruction, the fill character is only used if the first string is shorter than the second. With a CMPC5 instruction, the fill character may be used whenever the string lengths differ. As a result, a MOVC5 instruction followed by a CMPC5 instruction with identical operands will not necessarily yield an equal result. For example,

```
THREE:    .ASCII    "ABCDEF"
FOUR:     .BLKB     3

          .  .  .
          MOVC5     #6,THREE,#^A"*",#3,FOUR
          CMPC5     #6,THREE,#^A"*",#3,FOUR
```

The MOVC5 instruction will move ABC to string FOUR. However, the CMPC5 instruction will compare the string ABCDEF with ABC***, resulting in an unequal comparison.

As with the MOVC family, the operands of CMPC3 and CMPC5 instructions may overlap. For example, the instruction

```
CMPC3     #10,STRING,STRING+1
```

will yield an equal result only if the bytes in STRING + 1 through STRING + 9 are equal to the byte in STRING. (If the string contains AAAAABCDEF, R1 will point to the fifth "A" and R3 will point to the "B" when execution terminates.) Similarly, the instruction

```
CMPC5     #SIZE,BYTE_ARRAY,#128,#0,(SP)
```

will scan the byte array BYTE_ARRAY, leaving R1 with the address of the first byte that does not contain 128 decimal. (Since the second string operand has a length of zero, the operand (SP) was used as the address of the second operand.)

13.5 Other Character String Instructions
The SKPC, LOCC, and MATCHC Instructions

As noted in the previous section, the CMPC5 instruction can be used to skip over characters in a character string that are equal to the fill character. For example, consider the following:

```
STRING:  .ASCII     "     BEGINS WITH FIVE SPACES"
STRING_END:
LENGTH=STRING_END-STRING
         . . .
         CMPC5     #LENGTH,STRING,#^A" ",#0,(SP)
```

Since the fill character is a space character and the second string has a length of zero, the CMPC5 instruction first finds unequal bytes when the fill character is compared with the letter "B" in BEGINS. When the instruction terminates, R1 will point to the letter "B".

This effect can be obtained with the SKPC (SKiP Character) instruction that is part of the VAX architecture. For example, the instruction

```
SKPC      #^A" ",#LENGTH,STRING
```

will also leave R1 pointing to the letter "B". R0 will contain 23, the number of bytes remaining in the string (including the letter B) when the nonblank character was found. Unlike the CMPC5 instruction, the SKPC instruction always sets the N, V, and C bits to zero. The Z bit is set to indicate the value in R0. If a character not equal to the fill character is found in the string, R0 will contain the number of bytes remaining in the string and the Z bit is cleared. If all of the characters in the string are equal to the fill character, R0 will contain zero and the Z bit is set. R0 and R1 are the only registers used by SKPC for temporary storage.

The LOCC (LOCate Character) instruction is identical to the SKPC instruction except that it terminates on equality instead of inequality. LOCC is used to locate a particular character in a string. For example, the instruction

```
STRING:  .ASCII    "BEGINS WITH NO SPACES"
STRING_END:
LENGTH=STRING_END-STRING
         . . .
         LOCC      #^A" ",#LENGTH,STRING
```

will leave R1 pointing to the space character following the S in BEGINS. Like the SKPC instruction, the LOCC instruction sets the

Z bit depending on the value in R0. In the example above, R0 will contain 15 when the instruction terminates because there are 15 bytes (including the space character) remaining in the string. Thus, the Z bit will be cleared.

Locating a particular character in a character string is a fairly common operation. For example, the instruction

```
LOCC      #^A":",#LENGTH,STRING
```

can be used to search for a colon that terminates a label in an assembly language program. The same instruction can be used to search for the colon in a VAX/VMS file specification. In fact, a routine that parses a VMS file specification might use a variety of LOCC instructions to locate characters such as :, [,], ., and ;. Similarly, a routine that parses expressions in a higher-level language might use LOCC instructions to search for characters such as $=$, :, (,), $+$, $-$, $*$, and /.

The SKPC and LOCC instructions can be used to process a string of words that are separated by one or more separator characters. In the following example, the asterisk is used as the separator character. (For English text of course, the separator would be a space character.)

```
STRING:   .ASCII "**WORDS*SEPARATED***BY*****ASTERISKS**"
STRING_END:
LENGTH=STRING_END-STRING
          . . .
          SKPC    #^A"*",#LENGTH,STRING     ;R1 POINTS TO "W" OF "WORDS"
          LOCC    #^A"*",R0,(R1)            ;R1 POINTS TO "*" AFTER "WORDS"
          SKPC    #^A"*",R0,(R1)            ;R1 POINTS TO "S" OF "SEPARATED"
          LOCC    #^A"*",R0,(R1)            ;R1 POINTS TO "*" AFTER "SEPARATED"
          SKPC    #^A"*",R0,(R1)            ;R1 POINTS TO "B" OF "BY"
```

The comment on each line indicates the byte that R1 points to after the instruction is executed. Note how the results left in registers R0 and R1 by one instruction are used as input to the next instruction. The words in the string can be processed with the following loop:

```
          MOVZWL   #LENGTH,R0       ;INITIALIZE R0 TO LENGTH
          MOVAB    STRING,R1        ; AND R1 TO ADDRESS OF STRING
10$:      SKPC     #^A"*",R0,(R1)   ;SKIP *'s TO START OF NEXT WORD
          BEQL     20$              ;IF R0 IS ZERO, END OF STRING
          any code to be executed at beginning of a word
          LOCC     #^A"*",R0,(R1)   ;FIND * AT END OF WORD
          BEQL     20$              ;IF R0 IS ZERO, END OF STRING
          any code to be executed after end of a word
          BRB      10$
20$:      . . .
```

The MATCHC (MATCH Character substring) is similar in concept to the LOCC instruction. However, while LOCC locates the first occurrence of a particular character within a string, MATCHC locates the first occurrence of a particular substring within a string. Consider, for example, the following:

```
STRING:          .ASCII     "ABCDEFGHIJKLMNOPQRSTUVWXYZ"
LENGTH=26
SUB_STRING:      .ASCII     "DEF"
SUB_LENGTH=3

            . . .
            MATCHC     #SUB_LENGTH,SUB_STRING,#LENGTH,STRING
```

Notice that the first two operands specify the length and starting address of the substring that will be matched while the third and fourth operands specify the length and starting address of the string that will be searched. In this example, the substring DEF will be found inside the string. The instruction uses R0 through R3 for temporary storage. In this case, after the instruction is executed, R0 through R3 will contain the following:

- R0 Zero (the number of bytes remaining in the substring)
- R1 The address SUB_STRING + 3 (the address of the byte following the substring)
- R2 Twenty (the number of bytes remaining in the string following the match)
- R3 The address STRING + 6 (the address of the first byte following the match)

The condition codes N, V, and C are cleared and the Z bit is set according to the value in R0. In this case, R0 contains 0, and therefore, the Z bit will be set indicating a match has occurred.

If the substring is not found, R0 will contain the length of the substring (in this case 3) and R1 will point to the beginning of the substring. In addition, R2 will contain zero and R3 will point to the byte following the string. Since R0 is not equal to zero, the Z bit will be cleared.

Table Lookup Instructions

Four additional instructions resemble MOVC, LOCC, and SKPC instructions, except that they use an additional table or string of 256 bytes. The MOVC, LOCC, and SKPC instructions successively fetch bytes from a source string. (With the MOVC instruction, the fetched bytes are moved to a destination string. With LOCC or SKPC, the fetched bytes are compared with a character specified by a third operand.) The instructions described here are similar except that, after each byte is fetched from the source string, it is used as an index into a table of 256 bytes. The appropriate byte is fetched from the table and used in place of the byte fetched from the source string.

The following shows the operands of the MOVTC (MOVe Translated Characters) instruction. The operands of the MOVC5 instruction are included to show the similarity of the two instructions.

```
MOVC5    srclen,srcadr,fill,dstlen,dstadr
MOVTC    srclen,srcadr,fill,tbladr,dstlen,dstadr
```

Notice that the only difference between the MOVC5 instruction and the MOVTC instruction is the addition of the operand, tbladr, which specifies the starting address of the 256-byte table.

The MOVTC instruction can be used to perform character conversions such as ASCII to EBCDIC or EBCDIC to ASCII. It can be used to convert lowercase letters to uppercase letters or to convert spaces to zeros or vice versa. However, it can also be used for other purposes. Consider the following simple example which illustrates the operation of the MOVTC instruction.

```
CNT=1
TABLE:
            .REPT    255
            .BYTE    CNT
CNT=CNT+1
            .ENDR
            .BYTE    0
            . . .
ARRAY:      .BYTE    27,255,0,100,1
            . . .
            MOVTC    #5,ARRAY,#0,TABLE,#5,ARRAY
```

The 256-byte table contains 1, 2, 3, . . . , 254, 255, 0. Thus, the value in BYTE[I] is equal to $I + 1$. (The 256th byte is treated as a special case and set to zero.). The MOVTC instruction fetches each byte from the byte array ARRAY, uses the byte as an index to fetch a byte from the table (which is one greater than the byte from the array), and stores the byte from the table back into the array. As a result, the MOVTC instruction adds one to each byte in the array, so that the array contains 28,0,1,101,2 when the instruction terminates.

In using registers, the MOVTC instruction treats the table as a third character string. Thus, R0 and R1 are used for the length and address of the source string, R2 and R3 are used for the length (256) and address of the table, and R4 and R5 are used for the length and address of the destination string. When the MOVTC instruction terminates, the registers contain:

MOVTC   srclen,srcadr,fill,tbladr,   dstlen,dstadr
           R0=a R1=b   R3=adr R4=0 R5=c   (R2=0)

a = srclen − dstlen if srclen > dstlen, 0 otherwise
b = address one byte beyond last byte translated
c = address of byte following last byte of destination

As with the MOVC5 instruction, the MOVTC instruction sets the condition codes as though the pair of instructions

MOVTC   srclen,srcadr,fill,tbladr,dstlen,dstadr

CMPW   srclen,dstlen

had been executed, except that the Z bit is cleared.

     The MOVTUC (MOVe Translated Until Character) instruction operates in the same manner as the MOVTC instruction except that execution terminates when a particular character, called the **escape character,** is fetched from the table. The description of this instruction is:

MOVTUC   srclen,srcadr,esc,tbladr,   dstlen,dstadr
            R0=a R1=b   R3=adr R4=c R5=d   (R2=0)

MOVTC   srclen,srcadr,fill,tbladr,dstlen,dstadr

a = bytes remaining including escape if terminated, 0 otherwise
b = address of last byte fetched or address of byte following last byte
     in the string
c = number of bytes remaining in destination string.
d = address of first unmodified (unstored) byte

As the comparison with the MOVTC instruction shows, the fill character in the MOVTC instruction is replaced by the esc character in the MOVTUC instruction. Because there is no fill character, the instruction terminates if the characters in the source string are exhausted, leaving R1 pointing to the first byte following the end of the string. MOVTUC sets the condition codes in the same way as MOVTC (CMPW srclen,dstlen), except that the V bit is set if the instruction is terminated because a character equal to the escape character was fetched from the table.

The SCANC and SPANC instructions are similar to the LOCC and SKPC instructions except that SCANC and SPANC terminate when any one of a set of characters is located (SCANC) or a character outside the set is found (SPANC). The format of the SCANC and SPANC instructions is

SCANC   scrlen,srcadr,tbladr,mask
           R0=a R1=b R3=adr   (R2=0)
SPANC   srclen,srcadr,tbladr,mask
           R0=a R1=b R3=adr   (R2=0)

a = bytes remaining in string including byte that terminated execution
b = address of byte that terminated execution or scradr + scrlen

Bytes from the source string (specified by the first two operands) are successively used to index the table (specified by the third operand). Each byte fetched from the table is logically ANDed with the byte specified by the fourth operand (mask). The SCANC instruction terminates when either the result of the AND is nonzero or the characters in the source string are exhausted. SPANC terminates when the result of the AND is zero or when the source string is exhausted.

The eight-bit mask allows a great deal of flexibility. For example, characters can be classified on up to eight binary attributes, such as digit versus nondigit, upper case letter versus other characters, lower case letter versus other characters letter, and so forth. The table entry for each character is based on the eight binary attributes. By selecting an appropriate mask, the SCANC instruction can search for a character that possesses one or more of these attributes. (The SPANC instruction can be used to skip over the characters that possess one or more of these attributes.)

Exercise Set 1

1. Describe how the MOVC3 instruction could be implemented so that temporary storage for characters is not needed even if the strings overlap.

2. Write a macro that simulates the MOVC3 instruction using only the instructions described up to Chapter 8. (Your macro should handle overlap properly.) Write a main program which tests your macro by comparing its results with the results of a MOVC3 instruction.

3. Write a program that reads English sentences and produces a concordance. (A concordance is a sorted listing of the words in a body of text). You may assume that the words in the text are separated by one or more spaces, but that no other punctuation is involved. Also assume that no word is more than 20 characters long.

4. Rewrite the program in Exercise 3, above, assuming that the text contains realistic punctuation, including periods, commas, question marks, hyphens, apostrophes, and so forth.

5. Write a program that reads the text in Exercise 3 and prints out the text as a well-formatted paragraph. (There should be only one space between words in the output text and the maximum number of words should be placed in each line.) Note that there might be many spaces between words in the input text.

6. Modify the program in Exercise 5, above, by adding enough spaces between words to line up the right margin of the text.

*7. Write a program that reads any assembly language program and prints all symbolic names in the program. (Note that this requires that you partially parse an assembly language program).

*8. Combine Exercises 3 and 7 to create a program that prints a complete symbol table (without symbol values) for an assembly language program.

13.6 Packed Decimal Arithmetic
Packed Decimal Numbers

In business data processing, programmers prefer to specify numbers in terms of a fixed-length sequence of decimal digits with a fixed decimal point position. Business data processing languages, such as COBOL, make extensive use of this kind of number representation. Following are some reasons for using decimal numbers.

1. Input from punched cards and output to printed lines are in terms of fixed-length decimal fields.

2. Most numeric quantities in business data processing are used in simple calculations and it would be wasteful to convert decimal numbers to binary numbers in order to perform the calculations.

3. The fixed number of digits helps prevent errors such as issuing a check for $1,000,000.00 to petty cash.

4. Decimal fractions such as 0.20 cannot be represented exactly in binary.

5. Floating-point notations may produce unwanted accuracy. For example, most monetary calculations are rounded to the nearest cent and bookkeeping errors may occur if monetary calculations preserve fractions of a cent.

To avoid these and other problems, very early (first generation) computers designed for data processing allowed numbers to be represented as a string of decimal digits. As a general purpose computer that is designed for both data processing and scientific computation, the VAX architecture includes provisions for decimal numbers and decimal arithmetic. The general idea is to pack two decimal digits into each byte—hence the name **packed decimal numbers.** For example, the decimal number 12345678 could be represented in four bytes beginning at address ^X1000 as follows:

Content	Address
12	1000
34	1001
56	1002
78	1003

Each 8-bit byte is composed of two 4-bit **nibbles** (or **nybbles**) and each nibble contains a decimal digit. In byte ^X1000, for example, the nibble on the left contains ^X1 which represents the decimal digit one and the nibble on the right contains ^X2 which represents the decimal digit two.

If the content of bytes ^X1000 through ^X1003 is represented on a single line, the result is

Content				Address
78	56	34	12	1000

Because the most significant digits of the number (12 in this case) are stored in the byte with the lowest address (^X1000 in this case), packed decimal numbers may seem awkward to read in a memory dump. (Note that the longword beginning in ^X1000 is ^X78563412 and that this represents the packed decimal number 12345678.)

The packed decimal representation above must be modified to allow room for the sign of the number. The convention followed on the VAX is that the sign is stored in the right nibble of the highest addressed byte. This means that the highest addressed byte contains the low-order digit (the units digit) in the left nibble and the sign in the right nibble. Although the VAX allows the hexadecimal digits A, C, E, or F to represent a positive sign and B or D to represent a negative sign, the preferred representations are ˆXC for plus and ˆXD for minus. Thus, the decimal number 12345678 is represented as follows:

Content	Address
01	1000
23	1001
45	1002
67	1003
8C	1004

In a listing, this might appear as

Content	Address
8C 67 45 23 01	1000

The decimal number − 12345678 would be represented in five bytes as:

Content	Address
8D 67 45 23 01	1000

On the VAX, a packed decimal number is specified by two attributes—the starting address of the number and the length. However, unlike character strings, the length of a packed decimal number is specified in terms of decimal digits rather than bytes. Thus, the length of the packed decimal number 12345678 (or − 12345678) is eight, even though the number occupies five bytes.

Notice that the memory representation of the nine-digit packed decimal number, 012345678, is exactly the same as the representation of the eight-digit number, 12345678. Both numbers will be represented in five bytes that contain 8C, 67, 45, 23, and 01. However, the two numbers can be distinguished by their lengths (nine versus eight). In general, the length of a packed decimal number can vary from 0 to 31 decimal digits. Note that any packed decimal number with an even length (such as 12345678) will have an unused nibble in the high-order (lowest-addressed) byte. A decimal string of length zero consists of a single byte that contains the sign in the right nibble and an unused nibble on the left. A decimal string of length 31 consists of 16 bytes.

In assembly language, the directive .PACKED is used to reserve storage and initialize packed decimal numbers. The following assembly language listing illustrates the way in which the .PACKED directive is used. The first four lines define packed decimal numbers that have been previously described. On line 5, the symbol L_PACKE (Length of PACKed number E) follows the value 12345678. As a result, the .PACKE directive defines the symbol L_PACKE as the length of the packed decimal number PACKE. In this case, L_PACKE will be inserted into the symbol table with the value 8. On line 6, L_PACKF will be entered into the symbol table with the value 9. Finally, line 7 shows how space can be reserved (but not initialized) for a packed decimal number, PACKG, that has the same number of bytes as PACKE.

```
8C 67 45 23 01   0000    1 PACKA:   .PACKED   12345678
8D 67 45 23 01   0005    2 PACKB:   .PACKED   -12345678
              0D 000A    3 PACKC:   .PACKED   -0
              0C 000B    4 PACKD:   .PACKED   +0
8C 67 45 23 01   000C    5 PACKE:   .PACKED   12345678,L_PACKE
8C 67 45 23 01   0011    6 PACKF:   .PACKED   012345678,L_PACKF
        0000001A 0016    7 PACKG:   .BLKB     <L_PACKE+1>/2+1
                 001A    8          .END
```

Packed Decimal Instructions

The VAX architecture includes instructions for moving, comparing, and performing arithmetic operations on packed decimal numbers. The instruction formats for packed decimal instructions are similar to the formats for integer or floating-point instructions, except that operands for the lengths of the packed decimal numbers must be included. These instructions are as follows:

Opcode	Operands	Description
MOVP	len,srcadr,dstadr	dst ← src
CMPP3	len,srcadr,dstadr	tmp ← src − dst
CMPP4	src1len,src1adr,src2len,src2adr	tmp ← src − dst
ADDP4	srclen,srcadr,dstlen,dstadr	dst ← dst + scr
SUBP4	srclen,srcadr,dstlen,dstadr	dst ← dst + scr
ADDP6	src1len,src1adr,scr2len,scr2adr,dstlen,dstadr	dst ← scr2 + scr1
SUBP6	src1len,src1adr,scr2len,scr2adr,dstlen,dstadr	dst ← src2 − src1
MULP	src1len,src1adr,scr2len,scr2adr,dstlen,dstadr	dst ← src2*src1
DIVP	src1len,src1adr,scr2len,scr2adr,dstlen,dstadr	dst ← src2/src1

The packed decimal instructions make implied use of registers R0 through R5 just as the character string instructions do. Registers R0, R2, and (if needed) R4 are used for the lengths of the strings, and registers R1, R3, and (if needed) R5 are used for the addresses of the strings. After the instructions are executed, the even-numbered registers contain zero while the odd-numbered registers point to the starting address of the appropriate decimal string. For example, after an MOVP instruction is executed, R0 and R2 contain zero, R1 and R3 point to the starting address of the source and destination strings, and R4 and R5 are not modified or used. The addresses in the odd-numbered registers can be used as input to the next instruction.

These instructions set the N, Z, and V condition code bits in the expected manner. The V bit is set if decimal overflow occurs. Because there are no unsigned packed decimal numbers, the C bit is simply cleared except that the MOVC instruction preserves the value of the C bit.

There is one subtlety involved in setting the N and Z bits. Because of the way that the sign bit is represented in packed decimal numbers, packed decimal representations of both $+0$ and -0 exist. (Since the length of a packed decimal number can vary from 0 to 31 decimal digits, there are actually 64 different representations of zero.) The existence of representations for $+0$ and -0 has caused difficulty in some older computer architectures. (A branch-if-negative instruction would branch on -0 but not on $+0$ even though the two quantities are mathematically equal.) The VAX architecture includes two features to avoid this problem. First, a zero result is always represented as $+0$. For example, if a -0 source operand is moved with a MOVP instruction, $+0$ will be moved to the destination. However, it is possible to generate a result of -0 if decimal overflow occurs. The second feature solves this problem. If the result is -0, the VAX simply sets the N and Z bits as though the result were $+0$. Thus a result of $+0$ or -0 will clear the N bit and set the Z bit. As a result, programmers do not have to worry about the existence of representations for -0 except in the most unusual circumstances.

The ASHP, CVTLP, and CVTPL Instructions

In order to handle fractional quantities, packed decimal numbers are treated as fixed-point numbers. As explained in Chapter 10, this simply means that the decimal point is assumed to be at some fixed point within the number. It is the programmer's responsibility to keep track of the position of the assumed decimal point. In particular, the decimal points must be aligned before addition or subtraction. (As we saw in Chapter 10, the same problem arises in floating-point computations. However, that alignment is handled automatically by the floating-point instructions.) The alignment of packed decimal numbers could be handled by multiplying or dividing the numbers by powers of ten. However, multiplying or dividing a packed decimal number by powers of ten can be accomplished more quickly by shifting nibbles. This is accomplished with the ASHP (Arithmetic SHift Packed decimal) instruction.

The ASHP instruction requires six operands. In addition to the lengths and addresses for the source and destination strings, a byte parameter called CNT (the first parameter) specifies the amount of the shift in decimal digits. A positive CNT of n effectively multiplies the source by 10^n and places the result in the destination. A negative value divides the source by 10^n. The fourth operand is a byte operand that allows the division to be performed with rounding instead of truncation. For example, the following instruction converts a packed decimal number expressed in dollars to a number expressed in cents.

```
ASHP      #2,#DOLLAR_LEN,DOLLAR,#0,#CENTS_LEN,CENTS
```

A quantity expressed in cents could be converted to dollars with the instruction

```
ASHP      #-2,#CENTS_LEN,CENTS,#0,#DOLLAR_LEN,DOLLAR
```

This instruction will truncate in moving the packed decimal number CENTS to DOLLAR. Rounding can be achieved with the instruction

```
ASHP      #-2,#CENTS_LEN,CENTS,#5,#DOLLAR_LEN,DOLLAR
```

The fourth operand, #5, adds 50 to the packed decimal number beginning at CENTS before dividing by 100. The ASHP instruction uses R0 through R3 in the expected manner.

The MOVP instruction is designed to move a source packed decimal number to a destination packed decimal number that has the same length. The ASHP instruction (with the shift and round operands equal to zero) can be used to move packed decimal numbers between fields of differing lengths. For example, the instruction

```
ASHP      #0,#4,SOURCE,#0,#10,DEST
```

can be used to move a four-digit source packed decimal number to a ten-digit destination.

The VAX architecture provides a single pair of instructions for converting between packed decimal numbers and signed integers. These instructions are CVTLP (ConVerT Long to Packed) and CVTPL (ConVert Packed to Long). The description of these instructions is

```
CVTLP      longsrc,dstlen,dstadr
                 R2 = 0 R3 = a                         R0 = 0, R1 = 0
CVTPL      srclen,srcadr,longdst
                 R0 = 0 R1 = a                         R2 = 0, R3 = 0
```

a = address of the byte following last byte of packed decimal number

The longword convert instruction can easily be used to convert between byte or word integers and packed decimal numbers. For example, the following will convert a 16-bit signed integer in WORD to a five-digit packed decimal number.

```
CVTWL      WORD,LONG          ;CONVERT BINARY WORD TO LONG
CVTLP      LONG,#5,PACK_ADR   ;CONVERT LONG TO PACKED
```

Notice that overflow cannot occur because a 16-bit signed integer will always fit into a five-digit decimal field. Similarly, the following statements will convert a five-digit packed decimal number into a 16-bit binary integer. Note that overflow is possible.

```
CNTPL      #5,PACK_ADR,LONG   ;CONVERT PACKED TO LONG
CVTLW      LONG,WORD          ;CONVERT LONG TO WORD (OVERFLOW POSSIBLE)
```

Converting between packed decimal and signed quadwords is somewhat more involved. The following statements convert a signed quadword in QUAD to a 20-digit packed decimal number in PACKED_ANS.

```
PACKED_CONST:
        .PACKED  4294967286                ;CONSTANT 2**32
        . . .
        MOVL    QUAD,LONG_LOW               ;BREAK INTO TWO LONGS
        MOVL    QUAD+4,LONG_HIGH
        CVTLP   LONG_LOW,#10,PACKED_LOW ;PACK EACH LONGWORD
        CVTLP   LONG_HIGH,#10,PACKED_HIGH
;COMBINE TWO PACKED WITH LENGTH 10 INTO PACKED_ANS OF LENGTH 20
        MULP    #10,PACKED_CONST,#10,PACKED_HIGH,#20,PACKED_ANS
        ADDP4   #10,PACKED_LOW,#20,PACKED_ANS
        TSTL    LONG_LOW
        BGEQ    10$
        ADDP4   #10,PACKED_CONST,#10,PACKED_ANS
10$:    . . .
```

The first two instructions break the 64-bit quadword into the 32-bit longwords LONG_LOW and LONG_HIGH. If both longwords are positive (i.e., if bit 31 is zero), the conversion is straight forward. The longwords are converted to ten-digit packed decimal numbers, the high-order packed decimal number is multiplied by 2^{32} and moved to PACKED_ANS, and the low-order packed decimal number is added to PACKED_ANS.

If either or both longwords are negative, the algorithm is more complicated. For example, assume that bit 31 in LONG_LOW is equal to one and that bit 31 in LONG_HIGH is zero. Bit 31 in LONG_LOW represents the 2^{31} bit position in the 64-bit quadword. However, the CVTLP instruction treats the bit as a sign bit and PACKED_LOW becomes a negative number. After the first ADDP4 instruction, the swer is wrong for two reasons. First, the number in PACKED_LOW has been, in effect, subtracted from rather than added to PACKED_ANS. Second, since bit 31 is really a data bit that has not been treated as a data bit, the factor of 2^{31} needs to be added to the answer. It happens that the combined effect of these two effects always results in an answer that is too low by exactly 2^{32}. The last three instructions add 2^{32} to the answer if PACKED_LOW is negative. As an exercise, the reader is asked to demonstrate that the algorithm works for a variety of numbers.

13.7 Numeric Strings
Leading and Trailing Numeric Strings

Up to this point, we have considered four different representations for numbers—unsigned binary integers, signed binary integers, real or floating-point numbers, and packed decimal numbers. Arithmetic computations may be performed with any of these representations. In addition, numbers having any of these representations may be written to or read from intermediate storage devices such as magnetic disk or magnetic tape. However, such numbers cannot be written to or read from ASCII devices such as terminal keyboards, VDT terminal screens, or printers. Such devices require that numbers be represented as a string of ASCII characters.

In order to support ASCII devices, the VAX architecture includes a fifth representation for numbers called **numeric strings.** Basically, a numeric string is nothing more than a character string in which the characters are restricted to the set of ASCII digits, 0 through 9. In other words, the bytes in the string are restricted to the values of digits in ASCII, namely ^X30 through ^X39.

   Numbers have been represented as character strings since the earliest days of electronic computers. Because of differences between computers (including differences in the character codes used), a variety of representations for the sign of a number have evolved. As a result, the VAX architecture supports several methods for representing the sign of a numeric string. The simplest representation is a **leading separate numeric string.** This representation derives its name from the fact that the ASCII code for a plus sign (^X2B) or a minus sign (^X2D) is stored in a separate byte in front of the high-order digit. For example, the following shows how several leading separate numeric strings can be defined in assembly language.

```
STRING_1:   .ASCII      "+1234"      ;5 BYTES BUT LENGTH IS 4
STRING_2:   .ASCII      "-12345678   ;9 BYTES BUT LENGTH IS 8
STRING_3:   .ASCII      "+"          ;1 BYTE BUT LENGTH IS 0
STRING_4:   .ASCII      "-"          ;REPRESENTATION FOR MINUS ZERO
STRING_5:   .ASCII      "-0000"      ;ANOTHER MINUS ZERO BUT LENGTH IS 4
STRING_6:   .ASCII      " 1234"      ;SAME AS STRING_1 WITH SPACE FOR SIGN
```

   A leading separate numeric string is specified by two attributes—the starting address of the string (which is actually the address of the sign byte) and the length of the string. However, the length refers to **the number of digits** in the string which, because of the sign byte, is one less than the number of bytes in the string. As shown by STRING_6, a space character (^X20) can be substituted for the plus sign. However, the use of the plus sign is preferred.

   The rules for leading separate numeric strings are quite restrictive. For example, each of the following is illegal for the reason indicated.

```
BAD_1:   .ASCII      "1234"       ;NO SIGN
BAD_2:   .ASCII      ""           ;SIGN IS REQUIRED
BAD_3:   .ASCII      " +1234"     ;SPACE IN FRONT OF SIGN ILLEGAL
BAD_4:   .ASCII      "+123,456"   ;COMMA ILLEGAL
BAD_5:   .ASCII      "-1234,56"   ;DECIMAL POINT ILLEGAL
```

To be consistent with packed decimal numbers, the length of a leading separate numeric string must be between 0 and 31 digits. (Because of the byte for the sign, the number of bytes varies from 1 to 32.)

   The VAX supports a second format for numeric strings called **trailing numeric strings.** This format is derived from Hollerith punch card code. As noted in Chapter 9, a Hollerith card contains 12 rows that are called the 12, 11, 0, 1, 2, . . . , 8, and 9 rows respectively. The punches 0 through 9 are used to represent the digits 0 through 9; a

12 punch represents a plus sign; and an 11 punch represents a minus sign. Rather than use an additional column for the sign, the sign is included in the same column with the units digit. For example, to represent the number minus 12345, a 1, 2, 3, and 4 punch are punched into the first four columns and a 5 punch along with an 11 punch are punched into the fifth column. Since the sign punch is in the same column as the units digit, this representation is called **overpunch format.**

When punched-card codes were extended to include alphabetic characters, the letter "N" happened to be assigned the punch code consisting of an 11 punch along with a 5 punch. To enter the number minus 12345, an experienced keypunch operator could type "1234N". Similarly, since the character "E" consists of a 12 punch along with a 5 punch, the number plus 12345 was entered by punching "1234E".

As a result, the following are valid trailing numeric strings on the VAX.

```
TRAIL_1: .ASCII     "1234N"     ;PLUS 12345 IN OVERPUNCH FORMAT
TRAIL_2: .ASCII     "1234E"     ;MINUS 12345 IN OVERPUNCH FORMAT
```

In this format the last byte contains both the sign and the units digit. The left nibble of the byte specifies the sign and the right nibble specifies the units digit. To be more consistent with the way that characters are represented in EBCDIC (see Chapter 8), the VAX also supports a second format for trailing numeric strings called **zoned numeric format.** This format simply uses a different set of bits in the left nibble of the last byte to represent plus and minus signs.

In order to process the various ways in which the sign and units digit may be coded in a trailing numeric string, VAX instructions that manipulate trailing numeric strings use a 256-byte table to process the byte containing the units digit and the sign. For more information on either format of trailing numeric strings, the interested reader is referred to the *VAX Architecture Handbook.* For the remainder of this text, we will use the easier to understand leading separate numeric strings.

The CVTPS and CVTSP Instructions

The VAX architecture does not include any instructions for performing arithmetic operations on numeric strings. However, it does include instructions for converting a numeric string to packed decimal and vice versa. The instructions are CVTPS (ConVerT Packed to leading

Separate numeric) and CVTSP (ConVerT leading Separate numeric string to Packed). The description of these instructions is

CVTPS   src_len,src_adr,dst_len,dst_adr
          R0=0 R1=a R2=0 R3=a
CVTSP   src_len,src_adr,dst_len,dst_adr
          R0=0 R1=a R2=0 R3=a

a = the address of the byte following the last byte of the string

The N and Z bits are set depending on the sign and value of the packed decimal operand. The V bit is set if overflow occurs, and the C bit is always cleared.

The VAX architecture also includes instructions for converting trailing numeric strings. The CVTPT (ConVerT Packed to Trailing numeric) and CVTTP (ConVerT Trailing numeric to Packed) instructions have a similar operand format and operate in a similar manner as the CVTPS and CVTSP. Because there are a variety of ways to represent the sign of a trailing numeric string, the CVTPT and CVTTP instructions include an additional operand. This operand is the address of a 256-byte table that determines the representation of the sign. See the *VAX Architecture Handbook* for additional details.

Note that the CVTSP instruction will terminate with a reserved operand fault if the source string contains an illegal character. The source string must contain the ASCII code for plus, minus, or space in the first byte and ASCII codes for the digits 0–9 in all subsequent bytes. If the numbers to be converted contain leading blanks, the SKPC instruction can be used to skip over them.

The EDITPC Instruction

A programmer may want to write numbers in a wide variety of formats. Assume, for example, that a packed decimal field contains the number 12345. Further assume that this number is to be converted to a character string containing ten bytes. The following list shows a variety of possible formats for the resulting character string. The underscore character (_) is used to indicate a space character.

```
+000012345   _____12345   0000012345   ____+12345
$000012345   $____12345   ____$12345   $****12345
0012345 CR   0000123.45   ____123.45   ___+123.45
$***123.45   0123.45 CR   $___123.45   ___$123.45
```

Decimal points are included because, with the fixed-point representation described in Chapter 10, the decimal point could be assumed
to be anywhere within the packed decimal number.

The CVTPS instruction can be used to generate the first output
string (+000012345). In addition, the various table lookup instructions would be useful in producing the various character strings.
However, the problem is actually more complicated than it might
appear. Consider, for example, the format that produces the character
string ....123.45. If the number to be converted to a character string
is zero, the result ......0.00 is probably preferable to the result
....

To simplify the problem of converting packed decimal numbers
to character strings, the VAX architecture includes the instruction
EDITPC (EDIT Packed to Character string). The format of this instruction is

```
EDITPC    srclen,  srcadr,pattern,dstadr
          R0=len R1=a R3=b  R5=c                    (R2=R4=0)
```
a = first byte of the source string
b = last byte of the source or pattern string
c = first byte following the destination string

The first two operands are the length and address of the packed decimal number. The third operand, pattern, is the starting address of
a sequence of **edit pattern operators.** Each edit pattern operator is
one or two bytes in length and indicates how characters are to be
placed into the output character string. The last operand is the starting address of the character string. Notice that the length of the
character string is **not** an operand. This is because the length of the
packed decimal numbers, together with the edit pattern operators,
uniquely determine the length of the resulting character string.

The exact encoding of the edit pattern operators is described in
the *VAX Architecture Handbook*. To make the pattern operators easy
to use, the VAX macro library contains a set of macros to generate
the pattern operators. Consider, for example, the following:

```
PACKED:   .PACKED          0012345
PATTERN:
          EO$LOAD_FILL     #^A" "
          EO$MOVE          7
          EO$END
CHAR_7:   .BLKB            7
          . . .
          EDITPC           #7,PACKED,PATTERN,CHAR_7
```

The pattern contains three macros—EO$LOAD_FILL, EO$MOVE, and EO$END. The operation of EO$MOVE will be described first. The macro EO$MOVE generates a pattern operator called EO$MOVE which causes a certain number of decimal digits to be fetched from the packed decimal number, converted to ASCII characters, and stored in the destination string. In this case, the argument following EO$MOVE is 7, so all seven digits in PACKED will be converted. As a result, one would expect the string 0012345 to be stored in CHAR_7.

However, in many cases, it is desirable to eliminate leading zeros at the front of a number. To do this, the EDITPC instruction uses a one-bit storage area called the **significance bit.** As long as the digits fetched from the packed decimal number are zero, the significance bit remains zero. However, as soon as a nonzero digit is fetched, the significance bit is set to one (significance is set) and it remains set even if more zeros are subsequently fetched (these zeros are significant because they follow a nonzero digit). The EDITPC instruction also uses an 8-bit register that contains a character called the **fill character.** The purpose of the EO$LOAD_FILL macro is to load a character into the fill register.

The EO$LOAD FILL operator in the previous example loads the fill register with a space character. (The operand following EO$LOAD fill is #^A" ". The # character specifies an immediate operand, ^A indicates that the immediate operand is specified as an ASCII character, and " " indicates that the character is a space.) The EO$MOVE operator fetches digits from the packed decimal source as described previously. However, if significance is not set (because no nonzero digits have been fetched), digits from the source string are translated into the fill character (in this case a space). As a result, CHAR_7 will contain __12345 when execution terminates. Note that if the EO$LOAD_FILL operator is changed to EO$LOAD_FILL #^A"*", the result would have been **12345.

If the number PACKED were 0000000, significance would never be set, the fill character would be substituted for all seven digits, and the result would be _____. To correct this, the pattern should be changed to

```
PATTERN:
        EO$LOAD_FILL    #^A" "      ;FILL CHARACTER IS SPACE
        EO$MOVE         6           ;CONVERT 6, USE FILL TILL SIGNIFICANT
        EO$SET_SIGNIF               ;PRETEND NONZERO DIGIT FETCHED
        EO$MOVE         1           ;TRANSLATE 7 TH DIGIT REGARDLESS
        EO$END
```

The EO$SET_SIGNIF macro sets significance even if all of the digits fetched from the source string were zero. As a result, this pattern has the same effect as the previous pattern, except that a zero source is translated to _ _ _ _ _ _0.

In order to allow the sign of the number to be printed, the EDITPC instruction uses a second 8-bit register to contain the **sign character.** The sign register is just like the fill register except that three different pattern operators are used to load a character into the sign register. EO$LOAD_SIGN loads the sign register unconditionally, EO$LOAD_PLUS loads the sign register if and only if the packed decimal source is positive, and EO$LOAD_MINUS loads the sign register if the packed decimal source is negative. The operator EO$STORE_SIGN is used to insert the sign character in the output character string. Consider, for example, the following:

```
PACKED:.PACKED 0012345
PATTERN:
        EO$LOAD_FILL     #^A" "      ;FILL CHARACTER IS SPACE
        EO$LOAD_PLUS     #^A"+"      ;SIGN CHAR IS "+" IF PACKED IS PLUS
        EO$LOAD_MINUS    #^A"-"      ;SIGN CHAR IS "-" IF PACKED IS MINUS
        EO$STORE_SIGN                ;OUTPUT SIGN CHARACTER
        EO$MOVE          6           ;CONVERT 6, USE FILL TILL SIGNIFICANT
        EO$SET_SIGNIF                ;SET SIGNIFICANCE IF NOT SET
        EO$MOVE          1           ;CONVERT LAST DIGIT REGARDLESS
        EO$END
CHAR_7: .BLKB            8
        . . .
        EDITPC           #7,PACKED,PATTERN,CHAR_5
```

The string +_ _12345 will be produced. Note that if the packed decimal number were zero, the result would be +_ _ _ _ _ _0.

The EO$FLOAT and EO$END_FLOAT are used to float the sign character to the right so that it appears before the first significant digit of the number. EO$FLOAT is just like EO$MOVE except that, when the first significant digit is found, the sign character is placed in front of the digit. To handle the case where no significant digits are found, a series of one or more EO$FLOAT operators must be followed by a single EO$END_FLOAT operator which places the sign character into the string if and only if it was not already placed in the string by EO$FLOAT. For example, if the previous pat-tern string is replaced by the following string, the output will be _ _ +12345. If the packed number were zero, the output would be _ _ _ _ _ _+0.

```
EO$LOAD_FILL      #^A" "      ;FILL CHARACTER IS SPACE
EO$LOAD_PLUS      #^A"+"      ;SIGN CHAR IS "+" IF PACKED IS PLUS
EO$LOAD_MINUS     #^A"-"      ;SIGN CHAR IS "-" IF PACKED IS MINUS
EO$FLOAT          6           ;CONVERT 6, USE FILL TILL SIGNIFICANT
EO$END_FLOAT                  ;OUTPUT SIGN IF NEEDED
EO$SET_SIGNIF                 ;SET SIGNIFICANCE
EO$MOVE           1           ;CONVERT LAST DIGIT REGARDLESS
EO$END
```

The pattern operator EO$INSERT can be used to insert a particular character into the output string. (The operand is the character to be inserted.) Thus, EO$INSERT can be used to insert commas (1,234,567), decimal points (12345.67), or both (12,345.67) into the output string. EO$INSERT inserts the fill character if no significant digits have been detected so that zero can be printed without unneeded commas (_____0 rather than __,___0.) (If EO$SET_SIGNIF precedes EO$INSERT, the character will be inserted unconditionally.) See the *VAX Architecture Handbook* for additional details on these and other pattern operators.

13.8 Variable-Length Bit Strings

At times it is desirable to address strings of bits that do not necessarily begin at a byte boundry. Assume, for example, that a high-resolution television picture is digitized to form a 1000 by 1000 matrix, where each element of the matrix is a 10-bit number that indicates the brightness level at that point. Each of the 10-bit numbers could be stored in a word with 16 minus 10 or 6 bits unused. However, the unused bits represent wasted storage of 6 million bits or 750,000 bytes.

To avoid wasting bits, the 10-bit numbers can be packed together as follows:

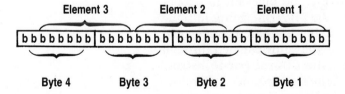

Fetching and storing the 10-bit fields is awkward with the instructions described to this point.

To solve these and other problems, the VAX architecture includes a data type called a **variable-length bit field.** A bit field is specified by three attributes:

1. A byte address that specifies the starting address of the storage area used for the bit fields (the address of byte 1 in the example).
2. A bit displacement that specifies the distance in bits between the starting address of the storage area and the starting address of the bit field (0 for element 1, 10 for element 2, 20 for element 3, and so on, in the example).
3. A length that specifies the length of the bit field in bits (10 in the example).

The starting address of the table can be generated by any of the addressing modes that generate a 32-bit address. (In addition, register addressing can be used.) This means that the bit string can be located in one of the processor registers. The bit displacement is a 32-bit signed longword displacement. Note that this displacement can be thought of as a 29-bit byte displacement that references the byte where the string begins followed by a 3-bit number that specifies the location of the string within the byte. The length is an unsigned byte that has a value from 0 to 32 (0 to 31 if the string is in a general register).

The VAX architecture includes instructions for extracting (fetching), comparing, and inserting (storing) bit fields. The formats of these instructions are

```
EXTV    disp,len,start,longdst
CMPV    disp,len,start,longsrc
INSV    longsrc,disp,len,start
```

In the operand fields, start refers to the starting address of the block of memory used for storing the bit fields, disp refers to the 32-bit displacement, and len is the byte operand that specifies the length. The EXTV instruction fetches the bit string and places it in a longword (longdst) with the low-order bit of the bit string going into the low-order bit of the longword. The bit string is treated as a signed number so the high-order bit of the bit string is propagated through the high-order bits of the longword destination. (An alternate instruction, EXTZV, propagates zero instead of the sign bit and is therefore used for unsigned bit fields.) Similarly, the CMPV instruction extends the bit string before comparing it with the longword. (The CMPZV instruction propagates zero instead of the sign.) The condition code bits are set in the expected manner, except that INSV leaves the condition codes unchanged.

The operation of these instructions is straightforward. In the following example, the EXTV instruction extracts bits 20 through 25 in R2 and places the sign-extended result in R4. The INSV instruction places the 6-bit string into bit positions 15 through 20 of R10.

```
EXTV    #20,#6,R2,R4
INSV    R4,#15,#6,R10
```

13.9 Queue Data Types and Instructions

The VAX architecture supports a data type called an **absolute queue.** A queue is a type of doubly linked list in that each element in a queue contains a pointer to the preceding element in the list as well as a pointer to the succeeding element of the list. In a queue, the last element in the list is succeeded by the first element of the list, forming a circular structure.

Consider, for example, the elements HEAD, A, B, C, and D.

```
HEAD:   .ADDRESS    C       ;FORWARD LINK
        .ADDRESS    B       ;BACKWARD LINK
        . . .
A:      .ADDRESS    D       ;FORWARD LINK
        .ADDRESS    C       ;BACKWARD LINK
        . . .
B:      .ADDRESS    HEAD    ;FORWARD LINK
        .ADDRESS    D       ;BACKWARD LINK
        . . .
C:      .ADDRESS    A       ;FORWARD LINK
        .ADDRESS    HEAD    ;BACKWARD LINK
        . . .
D:      .ADDRESS    B       ;FORWARD LINK
        .ADDRESS    A       ;BACKWARD LINK
```

Each element begins with two longword addresses. (Any data associated with an element can follow the two addresses.) The first address of each pair is a pointer to the succeeding element. Since address HEAD contains the address C, element C follows head. Similarly, address C contains the succeeding address A, so A follows C. In the forward direction, the order is HEAD, C, A, D, B, and then back to

HEAD. The second address in each element points to the preceding element. Since address HEAD+4 contains the preceding address B, element B precedes the element HEAD. In the backward direction, the order is B, D, A, C, HEAD.

This structure can be represented as follows:

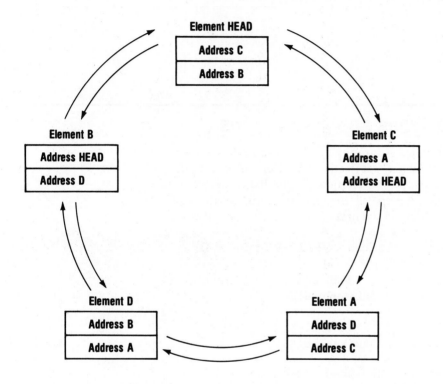

The VAX instruction set includes the instructions INSQUE (INSert element into QUEue) and REMQUE (REMove element from QUEue). The description of these instructions is

```
INSQUE    elemadr,headadr
REMQUE    headadr,elemadr
```

For example, the instruction INSQUE A,HEAD will insert the element A into the queue as the successor to HEAD. (The old successor of HEAD will be the successor of A.) The instruction REMQUE HEAD,E will remove the element HEAD from the queue and place the address of the element in longword E. For example, the five element structure shown above can be created as follows:

```
HEAD:      .ADDRESS   HEAD
           .ADDRESS   HEAD
           , , ,
A:         .BLKL      2
           , , ,
B:         .BLKL      2
           , , ,
C:         .BLKL      2
           , , ,
D:         .BLKL      2
           , , ,
           INSQUE     B,HEAD         ;QUEUE CONTAINS HEAD, B
           INSQUE     D,HEAD         ;QUEUE CONTAINS HEAD, D, B
           INSQUE     A,HEAD         ;QUEUE CONTAINS HEAD, A, D, B
           INSQUE     C,HEAD         ;QUEUE CONTAINS HEAD, C, A, D, B
```

Notice that an empty queue consists of a header element (HEAD) in which the two addresses both point to the header element. The five element structure HEAD, C, A, D, B is normally viewed as having a head element and four data elements.

Although the head element is considered to be a special element, it has the same structure as the other elements. As a result, the INSQUE instruction can be used to insert an element after any given element as long as the address of the given element is available. For example, in the structure HEAD, C, A, D, B, address HEAD + 4 contains the address B. As described in Chapter 7, the operand @HEAD + 4 specifies the address contained in HEAD + 4. As a result, the instruction

```
INSQUE    E,@HEAD+4
```

treats element B as the head of the list and inserts element E between elements B and HEAD, producing the structure HEAD, C, A, D, B, E.

Similar addressing techniques can be used with the REMQUE instruction. For example,

```
REMQUE    @HEAD,R0        ;REMOVE ITEM FOLLOWING HEAD
REMQUE    @HEAD+4,R0      ;REMOVE ITEM PRECEDING HEAD
```

A queue is a data structure in which the first item added is the first item removed (FIFO or First In, First Out). Queues are implemented easily by using instructions of the form INSQUE item, HEAD and REMQUE @HEAD + 4,dest which insert items after the head and remove items preceding the head. A queue contrasts with a stack, which uses a LIFO organization (Last In, First Out). However, the

VAX implementation of the queue is a more powerful data structure than a normal queue (or a stack) because it is based on a doubly linked list. As a result, the items included in the structure can be scattered around memory, the data following each element may have any length and may be easily changed, and elements may be easily inserted or removed at any point in the data structure.

In addition to absolute queues, the VAX supports **relative queues** in which the pointers are relative instead of absolute addresses. Instructions are available for inserting or removing elements that precede or succeed the head of the queues. See the *VAX Architecture Handbook* for additional details.

Exercise Set 2

1. Using the Newton-Raphson formula described in Chapter 12, compute the square root of 2 to at least 25 decimal places. However, the computations should be done using packed decimal numbers rather than floating-point numbers. Use the CVTPS instruction to print out the successive estimates.

2. Section 13.7 (p. 395) contained a program segment that converted a signed quadword to a 20-digit packed decimal number. Show how the algorithm operates with each of the following quadwords.

   a. ˆX 0 00000100 0000001   b. ˆX 0 00000008 0000000
   c. ˆX 8 00000000 0000000   d. ˆX 8 00000008 0000000
   e. ˆX 0 00000018 0000001   f. ˆX 8 00000018 0000001
   g. ˆX C0000000C0000000   h. ˆX C0000001C0000001

3. Write a subroutine that converts a signed integer longword to a leading separate numeric string. The string should have length 10 which means that it occupies 11 bytes. (Hint: Use the CVTLP and CVTPS instructions.)

4. Modify the subroutine in Exercise 3 so that leading zeros are suppressed and the sign is floated to the right so that it is in front of the first significant digit. (Positive zero should print as _____ +0.)

5. Write a subroutine that prints an F_FLOAT number in a FOR-TRAN F10.0 format. (An F10.0 number consists of a sign, 6 decimal digits, a decimal point, and 2 digits after the decimal point.) However, the space is used for a plus sign, leading zeros are suppressed, and the sign is floated to the first significant digit.

(Hint: Multiply the F_FLOAT number by 100, and then use the CVTFL, CVTLP, and EDITPC instructions.)

6. Write a program that reads a number represented as a character string of length 20 and converts the number to a G_ floating-point number. The character string begins with a plus or minus sign and contains a decimal point imbedded within 18 decimal digits (e.g., +00000000012345.6789). (Hint: Remove the decimal point and break the character string into two 9-digit leading separate numeric strings. Convert to two packed decimal numbers with the CVTSP instruction and then to two longword integers with the CVTPL instruction. Use the CVTLG instruction to convert the longwords, using appropriate scaling to obtain the G floating result.)

7. As in Exercise 3 on page 389, write a program that produces a concordance. However, your program should use a data structure in which each English word is represented by an element in a queue.

Elements Of VAX Architecture

14.1 Introduction

The **architecture** of a computer is the machine interface visible to the programmer. It includes such features as the machine language instruction set, the data types, the addressing modes, and so forth. The **implementation** of a computer is a particular arrangement of hardware elements that implement the functions of an architecture. A given architecture may be implemented many ways. A program capable of executing on one implementation of a given architecture should be capable of executing on any other implementation of that architecture.

For example, different members of the VAX computer family, such as the VAX-11/730, the VAX-11/750, the VAX-11/780, and others, represent different implementations of the VAX architecture. The members of the VAX computer family differ in price and performance capabilities. As technology changes, new implementations of the VAX architecture become available. Because these computers will support the same architecture, programs developed for earlier machines can be executed on newer machines.

The previous chapters have described those aspects of the VAX architecture that are apparent to normal user programs. This chapter describes the architectural features used by the operating system. In addition, we will look at the implementation of some of these architectural features. Concepts to be discussed are virtual memory, cache memory, systems privileges, bus structures, and hardware level input and output.

14.2 Memory Management and Virtual Memory

Introduction

From the earliest days of computers, the storage capability of the computer could be divided into fast memory and slow memory. The reason for having two different speeds of memory is that the slow memory may be orders of magnitude less expensive than the fast memory. As technology has progressed, the particular implementations of fast versus slow memory has changed. At present, most computers use semiconductor memory for the fast memory and disk drives for the slow memory. A typical VAX-11/780 system might have 8 megabytes of fast (semiconductor) memory and 1000 megabytes of the slower disk space. (As technological improvements make both kinds of memory less expensive, these numbers will increase on typical systems.)

As a general principle, fast or **main storage** is used for storing running programs and the data they are actively using. Slower or **mass storage** is used for storing **files** of programs and data which are being saved for later use. Two difficulties occur which complicate this simple scheme of allocating memory.

The first difficulty is that large problems often have memory requirements that exceed the amount of fast memory available. An early solution to this problem is through the use of **program overlays.** That is, these large programs are written so that the program is stored in the mass storage device, and portions are brought into main storage for execution. As one section finishes, another section is brought in and **overlays** the area of main storage which had been used by the previous section. In order for overlaying to operate efficiently, the programmer must be careful to divide the program into separate sections which execute successively without the kind of interaction which requires a lot of swapping back and forth between sections. Some early attempts to automate the overlaying process led to the development of what is now called **virtual memory.**

The second difficulty occurred as computers began to be used in a multiprogram environment. In order to make more efficient use of a computer system, it is usually desirable to have more than one program loaded into memory at a time. Then, if one program is idle, as happens when slow input or output is in progress, another program can then execute for a while, making use of the slack time. For example, a line printer may print 600 lines per minute, or 10 lines per second. While a program is waiting for one line to be printed so that it can print another, 100,000 or more instructions could be executed in some other program. The problem is more acute when the input/ output is to an **on line, interactive** terminal. Millions of instructions can be executed in the time it takes for the user to decide what character to type next. When a number of users have programs running concurrently in this way, it is called **time-sharing.** For this reason, an on line, interactive terminal is often referred to as a **time-shared** terminal.

As we have seen in previous chapters, a typical user's program is written to occupy some set of memory locations. On the VAX, programs are normally linked to start at memory location ^X200 and proceed to higher-numbered addresses. If these addresses referred to real memory addresses, there would be a problem. It is not possible to have two different programs occupying the same memory locations at the same time. In order to solve this problem, the VAX uses a mapping scheme so that user's addresses are mapped onto some other addresses in real memory. For example, your addresses ^X200, ^X201, ^X202, . . . might be mapped to address ^X3C600, ^X3C601, ^X3C602, . . . in the VAX memory. A different user would have addresses ^X200 . . . mapped to some other addresses in the VAX memory. Therefore, there would be no conflict.

An address mapping algorithm can be quite simple. One method uses a relocation register which contains an offset value. Whenever the program refers to an address, the offset value is automatically added to the address, to compute the actual address. In the above example, the relocation register would contain ^X3C400. Therefore, when the program refers to address ^X202, ^X3C400 is added, and actual address ^X3C602 is fetched. This addition is automatic, and the user's program is not aware of the operation. As far as the program can tell, it requested the contents of location ^X202 and it got the contents of location ^X202. The address ^X202 is the apparent address as far as the program is concerned. Such addresses are called **virtual** addresses after the idea of **virtual image** which appears in a mirror. The address ^X202 is the virtual address, ^X3C602 in the **real** address or **absolute machine address.** When another program is executing, there would be a different value in the relocation register and therefore a different mapping for virtual addresses to real addresses.

Some older computer systems had just one relocation register. Thus, all addresses in a program mapped to some contiguous block of real memory. As programs complete, and are replaced with other programs, there is a problem because not all programs are the same size. This can result in blocks of unused memory between programs. This is called the **memory fragmentation** problem. One solution to this is the **paged memory.** For example, memory on the VAX is organized into 512-byte pages. There is a relocation register for each page.

Thus, each page (or 512 bytes) of a program's virtual address space is mapped to some page of real memory. The pages in real memory are not necessarily contiguous, and are chosen by the operating system using some algorithm for finding free pages.

In addition to relocation and memory fragmentation, there is the problem of memory protection. When a number of users are sharing the use of a computer for unrelated purposes,* there must be some way of preventing one user from altering or even accessing the memory assigned to another user. In addition, all users should be prevented from altering and/or accessing the memory area reserved for the operating system.

The overall process of allocating memory, relocating programs, and implementing memory protection comes under the general category of **memory management.** Memory management involves both hardware and software. The allocation of memory and the loading of programs involve complex algorithms and are essentially software functions. The actual address mapping process is carried out using specially designed hardware in order that programs can run at full speed. The hardware portions of the memory management system include such devices as the relocation register(s) and the adder which automatically adds the contents of a relocation register to each virtual address generated by the program. In addition, the hardware memory management system implements protection schemes which restrict or prevent a user from having access to certain pages. More will be said about access restrictions later in the chapter.

Virtual Memory

In order for a system to be considered to be a full **virtual memory** system, it needs one more thing—automatic overlaying of pages. In the previous section, we discussed how a large program could use overlaying to bring pieces of itself in and out of main memory as needed. We also saw how a program can be divided into pages where each page has its own relocation register. Virtual memory combines these two concepts.

The VAX/VMS operating system, along with all the user programs running at a particular point in time, requires a set of memory pages that can be thought of as a very large program. In a multiuser system, there is usually not enough real memory to load all of the pages in the set into memory at one time. As a result, an overlaying scheme is needed so that users can get pages of their program into main memory.

---

* Sometimes users will share a computer for a common purpose, such as airline ticket reservations. In such cases, there is a controlled interaction between programs.

At a particular point in time, some of the pages in the set are actually in high speed memory. References to these pages are relocated using the relocation registers described previously. The pages that will not fit in memory are stored on a mass storage device such as a disk. When programs reference such a page, the memory management system must load the page into real memory and initialize the page's relocation register with an appropriate value. (In order to find an unused page in main memory, the memory management system may have to move some other page from main memory to the mass storage device.) In this way, virtual memory provides an automatic method for overlaying pages.

For example, as a program executes, it references various locations in memory. If these locations reside in pages that are currently in memory, information is fetched or stored using the relocation registers. If a referenced location is not in memory, the fetch or store operation is aborted. This situation is known as a **page fault.** When a page fault occurs, the memory management system employs an algorithm for loading the appropriate page into memory and initializing the appropriate relocation register so that locations in the page can be referenced.

When a page fault occurs, the relevant page must be read from the mass storage device and placed in main or **real** memory. If there are unused pages of real memory, a page can be assigned, but if the machine is being heavily used, there will probably not be any unused pages in main or real memory. This means that the memory management system must find a page to allocate to the program. To do this, the operating system uses some algorithm for picking a page that is not likely to be needed in the near future. This page is allocated to the program. However, before allocating the page, the operating system saves the old contents of the page on the mass storage device so that its original user can get the page back at some later time. The needed page is then read from the mass storage device into the page which has been made available. The appropriate relocation register is then set to address that page and the page is flagged as being available. Then, control is returned to the program that was interrupted by the page fault.

Now, let us look at a specific example which shows how the process might work with a program. When the program is loaded, the loader determines how much memory space the program needs.* For example, if the addresses run from ^X200 to ^X21FF, the program uses ^X2000 = 8192 bytes or ^X10 or 16 pages of memory. Note that

---

* With VAX/VMS, the program loading process is intimately connected with the implementation of virtual memory, and what would normally be called the loader is called the image activator. See Chapter 15.

this is a **virtual** memory assignment, since there is no guarantee of any particular assignment of pages of real memory. Since virtual pages may be moved in and out of real memory, a copy of the contents of the latest contents of the 16 pages is kept on the mass storage device.

Stepping ahead a bit, let us assume that the program has been executing for some time and attempts to access the contents of location ^X8C4. Perhaps the program is executing the instruction MOVL A,R0, and the location of A happens to be ^X8C4. Let us further suppose that the page containing ^X8C4 has been moved out of memory to the mass storage device or that it has never been loaded in the first place. In either case, there is no page of real memory assigned to the virtual addresses ^X800 through ^X9FF. As a result, the instruction MOVL A,R0 causes a page fault which in turn causes control to revert to the operating system.

Since ^X8C4 is a legal address for the program to use, the operating system must find a page of real memory. By whatever algorithm it uses (and this will be discussed later), the operating system may decide that the page of real memory starting at address ^X000A3C00 is a good page to assign to the program. Most likely, the page is already in use; perhaps by this program, perhaps by some other program.

Let us suppose that the real memory page starting at address ^X000A3C00 was assigned to the virtual page of some program. Then, before that page of real memory can be used, its contents must be saved on the mass storage device. Once the old contents has been saved, the memory page is available.

Finally, to resolve the page fault, the needed information can be loaded from the mass storage device into the now-available memory page. In this example, the page of information on the mass storage device would be copied into the memory page beginning at address ^X000A3C00. The page relocation register for this program is set to map virtual page ^X800 to the page of real memory starting at ^X000A3C00. At the same time, the page relocation register for the previous user must be set to indicate that the page no longer exists in real memory. The operating system can then return control to your program so that the instruction MOVL A,R0 can be executed successfully.

Needless to say, the process of page swapping can become quite complicated. Consider, for example, an instruction such as ADDL3 A,B,C. To execute this instruction, the processor must reference four items of information—the instruction itself as well as the operands A, B, and C. Since any of these four items could be in a page that no longer exists in real memory, a variety of page faults can occur as the instruction is executed.

The situation is actually more complicated than it may appear. For example, if the longword operand A is located at virtual address ^X9FE, then half the longword is in one page and the other half is in another. As a result, a reference to the longword A may cause as many as two page faults. A similar situation occurs when the instruction itself crosses page boundaries. This can cause a page fault as the instruction is being fetched. In any case, getting a virtual memory system to work correctly and efficiently is an extremely complex problem, involving both hardware and software design.

Paging Algorithms

In the above description, we referred to an algorithm for selecting a page to be moved to mass storage when a page fault occurs. When making a decision on what page to move out, it is important to pick a page that is unlikely to be needed right away. Poor choices on pages to move out could result in a page fault at every instruction. This would have the effect of your program running as slowly as if the mass storage device were the main memory.

The ideal choice for a page to move out would be a memory page which will not be needed for a long time. Unfortunately, it is not possible to predict such things in real time. Therefore, the algorithm must rely on probable choices. One such algorithm is to choose the least recently accessed page. The assumption is that if a page has not been used recently, it is unlikely to be needed soon. There may be cases where this assumption is not good, but on the average the premise is sound. However, the algorithm is expensive both in hardware and software. Determining which page was least recently used, would require each page register to have a clock which is automatically set at each access. Then a search would have to be made for the page register with the earliest clock setting.

One simple algorithm for selecting the page to swap out is to make a random choice. Another simple algorithm is to choose the pages in sequence. In practice, a simple algorithm may not be that much worse than a more complex and expensive algorithm. (Note that simple algorithms can be improved by weighting the probabilities in favor of choosing pages from lower priority programs.)

Cache Memory

The primary purpose of the virtual memory scheme described in the previous section is that the availability of memory to a program can be increased significantly by swapping between the fast, expensive, main memory and the slower, less expensive, disk memory. With proper use, a program can run with a page swapping virtual memory system almost as quickly as if it were run entirely in main memory. The question arises as to whether or not a similar trade-off could be made between main memory and a more expensive, superspeed memory. The effect could be almost as though the program were run from the faster memory.

Indeed, such a system can be made to operate and goes under the name of **cache memory.** Cache memory consists of a very high speed memory which is organized in blocks called **frames** (to distinguish them from virtual memory pages). Generally, frames are much smaller than pages. Depending upon the implementation, the frame size is characteristically in the range from tens to hundreds of bytes. In contrast, the page is characteristically in the range from hundreds to thousands of bytes.

As information from main memory is used by a program, the frames on which they reside are loaded into the cache. Therefore, if other data from that frame is needed, it is read directly from the cache, thus saving access time. When the program writes information, it is written to both the cache and main memory so that it will be available later from either memory. This is called a **write through.**

While main memory may be orders of magnitude faster than disk memory, the cache memory is only a few times faster than main memory. As a result, simplicity and speed are needed in the algorithms for loading frames, writing through, selecting the frame to overwrite, and determining if the data is in the cache to begin with. These algorithms must be directly implemented with high-speed logic or hardware since interrupting the program to execute software would nullify any speed advantage. As it is, the use of cache memory may improve the speed of a computer by two or three times.

14.3 Memory Management on the VAX
VAX Memory Organization

The previous section covered the general principles of memory management, virtual addressing, virtual memory, and cache memory. These principles are not peculiar to the VAX, but could apply to many computer designs. In this subsection we will look at some of the details of how memory management is handled on the VAX. Memory management includes both architectural features that operate in the same way on all VAX models as well as implementation features that may differ between models. For example, while the higher-end models of the VAX have extensive cache systems, the lower-end models have simple systems, or perhaps no cache at all. Since covering all the model-related peculiarities is a long and tedious topic, we will concentrate here on those things which apply to most or all models of the VAX.

One such principle is the partitioning of the virtual address space. The total virtual address space on the VAX is four gigabytes. This is broken down into pages which are the same size as the blocks or physical records on the disk. DEC keeps this figure to a standard of 512 bytes or 1/2K byte. Thus, in order to map all of virtual memory it would require approximately

4 gigabytes/.5K bytes per page = 8-million pages

or

8-million longword entries in the page table

These 8-million longword entries would occupy 8 × 4 = 32 megabytes of memory. This is not only much more real memory than most VAXs have, it is much more memory than most VAX implementations can accommodate. As a consequence it is not possible to produce a map for all virtual addresses in real memory. Fortunately, however, most applications have much more modest memory requirements. In any case, the page tables for user memory is actually stored in virtual memory. This allows the page tables themselves to be paged.

In order for page relocation registers to be easily located, they are kept in contiguous tables which can be searched with direct indexing from the high-order bits of the virtual address. In its simplest form this would restrict a program to using a contiguous set of virtual addresses starting at ^X00000000. To allow more flexibility, which helps deal with fixed-system areas as well as unknown quantities such as the program size and the stack, the 4-gigabyte virtual address space is divided into two 2-gigabyte areas called **process space** and **system space.** Process space consists of the virtual addresses ^X00000000 through ^X7FFFFFFF. System space consists of the rest, running from ^X80000000 through ^XFFFFFFFF. However, current VAX systems only use the first half of system space. (Those are the addresses in the range from ^X80000000 through ^XBFFFFFFF.) System space is used for permanently assigned system routines, stack space for system routines, and input/output functions which are described later in this chapter. Although users may have read access to some system routines in the system area, the area will be write protected from users.

Process space is allocated for each user's process or set of running programs. There needs to be a page table for each user's process area, and when control is exchanged from one user to another, the page tables are switched. This is part of what is called **context switching** which is described later in this section.

One problem that appears to occur when a user is assigned a contiguous area of memory is that the memory used by a program can grow with time. The VAX solves this problem by appending extra areas for growth at the end of the program so that the total space needed is still contiguous, while growing upward.

While a program's memory needs are making it grow upward, VAX programs make much use of the stack, and the stack grows downward or to lower-numbered addresses. To solve this problem, the VAX divides process space into two areas. The first is called **P0** space, or the **program region,** and is used primarily for programs and their data. The second is called **P1** space, or the **control region,** and is used primarily for the stack and some user-related system functions.

The P0 space runs from virtual address ^X00000000 to ^X3FFFFFFF and is assigned mapping space in the page table starting at ^X00000000 and working upward. If your program uses an address in P0 space which is higher than any mapped by the page table, a page fault occurs. If the operating system decides that you are entitled to that much space, your page table will be expanded to include that address and additional pages in virtual memory will be assigned to your program.

Since the stack pointer is decremented as information is placed on the stack, the P1 space maps in the opposite direction. P1 space extends from virtual addresses ^X40000000 through ^X7FFFFFFF, but is allocated backward starting at ^X7FFFFFFF and working toward lower-numbered addresses as more room is needed for the stack.

The Translation Buffer

In order to speed up the translation of virtual addresses to real addresses, a very high-speed memory called the **translator buffer** is used to hold the most frequently used addresses. This memory operates in a similar manner to cache for the address translation process. As with cache, the translation buffer is a very expensive piece of hardware which may or may not be implemented in different models of the VAX. However, also like the cache, the translation buffer is **transparent** to the programmer. That is, the programmer cannot tell that the computer has a cache or translation buffer except that program execution speed will be improved.

A design feature which exists in both the cache and the translation buffer in different forms is the **associative memory.** An ordinary, random access memory has an address decoder which transforms an address to a selection of one of the n memory locations. For example, a memory with four-million longwords would have an address decoder which selects one location from four-million possible locations. The reason that this works so simply is that the number of locations in the memory is exactly the same as the number of possible (allowable) addresses.

On the other hand, an associative memory has a relatively small number of locations which respond to selected addresses from a much larger address space. This means that there are more addresses than locations. As a result, some addresses do not correspond to a location. In other words, there is an incomplete mapping from addresses to data locations.

This is the same situation that arises with a translation buffer, since the buffer is only large enough to hold the most frequently used addresses. If the translation buffer were to be implemented in software, a search algorithm would be required involving numerous comparisons. Such a search would be slow and thus would defeat the purpose of having a translation buffer. To solve this problem, a page translation buffer is implemented in hardware using many comparitor circuits which operate in parallel, giving high-speed access to the stored data. A buffer (or memory) implemented with parallel hardware comparitors for high-speed searching is called an **associative memory.** Associative memory design techniques are used in various parts of large computer implementations, including page translation buffers and cache memory.

The Process Context

As each user logs into the system, resources are made available for the running of programs. The programs run must be thought of generally as including not only user programs, but also the system command processor and any system programs invoked by system commands such as COPY, DELETE, MACRO, LINK, and so forth.Whatever of these the user is executing is called the user's **process.** As far as the system is concerned, it is maintaining the operation of a number of processes. Some are user's processes; some are system's processes. The machine resources needed by each process include the following:

1. Some assignment of virtual addresses to real memory
2. A set of processor registers (R0, R1, R2, . . .)
3. Some other system registers for process control

These resources are called the **process context** and are assigned uniquely for each user.

Clearly, what your program has stored in virtual memory location ˆX8E4 is not the same as what somebody else's program has stored in virtual memory location ˆX8E4. Each program must have its own map for this virtual address so that each program accesses different real addresses. Similarly, your program uses R0, R1, etc., and so do other programs running at the same time. When the operating system switches control back and forth from one process to another, it must load the registers R0, R1, etc. with the correct values for that process and set the page table pointer and length registers (which specify the lengths of the P0 and P1 page tables) to give the proper virtual address assignments for that process. These values are kept in system memory, and the operation of saving one context and loading another is called **context switching.** There are instructions for implementing context switching very efficiently.

Because context switching or any operation involving memory mapping or other system functions can affect all users, these operations can only be executed by privileged programs. The different kinds of protections and privileges in the VAX are discussed later in this chapter.

Exercise Set 1

1. Write a short definition of the following terms:
   - **a.** Overlay
   - **b.** Virtual Address
   - **c.** Virtual Memory
   - **d.** Cache Memory
   - **e.** Page
   - **f.** Frame
   - **g.** Process Context

2. **a.** How is memory assigned in P0 space, P1 space?
   - **b.** What is the significance of the directions?
   - **c.** What are the names of P0 space and P1 space?
   - **d.** How is system space allocated?

*3. Choose some particular model of the VAX (perhaps the one you are using). Answer the following questions as they pertain to your model.
   - **a.** How much real memory does it have?
   - **b.** How much real memory is allowed on the model? (That is, the maximum that will fit.)
   - **c.** Does your model have a cache memory? If so, how long is it, and what is its organization?

d. Does your model have a page translation buffer? If so, how large is it, and what is its organization?

*4. a. Suppose you had a program which uses 1000 pages of virtual memory on a machine that has only 100 pages of real memory. Simulate page requests by generating random numbers between 1 and 1000. Write a program in any available language which will simulate such a system for 10,000 memory operations. Your program should simulate page swapping as faults occur and print out the number of faults and the average number of operations between faults.

b. Rerun the program modifying the probabilities so that the probability of choosing a page already mapped to real memory is ten times greater than that of choosing a page which causes a fault. How do the averages vary?

14.4 Protections and Privileges

In any multiuser system, it is necessary to have various systems of protections so that one user cannot interfere with another, either accidentally or intentionally. At the same time, it is necessary for well-debugged system processes to be able to transcend protection and other limitations so that they can do such things as load and unload user processes or even allow users' processes to interact with each other.

Access Modes

In order to simplify the grouping of privileges that a program can have, the VAX has four levels of privilege that can be in effect when a program executes. These levels are called **access modes,** because they control what kinds of operations the program has access to. From highest to lowest, the four access modes are

- Kernel
- Executive
- Supervisor
- User

As mentioned previously, the page relocation longwords have some extra bits which are used for memory protection. Some pages can be

used freely, some can be read from but not written to, others are not
accessible at all. This protection scheme operates through the access
modes so that different protections can exist for the different modes.
Thus, it is possible to set the bits for a page so that programs running
in user mode have no access, programs running in supervisor mode
have read access, and programs running in executive and kernel mode
have both read and write access. Note that the access modes form a
strict hierarchy. Therefore, a program running in a higher mode has
access to any privileges of the lower-access modes. If a user can read
a page, so can all the higher-mode programs. Similarly, note that the
privilege to write a location implies the privilege to read that location.
Table 14.1 shows how bits 27 through 30 of the page table entry are
used for assigning page access to the different modes. Note that there
are no entries in the table which allow a lower-level program more
access than a higher-level one.

In addition to the effect on memory access, the access mode also
affects instruction use. For example, the **reserved instruction** for reading or writing the processor control register and for loading or saving
process contexts can only be executed when in kernel mode. Any
attempt to execute these instructions while in any other mode causes
a **reserved instruction fault.** Reserved instructions are instructions
which require special privileges in order to use them.

Table 14.1 Memory protection codes

Code	Kernel	Executive	Supervisor	User
0000	none	none	none	none
0001	-----------------	not used -----	-----------------	-----------------
0010	Read/Write	none	none	none
0011	Read only	none	none	none
0100	Read/Write	Read/Write	Read/Write	Read/Write
0101	Read/Write	Read/Write	none	none
0110	Read/Write	Read only	none	none
0111	Read only	Read only	none	none
1000	Read/Write	Read/Write	Read/Write	none
1001	Read/Write	Read/Write	Read only	none
1010	Read/Write	Read only	Read only	none
1011	Read only	Read only	Read only	none
1100	Read/Write	Read/Write	Read/Write	Read only
1101	Read/Write	Read/Write	Read only	Read only
1110	Read/Write	Read only	Read only	Read only
1111	Read only	Read only	Read only	Read only

The VMS operating system is organized so that different kinds of operations occur at the different access modes. The following list describes the basic uses.

Mode	Uses
User	User programs, utilities, compilers, debuggers
Supervisor	The command interpreter
Executive	Calls to system service routines and RMS functions
Kernel	Virtual memory page management, process scheduling, hardware level input and output

The PROBE instruction

The PROBE instruction allows a program to test the legality of a memory operation before performing that operation. There are a number of reasons why such testing would be useful. The first is protection of the operating system. A user program may call a Record Manager System (RMS) routine which operates at a higher privilege such as executive mode. The user program may pass some addresses along as arguments. Suppose that the contents at those addresses were protected from user access, but not from executive access. The RMS routine could successfully make the illegal accesses for the user routine which called it.

To guard against this, a more privileged routine should **probe** all address arguments passed to it by a less privileged routine to make certain that the less privileged has legal access to those locations.

There are two PROBE instructions, one to test read access (**PROBER**) and the other to test write access (**PROBEW**). The instructions have three arguments:

1. Mode
2. Base address
3. Length

The mode gives the access mode to be tested:

- 0 for kernel
- 1 for executive
- 2 for supervisor
- 3 for user

However, the VAX saves the previous mode when a call to a more privileged mode changes the access mode. The PROBE instructions use whichever mode is higher, the specified mode, or the previous mode. (Note that the higher-numbered modes are less privileged.)

The base address and length allow the specification of an array of bytes. However, only the first and last address are checked, so arrays that span more than two pages should be checked in pieces.

For example, the instruction

```
PROBER    #3,#50,A
```

would check to see if a user's program has read access to the 50 bytes beginning with the address A. Similarly, the instruction

```
PROBEW    #3,#4,B
```

would check to see if a user's program has write access to the long-word B. For both instructions, the Z bit is used for testing accessibility. If $Z = 1$, access is illegal; if $Z = 0$, access is legal. Therefore, the PROBE instructions should be followed by an instruction of the sort

```
BEQL      NO_ACCESS
```

or

```
BNEQ      ACCESS_LEGAL
```

to complete the test.

Note that there are a few assumptions at work here. First, write access implies read access, and no-read access implies no-write access. Second, mode #3 or user mode is the lowest privileged. Therefore, the previous PROBE instructions test user mode access regardless of the previous mode value.

Processor Registers

In addition to the 16 general purpose processor registers (R0, R1, . . .) that we have been using, there are a number of special purpose registers in the VAX. These registers control the inner workings of the VAX, such as pointers to virtual memory page relocation tables. Note that since most of these registers are accessible only to kernel mode programs, we will only cover the more general principles. In addition, there are some registers which differ in their use from model to model of the VAX, or exist on some models but not on others.

One register of special note is called the **processor status longword** or PSL. This register contains fields of bits which contain various kinds of information about the status of the running process. For example, two of the bits give the process access level 0, 1, 2, or 3 for kernel mode, executive mode, supervisor mode, or user mode, respectively. Two more bits provide the previous mode used by the **PROBE** instructions. Four of the bits hold the condition codes, N, C, Z, and V bits.

Bits in the PSL are changed as a program executes. For example, any instruction which affects condition codes will write into the condition code bits. It is necessary to write into the PSL to change the access mode, and of course, that requires certain privileges. It is, however, possible to read the PSL using the instruction, MOVPSL. MOVPSL causes the contents of the PSL to be copied to a destination longword. The MOVPSL instruction can be used to determine your current or previous mode as well as some other status information. The following lists the use of the bits of the PSL, and the user is referred to the *VAX Architecture Handbook* for more detail.

Bit(s)	Use
0	C bit
1	V bit
2	Z bit
3	N bit
4	Trace bit, can be used for emulating single stepping of a program for debugging purposes
5	Integer overflow trap enable
6	Floating-point underflow trap enable
7	Decimal overflow trap enable
8–15	Must be zero
16–20	Interrupt priority level
21	Must be zero
22–23	Previous mode
24–25	Current mode
26	Interrupt stack flag
27	First part done flag, allows certain instructions which take a long time to execute to be interrupted part way through execution
28–29	Must be zero
30	Trace pending bit
31	Compatibility mode bit, when set, the VAX will execute PDP-11 instructions

Notice that the low-order 16 bits (bits 0–15) do not contain privileged information, and therefore may be modified by the user (except for bits 8–15 which are unused and must always be zero.) These 16 bits are sometimes referred to as the **processor status word** or PSW. The lower 8 bits of the PSW can be modified by setting or clearing the bits using BISPSW or BICPSW. For example, the instruction

```
BISPSW    #^X20
```

would set the integer overflow trap bit. The integer overflow trap causes the program to abort with an error message if any instruction causes the V bit to be set. Setting this bit would help assume the correctness of integer calculations, but would cause problems for any programs using unsigned arithmetic.

In order to speed up transfer from programs with different privilege and to aid in maintaining protection of the operating system, there are five different stacks in the system. These are the user stack, the supervisor stack, the executive stack, the kernel stack, and the interrupt stack. This means that there are five different stack pointers. When in a particular mode, the appropriate stack pointer is used whenever an instruction refers to SP, or does some implied push or pop operation. The first four stack pointers are selected by the current access mode. The interrupt stack pointer is used if bit 26 of the PSL is one. Normally, a program can only access its own stack pointer. However, there are two instructions MTPR and MFPR (Move to Processor Register and Move From Processor Register) which allow programs running in kernel mode to access all five stack pointers.

These instructions are also used to access the base and length registers which define the P0, P1, and system virtual address page tables. There are also a number of other registers accessible with these instructions, and the reader should refer to the *VAX Architecture Handbook* for the particular model of VAX being used.

14.5 Busses and Bus Structures

A **bus** is a common set of wires which is used to connect a computer processor to its memory and peripheral devices. Normally, a bus has many wires, one for each bit being transmitted or received. This allows those bits to be transmitted at the same time, which is much faster than sending one bit at a time down a single wire as is done with serial communications systems. Processors characteristically transmit address and control information on a bus and the memory or peripheral device which recognizes that address will respond by transmitting or receiving data from the data portion of the bus.

Usually even the simplest computers will have several different busses. However, some busses may be transparent to the user. For example, there is a bus inside the VAX processor which interconnects the processor registers. Such busses may be completely contained on a single printed circuit board, or even within a single integrated circuit chip.

On the other hand, there are busses which are used for transmitting data across various portions of the computer system, and it is important for users to know a little about these busses, since they affect system configuration and the use of peripherals. There are a number of different busses of this kind used by the different members of the VAX family of computers. Many of the VAX computers have more than one bus to accommodate different purposes. In the following sections, we will briefly describe the different busses used in the VAX family and show how they are used in different models of the VAX.

Synchronous Backplane Interconnect

The larger VAX-11 processors, such as the 780, the 782, and the 785, are connected to the memory and certain peripheral controllers by means of a high-speed synchronous bus called the **synchronous backplane interconnect,** or **SBI.** A synchronous bus operates on the ticks of a clock, and all devices on the bus must be able to respond at the speed of the clock. In the case of the VAX SBI, the clock cycle time is 200 nanoseconds where a nanosecond is 1/1,000,000,000 of a second. Data is transferred 32 bits at a time, and double transfers allow two groups of 32 bits to be transmitted based upon one address. This enhances the speed of the SBI and gives a rated transfer speed of 13.3-million bytes per second.

A high-speed synchronous bus such as the SBI is only usable over a short distance, and for interconnecting devices which are all able to operate at the synchronous speed. When the speeds of devices differ, a synchronous bus would have to operate at the speed of the slowest device on the bus. To avoid this problem, an asynchronous bus can be used. An asynchronous bus communicates with devices which respond at their own speeds and then signal completion of the transmission. This signaling back and forth is called **handshaking.**

Asynchronous Busses on the VAX

VAX family processors use several asynchronous busses for communication with peripheral devices. On the smaller members of the VAX family, the main bus may be one of these asynchronous busses, but on the larger VAX processors, these busses are connected into the SBI using **backplane adaptors.** These adapters have some small, high-speed, first-in-first-out storage devices called **silos.** The silos allow the adaptors to transmit data to the SBI in 64-bit chunks and therefore to take advantage of the high-speed double transfers of the SBI. The asynchronous busses were originally designed for use on various models of the PDP-11 or LSI-11 series of computers. As these computers have less storage capability than the VAX, the backplane adaptors have address mapping capabilities. The following list gives the main properties of these busses.

MASSBUS is a high-speed bus with a 16-bit data path. It is asynchronous for control information, and synchronous for data transmission. While it was originally designed for the PDP-11/70 computer system, it is used on some larger VAXs for interfacing to high-speed disk units such as the RP and RM disks. The data transfer rate of the MASSBUS can be as high as 2-million bytes per second.

UNIBUS is a fully asynchronous bus with a 16-bit data path. It was originally used on all the PDP-11 computers, except for the LSI-11 series. The UNIBUS allows the VAX to connect to any peripheral device which can be connected to the PDP-11 series computers and is used for most input/output, except for the high-speed disks connected to the MASSBUS. The lower-end VAX processors, such as the VAX-11/730, use the UNIBUS for all input and output. The data transfer rate of the UNIBUS can be as high as 1.5-million bytes per second.

Q-BUS is a low-cost, 16-bit, fully asynchronous bus which was originally designed for the LSI-11 family of computers as a low-cost alternative to the UNIBUS. Cost is reduced by using the same lines for both data and the lower 16 bits of the address. This means that data and addresses have to be transmitted at different times, thus it slows down the user somewhat but cuts the amount of circuitry for each peripheral controller nearly in half. The standard-size VAX computers do not use the Q-BUS directly. Nevertheless, large VAX computers, such as the VAX-11/780, have an LSI-11 contained internally for control of the operator console and system startup. Therefore, these models of the VAX have a Q-BUS even though it is not used during normal user operations. However, the MicroVAX series of computers are designed with the Q-BUS as the only external bus, which is used for both memory and peripheral devices.

14.6 Hardware Level Input/Output on the VAX

Unlike many computers, the VAX has no specific instructions for performing input or output. Instead, the VAX uses the ordinary data handling instructions such as MOV, ADD, INC, and so on, which activate input and output by referencing specifically reserved addresses.

One megabyte of the higher end of the real (as opposed to virtual) address space is reserved for input/output functions, and is not used for memory. Addresses in this area refer to locations in a UNIBUS or MASSBUS controller. (In the case of the MicroVAX, the addresses refer to locations in an input/output controller board which is plugged into the Q-BUS.) Specific addresses will locate registers in the device controllers. These device registers use bits or bit patterns to activate peripheral devices or to return status information. For example, a code placed in a command register may cause a tape unit to rewind. A bit in a status register may be used to indicate completion of an input/output operation, and another bit may be used to indicate an error. Each device has its own set of registers and its own method for interpreting the bits. The appropriate handbooks must be consulted for the specifics of each device.

It should be noted that the addresses of device registers are real addresses which must be mapped to virtual addresses so that programs can access them. However, since so much potential danger to the system would result from improper access to devices at the hardware level, these addresses are marked for kernel mode access only. (If a user had hardware access to a device such as a disk, the user could read, modify, or delete the files and directories on the disk, thus bypassing the VAX/VMS file protection system.)

Direct Memory Access

In order to achieve a high rate of performance, it is necessary to minimize the need for programs to operate on the input/output register. For example, if the VAX had to execute a MOVB instruction for every byte being transferred from a disk, it would completely tie up the CPU. In fact, the VAX is probably not fast enough to keep up with the faster disks in this manner. To avoid this problem, most input/output devices on the VAX operate in a **direct memory access** or **DMA** mode. That means that once started, the device is capable of reading from or writing into the VAX memory directly, without the need for attention from the running program, until the whole block of information has been transferred.

Direct memory access is accomplished partly through the controller for the input/output device, and partly through the I/O bus to backplane adaptor. Since both the MASSBUS and UNIBUS are 16-bit busses, they are only capable of transmitting words or bytes. Transferring these small units of information is inefficient for the

VAX which prefers the use of 32-bit transfers, or 64-bit double transfers. In order to take advantage of this gain in efficiency, the backplane adaptors have an internal memory called a **silo** which stores data and attempts to make all DMA transfers 64 bits long, in so far as is possible. (If the length of the block being transferred is not a multiple of 64 bits, there must be some odd transfer to complete the block.) A silo is a memory that operates in a manner which is opposite to that of a pushdown stack. In a pushdown stack, the last item placed in is the first to be removed. In the silo, the first placed in is the first to be removed. The size of the silos on current backplane adaptors is 64 bytes. This gives sufficient buffer space, so that the SBI can get a little behind, and then catch up as the SBI is used for various other tasks.

Interrupts

When a DMA or other input/output process is in progress, the central processor would be tied up excessively if it continuously had to check to see if the input/output process is complete. In order to solve this problem, modern computers use interrupts. An interrupt is an alarm that causes the processor to leave execution of the currrent program and begin execution of a special program called the **interrupt servicing routine.** In the process of interrupting a program, enough information is saved so that control can be returned to the interrupted program and it can continue on as if it had not been interrupted. On the VAX, this information consists of saving the PC and the Processor Status Longword (PSL) on the interrupt stack. Any other register that the interrupt routine uses must be saved by the interrupt routine itself.

Interrupt routines are located by longwords called **interrupt vectors** each of which specifies the starting addresses of a particular interrupt routine. This is called **vectored interrupting.** On the VAX, interrupt vectors and interrupt routines are in protected system memory space, and operate at kernel access mode. However, the VAX/VMS operating system provides methods for calling user-generated interrupt routines called **asynchronous system traps** or **AST**s. When set up properly, a user program can have input/output completion routines which are activated by a system interrupt. This allows a program to continue computations while waiting for input or output to complete. Readers should review Chapter 11 or consult the *VAX/VMS System Services Reference Manual* for more information on using ASTs.

Exceptions

Exceptions are like interrupts except that instead of being triggered by external events such as input/output completion, they are triggered by internally generated conditions such as overflow, illegal or reserved instructions or operands, or illegal memory references. For the most part, exceptions result in program termination with an error message. However, it is possible to have certain exceptions activate user-written procedures called **condition handlers.**

Exceptions are grouped into two categories, **traps** and **faults.** On a trap, the interruption occurs after the instruction has completed. The saved value of the PC would point to the next instruction to be executed. An example of a trap is the integer overflow trap. If the integer overflow trap bit is set in the PSL, a trap occurs wherever an integer instruction such as ADDL3 performs an operation that sets the V bit. The operation is completed, and the result (which may be correct for unsigned arithmetic) is stored at the destination.

A fault occurs if the instruction cannot be completed. In this case the PC is reset to its value prior to execution of the instruction. This allows the exception routine to examine the instruction and determine what the problem is. It may be possible for the exception routine to fix things up. For example, models of the VAX which do not have the G_ and H_ level floating-point instructions can use the reserved instruction fault to emulate the instructions in software. As far as the user is concerned, the program is being executed correctly, although more slowly than if the instruction had been implemented in hardware.

Interruptable Instructions

When the processor receives an interrupt request, the processor will be in the process of executing an instruction. Normally, the processor finishes executing this instruction before it transfers control to the interrupt servicing routine. However, complex instructions such as character string instructions described in Chapter 13 present a potential problem. Such instructions can have lengthy execution times and many higher priority events cannot wait until the execution of such instructions has been completed. (Even on a VAX computer system, it can take a significant fraction of a second to move 65536 bytes.)

To overcome this problem, instructions with potentially long execution times are designed so that they can be interrupted before instruction execution has been completed. Such instructions are called

interruptable instructions. When control returns to the interrupted program, execution of the interrupted instruction proceeds from the point at which the execution of the instruction was suspended.

When an interruptable instruction is interrupted part way through execution, it is necessary to save intermediate results so that execution can be resumed from the point at which it was interrupted. (If it were necessary to restart execution of the instruction from the beginning, a series of interrupts could delay completion of the instruction indefinitely.) Because the interruptable instructions use R0 through R5 for temporary storage as the instruction is executed, the interrupt process is fast and efficient. The interruptable instructions include the POLY instruction described in Chapter 12 as well as the character and packed decimal instructions described in Chapter 13.

Interlocks

When information is being modified by more than one process or device, there is a possibility that the information will be updated improperly. This is true of any storage device including main memory or disk. For example, assume that you owe a university a total of $2,001—$2,000 for tuition and $1 for library fines. If both payments happen to be processed at approximately the same time, the following could occur:

1. The Library's process fetches your current balance, $2,001.
2. The Bursar's process fetches your current balance, $2,001.
3. The Bursar's process computes your new balance as $1 ($2,001 minus your $2000 payment to the Bursar) and writes the new balance on the storage device.
4. The Library's process computes your new balance as $2,000 ($2,001 minus your $1 payment to the Library) and writes the new balance on the storage device, overwriting the amount ($1) just written by the Bursar's process.

As a result, you have made payments of $1 and $2,000 for a $2,001 bill, but the storage device shows that you still owe $2,000.

This same error can occur when processes and devices are modifying the same location in memory. Avoiding the error can be a difficulty in writing operating system software. The solution to this problem is to **interlock** information so that it cannot be accessed by one process while it is being modified by another process. In the example above, if your balance had been interlocked, the bursar's process could not have accessed your balance while the library's process was modifying it.

To support the operating system and other concurrent processes, the VAX architecture provides the following seven instructions.

Instruction		Description
ADAWI	add,sum	ADd Aligned Word Interlocked
BBCCI	off,adr,disp	Branch on Bit Clear and Clear Interlocked
BBSSI	off,adr,disp	Branch on Bit Set and Set Interlocked
INSQHI	entry,head	INSert into relative Queue at Head Interlocked
INSQTI	entry,head	INSert into relative Queue at Tail Interlocked
REMQHI	entry,head	REMove from relative Queue at Head Interlocked
REMQTI	entry,head	REMove from relative Queue at Tail Interlocked

See the *VAX Architecture Handbook* for additional details.

Exercise Set 2

1. Write a short definition of the following terms.
   a. Privilege
   b. Access Mode
   c. Processor Registers
   d. Bus
   e. UNIBUS
   f. MASSBUS
   g. Q-BUS
   h. Direct Memory Access
   i. Interrupt
   j. Trap
   k. Fault

2. Ignoring any implied restrictions, how many possible ways are there of assigning the access rights "none," "read only," and "read/write" to four access modes? Does Table 14.1 show all the possibilities of access rights that imply that higher modes can do the accesses that lower modes can? If not, what other possibilities are there?

3. For the particular VAX that you are using, what kinds of busses does it have? What input/output devices are on which bus? Are other busses available as optional equipment? If so, what are they, and what extra equipment is needed?

*4. Use the PROBER and PROBEW instructions to determine which locations of memory are available to users for reading, and what locations are available for writing. Print out a concise memory map of the entire virtual memory space. Use care in your format, since a printout of one line per memory page would require 8 million lines.

*5. Consult the *VAX/VMS System Services Reference Manual* to find how to generate an AST which will interrupt your program every ten seconds. Write a program which rings the bell on your terminal every ten seconds, but which does not waste computer time by continuously looping.

Advanced Assembly Language Topics

15.1 Introduction

One topic that becomes clear when studying assembly language is often hidden when using a higher-level language. This is the relationship between programs and data. We have seen in previous chapters that instructions (the program) and data utilize the same memory in the computer. In fact, this is true not only of the VAX, but also of most general purpose computers, both large and small.*

In effect, this means that there is little difference between programs and data. This chapter will look at the ramifications of this, and we will see how various parts of an operating system treat programs that people write as data. In fact, your program can always be thought of as data that are read by one of the various processors. These processors have all been used in the material in the previous chapters, but the processes have not been fully identified. This chapter will proceed in that direction. In addition, we will look at some topics involved with program manipulation, such as writing position-independent code.

---

* Some special purpose microcomputers, such as the Texas Instruments TMS-1000, have separate program and data areas. However, many of the principles described here still apply.

15.2 Program Format
General Forms

An assembly language or FORTRAN program normally goes through various stages of translation before it can be executed. At each stage, the program is treated as data in a specific form. We will look at each of these forms and their structures, as well as how the various processors deal with them.

On the VAX, assembly language programs and most higher-level language programs have the following forms:

1. Source code. This consists of the alphabetic strings that make up the statements of the language.

2. Object code. This is a translated program with all operations converted to binary VAX operation codes. However, although some addresses are translated into binary addresses, others are not. This is because the assembler (compiler) does not assign values to global symbols and also because program addresses may need to be relocated. As a consequence, information must be provided to tell the linker how to complete the program translation.

3. Executable image file. The linker takes one or more object files and relocates the program areas so that they all will each occupy unique areas of memory. Global symbols are assigned binary values. The result is an executable image file that contains binary codes which can be loaded into memory for the most part without further modification.

4. An activated program. This is a specified area of memory in the computer which contains a program that is ready for execution. The difference between an activated program and executable image file is that the activated program is assigned an execution area in the virtual memory, whereas the executable image file simply resides on some input/output or mass storage media. There is a program in the VAX/VMS system called the **image activator** which assigns a program from an executable image file to space in virtual memory. The way that this is done is closely related to the operation of virtual memory and is described in more detail in the section on virtual loading.

Source Code

Source code in the VAX consists of an indefinitely long string of ASCII characters. This string is broken into pieces called **statements** or **lines** or **records.** The exact format of a line of source code depends upon the language (such as assembly language, Pascal, or FORTRAN). However, each line is delimited by control information in the record structure of the file. Usually line lengths are limited to some fixed upper bound, such as 80 characters.

There are a number of processors that operate on source code. Processors are programs that, in effect, treat the source code as data, that is, a string of characters upon which to perform certain operations. Some of these programs perform relatively simple operations, such as the program for copying a file from one place to another. This program is used when you type a COPY command (see Appendix D). Other programs such as the editors (see Appendix E) or the assembler perform specific operations on the source text itself.

Source Editing

Editors, such as EDT and TECO, are generally used to create, modify, and update source code. However, editors are not keyed to any particular language; they can operate with **any** line-oriented ASCII text, including text which has nothing to do with programming such as straight English prose. The editors do recognize record and page delimiters as special, but the remaining characters in the record are just treated as ordinary data. The way the editors work is that they copy the entire text or a large block of text into memory as one big array of characters. (Large text files may not fit into allocated memory and must be broken into pages, each of which is edited separately. Some editors, like EDT, can move back and forth over pages. Others, like TECO, must progress from page to page in the forward direction only.) The various edit commands are interpreted to cause the editor to locate places in the array of characters and to insert or delete characters from the array. Insertion and deletion are often slow, because the entire tail end of the array may have to be recopied in order to make or take up space. However, the VAX is fast enough so that the user does not usually notice any delays unless inserts or deletes are repeated. When editing is finished, memory is then copied back out to a mass storage file.

The Assembly Process

We should already be somewhat familiar with the assembly process because it has been covered in various chapters from Chapter 4 on. However, certain points come into focus if we look at the process in terms of data operations. As with most processors, the assembler

```
    JSB    NEXT
          , , ,
NEXT:
```

Figure 15.1 A forward
reference

reads data from input files and and writes data to output files.* In its simplest operation, there is one input file that contains source code. There are **two** output files. The first receives the translated program in binary format, the **object file.** The second output file receives the listing. Both files receive similar information, but there are some differences; and the format is completely different, as we shall see in the next section.

As we have stated before, assembly on the VAX is a two-pass process. That is, the input file must be read all the way through by the assembler two times. This is because the assembler cannot assign addresses to locations that are defined further down in the program. These are known as **forward references,** and they occur in situations such as shown in Figure 15.1. The symbol NEXT is referred to by the JSB instruction. However, the code for this instruction cannot be assigned because the assembler has not yet read the line that defines NEXT. Although it might appear in this example that the assembler need only look ahead a little to resolve the forward reference, we must remember that forward references may often reach ahead many pages in a long program.

The solution used on the VAX is to look ahead once through the whole program. During this first pass, the symbol table is created. The assembler then uses a second pass to substitute numbers for names to create the machine language program. The remarkable thing is that in the VAX assembler, the processes for pass 1 and pass 2 are almost identical. The main difference is that during pass 1, all output is suppressed. If output were generated during pass 1, there would be an undefined symbol error message for each forward reference.

During the second pass, the same process is repeated. However, now there is already a complete symbol table created by the first pass. This symbol table will contain the resolved values of all forward references. The object file and listing can be output during the second pass, because there will not be any undefined symbols unless the programmer really left them undefined.

It should be noted that the VAX's use of a two-pass assembler is not the only solution to the forward reference problem. There are other solutions. One would be to insist that programmers avoid for-

---

* For our purposes here, we will consider a file to be a collection or string of data that comes from or goes to some input/output device such as the card reader, a line printer, a disk, or a tape.

ward references. Most users would not like this. Another solution is to produce code during the first pass, making note of forward references. Then, when forward references are resolved, the object file is corrected as dictated by the noted references. This is sometimes called a **one-and-a-half pass assembler.** Still another solution is to leave the resolution of forward references to another program such as the linker, the loader, or the processor itself through some indirect addressing scheme.

Data for the Assembler

As we stated before, the input and output files for the assembler are really data input and output for a program. Two of the three data files, namely the source and listing files, are meant for human users. Therefore these files are **character files** that can be printed as characters on a page. The reader should already be familiar with the appearance of both of these files. However, a file's appearance to a person is quite different from the way that the computer must access the data. We are used to looking at words, lines, and pages as single objects. The computer is much more restricted, so that alphabetic data must be processed by a program character by character, or at best in small strings of characters (perhaps up to eight at a time with a quadword operation on the VAX).

As the assembler reads the source file, it must be able to distinguish the various **fields** on a line. These are the label field, opcode field, operand field, and comments. There are two popular methods for identifying fields. One is to use fixed fields that start at particular character positions on a line. For example, FORTRAN statements occupy positions (columns) 7 through 72 of a line. Essentially, FORTRAN has this rule because the language was originally implemented in a punched card environment. Similarly, early IBM assemblers had fixed-field locations.

The second method to identify fields is to use punctuation such as the colons, semicolons, commas, spaces, and so on as used in the VAX assembly language. This method tends to be more desirable for more modern applications because input is from a terminal where character positions are less easily identifiable than with cards. As a consequence, many assemblers use a combination of partially fixed fields and punctuation. For example, the CDC COMPASS assembler requires labels to start in column 1, and opcodes to start later than column 1. Consequently, there is no need for a colon to distinguish labels from opcodes or operands.

We can now roughly outline the functions of the portion of the assembler that performs pass 1 and pass 2 in the VAX assembler. At each cycle of its process, the assembler fetches a line of source code and examines it character by character.* Initial spaces are ignored.** The first nonblank character is assumed to be the start of a symbol. The assembler stores successive characters until a punctuation character is found. This is usually a space, a colon, or an equal sign.

If the first nonblank character is a colon, it means that the accumulated symbol is a label, and an entry is made in the symbol table. If the first nonblank character is an equal sign, the assembler expects to see an expression that is evaluated and entered in the symbol table. If the first nonblank character is anything else, the assembler assumes that the accumulated symbol is an opcode, assembly directive, or macro name. Opcodes and assembly directives are grouped into classes. For example, ADDL2, MOVL, and SUBL2 are similar, and BRB, BEQL, and BNEQ are similar. Each class of opcode has a special subprocessor that deals appropriately with the operand field and generates object code. The entire line of code is then terminated either by an end of line or a semicolon. Comments are, in effect, ignored by the assembler.

If this is the second pass, the generated object code (if any) is written to the object file, and a listing line is generated. The listing line consists of the hexadecimal value of the object code (with relocation marks) and the address followed by the line number and the source code as it appears on the input line for each line of source code. This overall cycle repeats and is eventually terminated by processing the .END directive.

Macro Expansion

The macro processor is virtually a separate entity that is, in effect, an extension to assembly language. As described in Chapter 10, there are two parts to macro processing: macro definition and macro calling or expanding. When a macro is defined, the lines following .MACRO up through the corresponding .ENDM are copied to a macro definition area.

When the macro is called, its name is in the opcode field of an input line. This causes the macro expansion processor to be entered. The expansion processor copies the lines of alphabetic text in the definition area to an expansion area. While doing this, substitutable parameters are replaced by arguments in the calling line. In most cases, this is a character-string-for-character-string substitution with no interpretation.

---

* The string instructions described in Chapter 13 operate effectively in a character-by-character fashion.
** Horizontal tabs and spaces are treated essentially the same.

After the expansion is complete, control is returned to the subroutine that processes the assembly passes. However, there is a slight difference. If there is any code in the macro expansion area, lines are fetched from there rather than from the source file. Otherwise the process proceeds as before. This continues until the expansion area is empty, and then lines will again be taken from the source file. This action is the same on both passes.

If one of the lines of the macro expansion happens to be a macro call, the same expansion process occurs, except that the expanded macro is always added in front of whatever may be left in the expansion area. This allows macros to call macros, which call macros, and so on. There is no limit, except for the memory limit of the expansion area. Because the macro expansion area operates as a push down stack, macros can even be recursive and call themselves. Note that a recursive macro must have its call to itself in a conditional block so that the process will eventually terminate.

Exercise Set 1

1. Write a program that prints out the contents of ALL its own locations byte by byte (both instruction and data) in both hexadecimal and binary. The program should also print out the contents of the 16 general registers in hexadecimal and binary. For example, the printout might appear as

Address	Hex	Binary
00000200	AF	10101111
00000201	B0	10110000
. . .	. . .	. . .

a. Identify which parts of your program (if any) function as instructions only, data only, or both instructions and data. Why?

b. Does your printout have any strange features such as the hexadecimal and binary values disagreeing? Why? Can anything be done about this?

2. Write a simple editor program that operates somewhat like the BASIC language system editor.

a. Each line is preceded by a six-digit decimal number.

b. The lines can be entered in any order, but will be printed with increasing line numbers.

c. If a line is entered with a line number that is the same as an earlier line, the earlier line will be deleted.

d. A line number of 999999 terminates input and causes the edited data to be printed. For example, the input

```
000100    FIRST LINE
000070    SECOND LINE
000120    THIRD LINE
000130    FOURTH LINE
000120    FIFTH LINE
999999
```

would cause the following printout

```
000070    SECOND LINE
000100    FIRST LINE
000120    FIFTH LINE
000130    FOURTH LINE
```

3. The following instructions would be found in different groups because of the different operand structures they have.

```
CLRL    ADDL2    BRB     JMP
CALLS   RET      MOVAB   ACBL
```

a. Describe the operands of each instruction, being as general as possible.

b. Describe what the assembler would do in its operand processing.

4. Describe the functions of the following assembly directives. What processes would be performed during each pass?

```
.LIST    .WORD    .REPT    .ASCII
```

5. Hand assemble the following program step by step, and show the macro definition area and macro expansion area as each line is processed.

```
        .MACRO  FAC       A,N
        .IF     EQUAL,N
A=1
        .IF_FALSE
        FAC     A,N-1
A=A*N
        .ENDC
        .ENDM
        FAC     NUM,3
        .END
```

15.3 Object Code
Binary Files and Record Structure

Since the source code and listings are meant to communicate with people, they are generated as character files in ASCII. However, the object code is not generally intended to be seen by humans, but rather to be read into the computer during linking. As a result, it is preferable to use a data format that is better for machine use than ASCII. Character files are not very compact because they usually use spaces, tabs, and other punctuation to make the data readable (by humans). For example, a 16-bit binary number could be expressed as a four-digit hexadecimal number with one space to separate it from the next number. This would require five ASCII characters or five bytes of data. However, in its internal representation, a 16-bit binary number only occupies two bytes. Consequently, data items are much more compact and can be transmitted much more efficiently if they are kept in internal binary form. Files stored in this manner are called **binary files.**

Normally the large amounts (or potentially large amounts) of data that are stored in binary files need to be broken down into smaller pieces in the same way that character files are broken into lines. As we saw in Chapter 11, these identifiable strings of data are referred to as **records.** There are essentially two methods of segmenting a binary file: fixed-length records and variable-length records. With fixed-length records, there is an understanding that all records are exactly a certain fixed size. Consequently, there is no need to provide any control information to delineate the data.

In object files, as we shall see, there is a need for various kinds of data in differing amounts. As a consequence, variable-length records conserve space. There are two main ways to delimit variable-length records. These methods are analogous to what is done in higher-level languages for delimiting character strings. For example, the first method is to use a **length count** which is part of the data in the record. This is similar to what is done in FORTRAN with the H notation. (H stands for Hollerith.) For example,

```
17HHERE'S A MESSAGE.
```

The initial 17H defines the length of the message that can contain any characters.

The other method to delimit records uses control characters such as the carriage control/line feed used with ASCII text from a terminal. One problem with this method is that it becomes awkward to deal with text that itself contains control characters. This is especially important with binary files where any combination of bits can be valid information. One solution to this problem is to use double control characters to indicate a single control character in the text. This is used in FORTRAN when one wishes to use apostrophes to delimit a string that contains an apostrophe. The previous example can be rewritten

```
'HERE''S A MESSAGE.'
```

Two apostrophes in a row are treated as a single apostrophe of text. This method can be adapted for use with binary data and is used with some standard data transmission protocols such as BISYNC (a protocol used by IBM and others for computer networks). However, the VAX/VMS system uses the counting method for delimiting variable length records, as is shown in the following section.

Internal Record Format on the VAX

As was described in Chapter 11, files on the VAX are broken down into records which can be accessed randomly or sequentially. Records can have either a variable length or a fixed length. With a fixed-length record format, there is no need to delimit the beginnings or ends of records, because the fixed and known record byte count can be used. However, with variable-length records, there must be a scheme for determining the location of record boundaries.

Most of the mass storage devices on the VAX are set up so that information is written in physical blocks which are 512 bytes in length.* In order to ascertain the record format and access methods for the file, an extra block is written at the beginning of each file. Usually the user does not see this block, because it only contains control information. Among other things, this block contains bit codes which identify the record type and access method to be used for the remainder of the file. If you are curious, you can see what is in this block using the DUMP/HEADER or DUMP/HEADER/NOFORMATED command from a terminal or the batch stream.

The remaining blocks in the file contain the user's information, formatted as specified in the control block. If variable-record length is specified, as is usually the case, each record will be preceded with a 16-bit byte count. In addition, a byte of zero is added to the end of

---

* Some disks such as floppy disks are sectored for a smaller block size. However, in those cases, the VAX maintains compatibility by using several sectors to form a 512-byte block.

a record, if necessary, in order to ensure that records always have an
even number of bytes. Consequently the following records of text

```
Hello
This is
Some text
  + + +
```

would have the following structure in a record:

```
69 29 73 69 68 54 00 07 00 6F 6C 6C 65 48 00 05
. . .   00 74 78 45 74 20 65 6D 6F 53 00 09 00 73
```

Note that these records are listed from right to left as is the custom
with dumps and assembly listings on the VAX. Also note that because
each record happens to have an odd number of bytes, a 00 fill was
required for each record.

   Because the byte counts explicitly delimit the size of each record,
the individual bytes in the records do not have to contain ASCII codes,
but can contain any combination of bits. Some other systems, like
the DEC PDP-11 operating system, use control characters such as
carriage returns (^X0D) or line feed (^X0A) to delimit records. This
means that the text cannot contain any of these characters in the
middle of a record. As a result, these systems often have files classified
as character files or binary files. Character files delimit records with
control characters, and binary files use a byte count as described
above. The VAX/VMS system uses a byte count for both character
files and binary files thereby leaving little distinction between them.
Essentially, the difference on the VAX is that character files usually
have carriage control parameters in the control block. This information is originally specified in the **file access block** when the file is
created. See Chapter 11.

The Object Module

The **object module** is a formatted binary file that is produced by the
assembler during the assembly process. The object module contains
all the binary machine language produced by the assembler. However, additional information is needed. Recall that assembly language
programs are usually assembled so that they can be loaded at differing places in memory, and so that several modules for programs
and subroutines can be linked together.

   Therefore, the VAX object modules normally are made up of
three sections. The first provides general information about the pro-

gram and its use of global symbols. The second is the translated machine language, and the third section tells how the machine language must be modified in order to relocate the program to any memory area, and where global addresses or parameters must be provided. More specifically, these three sections are identified as the global symbol directory, the text, and the relocation directories.

Global symbol directory The global symbol directory is one or more records.* These records are made up of segments that

1. Specify the length of the program and the lengths of all program sections (as defined with .PSECT).
2. Specify the relative locations of all defined global symbols.
3. Name all undefined global symbols referred to in the program.
4. Provide miscellaneous information such as the program name from the .TITLE directive.

Text The translated binary language is called the text and consists of a number of records. Each record, which is called a text block, contains the relative address where the text is to be stored as well as some binary machine language.

Relocation directories Each text block is optionally followed by a record that contains coded directions for modifying the preceding text block. Some examples of the kinds of directions that are found in relocation directories follow:

1. Modify a given address in the preceding text block by adding the actual program origin. Recall that the assembler normally assigns an origin of ^X00000000 to program sections, and this is usually modified when the program is actually loaded.
2. Replace a given address in the text block with a computed displacement from the value of the program counter when the instruction is executed.
3. Replace an address with the actual location assigned to a global symbol.

There are other variations of these kinds of relocation, but they are too numerous to discuss here. Note that some of the instructions have to do with whether a byte, word, or longword is being modified.

---

* In order to keep records from getting too large, a large global symbol directory will require several records.

The binary records in the object module all contain codes that identify the type of record. In addition, there are codes to identify ends of sections, and the end of the module itself. This allows several modules to be concatenated (joined together) into a single file. Finally, sections will be added if the /DEBUG option is selected. These sections are necessary in order to preserve the symbol table and other information for the debugger.

The Linking Process

Linking several object modules together into a single, absolute, machine language program is essentially a two-pass process. This is required for the same reason that assembly uses two passes (see notes on page 438 *ff*). Global symbols may be used by one module, but not defined until a later module.

During the first pass of linking, space allocation and global symbol definition is performed. The information needed to do this is contained in the global symbol directories of the modules. As the linker reads through the global symbol directories, it can allocate space in the computer's memory based on the size information provided for each program section. Then actual addresses can be assigned, and global symbols can be assigned absolute addresses. It then becomes possible to perform the modifications specified in the relocation directories.

Thus, during the second pass, the text blocks are assigned actual, rather than relative, addresses. Specific locations are modified in accordance with the relocation directories. The result is absolute machine language that can be loaded directly into a specified area of the VAX virtual memory and executed without further modification as long as the program is completely self-contained and executed from location ^X200. If either of these is not the case, the output of the linker will need to be modified further to one degree or another.

Program Sections

Program sections are blocks of code in a program that are used for some particular purpose which requires that they have an integrity of their own. When producing handwritten code, a programmer could simulate the effect of program sections by writing different pieces of the program on different sheets of paper. Each sheet of paper simulates a program section. The programmer then arranges the sheets of paper by hand so that the code has the proper order. For example, definitions might be on one sheet, data blocks on a second, the main program on a third, internal subroutines on another. From time to time, while writing the program, the programmer might reference one sheet or another. When the program is complete, the programmer would enter the program from the properly ordered sheets.

When programs are generated automatically by some processor, such as the macro expander or the Pascal or FORTRAN compiler, it is often useful to partition code into different blocks. This can be done by making each block a program section. Code can be entered a few lines at a time into each program section using the .PSECT directive. When the program is linked, the blocks of code are rearranged so that they appear in the appropriate program sections.

For purposes of address allocation in the linker, program sections fall into two main categories. The first is concatenated sections. These are local blocks within a given program module that are not used by other program modules. They have names to distinguish them, but for the most part, the names are only used for grouping purposes. The other kind of program section is the overlaid section. Overlaid sections are like FORTRAN common blocks and contain data or instructions that are shared by several program modules. These sections have global names so that the linker will allocate the same space for identically named sections from other modules.

During the first pass of linking, the linker must allocate space for the program sections. Recall that the global symbol directory of a module has the size of each program section along with its type. Concatenated sections are placed one after the other, and space is allocated for each differently named, overlaid section. The linker now has a full memory map for this entire program, which can be printed upon request, and we are now ready for pass 2 of linking.

Subroutine Libraries

Most systems operate with a library of preassembled (compiled) subroutines. For example, in the VAX/VMS system, there are system libraries that contain the following kinds of subroutines:

1. Standard Pascal or FORTRAN or other language subroutines and functions like SIN, SQRT, EXP, and so on.
2. Internal Pascal or FORTRAN or other language subroutines and functions. These are automatically called by more complex statements such as READ and WRITE. In fact, some minicomputers do not have the sophisticated operations of the VAX. Therefore, simple operations such as multiplication and division might require a subroutine. In order to avoid confusion with

user subroutines, the internal subroutines all have odd global names containing underlines or dollar signs, such as PAS$FV_OUTPUT.

3. System subroutines. These are higher-level language or assembly language-callable subroutines for performing special VAX functions. There are Pascal and FORTRAN callable subroutines that allow the programmer to perform functions quite similar to most of the input/output macro described in Chapter 11. For example, a higher-level language program can perform queued input or output by calling the routine SYS$QIOW.

These subroutines are assembled into a special kind of object file that has features which aid in searching for global symbols. The way this is used is that at the normal end of pass 1 of linking, if there are any undefined global symbols, a library search is initiated. Recall that the global symbol directories contain lists of undefined global symbols as well as symbol definitions.

If there are any undefined global symbols, the library is searched for object modules that define these symbols. As such object modules are found, they are added to the program. Modules that do not define missing global symbols are not added because this would make the overall program larger than necessary.

Note, however, that the modules added to the program may themselves refer to undefined global symbols. These symbols have to be added to the list that is searched for, and additional modules may need to be included.

There are three ways that library subroutines are dealt with on the VAX/VMS operating system. First, there are system subroutines such as SYS$QIOW. These programs are permanently resident parts of the system and are assigned fixed addresses in system space. Consequently, all that the linker obtains for these references is the address. No code is added to the program.

The second method is used when a routine is needed and is added to the code generated by the linker. The size of your program will be increased to make room for the library subroutine and a copy of the linked program is included in the executable image file.

The third method is somewhere between the first two methods. In older computer systems, the second method was used for all non-system subroutines. This meant that if you had 100 programs which used the square root routine, you would have 100 copies of the square root routine in your file space. Worse yet, you would also have multiple copies of the larger input/output routines which are automatically called whenever your Pascal or FORTRAN program uses a

WRITELN or PRINT or similar statement. In order to save file space, there is only one executable image made for each of the more important of these subroutines. These images are kept in a **shareable image** library. As your program is readied for execution, the necessary shareable images are added to your executable image.

15.4 Executable Image Files

Whenever the RUN command is executed, the system will load your program using the .EXE or executable image file generated by the linker. Therefore, the .EXE file must have within it all the information necessary to load and run your program. The format of the .EXE file is actually quite complex, since it contains a considerable amount of information for altering addresses referred to or used in shareable images. However, if we ignore this complexity, we can simplify our discussion considerably. For the most part, the .EXE file is a byte-for-byte image of the user's program. There are two important exceptions. One is where shareable images are included. The other is when a program has large arrays of uninitialized data such as arrays specified with .BLKL, etc. The .EXE file contains codes for skipping over these areas in order to save file space. However, if we avoid shareable images and large arrays, we can simplify the format of .EXE files to the following. (Note that this discussion is based on the current version of VAX/VMS at the time of writing. There is no guarantee that this format will stay as described here. The reader is encouraged to obtain dumps of the .EXE files and to verify the format used.)

Because of the byte-for-byte nature of the .EXE files, one of the simple record structures is used. This is the sequential file with fixed-length records. The fixed-record size is 512 bytes, and these records are loaded into 512-byte blocks of memory. (Notice that 512 decimal is 200 in hexadecimal, and is also the size of physical blocks on most VAX mass storage devices.)

In addition to the program text, the control information in an execution file contains the following:

1. Size of the program
2. Starting address of the program
3. Location sizes and protective codes for program sections
4. Location of the stack and other system areas
5. Debugger information as required

This information is in the same fixed-length record structure as is the rest of the file. The overall format for the execution file is

1. Header record. This record contains such information as the highest address used for loading the program, the starting address (also called the transfer address), and the character string used for the name of the program in the .TITLE directive. (The name of a program is determined from the first symbol after the .TITLE directive. This is limited to 31 characters as are all symbols). The header record also contains other pieces of data which link this record to information contained in the later blocks.

2. A variable number of text records. These records contain the byte-for-byte contents of memory to be loaded by the loader. Program loading starts at address ^X200 and proceeds upward until the highest address is read, as specified in the header record.

3. Auxiliary information records. These records contain the program section information and the symbol table used by the debugger.

The format for the three pieces of information contained in the header record is as follows:

1. High address. This is a longword located ^X2C byte locations beyond the start of the record. This gives the highest address used for program text and in effect tells the loader how many records of text need to be read.

2. Transfer address. This is a longword located ^X34 byte locations beyond the start of the record. This gives the address which should be called in order to begin execution. Remember that your program is called with a CALLS or CALLG instruction. Therefore, the transfer location should contain a register-save mask word followed by the first executable instruction of your program.

3. Program name. This is a byte string starting ^X4C byte locations beyond the start of the record. The first byte of this string is a byte count giving the number of bytes in the name. This count must be less than or equal to 31. The remaining bytes are ASCII characters.

This simplified understanding of the header and text records is sufficient to be able to write a program which can load and execute the program. See Exercise 6 on page 459.

Virtual Loading

In a conventional architecture, the program text of an .EXE file would have to be read (or loaded) into memory prior to execution. However, in a virtual memory machine architecture, the loading process can be modified to take into account the fact that the entire program is not usually needed immediately. Note that in the virtual memory system, there is a table that has entries for each page. Each entry contains the following information:

1. Whether the virtual page is active, and thus is currently mapped to a page of real memory
2. If the page is active, what real memory it is mapped to
3. The location on the disk system for the block which is used for backing up the page

See Chapter 14.

When a user issues a RUN command, VAX/VMS runs a program called the **image activator.** The image activator does not load the program. The image activator copies the pages of the program to the virtual memory backup area on the disk, making modifications as needed. As previously noted, the program may require address modification. If a page is in a read-only section which requires no modification, the page can be mapped directly to the corresponding block of the .EXE file. The image activator also deactivates all page maps to real memory. Therefore, when execution of the program begins, a page fault will occur immediately, and it is the page fault handler that ultimately loads the user's program.

15.5 Program Execution
Hardware Operation

In Chapter 3, the instruction cycle was discussed in general terms. At this point, it is intended to extend the concept in more detail. Figure 15.2 shows a general flowchart for the instruction cycle of the VAX, or in fact most computers.

In the VAX there are instructions of different numbers of bytes. Consequently, it may seem that updating the program counter is not a well-defined operation. However, from the point of view of this flowchart, all instructions are assumed to be one byte long, but the execution of the instruction may require fetching additional bytes

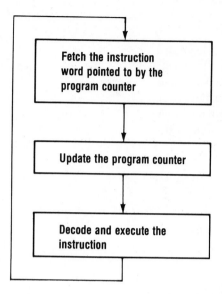

Figure 15.2 The instruc-
tion cycle

from the program. Consequently, updating the program counter means
PC←PC + 1.

Decoding the instruction essentially requires taking the one-byte
opcode and using it to select one of 256 pieces of circuitry as needed
to execute the particular operations specified for the instruction.
However, if every instruction were implemented without regard to
the implementation of any others, the processor would be extremely
expensive to build. In order to design a processor economically,
advantage must be taken of the fact that many instructions have
common functions. For example, most of the instructions on the VAX
use the same addressing modes. Therefore, a single piece of circuitry
can implement certain functions, such as addressing, for many different instructions. This operates in much the same way that subroutines operate in software.

In operation, each instruction activates a selected sequence of
actions from the various processing circuits in the processor. This
selected sequence of operations is referred to as the **micro program**
or **micro code** for the instruction. The micro program for some
instructions can be quite complex. For example, some instructions,
such as multiplication, are often implemented as repeated activations
of adding and shifting circuits. Thus, micro programs can, like regular
programs, incorporate loops. Of course, the use of loops will tend to
slow down an operation. As a result, in order to achieve high speed,

some big computers will incorporate expensive, high-speed, multiplication circuits which multiply binary numbers by doing Boolean operations, without any looping. However, some instructions, such as POLYF or POLYD, are far too complex to implement effectively without loops. Table 15.1 summarizes how multiplication is implemented on various kinds of systems.

In order to simplify decoding, instructions are often organized into groups, and similar numerical values will indicate membership in the group. For example, consider the following opcode list:

```
ADDF2    40        ADDF3    41
ADDD2    60        ADDD3    61
ADDB2    80        ADDB3    81
ADDW2    A0        ADDW3    A1
ADDL2    C0        ADDL3    C1
```

The more sense that can be made of the numeric value of opcodes, the simpler the decoding process. This can lower the cost and increase the speed of computers. However, the trend in large, modern computers is to have large numbers of complex instructions. As a result, there is a tendency to run out of possibilities and, therefore, choices. As a result, the numeric values of the opcodes may tend to lose their obvious meanings. What is often done is for the processor to use the opcode as an address into a read-only memory which contains a translation table converting 8-bit opcodes to longer ones which more directly relate to the micro code for that instruction.

Related to this is the fact that the VAX has more than 256 different instructions. This means that one byte is not sufficient for uniquely identifying all the instructions. The solution to this problem is that the opcodes ^XFD, ^XFE, and ^XFF are used as escape codes telling the processor to fetch a second byte for second-level decoding. This effectively allows the number of opcodes to increase without any particular limit. At present, little use is being made of the extended

Table 15.1 Implementation of Multiplication

Speed	Cost		Typical Processor
High	High	Hardware multiplier	VAX-11/780
Medium	Medium	Micro coded instruction with loops	PDP-11/23
Low	Low	Machine language subroutine with loops	Z80 or 6502

opcode space. All of the two-byte opcodes are used for the G and H floating-point operations and all of these use ^XFD as the escape code. (See Chapter 12.)

Position-Independent Code

One particular advantage of the VAX architecture lies in the ability to use the program counter as an ordinary displacement register. This allows addressing data and instructions relative to where the program is currently executing. The advantage of being able to do this is that when programs address their own locations relative to the program counter, the relative addresses do not change if the program is relocated.

For example, assume that a program is executing an instruction with the program counter equal to ^X0740 and that instruction is accessing data at ^X0A14; the relative location from the program counter is ^X0A14 − ^X0740 = ^X03D4. In fact, this is the same kind of addressing used with the VAX mode CF. (See Chapter 7, page 192 *ff.*) Now if the program is relocated ^X0200 locations higher, both the program counter and the data address will move to ^X0940 and ^X0C14, respectively, but the difference will remain at ^X03D4. As a result, this program could be loaded anywhere in memory without requiring this particular instruction to be modified. If the entire program is written this way, it is said to be in **position-independent code.** In order for a program to be in position-independent code, the programmer must take special care in using only those instructions and addressing modes that are position independent. The following set of rules gives the most important cases.

Rule 1 Addressing a location within your program. As shown before, all addresses in your program must be accessed using relative-mode addressing. However, since this is the normal mode, nothing special needs to be done. MOVL A,B works all right.

Rule 2 Addressing a fixed location in memory, or a device register at a fixed address. Relative mode no longer works, because the PC added to a fixed displacement will address different locations when the program is moved. However, absolute mode works, because this is followed by the actual (fixed) address. Absolute mode can be forced by placing @# before the address. For example, assume that PORG and PLOC are fixed locations in memory and that A is an address

inside your program. Then both TSTB @#PORG and
MOVB A,@#PLOC are position independent.

Rule 3 Branch and jump instructions. Branch instructions are
program-counter relative over a short range and give no
added problems. The jump instructions use general
operands and therefore use either relative or absolute mode,
depending on whether the jump is within the program
or to a fixed place in memory.

Rule 4 Addressing arrays in the program. Arrays cause a special
problem because the actual address is needed either
for register-deferred access, or index register mode
instructions. Recall that, in Chapter 7, several ways of
accessing locations in an array were presented. Index
register mode, CLRB A[R0] will be position independent
even though A is relocatable, because the effective address
is computed in two stages. First the address of A is
computed as an offset from the PC. Then the contents of
R0 are added to access the indexed location. Finally, the
deferred, displaced, and auto-increment modes were
presented where an address is placed in a general register.
Note that the normal way of getting an address into a
register is

```
MOVAB    A,R0
```

This is position independent if A is relocatable, but if A
is absolute, the instruction should be

```
MOVAB    @#A,R0
```

Note that because of the way addressing is handled
on the VAX, these rules are fairly easy to follow, so that
it is almost difficult to write a program that is not position
independent. However, care must also be taken with data.
Addresses often appear in arrays of data such as those of
descriptors and subroutine argument lists. If relocatable
addresses are assembled into data arrays, the program
will not be completely position independent. For example,
a program will not be position independent if it contains
an .ASCID directive. The solution is to avoid .ASCID by
using .ASCII and to set up the descriptor at execution
time. For example, the following could be done.

```
MSGD:     ,WORD    20$-10$,0
          ,LONG    0
10$:      ,ASCII   "MESSAGE TEXT"
20$:

            ,

            ,

            ,

          MOVAB    MSGD+8,MSGD+4

            ,

            ,

            ,
```

The MOVAB instruction, as shown, is position independent and will put the proper address into the descriptor. In order to avoid this problem and to simplify program writing, VAX/VMS provides a last-moment modification for .EXE files which allows .ASCID and .ADDRESS to be used in shareable images. As a result, .ASCID and .ADDRESS can be used in PIC program sections even though they are not, strictly speaking, position independent.

Position independent code can be very useful for operating system programs. For example, in the VAX/VMS system, the system programs are often capable of being loaded wherever there is free space. Many of these programs, such as input/output device handlers and user-service routines, are dynamically brought into memory as they are needed, using available space.

Exercise Set 2

1. Design a variable-length record file format that uses control characters instead of byte counts. All bit patterns must be allowable for data bytes.
2. Write a program that writes and reads files in the format you designed in Exercise 1, above.
3. Create a number of files with different kinds of record structures. This can be done with some simple FORTRAN programs using

various parameters in the OPEN statement or with assembly language programs using various $FAB and $RAB macros. Then use the DUMP/HEADER/NOFORMATED command to examine the control blocks on the files. Try to determine the significance of the different control codes used in the control block, and write a description of your hypothesis. Test your hypothesis by dumping other files or files generated by other students.

4. Write a program which reads dumps generated by the DUMP command and prints the file out in its original form. The program should work with normal character files as used for source programs. Your program can be written either in assembly language or a higher-level language. Notice that your program must be able to skip over page format and other irrelevant information found in these dumps.

5. Write a program that is in position-independent code. The program need only type out a few lines to show that it is working. The program then copies most of itself into an array elsewhere in memory, sets the area used by the original program to contain all zeros, and jumps to the relocated starting address to reexecute the typeout code to verify that it was indeed position independent. Note that data areas should be relocated along with the program. Be careful that data areas are position independent as well as the program. (See the comments on the .ASCID directive on pages 457–8.) Note, especially, that for $RAB and $FAB to be position independent, all address parameters must be supplied at execution time. This includes such parameters as NAM = <FILE.XYZ> and FAB = FABLOC.

*6. Write a program which begins with a large empty array, perhaps .BLKL 5000. This will be located at final linking to address ^X200. Write a program which can read in an .EXE file for a simple program, store its text records in the array, which begins at address ^X200, and execute it. Since programs are normally relocated to begin at ^X200, the program should be in the right place for execution.

Running Assembly Language Programs

A.1 An Assembly Language Program

This appendix shows how to run an assembly language program on a VAX/VMS computer system. The assembly language program to be run is shown below. This is the same program that was described in Chapter 1. When the program exits, the contents of DIF will be 8.

```
J:      .BLKL   1
K:      .BLKL   1
DIF:    .BLKL   1
        .ENTRY  ADDRESS,0
        MOVL    #20,J
        MOVL    #12,K
        MOVL    J,DIF
        SUBL2   K,DIF
        $EXIT_S
        .END    ADDRESS
```

A.2 Entering Programs on the VAX

Programs are entered on the VAX by using an interactive terminal. There are two basic types of terminals—**hard-copy** terminals and **video display (VDT)** terminals. Hard-copy terminals produce printed output (the hard copy) and resemble typewriters. A video display terminal resembles a keyboard attached to a small television set. Either type of terminal can be used to run assembly language programs.

This appendix will show how to run assembly language programs with either the batch or interactive systems. The next few sections are aimed at interactive users but should be read by batch users because many features are common to both batch and interactive use.

A.3 The Process of Logging into the VAX

Terminals may be connected to the VAX in a number of ways. For example, some terminals may be permanently connected to a VAX computer system. Such terminals can be used by simply turning them on. Other terminals may have to be connected to a VAX computer system via phone lines. It may be necessary to dial the correct phone number and then connect the phone to an acoustic coupler or modem. In any case, once the terminal is connected to the VAX, the user generally strikes the key marked RETURN, CARRIAGE RETURN, or CR. (It may be necessary to strike this key more than once.)

When the VAX/VMS system detects the return character, it initiates the log on sequence. It asks for the "Username" and "Password" that have been assigned. If the user is an authorized user, the VAX system will print a welcome message followed by a dollar sign. For a user called JOHNDOE with the password GUESS, the log on sequence might appear as follows:

```
Username: JOHNDOE
Password: __
        Welcome to VAX/VMS version Vx.x
$
```

The entries that are typed by the user in the lines above are underlined. This convention will be followed in the remainder of this appendix. Notice that the VAX system did not print the password GUESS. This is to prevent someone from seeing your password and using your account without authorization. Finally, the user must strike the return key after typing JOHNDOE and GUESS. Usually, nothing that the user types is processed by the VAX computer system until the return key is struck.

A.4 VAX/VMS Commands

The dollar sign ($) on the line after the welcome message is the VAX/VMS prompt character. VAX/VMS is the monitor program that coordinates and directs the execution of all other programs. The $ indicates that the user is communicating with VAX/VMS (as opposed to some other program) and that the user should enter a VAX/VMS **command.**

One of the VAX/VMS commands is the HELP command. If the user enters the command HELP, the following kind of information will be listed

```
$ HELP

Information available:

ACCOUNTING ALLOCATE   ANALYZE   APPEND    ASSIGN     ATTACH      BACKUP
BASIC      BLISS      CANCEL    CC        CLOSE      COBOL       CONTINUE
CONVERT    COPY       CORAL     CREATE    DBO        DDL
DEALLOCATE DEASSIGN   DEBUG     DECK      DEFINE     DELETE      DEPOSIT
DIFFERENCES           DIRECTORY DISMOUNT  DUMP       EDIT        EOD
EOJ        Errors     EXAMINE   EXIT      FDL        FORTRAN     GOTO
HELP       IF         INITIALIZE INQUIRE  JOB        Lexical     LIBRARY
LINK       Login      LOGOUT    MACRO     MAIL       MCR         MERGE
MESSAGE    MONITOR    MOUNT     ON        OPEN       PASCAL      PASSWORD
PATCH      PHONE      PLI       PRINT     Procedure  PURGE       Queues
READ       RENAME     REPLY     REQUEST   RMS        RTL         RUN
RUNOFF     SEARCH     SET       SHOW      SORT       SPAWN       Specify
START      STOP       SUBMIT    Symbol_Assign        SYNCHRONIZE
System     TECO       TYPE      UNLOCK    WAIT       WRITE

Topic?
$
```

In this and subsequent examples of printouts, the exact contents and format may differ from system to system.

After printing the list of VAX/VMS commands, the help command prints the message "Topic?". If the user types one of the commands listed above, the HELP command would have printed additional information about that command. In this case, however, the user struck the return key. This causes the help command to return control back to VAX/VMS. VAX/VMS, in turn, prompts the user by typing a dollar sign.

Only a small number of VAX/VMS commands are needed to run assembly language programs. The most important commands are COPY, CREATE, DELETE, DIRECTORY, EDIT, LINK, LOGOUT, MACRO, PRINT, PURGE, and TYPE. Additional details on these commands can be found in Appendix D.

A.5 Creating a File

Most of the important commands listed above manipulate **files** in some way. A file is simply an ordered collection of records (lines). Each of the files to be described here represents a program in some language. User files are generally stored on an auxiliary storage device called a disk. The DIRECTORY command is used to list the names of the user's disk files. As the following command shows, the user does not currently have any files.

```
$ DIR
No files found.
$
```

Notice that DIR rather than DIRECTORY was entered. Most VAX/VMS commands can be abbreviated to three or four letters.

Programmers can create files using a command called CREATE. The user types the command CREATE EXAMPLE.MAR followed by a carriage return, followed by the program, followed by Control Z. For example,

```
$ CREATE EXAMPLE.MAR
J:      .BLKL   1
K:      .BLKL   1
DIF:    .BLKL   1
        .ENTRY  ADDRESS,0
        MOVL    #20,J
        MOVL    #12,K
        MOVL    J,DIF
        SUBL2   K,DIF
        $EXIT_S
        .END    ADDRESS
^Z
$
```

In the CREATE command, EXAMPLE is the name that the user selected for the file. The characters .MAR after the file name designate the file type. In this case, the type MAR designates that this file is a MAcRo assembly language program. This file type should be used for VAX/VMS assembly language programs. The character control Z is typed by holding down the key marked CONTROL, or CTRL, as if it were a shift key and typing Z. The character control Z is a special character used to signal the end of the file.

When typing commands or programs, mistakes are often made. There are two ways of correcting mistakes. The first is to type the RUB OUT or DELETE key. This erases the previous character. If you are typing at a CRT terminal, you may actually see the character disappear. At a hard-copy terminal, a back slash is typed followed by the deleted character. You may erase all the way to the beginning of the line if you want. A second back slash is typed when you start typing again. For example, if you type

```
HEXY (delete)(delete) LLO
```

the effect would be the same as if you typed HELLO. A CRT terminal would display HELLO, but a hard-copy terminal would have

```
HEXY\YX\LLO
```

The second way to correct errors is to erase the entire line and start over by typing control U. (Hold down the CTRL key and type U).

After the file has been created in this fashion, the DIRECTORY command can be entered. The output will indicate that a file has indeed been created.

```
$ DIR

Directory DISK$USER:[JOHNDOE]

EXAMPLE.MAR;1

Total of 1 file.
```

The directory command indicates that a user called JOHNDOE has a file called EXAMPLE.MAR;1 on a disk called DISK$USER. The characters ";1" in the file name EXAMPLE.MAR;1 indicate the version number of the file. If this file were modified, the user would have two disk files—EXAMPLE.MAR;1 and EXAMPLE.MAR;2. When the version number is omitted from a VAX/VMS command, most com-

mands select the newest version of the file (that is, the one with the
largest version number). For example, the following TYPE command
will print the most recent version of the file EXAMPLE.MAR.

```
$ TYPE EXAMPLE.MAR
J:     .BLKL    1
K:     .BLKL    1
DIF:   .BLKL    1
       .ENTRY   ADDRESS,0
       MOVL     #20,J
       MOVL     #12,K
       MOVL     J,DIF
       SUBL2    K,DIF
       $EXIT_S
       .END     ADDRESS
$
```

The PRINT command can be used to list files on a high-speed line
printer.

The use of the CREATE command to enter programs has a problem in that it requires the user to be able to create the file without
making any mistakes. This is only practical for very small programs.
To enter larger programs, the user must be able to correct errors
without retyping the entire program. A program called a text editor
can make such corrections. One editor available on the VAX/VMS
system is called EDT. The EDT editor is described in more detail in
Appendix E. Appendix E also describes the special features of EDT
that can be used with VT52 and VT100/VT200 terminals.

A.6 Executing a Program

The assembly language program can be prepared for execution by
entering the following three VAX/VMS commands.

```
$ MACRO/DEBUG EXAMPLE
$ LINK/DEBUG EXAMPLE
$ RUN EXAMPLE

        VAX-11 DEBUG Version x.x

%DEBUG-I-INITIAL, language is MACRO, module set to '.MAIN.'
DBG>
```

The characters /DEBUG on the first two commands indicate that the user wishes to use a program called the **debugger** to provide a variety of services when the program is executed. The MACRO command causes the MACRO assembler to be executed. The assembler reads the assembly language program EXAMPLE.MAR and produces a type of machine language program called an **object module.** The LINK command causes a program called the **linker** to be executed. The linker reads the object module and creates a second type of machine language program called an **executable image,** which is ready to be executed. The RUN command causes the executable module to be executed under the control of the debugger.

After printing two information lines, the debugger prints the characters DBG>. This is the debugger's way of prompting the user to enter a debugger command. As one might expect by this time, the command HELP will cause the debugger to print a list of debugger commands. In this case, however, the user enters the GO command which causes the machine language version of the assembly language program to be executed. The results appear as follows:

```
DBG>GO
routine start at .MAIN.\ADDRESS
%DEBUG-I-EXITSTATUS, is '%SYSTEM-S-NORMAL, normal successful completion'
DBG>
```

The message, "normal successful completion" means that the program has executed down to the statement $EXIT_S without encountering an error.

The EXAMINE command can be used to print the contents of the various symbolic addresses (variables) in the program. For example, the command E/DEC J directs the debugger to Examine (type) in DECimal the number contained in J.

```
DBG>E/DEC J
.MAIN.\J: 20
DBG>E/DEC K
.MAIN.\K: 12
DBG>E/DEC DIF
.MAIN.\DIF: 8
DBG>
```

As the three Examine commands show, J, K, and DIF contain 20, 12, and 8, respectively, which is the expected result.

The EXIT command is used to return control from the DEBUG program back to VAX/VMS. If the user then enters a DIRECTORY command, the results will be

```
DBG>EXIT
$ DIR

Directory DISK$USE:[JOHNDOE]

EXAMPLE.EXE;1    EXAMPLE.MAR;1    EXAMPLE.OBJ;1

Total of 3 files.
```

In the directory above, EXAMPLE.MAR is the assembly language program that was created with the CREATE command. EXAMPLE.OBJ is the object module that was created by the MACRO command and EXAMPLE.EXE is the execution module that was created with the LINK command.

Finally, the VAX/VMS command LOGOUT is used to end the terminal session.

```
$ LOGOUT
JOHNDOE   logged out at 25-JUL-1985 11:56:50.32
```

A.7 Programming Errors and Debugging

The above example contained no errors. Normally, however, newly created programs contain errors and the programmer must locate the errors and correct them. Errors in assembly language programs may produce error messages from the assembler, the linker, or from VAX/VMS when the program is executed. Errors may, of course, simply produce wrong answers. The effects of several types of errors are shown below.

Assume that the third line of the program is incorrectly entered as

```
DIF     .BLKL   1
```

Notice that the colon (:) after the symbol DIF has been omitted. This error will generate the following error message from the assembler.

```
$ MACRO/DEBUG EXAMPLE
                                0008    3 DIF     .BLKL   1
%MACRO-E-UNRECSTMT, Unrecognized statement
```

A similar error message would be generated if the symbol MOVL on the fifth line of the program were misspelled as MOV. Assembly errors are usually easy to locate and correct because the assembler prints the statements that contain the errors.

The linker may also generate error messages. For example, assume that the seventh line of the program is entered as

```
MOVL    J,DIFF
```

Notice that the symbol DIF has been misspelled as DIFF. The assembler considers DIFF to be an undefined symbol. However, the assembler may not produce an error message because it may assume that the linker will find a definition for the symbol DIFF. When the linker is unable to find a definition for DIFF, it will print an error message. The output would appear as follows:

```
$ MACRO/DEBUG EXAMPLE
$ LINK/DEBUG EXAMPLE
%LINK-W-NUDFSYMS, 1 undefined symbol
%LINK-I-UDFSYM,    DIFF
%LINK-W-USEUNDEF, undefined symbol DIFF referenced
     B    in psect , BLANK , offset %X0000001A
          in module ,MAIN, file DISK$USER:[JOHNDOE]EXAMPLE,OBJ;1
```

Linker errors that result from undefined symbols are usually easy to find because the linker prints the undefined symbol.

Errors that occur during the execution of the machine language program can be much more difficult to find. For example, assume that the fifth line of the program is incorrectly entered as

```
MOVL    20,J
```

Notice that the number sign (#) has been omitted in front of the number 20. The program will assemble and link without error. However, when the program is executed, VAX/VMS will print an error message.

```
$ MACRO/DEBUG EXAMPLE
$ LINK/DEBUG EXAMPLE
$ RUN/DEBUG EXAMPLE


            VAX-11 DEBUG Version 3,2-1


%DEBUG-I-INITIAL, language is MACRO, module set to ',MAIN,'
DBG>GO
routine start at ,MAIN,\ADDRESS
%SYSTEM-F ACCVIO, access violation, reason mask=00, virtual address=00000014,
PC=0000020E, PSL=03C00000
```

This error tells the user that the number 20 was interpreted as an address. In the hexadecimal number system this is displayed as "virtual address = 00000014". See Chapters 2, 3, and 4.

An omitted number sign may also produce results that are wildly incorrect. Similar errors can be caused by failing to initialize a variable properly. In some cases, it is necessary to go through the assembly language program character by character to find an error. Debugging assembly language programs can be much more difficult than debugging programs that are written in higher-level languages.

The debugger STEP command can be used to help find these errors. Instead of the GO command, type STEP. This will cause one instruction to be executed (rather than the whole program). The debugger will display the effect on successive instructions. The STEP instruction can be executed repeatedly and the EXAMINE command can be used between steps for tracing progress of the program. If you step to a subroutine call, the subroutine is executed as one step. If you want to step through the subroutine use the command STEP/INTO.

A.8 Final Program Execution

When a program has been fully debugged, a final run without using the debugger may be desirable. (Until the input/output routines discussed in Chapter 5 are used, the debugger must be used for input and output.) To run without the debugger, drop the /DEBUG from the MACRO and LINK commands. It is probably also desirable at this time to obtain an assembly listing. This is accomplished by placing /LIST on the MACRO command. The commands then become

```
$ MACRO/LIST EXAMPLE
$ LINK EXAMPLE
$ RUN EXAMPLE
  program input and output
```

Note that /LIST does not cause anything to be printed. Rather, it produces a file EXAMPLE.LIS. This file contains the assembly listing which can be subsequently printed using the TYPE or PRINT commands.

A.9 Obtaining a Hard Copy

The problem with using a video display terminal is that there is no way of saving the output or showing it to a person who is not present at the time the output is generated. This presents a problem when a student wants to turn the assignment in to the instructor.

There are two simple methods for obtaining hard copy. The first is to run the program from a hard-copy terminal such as an LA36 or LA100. Often, computer centers have one hard-copy terminal in each group of terminals. The video display terminals are used for creating the files and debugging. Then a final run can be made using the hard-copy terminal. When using this method it is usually desirable to print a listing of the program. Use the pair of commands

```
$ MACRO/LIST EXAMPLE
$ TYPE EXAMPLE
```

The second method for obtaining hard copy is to submit your program through the batch system. Normally, output from batch jobs is printed on the system line printer. Batch jobs can be submitted by creating a command file. The command file consists of the VAX/VMS commands required to execute the job. Each VAX/VMS command is preceded by a $. Data for the program follows the $RUN command. Data lines must not begin with $. The command file should have the type .COM. As an example, you could create the following file called EXAMPLE.COM.

```
$ MACRO/LIST EXAMPLE
$ TYPE EXAMPLE
$ LINK EXAMPLE
$ RUN EXAMPLE
Data line #1
Data line #2
Data line #3
```

A command file can be executed before submission to see if it works by using the command

```
$ @EXAMPLE
```

Program output will appear at the terminal. If everything seems to be as expected, the program can be submitted to batch with the command

```
$ SUBMIT EXAMPLE
```

The output seen on the terminal when you typed @EXAMPLE will be directed to the system line printer.

Input/Output Routines

The following set of routines can be used as a simple way to accomplish input/output with assembly language programs. The routines can be used for either reading and printing numbers or reading and printing character strings. The routines either can be copied and assembled along with each user's program or can be assembled once and linked with the user's program through global symbols.

The package contains five subroutines, named IOINIT, RNUM, PNUM, RLINE, and PLINE. They are all called with the JSB instruction and have the following functions.

IOINIT

IOINIT is a program that initializes all four of the other routines. IOINIT is only called once, but **must be** called before any of the other routines can be used. The calling sequence is

```
JSB    IOINIT
```

IOINIT returns with all registers saved; its only apparent effect, other than allowing the other routines in this package to run, is that it prints a line showing that it ran successfully.

RNUM

RNUM reads a hexadecimal number from the system input file and leaves the result in R0. All other registers are unchanged. If you are running interactively, RNUM prompts with the request "Enter hex number - ". The calling sequence is

```
JSB    RNUM
```
result is left in R0

PNUM

PNUM prints the contents of R0 as a longword in both hexadecimal and decimal. All registers are unchanged. The calling sequence is

```
load number in R0
JSB    PNUM
```

RLINE

RLINE is a routine for reading a string of ASCII characters from system input and passing it to an array in your program. To call it you must provide the address of a byte array to receive the string and the size of the array. R0 must contain the address as a longword, and R1 contains the size as a word. RLINE will return with the array containing as many characters as there were in the line, and R1 will contain a word giving the actual number of characters read. This latter result can be from zero up to the given size of the array, but no larger. R0 will contain an error code word. If R0 contains the number 1, there was no error. Any other value means that there was an error. The most probable errors are that the buffer was too small or that you attempted to read past the end of the available input. All other registers are unchanged. The calling sequence for RLINE is

```
load buffer address in R0 and
maximum buffer size in R1
JSB RLINE
R0 contains the error code
R1 contains the number of characters read
```

PLINE

PLINE is a program for printing a line of ASCII text on the system output file. R0 must contain the address of the character array and R1 is a word giving the number of characters. All registers are saved. As PLINE provides a carriage return and line feed with each line, the output string should not contain these control characters unless extra lines are being printed. The calling sequence is

```
load buffer address in R0 and
number of characters in R1
JSB PLINE
```

Program Listing

The following lines can be typed at the end of the user's program just before the .END directive, in order to use these routines in the program. The comments are provided to take some of the mystery from the program. However, it is not expected that the programs be fully understandable until Chapters 1 through 11 have been covered. If desired, you can omit the comments from these lines to shorten the typing effort. The program can be assembled as a separate module, and the pre-assembled object file can be linked with the main program.

```
RNUMBUFSIZ=80                                ;SET BUFFER SIZES TO 80
PNUMBUFSIZ=80
                .PSECT  IOROUTINE,LONG       ;FABS AND RABS LONGWORD ALIGNED
RNUMFILE:       $FAB    FNM=<SYS$INPUT>
PNUMFILE:       $FAB    FNM=<SYS$OUTPUT>,RAT=<CR>
RNUMIREC:       $RAB    FAB=RNUMFILE,UBF=RNUMBUF,USZ=RNUMBUFSIZ,-
                        PBF=RNUMPRO,PSZ=RNUMPROL-RNUMPRO,ROP=<PMT>
PNUMOREC:       $RAB    FAB=PNUMFILE,RBF=PNUMOUT
RLINEREC:       $RAB    FAB=RNUMFILE,-
                        PBF=RLINEPRO,PSZ=RLINEPROL-RLINEPRO,ROP=<PMT>
PLINEREC:       $RAB    FAB=PNUMFILE

PNUMTEMP:       .BLKL   1                    ;TEMPORARY STORAGE AND BUFFERS
PNUMOUT:        .BLKB   PNUMBUFSIZ
RNUMBUF:        .BLKB   RNUMBUFSIZ

;CHARACTER STRINGS AND DESCRIPTORS

PNUMSTR:        .ASCID  "Output !XL(hex) !SL(decimal)"
IOINITSTR:      .ASCID  "Input and output initialized on !%D,"
RNUMPRO:        .ASCII  "Enter hex number - "
RNUMPROL:
RLINEPRO:       .ASCII  "Enter line - "
RLINEPROL:
PNUMDES:        .LONG   PNUMBUFSIZ
                .LONG   PNUMOUT
```

(continued)

```
;INITIALIZATION ROUTINE

IOINIT::
        PUSHR       #^M<R0,R1>                      ;SAVE REGISTERS
        $OPEN       FAB=RNUMFILE                    ;OPEN INPUT FILE
        $CREATE     FAB=PNUMFILE                    ;OPEN OUTPUT FILE
        $FAO_S      CTRSTR=IOINITSTR,OUTBUF=PNUMDES,-              ;FORMAT
                    OUTLEN=PNUMOREC+RAB$W_RSZ,P1=#0               ;MESSAGE
        $CONNECT RAB=PNUMOREC          ;CONNECT THE MESSAGE RAB
        $PUT        RAB=PNUMOREC       ;AND PRINT THE INITIALIZATION MESSAGE
        POPR        #^M<R0,R1>         ;RESTORE REGISTERS
        RSB                            ;AND RETURN

;PRINT NUMBER ROUTINE

PNUM::
        PUSHR       #^M<R0,R1>         ;SAVE REGISTERS
        MOVL        R0,PNUMTEMP        ;GET THE NUMBER AND CONVERT IT
        $FAO_S      CTRSTR=PNUMSTR,OUTBUF=PNUMDES,OUTLEN=PNUMOREC+RAB$W_RSZ,-
                    P1=PNUMTEMP,P2=PNUMTEMP
        $CONNECT         RAB=PNUMOREC  ;CONNECT THE OUTPUT RAB
        $PUT        RAB=PNUMOREC       ;AND PRINT IT
        POPR        #^M<R0,R1>         ;RESTORE REGISTERS
        RSB                            ;AND RETURN

;READ NUMBER ROUTINE

RNUM::
        PUSHR       #^M<R1>            ;SAVE R1
        $CONNECT         RAB=RNUMIREC  ;CONNECT THE INPUT RAB
        $GET        RAB=RNUMIREC       ;READ A NUMBER
        CLRL        R0                 ;CLEAR THE CONVERSION REGISTER
        MOVAB       RNUMBUF,R1         ;POINT TO NUMBER BUFFER
10$:    DECW        RNUMIREC+RAB$W_RSZ ;DECREMENT CHARACTER COUNT
        BLSS        30$                ;AND EXIT IF IT WAS ZERO
        ASHL        #4,R0,R0           ;MULTIPLY COUNT SO FAR BY 16
        SUBB2       #48,(R1)           ;CONVERT ASCII DIGIT TO BINARY
        CMPB        (R1),#10           ;GREATER THAN 10?
        BLSS        20$                ;NO
        SUBB2       #65-48-10,(R1)     ;YES, SO SET ASCII "A" TO 10
20$:    BICB        #^XF0,(R1)         ;JUST TO BE SAFE
        BISB        (R1)+,R0           ;ADD INTO ACCUMULATED NUMBER
        BRB         10$                ;LOOP FOR MORE DIGITS
30$:    POPR        #^M<R1>            ;RESTORE R1
        RSB                            ;AND RETURN
```

(continued)

```
;READ LINE ROUTINE

RLINE::
        MOVL      R0,RLINEREC+RAB$L_UBF   ;SET UP ADDRESS OF THE BUFFER
        MOVW      R1,RLINEREC+RAB$W_USZ   ;AND ITS MAXIMUM SIZE
        $CONNECT RAB=RLINEREC             ;CONNECT THE RAB
        $GET      RAB=RLINEREC            ;READ A LINE
        MOVZWL    RLINEREC+RAB$W_RSZ,R1   ;RETURN THE REAL SIZE
        RSB                               ;AND ERROR CODE IN R0

;PRINT LINE ROUTINE

PLINE::
        PUSHR     #^M<R0,R1>              ;SAVE REGISTERS
        MOVL      R0,PLINEREC+RAB$L_RBF   ;GET BUFFER ADDRESS
        MOVW      R1,PLINEREC+RAB$W_RSZ   ;AND LINE LENGTH
        $CONNECT RAB=PLINEREC             ;CONNECT THE OUTPUT RAB
        $PUT      RAB=PLINEREC            ;AND PRINT THE LINE
        POPR      #^M<R0,R1>              ;RESTORE REGISTERS
        RSB                               ;AND RETURN
```

Input/Output Routines Using Higher-Level Languages

A convenient method for performing input and output on the VAX is to use the input and output features of higher-level languages. The following set of routines perform the same functions as the input/output routines shown in Appendix B. However, they make use of subroutines, procedures, and functions written in FORTRAN, BASIC, and Pascal. In order to make the calling sequences identical to those used in the routines of Appendix B, an assembly language program is included which converts the calling sequences to the form necessary for the higher-level languages. Chapter 9 explains these calling sequences. One thing to note is that the higher-level language systems all take care of their own input/output initialization. As a consequence, the routine IOINIT is not necessary. However, for compatibility, a dummy IOINIT routine was included which does nothing except return.

Assembly Language Routine

The following routine is used to call the higher-level language routines for all three languages. It can be included as part of your main program or assembled separately and linked to your main program along with the higher-level language routines.

```
;
; THIS PROGRAM DOES THE SAME AS RNUM, PNUM, ETC.
; CALLING ROUTINES WRITTEN IN HIGHER LEVEL LANGUAGES
;
          .EXTERNAL       FRNUM,FPNUM,FRSTR,FPSTR
;
IOINIT::
          RSB                             ;NO NEED FOR IOINIT
;
RNUM::
          PUSHR     #^M<R1>               ;SAVE R1
          CALLS     #0,FRNUM              ;CALL HIGH LEVEL RNUM
          POPR      #^M<R1>               ;RESTORE R1
          RSB                             ;RESULT IS IN R0
;
PNUM::
          PUSHR     #^M<R1>               ;SAVE R1
          PUSHL     R0                    ;PUT ARGUMENT ON THE STACK
          PUSHAL    (SP)                  ;PUT ADDRESS ON THE STACK
          CALLS     #1,FPNUM              ;CALL HIGH LEVEL PNUM
          MOVL      (SP)+,R0              ;RESTORE R0
          POPR      #^M<R1>               ;RESTORE R1
          RSB
;
RLINE::
          PUSHL     R0                    ;PUT ADDRESS IN DESCRIPTOR
          MOVZWL    R1,-(SP)              ;AND LENGTH ALL ON STACK
          PUSHAL    (SP)                  ;DESCRIPTOR ARGUMENT
          CALLS     #1,FRSTR              ;READ THE STRING
          ADDL2     #8,SP                 ;POP THE DESCRIPTOR
          MOVZWL    R0,R1                 ;LEAVE LENGTH IN R1
          MOVL      #1,R0                 ;AND NORMAL FLAG IN R0
          RSB
;
PLINE::
          PUSHR     #^M<R0,R1>            ;SAVE R0 AND R1
          PUSHL     R0                    ;PUT ADDRESS IN DESCRIPTOR
          MOVZWL    R1,-(SP)              ;AND LENGTH ALL ON STACK
          PUSHAL    (SP)                  ;DESCRIPTOR ARGUMENT
          CALLS     #1,FPSTR              ;READ THE STRING
          ADDL2     #8,SP                 ;POP THE DESCRIPTOR
          POPR      #^M<R0,R1>            ;RESTORE R0 AND R1
          RSB
```

FORTRAN Routines

The following subroutines and functions are compiled and linked with the assembly language main program and the above assembly language calling programs. The effect of using this program is essentially identical to the input/output routines of Appendix B, except for some slight formatting differences.

```
INTEGER FUNCTION FRNUM()
TYPE '(''$Enter hex number -'')'
ACCEPT '(BN,Z8)',FRNUM
RETURN
END


SUBROUTINE FPNUM(N)
INTEGER N
TYPE '('' Output ''Z9.8''(hex)''I14''(decimal)'')',N,N
RETURN
END


INTEGER FUNCTION FRSTR(S)
INTEGER M,MINO,LEN
CHARACTER *(*) S
TYPE '(''$Enter line -'')'
ACCEPT '(Q,A)',M,S
FRSTR=MINO(M,LEN(S))
RETURN
END


SUBROUTINE FPSTR(S)
CHARACTER *(*) S
TYPE '(1X,A)',S
RETURN
END
```

BASIC Routines

The following routines are written in VAX/VMS extended BASIC and again produce the same results. However, since BASIC does not recognize hexadecimal format, numerical input and output is exclusively in decimal. To convert to or from hexadecimal would require rather lengthy conversion routines, and thus obviate the benefit of using higher-level languages rather than assembly language.

```
100      FUNCTION INTEGER FRNUM
110      INPUT "Enter decimal number - ";X%
120      FRNUM=X%
130      FUNCTIONEND

200      SUB FPNUM(N%)
210      PRINT "Output ";N%;"(decimal)"
220      SUBEND

300      FUNCTION INTEGER FRSTR(S$)
310      LINPUT "Enter line - ";S$
320      FRSTR=LEN(S$)
330      FUNCTIONEND

400      SUB FPSTR(S$)
410      PRINT S$
420      SUBEND
```

Pascal Routines

The following routines are written in VAX/VMS extended Pascal.
Since Pascal does not have a simple method for implementing variable-length character strings, the routines RLINE and PLINE were
not incorporated into this example.

```
MODULE PRPNUM (INPUT, OUTPUT);
[GLOBAL] FUNCTION FRNUM:INTEGER;
VAR N : INTEGER;
 BEGIN
 WRITE ('Enter decimal number - ');
 READLN (N);
 FRNUM := N;
 END;
[GLOBAL] PROCEDURE FPNUM (N : INTEGER);
 BEGIN
 WRITELN ('Output - ',N,'(decimal)');
 END;
END.
```

VAX/VMS File Management

D.1 Files

Information on the VAX is stored in blocks called **files**. Files can consist of various kinds and amounts of information. Files could be very small or very large. The unit of measurement for files in the VAX/VMS system is a **block** of 512 characters. Each user is limited to a quota of some number of blocks for files. The kinds of information in files can be thought of as being in two forms: character data and noncharacter data. Character data can be printed and looked at as a meaningful printout. Noncharacter data is intended for reading by the computer only, and an attempt to print noncharacter data will give a garbage printout and may hang the computer terminal.

Files are identified within a user's directory by a file name which has three parts. These are: the name (proper), the type, and the version number. The appearance of a file name would be

```
DATA.TXT;5
```

The name is DATA; the type is TXT; the version number is 5.

Note that period and semicolon are used for separating the parts of the name. The name is something you (or the file's creator) makes up to identify the file uniquely. Names are strings of from 1 to 39 letters or numbers. Examples of possible file names are

```
X
132
R2D2
XYZ123AAA
```

The type is normally a three-letter code which is used by the system for indicating the intended use for the file*. When used in the intended context, the type need not be specified. Examples of types are

Type	Intended use
.MAR	MACRO assembly language program
.OBJ	Compiled object file
.EXE	Executable image file
.LIS	Listing file
.PAS	Pascal program
.FOR	FORTRAN program
.	.
.	.
.	.

The version number is assigned so that you can create a new version of a file without destroying the old version. Normally, the user does not explicitly refer to versions. A reference without a version number refers to the latest version, and if you create a new version, it will be numbered one higher than the latest version created so far.

D.2 Directories

To avoid problems that could arise if several users accidently used the same name for two different files, files are cataloged in directories. Every user has his own directory which was assigned by the system manager to be associated with the log in name. Directory names can have up to 39 letters and are enclosed in square brackets, such as

[SMITH]

Users can (and are encouraged to) create subdirectories. These are named with a second (or third, or fourth, etc.) name separated by period. For example,

[SMITH.HOMEWORK.CIS72]

---

* Older versions of VAX/VMS restricted file names to 9 characters and file types to 3 characters. Version 4, however, allows both names and types to have as many as 39 characters.

would indicate subsubdirectory CIS72 in subdirectory HOMEWORK in directory SMITH. In order to give a system-wide name for a file, it is necessary to specify the directory as well as the file name. An example of such a full file name is

```
[SMITH.HOMEWORK.CIS72]DATA.TXT;5
```

Since this is a lot to type, the VAX allows you to specify a default directory. Then the default directory is assumed unless a different directory is specifically named. Thus, if the default directory is [SMITH.HOMEWORK.CIS72], the previous file could be accessed as simply

```
DATA.TXT
```

This assumes that version 5 is the most recent version.

D.3 Looking at a File

As we said earlier, if a file is a character file, it can be typed or printed. To type a file, use the system command

```
$ TYPE filename
```

Note that the VAX types the dollar sign, you type the rest. All commands must end with a carriage return. For example, if you want to see what is contained in the file TEST.TXT type

```
$ TYPE TEXT.TXT
```

When you type this command, the information will start appearing on the screen. Unless you can read very rapidly, you may have difficulty reading the information as fast as the VAX can type. To allow for this, you can stop the display by keying control S to the VAX. You do this by holding down the key marked CONTROL or CTRL (on the lower left of your keyboard) and then keying S. The display will stop until you restart it by typing control Q.

If you want to keep a paper printout of the file, use the PRINT command instead of TYPE. This will cause the file to be printed on the system line printer. The printout will be preceded by a banner page that identifies both the user and the file being printed.

D.4 Looking at a Directory

The command DIRECTORY (or DIR for short) can be used to see the names and versions of all the files in your directory. As with TYPE or any command or program which outputs to the screen, control S and control Q can be used to stop or restart the typing. There are many variations of the DIRECTORY command which produce modified directories. The following list gives some of the most useful variations.

Command	Results
`DIRECTORY/PRINT`	Produce the directory on the printer
`DIRECTORY/SINCE=TODAY`	Show files created today
`DIRECTORY/SINCE=5-JUL-1985`	Show files created since 5-July-1985 (Note: the full year must be typed.)
`DIRECTORY/SINCE=10:30`	Show files created since 10:30 this morning. (Note: the VAX uses 24-hour time; therefore, 1:30 PM is 13:30.)
`DIRECTORY [SMITH.HOMEWORK.CIS72]`	Show files in directory [SMITH.HOMEWORK.CIS72]
`DIRECTORY TEXT`	Show files with name TEXT
`DIRECTORY .TXT`	Show files with type .TXT

Other variations are shown in the section on "Wild Cards." Note that most commands can be abbreviated to three or four letters, e.g., DIR/PRI. If you overabbreviate, the VAX tells you that you have an ambiguous command.

D.5 Copying Files

The copy command allows you to make a copy of a file. The command would make a copy of the file TEXT.TXT in directory [SMITH] and place it in the current directory with the name DATA.TXT. This command is useful for getting a file from another directory, but it can be used just to make a working copy of a file in your current directory.

```
$ COPY file-1  file-2
```

copies file-1 to file-2. For example,

```
$ COPY [SMITH]TEXT.TXT DATA.TXT
```

D.6 Using Subdirectories

When you log into your account, you are in the default directory that was set up for you by the system manager. If you have many files, it is usually best to keep as few files as possible in your default directory. This means that you should create a subdirectory for each of your projects, and perhaps subsubdirectories for subprojects. Let us suppose that your log in directory is [SMITH]. Then your subdirectories might be

```
[SMITH.HOMEWORK]
[SMITH.PROJECT]
[SMITH.LISTINGS]
[SMITH.DATA]
```

To set one of these subdirectories to be the current directory, type the command

```
$ SET DEFAULT [SMITH.HOMEWORK]
```

It is useful now to use the DIRECTORY command to verify that you are operating in the correct subdirectory.

D.7 Creating a Subdirectory

It is usually a good idea to create subdirectories for each of your projects. Then the files you create for one project will not interfere with the files you create for another project. If need be, you can always use the COPY command to get copies of files from one directory to another. As an example, to create a subdirectory named [SMITH.HOMEWORK], use the command

```
$ CREATE/DIRECTORY [SMITH.HOMEWORK]
```

D.8 Wild Cards

Copying a large number of files could require a lot of typing. Suppose you wanted to copy 100 files. It would take a long time to type all the copy commands. The use of wild cards allows the wholesale copy-

ing of files. In this case the way a wild card works is that the asterisk
(*) symbol can be used to represent any character string. Thus, for
example, V* means any name beginning with V. The asterisk all by
itself means any name at all. Therefore, the following command could
be used to copy the most recent version of all files in one subdirectory
to another:

$ COPY [SMITH.DATA]*.* [SMITH.PROJECT]*.*

The wild card asterisk can be used in the name, type, and version-
number fields.

In addition to the COPY command, wild card symbols can be
used in the TYPE, PRINT, and DIRECTORY commands. For example,
consider the following wild card definitions

Symbol	Meaning
*.OBJ	The most recent version of any file of type .OBJ (e.g., SAMPLE.OBJ, PROG.OBJ, etc.)
PROG.*	The most recent version of all files with the name PROG. (e.g., PROG.MAR, PROG.OBJ, etc.)
P*.MAR	Every assembly language program beginning with the letter P
SAMPLE.MAR;*	All versions of SAMPLE.MAR

While it is possible to use wild cards in directory names, it is a
bit more complicated. The possible wild card symbols are

Symbol	Meaning
*	Any string
. at the beginning	The current directory
- at the beginning	The next higher-level directory
...	All sequences of directory names

As an example of how these wild card symbols operate, consider
the following DIRECTORY commands executed while in
[SMITH.HOMEWORK]

Command	Files Listed
DIRECTORY [SMITH.*]	All files in any subdirectory of [SMITH]
DIRECTORY [.CIS72]	All files in [SMITH.HOMEWORK.CIS72]
DIRECTORY [-.PROJECT]	All files in [SMITH.PROJECT]
DIRECTORY [SMITH...]	All files in [SMITH] and all subdirectories of [SMITH] plus all subsubdirectories, etc.

D.9 Housekeeping

As files are repeatedly edited and new versions are created, you can end up with a plethora of versions. In addition, some files become obsolete and useless. If everything is kept and useless files are never cleaned out, your quota of file space will soon be filled up. In order to help you keep house and get rid of obsolete files, there are two commands, PURGE and DELETE. The simplest command is PURGE. This gets rid of all but the most recent version of file. Examples are

Command	Files purged
PURGE	All files in current directory
PURGE NAME.TXT	The file NAME.TXT in the current directory
PURGE *.OBJ	All files of type .OBJ in the current directory

Sometimes, for safety sake you may want to keep a few versions of a file, in case you botched up your last edit. This can be done with the command

$ PURGE/KEEP=5

Which will delete all but the last five versions of all files in the default directory. To keep the overall system in order, the system manager may periodically do a PURGE/KEEP=5, or some other number, for all files in the whole system.

The second command is DELETE. It is used to delete specific files by name. When you use this you must explicitly state the name, type, and version number, although you can use wild cards. Examples are

Command	Files Deleted
DELETE NAME.TXT;17	Delete version 17 of NAME.TXT. This command is useful to delete the most recent version after you botched up an edit.
DELETE *.OBJ;*	Delete all files of type .OBJ
DELETE *.*;*	All files in the default directory—Look out!!
DELETE/CONFIRM *.*;*	All files in your directory, but the VAX will ask you to answer Y or N before deleting each file.
DELETE NAME.TXT;0	Delete the most recent version of NAME.TXT. (Note: version number 0 is a code for the most recent version.)
DELETE NAME.TXT;-3	Delete the version three earlier than the most recent of file NAME.TXT

Finally, we come to the task of deleting a directory. Suppose that you are done with directory [SMITH.PROJECT.TEXT]. How do you get rid of it once and for all? Use the following commands:

Command	**Results**
`SET DEFAULT [SMITH.PROJECT.TEXT]`	Get to the directory you want to delete
`DELETE *.*;*`	Delete all the files in the directory
`SET DEFAULT [-]`	Get back to the previous directory, namely [SMITH.PROJECT]
`SET PROTECT=(OWNER=D) TEXT.DIR`	Allow the directory file to be deleted
`DELETE TEXT.DIR`	Delete the directory

Using the EDT Editor

E.1 Function of the Editor

As we saw in Appendix D, unless you are using the batch system, programs must reside in a file such as PROG.MAR (or PROG.FOR for FORTRAN programs or PROG.PAS for Pascal programs). Although it is possible to create programs using the CREATE command, there are difficulties in doing so. For example, you could enter the command

```
CREATE PROG.MAR
```

You would then type your entire program and signal the end by typing control Z. However, if there were any mistakes in your program, you would have no choice but to retype the entire program. The EDT editor allows you to enter and modify programs so that correcting mistakes or adding features to programs is relatively easy.

The EDT editor is used for creating and modifying strings of text. This text is considered to be an arbitrary string of characters. No distinction is made as to whether the text constitutes a valid MACRO program, a FORTRAN or PASCAL program, a nursery rhyme, or whatever. In fact, many people use the EDT editor for dealing with English prose, such as business letters. The growing use of computers for this purpose comes under the general name of **word processing.** The important point to remember is that the editor does not know that you are writing MACRO programs, therefore symbols such as .TITLE, .END, colon, semicolon, and so on, have no recognizable meaning.

There are a number of editors available on the VAX. EDT, SOS, and TECO are the most popular editors. Of these, EDT is perhaps the simplest to use, especially if you are using a sophisticated video display terminal, such as a VT52, or a terminal in the VT100 or VT200 family, or any terminal that is compatible with these.

E.2 Using the EDT Editor in Screen Mode

In screen mode, the EDT editor displays the information that you are typing on the face of your VT52 or VT100/VT200-compatible terminal. As you enter text, delete text, or make any kind of change, you see the change occur on the screen before you to the form it will have in the final text.*

In order to use the EDT editor, type the command

```
EDIT/EDT PROGRAM.MAR**
```

where PROGRAM.MAR is the name of the program file to be edited. If the file PROGRAM.MAR already exists, the first line of the file will be typed, followed by an asterisk. If this is a new file you are trying to create, the message "Input file does not exist." followed by [EOB], followed by asterisk, will be typed. This is not an error message; it is simply information advising you that you are creating a new file. The symbol [EOB] will appear from time to time; it means End Of Buffer and marks the end of the editable text.

In either case, the asterisk indicates that EDT is in the line edit mode which is described in Section E.4. In order to change to screen mode enter the command CHANGE followed by carriage return. At this command, the first 22 lines of your program (or as many as there are up to 22) are displayed on the screen. At this point, there will be a flashing **cursor** mark in the upper left-hand corner indicating that EDT is ready to make insertions or deletions at that point.

Unless your program is short (no more than 24 lines), it cannot be displayed on the terminal screen in its entirety. Therefore, a **window** is displayed of the 24 lines surrounding the place where insertions or deletions are being made. Insertions and deletions can be

---

* In order for EDT to keep your screen up-to-date, lines or parts of lines are constantly being retyped by the processor. This means that performance will degrade considerably if you are operating at low baud rates (data transmission rates). The minimum recommended baud rate is 1200 (120 characters per second). However, EDT screen mode can be used at 300 baud if the display window is reduced with the commands SET LINES 8 and SET CURSOR 4:6 which are issued before the CHANGE command.

** The qualifier /EDT is not necessary if your system defaults to the EDT editor.

made at any point in the text. The place where a change occurs is marked by a flashing mark called the **cursor**. The cursor can be moved around with the arrow keys and in other ways as well. The window is usually adjusted so that the cursor is on the line about two-thirds of the way down your screen. Of course, if the cursor is on the first few lines or the last few lines of your program, the cursor may be placed higher or lower on the window. Figure E.1 shows how the screen might appear. This program contains some intentional errors which will be corrected.

Insertions and Deletions

In order to correct the errors in the program section shown in Figure E.1, it is first necessary to read and locate the errors. The first error noticed is that the second line reads

```
MSG2:       .ASCID        "NOW IS TIME"
```

It should read

```
MSG2:       .ASCID        "NOW IS THE TIME"
```

In order to make this change, we must insert the word THE after IS. To do this, we must first move the cursor to that point. This can be done with the arrow keys. There are four keys with arrows (left, right, up, and down). Since the cursor position is too low, type the up arrow 15 times to get it to the second line of Figure E.1. Note that as the cursor is moved up, the window will be readjusted to keep the cursor as near the lower two-thirds of the screen as possible. Therefore, new lines will appear at the top, and lines will disappear at the bottom. This is called **scrolling upward**. Once the first line of the program appears on the screen, no more scrolling takes place, and the cursor will move up the screen, above the lower two-thirds of the screen. Also note that some lines are shorter than the horizontal position of the cursor. As a result, the cursor will drop back and forth, trying to keep its original horizontal position, but not going beyond the end of any line.

After typing the up arrow 15 times, the cursor will be on the right line, but in the wrong place. It will be flashing over the E in TIME, and will appear as follows

```
MSG2:    .ASCID   "NOW IS TIME"
                            ↑
                            └─ cursor
```

```
MSG1:   .ASCID  "THESE ARE SOME MESSAGES"
MSG2:   .ASCID  "NOW IS TIME"
MSG3:   .ASCID  "FOR ALL MEN TO TO COME"
MSG4:   .ASCID  "COME TWO THE AID OF HIS"
MSG5:   .ASCID  "PARTY"
;THE PRECEDING ARE SOME RANDOM MESSAGES
        .ENTRY  START
        MOVAB   MSG1,R0
        JSB     PMESG
        MOVAB   MSG2,R0
        JSB     PMESG
        MOVAB   MSG3,R0
        JSB     PMESG
        MOVAB   MSG5,R0
        JSB     PMESG
        $EXIT_S
;HERE IS A SUBROUTINE FOR PRINTING THE MESSAGES
PMESG:  TSTB    OPENFLAG         ┗━━━━━━━━━━flashing cursor mark
        BNEQ    10$
        JSB     OPENFILE
        DECB    OPENFLAG
10$:    MOVW    2(R0),FILEFAB+FAB$W_RSZ
```

Figure E.1 CRT display from the EDT editor

Now type the left arrow three times, and it will appear over the T in TIME.

```
MSG2:   .ASCID  "NOW IS TIME"
                        ┗━━━ cursor
```

We are now ready to insert characters. As characters are typed they will be inserted just ahead of the character at the cursor. If the characters T H E space are typed, Figure E.2 shows how the line will be redisplayed on the screen as each character is typed. Notice in Figure E.2 how the cursor moves with the typing of each character. As a result the characters of text are inserted in the right place and in the right order. Also note that spaces and tabs are very much a part of the text and must be inserted in their appropriate places.

The next error is in the line

```
MESG3:  .ASCID          "FOR ALL MEN TO TO COME"
```

```
              MSG2:    .ASCID    "NOW IS TIME"                        Figure E.2 Inserting a
                                        └──────────cursor             string

Type T        MSG2:    .ASCID    "NOW IS TTIME"
                                         └──────────cursor

Type H        MSG2:    .ASCID    "NOW IS THTIME"
                                          └──────────cursor

Type E        MSG2:    .ASCID    "NOW IS THETIME"
                                           └──────────cursor

Type space    MSG2:    .ASCID    "NOW IS THE TIME"
                                            └──────────cursor
```

First the word GOOD is missing; it should read . . . ALL *GOOD* MEN. . . .
Again, the cursor must be moved, this time with the down arrow and
the left arrow. Then the word GOOD can be inserted as was done
with the word THE in the previous example.

However, there is still another error on this line; TO appears
twice. We must delete one of them. To delete text, first the cursor
must be moved just to the right of the character to be deleted. Then
the delete key will remove characters to the left in a way similar to
the way the delete key removes characters in the normal typing mode
outside the editor. The main difference is that with EDT, we can
delete from anywhere in a line by positioning the cursor correctly.
In this case, the right arrow can be used to move the cursor just after
the O in the first TO. (Either TO could be deleted. It does not matter,
except that the first TO was closer and required fewer right arrow
moves to get there.) Figure E.3 shows what the line would look like
after each delete. Note that the delete key was typed three times. The
extra time was to get rid of the extra space that went along with the
TO.

With what is known so far, the reader should easily be able to
correct the rest of the errors since all editing is simply a matter of
finding the right place in the text and either inserting or deleting
characters. However, if all EDT editing were restricted to use of the
five control keys described so far (four arrows and delete) we would
soon wear our fingers to the bone typing these keys to edit any sizable
amount of text. These keys do "retail" editing; there are other keys
for "wholesale" editing, such as delete word, delete line, or delete

Figure E.3 Deleting Text

```
          MSG3:     .ASCID    "FOR ALL GOOD MEN TO TO COME"TIME"
                                                     └─cursor
```

```
Delete    MSG3:     .ASCID    "FOR ALL GOOD MEN T TO COME"
                                                 ↑
                                                 └──cursor
```

```
Delete    MSG3:     .ASCID    "FOR ALL GOOD MEN  TO COME"
                                                 ↑
                                                 └──────cursor
```

```
Delete    MSG3:     .ASCID    "FOR ALL GOOD MEN TO COME"
                                                 ↑
                                                 └───────cursor
```

whole sections. Some of these commands will be described in the next section; others will be left for the reader to learn on his or her own.

E.3 Keypad Commands

Use of the keypad provides another means of editing a program. Keypad commands can be invoked by use of the numeric keypad on the right-hand side of the keyboard. The numeric keypads on these terminals operate in one of two modes. The first is normal mode, where the keys just duplicate the ability to type numbers. When a terminal is used primarily for entering numeric data, use of these keys can speed up data entry, since the layout is essentially the same as is found on many adding machines. The second mode is the special character mode, where these keys produce their own character codes which are not like any other keys on the keyboard.* When using the EDT screen editor, the keypad will be in the special character mode.

Since there are more editor functions provided than there are keys, most of the keys have two functions: the primary function and the secondary function. In order to get the primary function, just type the key. For example, the primary function of the 2 key is to move

---

* In the special character mode, these keys transmit a sequence of characters starting with the ASCII control character, escape. For example, the 1 key will cause <esc>?q to be transmitted on a VT52 or <esc>Oq to be transmitted on the VT100 or VT200 terminals.

the cursor to the end of a line. If you use this key, it can save a lot of typing of the right arrows. The secondary function of the 2 key is to delete everything from the cursor to the end of the line. (This is sort of the reverse of control U used in normal type mode to delete everything to the left.) To get the secondary function of the 2 key, you must first type a special key called the **gold** key. On the VT100/VT200, the gold key is the key marked PF1, on the VT52 it is the key that is colored blue. In either case, it is the key in the upper left-hand corner of the numeric keypad. Figures E.4 and E.5 show the keypad layouts on the VT52 and VT100/VT200. It is even possible to purchase replacement keytops which have the EDT functions embossed on them. If you are not so lucky as to have the embossed keytops, you can type a special key called the **help** key which is right next to the gold key. (This is the red key on the VT52 or the PF2 key on the VT100/VT200.) Press this, and your text will disappear from the screen. (Don't worry; it is still in the computer.) Then a replica of Figure E.4 or E.5 will appear on the screen to help locate the proper function.

It is not the intention here to give a full description of the keypad editor functions. The best way to learn the editor is to try out the different functions and see what happens. (The VAX tends to back up files pretty well so that experimenting can be done without too much risk.) Therefore, each of the keypad functions will be described in a few sentences. More information is available in the *VAX/VMS EDT— Editor Manual* and through use of the HELP command. The functions will not be described by key because this differs between the VT52 and the VT100/VT200. In fact, since the VT52 has fewer keys, some of the functions are not available from its keypad. Figure E.4 or E.5

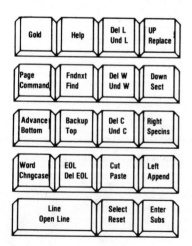

Figure E.4 VT52 keypad commands

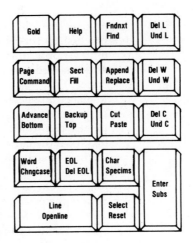

Figure E.5 VT100/VT200 keypad commands

will identify the right key to use. The upper line is for the primary function; the lower line is the secondary function and requires use of the gold key.

Press	Results
GOLD	Sets the next function to its secondary set.
HELP	Displays the keyboard picture and other help messages.
FIND NEXT	Searches for the next occurrence of a string match in the selected direction.
FIND	Sets a "search" string and searches for it.
DELETE LINE	Deletes the line to the right of the cursor.
UNDELETE LINE	Restores the last line deleted. This can be used in case a line is accidently deleted. It can also be used to make copies of a line, by deleting it and undeleting it several times.
PAGE	Moves the cursor one page in the selected direction, that is, to the next form feed character.
COMMAND	Allows the typing of an editor command.
SECTION	Moves the cursor sixteen lines in the selected direction.

(continued)

Press	Results
FILL	Adjusts line lengths in word processing. This is not normally used for programming.
APPEND	Adds marked text to the paste buffer.
REPLACE	Replaces a selected range with the paste buffer.
DELETE WORD	Deletes one word. A word is the text from the cursor position to the next space, tab, or line termination.
UNDELETE WORD	Reinserts the last word deleted.
ADVANCE	Selects the direction of motion for the page, line, word, character, and search functions to be forward.
BOTTOM	Moves the cursor to the bottom of the text.
BACKUP	Selects the direction of motion for the page, line, word, character and search functions to be backward.
TOP	Moves the cursor to the top of the text.
CUT	Moves marked text to the paste buffer, and then deletes the marked text.
PASTE	Copies the paste buffer into the text at the cursor position.
DELETE CHARACTER	Deletes one character in the forward direction. This is the opposite of the delete key which deletes to the left.
UNDELETE CHARACTER	Reinserts the last deleted character.
WORD	Moves the cursor one word in the selected direction until the next space, tab, or end of line.
CHANGE CASE	Changes text from upper to lower case and vice versa.
END OF LINE	Moves the cursor to the end of the current line (or previous line depending upon ADVANCE or BACKUP mode).
DELETE TO END OF LINE	Deletes all the characters to the right of the cursor up to the end of the line, but not the carriage return/line feed at the end of the line. That is the only difference between DELETE TO END OF LINE and DELETE LINE.

Press	Results
MOVE CHARACTER	Moves the cursor one character position in the selected direction.
SPECIAL CHARACTER INSERT	Allows control characters to be inserted in the text.
ENTER	Enters a command.
SUBSTITUTE	Substitutes the paste buffer for the string found and then does a FIND NEXT (used after FIND).
BEGINNING OF LINE	Moves the cursor to the beginning of the next or previous line, depending upon direction selected.
OPEN LINE	Inserts a blank line in the text and leaves the cursor at the beginning of the line. This makes typing easier when inserting a line into the body of the text.
SELECT	Marks one end of a selected area. The cursor marks the other end. Selected areas are used for cutting and pasting. On a VT100/VT200, selected text is displayed in reverse video.
RESET	Turns off a selected area.

Two of the most important commands are the FIND and FIND NEXT. In a large program it can become quite tiresome finding the errors by stepping the cursor through with the arrows. A better method is to have the editor search for some character string which will locate the place that needs editing. For example, suppose that the assembler tells you that you have used the undefined operation code MOVX somewhere in your program. You can enter the editor and invoke FIND. This is PF1–PF3 on a VT100/VT200, or Blue–8 on a VT52. The bottom of the screen will then request "Search for:". You then type the string you want to search for; in this case type MOVX. Then type either FORWARD or BACK (4 or 5 on either terminal) depending on whether you want to search forward or backward in the file. The editor will then search until MOVX is found. You can then use the arrows to position the cursor to the X, delete it, and type L,W, or B, or whatever was appropriate. If this error occurred more than once, subsequent occurrences of MOVX could be searched for by using the FIND NEXT key (PF3 on the VT100/VT200 or 8 on the VT52).

Another important operation is the ability to enter general edit commands. Although there are a number of such commands, there is only one crucial one, EXIT. The EXIT command is needed to tell EDT that the editing session is done and that the new file is to be saved. Until this command is executed none of your editing will have a permanent effect. To enter the command mode type GOLD–7 on either terminal. The prompt "Command:" will then be displayed at the bottom of the screen. Type EXIT and then strike the ENTER key. EDT will now exit, and you will return to the VAX/VMS system. If you now enter the VAX/VMS DIRECTORY command, you will see that there is a new version of the file with a version number one higher than the last version. For example if this is the fifth time that the file was edited, the directory might show

```
.
.
.
PROGRAM.MAR;3
PROGRAM.MAR;4
PROGRAM.MAR;5
```

(See Appendix D for use of the PURGE command to get rid of old versions.) The edited output will be found in PROGRAM.MAR;5. The unedited file still resides in PROGRAM.MAR;4 and can be recovered in case you accidently botched up the edit.

E.4 Editing from a Hard-Copy Terminal

If you are not fortunate enough to have a VT52 or VT100/VT200-compatible CRT terminal to edit with, things become somewhat more complicated. The assumption then is that you are working from a hard-copy or printing terminal. On a hard-copy terminal you cannot see the text change before your eyes because once something is printed, it is printed and cannot change. As a result, editing with EDT must be done in a line-by-line fashion. Although there are a considerable number of commands provided by EDT to facilitate line editing, it is possible to get by with just a few basic commands which will be described here.

In order to start editing a file, type the VAX/VMS command:

```
EDIT/EDT PROGRAM.MAR*
```

where PROGRAM.MAR is the name of your program file. If this is the first time that you have used this file, the message "Input file does

---

* The qualifier /EDT is not necessary if your system defaults to the EDT editor.

not exist." then [EOB] will be displayed, followed by an asterisk. The
message "Input file does not exist." looks like an error message, but
it really is just advising you that you are creating a new file. The line

```
[EOB]
```

means that the only text you have is the End Of Buffer mark.

If this is not the first time you are using this file, an input file
will exist, so there will be no message. The first line of your program
will be displayed with a line number of 1. For example,

```
1       .TITLE   MY PROGRAM
*
```

Note again that there is an asterisk. The asterisk is a prompt advising
that EDT is expecting you to type an EDT command.

A basic set of EDT commands which can start a person editing
follows. Other commands and variations of these commands can be
learned for more efficient use of the editor.

INSERT When creating a new file or adding missing lines to a program,
the INSERT command can be used. After the asterisk, type INSERT*
followed by carriage return. EDT will return with a blank line, but
indented. This is the prompt to start entering text. From now on,
everything typed will be inserted into the text as you type it. Note
that each line will be indented. The indents are not part of the text.
They are simply prompts so that you know that the VAX is still alive.
When you have inserted all that you want, type control Z. (Hold the
control key down and type Z.) EDT will then prompt with an asterisk
showing that it is back in command mode. In general, the prompts
are asterisk for command mode and indent for insert mode.

TYPE After making insertions or other kinds of modifications, it is
usual to want to see what the file looks like. This is done with the
TYPE command. The TYPE command must be followed by a **range**
code that tells which lines you want typed. If you do not specify a
range, just the **current** line is typed. The current line is the line where
editing is about to take place. Whenever you insert text, it will be
just in front of the current line.

---

* All the commands and keywords described in this section (except EXIT and RESE-
QUENCE.) can be abbreviated to one letter. Thus, INSERT can be entered as just I.
Similarly, the commands TYPE, FIND, DELETE, and SUBSTITUTE and the key-
words BEGIN and END can be abbreviated as: T, F, D, S, B, and E.

If you want to type the entire program, the range BEGIN:END can be specified with the command

```
TYPE BEGIN:END
```

Notice that when the lines are typed, line numbers are appended on the left. These are not part of the text, and are used only for editing purposes. For example, if lines were inserted in an empty file as is done when creating a file, a TYPE BEGIN:END command might produce the following:

```
1        .TITLE    PROGRAM
2        .ASCII    "HERE ARE JUST"
3        .ASCII    "A FEW LINES"
[EOB]
*
```

Ranges can also be specified using line numbers. For example, TYPE 1:2 to type line 1 through 2 or just a single line number to type a single line. For example, TYPE 2.

Another thing to note is that after executing a TYPE command, the current line becomes the first of the lines typed. Thus, TYPE 2:3 will set line 2 to be the current line. That means that an INSERT command will now insert text between lines 1 and 2. If insertions are made between two such consecutively numbered lines, EDT will generate line numbers that are decimal fractions (e.g., 1.1, 1.2, 1.3, and so forth). These fractional line numbers can be used to specify a range, just as the whole numbers can. For example,

```
TYPE 1.2:1.3
```

would cause all the lines from 1.2 through 1.3 to be typed. Then line 1.2 would become the current line. Insertions would therefore occur between lines 1.1 and 1.2 and would get line numbers 1.11, 1.12, 1.13, and so forth.

One more useful feature is the **dot symbol**. The dot symbol or period refers to the current line and can be used in expressions. Thus, .−3 means three lines prior to the current line and .+3 means three lines after the current line. The command TYPE .−3,.+3 will type from three lines before to three lines after the current line.

FIND In order to use the INSERT command, the current line must be set to the line in front of which the text is to be inserted. In other words, if text is to be inserted between lines 1.11 and 1.12, the current line must be set to 1.12. This can be done with the FIND command.

The FIND command is followed by a line designation which identifies the line to be located. Any of the line designations described in the section on the TYPE command can be used. For example, the following find commands locate the current lines as described.

Command	Current Line
FIND 1.12	Line 1.12
FIND BEGIN	The first line
FIND END	The [EOB]
FIND .+4	Four lines after the current line from which the command is entered

In addition, a quoted string can be used as a line specifier. This causes EDT to search for the first line containing the specified character string. For example, the command FIND ".BLKL" will cause EDT to search forward in your file for the first line after the current line that contains the character string .BLKL. Sometimes it is useful to search in the reverse direction; that is, to search for a line earlier than the current line. To search upward, the quoted string must be preceded by a minus sign, as with the command FIND −".BLKL".

When using the search feature, it is important to pick a string which is long enough to be unique, or you may find the wrong line. In fact, ".BLKL" may not be so good, because your program may have many lines with the string .BLKL in them. A better choice might be

FIND ".BLKL (tab) 23"

Here "tab" refers to the tab character which can be in the quoted string just as any other character in your program.

After using the find command, it is usually a good idea to type the current line to make sure that you are at the right place. This can be done with the TYPE command with no range specification. This might appear as

FIND ".BLKL (tab) 23" *
TYPE

This will cause the line found to be typed.

---

* This can be abbreviated by formatting the quoted string directly on the TYPE command as TYPE ".BLKL (tab) 23". Then the FIND command will be unnecessary.

DELETE Lines that are in error need to be removed from the program. This is done with the DELETE command. The DELETE command specifies a range of numbers, just as the TYPE command does. All the lines in the range will be deleted. If you delete too much, you will have to reenter the lines. Therefore, it is usually a good idea to type the range before you delete it. For example, the following pair of lines could be used

```
TYPE 1,2:1,22
DELETE 1,2:1,22
```

If you type the range of lines on the DELETE exactly as it appeared on the TYPE, you will know exactly which lines were deleted. It is also possible to have EDT query you about each line as you delete it by using the DELETE/VERIFY command.

SUBSTITUTE If an error occurs on a line, the usual thing to do would be to delete the line and then insert the correction. However, if it is a long line, with only one small error somewhere, there is a better way. Suppose the line with the error reads

```
MESG: .ASCII" THIS IS A LONG MESSAGE"
```

and it should read .ASCI*D* instead of .ASCI*I*. The SUBSTITUTE command allows you to tell EDT precisely that. After using the FIND command to locate the line, enter the command:

```
SUBSTITUTE /.ASCII/.ASCID/
```

Notice that the wrong string is specified first and the correct string second. As with the FIND command, it is important to make the matching string long enough to be unique. The command SUBSTITUTE /II/ID/ would work, but SUBSTITUTE /I/D/ would replace the wrong I giving .ASCDI.

RESEQUENCE As insertions are made, more and more fractional line numbers will be generated. This may make finding a line confusing. The RESEQUENCE command will renumber all the lines with whole numbers starting at 1. It is often a good idea after resequencing to retype the entire program so that lines can be found. Resequencing occurs automatically when you start to edit a file, unless special measures are taken to save line numbers.

EXIT After you finish editing, the command EXIT must be typed. If you exit any other way, such as by typing control Y you could lose all of your edits.

Although the EDT editor sounds complicated, it will become easy to use with practice.

VAX-11 Programming Card

SUMMARY OF GENERAL MODE ADDRESSING

General Register Addressing

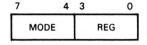

7	4	3	0
MODE		REG	

Hex	Dec	Name	Assembler	r	m	w	a	v	PC	SP	AP& FP	Indexable
0-3	0-3	literal	S^#literal	y	f	f	f	f	–	–	–	f
4	4	indexed	i[Rx]	y	y	y	y	y	f	y	y	f
5	5	register	Rn	y	y	y	f	y	u	uq	uo	f
6	6	register deferred	(Rn)	y	y	y	y	y	u	y	y	y
7	7	autodecrement	– (Rn)	y	y	y	y	y	u	y	y	ux
8	8	autoincrement	(Rn) +	y	y	y	y	y	p	y	y	ux
9	9	autoincrement deferred	@(Rn) +	y	y	y	y	y	p	y	y	ux
A	10	byte displacement	B^D(Rn)	y	y	y	y	y	p	y	y	y
B	11	byte displacement deferred	@B^D(Rn)	y	y	y	y	y	p	y	y	y
C	12	word displacement	W^D(Rn)	y	y	y	y	y	p	y	y	y
D	13	word displacement deferred	@W^D(Rn)	y	y	y	y	y	p	y	y	y
E	14	longword displacement	L^D(Rn)	y	y	y	y	y	p	y	y	y
F	15	longword displacement deferred	@L^D(Rn)	y	y	y	y	y	p	y	y	y

504

Program Counter Addressing (reg = 15)

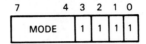

Hex	Dec	Name	Assembler	r	m	w	a	v	Indexable?
8	8	immediate	I∧#constant	y	u	u	y	y	u
9	9	absolute	@#address	y	y	y	y	y	y
A	10	byte relative	B∧address	y	y	y	y	y	y
B	11	byte relative deferred	@B∧address	y	y	y	y	y	y
C	12	word relative	W∧address	y	y	y	y	y	y
D	13	word relative deferred	@W∧address	y	y	y	y	y	y
E	14	long word relative	L∧address	y	y	y	y	y	y
F	15	long word relative deferred	@L∧address	y	y	y	y	y	y

Key:

D	–	displacement
i	–	any indexable addressing mode
–	–	logically impossible
f	–	reserved addressing mode fault
p	–	Program Counter addressing
u	–	UNPREDICTABLE
uq	–	UNPREDICTABLE for quad, octa, D_floating, G_floating, and H_floating (and field if position + size greater than 32)
uo	–	UNPREDICTABLE for octa, and H format
ux	–	UNPREDICTABLE for index register same as base register
y	–	yes, always valid addressing mode
r	–	read access
m	–	modify access
w	–	write access
a	–	address access
v	–	field access
Rn	–	general register, n = 0–15
Rx	–	general register, x = 0–14

OPERAND SPECIFIER NOTATION

Operand specifiers are described in the following way:

<name>.<access type><data type>

where:

1. Name is a suggestive name for the operand in the context of the instruction. The name is often abbreviated.

2. Access type is a letter denoting the operand specifier access type:

    a – Calculate the effective address of the specified operand. Address is returned in a longword which is the actual instruction operand. Context of address calculation is given by <data type>; i.e. size to be used in autoincrement, autodecrement, and indexing.

    b – No operand reference. Operand specifier is a branch displacement. Size of branch displacement is given by <data type>.

    m – Operand is read, potentially modified and written. Note that this is NOT an indivisible memory operation. Also note that if the operand is not actually modified, it may not be written back. However, modify type operands are always checked for both read and write accessibility.

    r – Operand is read only.

    v – Calculate the effective address of the specified operand. If the effective address is in memory, the address is returned in a longword which is the actual instruction operand. Context of address calculation is given by <data type>. If the effective address is Rn, the operand is in Rn or R[n + 1]'Rn.

    w – Operand is written only.

3. Data type is a letter denoting the data type of the operand:

    b – byte   o – octaword
    d – D_floating   q – quadword
    f – F_floating   w – word
    g – G_floating   x – first data type specified by instruction
    h – H_floating   y – second data type specified by instruction
    i – longword   * – multiple longwords (used only on implied operands)

4. Implied operands, that is, locations accessed by the instruction but not specified in and operand, are denoted in enclosing brackets [   ].

Condition Codes Legend

. = conditionally cleared/set
− = not affected
0 = cleared
1 = set

INSTRUCTION SET

OP	Mnemonic	Description	Arguments	Cond. Codes N Z V C
9D	ACBB	Add compare and branch byte	limit.rb, add.rb, index.mb, displ.bw	. . . -
6F	ACBD	Add compare and branch D_floating	limit.rd, add.rd, index.md, displ.bw	. . . -
4F	ACBF	Add compare and branch F_floating	limit.rf, add.rf, index.mf, displ.bw	. . . -
4FFD	ACBG	Add compare and branch G_floating	limit.rg, add.rg, index.mg, displ.bw	. . . -
6FFD	ACBH	Add compare and branch H_floating	limit.rh, add.rh, index.mh, displ.bw	. . . -
F1	ACBL	Add compare and branch long	limit.rl, add.rl, index.ml, displ.bw	. . . -
3D	ACBW	Add compare and branch word	limit.rw, add.rw, index.mw, displ.bw	. . . -
58	ADAWI	Add aligned word interlocked	add.rw, sum.mw	. . . .
80	ADDB2	Add byte 2-operand	add.rb, sum.mb	. . . .
81	ADDB3	Add byte 3-operand	add1.rb, add2.rb, sum.wb	. . . .
60	ADDD2	Add D_floating 2-operand	add.rd, sum.md	. . . 0
61	ADDD3	Add D_floating 3-operand	add1.rd, add2.rd, sum.wd	. . . 0
40	ADDF2	Add F_floating 2-operand	add.rf, sum.mf	. . . 0
41	ADDF3	Add F_floating 3-operand	add1.rf, add2.rf, sum.wf	. . . 0
40FD	ADDG2	Add G_floating 2-operand	add.rg, sum.mg	. . . 0
41FD	ADDG3	Add G_floating 3-operand	add1.rg, add2.rg, sum.wg	. . . 0
60FD	ADDH2	Add H_floating 2-operand	add.rh, sum.mh	. . . 0
61FD	ADDH3	Add H_floating 3-operand	add1.rh, add2.rh, sum.wh	. . . 0
C0	ADDL2	Add long 2-operand	add.rl, sum.ml	. . . .
C1	ADDL3	Add long 3-operand	add1.rl, add2.rl, sum.wl	. . . .
20	ADDP4	Add packed 4-operand	addlen.rw, addaddr.ab, sumlen.rw, sumaddr.ab, [R0-3.wl]	. . . 0
21	ADDP6	Add packed 6-operand	add1len.rw, add1addr.ab, add2len.rw, add2addr.ab, sumlen.rw, sumaddr.ab, [R0-5.wl]	. . . 0
A0	ADDW2	Add word 2-operand	add.rw, sum.mw	. . . .
A1	ADDW3	Add word 3-operand	add1.rw, add2.rw, sum.ww	. . . .
D8	ADWC	Add with carry	add.rl, sum.ml	. . . .
F3	AOBLEQ	Add one and branch on less or equal	limit.rl, index.ml, displ.bb	. . . -
F2	AOBLSS	Add one and branch on less	limit.rl, index.ml, displ.bb	. . . -
78	ASHL	Arithmetic shift long	count.rb, src.rl, dst.wl	. . . 0
F8	ASHP	Arithmetic shift and round packed	count.rb, srclen.rw, srcaddr.ab, round.rb, dstlen.rw, dstaddr.ab, [R0-3.wl]	. . . 0
79	ASHQ	Arithmetic shift quad	count.rb, src.rq, dst.wq	. . . 0
E1	BBC	Branch on bit clear	pos.rl, base.vb, displ.bb, [field.rv]	- - - -
E5	BBCC	Branch on bit clear and clear	pos.rl, base.vb, displ.bb, [field.mv]	- - - -
E7	BBCCI	Branch on bit clear and clear interlocked	pos.rl, base.vb, displ.bb, [field.mv]	- - - -
E3	BBCS	Branch on bit clear and set	pos.rl, base.vb, displ.bb, [field.mv]	- - - -
E0	BBS	Branch on bit set	pos.rl, base.vb, displ.bb, [field.rv]	- - - -
E4	BBSC	Branch on bit set and clear	pos.rl, base.vb, displ.bb, [field.mv]	- - - -
E2	BBSS	Branch on bit set and set	pos.rl, base.vb, displ.bb, [field.mv]	- - - -
E6	BBSSI	Branch on bit set and set interlocked	pos.rl, base.vb, displ.bb, [field.mv]	- - - -
1E	BCC	Branch on carry clear	displ.bb	- - - -
1F	BCS	Branch on carry set	displ.bb	- - - -
13	BEQL	Branch on equal	displ.bb	- - - -
13	BEQLU	Branch on equal unsigned	displ.bb	- - - -
18	BGEQ	Branch on greater or equal	displ.bb	- - - -
1E	BGEQU	Branch on greater or equal unsigned	displ.bb	- - - -
14	BGTR	Branch on greater	displ.bb	- - - -
1A	BGTRU	Branch on greater unsigned	displ.bb	- - - -

OP	Mnemonic	Description	Arguments	N	Z	V	C
				Cond. Codes			
8A	BICB2	Bit clear byte 2-operand	mask.rb, dst.mb	.	.	0	-
8B	BICB3	Bit clear byte 3-operand	mask.rb, src.rb, dst.wb	.	.	0	-
CA	BICL2	Bit clear long 2-operand	mask.rl, dst.ml	.	.	0	-
CB	BICL3	Bit clear long 3-operand	mask.rl, src.rl, dst.wl	.	.	0	-
B9	BICPSW	Bit clear processor status word	mask.rw	.	.	.	.
AA	BICW2	Bit clear word 2-operand	mask.rw, dst.mw	.	.	0	-
AB	BICW3	Bit clear word 3-operand	mask.rw, src.rw, dst.ww	.	.	0	-
88	BISB2	Bit set byte 2-operand	mask.rb, dst.mb	.	.	0	-
89	BISB3	Bit set byte 3-operand	mask.rb, src.rb, dst.wb	.	.	0	-
C8	BISL2	Bit set long 2-operand	mask.rl, dst.ml	.	.	0	-
C9	BISL3	Bit set long 3-operand	mask.rl, src.rl, dst.wl	.	.	0	-
B8	BISPSW	Bit set processor status word	mask.rw	.	.	.	.
A8	BISW2	Bit set word 2-operand	mask.rw, dst.mw	.	.	0	-
A9	BISW3	Bit set word 3-operand	mask.rw, src.rw, dst.ww	.	.	0	-
93	BITB	Bit test byte	mask.rb, src.rb	.	.	0	-
D3	BITL	Bit test long	mask.rl, src.rl	.	.	0	-
B3	BITW	Bit test word	mask.rw, src.rw	.	.	0	-
E9	BLBC	Branch on low bit clear	src.rl, displ.bb	-	-	-	-
E8	BLBS	Branch on low	src.rl, displ.bb	-	-	-	-
15	BLEQ	Branch on less or equal	displ.bb	-	-	-	-
1B	BLEQU	Branch on less or equal unsigned	displ.bb	-	-	-	-
19	BLSS	Branch on less	displ.bb				
1F	BLSSU	Branch on less unsigned	displ.bb	-	-	-	-
12	BNEQ	Branch on not equal	displ.bb	-	-	-	-
12	BNEQU	Branch on not equal unsigned	displ.bb	-	-	-	-
03	BPT	Break point fault	[–(KSP).w*]	0	0	0	0
11	BRB	Branch with byte displacement	displ.bb	-	-	-	-
31	BRW	Branch with word displacement	displ.bw	-	-	-	-
10	BSBB	Branch to subroutine with byte displacement	displ.bb, [–(SP).wl]	-	-	-	-
30	BSBW	Branch to subroutine with word displacement	displ.bw, [–(SP).wl]	-	-	-	-
FDFF	BUGL	VMS bugcheck		0	0	0	0
FEFF	BUGW	VMS bugcheck		0	0	0	0
1C	BVC	Branch on overflow clear	displ.bb	-	-	-	-
1D	BVS	Branch on overflow set	displ.bb	-	-	-	-
FA	CALLG	Call with general argument list	arglist.ab, dst.ab, [–(SP).w*]	0	0	0	0
FB	CALLS	Call with argument list on stack	numarg.rl, dst.ab, [–(SP).w*]	0	0	0	0
8F	CASEB	Case byte	selector.rb, base.rb, limit.rb, displ.bw-list	.	.	0	.
CF	CASEL	Case long	selector.rl, base.rl, limit.rl, displ.bw-list	.	.	0	.
AF	CASEW	Case word	selector.rw, base.rw, limit.rw, displ.bw-list	.	.	0	.
BD	CHME	Change mode to executive	param.rw, [–(ySP).w*] y=MINU(E, PSL*current-mode*)	0	0	0	0
BC	CHMK	Change mode to kernel	param.rw, [–(KSP).w*]	0	0	0	0
BE	CHMS	Change mode to supervisor	param.rw, [–(ySP).w*] y=MINU(S, PSL*current-mode*)	0	0	0	0
BF	CHMU	Change mode to user	param.rw, [–(SP).w*]	0	0	0	0
94	CLRB	Clear byte	dst.wb	0	1	0	-
7C	CLRD	Clear D_floating	dst.wd	0	1	0	-
D4	CLRF	Clear F_floating	dst.wf	0	1	0	-
7C	CLRG	Clear G_floating	dst.wg	0	1	0	-
7CFD	CLRH	Clear H_floating	dst.wh	0	1	0	-

OP	Mnemonic	Description	Arguments	Cond. Codes			
				N	Z	V	C
D4	CLRL	Clear long	dst.wl	0	1	0	-
7CFD	CLRO	Clear octaword	dst.wo	0	1	0	-
7C	CLRQ	Clear quad	dst.wq	0	1	0	-
B4	CLRW	Clear word	dst.ww	0	1	0	-
91	CMPB	Compare byte	src1.rb, src2.rb	.	.	0	.
29	CMPC3	Compare character 3-operand	len.rw, src1addr.ab, src2addr.ab, [R0-3.wl]	.	.	0	.
2D	CMPC5	Compare character 5-operand	src1len.rw, src1addr.ab, fill.rb, src2len.rw, src2addr.ab, [R0-3.wl]	.	.	0	.
71	CMPD	Compare D_floating	src1.rd, src2.rd	.	.	0	0
51	CMPF	Compare F_floating	src1.rf, src2.rf	.	.	0	0
51FD	CMPG	Compare G_floating	src1.rg, src2.rg	.	.	0	0
71FD	CMPH	Compare H_floating	src1.rh, src2.rh	.	.	0	0
D1	CMPL	Compare long	src1.rl, src2.r1	.	.	0	.
35	CMPP3	Compare packed 3-operand	len.rw, src1addr.ab, src2addr.ab, [R0-3.wl]	.	.	0	0
37	CMPP4	Compare packed 4-operand	src1len.rw, src1addr.ab, src2len.rw, src2addr.ab, [R0-3.wl]	.	.	0	0
EC	CMPV	Compare field	pos.rl, size.rb, base.vb, [field.rv], src.rl	.	.	0	.
B1	CMPW	Compare word	src1.rw, src2.rw	.	.	0	.
ED	CMPZV	Compare zero-extended field	pos.rl, size.rb, base.vb, [field.rv], src.rl	.	.	0	.
0B	CRC	Calculate cyclic redundancy check	tbl.ab, initialcrc.rl, strlen.rw, stream.ab, [R0-3.wl]	.	.	0	0
6C	CVTBD	Convert byte to D_floating	src.rb, dst.wd	.	.	.	0
4C	CVTBF	Convert byte to F_floating	src.rb, dst.wf	.	.	.	0
4CFD	CVTBG	Convert byte to G_floating	src.rb, dst.wg	.	.	.	0
6CFD	CVTBH	Convert byte to H_floating	src.rb, dst.wh	.	.	.	0
98	CVTBL	Convert byte to long	src.rb, dst.wl	.	.	.	0
99	CVTBW	Convert byte to word	src.rb, dst.ww	.	.	.	0
68	CVTDB	Convert D_floating to byte	src.rd, dst.wb	.	.	.	0
76	CVTDF	Convert D_floating to F_floating	src.rd, dst.wf	.	.	.	0
32FD	CVTDH	Convert D_floating to H_floating	src.rd, dst.wh	.	.	.	0
6A	CVTDL	Convert D_floating to long	src.rd, dst.wl	.	.	.	0
69	CVTDW	Convert D_floating to word	src.rd, dst.ww	.	.	.	0
48	CVTFB	Convert F_floating to byte	src.rf, dst.wb	.	.	.	0
56	CVTFD	Convert F_floating to D_floating	src.rf, dst.wd	.	.	.	0
99FD	CVTFG	Convert F_floating to G_floating	src.rf, dst.wg	.	.	.	0
98FD	CVTFH	Convert F_floating to H_floating	src.rf, dst.wh	.	.	.	0
4A	CVTFL	Convert F_floating to long	src.rf, dst.wl	.	.	.	0
49	CVTFW	Convert F_floating to word	src.rf, dst.ww	.	.	.	0
48FD	CVTGB	Convert G_floating to byte	src.rg, dst.wb	.	.	.	0
33FD	CVTGF	Convert G_floating to F_floating	src.rg, dst.wf	.	.	.	0
56FD	CVTGH	Convert G_floating to H_floating	src.rg, dst.wh	.	.	.	0
4AFD	CVTGL	Convert G_floating to longword	src.rg, dst.wl	.	.	.	0
49FD	CVTGW	Convert G_floating to word	src.rg, dst.ww	.	.	.	0
68FD	CVTHB	Convert H_floating to byte	src.rh, dst.wb	.	.	.	0
F7FD	CVTHD	Convert H_floating to D_floating	srd.rh, dst.wd	.	.	.	0
F6FD	CVTHF	Convert H_floating to F_floating	src.rh, dst.wf	.	.	.	0
76FD	CVTHG	Convert H_floating to G_floating	srd.rh, dst.wg	.	.	.	0
6AFD	CVTHL	Convert H_floating to longword	srd.rh, dst.wl	.	.	.	0
69FD	CVTHW	Convert H_floating to word	src.rh, dst.ww	.	.	.	0
F6	CVTLB	Convert long to byte	src.rl, dst.wb	.	.	.	0
6E	CVTLD	Convert long to D_floating	src.rl, dst.wd	.	.	.	0
4E	CVTLF	Convert long to F_floating	src.rl, dst.wf	.	.	.	0
4EFD	CVTLG	Convert longword to G_floating	src.rl, dst.wg	.	.	.	0

OP	Mnemonic	Description	Arguments	Cond. Codes N Z V C
6EFD	CVTLH	Convert longword to H_floating	src.rl, dst.wh	. . . 0
F9	CVTLP	Convert long to packed	src.rl, dstlen.rw, dstaddr.ab, [R0-3.wl]	. . . 0
F7	CVTLW	Convert long to word	src.rl, dst.ww	. . . 0
36	CVTPL	Convert packed to long	srclen.rw, srcaddr.ab, [R0-3.wl], dst.wl	. . . 0
08	CVTPS	Convert packed to leading separate	srclen.rw, srcaddr.ab, dstlen.rw, dstaddr.ab, [R0-3.wl]	. . . 0
24	CVTPT	Convert packed to trailing	srclen.rw, srcaddr.ab, tbladdr.ab, dstlen.rw, dstaddr.ab, [R0-3.wl]	. . . 0
6B	CVTRDL	Convert rounded D_floating to long	src.rd, dst.wl	. . . 0
4B	CVTRFL	Convert rounded F_floating to long	src.rf, dst.wl	. . . 0
4BFD	CVTRGL	Convert rounded G_floating to long	src.rg, dst.wl	. . . 0
6BFD	CVTRHL	Convert rounded H_floating to long	src.rh, dst.wl	. . . 0
09	CVTSP	Convert leading separate to packed	srclen.rw, srcaddr.ab, dstlen.rw, dstaddr.ab, [R0-3.wl]	. . . 0
26	CVTTP	Convert trailing to packed	srclen.rw, srcaddr.ab, tbladdr.ab, dstlen.rw, dstaddr.ab, [R0-3.wl]	. . . 0
33	CVTWB	Convert word to byte	src.rw, dst.wb	. . . 0
6D	CVTWD	Convert word to D_floating	src.rw, dst.wd	. . . 0
4D	CVTWF	Convert word to F_floating	src.rw, dst.wf	. . . 0
4DFD	CVTWG	Convert word to G_floating	src.rw, dst.wg	. . . 0
6DFD	CVTWH	Convert word to H_floating	src.rw, dst.wh	. . . 0
32	CVTWL	Convert word to long	src.rw, dst.wl	. . . 0
97	DECB	Decrement byte	dif.mb	. . . .
D7	DECL	Decrement long	dif.ml	. . . .
B7	DECW	Decrement word	dif.mw	. . . .
86	DIVB2	Divide byte 2-operand	divr.rb, quo.mb	. . . 0
87	DIVB3	Divide byte 3-operand	divr.rb, divd.rb, quo.wb	. . . 0
66	DIVD2	Divide D_floating 2-operand	divr.rd, quo.md	. . . 0
67	DIVD3	Divide D_floating 3-operand	divr.rd, divd.rd, quo.wd	. . . 0
46	DIVF2	Divide F_floating 2-operand	divr.rf, quo.mf	. . . 0
47	DIVF3	Divide F_floating 3-operand	divr.rf, divd.rf, quo.wf	. . . 0
46FD	DIVG2	Divide G_floating 2-operand	divr.rg, quo.mg	. . . 0
47FD	DIVG3	Divide G_floating 3-operand	divr.rg, divd.rg, quo.wg	. . . 0
66FD	DIVH2	Divide H_floating 2-operand	divr.rh, quo.mh	. . . 0
67FD	DIVH3	Divide H_floating 3-operand	divr.rh, divd.rh, quo.wh	. . . 0
C6	DIVL2	Divide long 2-operand	divr.rl, quo.ml	. . . 0
C7	DIVL3	Divide long 3-operand	divr.rl, divd.rl, quo.wl	. . . 0
27	DIVP	Divide packed	divrlen.rw, divraddr.ab, divdlen.rw, divdaddr.ab, quolen.rw, quoaddr.ab, [R0-5.wl, − 16(SP): − 1(SP).wb]	. . . 0
A6	DIVW2	Divide word 2-operand	divr.rw, quo.mw	. . . 0
A7	DIVW3	Divide word 3-operand	divr.rw, divd.rw, quo.ww	. . . 0
38	EDITPC	Edit packed to character string	srclen.rw, srcaddr.ab, pattern.ab, dstaddr.ab, [R0-5.wl]	. . . .
7B	EDIV	Extended divide	divr.rl, divd.rq, quo.wl, rem.wl	. . . 0
74	EMODD	Extended modulus D_floating	mulr.rd, mulrx.rb, muld.rd, int.wl, fract.wd	. . . 0
54	EMODF	Extended modulus F_floating	mulr.rf, mulrx.rb, muld.rf, int.wl, fract.wf	. . . 0
54FD	EMODG	Extended modulus G_floating	mulr.rg, mulrx.rw, muld.rg, int.wl, fract.wg	. . . 0
74FD	EMODH	Extended modulus H_floating	mulr.rh, mulrx.rw, muld.rh, int.wl, fract.wh	. . . 0
7A	EMUL	Extended multiply	mulr.rl, muld.rl, add.rl, prod.wq	. . 0 0
FD	ESCD	Escape D		. . . .
FE	ESCE	Escape E		. . . .
FF	ESCF	Escape F		. . . .
EE	EXTV	Extract field	pos.rl, size.rb, base.vb, [field.rv], dst.wl	. . 0 -

OP	Mnemonic	Description	Arguments	N	Z	V	C
EF	EXTZV	Extract zero-extended field	pos.rl, size.rb, base.vb, [field.rv], dst.wl	.	.	0	-
EB	FFC	Find first clear bit	startpos.rl, size.rb, base.vb, [field.rv], findpos.wl	0	.	0	0
EA	FFS	Find first set bit	startpos.rl, size.rb, base.vb, [field.rv], findpos.wl	0	.	0	0
00	HALT	Halt (kernel mode only)	[−(KSP).w*]	.	.	.	.
96	INCB	Increment byte	sum.mb	.	.	.	.
D6	INCL	Increment long	sum.ml	.	.	.	.
B6	INCW	Increment word	sum.mw	.	.	.	.
0A	INDEX	Index calculation	subscript.rl, low.rl, high.rl, size.rl, entry.rl, addr.wl	.	.	0	0
5C	INSQHI	Insert at head of queue, interlocked	entry.ab, header.aq	0	.	0	.
5D	INSQTI	Insert at tail of queue, interlocked	entry.ab, header.aq	0	.	0	.
0E	INSQUE	Insert into queue	entry.ab, addr.wl	.	.	0	.
F0	INSV	Insert field	src.rl, pos.rl, size.rb, base.vb, [field.wv]	-	-	-	-
17	JMP	Jump	dst.ab	-	-	-	-
16	JSB	Jump to subroutine	dst.ab, [−(SP) + .wl]	-	-	-	-
06	LDPCTX	Load process context (kernel mode only)	[PCB.r*, −(KSP).w*]	-	-	-	-
3A	LOCC	Locate character	char.rb, len.rw, addr.ab, [R0-1.wl]	0	.	0	0
39	MATCHC	Match characters	len1.rw, addr1.ab, len2.rw, addr2.ab, [R0-3.wl]	0	.	0	0
92	MCOMB	Move complemented byte	src.rb, dst.wb	.	.	0	-
D2	MCOML	Move complemented long	src.rl, dst.wl	.	.	0	-
B2	MCOMW	Move complemented word	src.rw, dst.ww	.	.	0	-
DB	MFPR	Move from processor register (kernel mode only)	procreg.rl, dst.wl	.	.	0	-
8E	MNEGB	Move negated byte	src.rb, dst.wb	.	.	.	.
72	MNEGD	Move negated D_floating	src.rd, dst.wd	.	.	0	0
52	MNEGF	Move negated F_floating	src.rf, dst.wf	.	.	0	0
52FD	MNEGG	Move negated G_floating	src.rg, dst.wg	.	.	0	0
72FD	MNEGH	Move negated H_floating	src.rh, dst.wh	.	.	0	0
CE	MNEGL	Move negated long	src.rl, dst.wl	.	.	.	.
AE	MNEGW	Move negated word	src.rw, dst.ww	.	.	.	.
9E	MOVAB	Move address of byte	src.ab, dst.wl	.	.	0	-
7E	MOVAD	Move address of D_floating	src.aq, dst.wl	.	.	0	-
DE	MOVAF	Move address of F_floating	src.al, dst.wl	.	.	0	-
7E	MOVAG	Move address of G_floating	src.aq, dst.wl	.	.	0	-
7EFD	MOVAH	Move address of H_floating	src.ao, dst.w l	.	.	0	-
DE	MOVAL	Move address of long	src.al, dst.wl	.	.	0	-
7EFD	MOVAO	Move address of octaword	src.ao, dst.wl	.	.	0	-
7E	MOVAQ	Move address of quad	src.aq, dst.wl	.	.	0	-
3E	MOVAW	Move address of word	src.aw, dst.wl	.	.	0	-
90	MOVB	Move byte	src.rb, dst.wb	.	.	0	-
28	MOVC3	Move character 3-operand	len.rw, srcaddr.ab, dstaddr.ab, [R0-5.wl]	0	1	0	0
2C	MOVC5	Move character 5-operand	srclen.rw, srcaddr.ab, fill.rb, dstlen.rw, dstaddr.ab, [R0-5.wl]	.	.	0	.
70	MOVD	Move D_floating	src.rd, dst.wd	.	.	0	-
50	MOVF	Move F_floating	src.rf, dst.wf	.	.	0	-
50FD	MOVG	Move G_floating	src.rg, dst.wg	.	.	0	-
70FD	MOVH	Move H_floating	src.rh, dst.wh	.	.	0	-
D0	MOVL	Move long	src.rl, dst.wl	.	.	0	-
7DFD	MOVO	Move octaword	src.ro, dst.wo	.	.	0	-

OP	Mnemonic	Description	Arguments	N	Z	V	C
34	MOVP	Move packed	len.rw, srcaddr.ab, dstaddr.ab, [R0-3.wl]	.	.	0	-
DC	MOVPSL	Move processor status longword	dst.wl	-	-	-	-
7D	MOVQ	Move quad	src.rq, dst.wq	.	.	0	-
2E	MOVTC	Move translated characters	srclen.rw, srcaddr.ab, fill.rb, tbladdr.ab, dstlen.rw, dstaddr.ab, [R0-5.wl]	.	.	0	.
2F	MOVTUC	Move translated until character	srclen.rw, srcaddr.ab, escape.rb, tbladdr.ab, dstlen.rw, dstaddr.ab, [R0-5.wl]	.	.	.	.
B0	MOVW	Move word	src.rw, dst.ww	.	.	0	-
9A	MOVZBL	Move zero-extended byte to long	src.rb, dst.wl	0	.	0	-
9B	MOVZBW	Move zero-extended byte to word	src.rb, dst.ww	0	.	0	-
3C	MOVZWL	Move zero-extended word to long	src.rw, dst.wl	0	.	0	-
DA	MTPR	Move to processor register (kernel mode only)	src.rl, procreg.wl	.	.	0	-
84	MULB2	Multiply byte 2-operand	mulr.rb, prod.mb	.	.	.	0
85	MULB3	Multiply byte 3-operand	mulr.rb, muld.rb, prod.wb	.	.	.	0
64	MULD2	Multiply D_floating 2-operand	mulr.rd, prod.md	.	.	.	0
65	MULD3	Multiply D_floating 3-operand	mulr.rd, muld.rd, prod.wd	.	.	.	0
44	MULF2	Multiply F_floating 2-operand	mulr.rf, prod.mf	.	.	.	0
45	MULF3	Multiply F_floating 3-operand	mulr.rf, muld.rf, prod.wf	.	.	.	0
44FD	MULG2	Multiply G_floating 2-operand	mulr.rg, prod.mg	.	.	.	0
45FD	MULG3	Multiply G_floating 3-operand	mulr.rg, muld.rg, prod.wg	.	.	.	0
64FD	MULH2	Multiply G_floating 2-operand	mulr.rh, prod.mh	.	.	.	0
65FD	MULH3	Multiply H_floating 3-operand	mulr.rh, muld.rh, prod.wh	.	.	.	0
C4	MULL2	Multiply long 2-operand	mulr.rl, prod.ml	.	.	.	0
C5	MULL3	Multiply long 3-operand	mulr.rl, muld.rl, prod.wl	.	.	.	0
25	MULP	Multiply packed	mulrlen.rw, mulradr.ab, muldlen.rw, muldadr.ab, prodlen.rw, prodadr.ab, [R0-5.wl]	.	.	.	0
A4	MULW2	Multiply word 2-operand	mulr.rw, prod.mw	.	.	.	0
A5	MULW3	Multiply word 3-operand	mulr.rw, muld.rw, prod.ww	.	.	.	0
01	NOP	No operation		-	-	-	-
75	POLYD	Evaluate polynomial D_floating	arg.rd, degree.rw, tbladdr.ab, [R0-5.wl]	.	.	.	0
55	POLYF	Evaluate polynomial F_floating	arg.rf, degree.rw, tbladdr.ab, [R0-3.wl]	.	.	.	0
55FD	POLYG	Evaluate polynomial G_floating	arg.rg, degree.rw, tbladdr.ab, [R0-5.wl]	.	.	.	0
75FD	POLYH	Evaluate polynomial H_floating	arg.rh, degree.rw, tbladdr.ab, [R0-5.wl, −16(SP):−1(SP).wl]	.	.	.	0
BA	POPR	Pop registers	mask.rw, [(SP)+.r*]	-	-	-	-
0C	PROBER	Probe read access	mode.rb, len.rw, base.ab	0	.	0	-
0D	PROBEW	Probe write access	mode.rb, len.rw, base.ab	0	.	0	-
9F	PUSHAB	Push address of byte	src.ab, [−(SP).wl]	.	.	0	-
7F	PUSHAD	Push address of D_floating	src.aq, [−(SP).wl]	.	.	0	-
DF	PUSHAF	Push address of F_floating	src.al, [−(SP).wl]	.	.	0	-
7F	PUSHAG	Push address of G_floating	src.aq, [−(SP).wl]	.	.	0	-
7FFD	PUSHAH	Push address of H_floating	src.ao, [−(SP).wl]	.	.	0	-
DF	PUSHAL	Push address of long	src.al, [−(SP).wl]	.	.	0	-
7FFD	PUSHAO	Push address of octaword	src.ao, [−(SP).wl]	.	.	0	-
7F	PUSHAQ	Push address of quad	src.aq, [−(SP).wl]	.	.	0	-
3F	PUSHAW	Push address of word	src.aw, [−(SP).wl]	.	.	0	-
DD	PUSHL	Push long	src.rl, [−(SP).wl]	.	.	0	-
BB	PUSHR	Push registers	mask.rw, [−(SP).w*]	-	-	-	-
02	REI	Return from exception or interrupt	[(SP)+.r*]	.	.	.	.
5E	REMQHI	Remove from head of queue, interlocked	header.aq, addr.wl	0	.	.	.

OP	Mnemonic	Description	Arguments	N	Z	V	C
				Cond. Codes

OP	Mnemonic	Description	Arguments	N	Z´	V	C
5F	REMQTI	Remove from tail of queue, interlocked	header.aq, addr.wl	0	.	.	.
0F	REMQUE	Remove from queue	entry.ab, addr.wl	.	.	.	.
04	RET	Return from procedure	[(SP) + .r*]	.	.	.	.
9C	ROTL	Rotate long	count.rb, src.rl, dst.wl	.	.	0	-
05	RSB	Return from subroutine	[(SP) + .rl]	-	-	-	-
57	Reserved	Reserved					
5A	Reserved	Reserved					
5B	Reserved	Reserved					
77	Reserved	Reserved					
FE	Reserved	Reserved					
FF	Reserved	Reserved					
D9	SBWC	Subtract with carry	sub.rl, dif.ml	.	.	.	.
2A	SCANC	Scan for character	len.rw, addr.ab, tbladdr.ab, mask.rb, [R0-3.wl]	0	.	0	0
3B	SKPC	Skip character	char.rb, len.rw, addr.ab. [R0-1.wl]	0	.	0	0
F4	SOBGEQ	Subtract one and branch on greater or equal	index.ml, displ.bb	.	.	.	-
F5	SOBGTR	Subtract one and branch on greater	index.ml, displ.bb	.	.	.	-
2B	SPANC	Span characters	len.rw, addr.ab, tbladdr.ab, mask.rb, [R0-3.wl]	0	.	0	0
82	SUBB2	Subtract byte 2-operand	sub.rb, dif.mb	.	.	.	.
83	SUBB3	Subtract byte 3-operand	sub.rb, min.rb, dif.wb	.	.	.	.
62	SUBD2	Subtract D_floating 2-operand	sub.rd, dif.md	.	.	.	0
63	SUBD3	Subtract D_floating 3-operand	sub.rd, min.rd, dif.wd	.	.	.	0
42	SUBF2	Subtract F_floating 2-operand	sub.rf, dif.mf	.	.	.	0
43	SUBF3	Subtract F_floating 3-operand	sub.rf, min.rf, dif.wf	.	.	.	0
42FD	SUBG2	Subtract G_floating 2-operand	sub.rg, dif.mg	.	.	.	0
43FD	SUBG3	Subtract G_floating 3-operand	sub.rg, min.rg, dif.wg	.	.	.	0
62FD	SUBH2	Subtract H_floating 2-operand	sub.rh, dif.mh	.	.	.	0
63FD	SUBH3	Subtract H_floating 3-operand	sub.rh, min.rh, dif.wh	.	.	.	0
C2	SUBL2	Subtract long 2-operand	sub.rl, dif.ml	.	.	.	.
C3	SUBL3	Subtract long 3-operand	sub.rl, min.rl, dif.wl	.	.	.	.
22	SUBP4	Subtract packed 4-operand	sublen.rw, subaddr.ab, diflen.rw, difaddr.ab, [R0-3.wl]	.	.	.	0

OP	Mnemonic	Description	Arguments	Cond. Codes N Z V C
23	SUBP6	Subtract packed 6-operand	sublen.rw, subaddr.ab, minlen.rw, minaddr.ab, diflen.rw, difaddr.ab, [R0-5.wl]	. . . 0
A2	SUBW2	Subtract word 2-operand	sub.rw, dif.mw	. . . .
A3	SUBW3	Subtract word 3-operand	sub.rw, min.rw, dif.ww	. . . .
07	SVPCTX	Save process context (kernel mode only)	[(SP) + .r*, ¬(KSP).w*]	- - - -
95	TSTB	Test byte	src.rb	. . 0 0
73	TSTD	Test D_floating	src.rd	. . 0 0
53	TSTF	Test F_floating	src.rf	. . 0 0
53FD	TSTG	Test G_floating	src.rg	. . 0 0
73FD	TSTH	Test H_floating	src.rh	. . 0 0
D5	TSTL	Test long	src.rl	. . 0 0
B5	TSTW	Test word	src.rw	. . 0 0
FC	XFC	Extended function call	user defined operands	0 0 0 0
8C	XORB2	Exclusive or byte 2-operand	mask.rb, dst.mb	. . 0 -
8D	XORB3	Exclusive or byte 3-operand	mask.rb, src.rb, dst.wb	. . 0 -
CC	XORL2	Exclusive or long 2-operand	mask.rl., dst.ml	. . 0 -
CD	XORL3	Exclusive or long 3-operand	mask.rl, src.rl, dst.wl	. . 0 -
AC	XORW2	Exclusive or word 2-operand	mask.rw, dst.mw	. . 0 -
AD	XORW3	Exclusive or word 3-operand	mask.rw, src.rw, dst.ww	. . 0 -

INSTRUCTIONS

Numeric Order

00	HALT	10	BSBB	1E	BCC	2C	MOVC5	3A	LOCC		
01	NOP	11	BRB	1E	BGEQU	2D	CMPC5	3B	SKPC		
02	REI	12	BNEQ	1F	BCS	2E	MOVTC	3C	MOVZWL		
03	BPT	12	BNEQU	1F	BLSSU	2F	MOVTUC	3D	ACBW		
04	RET	13	BEQL	20	ADDP4	30	BSBW	3E	MOVAW		
05	RSB	13	BEQLU	21	ADDP6	31	BRW	3F	PUSHAW		
06	LDPCTX	14	BGTR	22	SUBP4	32	CVTWL	40	ADDF2		
07	SVPCTX	15	BLEQ	23	SUBP6	32FD	CVTDH	40FD	ADDG2		
08	CVTPS	16	JSB	24	CVTPT	33	CVTWB	41	ADDF3		
09	CVTSP	17	JMP	25	MULP	33FD	CVTGF	41FD	ADDG3		
0A	INDEX	18	BGEQ	26	CVTTP	34	MOVP	42	SUBF2		
0B	CRC	19	BLSS	27	DIVP	35	CMPP3	42FD	SUBG2		
0C	PROBER	1A	BGTRU	28	MOVC3	36	CVTPL	43	SUBF3		
0D	PROBEW	1B	BLEQU	29	CMPC3	37	CMPP4	43FD	SUBG3		
0E	INSQUE	1C	BVC	2A	SCANC	38	EDITPC	44	MULF2		
0F	REMQUE	1D	BVS	2B	SPANC	39	MATCHC	44FD	MULG2		

45	MULF3	4E	CVTLF	57	Reserved	65	MULD3	6E	CVTLD		
45FD	MULG3	4EFD	CVTLG	58	ADAWI	65FD	MULH3	6EFD	CVTLH		
46	DIVF2	4F	ACBF	5A	Reserved	66	DIVD2	6F	ACBD		
46FD	DIVG2	4FFD	ACBG	5B	Reserved	66FD	DIVH2	6FFD	ACBH		
47	DIVF3	50	MOVF	5C	INSQHI	67	DIVD3	70	MOVD		
47FD	DIVG3	50FD	MOVG	5D	INSQTI	67FD	DIVH3	70FD	MOVH		
48	CVTFB	51	CMPF	5E	REMQHI	68	CVTDB	71	CMPD		
48FD	CVTGB	51FD	CMPG	5F	REMQTI	68FD	CVTHB	71FD	CMPH		
49	CVTFW	52	MNEGF	60	ADDD2	69	CVTDW	72	MNEGD		
49FD	CVTGW	52FD	MNEGG	60FD	ADDH2	69FD	CVTHW	72FD	MNEGH		
4A	CVTFL	53	TSTF	61	ADDD3	6A	CVTDL	73	TSTD		
4AFD	CVTGL	53FD	TSTG	61FD	ADDH3	6AFD	CVTHL	73FD	TSTH		
4B	CVTRFL	54	EMODF	62	SUBD2	6B	CVTRDL	74	EMODD		
4BFD	CVTRGL	54FD	EMODG	62FD	SUBH2	6BFD	CVTRHL	74FD	EMODH		
4C	CVTBF	55	POLYF	63	SUBD3	6C	CVTBD	75	POLYD		
4CFD	CVTBG	55FD	POLYG	63FD	SUBH3	6CFD	CVTBH	75FD	POLYH		
4D	CVTWF	56	CVTFD	64	MULD2	6D	CVTWD	76	CVTDF		
4DFD	CVTWG	56FD	CVTGH	64FD	MULH2	6DFD	CVTWH	76FD	CVTHG		

77	Reserved	7F	PUSHAG	8E	MNEGB	9E	MOVAB	B0	MOVW		
78	ASHL	7F	PUSHAQ	8F	CASEB	9F	PUSHAB	B1	CMPW		
79	ASHQ	7FFD	PUSHAH	90	MOVB	A0	ADDW2	B2	MCOMW		
7A	EMUL	7FFD	PUSHAO	91	CMPB	A1	ADDW3	B3	BITW		
7B	EDIV	80	ADDB2	92	MCOMB	A2	SUBW2	B4	CLRW		
7C	CLRD	81	ADDB3	93	BITB	A3	SUBW3	B5	TSTW		
7C	CLRG	82	SUBB2	94	CLRB	A4	MULW2	B6	INCW		
7C	CLRQ	83	SUBB3	95	TSTB	A5	MULW3	B7	DECW		
7CFD	CLRH	84	MULB2	96	INCB	A6	DIVW2	B8	BISPSW		
7CFD	CLRO	85	MULB3	97	DECB	A7	DIVW3	B9	BICPSW		
7D	MOVQ	86	DIVB2	98	CVTBL	A8	BISW2	BA	POPR		
7DFD	MOVO	87	DIVB3	98FD	CVTFH	A9	BISW3	BB	PUSHR		
7E	MOVAD	88	BISB2	99	CVTBW	AA	BICW2	BC	CHMK		
7E	MOVAG	89	BISB3	99FD	CVTFG	AB	BICW3	BD	CHME		
7E	MOVAQ	8A	BICB2	9A	MOVZBL	AC	XORW2	BE	CHMS		
7EFD	MOVAH	8B	BICB3	9B	MOVZBW	AD	XORW3	BF	CHMU		
7EFD	MOVAO	8C	XORB2	9C	ROTL	AE	MNEGW	C0	ADDL2		
7F	PUSHAD	8D	XORB3	9D	ACBB	AF	CASEW	C1	ADDL3		

Numeric Order

C2	SUBL2	D4	CLRF	E3	BBCS	F5	SOBGTR
C3	SUBL3	D4	CLRL	E4	BBSC	F6	CVTLB
C4	MULL2	D5	TSTL	E5	BBCC	F6FD	CVTHF
C5	MULL3	D6	INCL	E6	BBSSI	F7	CVTLW
C6	DIVL2	D7	DECL	E7	BBCCI	F7FD	CVTHD
C7	DIVL3	D8	ADWC	E8	BLBS	F8	ASHP
C8	BISL2	D9	SBWC	E9	BLBC	F9	CVTLP
C9	BISL3	DA	MTPR	EA	FFS	FA	CALLG
CA	BICL2	DB	MFPR	EB	FFC	FB	CALLS
CB	BICL3	DC	MOVPSL	EC	CMPV	FC	XFC
CC	XORL2	DD	PUSHL	ED	CMPZV	FD	ESCD
CD	XORL3	DE	MOVAF	EE	EXTV	FDFF	BUGL
CE	MNEGL	DE	MOVAL	EF	EXTZV	FE	ESCE
CF	CASEL	DF	PUSHAF	F0	INSV	FE	Reserved
D0	MOVL	DF	PUSHAL	F1	ACBL	FEFF	BUGW
D1	CMPL	E0	BBS	F2	AOBLSS	FF	ESCF
D2	MCOML	E1	BBC	F3	AOBLEQ	FF	Reserved
D3	BITL	E2	BBSS	F4	SOBGEQ		

Hexadecimal to Decimal Conversion Table

	8		7		6		5		4		3		2		1
HEX	DEC	HEX	DEC	HEX	DEC	HEX	DEC	HEX	DEC	HEX	DEC	HEX	DEC	HEX	DEC
0	0	0	0	0	0	0	0	0	0	0	0	0	0	0	0
1	268,435,456	1	16,777,216	1	1,048,576	1	65,536	1	4,096	1	256	1	16	1	1
2	536,870,912	2	33,554,432	2	2,097,152	2	131,072	2	8,192	2	512	2	32	2	2
3	805,306,368	3	50,331,648	3	3,145,728	3	196,608	3	12,288	3	768	3	48	3	3
4	1,073,741,824	4	67,108,864	4	4,194,304	4	262,144	4	16,384	4	1,024	4	64	4	4
5	1,342,177,280	5	83,886,080	5	5,242,880	5	327,680	5	20,480	5	1,280	5	80	5	5
6	1,610,612,736	6	100,663,296	6	6,291,456	6	393,216	6	24,576	6	1,536	6	96	6	6
7	1,879,048,192	7	117,440,512	7	7,340,032	7	458,752	7	28,672	7	1,792	7	112	7	7
8	2,147,483,648	8	134,217,728	8	8,388,608	8	524,288	8	32,768	8	2,048	8	128	8	8
9	2,415,929,104	9	150,994,994	9	9,437,184	9	589,824	9	36,864	9	2,304	9	144	9	9
A	2,684,354,560	A	167,772,160	A	10,485,760	A	655,360	A	40,960	A	2,560	A	160	A	10
B	2,952,790,016	B	184,549,376	B	11,534,336	B	720,896	B	45,056	B	2,816	B	176	B	11
C	3,221,225,472	C	201,326,592	C	12,582,912	C	786,432	C	49,152	C	3,072	C	192	C	12
D	3,489,660,928	D	218,103,808	D	12,631,488	D	851,968	D	53,248	D	3,328	D	208	D	13
E	3,758,096,384	E	234,881,024	E	14,680,064	E	917,504	E	57,344	E	3,584	E	224	E	14
F	4,026,531,840	F	251,685,240	F	15,728,640	F	983,040	F	61,440	F	3,840	F	240	F	15

DATA TYPES

BYTE

```
 7              0
┌──────────────┐
│              │ :A
└──────────────┘
```

WORD

```
 1
 5                         0
┌──────────────────────────┐
│                          │ :A
└──────────────────────────┘
```

LONGWORD

```
 3
 1                                      0
┌────────────────────────────────────────┐
│                                        │ :A
└────────────────────────────────────────┘
```

QUADWORD

```
 3
 1                                      0
┌────────────────────────────────────────┐
│                                        │ :A
├────────────────────────────────────────┤
│                                        │ :A+4
└────────────────────────────────────────┘
 6                                      3
 3                                      2
```

MK4675

OCTAWORD

```
 3
 1                                      0
┌────────────────────────────────────────┐
│                                        │ :A
├────────────────────────────────────────┤
│                                        │ :A+4
├────────────────────────────────────────┤
│                                        │ :A+8
├────────────────────────────────────────┤
│                                        │ :A+12
└────────────────────────────────────────┘
 1                                      9
 2                                      6
 7
```

F __ FLOATING

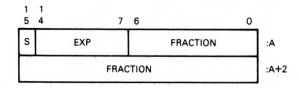

D __ FLOATING

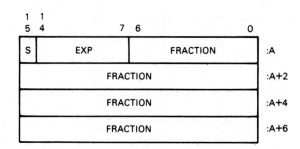

MK4676

G __ FLOATING

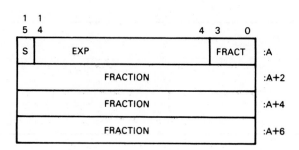

H — FLOATING

```
 1  1
 5  4                                    0
┌───┬──────────────────────────────────┐
│ S │           EXPONENT               │  :A
├───┴──────────────────────────────────┤
│              FRACTION                │  :A+2
├──────────────────────────────────────┤
│              FRACTION                │  :A+4
├──────────────────────────────────────┤
│              FRACTION                │  :A+6
├──────────────────────────────────────┤
│              FRACTION                │  :A+8
├──────────────────────────────────────┤
│              FRACTION                │  :A+10
├──────────────────────────────────────┤
│              FRACTION                │  :A+12
├──────────────────────────────────────┤
│              FRACTION                │  :A+14
└──────────────────────────────────────┘
```
                                        MK4679

Variable Length Bit Field

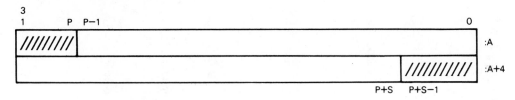

```
 3
 1       P   P−1                                      0
┌────────┬──────────────────────────────────────────┐
│////////│                                           │  :A
├────────┴────────────────────────┬──────────────────┤
│                                 │//////////////////│  :A+4
└─────────────────────────────────┴──────────────────┘
                                  P+S    P+S−1
```

P = STARTING LOCATION OF BIT FIELD
S = SIZE OF FIELD

                                        MK4680

Character String

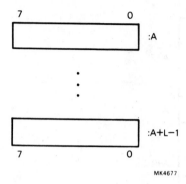

MK4677

Trailing Numeric String

Representation of Least Significant Digit and Sign

	Zoned Numeric Format				Overpunch Format		
Digit	Decimal	Hex	ASCII Char	Decimal	Hex	ASCII Character Norm	Alt.
0	48	30	0	123	7B	{	0 [?
1	49	31	1	65	41	A	1
2	50	32	2	66	42	B	2
3	51	33	3	67	43	C	3
4	52	34	4	68	44	D	4
5	53	35	5	69	45	E	5
6	54	36	6	70	46	F	6
7	55	37	7	71	47	G	7
8	56	38	8	72	48	H	8
9	57	39	9	73	49	I	9

Zoned Numeric Format

Digit	Decimal	Hex	ASCII Char
−0	112	70	p
−1	113	71	q
−2	114	72	r
−3	115	73	s
−4	116	74	t
−5	117	75	u
−6	118	76	v
−7	119	77	w
−8	120	78	x
−9	121	79	y

Overpunch Format

Decimal	Hex	ASCII Character Norm	Alt.
125	7D	}	] ! :
74	4A	J	
75	4B	K	
76	4C	L	
77	4D	M	
78	4E	N	
79	4F	O	
80	50	P	
81	51	Q	
82	52	R	

Leading Separate Numeric String Sign Representation

Sign	Decimal	Hex	ASCII Character
+	43	2B	+
+	32	20	<blank>
-	45	2D	-

The preferred representation for " + " is ASCII " + ".

Packed Decimal String

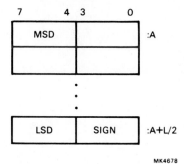

MK4678

Packed Decimal Sign Nibble Representation

Sign	Decimal	Hex
+	10, 12, 14 or 15	A, C, E, or F
−	11 or 13	B or D

The preferred sign representation is 12 for " + " and 13 for " − ".

ASSEMBLER NOTATION FOR ADDRESSING MODES

S∧#5	forced short literal
#5	optimized short literal
R10	register
(R10)	register deferred
−(R10)	autodecrement
(R10)+	autoincrement
#START	immediate
I∧#1	forced immediate
@(R10)+	autoincrement deferred
@#START	absolute
1(R10)	optimized byte displacement
0(R10)	optimized register deferred
@1(R10)	optimized byte displacement deferred
@(R10)	implied byte displacement deferred
START	optimized pc relative
@START	optimized pc relative deferred
1234(R10)	optimized word displacement
@1234(R10)	optimized word displacement deferred
12345678(R10)	longword displacement
@12345678(R10)	longword displacement deferred
B∧12(R10)	forced byte displacement
B∧START	forced byte pc relative
@B∧12(R10)	forced byte displacement deferred
@B∧START	forced byte pc relative deferred
W∧12(R10)	forced word displacement
W∧START	forced word pc relative
@W∧12(R10)	forced word displacement deferred
@W∧START	forced word pc relative deferred
L∧12(R10)	forced longword displacement
L∧START	forced longword pc relative
@L∧12(R10)	forced longword displacement deferred
@L∧START	forced longword pc relative deferred
(R10)[R11]	register deferred index
−(R10)[R11]	autodecrement indexed
(R10)+[R11]	autoincrement indexed
@(R10)+[R11]	autoincrement deferred indexed

@#START[R11]	absolute indexed
1(R10)[R11]	optimized byte displacement indexed
0(R10)[R11]	optimized register deferred indexed
@1(R10)[R11]	optimized byte displacement deferred indexed
@(R10)[R11]	implied byte displacement deferred indexed
1234(R10)[R11]	optimized word displacement indexed
@1234(R10)[R11]	optimized word displacement deferred indexed
12345678(R10)[R11]	longword displacement indexed
@12345678(R10)[R11]	longword displacement deferred indexed
START[R11]	optimized pc relative indexed
@START[R11]	optimized pc relative deferred indexed
B^12(R10)[R11]	forced byte displacement indexed
B^START[R11]	forced byte pc relative indexed
@B^12(R10)[R11]	forced byte displacement deferred indexed
@B^START[R11]	forced byte pc relative deferred indexed
W^12(R10)[R11]	forced word displacement indexed
W^START[R11]	forced word pc relative indexed
@W^12(R10)[R11]	forced word displacement deferred indexed
@W^START[R11]	forced word pc relative deferred indexed
L^12(R10)[R11]	forced longword displacement indexed
L^START[R11]	forced longword pc relative indexed
@L^12(R10)[R11]	forced longword displacement deferred indexed
@L^START[R11]	forced longword pc relative deferred

PROCESSOR STATUS LONGWORD

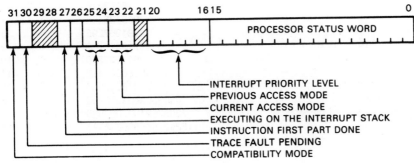

MK4790

PROCESSOR STATUS WORD

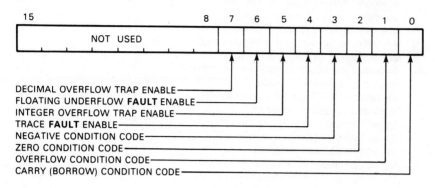

MK4791

POWERS OF 2

2^n	n
256	8
512	9
1024	10
2048	11
4096	12
8192	13
16384	14
32768	15
65536	16
131072	17
262144	18
524288	19
1048576	20
2097152	21
4194304	22
8388608	23
16777216	24

POWERS OF 16

16^n	n
1	0
16	1
256	2
4096	3
65536	4
1048576	5
16777216	6
268435456	7
4294967296	8
68719476736	9
1099511627776	10
17592186044416	11
281474976710656	12
4503599627370496	13
72057594037927936	14
1152921504606846976	15

STACK FRAME FORMAT

CONDITION HANDLER (INITIALLY 0)					:(FP)

SPA	S	0	MASK<11:0>	SAVED PSW <14:5>	0
SAVED AP					
SAVED FP					
SAVED PC					
SAVED R0					

⋮   ⋮

SAVED R11

(0 TO 3 BYTES SPECIFIED BY SPA, STACK POINTER ALIGNMENT)
S = SET IF CALLS; CLEAR IF CALLG.

TK-10860

ARGUMENT LIST FORMAT:

The argument count N is an unsigned byte contained in the first byte of the list. The high order 24 bits of the first longword are reserved for future use and must be zero.

0	N	:(AP)
N LONGWORDS OF ARGUMENT LIST		

Hexadecimal–ASCII Conversion

Hexadecimal – ASCII Conversion

HEX Code	ASCII Char	HEX Code	ASCII Char	HEX Code	ASCII Char	HEX Code	ASCII Char
00	NUL	20	SP	40	(a	60	
01	SOH	21	!	41	A	61	a
02	STX	22	"	42	B	62	b
03	ETX	23	#	43	C	63	c
04	EOT	24	$	44	D	64	d
05	ENQ	25	%	45	E	65	e
06	ACK	26	&	46	F	66	f
07	BEL	27	'	47	G	67	g
08	BS	28	(	48	H	68	h
09	HT	29	)	49	I	69	i
0A	LF	2A	*	4A	J	6A	j
0B	VT	2B	+	4B	K	6B	k
0C	FF	2C	,	4C	L	6C	l
0D	CR	2D	-	4D	M	6D	m
0E	SO	2E	.	4E	N	6E	n
0F	SI	2F	/	4F	O	6F	o
10	DLE	30	0	50	P	70	p
11	DC1	31	1	51	Q	71	q
12	DC2	32	2	52	R	72	r
13	DC3	33	3	53	S	73	s
14	DC4	34	4	54	T	74	t
15	NAK	35	5	55	U	75	u
16	SYN	36	6	56	V	76	v
17	ETB	37	7	57	W	77	w
18	CAN	38	8	58	X	78	x
19	EM	39	9	59	Y	79	y
1A	SUB	3A	:	5A	Z	7A	z
1B	ESC	3B	;	5B	[	7B	{
1C	FS	3C	<	5C	\	7C	l
1D	GS	3D	=	5D	]	7D	}
1E	RS	3E	>	5E	^	7E	~
1F	US	3F	?	5F	–	7F	DEL

Answers
to Selected Exercises

Chapter 1
Exercise Set 1, page 8

1. **a.** Herman Hollerith invented punched card data processing. His equipment was used to tabulate the 1890 United States census.

   b. Howard Aiken completed the first large scale digital computer in 1944. Since the Mark I used electromechanical devices such as relays, it was much slower than the electronic computers that followed it.

   c. Presper Eckert is the coinventor (with John Mauchly) of the electronic digital computer. Eckert and Mauchly completed the first electronic computer, ENIAC, in 1946.

   d. John Mauchly is the coinventor (with Presper Eckert) of the electronic digital computer.

   e. John von Neumann was a legendary mathematician whose name is intimately connected with the development of digital computers in the 1940's and early 1950's.

   f. John Backus lead the group at International Business Machines (IBM) that developed one of the first higher level languages, FORTRAN. FORTRAN (FORmula TRANslation), developed beginning in 1954, was designed to perform complex mathematical calculations.

3. Vacuum-tube computers are larger, consume more energy, are slower, are more expensive, and are less reliable than their later counterparts.

Exercise Set 2, pages 16-18

```
7. J:     .BLKL    1
   K:     .BLKL    1
          .ENTRY   START,0
          MOVL     $50,J
          MULL3    $32,J,K
          $EXIT_S
          .END     START
```

Chapter 2
Exercise Set 1, pages 32-34

2.

Dec	Hex	Binary	Dec	Hex	Binary	Dec	Hex	Binary	Dec	Hex	Binary
101	65	1100101	126	7E	1111110	151	97	10010111	176	B0	10110000
102	66	1100110	127	7F	1111111	152	98	10011000	177	B1	10110001
103	67	1100111	128	80	10000000	153	99	10011001	178	B2	10110010
104	68	1101000	129	81	10000001	154	9A	10011010	179	B3	10110011
105	69	1101001	130	82	10000010	155	9B	10011011	180	B4	10110100
106	6A	1101010	131	83	10000011	156	9C	10011100	181	B5	10110101
107	6B	1101011	132	84	10000100	157	9D	10011101	182	B6	10110110
108	6C	1101100	133	85	10000101	158	9E	10011110	183	B7	10110111
109	6D	1101101	134	86	10000110	159	9F	10011111	184	B8	10111000
110	6E	1101110	135	87	10000111	160	A0	10100000	185	B9	10111001
111	6F	1101111	136	88	10001000	161	A1	10100001	186	BA	10111010
112	70	1110000	137	89	10001001	162	A2	10100010	187	BB	10111011
113	71	1110001	138	8A	10001010	163	A3	10100011	188	BC	10111100
114	72	1110010	139	8B	10001011	164	A4	10100100	189	BD	10111101
115	73	1110011	140	8C	10001100	165	A5	10100101	190	BE	10111110
116	74	1110100	141	8D	10001101	166	A6	10100110	191	BF	10111111
117	75	1110101	142	8E	10001110	167	A7	10100111	192	C0	11000000
118	76	1110110	143	8F	10001111	168	A8	10101000	193	C1	11000001
119	77	1110111	144	90	10010000	169	A9	10101001	194	C2	11000010
120	78	1111000	145	91	10010001	170	AA	10101010	195	C3	11000011
121	79	1111001	146	92	10010010	171	AB	10101011	196	C4	11000100
122	7A	1111010	147	93	10010011	172	AC	10101100	197	C5	11000101
123	7B	1111011	148	94	10010100	173	AD	10101101	198	C6	11000110
124	7C	1111100	149	95	10010101	174	AE	10101110	199	C7	11000111
125	7D	1111101	150	96	10010110	175	AF	10101111	200	C8	11001000

3. a. 1000   **b.** 1011   **c.** 1010
  d. 100001   **e.** 100100   **f.** 100010
    g. 10001000   **h.** 1001011111   **i.** 1100001111101

4. **a.** 10   **b.** 1   **c.** 0
  d. 1101   **e.** 10010   **f.** 11000
  g. 101110   **h.** 11111011   **i.** 1001001001

5. **a.** 5   **b.** 26   **c.** 58
  d. 46   **e.** 51   **f.** 93
  g. 99   **h.** 111   **i.** 229
  j. 939   **k.** 2977   **l.** 12974

6. **a.** ^X5   **b.** ^X1A   **c.** ^X3A
  d. ^X2E   **e.** ^X33   **f.** ^X5D
  g. ^X63   **h.** ^X6F   **i.** ^XE5
  j. ^X3AB   **k.** ^XBA1   **l.** ^X32AE

7. **a.** ^XB1   **b.** ^FD   **c.** ^X18D
  d. ^XAFD   **e.** ^X981   **f.** ^X1B18
  g. ^XA82F   **h.** ^X85FC   **i.** ^X3B88

8. **a.** ^X4D   **b.** ^XC9   **c.** ^X39
  d. ^X9F9   **e.** ^X247   **f.** ^X1FE
  g. ^XA343   **h.** ^XBFE   **i.** ^X1B8A

9. **a.** 10   **b.** 16   **c.** 256
  d. 31   **e.** 42   **f.** 69
  g. 164   **h.** 200   **i.** 218
  j. 4,980   **k.** 6,717   **l.** 62,430

10. **a.** 1010   **b.** 1111   **c.** 11000
  d. 100101   **e.** 101010   **f.** 110011
  g. 1010101   **h.** 1100001   **i.** 10000000
  j. 1111101000   **k.** 110111100011   **l.** 1011101101111

11. **a.** ^XA   **b.** ^XF   **c.** ^X18
  d. ^X25   **e.** ^X2A   **f.** ^X33
  g. ^X55   **h.** ^X61   **i.** ^X80
  j. ^X3E8   **k.** ^XDE3   **l.** ^X176F

Exercise Set 2, pages 46–48

2. **a.** 00001000 no carry (3+5=8)
  b. 00000111 carry (11+{-4}=7)
  c. 11110111 carry ({-3}+{-6})=-9)
  d. 11101011 carry ({-20}+{-1}=-21)
  e. 00000010 carry (39+{-37}=2)
  f. 11000010 no carry ({-99}+37=-62)

3. **a.** 11111110 borrow (3-5=-2)
    b. 00001111 borrow (11-{-4}=15)
    c. 00000011 no borrow ({-3}-{-6}=3)
    d. 11101101 borrow ({-20}-{-1}=-19)
    e. 01001100 borrow (39-{-37}=76)
    f. 01111000 no borrow ({-99}-37=120) overflow

4. **a.** ^X08 no carry   **b.** ^X07 carry   **c.** ^XF7 carry
    d. ^XEB carry   **e.** ^X02 carry   **f.** ^XC2 no carry

5. **a.** ^XFE borrow   **b.** ^X0F borrow   **c.** ^X03 no borrow
    d. ^XED borrow   **e.** ^X04 borrow   **f.** ^X78 no borrow

7. **a.** ^X37
    b. ^XA1
    c. ^X7C
    d. ^XEF
    e. ^X39E5
    f. ^XABF2
    g. ^X3BEF58D1
    h. ^XDE698E5E

8. **a.** 1   **b.** -1   **c.** 15   **d.** 26
    e. -6   **f.** -96   **g.** 122   **h.** -125

9. **a.** 1   **b.** 255   **c.** 15   **d.** 26
    e. 250   **f.** 160   **g.** 122   **h.** 131

Chapter 3

Exercise Set 1, pages 65–66

1. **a.** ^X9F90
    b. ^X349F
    c. ^X0BCD
    d. ^X12349F90
    e. ^X00123494
    f. ^XCDEF9F00

3.   Byte   Address

    a. 1F   00000203
    b. 24   00000201
    c. 1E   00000202
    d. 1A   00000200
    e. 00   00000203

Exercise Set 2, pages 72–73

1.   Contents   Address
   a. 0000000F   0000020B
   b. 00000200   0000020B
   c. 00000000   00000204
   d. 0000020B   00000204
   e. 00000002   0000020C
   f. 00000110   00000204
   g. 000000E0   00000204
   h 0000000F   0000020B
        FFFFFFFF   0000020C

2. Contents   Address
   00000020   00000200
   00000040   00000204
   00000060   00000208
   00000051   0000020C

Chapter 4
Exercise Set 1, pages 94–95

3. **A:** ^X14
   B: ^X80
   C: ^X80
   D: ^X0080
   E: ^XFF80
   F: ^X00000128
   G: ^X80
   H: ^X00001000

Chapter 6
Exercise Set 1, pages 152–153

1. **a.** 253,253   **b.** 65533,-3   **c.** 32767,32767
   d. 63254,-2282   **e.** 32768,-32768   **f.** 32769,-32767
   g. 33021,-32515   **h.** 30293,30293   **i.** 28399,28399

2.   N Z V C
   a. ^XFF03   1 0 0 1
   b. ^X0003   0 0 0 1

```
c.  ^X8001    1 0 0 1
d.  ^X08EA    0 0 0 1
e.  ^X8000    1 0 1 1
f.  ^X7FFF    0 0 0 1
g.  ^X7F03    0 0 0 1
h.  ^X89AB    1 0 0 1
i.  ^X9111    1 0 0 1
```

```
3.                N Z V C
a.  ^X0217    0 0 0 0
b.  ^XEA46    1 0 1 0
c.  ^X6E48    0 0 0 1
d.  ^XFFFE    1 0 0 1
e.  ^X0000    0 1 0 1
f.  ^X45AF    0 0 0 1
```

7. (lettered bits are set)

	INCL	DECL	INCW	DECW
	N Z V C	N Z V C	N Z V C	N Z V C
a.	1 0 1 0	0 0 0 0	0 1 0 1	1 0 0 0
b.	1 0 0 0	0 0 1 0	0 0 0 0	1 0 0 1
c.	0 1 0 1	1 0 0 0	0 1 0 1	1 0 0 0
d.	0 0 0 0	1 0 0 1	0 0 0 0	1 0 0 1
e.	0 0 0 0	0 1 0 0	0 0 0 0	0 1 0 0
f.	1 0 0 0	1 0 0 0	0 0 0 0	0 1 0 0

Exercise Set 2, pages 167–168

```
1. a.  ^X03AC    b.  ^X85E0 (overflow)   c.  ^XFFFF
   d.  ^FFFE     e.  ^X0001              f.  ^XFFFF (overflow)
```

```
2. a.  ^X0050    b.  ^X0000              c.  invalid (trap)
   d.  ^X0000    e.  ^X0001              f.  invalid (V-bit set)
```

Chapter 7
Exercise Set 1, pages 177–178

```
1. a.  ^X0000C4E0 <=0    b.  ^X0000C4F8 <=0
   c.  ^X000010E4 <=0    d.  ^X0000112C <=0
   e.  ^X00001111 <=0    f.  ^X0000040E <=0
   g.  ^X00000E24 <=0    h.  ^X000002F8 <=0
   i.  ^X0000FFC4 <=0    j.  ^X0000005C <=0
```

Exercise Set 2, pages 201–202

	R0 Value	Contents	Address		R0 Value	Contents	Address
a.	00000000			**b.**	no change	00000000	00001200
c.	00001204	00000000	00001200	**d.**	000011FC	00000000	000011FC
e.	no change	00001200	00001200	**f.**	0000120C		
g.	00001208	0000120C	00001204	**h.**	00001204	0000120C	00001204
i.	no change	no change	00001200	**j.**	000011F8	000011F4	000011F8
k.	000011F4			**l.**	00001208	000011F4	00001208

Chapter 8

Exercise Set 2, pages 231–233

			N Z V C
1.	**a.**	B = ^XFFFFFFFF	1 0 0 -
	b.	C = ^X10305070	0 0 0 -
	c.	A = ^X0D0B0907	0 0 0 -
	d.	C = ^XF2F4F6F8	1 0 0 -
	e.	no change	0 0 0 -
	f.	no change	0 0 0 -

10. a. A = old B   B = old A   **b.** B = 0
    c. B = -A   **d.** B = -A
    e. C = A + B

Chapter 9

Exercise Set 1, pages 243–244

1. 00000005
00004212

2. a. 7FFC8FF4 <= ^X00000256
    SP <= ^X7FFC8FF4
  b. R1 <= ^X00000005
    SP <=^X7FFC8FFC
  c. SP <= ^X7FFC9000
  d. 7FFC8FF4 <= ^X000004E6 to ^X000004E9
    SP <= ^X7FFC8FF4
    PC <= ^X0000067F

e. 7FFC8FF4 <= ^X000004E5
    SP <= ^X7FFC8FF4
    PC <= ^X00000256
f. SP <= ^X7FFC8FFC
    PC <= ^X00000005
g. SP <= ^X7FFC8FF4
h. ^X7FFC8FF4 <= ^X00000005
    SP <= ^X7FFC8FF4
i. ^X7FFC8FF4 <= ^XFFFFF624
    ^X7FFC8FF0 <= ^X00000256
    SP <= ^X7FFC8FF0
j. R1 <= ^X00000005
    R2 <= ^X00004212
    SP <= ^X7FFC9000

Chapter 10
Exercise Set 1, pages 277–278

3. **a.** 11   **b.** 25
    c. 3   **d.** 1
    e. 3   **f.** 22
    g. 25   **h.** 13

4. **a.** relocatable   **b.** relocatable
    c. absolute   **d.** complex
    e. absolute   **f.** absolute
    g. complex   **h.** relocatable

5. The misplaced statements are:
    B: .BLKL   D-C
    K=J
    J=I+5

    The statements flagged with errors are:
    A: .BLKL   K
    B: .BLKL   D-C
    D: .BLKL   K+I
    K=J

6. I=3
    J=I+5
    K=J
    A: .BLKL   K

```
C:      .BLKL    I
D:      .BLKL    K+I
B:      .BLKL    D-C
```

Exercise Set 2, pages 287–290

2. a. nothing   **b.** MOVL   #3,W
  c. MOVL   R,RO **d.** MOVL   H,Q
  e. nothing   **f.** MOVL   I,J
                    MOVL   G,F

Exercise Set 3, pages 298–299

1. a. PROB EXP=A,TOTAL=B,SUB=C,MAC=D
  b. PROB EXP=A+5,TOTAL=B(R5)[R3],SUM=-(SP),MAX=#27
  c. PROB EXP=A,MAX=D
  d. PROB TOTAL=R5,SUM=<A,B>,MAX=LONGSYMBOL
  e. PROB SUM=(SP)+
  f. PROB EXP=<A,B,C,D>

2. a. SECOND   A,B,C,D
  b. SECOND   C,A,B,D
  c. SECOND   ADS,ORK,W,CHAN
  d. SECOND   ,(R5+,,-(SP)   This looks weird, but could be OK
  e. SECOND   <A,B>
  f. SECOND   ,,,<A,B>

```
5.  .MACRO    ADD    A=X,B=#100,C=(R1)+,D=#0,ANS=RO
    ADDL3     A,B,ANS
    ADDL2     C,ANS
    ADDL2     D,ANS
    .ENDM     ADD
```

Chapter 12
Exercise Set 1, pages 352–353

1. a. 51500000 **b.** 53374000
  c. 51314159 **d.** 47500000
  e. 73803500 **f.** 35492300
  g. 69849600 **h.** 41954200

2. a. 3.00000E 00   **b.**   -7.42000E 02
      3   -742

c. 8.94026E-01   d. 8.05216E-06
   .894026   .00000805216
e. -2.93465E 05   f. -1.00000E 06
   -293.465   -1,000,000
g. 9.50125E-13   h. -7.90881E 13
   .000000000000950125   -79088100000000

Exercise Set 2, pages 369-372

1. a. ^X00004080   b. ^X0000C220   c. ^X000043C8
   b. ^X00004000   e. ^XCCCD3ECC   f. ^XD70ABD23

2. a. 1.0   b. 0.5
   c. 0.25   d. 1.8446744E 19 or 2.0**64
   e. -1.0   f. 0.2

3.   D_floating for Exercise 2

   a. 00000000 00004080   1.0
   b. 00000000 0000C220   -10.0
   c. 00000000 000043C8   100.0
   d. 00000000 00004000   0.5
   e. CCCDCCCC CCCC3ECC   0.1
   f. A3D73D70 D70ABD23   -0.01

        D_floating for Exercise 2

   a. 00000000 00004080   1.0
   b. 00000000 00004000   0.5
   c. 00000000 00003F80   0.25
   d. 00000000 00006080   2.0**64
   e. 00000000 0000C080   -1.0
   f. CCCDCCCC CCCC3F4C   0.2

        G_floating for Exercise 1

   a. 00000000 00004010   1.0
   b. 00000000 0000C044   -10.0
   c. 00000000 00004079   100.0
   d. 00000000 00004000   0.5
   e. 999A9999 99993FD9   0.1
   f. 147B47AE 7AE1BFA4   -0.01

        G_floating for Exercise 2

   a. 00000000 00004010   1.0
   b. 00000000 00004000   0.5

c. 00000000 00003FF0   0.25
d. 00000000 00004410   2.0**64
e. 00000000 0000C010   -1.0
f. 999A9999 99993FE9   0.2

H_floating for Exercise 2

a. 00000000 00000000 00000000 00004001   1.0
b. 00000000 00000000 00000000 4000C004   -10.0
c. 00000000 00000000 00000000 90000407   100.0
d. 00000000 00000000 00000000 00004000   0.5
e. 999A9999 99999999 99999999 99993FFD   0.1
f. 147B47AE 7AE1AE14 E147147A 47AEBFFA   -0.01

H_floating for Exercise 2

a. 00000000 00000000 00000000 00004001   1.0
b. 00000000 00000000 00000000 00004000   0.5
c. 00000000 00000000 00000000 00003FFF   0.25
d. 00000000 00000000 00000000 00004041   2.0**64
e. 00000000 00000000 00000000 0000C001   -1.0
f. 999A9999 99999999 99999999 99993FFE   0.2

Chapter 14
Exercise Set 1, pages 421–422

1. **a.** Overlay – An overlay is a portion of code which is brought from slower memory into main memory when needed to allow the machine to run more code than it could actually hold at one time.
   b. Virtual Address – A virtual address is the address the program assumes it is fetching from or storing to.
   The actual address may be different because of relocation.
   c. Virtual Memory – A virtual memory system is a scheme for automatically overlaying the high speed memory of a computer with pages from a mass storage device. This greatly extends the effective memory space available to programs.
   d. Cache Memory – Cache memory is a very high speed memory used to buffer requests from main memory.
   e. Page – A page is the unit of memory swapped by the virtual memory system. On the VAX, pages consist of 512 bytes.
   f. Frame – A frame is the unit of memory buffered by the cache memory.
   g. Process Context – The machine resources needed by a process for the running of a program.

2. PO, or the program region is designated for programs and their data, and
    it is assigned virtual addresses working upwards from ^X00000000 to
    ^X3FFFFFFF. P1, or the control region, is assigned to handle the stack
    and other user related functions and runs downwards from X^7FFFFFFF
    to X^40000000 in memory. Such assignment of memory allows both areas
    to grow. System space is allocated from virtual address ^X80000000 to
    ^XFFFFFFFF. However, current implementations do not allow use of the
    area above ^XBFFFFFFF.

Exercise Set 2, pages 434–435

1. **a.** Privilege – The level to which a program has access to the resources
    of a computer system.
   b. Access Mode – Specifies the level of privilege that a program currently
    has for access to memory and instructions. On the VAX, there are four
    access modes–kern, executive, supervisor, and user.
   c. Processor Registers – Storage areas inside the processor. These include
    the sixteen general purpose registers as well as special registers such
    as the PSL.
   d. Bus – A common set of wires that is used to connect a computer pro-
    cessor to its memory and peripheral devices.
   e. UNIBUS – An asynchronous bus with a 16-bit data path used for inter-
    facing VAX computers to many input/output devices.
   f. MASSBUS – A bus with a 16-bit data path used for interfacing some
    VAX computers to high speed input/output devices.
   g. Q-BUS – A lower cost 16-bit asynchronous bus used on the Micro-VAX.
   h. Direct Memory Access – A technique that allows input/output devices
    to fetch from or store into a computer memory without processor
    intervention.
   i. Interrupt – A transfer of program control caused by a signal from an
    input/output device.
   j. Trap – A transfer of program control caused by an error condition in
    the running program. Traps occur after instruction execution has been
    completed and the saved program counter points to the next instruction
    after the instruction that caused the trap.
   k. Fault – A transfer of program control caused by an error condition in
    the running program. Faults occur before instruction execution has
    been completed and the saved program counter points to the operation
    code which caused the fault.
2. **a.** Fifteen ways.
   b. Yes.

Chapter 15
Exercise Set 1, pages 442–443

4. .LIST – Controls the format of the listing generated during pass two. There is no effect during pass two.

.WORD – Reserves space and initializes memory for one or more words. During pass one, space is reserved by incrementing the location counter by the appropriate amount. During pass two, object code is generated from the list of expressions in the operand field. In addition the location counter is updated as in pass one.

.REPT – Instructs the assembler to repeat the following code until a .ENDR is reached as many times as is specified in the operand field. The effect is the same on both passes.

.ASCII – Reserves space and initializes memory for zero or more ASCII characters. During pass one, space is reserved by incrementing the location counter by the appropriate amount. During pass two, object code is generated from the string of ASCII characters in the operand field. In addition the location counter is updated as in pass one.

Index

Operation Code Index

Legend: x is 2 or 3
            f is floating point (D, F, G, or H)